Thinking
in
Java

Bruce Eckel

ISBN 0-13-659723-8

Comments from readers:

Much better than any other Java book I've seen. Make that "by an order of magnitude"... very complete, with excellent right-to-the-point examples and intelligent, not dumbed-down, explanations ... In contrast to many other Java books I found it to be unusually mature, consistent, intellectually honest, well-written and precise. IMHO, an ideal book for studying Java. **Anatoly Vorobey, Technion University, Haifa, Israel**

One of the absolutely best programming tutorials I've seen for any language. **Joakim Ziegler, FIX sysop**

Thank you for your wonderful, wonderful book on Java. **Dr. Gavin Pillay, Registrar, King Edward VIII Hospital, South Africa**

Thank you again for your awesome book. I was really floundering (being a non-C programmer), but your book has brought me up to speed as fast as I could read it. It's really cool to be able to understand the underlying principles and concepts from the start, rather than having to try to build that conceptual model through trial and error. Hopefully I will be able to attend your seminar in the not-too-distant future. **Randall R. Hawley, Automation Technician, Eli Lilly & Co.**

The best computer book writing I have seen. **Tom Holland**

This is one of the best books I've read about a programming language... Chapter 16 on design patterns is one of the most interesting things I've read in a long time. **Ilan Finci, graduate student and teaching assistant, Institute of Computer Science, The Hebrew University of Jerusalem, Israel**

The best book ever written on Java. **Ravindra Pai, Oracle Corporation, SUNOS product line**

This is the best book on Java that I have ever found! You have done a great job. Your depth is amazing. I will be purchasing the book when it is published. I have been learning Java since October 96. I have read a few books, and consider yours a "MUST READ." These past few months we have been focused on a product written entirely in Java. Your book has helped solidify topics I was shaky on and has expanded my knowledge base. I have even used some of your explanations as information in interviewing contractors to help our team. I have found how much Java knowledge they have by asking them about things I have learned from reading your book (e.g. the difference between arrays and Vectors). Your book is great! **Steve Wilkinson, Senior Staff Specialist, MCI Telecommunications**

Great book. Best book on Java I have seen so far. **Jeff Sinclair, Software Engineer, Kestral Computing**

Thank you for *Thinking in Java*. It's time someone went beyond mere language description to a thoughtful, penetrating analytic tutorial that doesn't kowtow to The Manufacturers. I've read almost all the others– only yours and Patrick Winston's have found a place in my heart. I'm already recommending it to customers. Thanks again. **Richard Brooks, Java Consultant, Sun Professional Services, Dallas**

Other books cover the WHAT of Java (describing the syntax and the libraries) or the HOW of Java (practical programming examples). *Thinking in Java* is the only book I know that explains the WHY of Java; why it was designed the way it was, why it works the way it does, why it sometimes doesn't work, why it's better than C++, why it's not. Although it also does a good job of teaching the what and how of the language, *Thinking in Java* is definitely the thinking person's choice in a Java book. **Robert S. Stephenson**

Thanks for writing a great book. The more I read it the better I like it. My students like it, too. **Chuck Iverson**

I just want to commend you for your work on *Thinking in Java*. It is people like you that dignify the future of the Internet and I just want to thank you for your effort. It is very much appreciated. **Patrick Barrell, Network Officer Mamco-QAF Mfg. Inc.**

Most of the Java books out there are fine for a start, and most just have beginning stuff and a lot of the same examples. Yours is by far the best advanced thinking book I've seen. Please publish it soon! ... I also bought *Thinking in C++* just because I was so impressed with *Thinking in Java*. **George Laframboise, LightWorx Technology Consulting, Inc.**

I wrote to you earlier about my favorable impressions regarding your *Thinking in C++* (a book that stands prominently on my shelf here at work). And today I've been able to delve into Java with your e-book in my virtual hand, and I must say (in my best Chevy Chase from "Modern Problems") "I like it!" Very informative and explanatory, without reading like a dry textbook. You cover the most important yet the least covered concepts of Java development: the whys. **Sean Brady**

Your examples are clear and easy to understand. You took care of many important details of Java that can't be found easily in the weak Java documentation. And you don't waste the reader's time with the basic facts a programmer already knows. **Kai Engert, Innovative Software, Germany**

I'm a great fan of your *Thinking in C++* and have recommended it to associates. As I go through the electronic version of your Java book, I'm finding that you've retained the same high level of writing. Thank you! **Peter R. Neuwald**

VERY well-written Java book ... I think you've done a GREAT job on it. As the leader of a Chicago-area Java special interest group, I've favorably mentioned your book and website several times at our recent meetings. I would like to use *Thinking in Java* as the basis for a part of each monthly SIG meeting, in which we review and discuss each chapter in succession. **Mark Ertes**

I really appreciate your work and your book is good. I recommend it here to our users and Ph.D. students. **Hugues Leroy // Irisa-Inria Rennes France, Head of Scientific Computing and Industrial Tranfert**

OK, I've only read about 40 pages of *Thinking in Java*, but I've already found it to be the most clearly-written and presented programming book I've come across ... and I'm a writer, myself, so I am probably a little critical. I have *Thinking in C++* on order and can't wait to crack it – I'm fairly new to programming and am hitting learning curves head-on everywhere. So this is just a quick note to say thanks for your excellent work. I had begun to burn a little low on enthusiasm from slogging through the mucky, murky prose of most computer books – even ones that came with glowing recommendations. I feel a whole lot better now. **Glenn Becker, Educational Theatre Association**

Thank you for making your wonderful book available. I have found it immensely useful in finally understanding what I experienced as confusing in Java and C++. Reading your book has been very satisfying, **Felix Bizaoui, Twin Oaks Industries, Louisa, Va.**

I must congratulate you on an excellent book. I decided to have a look at *Thinking in Java* based on my experience with *Thinking in C++*, and I was not disappointed. **Jaco van der Merwe, Software Specialist, DataFusion Systems Ltd, Stellenbosch, South Africa**

This has to be one of the best Java books I've seen. **E.F. Pritchard, Senior Software Engineer, Cambridge Animation Systems Ltd., United Kingdom**

Your book makes all the other Java books I've read or flipped through seem doubly useless and insulting. **Brett g Porter, Senior Programmer, Art & Logic**

I have been reading your book for a week or two and compared to the books I have read earlier on Java, your book seems to have given me a great start. I have recommended this book to lot of my friends and they have rated it excellent. Please accept my congratulations for coming out with an excellent book. **Rama Krishna Bhupathi, Software Engineer, TCSI Corporation, San Jose**

Just wanted to say what a "brilliant" piece of work your book is. I've been using it as a major reference for in-house Java work. I find that the table of contents is just right for quickly locating the section that is required. It's also nice to see a book that is not just a rehash of the API nor treats the programmer like a dummy. **Grant Sayer, Java Components Group Leader, Ceedata Systems Pty Ltd, Australia**

Wow! A readable, in-depth Java book. There are a lot of poor (and admittedly a couple of good) Java books out there, but from what I've seen yours is definitely one of the best. **John Root, Web Developer, Department of Social Security, London**

I've *just* started *Thinking in Java*. I expect it to be very good because I really liked *Thinking in C++* (which I read as an experienced C++ programmer, trying to stay ahead of the curve). I'm somewhat less experienced in Java, but expect to be very satisfied. You are a wonderful author. **Kevin K. Lewis, Technologist, ObjectSpace, Inc.**

I think it's a great book. I learned all I know about Java from this book. Thank you for making it available for free over the Internet. If you wouldn't have I'd know nothing about Java at all. But the best thing is that your book isn't a commercial brochure for Java. It also shows the bad sides of Java. YOU have done a great job here. **Frederik Fix, Belgium**

I have been hooked to your books all the time. A couple of years ago, when I wanted to start with C++, it was *C++ Inside & Out* which took me around the fascinating world of C++. It helped me in getting better opportunities in life. Now, in pursuit of more knowledge and when I wanted to learn Java, I bumped into *Thinking in Java* – No doubts in my mind as to whether I need some other book. Just fantastic. It is more like rediscovering myself as I get along with the book. It is just a month since I started with Java, and heartfelt thanks to you, I am understanding it better now. **Anand Kumar S. - Software Engineer – Computervision, India**

Your book stands out as an excellent general introduction. **Peter Robinson, University of Cambridge Computer Laboratory**

It's by far the best material I have come across to help me learn Java and I just want you to know how lucky I feel to have found it. THANKS! **Chuck Peterson, Product Leader, Internet Product Line, IVIS International**

The book is great. It's the third book on Java I've started and I'm about two-thirds of the way through it now. I plan to finish this one. I found out about it because it is used in some internal classes at Lucent Technologies and a friend told me the book was on the Net. Good work. **Jerry Nowlin, MTS, Lucent Technologies**

Of the six or so Java books I've accumulated to date, your *Thinking in Java* is by far the best and clearest. **Michael Van Waas, Ph.D., President, TMR Associates**

I just want to say thanks for *Thinking in Java*. What a wonderful book you've made here! Not to mention downloadable for free! As a student I find your books invaluable (I have a copy of *C++ Inside Out*, another great book about C++), because they not only teach me the how-to, but also the whys, which are of course very important in building a strong foundation in languages such as C++ or Java. I have quite a lot of friends here who love programming just as I do, and I've told them about your books. They think it's great! Thanks again! By the way, I'm Indonesian and I live in Java. **Ray Frederick Djajadinata, Student at Trisakti University, Jakarta**

The mere fact that you have made this work free over the Net puts me into shock. I thought I'd let you know how much I appreciate and respect what you're doing. **Shane LeBouthillier, Computer Engineering student, University of Alberta, Canada**

I have to tell you how much I look forward to reading your monthly column. As a newbie to the world of object oriented programming, I appreciate the time and thoughtfulness that you give to even the most elementary topic. I have downloaded your book, but you can bet that I will purchase the hard copy when it is published. Thanks for all of your help. **Dan Cashmer, B. C. Ziegler & Co.**

Just want to congratulate you on a job well done. First I stumbled upon the PDF version of *Thinking in Java*. Even before I finished reading it, I ran to the store and found *Thinking in C++*. Now, I have been in the computer business for over eight years, as a consultant, software engineer, teacher/trainer, and recently as self-employed, so I'd like to think that I have seen enough (not "have seen it all," mind you, but enough). However, these books cause my girlfriend to call me a "geek." Not that I have anything against the concept - it is just that I thought this phase was well beyond me. But I find myself truly enjoying both books, like no other computer book I have touched or bought so far. Excellent writing style, very nice introduction of every new topic, and lots of wisdom in the books. Well done. **Simon Goland, simonsez@smartt.com, Simon Says Consulting, Inc.**

I must say that your *Thinking in Java* is great! That is exactly the kind of documentation I was looking for. Especially the sections about good and poor software design using Java 1.1. **Dirk Duehr, Lexikon Verlag, Bertelsmann AG, Germany**

Thank you for writing two great books (*Thinking in C++*, *Thinking in Java*). You have helped me immensely in my progression to object oriented programming. **Donald Lawson, DCL Enterprises**

Thank you for taking the time to write a really helpful book on Java. If teaching makes you understand something, by now you must be pretty pleased with yourself. **Dominic Turner, GEAC Support**

It's the best Java book I have ever read - and I read some. **Jean-Yves MENGANT, Chief Software Architect NAT-SYSTEM, Paris, France**

Thinking in Java gives the best coverage and explanation. Very easy to read, and I mean the code fragments as well. **Ron Chan, Ph.D., Expert Choice, Inc., Pittsburgh PA**

Your book is great. I have read lots of programming books and your book still adds insights to programming in my mind. **Ningjian Wang, Information System Engineer, The Vanguard Group**

Thinking in Java is an excellent and readable book. I recommend it to all my students. **Dr. Paul Gorman, Department of Computer Science, University of Otago, Dunedin, New Zealand**

You make it possible for the proverbial free lunch to exist, not just a soup kitchen type of lunch but a gourmet delight for those who appreciate good software and books about it. **Jose Suriol, Scylax Corporation**

Thanks for the opportunity of watching this book grow into a masterpiece! IT IS THE BEST book on the subject that I've read or browsed. **Jeff Lapchinsky, Programmer, Net Results Technologies**

Your book is concise, accessible and a joy to read. **Keith Ritchie, Java Research & Development Team, KL Group Inc.**

It truly is the best book I've read on Java! **Daniel Eng**

The best book I have seen on Java! **Rich Hoffarth, Senior Architect, West Group**

Thank you for a wonderful book. I'm having a lot of fun going through the chapters. **Fred Trimble, Actium Corporation**

You have mastered the art of slowly and successfully making us grasp the details. You make learning VERY easy and satisfying. Thank you for a truly wonderful tutorial. **Rajesh Rau, Software Consultant**

Thinking in Java rocks the free world! **Miko O'Sullivan, President, Idocs Inc.**

About *Thinking in C++*:

Best Book! Winner of the
1995 Software Development Magazine Jolt Award!

"This book is a tremendous achievement. You owe it to yourself
to have a copy on your shelf. The chapter on iostreams is the
most comprehensive and understandable treatment of that
subject I've seen to date."

Al Stevens
Contributing Editor, *Doctor Dobbs Journal*

"Eckel's book is the only one to so clearly explain how to
rethink program construction for object orientation. That the
book is also an excellent tutorial on the ins and outs of C++ is
an added bonus."

Andrew Binstock
Editor, *Unix Review*

"Bruce continues to amaze me with his insight into C++, and
Thinking in C++ is his best collection of ideas yet. If you want
clear answers to difficult questions about C++, buy this
outstanding book."

Gary Entsminger
Author, *The Tao of Objects*

"Thinking in C++ patiently and methodically explores the
issues of when and how to use inlines, references, operator
overloading, inheritance, and dynamic objects, as well as
advanced topics such as the proper use of templates, exceptions
and multiple inheritance. The entire effort is woven in a fabric
that includes Eckel's own philosophy of object and program
design. A must for every C++ developer's bookshelf, Thinking
in C++ is the one C++ book you must have if you're doing
serious development with C++."

Richard Hale Shaw
Contributing Editor, PC Magazine

Thinking
in
Java

Bruce Eckel
President, MindView Inc.

Prentice Hall PTR
Upper Saddle River, New Jersey 07458
http://www.phptr.com

Library of Congress Cataloging-in-Publication Data

```
Eckel, Bruce.
   Thinking in Java / Bruce Eckel.
       p.    cm.
   Includes index.
   ISBN 0-13-659723-8
   1. Java (Computer program language) I. Title.
QA76.73.J38E25 1998
005.13'3--dc21                              97-52713
                                               CIP
```

Editorial/Production Supervision: Craig Little
Acquisitions Editor: Jeffrey Pepper
Manufacturing Manager: Alexis R. Heydt
Marketing Manager: Miles Williams
Cover Design Director: Jerry Votta
Cover Design: Daniel Will-Harris
Interior Design: Daniel Will-Harris, www.will-harris.com

 © 1998 by Prentice Hall PTR
Prentice-Hall Inc.
A Simon & Schuster Company
Upper Saddle River, NJ 07458

Prentice Hall books are widely used by corporations and government agencies for training, marketing, and resale. The publisher offers discounts on this book when ordered in bulk quantities. For more information, contact the Corporate Sales Department at 800-382-3419, fax: 201-236-7141, email: *corpsales@prenhall.com* or write: Corporate Sales Department, Prentice Hall PTR, One Lake Street, Upper Saddle River, New Jersey 07458.

Java is a registered trademark of Sun Microsystems, Inc. Windows 95 and Windows NT are trademarks of Microso Corporation. All other product names and company names mentioned herein are the property of their respective owners.

Printed in the United States of America
10 9

ISBN 0-13-659723-8

Prentice-Hall International (UK) Limited, *London*
Prentice-Hall of Australia Pty. Limited, *Sydney*
Prentice-Hall Canada Inc., *Toronto*
Prentice-Hall Hispanoamericana, S.A., *Mexico*
Prentice-Hall of India Private Limited, *New Delhi*
Prentice-Hall of Japan, Inc., *Tokyo*
Simon & Schuster Asia Pte. Ltd., *Singapore*
Editora Prentice-Hall do Brasil, Ltda., *Rio de Janeiro*

Bruce Eckel's Hands-On Java Seminar Multimedia CD
It's like coming to the seminar!
Available at http://www.BruceEckel.com

- Overhead slides and synchronized audio for all the lectures. Just play it to see and hear the lectures!
- Entire set of lectures are indexed so you can rapidly locate the discussion of the subject you're interested in.
- Special screen-formatted electronic version of *Thinking in Java* with hyperlinked index and table of contents.

Dedication

To the person who, even now,
is creating the next great computer language

Overview

What's Inside

10: The Java IO system   439

11: Run-time type identification   515

12: Passing and returning objects   541

Foreword

I suggested to my brother Todd, who is making the leap from hardware into programming, that the next big revolution will be in genetic engineering.

We'll have microbes designed to make food, fuel and plastic; they'll clean up pollution and in general allow us to master the manipulation of the physical world for a fraction of what it costs now. I claimed that it would make the computer revolution look small in comparison.

Then I realized I was making a mistake common to science fiction writers: getting lost in the technology (which is of course easy to do in science fiction). An experienced writer knows that the story is never about the things; it's about the people. Genetics will have a very large impact on our lives, but I'm not so sure it will dwarf the computer revolution – or at least the information revolution. Information is about talking to each other: yes, cars and shoes and especially genetic cures are important, but in the end those are just trappings. What truly matters is how we relate to the world. And so much of that is about communication.

This book is a case in point. A majority of folks thought I was very bold or a little crazy to put the entire thing up on the Web. "Why would anyone buy it?" they asked. If I had been of a more conservative nature I wouldn't have done it, but I really didn't want to write another computer book in the same old way. I didn't know what would happen but it turned out to be the smartest thing I've ever done with a book.

For one thing, people started sending in corrections. This has been an amazing process, because folks have looked into every nook and cranny and caught both technical and grammatical errors, and I've been able to eliminate bugs of all sorts that I know would have otherwise slipped through. People have been simply terrific about this, very often saying "Now, I don't mean this in a critical way" and then giving me a collection of errors I'm sure I never would have found. I feel like this has been a kind of group process and it has really made the book into something special.

But then I started hearing "OK, fine, it's nice you've put up an electronic version, but I want a printed and bound copy from a real publisher." I tried very hard to make it easy for everyone to print it out in a nice looking format but it didn't stem the demand for the published book. Most people don't want to read the entire book on screen, and hauling around a sheaf of papers, no matter how nicely printed, didn't appeal to them either (plus I think it's not so cheap in terms of laser printer toner). It seems that the computer revolution won't put publishers out of business, after all. However, one student suggested this may become a model for future publishing: books will be published on the Web first, and only if sufficient interest warrants it will the book be put on paper. Currently, the great majority of books of all kinds are financial failures, and perhaps this new approach could make the publishing industry more profitable.

This book became an enlightening experience for me in another way. I originally approached Java as "just another programming language," which in many senses it is. But as time passed and I studied it more deeply, I began to see that the fundamental intention of the language is different than in all the other languages I have seen.

Programming is about managing complexity: the complexity of the problem you want to solve laid upon the complexity of the machine in which it is solved. Because of this complexity, most of our programming projects fail. And yet of all the programming languages that I am aware, none of them have gone all out and decided that their main design goal would be to conquer the complexity of developing and maintaining programs. Of course, many language design decisions were made with complexity in mind, but at some point there were always some other issues that were considered essential to be added into the mix. Inevitably, those other issues are what causes programmers to eventually "hit the wall" with that language. For example, C++ had to be backwards-compatible with C (to allow easy migration for C programmers), as well as efficient. Those are both very useful goals and account for much of the success of C++, but they also expose extra complexity that prevents some projects from being finished (certainly, you can blame programmers and management, but if a language can help by catching your mistakes, why shouldn't it?). As another example, Visual Basic (VB) was tied to BASIC, which wasn't really designed to be an extensible language, so all the extensions piled upon VB have produced some truly horrible and un-maintainable syntax. On the other hand, C++, VB and other languages like Smalltalk had some of their design efforts focused on the issue of complexity and as a result are remarkably successful in solving certain types of problems.

What has impressed me most as I have come to understand Java is what seems like an unflinching goal of reducing complexity *for the programmer*. As if to say "we don't care about anything except reducing the time and difficulty of producing robust code." In the early days, this goal has resulted in code that doesn't run very fast (although there have been many promises made about how quickly Java will someday run) but it has indeed produced amazing reductions in development time; half or less of the time that it takes to create an equivalent C++ program. This result alone can save incredible amounts of time and money, but Java doesn't stop there. It goes on to wrap all the complex tasks that have become important, such as multithreading and network programming, in language features or libraries that can at times make those tasks trivial. And finally, it tackles some really big complexity problems: cross-platform programs, dynamic code changes, and even security, each of which can fit on your complexity spectrum anywhere from "impediment" to "show-stopper." So despite the performance problems we've seen, the promise of Java is tremendous: it can make us significantly more productive programmers.

One of the places I see the greatest impact for this is on the Web. Network programming has always been hard, and Java makes it easy (and they're working on making it easier all the time). Network programming is how we talk to each other more effectively and cheaply than we ever have with telephones (email alone has revolutionized many businesses). As we talk to each other more, amazing things begin to happen, possibly more amazing even than the promise of genetic engineering.

In all ways: creating the programs, working in teams to create the programs, building user interfaces so the programs can communicate with the user, running the programs on different types of machines, and easily writing programs that communicate across the Internet – Java increases the communication bandwidth *between people*. And I think that perhaps the results of the communication revolution will not be seen from the effects of moving large quantities of bits around. We shall see the true revolution because we will all be able to talk to each other more easily – one-on-one, but also in groups and as a planet. I've heard it suggested that the next revolution is the formation of a kind of global mind which results from enough people and enough interconnectedness. Java may or may not be the tool that foments that revolution, but at least the possibility has made me feel like I'm doing something meaningful here by attempting to teach the language.

Introduction

Like any human language, Java provides a way to express concepts. If successful, this medium of expression will be significantly easier and more flexible than the alternatives as problems grow larger and more complex.

You can't look at Java as just a collection of features; some of the features make no sense in isolation. You can use the sum of the parts only if you are thinking about *design*, not simply coding. And to understand Java in this way, you must understand the problems with it and with programming in general. This book discusses programming problems, why they are problems, and the approach Java has taken to solve them. Thus, the set of features I explain in each chapter are based on the way I see a particular type of problem being solved with the language. In this way I hope to move you, a little at a time, to the point where the Java mindset becomes your native tongue.

Throughout, I'll be taking the attitude that you want to build a model in your head that allows you to develop a deep understanding of the language; if you encounter a puzzle you'll be able to feed it to your model and deduce the answer.

Prerequisites

This book assumes that you have some programming familiarity; you understand that a program is a collection of statements, the idea of a subroutine/function/macro, control statements such as "if" and looping constructs such as "while," etc. However, you might have learned this in many places, such as programming with a macro language or working with a tool like Perl. As long as you've programmed to the point where you feel comfortable with the basic ideas of programming, you'll be able to work through this book. Of course, the book will be *easier* for the C programmers and more so for the C++ programmers, but don't count yourself out if you're not experienced with those languages (but come willing to work hard). I'll be introducing the concepts of object-oriented programming and Java's basic control mechanisms, so you'll be exposed to those, and the first exercises will involve the basic control-flow statements.

Although references will often be made to C and C++ language features, these are not intended to be insider comments, but instead to help all programmers put Java in perspective with those languages, from which, after all, Java is descended. I will attempt to make these references simple and to explain anything that I think a non- C/C++ programmer would not be familiar with.

Learning Java

At about the same time that my first book *Using C++* (Osborne/McGraw-Hill 1989) came out, I began teaching that language. Teaching programming languages has become my profession; I've seen nodding heads, blank faces, and puzzled expressions in audiences all over the world since 1989. As I began giving in-house training with smaller groups of people, I discovered something during the exercises. Even those people who were smiling and nodding were confused about many issues. I found out, by chairing the C++ track at the Software Development Conference for the past few years (and now also the Java track), that I and other speakers tended to give the typical audience too many topics too fast. So eventually, through both variety in the audience level and the way that I presented the material, I would end up losing some portion of the audience. Maybe it's asking too much, but because I am one of those

---

people resistant to traditional lecturing (and for most people, I believe, such resistance results from boredom), I wanted to try to keep everyone up to speed.

For a time, I was creating a number of different presentations in fairly short order. Thus, I ended up learning by experiment and iteration (a technique that also works well in Java program design). Eventually I developed a course using everything I had learned from my teaching experience – one that I would be happy giving for a long time. It tackles the learning problem in discrete, easy-to-digest steps and in a hands-on seminar (the ideal learning situation), there are exercises following each of the short lessons. I now give this course in public Java seminars, which you can find out about at *http://www.BruceEckel.com*. (The introductory seminar is also available as a CD ROM. Information is available at the same Web site.)

The feedback that I get from each seminar helps me change and refocus the material until I think it works well as a teaching medium. But this book isn't just a seminar handout – I tried to pack as much information as I could within these pages and structured it to draw you through onto the next subject. More than anything, the book is designed to serve the solitary reader who is struggling with a new programming language.

Goals

Like my previous book *Thinking in C++*, this book has come to be structured around the process of teaching the language. In particular, my motivation is to create something that provides me with a way to teach the language in my own seminars. When I think of a chapter in the book, I think in terms of what makes a good lesson during a seminar. My goal is to get bite-sized pieces that can be taught in a reasonable amount of time, followed by exercises that are feasible to accomplish in a classroom situation.

My goals in this book are to:

1.   Present the material one simple step at a time so that you can easily digest each concept before moving on.

2.   Use examples that are as simple and short as possible. This sometimes prevents me from tackling "real world" problems, but I've found that beginners are usually happier when they can understand every detail of an example rather than being

---

impressed by the scope of the problem it solves. Also, there's a severe limit to the amount of code that can be absorbed in a classroom situation. For this I will no doubt receive criticism for using "toy examples," but I'm willing to accept that in favor of producing something pedagogically useful.

3. Carefully sequence the presentation of features so that you aren't seeing something that you haven't been exposed to. Of course, this isn't always possible; in those situations, a brief introductory description is given.

4. Give you what I think is important for you to understand about the language, rather than everything I know. I believe there is an information importance hierarchy, and that there are some facts that 95 percent of programmers will never need to know and just confuses people and adds to their perception of the complexity of the language. To take an example from C, if you memorize the operator precedence table (I never did), you can write clever code. But if you need to think about it, it will also confuse the reader/maintainer of that code. So forget about precedence, and use parentheses when things aren't clear.

5. Keep each section focused enough so that the lecture time – and the time between exercise periods – is small. Not only does this keep the audience's minds more active and involved during a hands-on seminar, but it gives the reader a greater sense of accomplishment.

6. Provide you with a solid foundation so that you can understand the issues well enough to move on to more difficult coursework and books.

Online documentation

The Java language and libraries from Sun Microsystems (a free download) come with documentation in electronic form, readable using a Web browser, and virtually every third party implementation of Java has this or an equivalent documentation system. Almost all the books published on Java have duplicated this documentation. So you either already have it or you can download it, and unless necessary, this book will not repeat that documentation because it's usually much faster if you find the class descriptions with your Web browser than if you look them up in a book. (Plus it will be up-to-date.) This book will provide extra descriptions of the classes only when it's necessary to supplement the documentation so you can understand a particular example.

Chapters

This book was designed with one thing in mind: the way people learn the Java language. Seminar audience feedback helped me understand which parts were difficult and needed illumination. In the areas where I got ambitious and included too many features all at once, I came to know – through the process of presenting the material – that if you include a lot of new features, you need to explain them all, and this easily compounds the student's confusion. As a result, I've taken a great deal of trouble to introduce the features as few at a time as possible.

The goal, then, is for each chapter to teach a single feature, or a small group of associated features, in such a way that no additional features are relied upon. That way you can digest each piece in the context of your current knowledge before moving on.

Here is a brief description of the chapters contained in the book, which correspond to lectures and exercise periods in my hands-on seminars.

Chapter 1: ***Introduction to objects***
This chapter is an overview of what object-oriented programming is all about, including the answer to the basic question "What's an object?", interface vs. implementation, abstraction and encapsulation, messages and functions, inheritance and composition, and the all-important polymorphism. You'll also be introduced to issues of object creation such as constructors, where the objects live, where to put them once they're created, and the magical garbage collector that cleans up the objects that are no longer needed. Other issues will be introduced, including error handling with exceptions, multithreading for responsive user interfaces, and networking and the Internet. You'll also learn about what makes Java special, why it's been so successful, and about object-oriented analysis and design.

Chapter 2: ***Everything is an object***
This chapter moves you to the point where you can write your first Java program, so it must give an overview of the essentials, including the concept of a "handle" to an object; how to create an object; an introduction to primitive types and arrays; scoping

and the way objects are destroyed by the garbage collector; how everything in Java is a new data type (class) and how to create your own classes; functions, arguments, and return values; name visibility and using components from other libraries; the **static** keyword; comments and embedded documentation.

Chapter 3:   *Controlling program flow*
This chapter begins with all of the operators that come to Java from C and C++. In addition, you'll discover common operator pitfalls, casting, promotion, and precedence. This is followed by the basic control-flow and selection operations that you get with virtually any programming language: choice with if-else; looping with for and while; quitting a loop with break and continue as well as Java's labeled break and labeled continue (which account for the "missing goto" in Java); and selection using switch. Although much of this material has common threads with C and C++ code, there are some differences. In addition, all the examples will be full Java examples so you'll get more comfortable with what Java looks like.

Chapter 4:   *Initialization and cleanup*
This chapter begins by introducing the constructor, which guarantees proper initialization. The definition of the constructor leads into the concept of function overloading (since you might want several constructors). This is followed by a discussion of the process of cleanup, which is not always as simple as it seems. Normally, you just drop an object when you're done with it and the garbage collector eventually comes along and releases the memory. This portion explores the garbage collector and some of its idiosyncrasies. The chapter concludes with a closer look at how things are initialized: automatic member initialization, specifying member initialization, the order of initialization, **static** initialization and array initialization.

Chapter 5:   *Hiding the implementation*
This chapter covers the way that code is packaged together, and why some parts of a library are exposed while other parts are hidden. It begins by looking at the **package** and **import** keywords, which perform file-level packaging and allow you to build libraries of classes. The subject of directory paths and file names is also examined. The remainder of the chapter looks at the **public**, **private**, and **protected** keywords, the concept of

"friendly" access, and what the different levels of access control mean when used in various contexts.

Chapter 6: *Reusing classes*

The concept of inheritance is standard in virtually all OOP languages. It's a way to take an existing class and add to its functionality (as well as change it, the subject of Chapter 7). Inheritance is often a way to reuse code by leaving the "base class" the same, and just patching things here and there to produce what you want. However, inheritance isn't the only way to make new classes from existing ones. You can also embed an object inside your new class with *composition*. In this chapter you'll learn about these two ways to reuse code in Java, and how to apply them.

Chapter 7: *Polymorphism*

On your own, you might take nine months to discover and understand polymorphism, a cornerstone of OOP. Through small, simple examples you'll see how to create a family of types with inheritance and manipulate objects in that family through their common base class. Java's polymorphism allows you to treat all objects in this family generically, which means the bulk of your code doesn't rely on specific type information. This makes your programs extensible, so building programs and code maintenance is easier and cheaper. In addition, Java provides a third way to set up a reuse relationship through the *interface*, which is a pure abstraction of the interface of an object. Once you've seen polymorphism, the interface can be clearly understood. This chapter also introduces Java 1.1 *inner classes*.

Chapter 8: *Holding your objects*

It's a fairly simple program that has only a fixed quantity of objects with known lifetimes. In general, your programs will always be creating new objects at a variety of times that will be known only while the program is running. In addition, you won't know until run-time the quantity or even the exact type of the objects you need. To solve the general programming problem, you need to create any number of objects, anytime, anywhere. This chapter explores in depth the tools that Java supplies to hold objects while you're working with them: the simple arrays and more sophisticated collections (data structures) such as **Vector** and **Hashtable**. Finally, the new and improved Java 1.2 collections library is explored in depth.

Chapter 9: ***Error handling with exceptions***

The basic philosophy of Java is that badly-formed code will not be run. As much as possible, the compiler catches problems, but sometimes the problems – either programmer error or a natural error condition that occurs as part of the normal execution of the program – can be detected and dealt with only at run-time. Java has *exception handling* to deal with any problems that arise while the program is running. This chapter examines how the keywords **try**, **catch**, **throw**, **throws**, and **finally** work in Java; when you should throw exceptions and what to do when you catch them. In addition, you'll see Java's standard exceptions, how to create your own, what happens with exceptions in constructors, and how exception handlers are located.

Chapter 10: ***The Java IO system***

Theoretically, you can divide any program into three parts: input, process, and output. This implies that IO (input/output) is a pretty important part of the equation. In this chapter you'll learn about the different classes that Java provides for reading and writing files, blocks of memory, and the console. The distinction between "old" IO and "new" Java 1.1 IO will be shown. In addition, this section examines the process of taking an object, "streaming" it (so that it can be placed on disk or sent across a network) and reconstructing it, which is handled for you in Java version 1.1. Also, Java 1.1's compression libraries, which are used in the Java ARchive file format (JAR), are examined.

Chapter 11: ***Run-time type identification***

Java run-time type identification (RTTI) lets you find the exact type of an object when you have a handle to only the base type. Normally, you'll want to intentionally ignore the exact type of an object and let Java's dynamic binding mechanism (polymorphism) implement the correct behavior for that type. But occasionally it is very helpful to know the exact type of an object for which you have only a base handle. Often this information allows you to perform a special-case operation more efficiently. This chapter explains what RTTI is for, how to use it and how to get rid of it when it doesn't belong there. In addition, the Java 1.1 *reflection* feature is introduced.

Chapter 12: ***Passing and returning objects***

Since the only way you talk to objects in Java is through "handles," the concepts of passing an object into a function and

---

returning an object from a function have some interesting consequences. This chapter explains what you need to know to manage objects when you're moving in and out of functions, and also shows the **String** class, which uses a different approach to the problem.

Chapter 13: *Creating windows and applets*

Java comes with the *Abstract Window Toolkit* (AWT), which is a set of classes that handle windowing in a portable fashion; these windowing programs can either be applets or stand-alone applications. This chapter is an introduction to the AWT and the creation of World Wide Web applets. We'll also look at pros and cons of the AWT and the GUI improvements introduced in Java 1.1. The important "Java Beans" technology is introduced. This is fundamental for the creation of Rapid–Application Development (RAD) program-building tools. Finally, the new Java 1.2 "Swing" library is introduced – this provides a dramatic improvement in UI components for Java.

Chapter 14: *Multiple threads*

Java provides a built-in facility to support multiple concurrent subtasks, called *threads*, running within a single program. (Unless you have multiple processors on your machine, this is only the *appearance* of multiple subtasks.) Although these can be used anywhere, threads are most powerful when trying to create a responsive user interface so, for example, a user isn't prevented from pressing a button or entering data while some processing is going on. This chapter looks at the syntax and semantics of multithreading in Java.

Chapter 15: *Network programming*

All the Java features and libraries seem to really come together when you start writing programs to work across networks. This chapter explores communication across the Internet, and the classes that Java provides to make this easier. It also shows you how to create a Java applet that talks to a *common gateway interface* (CGI) program, shows you how to write CGI programs in C++ and covers Java 1.1's *Java DataBase Connectivity* (JDBC) and *Remote Method Invocation* (RMI).

Chapter 16: *Design patterns*

This chapter introduces the very important and yet non-traditional "patterns" approach to program design. An example of the design evolution process is studied, starting with an initial solution and moving through the logic and process of evolving the solution to more appropriate designs. You'll see one way that a design can materialize over time.

Chapter 17: *Projects*

This chapter includes a set of projects that build on the material presented in this book, or otherwise didn't fit in earlier chapters. These projects are significantly more complex than the examples in the rest of the book, and they often demonstrate new techniques and uses of class libraries.

There are subjects that didn't seem to fit within the core of the book, and yet I find that I discuss them during seminars. These are placed in the appendices.

Appendix A: *Using non-Java code*

A totally portable Java program has serious drawbacks: speed and the inability to access platform-specific services. When you know the platform that you're running on, it's possible to dramatically speed up certain operations by making them *native methods*, which are functions that are written in another programming language (currently, only C/C++ is supported). There are other ways that Java supports non-Java code, including CORBA. This appendix gives you enough of an introduction to these features that you should be able to create simple examples that interface with non-Java code.

Appendix B: *Comparing C++ and Java*

If you're a C++ programmer, you already have the basic idea of object-oriented programming, and the syntax of Java no doubt looks very familiar to you. This makes sense because Java was derived from C++. However, there are a surprising number of differences between C++ and Java. These differences are intended to be significant improvements, and if you understand the differences you'll see why Java is such a beneficial programming language. This appendix takes you through the important features that make Java distinct from C++.

Appendix C: *Java programming guidelines*

This appendix contains suggestions to help guide you while performing low-level program design and writing code.

Appendix D: *Performance*

This will allow you to find bottlenecks and improve speed in your Java program.

Appendix E: ***A bit about garbage collection***
This appendix describes the operation and approaches that are used to implement garbage collection.

Appendix F: ***Recommended reading***
A list of some of the Java books I've found particularly useful.

Exercises

I've discovered that simple exercises are exceptionally useful during a seminar to complete a student's understanding, so you'll find a set at the end of each chapter.

Most exercises are designed to be easy enough that they can be finished in a reasonable amount of time in a classroom situation while the instructor observes, making sure that all the students are absorbing the material. Some exercises are more advanced to prevent boredom for experienced students. The majority are designed to be solved in a short time and test and polish your knowledge. Some are more challenging, but none present major challenges. (Presumably, you'll find those on your own – or more likely they'll find you).

Multimedia CD ROM

To accompany this book a Multimedia CD ROM is available separately, but this is not like the CDs that you'll usually find packaged with books. Those often only contain the source code for the book. (The code for this book is freely downloadable from the Web site www.BruceEckel.com.) This CD ROM is a separate product and contains the entire contents of the week-long "Hands-On Java" training seminar. This is more than 15 hours of lectures given by Bruce Eckel, synchronized with 500 slides of information. The seminar is based on this book so it is an ideal accompaniment.

The CD ROM contains two versions of this book:

1. A printable version identical to the one available for download.

2. For easy on-screen viewing and reference, a screen-formatted and hyperlinked version which is available exclusively on the CD-ROM. These hyperlinks include:

   • 230 chapter, section, and sub-heading links

- 3600 index links

The CD ROM contains over 600MB of content. We believe that it sets a new standard for value.

The CD ROM contains everything in the printable version of the book and everything (with the important exception of personalized attention!) from the five-day full-immersion training seminars. We believe that it sets a new standard for quality.

The CD ROM is available only by ordering directly from the Web site www.BruceEckel.com.

Source code

All the source code for this book is available as copyrighted freeware, distributed as a single package, by visiting the Web site *http://www.BruceEckel.com*. To make sure that you get the most current version, this is the official site for distribution of the code and the electronic version of the book. You can find mirrored versions of the electronic book and the code on other sites (some of these sites are found at *http://www.BruceEckel.com*), but you should check the official site to ensure that the mirrored version is actually the most recent edition. You may distribute the code in classroom and other educational situations.

The primary goal of the copyright is to ensure that the source of the code is properly cited, and to prevent you from republishing the code in print media without permission. (As long as the source is cited, using examples from the book in most media is generally not a problem.)

In each source code file you will find the following copyright notice:

```
//////////////////////////////////////////////////
// Copyright (c) Bruce Eckel, 1998
// Source code file from the book "Thinking in Java"
// All rights reserved EXCEPT as allowed by the
// following statements: You can freely use this file
// for your own work (personal or commercial),
// including modifications and distribution in
// executable form only. Permission is granted to use
// this file in classroom situations, including its
// use in presentation materials, as long as the book
// "Thinking in Java" is cited as the source.
// Except in classroom situations, you cannot copy
```

```
// and distribute this code; instead, the sole
// distribution point is http://www.BruceEckel.com
// (and official mirror sites) where it is
// freely available. You cannot remove this
// copyright and notice. You cannot distribute
// modified versions of the source code in this
// package. You cannot use this file in printed
// media without the express permission of the
// author. Bruce Eckel makes no representation about
// the suitability of this software for any purpose.
// It is provided "as is" without express or implied
// warranty of any kind, including any implied
// warranty of merchantability, fitness for a
// particular purpose or non-infringement. The entire
// risk as to the quality and performance of the
// software is with you. Bruce Eckel and the
// publisher shall not be liable for any damages
// suffered by you or any third party as a result of
// using or distributing software. In no event will
// Bruce Eckel or the publisher be liable for any
// lost revenue, profit, or data, or for direct,
// indirect, special, consequential, incidental, or
// punitive damages, however caused and regardless of
// the theory of liability, arising out of the use of
// or inability to use software, even if Bruce Eckel
// and the publisher have been advised of the
// possibility of such damages. Should the software
// prove defective, you assume the cost of all
// necessary servicing, repair, or correction. If you
// think you've found an error, please email all
// modified files with clearly commented changes to:
// Bruce@EckelObjects.com. (Please use the same
// address for non-code errors found in the book.)
//////////////////////////////////////////////////
```

You may use the code in your projects and in the classroom (including your presentation materials) as long as the copyright notice that appears in each source file is retained.

Coding standards

In the text of this book, identifiers (function, variable and class names) will be set in **bold**. Most keywords will also be set in bold, except for those keywords that are used so much that the bolding can become tedious, such as "class."

I use a particular coding style for the examples in this book. This style seems to be supported by most Java development environments. It was developed over a number of years, and was inspired by Bjarne Stroustrup's style in his original *The C++ Programming Language* (Addison-Wesley, 1991; 2nd ed.). The subject of formatting style is good for hours of hot debate, so I'll just say I'm not trying to dictate correct style via my examples; I have my own motivation for using the style that I do. Because Java is a free-form programming language, you can continue to use whatever style you're comfortable with.

The programs in this book are files that are included by the word processor in the text, directly from compiled files. Thus, the code files printed in the book should all work without compiler errors. The errors that *should* cause compile-time error messages are commented out with the comment //! so they can be easily discovered and tested using automatic means. Errors discovered and reported to the author will appear first in the distributed source code and later in updates of the book (which will also appear on the Web site *http://www.BruceEckel.com*).

Java versions

Although I test the code in this book with several different vendor implementations of Java, I generally rely on the Sun implementation as a reference when determining whether behavior is correct.

By the time you read this, Sun will have released three major versions of Java: 1.0, 1.1 and 1.2 (Sun says it will make a major release about every nine months!). Version 1.1 represents a significant change to the language and should probably have been labeled 2.0. (And if 1.1 is such a big change from 1.0, I shudder to think what will justify the number 2.0.) However, it's version 1.2 that seems to finally bring Java into the prime time, in particular where user interface tools are concerned.

This book covers versions 1.0, 1.1 and selected parts of 1.2, although in situations where a new approach is clearly superior to the old, I definitely favor the new approach, often choosing to teach the better approach and completely ignore the old approach. However, there are some cases where it's unavoidable to teach the old approach before the new, in particular with the AWT, since not only is there a lot of old Java 1.0 code out there, but some platforms still support only Java 1.0. I will try to be scrupulous about pointing out which features belong to which version.

One thing you'll notice is that I don't use the sub-revision numbers. At this writing, the released version of 1.0 from Sun was 1.02 and the released version of 1.1 was 1.1.5 (Java 1.2 was in beta). In this book I will refer to Java 1.0, Java 1.1 and Java 1.2 only, to guard against typographical errors produced by further sub-revisioning of these products.

Seminars and mentoring

My company provides five-day, hands-on, public and in-house training seminars based on the material in this book. Selected material from each chapter represents a lesson, which is followed by a monitored exercise period so each student receives personal attention. The lectures and slides for the introductory seminar are also captured on CD-ROM to provide at least some of the experience of the seminar without the travel and expense. For more information, go to:

http://www.BruceEckel.com
or email:
Bruce@EckelObjects.com

My company also provides consulting services to help guide your project through its development cycle – especially your company's first Java project.

Errors

No matter how many tricks a writer uses to detect errors, some always creep in and these often leap off the page for a fresh reader. If you discover anything you believe to be an error, please send the original source file (which you can find at ***http://www.BruceEckel.com***) with a clearly commented error (following the form shown on the Web page) and suggested correction via electronic mail to **Bruce@EckelObjects.com** so that it might be fixed in the electronic version on the Web site and in the next printing of the book. When you submit a correction, please use the following format:

1. Put "TIJ Correction" (and nothing else) as the subject line – this way my email program can route it to the right directory.

2. In the body of your email, please use the form:

```
find: one-line string to search for
```

```
comment:
multi-line comment, best starting with "here's how
I think it should read"
###
```

Where the '###' is to indicate the end of comment. This way, my correction tools can do a "find" using the original text, and your suggested correction will pop up in a window next to it.

Suggestions for additional exercises or requests to cover specific topics in the next edition are welcome. Your help is appreciated.

Note on the cover design

The cover of *Thinking in Java* is inspired by the American Arts & Crafts Movement, which began near the turn of the century and reached its zenith between 1900 and 1920. It began in England as a reaction to both the machine production of the Industrial Revolution and the highly ornamental style of the Victorian era. Arts & Crafts emphasized spare design, the forms of nature as seen in the art nouveau movement, hand-crafting, and the importance of the individual craftsperson, and yet it did not eschew the use of modern tools. There are many echoes with the situation we have today: the impending turn of the century, the evolution from the raw beginnings of the computer revolution to something more refined and meaningful to individual persons, and the emphasis on software craftsmanship rather than just manufacturing code.

I see Java in this same way: as an attempt to elevate the programmer away from an operating-system mechanic and towards being a "software craftsman."

Both the author and the book/cover designer (who have been friends since childhood) find inspiration in this movement, and both own furniture, lamps and other pieces that are either original or inspired by this period.

The other theme in this cover suggests a collection box that a naturalist might use to display the insect specimens that he or she has preserved. These insects are objects, placed within the box objects which are themselves placed within the "cover object," which illustrates the fundamental concept of aggregation in object-oriented programming. Of course, a programmer cannot help but make the association with "bugs," and here the bugs have been captured and presumably killed in a

---

Thinking in Java

specimen jar, and finally confined within a small display box, as if to imply Java's ability to find, display and subdue bugs (which is truly one of its most powerful attributes).

Acknowledgements

First of all, thanks to the Doyle Street Cohousing Community for putting up with me for the two years that it took me to write this book (and for putting up with me at all). Thanks very much to Kevin and Sonda Donovan for subletting their great place in gorgeous Crested Butte, Colorado for the summer while I worked on the book. Also thanks to the friendly residents of Crested Butte and the Rocky Mountain Biological Laboratory who made me feel so welcome. The World Gym in Emeryville and its enthusiastic staff helped keep me sane during the final months of the book.

This is my first experience using an agent, and I'm not looking back. Thanks to Claudette Moore at Moore Literary Agency for her tremendous patience and perseverance in getting me exactly what I wanted.

My first two books were published with Jeff Pepper as editor at Osborne/McGraw-Hill. Jeff appeared at the right place and the right time at Prentice-Hall and has cleared the path and made all the right things happen to make this the most pleasant publishing experience I've ever had. Thanks, Jeff – it means a lot to me.

I'm especially indebted to Gen Kiyooka and his company Digigami, who have graciously provided my Web server, and to Scott Callaway who has maintained it. This has been an invaluable aid while I was learning about the Web.

Thanks to Cay Horstmann (co-author of *Core Java*, Prentice Hall 1997), D'Arcy Smith (Symantec), and Paul Tyma (co-author of *Java Primer Plus*, The Waite Group 1996), for helping me clarify concepts in the language.

Thanks to people who have spoken in my Java track at the Software Development Conference, and students in my seminars, who ask the questions I need to hear in order to make the material more clear.

Special thanks to Larry and Tina O'Brien, who turned this book and my seminar into a teaching CD ROM. (You can find out more at *http://www.BruceEckel.com.*)

Lots of people sent in corrections and I am indebted to them all, but particular thanks go to: Kevin Raulerson (found tons of great bugs), Bob

Resendes (simply incredible), John Pinto, Joe Dante, Joe Sharp (all three were fabulous), David Combs (many grammar and clarification corrections), Dr. Robert Stephenson, Franklin Chen, Zev Griner, David Karr, Leander A. Stroschein, Steve Clark, Charles A. Lee, Austin Maher, Dennis P. Roth, Roque Oliveira, Douglas Dunn, Dejan Ristic, Neil Galarneau, David B. Malkovsky, Steve Wilkinson, and a host of others.

Prof. Ir. Marc Meurrens put in a great deal of effort to publicize and make the book available in Europe.

There have been a spate of smart technical people in my life who have become friends and have also been both influential and unusual in that they're vegetarians, do yoga and practice other forms of spiritual enhancement, which I find quite inspirational and instructional. They are Kraig Brockschmidt, Gen Kiyooka and Andrea Provaglio, who helps in the understanding of Java and programming in general in Italy.

It's not that much of a surprise to me that understanding Delphi helped me understand Java, since there are many concepts and language design decisions in common. My Delphi friends provided assistance by helping me gain insight into that marvelous programming environment. They are Marco Cantu (another Italian – perhaps being steeped in Latin gives one aptitude for programming languages?), Neil Rubenking (who used to do the yoga/vegetarian/Zen thing but discovered computers) and of course Zack Urlocker, a long-time pal whom I've traveled the world with.

My friend Richard Hale Shaw's insights and support have been very helpful (and Kim's, too). Richard and I spent many months giving seminars together and trying to work out the perfect learning experience for the attendees. Thanks also to KoAnn Vikoren, Eric Faurot, Deborah Sommers, Julie Shaw, Nicole Freeman, Cindy Blair, Barbara Hanscome, Regina Ridley, Alex Dunne, and the rest of the cast and crew at MFI.

The book design, cover design, and cover photo were created by my friend Daniel Will-Harris, noted author and designer (*http://www.Will-Harris.com*), who used to play with rub-on letters in junior high school while he awaited the invention of computers and desktop publishing, and complained of me mumbling over my algebra problems. However, I produced the camera-ready pages myself, so the typesetting errors are mine. Microsoft® Word 97 for Windows was used to write the book and to create camera-ready pages. The body typeface is *Bitstream Carmina* and the headlines are in *Bitstream Calligraph 421* (*www.bitstream.com*). The symbols at the start of each chapter are *Leonardo Extras* from P22 (*http://www.p22.com*). The cover typeface is *ITC Rennie Mackintosh*.

Thanks to the vendors who supplied me with compilers: Borland, Microsoft, Symantec, Sybase/Powersoft/Watcom, and of course, Sun.

A special thanks to all my teachers and all my students (who are my teachers as well). The most fun writing teacher was Gabrielle Rico (author of *Writing the Natural Way*, Putnam 1983). I'll always treasure the terrific week at Esalen.

The supporting cast of friends includes, but is not limited to: Andrew Binstock, Steve Sinofsky, JD Hildebrandt, Tom Keffer, Brian McElhinney, Brinkley Barr, Bill Gates at *Midnight Engineering Magazine*, Larry Constantine and Lucy Lockwood, Greg Perry, Dan Putterman, Christi Westphal, Gene Wang, Dave Mayer, David Intersimone, Andrea Rosenfield, Claire Sawyers, more Italians (Laura Fallai, Corrado, Ilsa, and Cristina Giustozzi), Chris and Laura Strand, the Almquists, Brad Jerbic, Marilyn Cvitanic, the Mabrys, the Haflingers, the Pollocks, Peter Vinci, the Robbins Families, the Moelter Families (and the McMillans), Michael Wilk, Dave Stoner, Laurie Adams, the Cranstons, Larry Fogg, Mike and Karen Sequeira, Gary Entsminger and Allison Brody, Kevin Donovan and Sonda Eastlack, Chester and Shannon Andersen, Joe Lordi, Dave and Brenda Bartlett, David Lee, the Rentschlers, the Sudeks, Dick, Patty, and Lee Eckel, Lynn and Todd, and their families. And of course, Mom and Dad.

1: Introduction to objects

Why has object-oriented programming had such a sweeping impact on the software development community?

Object-oriented programming appeals at multiple levels. For managers, it promises faster and cheaper development and maintenance. For analysts and designers, the modeling process becomes simpler and produces a clear, manageable design. For programmers, the elegance and clarity of the object model and the power of object-oriented tools and libraries makes programming a much more pleasant task, and programmers experience an increase in productivity. Everybody wins, it would seem.

If there's a downside, it is the expense of the learning curve. Thinking in objects is a dramatic departure from thinking procedurally, and the process of *designing* objects is much more challenging than procedural design, especially if you're trying to create reusable objects. In the past, a novice practitioner of object-oriented programming was faced with a choice between two daunting tasks:

1. Choose a language such as Smalltalk in which you had to learn a large library before becoming productive.

2. Choose C++ with virtually no libraries at all,[1] and struggle through the depths of the language in order to write your own libraries of objects.

It is, in fact, difficult to design objects well – for that matter, it's hard to design *anything* well. But the intent is that a relatively few experts design the best objects for others to consume. Successful OOP languages incorporate not just language syntax and a compiler, but an entire development environment *including* a significant library of well-designed, easy to use objects. Thus, the primary job of most programmers is to use existing objects to solve their application problems. The goal of this chapter is to show you what object-oriented programming is and how simple it can be.

This chapter will introduce many of the ideas of Java and object-oriented programming on a conceptual level, but keep in mind that you're not expected to be able to write full-fledged Java programs after reading this chapter. All the detailed descriptions and examples will follow throughout the course of this book.

The progress of abstraction

All programming languages provide abstractions. It can be argued that the complexity of the problems you can solve is directly related to the kind and quality of abstraction. By "kind" I mean: what is it that you are abstracting? Assembly language is a small abstraction of the underlying machine. Many so-called "imperative" languages that followed (such as FORTRAN, BASIC, and C) were abstractions of assembly language. These languages are big improvements over assembly language, but their primary abstraction still requires you to think in terms of the structure of the computer rather than the structure of the problem you are trying to solve. The programmer must establish the association between the machine model (in the "solution space") and the model of the problem

---

[1] Fortunately, this has change significantly with the advent of third-party libraries and the Standard C++ library.

that is actually being solved (in the "problem space"). The effort required to perform this mapping, and the fact that it is extrinsic to the programming language, produces programs that are difficult to write and expensive to maintain, and as a side effect created the entire "programming methods" industry.

The alternative to modeling the machine is to model the problem you're trying to solve. Early languages such as LISP and APL chose particular views of the world ("all problems are ultimately lists" or "all problems are algorithmic"). PROLOG casts all problems into chains of decisions. Languages have been created for constraint-based programming and for programming exclusively by manipulating graphical symbols. (The latter proved to be too restrictive.) Each of these approaches is a good solution to the particular class of problem they're designed to solve, but when you step outside of that domain they become awkward.

The object-oriented approach takes a step farther by providing tools for the programmer to represent elements in the problem space. This representation is general enough that the programmer is not constrained to any particular type of problem. We refer to the elements in the problem space and their representations in the solution space as "objects." (Of course, you will also need other objects that don't have problem-space analogs.) The idea is that the program is allowed to adapt itself to the lingo of the problem by adding new types of objects, so when you read the code describing the solution, you're reading words that also express the problem. This is a more flexible and powerful language abstraction than what we've had before. Thus OOP allows you to describe the problem in terms of the problem, rather than in the terms of the solution. There's still a connection back to the computer, though. Each object looks quite a bit like a little computer; it has a state, and it has operations you can ask it to perform. However, this doesn't seem like such a bad analogy to objects in the real world; they all have characteristics and behaviors.

Alan Kay summarized five basic characteristics of Smalltalk, the first successful object-oriented language and one of the languages upon which Java is based. These characteristics represent a pure approach to object-oriented programming:

1. **Everything is an object.** Think of an object as a fancy variable; it stores data, but you can also ask it to perform operations on itself by making requests. In theory, you can take any conceptual component in the problem you're trying to solve (dogs, buildings, services, etc.) and represent it as an object in your program.
2. **A program is a bunch of objects telling each other what to do by sending messages**. To make a request of an object, you "send a

message" to that object. More concretely, you can think of a message as a request to call a function that belongs to a particular object.

3. **Each object has its own memory made up of other objects**. Or, you make a new kind of object by making a package containing existing objects. Thus, you can build up complexity in a program while hiding it behind the simplicity of objects.

4. **Every object has a type**. Using the parlance, each object is an *instance* of a *class*, where "class" is synonymous with "type." The most important distinguishing characteristic of a class is "what messages can you send to it?"

5. **All objects of a particular type can receive the same messages**. This is actually a very loaded statement, as you will see later. Because an object of type circle is also an object of type shape, a circle is guaranteed to receive shape messages. This means you can write code that talks to shapes and automatically handle anything that fits the description of a shape. This *substitutability* is one of the most powerful concepts in OOP.

Some language designers have decided that object-oriented programming itself is not adequate to easily solve all programming problems, and advocate the combination of various approaches into *multiparadigm* programming languages.[2]

An object has an interface

Aristotle was probably the first to begin a careful study of the concept of type. He was known to speak of "the class of fishes and the class of birds." The concept that all objects, while being unique, are also part of a set of objects that have characteristics and behaviors in common was directly used in the first object-oriented language, Simula-67, with its fundamental keyword **class** that introduces a new type into a program (thus *class* and *type* are often used synonymously[3]).

Simula, as its name implies, was created for developing simulations such as the classic "bank teller problem." In this, you have a bunch of tellers, customers, accounts, transactions, etc. The members (elements) of each class share some commonality: every account has a balance, every teller can accept a deposit, etc. At the same time, each member has its own

---

[2] See *Multiparadigm Programming in Leda* by Timothy Budd (Addison-Wesley 1995).

[3] Some people make a distinction, stating that type determines the interface while class is a particular implementation of that interface.

---

state; each account has a different balance, each teller has a name. Thus the tellers, customers, accounts, transactions, etc. can each be represented with a unique entity in the computer program. This entity is the object, and each object belongs to a particular class that defines its characteristics and behaviors.

So, although what we really do in object-oriented programming is create new data types, virtually all object-oriented programming languages use the "class" keyword. When you see the word "type" think "class" and vice versa.

Once a type is established, you can make as many objects of that type as you like, and then manipulate those objects as the elements that exist in the problem you are trying to solve. Indeed, one of the challenges of object-oriented programming is to create a one-to-one mapping between the elements in the *problem space* (the place where the problem actually exists) and the *solution space* (the place where you're modeling that problem, such as a computer).

But how do you get an object to do useful work for you? There must be a way to make a request of that object so it will do something, such as complete a transaction, draw something on the screen or turn on a switch. And each object can satisfy only certain requests. The requests you can make of an object are defined by its *interface*, and the type is what determines the interface. The idea of type being equivalent to interface is fundamental in object-oriented programming.

A simple example might be a representation of a light bulb:

Type Name	**Light**
	on( )
Interface	**off( )**
	brighten( )
	dim( )

```
Light lt = new Light();
lt.on();
```

The name of the type/class is **Light**, and the requests that you can make of a **Light** object are to turn it on, turn it off, make it brighter or make it

---

dimmer. You create a "handle" for a **Light** simply by declaring a name (**lt**) for that identifier, and you make an object of type **Light** with the **new** keyword, assigning it to the handle with the = sign. To send a message to the object, you state the handle name and connect it to the message name with a period (dot). From the standpoint of the user of a pre-defined class, that's pretty much all there is to programming with objects.

The hidden implementation

It is helpful to break up the playing field into *class creators* (those who create new data types) and *client programmers*[4] (the class consumers who use the data types in their applications). The goal of the client programmer is to collect a toolbox full of classes to use for rapid application development. The goal of the class creator is to build a class that exposes only what's necessary to the client programmer and keeps everything else hidden. Why? If it's hidden, the client programmer can't use it, which means that the class creator can change the hidden portion at will without worrying about the impact to anyone else.

The interface establishes *what* requests you can make for a particular object. However, there must be code somewhere to satisfy that request. This, along with the hidden data, comprises the *implementation*. From a procedural programming standpoint, it's not that complicated. A type has a function associated with each possible request, and when you make a particular request to an object, that function is called. This process is often summarized by saying that you "send a message" (make a request) to an object, and the object figures out what to do with that message (it executes code).

In any relationship it's important to have boundaries that are respected by all parties involved. When you create a library, you establish a relationship with the client programmer, who is another programmer, but one who is putting together an application or using your library to build a bigger library.

If all the members of a class are available to everyone, then the client programmer can do anything with that class and there's no way to force any particular behaviors. Even though you might really prefer that the client programmer not directly manipulate some of the members of your

---

[4] I'm indebted to my friend Scott Meyers for this term.

class, without access control there's no way to prevent it. Everything's naked to the world.

There are two reasons for controlling access to members. The first is to keep client programmers' hands off portions they shouldn't touch – parts that are necessary for the internal machinations of the data type but not part of the interface that users need to solve their particular problems. This is actually a service to users because they can easily see what's important to them and what they can ignore.

The second reason for access control is to allow the library designer to change the internal workings of the structure without worrying about how it will affect the client programmer. For example, you might implement a particular class in a simple fashion to ease development, and then later decide you need to rewrite it to make it run faster. If the interface and implementation are clearly separated and protected, you can accomplish this and require only a relink by the user.

Java uses three explicit keywords and one implied keyword to set the boundaries in a class: **public**, **private**, **protected** and the implied "friendly," which is what you get if you don't specify one of the other keywords. Their use and meaning are remarkably straightforward. These *access specifiers* determine who can use the definition that follows. **public** means the following definition is available to everyone. The **private** keyword, on the other hand, means that no one can access that definition except you, the creator of the type, inside function members of that type. **private** is a brick wall between you and the client programmer. If someone tries to access a private member, they'll get a compile-time error. "Friendly" has to do with something called a "package," which is Java's way of making libraries. If something is "friendly" it's available only within the package. (Thus this access level is sometimes referred to as "package access.") **protected** acts just like **private**, with the exception that an inheriting class has access to **protected** members, but not **private** members. Inheritance will be covered shortly.

Reusing the implementation

Once a class has been created and tested, it should (ideally) represent a useful unit of code. It turns out that this reusability is not nearly so easy to achieve as many would hope; it takes experience and insight to achieve a good design. But once you have such a design, it begs to be reused.

Code reuse is arguably the greatest leverage that object-oriented programming languages provide.

The simplest way to reuse a class is to just use an object of that class directly, but you can also place an object of that class inside a new class. We call this "creating a member object." Your new class can be made up of any number and type of other objects, whatever is necessary to achieve the functionality desired in your new class. This concept is called *composition*, since you are composing a new class from existing classes. Sometimes composition is referred to as a "has-a" relationship, as in "a car has a trunk."

Composition comes with a great deal of flexibility. The *member objects* of your new class are usually private, making them inaccessible to client programmers using the class. This allows you to change those members without disturbing existing client code. You can also change the member objects *at run time*, which provides great flexibility. Inheritance, which is described next, does not have this flexibility since the compiler must place restrictions on classes created with inheritance.

Because inheritance is so important in object-oriented programming it is often highly emphasized, and the new programmer can get the idea that inheritance should be used everywhere. This can result in awkward and overcomplicated designs. Instead, you should first look to composition when creating new classes, since it is simpler and more flexible. If you take this approach, your designs will stay cleaner. It will be reasonably obvious when you need inheritance.

Inheritance: reusing the interface

By itself, the concept of an object is a convenient tool. It allows you to package data and functionality together by *concept*, so you can represent an appropriate problem-space idea rather than being forced to use the idioms of the underlying machine. These concepts are expressed in the primary idea of the programming language as a data type (using the **class** keyword).

It seems a pity, however, to go to all the trouble to create a data type and then be forced to create a brand new one that might have similar functionality. It's nicer if we can take the existing data type, clone it and make additions and modifications to the clone. This is effectively what you get with *inheritance*, with the exception that if the original class (called the *base* or *super* or *parent* class) is changed, the modified "clone" (called the *derived* or *inherited* or *sub* or *child* class) also reflects the appropriate changes. Inheritance is implemented in Java with the **extends** keyword. You make a new class and you say that it **extends** an existing class.

When you inherit you create a new type, and the new type contains not only all the members of the existing type (although the **private** ones are hidden away and inaccessible), but more importantly it duplicates the interface of the base class. That is, all the messages you can send to objects of the base class you can also send to objects of the derived class. Since we know the type of a class by the messages we can send to it, this means that the derived class *is the same type as the base class*. This type equivalence via inheritance is one of the fundamental gateways in understanding the meaning of object-oriented programming.

Since both the base class and derived class have the same interface, there must be some implementation to go along with that interface. That is, there must be a method to execute when an object receives a particular message. If you simply inherit a class and don't do anything else, the methods from the base-class interface come right along into the derived class. That means objects of the derived class have not only the same type, they also have the same behavior, which doesn't seem particularly interesting.

You have two ways to differentiate your new derived class from the original base class it inherits from. The first is quite straightforward: you simply add brand new functions to the derived class. These new functions are not part of the base class interface. This means that the base class simply didn't do as much as you wanted it to, so you add more functions. This simple and primitive use for inheritance is, at times, the perfect solution to your problem. However, you should look closely for the possibility that your base class might need these additional functions.

Overriding base-class functionality

Although the **extends** keyword implies that you are going to add new functions to the interface, that's not necessarily true. The second way to differentiate your new class is to *change* the behavior of an existing base-class function. This is referred to as *overriding* that function.

To override a function, you simply create a new definition for the function in the derived class. You're saying "I'm using the same interface function here, but I want it to do something different for my new type."

Is-a vs. is-like-a relationships

There's a certain debate that can occur about inheritance: Should inheritance override *only* base-class functions? This means that the derived type is *exactly* the same type as the base class since it has exactly the same interface. As a result, you can exactly substitute an object of the derived class for an object of the base class. This can be thought of as *pure substitution*. In a sense, this is the ideal way to treat inheritance. We often refer to the relationship between the base class and derived classes in this case as an *is-a* relationship, because you can say "a circle *is a* shape." A test for inheritance is whether you can state the is-a relationship about the classes and have it make sense.

There are times when you must add new interface elements to a derived type, thus extending the interface and creating a new type. The new type can still be substituted for the base type, but the substitution isn't perfect in a sense because your new functions are not accessible from the base type. This can be described as an *is-like-a* relationship; the new type has the interface of the old type but it also contains other functions, so you can't really say it's exactly the same. For example, consider an air conditioner. Suppose your house is wired with all the controls for cooling; that is, it has an interface that allows you to control cooling. Imagine that the air conditioner breaks down and you replace it with a heat pump, which can both heat and cool. The heat pump *is-like-an* air conditioner, but it can do more. Because your house is wired only to control cooling, it is restricted to communication with the cooling part of the new object. The interface of the new object has been extended, and the existing system doesn't know about anything except the original interface.

When you see the substitution principle it's easy to feel like that's the only way to do things, and in fact it is nice if your design works out that way. But you'll find that there are times when it's equally clear that you must add new functions to the interface of a derived class. With inspection both cases should be reasonably obvious.

Interchangeable objects with polymorphism

Inheritance usually ends up creating a family of classes, all based on the same uniform interface. We express this with an inverted tree diagram:[5]

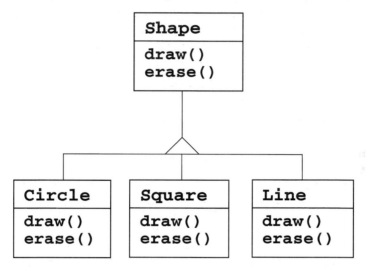

One of the most important things you do with such a family of classes is to treat an object of a derived class as an object of the base class. This is important because it means you can write a single piece of code that ignores the specific details of type and talks just to the base class. That code is then *decoupled* from type-specific information, and thus is simpler to write and easier to understand. And, if a new type – a **Triangle**, for example – is added through inheritance, the code you write will work just as well for the new type of **Shape** as it did on the existing types. Thus the program is *extensible*.

Consider the above example. If you write a function in Java:

```
void doStuff(Shape s) {
    s.erase();
    // ...
    s.draw();
```

---

[5] This uses the *Unified Notation*, which will primarily be used in this book.

```
    }
```

This function speaks to any **Shape**, so it is independent of the specific type of object it's drawing and erasing. If in some other program we use the **doStuff( )** function:

```
Circle c = new Circle();
Triangle t = new Triangle();
Line l = new Line();
doStuff(c);
doStuff(t);
doStuff(l);
```

The calls to **doStuff( )** automatically work right, regardless of the exact type of the object.

This is actually a pretty amazing trick. Consider the line:

```
doStuff(c);
```

What's happening here is that a **Circle** handle is being passed into a function that's expecting a **Shape** handle. Since a **Circle** *is* a **Shape** it can be treated as one by **doStuff( )**. That is, any message that **doStuff( )** can send to a **Shape**, a **Circle** can accept. So it is a completely safe and logical thing to do.

We call this process of treating a derived type as though it were its base type *upcasting*. The name *cast* is used in the sense of casting into a mold and the *up* comes from the way the inheritance diagram is typically arranged, with the base type at the top and the derived classes fanning out downward. Thus, casting to a base type is moving up the inheritance diagram: upcasting.

An object-oriented program contains some upcasting somewhere, because that's how you decouple yourself from knowing about the exact type you're working with. Look at the code in **doStuff( )**:

```
s.erase();
// ...
s.draw();
```

Notice that it doesn't say "If you're a **Circle**, do this, if you're a **Square**, do that, etc." If you write that kind of code, which checks for all the possible types a **Shape** can actually be, it's messy and you need to change it every time you add a new kind of **Shape**. Here, you just say "You're a shape, I know you can **erase( )** yourself, do it and take care of the details correctly."

Dynamic binding

What's amazing about the code in **doStuff( )** is that somehow the right thing happens. Calling **draw( )** for **Circle** causes different code to be executed than when calling **draw( )** for a **Square** or a **Line**, but when the **draw( )** message is sent to an anonymous **Shape**, the correct behavior occurs based on the actual type that the **Shape** handle happens to be connected to. This is amazing because when the Java compiler is compiling the code for **doStuff( )**, it cannot know exactly what types it is dealing with. So ordinarily, you'd expect it to end up calling the version of **erase( )** for **Shape**, and **draw( )** for **Shape** and not for the specific **Circle**, **Square**, or **Line**. And yet the right thing happens. Here's how it works.

When you send a message to an object even though you don't know what specific type it is, and the right thing happens, that's called *polymorphism*. The process used by object-oriented programming languages to implement polymorphism is called *dynamic binding*. The compiler and run-time system handle the details; all you need to know is that it happens and more importantly how to design with it.

Some languages require you to use a special keyword to enable dynamic binding. In C++ this keyword is **virtual**. In Java, you never need to remember to add a keyword because functions are automatically dynamically bound. So you can always expect that when you send a message to an object, the object will do the right thing, even when upcasting is involved.

Abstract base classes and interfaces

Often in a design, you want the base class to present *only* an interface for its derived classes. That is, you don't want anyone to actually create an object of the base class, only to upcast to it so that its interface can be used. This is accomplished by making that class *abstract* using the **abstract** keyword. If anyone tries to make an object of an **abstract** class, the compiler prevents them. This is a tool to enforce a particular design.

You can also use the **abstract** keyword to describe a method that hasn't been implemented yet – as a stub indicating "here is an interface function for all types inherited from this class, but at this point I don't have any implementation for it." An **abstract** method may be created only inside an **abstract** class. When the class is inherited, that method must be implemented, or the inherited class becomes **abstract** as well. Creating an **abstract** method allows you to put a method in an interface without being forced to provide a possibly meaningless body of code for that method.

The **interface** keyword takes the concept of an **abstract** class one step further by preventing any function definitions at all. The **interface** is a very useful and commonly-used tool, as it provides the perfect separation of interface and implementation. In addition, you can combine many interfaces together, if you wish. (You cannot inherit from more than one regular **class** or **abstract class**.)

Object landscapes and lifetimes

Technically, OOP is just about abstract data typing, inheritance and polymorphism, but other issues can be at least as important. The remainder of this section will cover these issues.

One of the most important factors is the way objects are created and destroyed. Where is the data for an object and how is the lifetime of the object controlled? There are different philosophies at work here. C++ takes the approach that control of efficiency is the most important issue, so it gives the programmer a choice. For maximum run-time speed, the storage and lifetime can be determined while the program is being written, by placing the objects on the stack (these are sometimes called *automatic* or *scoped* variables) or in the static storage area. This places a priority on the speed of storage allocation and release, and control of these can be very valuable in some situations. However, you sacrifice flexibility because you must know the exact quantity, lifetime and type of objects *while* you're writing the program. If you are trying to solve a more general problem such as computer-aided design, warehouse management or air-traffic control, this is too restrictive.

The second approach is to create objects dynamically in a pool of memory called the *heap*. In this approach you don't know until run time how many objects you need, what their lifetime is or what their exact type is. Those are determined at the spur of the moment while the program is running. If you need a new object, you simply make it on the heap at the point that you need it. Because the storage is managed dynamically, at run time, the amount of time required to allocate storage on the heap is significantly longer than the time to create storage on the stack. (Creating storage on the stack is often a single assembly instruction to move the stack pointer down, and another to move it back up.) The dynamic approach makes the generally logical assumption that objects tend to be complicated, so the extra overhead of finding storage and releasing that storage will not have an important impact on the creation of an object. In addition, the greater flexibility is essential to solve the general programming problem.

C++ allows you to determine whether the objects are created while you write the program or at run time to allow the control of efficiency. You might think that since it's more flexible, you'd always want to create objects on the heap rather than the stack. There's another issue, however, and that's the lifetime of an object. If you create an object on the stack or in static storage, the compiler determines how long the object lasts and can automatically destroy it. However, if you create it on the heap the compiler has no knowledge of its lifetime. A programmer has two options for destroying objects: you can determine programmatically when to destroy the object, or the environment can provide a feature called a *garbage collector* that automatically discovers when an object is no longer in use and destroys it. Of course, a garbage collector is much more convenient, but it requires that all applications must be able to tolerate the existence of the garbage collector and the other overhead for garbage collection. This does not meet the design requirements of the C++ language and so it was not included, but Java does have a garbage collector (as does Smalltalk; Delphi does not but one could be added. Third-party garbage collectors exist for C++).

The rest of this section looks at additional factors concerning object lifetimes and landscapes.

Collections and iterators

If you don't know how many objects you're going to need to solve a particular problem, or how long they will last, you also don't know how to store those objects. How can you know how much space to create for those objects? You can't, since that information isn't known until run time.

The solution to most problems in object-oriented design seems flippant: you create another type of object. The new type of object that solves this particular problem holds handles to other objects. Of course, you can do the same thing with an array, which is available in most languages. But there's more. This new object, generally called a *collection* (also called a *container*, but the AWT uses that term in a different sense so this book will use "collection"), will expand itself whenever necessary to accommodate everything you place inside it. So you don't need to know how many objects you're going to hold in a collection. Just create a collection object and let it take care of the details.

Fortunately, a good OOP language comes with a set of collections as part of the package. In C++, it's the Standard Template Library (STL). Object Pascal has collections in its Visual Component Library (VCL). Smalltalk has a very complete set of collections. Java also has collections in its standard library. In some libraries, a generic collection is considered good enough for all needs, and in others (C++ in particular) the library has different types of collections for different needs: a vector for consistent access to all elements, and a linked list for consistent insertion at all elements, for example, so you can choose the particular type that fits your needs. These may include sets, queues, hash tables, trees, stacks, etc.

All collections have some way to put things in and get things out. The way that you place something into a collection is fairly obvious. There's a function called "push" or "add" or a similar name. Fetching things out of a collection is not always as apparent; if it's an array-like entity such as a vector, you might be able to use an indexing operator or function. But in many situations this doesn't make sense. Also, a single-selection function is restrictive. What if you want to manipulate or compare a set of elements in the collection instead of just one?

The solution is an *iterator*, which is an object whose job is to select the elements within a collection and present them to the user of the iterator. As a class, it also provides a level of abstraction. This abstraction can be used to separate the details of the collection from the code that's accessing that collection. The collection, via the iterator, is abstracted to be simply a sequence. The iterator allows you to traverse that sequence without worrying about the underlying structure – that is, whether it's a vector, a linked list, a stack or something else. This gives you the flexibility to easily change the underlying data structure without disturbing the code in your program. Java began (in version 1.0 and 1.1) with a standard iterator, called **Enumeration**, for all of its collection classes. Java 1.2 has added a much more complete collection library which contains an iterator called **Iterator** that does more than the older **Enumeration**.

From the design standpoint, all you really want is a sequence that can be manipulated to solve your problem. If a single type of sequence satisfied all of your needs, there'd be no reason to have different kinds. There are two reasons that you need a choice of collections. First, collections provide different types of interfaces and external behavior. A stack has a different interface and behavior than that of a queue, which is different than that of a set or a list. One of these might provide a more flexible solution to your problem than the other. Second, different collections have different efficiencies for certain operations. The best example is a vector and a list. Both are simple sequences that can have identical interfaces and external behaviors. But certain operations can have radically different costs. Randomly accessing elements in a vector is a constant-time operation; it takes the same amount of time regardless of the element you select. However, in a linked list it is expensive to move through the list to randomly select an element, and it takes longer to find an element if it is further down the list. On the other hand, if you want to insert an element in the middle of a sequence, it's much cheaper in a list than in a vector. These and other operations have different efficiencies depending upon the underlying structure of the sequence. In the design phase, you might start with a list and, when tuning for performance, change to a vector. Because of the abstraction via iterators, you can change from one to the other with minimal impact on your code.

In the end, remember that a collection is only a storage cabinet to put objects in. If that cabinet solves all of your needs, it doesn't really matter *how* it is implemented (a basic concept with most types of objects). If you're working in a programming environment that has built-in overhead due to other factors (running under Windows, for example, or the cost of a garbage collector), then the cost difference between a vector and a linked list might not matter. You might need only one type of sequence. You can even imagine the "perfect" collection abstraction, which can automatically change its underlying implementation according to the way it is used.

The singly-rooted hierarchy

One of the issues in OOP that has become especially prominent since the introduction of C++ is whether all classes should ultimately be inherited from a single base class. In Java (as with virtually all other OOP languages) the answer is "yes" and the name of this ultimate base class is simply **Object**. It turns out that the benefits of the *singly-rooted hierarchy* are many.

All objects in a singly-rooted hierarchy have an interface in common, so they are all ultimately the same type. The alternative (provided by C++) is that you don't know that everything is the same fundamental type. From a backwards-compatibility standpoint this fits the model of C better and can be thought of as less restrictive, but when you want to do full-on object-oriented programming you must then build your own hierarchy to provide the same convenience that's built into other OOP languages. And in any new class library you acquire, some other incompatible interface will be used. It requires effort (and possibly multiple inheritance) to work the new interface into your design. Is the extra "flexibility" of C++ worth it? If you need it – if you have a large investment in C – it's quite valuable. If you're starting from scratch, other alternatives such as Java can often be more productive.

All objects in a singly-rooted hierarchy (such as Java provides) can be guaranteed to have certain functionality. You know you can perform certain basic operations on every object in your system. A singly-rooted hierarchy, along with creating all objects on the heap, greatly simplifies argument passing (one of the more complex topics in C++).

A singly-rooted hierarchy makes it much easier to implement a garbage collector. The necessary support can be installed in the base class, and the garbage collector can thus send the appropriate messages to every object in the system. Without a singly-rooted hierarchy and a system to manipulate an object via a handle, it is difficult to implement a garbage collector.

Since run-time type information is guaranteed to be in all objects, you'll never end up with an object whose type you cannot determine. This is especially important with system level operations, such as exception handling, and to allow greater flexibility in programming.

You may wonder why, if it's so beneficial, a singly-rooted hierarchy isn't it in C++. It's the old bugaboo of efficiency and control. A singly-rooted hierarchy puts constraints on your program designs, and in particular it was perceived to put constraints on the use of existing C code. These constraints cause problems only in certain situations, but for maximum flexibility there is no requirement for a singly-rooted hierarchy in C++. In Java, which started from scratch and has no backward-compatibility issues with any existing language, it was a logical choice to use the singly-rooted hierarchy in common with most other object-oriented programming languages.

Collection libraries and support for easy collection use

Because a collection is a tool that you'll use frequently, it makes sense to have a library of collections that are built in a reusable fashion, so you can take one off the shelf and plug it into your program. Java provides such a library, although it is fairly limited in Java 1.0 and 1.1 (the Java 1.2 collections library, however, satisfies most needs).

Downcasting vs. templates/generics

To make these collections reusable, they contain the one universal type in Java that was previously mentioned: **Object**. The singly-rooted hierarchy means that everything is an **Object**, so a collection that holds **Object**s can hold anything. This makes it easy to reuse.

To use such a collection, you simply add object handles to it, and later ask for them back. But, since the collection holds only **Object**s, when you add your object handle into the collection it is upcast to **Object**, thus losing its identity. When you fetch it back, you get an **Object** handle, and not a handle to the type that you put in. So how do you turn it back into something that has the useful interface of the object that you put into the collection?

Here, the cast is used again, but this time you're not casting *up* the inheritance hierarchy to a more general type, you cast *down* the hierarchy to a more specific type. This manner of casting is called *downcasting*. With upcasting, you know, for example, that a **Circle** is a type of **Shape** so it's safe to upcast, but you don't know that an **Object** is necessarily a **Circle** or a **Shape** so it's hardly safe to downcast unless you know that's what you're dealing with.

It's not completely dangerous, however, because if you downcast to the wrong thing you'll get a run-time error called an *exception*, which will be described shortly. When you fetch object handles from a collection, though, you must have some way to remember exactly what they are so you can perform a proper downcast.

Downcasting and the run-time checks require extra time for the running program, and extra effort from the programmer. Wouldn't it make sense to somehow create the collection so that it knows the types that it holds, eliminating the need for the downcast and possible mistake? The solution is *parameterized types*, which are classes that the compiler can automatically customize to work with particular types. For example, with a parameterized collection, the compiler could customize that collection so that it would accept only **Shape**s and fetch only **Shape**s.

Parameterized types are an important part of C++, partly because C++ has no singly-rooted hierarchy. In C++, the keyword that implements parameterized types is **template**. Java currently has no parameterized types since it is possible for it to get by – however awkwardly – using the singly-rooted hierarchy. At one point the word **generic** (the keyword used by Ada for its templates) was on a list of keywords that were "reserved for future implementation." Some of these seemed to have mysteriously slipped into a kind of "keyword Bermuda Triangle" and it's difficult to know what might eventually happen.

The housekeeping dilemma: who should clean up?

Each object requires resources in order to exist, most notably memory. When an object is no longer needed it must be cleaned up so that these resources are released for reuse. In simple programming situations the question of how an object is cleaned up doesn't seem too challenging: you create the object, use it for as long as it's needed, and then it should be destroyed. It's not too hard, however, to encounter situations in which the situation is more complex.

Suppose, for example, you are designing a system to manage air traffic for an airport. (The same model might also work for managing crates in a warehouse, or a video rental system, or a kennel for boarding pets.) At first it seems simple: make a collection to hold airplanes, then create a new airplane and place it in the collection for each airplane that enters the air-traffic-control zone. For cleanup, simply delete the appropriate airplane object when a plane leaves the zone.

But perhaps you have some other system to record data about the planes; perhaps data that doesn't require such immediate attention as the main controller function. Maybe it's a record of the flight plans of all the small planes that leave the airport. So you have a second collection of small planes, and whenever you create a plane object you also put it in this collection if it's a small plane. Then some background process performs operations on the objects in this collection during idle moments.

Now the problem is more difficult: how can you possibly know when to destroy the objects? When you're done with the object, some other part of the system might not be. This same problem can arise in a number of other situations, and in programming systems (such as C++) in which you must explicitly delete an object when you're done with it this can become quite complex.[6]

---

[6] Note that this is true only for objects that are created on the heap, with **new**. However, the problem described, and indeed any general programming problem, requires objects to be created on the heap.

With Java, the garbage collector is designed to take care of the problem of releasing the memory (although this doesn't include other aspects of cleaning up an object). The garbage collector "knows" when an object is no longer in use, and it then automatically releases the memory for that object. This, combined with the fact that all objects are inherited from the single root class **Object** and that you can create objects only one way, on the heap, makes the process of programming in Java much simpler than programming in C++. You have far fewer decisions to make and hurdles to overcome.

Garbage collectors
vs. efficiency and flexibility

If all this is such a good idea, why didn't they do the same thing in C++? Well of course there's a price you pay for all this programming convenience, and that price is run-time overhead. As mentioned before, in C++ you can create objects on the stack, and in this case they're automatically cleaned up (but you don't have the flexibility of creating as many as you want at run-time). Creating objects on the stack is the most efficient way to allocate storage for objects and to free that storage. Creating objects on the heap can be much more expensive. Always inheriting from a base class and making all function calls polymorphic also exacts a small toll. But the garbage collector is a particular problem because you never quite know when it's going to start up or how long it will take. This means that there's an inconsistency in the rate of execution of a Java program, so you can't use it in certain situations, such as when the rate of execution of a program is uniformly critical. (These are generally called *real time* programs, although not all real-time programming problems are this stringent.)[7]

The designers of the C++ language, trying to woo C programmers (and most successfully, at that), did not want to add any features to the language that would impact the speed or the use of C++ in any situation where C might be used. This goal was realized, but at the price of greater complexity when programming in C++. Java is simpler than C++, but the tradeoff is in efficiency and sometimes applicability. For a significant portion of programming problems, however, Java is often the superior choice.

---

[7] According to a technical reader for this book, one existing real-time Java implementation (www.newmonics.com) has guarantees on garbage collector performance.

Exception handling: dealing with errors

Ever since the beginning of programming languages, error handling has been one of the most difficult issues. Because it's so hard to design a good error-handling scheme, many languages simply ignore the issue, passing the problem on to library designers who come up with halfway measures that can work in many situations but can easily be circumvented, generally by just ignoring them. A major problem with most error-handling schemes is that they rely on programmer vigilance in following an agreed-upon convention that is not enforced by the language. If the programmer is not vigilant, which is often if they are in a hurry, these schemes can easily be forgotten.

Exception handling wires error handling directly into the programming language and sometimes even the operating system. An exception is an object that is "thrown" from the site of the error and can be "caught" by an appropriate *exception handler* designed to handle that particular type of error. It's as if exception handling is a different, parallel path of execution that can be taken when things go wrong. And because it uses a separate execution path, it doesn't need to interfere with your normally-executing code. This makes that code simpler to write since you aren't constantly forced to check for errors. In addition, a thrown exception is unlike an error value that's returned from a function or a flag that's set by a function in order to indicate an error condition, These can be ignored. An exception cannot be ignored so it's guaranteed to be dealt with at some point. Finally, exceptions provide a way to reliably recover from a bad situation. Instead of just exiting you are often able to set things right and restore the execution of a program, which produces much more robust programs.

Java's exception handling stands out among programming languages, because in Java, exception-handling was wired in from the beginning and you're *forced* to use it. If you don't write your code to properly handle exceptions, you'll get a compile-time error message. This guaranteed consistency makes error-handling much easier.

It's worth noting that exception handling isn't an object-oriented feature, although in object-oriented languages the exception is normally represented with an object. Exception handling existed before object-oriented languages.

Multithreading

A fundamental concept in computer programming is the idea of handling more than one task at a time. Many programming problems require that the program be able to stop what it's doing, deal with some other problem and return to the main process. The solution has been approached in many ways. Initially, programmers with low-level knowledge of the machine wrote interrupt service routines and the suspension of the main process was initiated through a hardware interrupt. Although this worked well, it was difficult and non-portable, so it made moving a program to a new type of machine slow and expensive.

Sometimes interrupts are necessary for handling time-critical tasks, but there's a large class of problems in which you're simply trying to partition the problem into separately-running pieces so that the whole program can be more responsive. Within a program, these separately-running pieces are called *threads* and the general concept is called *multithreading*. A common example of multithreading is the user interface. By using threads, a user can press a button and get a quick response rather than being forced to wait until the program finishes its current task.

Ordinarily, threads are just a way to allocate the time of a single processor. But if the operating system supports multiple processors, each thread can be assigned to a different processor and they can truly run in parallel. One of the convenient features of multithreading at the language level is that the programmer doesn't need to worry about whether there are many processors or just one. The program is logically divided into threads and if the machine has more than one processor then the program runs faster, without any special adjustments.

All this makes threading sound pretty simple. There is a catch: shared resources. If you have more than one thread running that's expecting to access the same resource you have a problem. For example, two processes can't simultaneously send information to a printer. To solve the problem, resources that can be shared, such as the printer, must be locked while they are being used. So a thread locks a resource, completes its task and then releases the lock so that someone else can use the resource.

Java's threading is built into the language, which makes a complicated subject much simpler. The threading is supported on an object level, so one thread of execution is represented by one object. Java also provides limited resource locking. It can lock the memory of any object (which is, after all, one kind of shared resource) so that only one thread can use it at a time. This is accomplished with the **synchronized** keyword. Other types of resources must be locked explicitly by the programmer, typically by creating an object to represent the lock that all threads must check before accessing that resource.

Persistence

When you create an object, it exists for as long as you need it, but under no circumstances does it exist when the program terminates. While this makes sense at first, there are situations in which it would be incredibly useful if an object could exist and hold its information even while the program *wasn't* running. Then the next time you started the program, the object would be there and it would have the same information it had the previous time the program was running. Of course you can get a similar effect now by writing the information to a file or to a database, but in the spirit of making everything an object it would be quite convenient to be able to declare an object *persistent* and have all the details taken care of for you.

Java 1.1 provides support for "lightweight persistence," which means that you can easily store objects on disk and later retrieve them. The reason it's "lightweight" is that you're still forced to make explicit calls to do the storage and retrieval. In some future release more complete support for persistence might appear.

Java and the Internet

If Java is, in fact, yet another computer programming language, you may question why it is so important and why it is being promoted as a revolutionary step in computer programming. The answer isn't immediately obvious if you're coming from a traditional programming perspective. Although Java will solve traditional stand-alone programming problems, the reason it is important is that it will also solve programming problems on the World Wide Web.

What is the Web?

The Web can seem a bit of a mystery at first, with all this talk of "surfing," "presence" and "home pages." There has even been a growing reaction against "Internet-mania," questioning the economic value and outcome of such a sweeping movement. It's helpful to step back and see what it really is, but to do this you must understand client/server systems, another aspect of computing that's full of confusing issues.

Client/Server computing

The primary idea of a client/server system is that you have a central repository of information – some kind of data, typically in a database – that you want to distribute on demand to some set of people or machines. A key to the client/server concept is that the repository of information is *centrally located* so that it can be changed and so that those changes will propagate out to the information consumers. Taken together, the information repository, the software that distributes the information and the machine(s) where the information and software reside is called the *server*. The software that resides on the remote machine, and that communicates with the server, fetches the information, processes it, and displays it on the remote machine is called the *client*.

The basic concept of client/server computing, then, is not so complicated. The problems arise because you have a single server trying to serve many clients at once. Generally a database management system is involved so the designer "balances" the layout of data into tables for optimal use. In addition, systems often allow a client to insert new information into a server. This means you must ensure that one client's new data doesn't walk over another client's new data, or that data isn't lost in the process of adding it to the database. (This is called *transaction processing*.) As client software changes, it must be built, debugged and installed on the client machines, which turns out to be more complicated and expensive than you might think. It's especially problematic to support multiple types of computers and operating systems. Finally, there's the all-important performance issue: you might have hundreds of clients making requests of your server at any one time, and so any small delay is crucial. To minimize latency, programmers work hard to offload processing tasks, often to the client machine but sometimes to other machines at the server site using so-called *middleware*. (Middleware is also used to improve maintainability.)

So the simple idea of distributing information to people has so many layers of complexity in implementing it that the whole problem can seem hopelessly enigmatic. And yet it's crucial: client/server computing accounts for roughly half of all programming activities. It's responsible for everything from taking orders and credit-card transactions to the distribution of any kind of data – stock market, scientific, government – you name it. What we've come up with in the past is individual solutions to individual problems, inventing a new solution each time. These were hard to create and hard to use and the user had to learn a new interface for each one. The entire client/server problem needs to be solved in a big way.

The Web as a giant server

The Web is actually one giant client-server system. It's a bit worse than that, since you have all the servers and clients coexisting on a single network at once. You don't need to know that, since all you care about is connecting to and interacting with one server at a time (even though you might be hopping around the world in your search for the correct server).

Initially it was a simple one-way process. You made a request of a server and it handed you a file, which your machine's browser software (i.e. the client) would interpret by formatting onto your local machine. But in short order people began wanting to do more than just deliver pages from a server. They wanted full client/server capability so that the client could feed information back to the server, for example, to do database lookups on the server, to add new information to the server or to place an order (which required more security than the original systems offered). These are the changes we've been seeing in the development of the Web.

The Web browser was a big step forward: the concept that one piece of information could be displayed on any type of computer without change. However, browsers were still rather primitive and rapidly bogged down by the demands placed on them. They weren't particularly interactive and tended to clog up both the server and the Internet because any time you needed to do something that required programming you had to send information back to the server to be processed. It could take many seconds or minutes to find out you had misspelled something in your request. Since the browser was just a viewer it couldn't perform even the simplest computing tasks. (On the other hand, it was safe, since it couldn't execute any programs on your local machine that contained bugs or viruses.)

To solve this problem, different approaches have been taken. To begin with, graphics standards have been enhanced to allow better animation and video within browsers. The remainder of the problem can be solved only by incorporating the ability to run programs on the client end, under the browser. This is called *client-side programming*.

Client-side programming[8]

The Web's initial server-browser design provided for interactive content, but the interactivity was completely provided by the server. The server produced static pages for the client browser, which would simply interpret and display them. Basic HTML contains simple mechanisms for data gathering: text-entry boxes, check boxes, radio boxes, lists and drop-down lists, as well as a button that can only be programmed to reset the data on the form or "submit" the data on the form back to the server. This submission passes through the *Common Gateway Interface* (CGI) provided on all Web servers. The text within the submission tells CGI what to do with it. The most common action is to run a program located on the server in a directory that's typically called "cgi-bin." (If you watch the address window at the top of your browser when you push a button on a Web page, you can sometimes see "cgi-bin" within all the gobbledygook there.) These programs can be written in most languages. Perl is a common choice because it is designed for text manipulation and is interpreted, so it can be installed on any server regardless of processor or operating system.

Many powerful Web sites today are built strictly on CGI, and you can in fact do nearly anything with it. The problem is response time. The response of a CGI program depends on how much data must be sent as well as the load on both the server and the Internet. (On top of this, starting a CGI program tends to be slow.) The initial designers of the Web did not foresee how rapidly this bandwidth would be exhausted for the kinds of applications people developed. For example, any sort of dynamic graphing is nearly impossible to perform with consistency because a GIF file must be created and moved from the server to the client for each version of the graph. And you've no doubt had direct experience with something as simple as validating the data on an input form. You press the submit button on a page; the data is shipped back to the server; the server starts a CGI program that discovers an error, formats an HTML page informing you of the error and sends the page back to you; you must then back up a page and try again. Not only is this slow, it's not elegant.

The solution is client-side programming. Most machines that run Web browsers are powerful engines capable of doing vast work, and with the

---

[8] The material in this section is adapted from an article by the author that originally appeared on Mainspring, at *www.mainspring.com*. Used with permission.

original static HTML approach they are sitting there, just idly waiting for the server to dish up the next page. Client-side programming means that the Web browser is harnessed to do whatever work it can, and the result for the user is a much speedier and more interactive experience at your Web site.

The problem with discussions of client-side programming is that they aren't very different from discussions of programming in general. The parameters are almost the same, but the platform is different: a Web browser is like a limited operating system. In the end, it's still programming and this accounts for the dizzying array of problems and solutions produced by client-side programming. The rest of this section provides an overview of the issues and approaches in client-side programming.

Plug-ins

One of the most significant steps forward in client-side programming is the development of the plug-in. This is a way for a programmer to add new functionality to the browser by downloading a piece of code that plugs itself into the appropriate spot in the browser. It tells the browser "from now on you can perform this new activity." (You need to download the plug-in only once.) Some fast and powerful behavior is added to browsers via plug-ins, but writing a plug-in is not a trivial task and isn't something you'd want to do as part of the process of building a particular site. The value of the plug-in for client-side programming is that it allows an expert programmer to develop a new language and add that language to a browser *without the permission of the browser manufacturer*. Thus, plug-ins provide the back door that allows the creation of new client-side programming languages (although not all languages are implemented as plug-ins).

Scripting languages

Plug-ins resulted in an explosion of scripting languages. With a scripting language you embed the source code for your client-side program directly into the HTML page and the plug-in that interprets that language is automatically activated while the HTML page is being displayed. Scripting languages tend to be reasonably simple to understand, and because they are simply text that is part of an HTML page they load very quickly as part of the single server hit required to procure that page. The trade-off is that your code is exposed for everyone to see (and steal) but generally you aren't doing amazingly sophisticated things with scripting languages so it's not too much of a hardship.

This points out that scripting languages are really intended to solve specific types of problems, primarily the creation of richer and more interactive graphical user interfaces (GUIs). However, a scripting language might solve 80 percent of the problems encountered in client-side programming. Your problems might very well fit completely within that 80 percent, and since scripting languages tend to be easier and faster to develop, you should probably consider a scripting language before looking at a more involved solution such as Java or ActiveX programming.

The most commonly-discussed scripting languages are JavaScript (which has nothing to do with Java; it's named that way just to grab some of Java's marketing momentum), VBScript (which looks like Visual Basic) and Tcl/Tk, which comes from the popular cross-platform GUI-building language. There are others out there and no doubt more in development.

JavaScript is probably the most commonly supported. It comes built into both Netscape Navigator and the Microsoft Internet Explorer (IE). In addition, there are probably more JavaScript books out than for the other languages, and some tools automatically create pages using JavaScript. However, if you're already fluent in Visual Basic or Tcl/Tk, you'll be more productive using those scripting languages rather than learning a new one. (You'll have your hands full dealing with the Web issues already.)

Java

If a scripting language can solve 80 percent of the client-side programming problems, what about the other 20 percent – the "really hard stuff?" The most popular solution today is Java. Not only is it a powerful programming language built to be secure, cross-platform and international, but Java is being continuously extended to provide language features and libraries that elegantly handle problems that are difficult in traditional programming languages, such as multithreading, database access, network programming and distributed computing. Java allows client-side programming via the *applet*.

An applet is a mini-program that will run only under a Web browser. The applet is downloaded automatically as part of a Web page (just as, for example, a graphic is automatically downloaded). When the applet is activated it executes a program. This is part of its beauty – it provides you with a way to automatically distribute the client software from the server at the time the user needs the client software, and no sooner. They get the latest version of the client software without fail and without difficult re-installation. Because of the way Java is designed, the programmer needs to create only a single program, and that program automatically works with all computers that have browsers with built-in Java interpreters. (This safely includes the vast majority of machines.) Since Java is a full-fledged programming language, you can do as much work as possible on the client before and after making requests of the server. For example, you won't need to send a request form across the Internet to discover that you've gotten a date or some other parameter wrong, and your client computer can quickly do the work of plotting data instead of waiting for the server to make a plot and ship a graphic image back to you. Not only do you get the immediate win of speed and responsiveness, but the general network traffic and load upon servers can be reduced, preventing the entire Internet from slowing down.

One advantage a Java applet has over a scripted program is that it's in compiled form, so the source code isn't available to the client. On the other hand, a Java applet can be decompiled without too much trouble, and hiding your code is often not an important issue anyway. Two other factors can be important. As you will see later in the book, a compiled Java applet can comprise many modules and take multiple server "hits" (accesses) to download. (In Java 1.1 this is minimized by Java archives, called JAR files, that allow all the required modules to be packaged together for a single download.) A scripted program will just be integrated into the Web page as part of its text (and will generally be smaller and reduce server hits). This could be important to the responsiveness of your Web site. Another factor is the all-important learning curve. Regardless of what you've heard, Java is not a trivial language to learn. If you're a Visual Basic programmer, moving to VBScript will be your fastest solution and since it will probably solve most typical client/server problems you might be hard pressed to justify learning Java. If you're experienced with a scripting language you will certainly benefit from looking at JavaScript or VBScript before committing to Java, since they might fit your needs handily and you'll be more productive sooner.

ActiveX

To some degree, the competitor to Java is Microsoft's ActiveX, although it takes a completely different approach. ActiveX is originally a Windows-only solution, although it is now being developed via an independent consortium to become cross-platform. Effectively, ActiveX says "if your program connects to its environment just so, it can be dropped into a Web page and run under a browser that supports ActiveX." (IE directly supports ActiveX and Netscape does so using a plug-in.) Thus, ActiveX does not constrain you to a particular language. If, for example, you're already an experienced Windows programmer using a language such as C++, Visual Basic, or Borland's Delphi, you can create ActiveX components with almost no changes to your programming knowledge. ActiveX also provides a path for the use of legacy code in your Web pages.

Security

Automatically downloading and running programs across the Internet can sound like a virus-builder's dream. ActiveX especially brings up the thorny issue of security in client-side programming. If you click on a Web site, you might automatically download any number of things along with the HTML page: GIF files, script code, compiled Java code, and ActiveX components. Some of these are benign; GIF files can't do any harm, and scripting languages are generally limited in what they can do. Java was also designed to run its applets within a "sandbox" of safety, which prevents it from writing to disk or accessing memory outside the sandbox.

ActiveX is at the opposite end of the spectrum. Programming with ActiveX is like programming Windows – you can do anything you want. So if you click on a page that downloads an ActiveX component, that component might cause damage to the files on your disk. Of course, programs that you load onto your computer that are not restricted to running inside a Web browser can do the same thing. Viruses downloaded from Bulletin-Board Systems (BBSs) have long been a problem, but the speed of the Internet amplifies the difficulty.

The solution seems to be "digital signatures," whereby code is verified to show who the author is. This is based on the idea that a virus works because its creator can be anonymous, so if you remove the anonymity individuals will be forced to be responsible for their actions. This seems like a good plan because it allows programs to be much more functional, and I suspect it will eliminate malicious mischief. If, however, a program has an unintentional bug that's destructive it will still cause problems.

The Java approach is to prevent these problems from occurring, via the sandbox. The Java interpreter that lives on your local Web browser examines the applet for any untoward instructions as the applet is being loaded. In particular, the applet cannot write files to disk or erase files (one of the mainstays of the virus). Applets are generally considered to be safe, and since this is essential for reliable client-server systems, any bugs that allow viruses are rapidly repaired. (It's worth noting that the browser software actually enforces these security restrictions, and some browsers allow you to select different security levels to provide varying degrees of access to your system.)

You might be skeptical of this rather draconian restriction against writing files to your local disk. For example, you may want to build a local database or save data for later use offline. The initial vision seemed to be that eventually everyone would be online to do anything important, but that was soon seen to be impractical (although low-cost "Internet appliances" might someday satisfy the needs of a significant segment of users). The solution is the "signed applet" that uses public-key encryption to verify that an applet does indeed come from where it claims it does. A signed applet can then go ahead and trash your disk, but the theory is that since you can now hold the applet creator accountable they won't do vicious things. Java 1.1 provides a framework for digital signatures so that you will eventually be able to allow an applet to step outside the sandbox if necessary.

Digital signatures have missed an important issue, which is the speed that people move around on the Internet. If you download a buggy program and it does something untoward, how long will it be before you discover the damage? It could be days or even weeks. And by then, how will you track down the program that's done it (and what good will it do at that point?).

Internet vs. Intranet

The Web is the most general solution to the client/server problem, so it makes sense that you can use the same technology to solve a subset of the problem, in particular the classic client/server problem within a company. With traditional client/server approaches you have the problem of multiple different types of client computers, as well as the difficulty of installing new client software, both of which are handily solved with Web browsers and client-side programming. When Web technology is used for an information network that is restricted to a particular company, it is referred to as an *Intranet*. Intranets provide much greater security than the Internet, since you can physically control access to the servers within your company. In terms of training, it seems that once people understand the general concept of a browser it's much easier for them to deal with differences in the way pages and applets look, so the learning curve for new kinds of systems seems to be reduced.

The security problem brings us to one of the divisions that seems to be automatically forming in the world of client-side programming. If your program is running on the Internet, you don't know what platform it will be working under and you want to be extra careful that you don't disseminate buggy code. You need something cross-platform and secure, like a scripting language or Java.

If you're running on an Intranet, you might have a different set of constraints. It's not uncommon that your machines could all be Intel/Windows platforms. On an Intranet, you're responsible for the quality of your own code and can repair bugs when they're discovered. In addition, you might already have a body of legacy code that you've been using in a more traditional client/server approach, whereby you must physically install client programs every time you do an upgrade. The time wasted in installing upgrades is the most compelling reason to move to browsers because upgrades are invisible and automatic. If you are involved in such an Intranet, the most sensible approach to take is ActiveX rather than trying to recode your programs in a new language.

When faced with this bewildering array of solutions to the client-side programming problem, the best plan of attack is a cost-benefit analysis. Consider the constraints of your problem and what would be the fastest way to get to your solution. Since client-side programming is still programming, it's always a good idea to take the fastest development approach for your particular situation. This is an aggressive stance to prepare for inevitable encounters with the problems of program development.

Server-side programming

This whole discussion has ignored the issue of server-side programming. What happens when you make a request of a server? Most of the time the request is simply "send me this file." Your browser then interprets the file in some appropriate fashion: as an HTML page, a graphic image, a Java applet, a script program, etc. A more complicated request to a server generally involves a database transaction. A common scenario involves a request for a complex database search, which the server then formats into an HTML page and sends to you as the result. (Of course, if the client has more intelligence via Java or a scripting language, the raw data can be sent and formatted at the client end, which will be faster and less load on the server.) Or you might want to register your name in a database when you join a group or place an order, which will involve changes to that database. These database requests must be processed via some code on the server side, which is generally referred to as *server-side programming*. Traditionally, server-side programming has been performed using Perl and CGI scripts, but more sophisticated systems have been appearing. These include Java-based Web servers that allow you to perform all your server-side programming in Java by writing what are called *servlets*.

A separate arena: applications

Most of the brouhaha over Java has been about applets. Java is actually a general-purpose programming language that can solve any type of problem, at least in theory. And as pointed out previously, there might be more effective ways to solve most client/server problems. When you move out of the applet arena (and simultaneously release the restrictions, such as the one against writing to disk) you enter the world of general-purpose applications that run standalone, without a Web browser, just like any ordinary program does. Here, Java's strength is not only in its portability, but also its programmability. As you'll see throughout this book, Java has many features that allow you to create robust programs in a shorter period than with previous programming languages.

Be aware that this is a mixed blessing. You pay for the improvements through slower execution speed (although there is significant work going on in this area). Like any language, Java has built-in limitations that might make it inappropriate to solve certain types of programming problems. Java is a rapidly-evolving language, however, and as each new release comes out it becomes more and more attractive for solving larger sets of problems.

Analysis and Design

The object-oriented paradigm is a new and different way of thinking about programming and many folks have trouble at first knowing how to approach a project. Now that you know that everything is supposed to be an object, you can create a "good" design, one that will take advantage of all the benefits that OOP has to offer.

Books on OOP analysis and design are coming out of the woodwork. Most of these books are filled with lots of long words, awkward prose and important-sounding pronouncements.[9] I come away thinking the book would be better as a chapter or at the most a very short book and feeling annoyed that this process couldn't be described simply and directly. (It disturbs me that people who purport to specialize in

---

[9] The best introduction is still Grady Booch's *Object-Oriented Design with Applications*, 2nd edition, Wiley & Sons 1996. His insights are clear and his prose is straightforward, although his notations are needlessly complex for most designs. (You can easily get by with a subset.)

managing complexity have such trouble writing clear and simple books.) After all, the whole point of OOP is to make the process of software development easier, and although it would seem to threaten the livelihood of those of us who consult because things are complex, why not make it simple? So, hoping I've built a healthy skepticism within you, I shall endeavor to give you my own perspective on analysis and design in as few paragraphs as possible.

Staying on course

While you're going through the development process, the most important issue is this: don't get lost. It's easy to do. Most of these methodologies are designed to solve the largest of problems. (This makes sense; these are the especially difficult projects that justify calling in that author as consultant, and justify the author's large fees.) Remember that most projects don't fit into that category, so you can usually have a successful analysis and design with a relatively small subset of what a methodology recommends. But some sort of process, no matter how limited, will generally get you on your way in a much better fashion than simply beginning to code.

That said, if you're looking at a methodology that contains tremendous detail and suggests many steps and documents, it's still difficult to know when to stop. Keep in mind what you're trying to discover:

1. What are the objects? (How do you partition your project into its component parts?)

2. What are their interfaces? (What messages do you need to be able to send to each object?)

If you come up with nothing more than the objects and their interfaces then you can write a program. For various reasons you might need more descriptions and documents than this, but you can't really get away with any less.

The process can be undertaken in four phases, and a phase 0 which is just the initial commitment to using some kind of structure.

Phase 0: Let's make a plan

The first step is to decide what steps you're going to have in your process. It sounds simple (in fact, *all* of this sounds simple) and yet, often, people don't even get around to phase one before they start coding. If your plan is "let's jump in and start coding," fine. (Sometimes that's appropriate when you have a well-understood problem.) At least agree that this is the plan.

You might also decide at this phase that some additional process structure is necessary but not the whole nine yards. Understandably enough, some programmers like to work in "vacation mode" in which no structure is imposed on the process of developing their work: "It will be done when it's done." This can be appealing for awhile, but I've found that having a few milestones along the way helps to focus and galvanize your efforts around those milestones instead of being stuck with the single goal of "finish the project." In addition, it divides the project into more bite-sized pieces and make it seem less threatening.

When I began to study story structure (so that I will someday write a novel) I was initially resistant to the idea, feeling that when I wrote I simply let it flow onto the page. What I found was that when I wrote about computers the structure was simple enough so I didn't need to think much about it, but I was still structuring my work, albeit only semi-consciously in my head. So even if you think that your plan is to just start coding, you still go through the following phases while asking and answering certain questions.

Phase 1: What are we making?

In the previous generation of program design (procedural design), this would be called "creating the *requirements analysis* and *system specification*." These, of course, were places to get lost: intimidatingly-named documents that could become big projects in their own right. Their intention was good, however. The requirements analysis says "Make a list of the guidelines we will use to know when the job is done and the customer is satisfied." The system specification says "Here's a description of *what* the program will do (not *how*) to satisfy the requirements." The requirements analysis is really a contract between you and the customer (even if the customer works within your company or is some other object or system). The system specification is a top-level exploration into the problem and in some sense a discovery of whether it can be done and how long it will take. Since both of these will require consensus among people, I think it's best to keep them as bare as possible – ideally, to lists and basic diagrams – to save time. You might have other constraints that require you to expand them into bigger documents.

It's necessary to stay focused on the heart of what you're trying to accomplish in this phase: determine what the system is supposed to do. The most valuable tool for this is a collection of what are called "use-cases." These are essentially descriptive answers to questions that start with "What does the system do if …" For example, "What does the auto-teller do if a customer has just deposited a check within 24 hours and there's not enough in the account without the check to provide the desired withdrawal?" The use-case then describes what the auto-teller does in that case.

You try to discover a full set of use-cases for your system, and once you've done that you've got the core of what the system is supposed to do. The nice thing about focusing on use-cases is that they always bring you back to the essentials and keep you from drifting off into issues that aren't critical for getting the job done. That is, if you have a full set of use-cases you can describe your system and move onto the next phase. You probably won't get it all figured out perfectly at this phase, but that's OK. Everything will reveal itself in the fullness of time, and if you demand a perfect system specification at this point you'll get stuck.

It helps to kick-start this phase by describing the system in a few paragraphs and then looking for nouns and verbs. The nouns become the objects and the verbs become the methods in the object interfaces. You'll be surprised at how useful a tool this can be; sometimes it will accomplish the lion's share of the work for you.

Although it's a black art, at this point some kind of scheduling can be quite useful. You now have an overview of what you're building so you'll probably be able to get some idea of how long it will take. A lot of factors come into play here: if you estimate a long schedule then the company might not decide to build it, or a manager might have already decided how long the project should take and will try to influence your estimate. But it's best to have an honest schedule from the beginning and deal with the tough decisions early. There have been a lot of attempts to come up with accurate scheduling techniques (like techniques to predict the stock market), but probably the best approach is to rely on your experience and intuition. Get a gut feeling for how long it will really take, then double that and add 10 percent. Your gut feeling is probably correct; you *can* get something working in that time. The "doubling" will turn that into something decent, and the 10 percent will deal with final polishing and details. However you want to explain it, and regardless of the moans and manipulations that happen when you reveal such a schedule, it just seems to work out that way.

Phase 2: How will we build it?

In this phase you must come up with a design that describes what the classes look like and how they will interact. A useful diagramming tool that has evolved over time is the *Unified Modeling Language* (UML). You can get the specification for UML at *www.rational.com*. UML can also be helpful as a descriptive tool during phase 1, and some of the diagrams you create there will probably show up unmodified in phase 2. You don't need to use UML, but it can be helpful, especially if you want to put a diagram up on the wall for everyone to ponder, which is a good idea. An alternative to UML is a textual description of the objects and their interfaces (as I described in *Thinking in C++*), but this can be limiting.

The most successful consulting experiences I've had when coming up with an initial design involves standing in front of a team, who hadn't built an OOP project before, and drawing objects on a whiteboard. We talked about how the objects should communicate with each other, and erased some of them and replaced them with other objects. The team (who knew what the project was supposed to do) actually created the design; they "owned" the design rather than having it given to them. All I was doing was guiding the process by asking the right questions, trying out the assumptions and taking the feedback from the team to modify those assumptions. The true beauty of the process was that the team learned how to do object-oriented design not by reviewing abstract examples, but by working on the one design that was most interesting to them at that moment: theirs.

You'll know you're done with phase 2 when you have described the objects and their interfaces. Well, most of them – there are usually a few that slip through the cracks and don't make themselves known until phase 3. But that's OK. All you are concerned with is that you eventually discover all of your objects. It's nice to discover them early in the process but OOP provides enough structure so that it's not so bad if you discover them later.

Phase 3: Let's build it!

If you're reading this book you're probably a programmer, so now we're at the part you've been trying to get to. By following a plan – no matter how simple and brief – and coming up with design structure before coding, you'll discover that things fall together far more easily than if you dive in and start hacking, and this provides a great deal of satisfaction. Getting code to run and do what you want is fulfilling, even like some kind of drug if you look at the obsessive behavior of some programmers. But it's my experience that coming up with an elegant solution is deeply satisfying at an entirely different level; it feels closer to art than technology. And elegance always pays off; it's not a frivolous pursuit. Not only does it give you a program that's easier to build and debug, but it's also easier to understand and maintain, and that's where the financial value lies.

After you build the system and get it running, it's important to do a reality check, and here's where the requirements analysis and system specification comes in. Go through your program and make sure that all the requirements are checked off, and that all the use-cases work the way they're described. Now you're done. Or are you?

Phase 4: Iteration

This is the point in the development cycle that has traditionally been called "maintenance," a catch-all term that can mean everything from "getting it to work the way it was really supposed to in the first place" to "adding features that the customer forgot to mention before" to the more traditional "fixing the bugs that show up" and "adding new features as the need arises." So many misconceptions have been applied to the term "maintenance" that it has taken on a slightly deceiving quality, partly because it suggests that you've actually built a pristine program and that all you need to do is change parts, oil it and keep it from rusting. Perhaps there's a better term to describe what's going on.

The term is *iteration*. That is, "You won't get it right the first time, so give yourself the latitude to learn and to go back and make changes." You might need to make a lot of changes as you learn and understand the problem more deeply. The elegance you'll produce if you iterate until you've got it right will pay off, both in the short and the long run.

What it means to "get it right" isn't just that the program works according to the requirements and the use-cases. It also means that the internal structure of the code makes sense to you, and feels like it fits together well, with no awkward syntax, oversized objects or ungainly exposed bits of code. In addition, you must have some sense that the program structure will survive the changes that it will inevitably go through during its lifetime, and that those changes can be made easily and cleanly. This is no small feat. You must not only understand what you're building, but also how the program will evolve (what I call the *vector of change*). Fortunately, object-oriented programming languages are particularly adept at supporting this kind of continuing modification – the boundaries created by the objects are what tend to keep the structure from breaking down. They are also what allow you to make changes that would seem drastic in a procedural program without causing earthquakes throughout your code. In fact, support for iteration might be the most important benefit of OOP.

With iteration, you create something that at least approximates what you think you're building, and then you kick the tires, compare it to your requirements and see where it falls short. Then you can go back and fix it by redesigning and re-implementing the portions of the program that didn't work right.[10] You might actually need to solve the problem, or an aspect of the problem, several times before you hit on the right solution. (A study of *Design Patterns*, described in Chapter 16, is usually helpful here.)

Iteration also occurs when you build a system, see that it matches your requirements and then discover it wasn't actually what you wanted. When you see the system, you realize you want to solve a different problem. If you think this kind of iteration is going to happen, then you owe it to yourself to build your first version as quickly as possible so you can find out if it's what you want.

Iteration is closely tied to *incremental development*. Incremental development means that you start with the core of your system and implement it as a framework upon which to build the rest of the system piece by piece. Then you start adding features one at a time. The trick to this is in designing a framework that will accommodate all the features you plan to add to it. (See Chapter 16 for more insight into this issue.) The advantage is that once you get the core framework working, each feature you add is like a small project in itself rather than part of a big project. Also, new features that are incorporated later in the development or maintenance phases can be added more easily. OOP supports incremental development because if your program is designed well, your increments will turn out to be discreet objects or groups of objects.

Plans pay off

Of course you wouldn't build a house without a lot of carefully-drawn plans. If you build a deck or a dog house, your plans won't be so elaborate but you'll still probably start with some kind of sketches to guide you on your way. Software development has gone to extremes. For a long time, people didn't have much structure in their development, but

---

[10] This is something like "rapid prototyping," where you were supposed to build a quick-and-dirty version so that you could learn about the system, and then throw away your prototype and build it right. The trouble with rapid prototyping is that people didn't throw away the prototype, but instead built upon it. Combined with the lack of structure in procedural programming, this often leads to messy systems that are expensive to maintain.

then big projects began failing. In reaction, we ended up with methodologies that had an intimidating amount of structure and detail. These were too scary to use – it looked like you'd spend all your time writing documents and no time programming. (This was often the case.) I hope that what I've shown you here suggests a middle path – a sliding scale. Use an approach that fits your needs (and your personality). No matter how minimal you choose to make it, *some* kind of plan will make a big improvement in your project as opposed to no plan at all. Remember that, by some estimates, over 50 percent of projects fail.

Java vs. C++?

Java looks a lot like C++, and so naturally it would seem that C++ will be replaced by Java. But I'm starting to question this logic. For one thing, C++ still has some features that Java doesn't, and although there have been a lot of promises about Java someday being as fast or faster than C++ the breakthroughs haven't happened yet (it's getting steadily faster, but still hasn't touched C++). Also, there seems to be a perking interest in C++ in many fields, so I don't think that language is going away any time soon. (Languages seem to hang around. Speaking at one of my "Intermediate/Advanced Java Seminars," Allen Holub asserted that the two most commonly-used languages are Rexx and COBOL, in that order.)

I'm beginning to think that the strength of Java lies in a slightly different arena than that of C++. C++ is a language that doesn't try to fit a mold. Certainly it has been adapted in a number of ways to solve particular problems, especially with tools like Microsoft Visual C++ and Borland C++ Builder (a particular favorite of mine). These combine libraries, component models and code generation tools to solve the problem of developing windowed end-user applications (for Microsoft Windows). And yet, what do the vast majority of Windows developers use? Microsoft's Visual Basic (VB). This despite the fact that VB produces the kind of code that becomes unmanageable when the program is only a few pages long (and syntax that can be positively mystifying). As successful and popular as VB is, from a language design viewpoint it's a mountain of hacks. It would be nice to have the ease and power of VB without the resulting unmanageable code. And that's where I think Java will shine: as the "next VB." You may or may not shudder to hear this, but think about it: so much of Java is designed to make it easy for the programmer to solve application-level problems like networking and cross-platform UI, and yet it has a language design intended to allow the creation of very large and flexible bodies of code. Add to this the fact that Java has the most robust type checking and error-handling systems I've ever seen in a language and you have the makings of a significant leap forward in programming productivity.

Should you use Java instead of C++ for your project? Other than Web applets, there are two issues to consider. First, if you want to use a lot of existing libraries (and you'll certainly get a lot of productivity gains there), or if you have an existing C or C++ code base, Java might slow your development down rather than speeding it up. If you're developing all your code primarily from scratch, then the simplicity of Java over C++ will shorten your development time.

The biggest issue is speed. Interpreted Java has been slow, even 20 to 50 times slower than C in the original Java interpreters. This has improved quite a bit over time, but it will still remain an important number. Computers are about speed; if it wasn't significantly faster to do something on a computer then you'd do it by hand. (I've even heard it suggested that you start with Java, to gain the short development time, then use a tool and support libraries to translate your code to C++, if you need faster execution speed.)

The key to making Java feasible for most non-Web development projects is the appearance of speed improvements like so-called "just-in time" (JIT) compilers and possibly even native code compilers (two of which exist at this writing). Of course, native-code compilers will eliminate the touted cross-platform execution of the compiled programs, but they will also bring the speed of the executable closer to that of C and C++. And cross compiling programs in Java should be a lot easier than doing so in C or C++. (In theory, you just recompile, but that promise has been made before for other languages.)

You can find comparisons of Java and C++, observations about Java realities and practicality and coding guidelines in the appendices.

2: Everything
is an object

Although it is based on C++, Java is more of a "pure" object-oriented language.

Both C++ and Java are hybrid languages, but in Java the designers felt that the hybridization was not as important as it was in C++. A hybrid language allows multiple programming styles; the reason C++ is hybrid is to support backward compatibility with the C language. Because C++ is a superset of the C language, it includes many of that language's undesirable features which can make some aspects of C++ overly complicated.

The Java language assumes that you want to do only object-oriented programming. This means that before you can begin you must shift your mindset into an object-oriented world (unless it's already there). The benefit of this initial effort is the ability to program in a language that is simpler to learn and to use than many other OOP languages. In this chapter we'll see the basic components of a Java program and we'll learn that everything in Java is an object, even a Java program.

You manipulate objects with handles

Each programming language has its own means of manipulating data. Sometimes the programmer must constantly be aware of what type of manipulation is going on. Are you manipulating the object directly or are you dealing with some kind of indirect representation (a pointer in C or C++) that must be treated with a special syntax?

All this is simplified in Java. You treat everything as an object, so there is a single consistent syntax that you use everywhere. Although you *treat* everything as an object, the identifier you manipulate is actually a "handle" to an object. (You might see this called a *reference* or even a pointer in other discussions of Java.) You might imagine this scene as a television (the object) with your remote control (the handle). As long as you're holding this handle, you have a connection to the television, but when someone says "change the channel" or "lower the volume," what you're manipulating is the handle, which in turn modifies the object. If you want to move around the room and still control the television, you take the remote/handle with you, not the television.

Also, the remote control can stand on its own, with no television. That is, just because you have a handle doesn't mean there's necessarily an object connected to it. So if you want to hold a word or sentence, you create a **String** handle:

```
String s;
```

But here you've created *only* the handle, not an object. If you decided to send a message to **s** at this point, you'll get an error (at run-time) because **s** isn't actually attached to anything (there's no television). A safer practice, then, is always to initialize a handle when you create it:

```
String s = "asdf";
```

However, this uses a special case: strings can be initialized with quoted text. Normally, you must use a more general type of initialization for objects.

Thinking in Java

You must create all the objects

When you create a handle, you want to connect it with a new object. You do so, in general, with the **new** keyword. **new** says, "Make me a new one of these objects." So in the above example, you can say:

```
String s = new String("asdf");
```

Not only does this mean "Make me a new **String**," but it also gives information about *how* to make the **String** by supplying an initial character string.

Of course, **String** is not the only type that exists. Java comes with a plethora of ready-made types. What's more important is that you can create your own types. In fact, that's the fundamental activity in Java programming, and it's what you'll be learning about in the rest of this book.

Where storage lives

It's useful to visualize some aspects of how things are laid out while the program is running, in particular how memory is arranged. There are six different places to store data:

1. **Registers**. This is the fastest storage because it exists in a place different than that of other storage: inside the processor. However, the number of registers is severely limited, so registers are allocated by the compiler according to its needs. You don't have direct control, nor do you see any evidence in your programs that registers even exist.

2. **The stack**. This lives in the general RAM (random-access memory) area, but has direct support from the processor via its *stack pointer*. The stack pointer is moved down to create new memory and moved up to release that memory. This is an extremely fast and efficient way to allocate storage, second only to registers. The Java compiler must know, while it is creating the program, the exact size and lifetime of all the data that is stored on the stack, because it must generate the code to move the stack pointer up and down. This constraint places limits on the flexibility of your programs, so while

some Java storage exists on the stack – in particular, object handles – Java objects are not placed on the stack.

3. **The heap**. This is a general-purpose pool of memory (also in the RAM area) where all Java objects live. The nice thing about the heap is that, unlike the stack, the compiler doesn't need to know how much storage it needs to allocate from the heap or how long that storage must stay on the heap. Thus, there's a great deal of flexibility in using storage on the heap. Whenever you need to create an object, you simply write the code to create it using **new** and the storage is allocated on the heap when that code is executed. And of course there's a price you pay for this flexibility: it takes more time to allocate heap storage.

4. **Static storage**. "Static" is used here in the sense of "in a fixed location" (although it's also in RAM). Static storage contains data that is available for the entire time a program is running. You can use the **static** keyword to specify that a particular element of an object is static, but Java objects themselves are never placed in static storage.

5. **Constant storage**. Constant values are often placed directly in the program code, which is safe since they can never change. Sometimes constants are cordoned off by themselves so that they can be optionally placed in read-only memory (ROM).

6. **Non-RAM storage**. If data lives completely outside a program it can exist while the program is not running, outside the control of the program. The two primary examples of this are *streamed objects*, in which objects are turned into streams of bytes, generally to be sent to another machine, and *persistent objects*, in which the objects are placed on disk so they will hold their state even when the program is terminated. The trick with these types of storage is turning the objects into something that can exist on the other medium, and yet can be resurrected into a regular RAM-based object when necessary. Java 1.1 provides support for *lightweight persistence*, and future versions of Java might provide more complete solutions for persistence.

Special case: primitive types

There is a group of types that gets special treatment; you can think of these as "primitive" types that you use quite often in your programming. The reason for the special treatment is that to create an object with **new**, especially a small, simple variable, isn't very efficient because **new** places objects on the heap. For these types Java falls back on the approach taken by C and C++. That is, instead of creating the variable using **new**, an "automatic" variable is created that *is not a handle*. The variable holds the value, and it's placed on the stack so it's much more efficient.

Java determines the size of each primitive type. These sizes don't change from one machine architecture to another as they do in most languages. This size invariance is one reason Java programs are so portable.

Primitive type	Size	Minimum	Maximum	Wrapper type
boolean	1–bit	–	–	**Boolean**
char	16–bit	Unicode 0	Unicode $2^{16} - 1$	**Character**
byte	8–bit	-128	$+127$	**Byte**[1]
short	16–bit	-2^{15}	$+2^{15} - 1$	**Short**[1]
int	32–bit	-2^{31}	$+2^{31} - 1$	**Integer**
long	64–bit	-2^{63}	$+2^{63} - 1$	**Long**
float	32–bit	IEEE754	IEEE754	**Float**
double	64–bit	IEEE754	IEEE754	**Double**
void	–	–	–	**Void**[1]

All numeric types are signed, so don't go looking for unsigned types.

The primitive data types also have "wrapper" classes for them. That means that if you want to make a non-primitive object on the heap to represent that primitive type, you use the associated wrapper. For example:

```
char c = 'x';
Character C = new Character(c);
```

or you could also use:

```
Character C = new Character('x');
```

The reasons for doing this will be shown in a later chapter.

High-precision numbers

Java 1.1 has added two classes for performing high-precision arithmetic: **BigInteger** and **BigDecimal**. Although these approximately fit into the same category as the "wrapper" classes, neither one has a primitive analogue.

---

[1] In Java version 1.1 only, not in 1.0.

Both classes have methods that provide analogues for the operations that you perform on primitive types. That is, you can do anything with a **BigInteger** or **BigDecimal** that you can with an **int** or **float**, it's just that you must use method calls instead of operators. Also, since there's more involved, the operations will be slower. You're exchanging speed for accuracy.

BigInteger supports arbitrary-precision integers. This means that you can accurately represent integral values of any size without losing any information during operations.

BigDecimal is for arbitrary-precision fixed-point numbers; you can use these for accurate monetary calculations, for example.

Consult your online documentation for details about the constructors and methods you can call for these two classes.

Arrays in Java

Virtually all programming languages support arrays. Using arrays in C and C++ is perilous because those arrays are only blocks of memory. If a program accesses the array outside of its memory block or uses the memory before initialization (common programming errors) there will be unpredictable results.[2]

One of the primary goals of Java is safety, so many of the problems that plague programmers in C and C++ are not repeated in Java. A Java array is guaranteed to be initialized and cannot be accessed outside of its range. The range checking comes at the price of having a small amount of memory overhead on each array as well as verifying the index at run time, but the assumption is that the safety and increased productivity is worth the expense.

When you create an array of objects, you are really creating an array of handles, and each of those handles is automatically initialized to a special value with its own keyword: **null**. When Java sees **null**, it recognizes that the handle in question isn't pointing to an object. You must assign an object to each handle before you use it, and if you try to use a handle that's still **null**, the problem will be reported at run-time. Thus, typical array errors are prevented in Java.

---

[2] In C++ you should often use the safer containers in the Standard Template Library as an alternative to arrays.

You can also create an array of primitives. Again, the compiler guarantees initialization because it zeroes the memory for that array.

Arrays will be covered in detail in later chapters.

You never need to destroy an object

In most programming languages, the concept of the lifetime of a variable occupies a significant portion of the programming effort. How long does the variable last? If you are supposed to destroy it, when should you? Confusion over variable lifetimes can lead to a lot of bugs, and this section shows how Java greatly simplifies the issue by doing all the cleanup work for you.

Scoping

Most procedural languages have the concept of *scope*. This determines both the visibility and lifetime of the names defined within that scope. In C, C++ and Java, scope is determined by the placement of curly braces {}. So for example:

```
{
    int x = 12;
    /* only x available */
    {
        int q = 96;
        /* both x & q available */
    }
    /* only x available */
    /* q "out of scope" */
}
```

A variable defined within a scope is available only to the end of that scope.

Indentation makes Java code easier to read. Since Java is a free form language, the extra spaces, tabs and carriage returns do not affect the resulting program.

Note that you *cannot* do the following, even though it is legal in C and C++:

```
{
  int x = 12;
  {
    int x = 96; /* illegal */
  }
}
```

The compiler will announce that the variable **x** has already been defined. Thus the C and C++ ability to "hide" a variable in a larger scope is not allowed because the Java designers thought that it led to confusing programs.

Scope of objects

Java objects do not have the same lifetimes as primitives. When you create a Java object using **new**, it hangs around past the end of the scope. Thus if you use:

```
{
  String s = new String("a string");
} /* end of scope */
```

the handle **s** vanishes at the end of the scope. However, the **String** object that **s** was pointing to is still occupying memory. In this bit of code, there is no way to access the object because the only handle to it is out of scope. In later chapters you'll see how the handle to the object can be passed around and duplicated during the course of a program.

It turns out that because objects created with **new** stay around for as long as you want them, a whole slew of programming problems simply vanish in C++ and Java. The hardest problems seem to occur in C++ because you don't get any help from the language in making sure that the objects are available when they're needed. And more importantly, in C++ you must make sure that you destroy the objects when you're done with them.

That brings up an interesting question. If Java leaves the objects lying around, what keeps them from filling up memory and halting your program? This is exactly the kind of problem that would occur in C++. This is where a bit of magic happens. Java has a *garbage collector*, which looks at all the objects that were created with **new** and figures out which ones are not being referenced anymore. Then it releases the memory for those objects, so the memory can be used for new objects. This means that you never need to worry about reclaiming memory yourself. You simply create objects, and when you no longer need them they will go away by themselves. This eliminates a certain class of programming problem: the so-called "memory leak," in which a programmer forgets to release memory.

Creating new data types: class

If everything is an object, what determines how a particular class of object looks and behaves? Put another way, what establishes the *type* of an object? You might expect there to be a keyword called "type" and that certainly would have made sense. Historically, however, most object-oriented languages have used the keyword **class** to mean "I'm about to tell you what a new type of object looks like." The **class** keyword (which is so common that it will not be emboldened throughout the book) is followed by the name of the new type. For example:

```
class ATypeName { /* class body goes here */ }
```

This introduces a new type, so you can now create an object of this type using **new**:

```
ATypeName a = new ATypeName();
```

In **ATypeName**, the class body consists only of a comment (the stars and slashes and what is inside, which will be discussed later in this chapter) so there is not too much that you can do with it. In fact, you cannot tell it to do much of anything (that is, you cannot send it any interesting messages) until you define some methods for it.

Fields and methods

When you define a class (and all you do in Java is define classes, make objects of those classes and send messages to those objects), you can put two types of elements in your class: data members (sometimes called *fields*) and member functions (typically called *methods*). A data member is an object (that you communicate with via its handle) of any type. It can also be one of the primitive types (which isn't a handle). If it is a handle to an object, you must initialize that handle to connect it to an actual object (using **new**, as seen earlier) in a special function called a *constructor* (described fully in Chapter 4). If it is a primitive type you can initialize it directly at the point of definition in the class. (As you'll see later, handles can also be initialized at the point of definition.)

Each object keeps its own storage for its data members; the data members are not shared among objects. Here is an example of a class with some data members:

```
class DataOnly {
    int i;
    float f;
    boolean b;
}
```

This class doesn't *do* anything, but you can create an object:

```
DataOnly d = new DataOnly();
```

You can assign values to the data members, but you must first know how to refer to a member of an object. This is accomplished by stating the name of the object handle, followed by a period (dot), followed by the name of the member inside the object (**objectHandle.member**). For example:

```
d.i = 47;
d.f = 1.1f;
d.b = false;
```

It is also possible that your object might contain other objects that contain data you'd like to modify. For this, you just keep "connecting the dots." For example:

```
myPlane.leftTank.capacity = 100;
```

The **DataOnly** class cannot do much of anything except hold data, because it has no member functions (methods). To understand how those work, you must first understand *arguments* and *return values*, which will be described shortly.

Default values for primitive members

When a primitive data type is a member of a class, it is guaranteed to get a default value if you do not initialize it:

Primitive type	Default
Boolean	**false**
Char	**'\u0000' (null)**
byte	**(byte)0**
short	**(short)0**
int	**0**

Primitive type	Default
long	**0L**
float	**0.0f**
double	**0.0d**

Note carefully that the default values are what Java guarantees when the variable is used *as a member of a class*. This ensures that member variables of primitive types will always be initialized (something C++ doesn't do), reducing a source of bugs.

However, this guarantee doesn't apply to "local" variables – those that are not fields of a class. Thus, if within a function definition you have:

```
int x;
```

Then **x** will get some random value (as in C and C++); it will not automatically be initialized to zero. You are responsible for assigning an appropriate value before you use **x**. If you forget, Java definitely improves on C++: you get a compile-time error telling you the variable might not have been initialized. (Many C++ compilers will warn you about uninitialized variables, but in Java these are errors.)

Methods, arguments and return values

Up until now, the term *function* has been used to describe a named subroutine. The term that is more commonly used in Java is *method*, as in "a way to do something." If you want, you can continue thinking in terms of functions. It's really only a syntactic difference, but from now on "method" will be used in this book rather than "function."

Methods in Java determine the messages an object can receive. In this section you will learn how simple it is to define a method.

The fundamental parts of a method are the name, the arguments, the return type, and the body. Here is the basic form:

```
returnType methodName( /* argument list */ ) {
  /* Method body */
}
```

The return type is the type of the value that pops out of the method after you call it. The method name, as you might imagine, identifies the method. The argument list gives the types and names for the information you want to pass into the method.

Methods in Java can be created only as part of a class. A method can be called only for an object,[3] and that object must be able to perform that method call. If you try to call the wrong method for an object, you'll get an error message at compile time. You call a method for an object by naming the object followed by a period (dot), followed by the name of the method and its argument list, like this: **objectName.methodName(arg1, arg2, arg3)**. For example, suppose you have a method **f( )** that takes no arguments and returns a value of type **int**. Then, if you have an object called **a** for which **f( )** can be called, you can say this:

```
int x = a.f();
```

The type of the return value must be compatible with the type of **x**.

This act of calling a method is commonly referred to as *sending a message to an object*. In the above example, the message is **f( )** and the object is **a**. Object-oriented programming is often summarized as simply "sending messages to objects."

The argument list

The method argument list specifies what information you pass into the method. As you might guess, this information – like everything else in Java – takes the form of objects. So, what you must specify in the argument list are the types of the objects to pass in and the name to use for each one. As in any situation in Java where you seem to be handing objects around, you are actually passing handles.[4] The type of the handle must be correct, however. If the argument is supposed to be a **String**, what you pass in must be a string.

Consider a method that takes a string as its argument. Here is the definition, which must be placed within a class definition for it to compile:

---

[3] **static** methods, which you'll learn about soon, can be called *for the class*, without an object.

[4] With the usual exception of the aforementioned "special" data types **boolean, char, byte, short, int, long, float,** and **double**. In general, though, you pass objects, which really means you pass handles to objects.

```
int storage(String s) {
  return s.length() * 2;
}
```

This method tells you how many bytes are required to hold the information in a particular **String**. (Each **char** in a **String** is 16 bits, or two bytes, long, to support Unicode characters.) The argument is of type **String** and is called **s**. Once **s** is passed into the method, you can treat it just like any other object. (You can send messages to it.) Here, the **length( )** method is called, which is one of the methods for **Strings**; it returns the number of characters in a string.

You can also see the use of the **return** keyword, which does two things. First, it means "leave the method, I'm done." Second, if the method produces a value, that value is placed right after the **return** statement. In this case, the return value is produced by evaluating the expression **s.length( ) * 2**.

You can return any type you want, but if you don't want to return anything at all, you do so by indicating that the method returns **void**. Here are some examples:

```
boolean flag() { return true; }
float naturalLogBase() { return 2.718; }
void nothing() { return; }
void nothing2() {}
```

When the return type is **void**, then the **return** keyword is used only to exit the method, and is therefore unnecessary when you reach the end of the method. You can return from a method at any point, but if you've given a non-**void** return type then the compiler will ensure that you return the appropriate type of value regardless of where you return.

At this point, it can look like a program is just a bunch of objects with methods that take other objects as arguments and send messages to those other objects. That is indeed much of what goes on, but in the following chapter you'll learn how to do the detailed low-level work by making decisions within a method. For this chapter, sending messages will suffice.

Building a Java program

There are several other issues you must understand before seeing your first Java program.

Name visibility

A problem in any programming language is the control of names. If you use a name in one module of the program, and another programmer uses the same name in another module, how do you distinguish one name from another and prevent the two names from "clashing"? In C this is a particular problem because a program is often an unmanageable sea of names. C++ classes (on which Java classes are based) nest functions within classes so they cannot clash with function names nested within other classes. However, C++ still allowed global data and global functions, so clashing was still possible. To solve this problem, C++ introduced *namespaces* using additional keywords.

Java was able to avoid all of this by taking a fresh approach. To produce an unambiguous name for a library, the specifier used is not unlike an Internet domain name. In fact, the Java creators want you to use your Internet domain name in reverse since those are guaranteed to be unique. Since my domain name is **BruceEckel.com**, my utility library of foibles would be named **com.bruceeckel.utility.foibles**. After your reversed domain name, the dots are intended to represent subdirectories.

In Java 1.0 and Java 1.1 the domain extension **com**, **edu**, **org**, **net**, etc., was capitalized by convention, so the library would appear: **COM.bruceeckel.utility.foibles**. Partway through the development of Java 1.2, however, it was discovered that this caused problems and so now the entire package name is lowercase.

This mechanism in Java means that all of your files automatically live in their own namespaces, and each class within a file automatically has a unique identifier. (Class names within a file must be unique, of course.) So you do not need to learn special language features to solve this problem – the language takes care of it for you.

Using other components

Whenever you want to use a predefined class in your program, the compiler must know how to locate it. Of course, the class might already exist in the same source code file that it's being called from. In that case, you simply use the class – even if the class doesn't get defined until later in the file. Java eliminates the "forward referencing" problem so you don't need to think about it.

What about a class that exists in some other file? You might think that the compiler should be smart enough to simply go and find it, but there is a problem. Imagine that you want to use a class of a particular name,

---

but the definition for that class exists in more than one file. Or worse, imagine that you're writing a program, and as you're building it you add a new class to your library that conflicts with the name of an existing class.

To solve this problem, you must eliminate all potential ambiguities. This is accomplished by telling the Java compiler exactly what classes you want using the **import** keyword. **import** tells the compiler to bring in a *package*, which is a library of classes. (In other languages, a library could consist of functions and data as well as classes, but remember that all code in Java must be written inside a class.)

Most of the time you'll be using components from the standard Java libraries that come with your compiler. With these, you don't need to worry about long, reversed domain names; you just say, for example:

```
import java.util.Vector;
```

to tell the compiler that you want to use Java's **Vector** class. However, **util** contains a number of classes and you might want to use several of them without declaring them all explicitly. This is easily accomplished by using '*' to indicate a wildcard:

```
import java.util.*;
```

It is more common to import a collection of classes in this manner than to import classes individually.

The **static** keyword

Ordinarily, when you create a class you are describing how objects of that class look and how they will behave. You don't actually get anything until you create an object of that class with **new**, and at that point data storage is created and methods become available.

But there are two situations in which this approach is not sufficient. One is if you want to have only one piece of storage for a particular piece of data, regardless of how many objects are created, or even if no objects are created. The other is if you need a method that isn't associated with any particular object of this class. That is, you need a method that you can call even if no objects are created. You can achieve both of these effects with the **static** keyword. When you say something is **static**, it means that data or method is not tied to any particular object instance of that class. So even if you've never created an object of that class you can call a **static** method or access a piece of **static** data. With ordinary, non-**static** data and methods you must create an object and use that object to access the data or method, since non-**static** data and methods must know the particular object they are working with. Of course, since **static** methods don't need any objects to be created before they are used, they cannot *directly* access non-**static** members or methods by simply calling those other members without referring to a named object (since non-**static** members and methods must be tied to a particular object).

Some object-oriented languages use the terms *class data* and *class methods*, meaning that the data and methods exist only for the class as a whole, and not for any particular objects of the class. Sometimes the Java literature uses these terms too.

To make a data member or method **static**, you simply place the keyword before the definition. For example, this produces a **static** data member and initializes it:

```
class StaticTest {
    static int i = 47;
}
```

Now even if you make two **StaticTest** objects, there will still be only one piece of storage for **StaticTest.i.** Both objects will share the same **i.** Consider:

```
StaticTest st1 = new StaticTest();
StaticTest st2 = new StaticTest();
```

At this point, both **st1.i** and **st2.i** have the same value of 47 since they refer to the same piece of memory.

There are two ways to refer to a **static** variable. As indicated above, you can name it via an object, by saying, for example, **st2.i.** You can also refer to it directly through its class name, something you cannot do with a non-static member. (This is the preferred way to refer to a **static** variable since it emphasizes that variable's **static** nature.)

```
StaticTest.i++;
```

The **++** operator increments the variable. At this point, both **st1.i** and **st2.i** will have the value 48.

Similar logic applies to static methods. You can refer to a static method either through an object as you can with any method, or with the special additional syntax **classname.method( )**. You define a static method in a similar way:

```
class StaticFun {
```

```
        static void incr() { StaticTest.i++; }
    }
```

You can see that the **StaticFun** method **incr( )** increments the **static** data **i**. You can call **incr( )** in the typical way, through an object:

```
    StaticFun sf = new StaticFun();
    sf.incr();
```

Or, because **incr( )** is a static method, you can call it directly through its class:

```
    StaticFun.incr();
```

While **static**, when applied to a data member, definitely changes the way the data is created (one for each class vs. the non-**static** one for each object), when applied to a method it's not so dramatic. An important use of **static** for methods is to allow you to call that method without creating an object. This is essential, as we will see, in defining the **main( )** method that is the entry point for running an application.

Like any method, a **static** method can create or use named objects of its type, so a **static** method is often used as a "shepherd" for a flock of instances of its own type.

Your first Java program

Finally, here's the program.[5] It prints out information about the system that it's running on using various methods of the **System** object from the Java standard library. Note that an additional style of comment is introduced here: the '//', which is a comment until the end of the line:

---

[5] Some programming environments will flash programs up on the screen and close them before you've had a chance to see the results. You can put in the following bit of code at the end of **main( )** to pause the output:

```
    try {
        Thread.currentThread().sleep(5 * 1000);
    } catch(InterruptedException e) {}
    }
```

This will pause the output for five seconds. This code involves concepts that will not be introduced until much later in the book, so you won't understand it until then, but it will do the trick.

```
// Property.java
import java.util.*;

public class Property {
  public static void main(String[] args) {
    System.out.println(new Date());
    Properties p = System.getProperties();
    p.list(System.out);
    System.out.println("--- Memory Usage:");
    Runtime rt = Runtime.getRuntime();
    System.out.println("Total Memory = "
                       + rt.totalMemory()
                       + " Free Memory = "
                       + rt.freeMemory());
  }
}
```

At the beginning of each program file, you must place the **import** statement to bring in any extra classes you'll need for the code in that file. Note that it is "extra." That's because there's a certain library of classes that are automatically brought into every Java file: **java.lang**. Start up your Web browser and look at the documentation from Sun. (If you haven't downloaded it from *java.sun.com* or otherwise installed the Java documentation, do so now). If you look at the **packages.html** file, you'll see a list of all the different class libraries that come with Java. Select **java.lang**. Under "Class Index" you'll see a list of all the classes that are part of that library. Since **java.lang** is implicitly included in every Java code file, these classes are automatically available. In the list, you'll see **System** and **Runtime**, which are used in **Property.java**. There's no **Date** class listed in **java.lang**, which means you must import another library to use that. If you don't know the library where a particular class is, or if you want to see all of the classes, you can select "Class Hierarchy" in the Java documentation. In a Web browser, this takes awhile to construct, but you can find every single class that comes with Java. Then you can use the browser's "find" function to find **Date**. When you do you'll see it listed as **java.util.Date**, which lets you know that it's in the **util** library and that you must **import java.util.*** in order to use **Date**.

If you look at the documentation starting from the **packages.html** file (which I've set in my Web browser as the default starting page), select **java.lang** and then **System**. You'll see that the **System** class has several fields, and if you select **out** you'll discover that it's a **static PrintStream** object. Since it's **static** you don't need to create anything. The **out** object is always there and you can just use it. What you can do with this **out** object is determined by the type it is: a **PrintStream**. Conveniently, **PrintStream** is shown in the description as a hyperlink, so if you click on that you'll see a list of all the methods you can call for **PrintStream**. There are quite a few and these will be covered later in the book. For now all we're interested in is **println( )**, which in effect means "print out what I'm giving you to the console and end with a new line." Thus, in any Java program you write you can say **System.out.println("things")** whenever you want to print something to the console.

The name of the class is the same as the name of the file. When you're creating a stand-alone program such as this one, one of the classes in the file must have the same name as the file. (The compiler complains if you don't do this.) That class must contain a method called **main( )** with the signature shown:

```
public static void main(String[] args) {
```

The **public** keyword means that the method is available to the outside world (described in detail in Chapter 5). The argument to **main( )** is an array of **String** objects. The **args** won't be used in this program, but they need to be there because they hold the arguments invoked on the command line.

The first line of the program is quite interesting:

```
System.out.println(new Date());
```

Consider the argument: a **Date** object is being created just to send its value to **println( )**. As soon as this statement is finished, that **Date** is unnecessary, and the garbage collector can come along and get it anytime. We don't need to worry about cleaning it up.

The second line calls **System.getProperties( )**. If you consult the online documentation using your Web browser, you'll see that **getProperties( )** is a **static** method of class **System**. Because it's **static**, you don't need to create any objects in order to call the method; a **static** method is always available whether an object of its class exists or not. When you call **getProperties( )**, it produces the system properties as an object of class **Properties**. The handle that comes back is stored in a **Properties** handle called **p**. In line three, you can see that the **Properties** object has a method called **list( )** that sends its entire contents to a **PrintStream** object that you pass as an argument.

The fourth and sixth lines in **main( )** are typical print statements. Note that to print multiple **String** values, we simply separate them with '**+**' signs. However, there's something strange going on here. The '**+**' sign doesn't mean addition when it's used with **String** objects. Normally, you wouldn't ascribe any meaning to '**+**' when you think of strings. However, the Java **String** class is blessed with something called "operator overloading." That is, the '**+**' sign, only when used with **String** objects, behaves differently from the way it does with everything else. For **String**s, it means "concatenate these two strings."

But that's not all. If you look at the statement:

```
System.out.println("Total Memory = "
                + rt.totalMemory()
                + " Free Memory = "
                + rt.freeMemory());
```

totalMemory( ) and **freeMemory( )** return *numerical values*, and not **String** objects. What happens when you "add" a numerical value to a **String**? The compiler sees the problem and magically calls a method that turns that numerical value (**int**, **float**, etc.) into a **String**, which can then be "added" with the plus sign. This *automatic type conversion* also falls into the category of operator overloading.

Much of the Java literature states vehemently that operator overloading (a feature in C++) is bad, and yet here it is! However, this is wired into the compiler, only for **String** objects, and you can't overload operators for any of the code you write.

The fifth line in **main( )** creates a **Runtime** object by calling the **static** method **getRuntime( )** for the class **Runtime**. What's returned is a handle to a **Runtime** object; whether this is a static object or one created with **new** doesn't need to concern you, since you can use the objects without worrying about who's responsible for cleaning them up. As shown, the **Runtime** object can tell you information about memory usage.

Comments and embedded documentation

There are two types of comments in Java. The first is the traditional C-style comment that was inherited by C++. These comments begin with a /* and continue, possibly across many lines, until a */. Note that many programmers will begin each line of a continued comment with a *, so you'll often see:

```
/*  This is
 *   A comment that continues
 *   Across lines
 */
```

Remember, however, that everything inside the /* and */ is ignored so it's no different to say:

```
/*  This is a comment that
continues across lines */
```

The second form of comment comes from C++. It is the single-line comment, which starts at a // and continues until the end of the line. This type of comment is convenient and commonly used because it's easy. You don't need to hunt on the keyboard to find / and then * (you just press the same key twice), and you don't need to close the comment. So you will often see:

```
// this is a one-line comment
```

Comment documentation

One of the thoughtful parts of the Java language is that the designers didn't consider writing code to be the only important activity – they also thought about documenting it. Possibly the biggest problem with documenting code has been maintaining that documentation. If the documentation and the code are separate, it becomes a hassle to change the documentation every time you change the code. The solution seems simple: link the code to the documentation. The easiest way to do this is to put everything in the same file. To complete the picture, however, you need a special comment syntax to mark special documentation and a tool to extract those comments and put them in a useful form. This is what Java has done.

The tool to extract the comments is called *javadoc*. It uses some of the technology from the Java compiler to look for special comment tags you put in your programs. It not only extracts the information marked by these tags, but it also pulls out the class name or method name that adjoins the comment. This way you can get away with the minimal amount of work to generate decent program documentation.

The output of javadoc is an HTML file that you can view with your Web browser. This tool allows you to create and maintain a single source file and automatically generate useful documentation. Because of javadoc we have a standard for creating documentation, and it's easy enough that we can expect or even demand documentation with all Java libraries.

Syntax

All of the javadoc commands occur only within /** comments. The comments end with */ as usual. There are two primary ways to use javadoc: embed HTML, or use "doc tags." Doc tags are commands that start with a '@' and are placed at the beginning of a comment line. (A leading '*', however, is ignored.)

There are three "types" of comment documentation, which correspond to the element the comment precedes: class, variable, or method. That is, a class comment appears right before the definition of a class; a variable comment appears right in front of the definition of a variable and a method comment appears right in front of the definition of a method. As a simple example:

```
/** A class comment */
public class docTest {
  /** A variable comment */
  public int i;
  /** A method comment */
  public void f() {}
}
```

Note that javadoc will process comment documentation for only **public** and **protected** members. Comments for **private** and "friendly" (see Chapter 5) members are ignored and you'll see no output. (You can use the -**private** flag to include **private** members as well.) This makes sense, since only **public** and **protected** members are available outside the file, which is the client programmer's perspective. However, all **class** comments are included in the output.

The output for the above code is an HTML file that has the same standard format as all the rest of the Java documentation, so users will be comfortable with the format and can easily navigate your classes. It's worth entering the above code, sending it through javadoc and viewing the resulting HTML file to see the results.

Embedded HTML

Javadoc passes HTML commands through to the generated HTML document. This allows you full use of HTML; however, the primary motive is to let you format code, such as:

```
/**
* <pre>
* System.out.println(new Date());
* </pre>
*/
```

You can also use HTML just as you would in any other Web document to format the regular text in your descriptions:

```
/**
* You can <em>even</em> insert a list:
* <ol>
* <li> Item one
* <li> Item two
* <li> Item three
* </ol>
*/
```

Note that within the documentation comment, asterisks at the beginning of a line are thrown away by javadoc, along with leading spaces. Javadoc reformats everything so that it conforms to the standard documentation appearance. Don't use headings such as **<h1>** or **<hr>** as embedded HTML because javadoc inserts its own headings and yours will interfere with them.

All types of comment documentation – class, variable, and method – can support embedded HTML.

@see: referring to other classes

All three types of comment documentation can contain **@see** tags, which allow you to refer to the documentation in other classes. Javadoc will generate HTML with the **@see** tags hyperlinked to the other documentation. The forms are:

```
@see classname
@see fully-qualified-classname
@see fully-qualified-classname#method-name
```

Each one adds a hyperlinked "See Also" entry to the generated documentation. Javadoc will not check the hyperlinks you give it to make sure they are valid.

Class documentation tags

Along with embedded HTML and **@see** references, class documentation can include tags for version information and the author's name. Class documentation can also be used for *interfaces* (described later in the book).

@version

This is of the form:

```
@version version-information
```

in which **version-information** is any significant information you see fit to include. When the **-version** flag is placed on the javadoc command line, the version information will be called out specially in the generated HTML documentation.

@author

This is of the form:

```
@author author-information
```

in which **author-information** is, presumably, your name, but it could also include your email address or any other appropriate information. When the **-author** flag is placed on the javadoc command line, the author information will be called out specially in the generated HTML documentation.

You can have multiple author tags for a list of authors, but they must be placed consecutively. All the author information will be lumped together into a single paragraph in the generated HTML.

Variable documentation tags

Variable documentation can include only embedded HTML and **@see** references.

Method documentation tags

As well as embedded documentation and @**see** references, methods allow documentation tags for parameters, return values, and exceptions.

@param

This is of the form:

```
@param parameter-name description
```

in which **parameter-name** is the identifier in the parameter list, and **description** is text that can continue on subsequent lines. The description is considered finished when a new documentation tag is encountered. You can have any number of these, presumably one for each parameter.

@return

This is of the form:

```
@return description
```

in which **description** gives you the meaning of the return value. It can continue on subsequent lines.

@exception

Exceptions will be described in Chapter 9, but briefly they are objects that can be "thrown" out of a method if that method fails. Although only one exception object can emerge when you call a method, a particular method might produce any number of different types of exceptions, all of which need descriptions. So the form for the exception tag is:

```
@exception fully-qualified-class-name description
```

in which **fully-qualified-class-name** gives an unambiguous name of an exception class that's defined somewhere, and **description** (which can continue on subsequent lines) tells you why this particular type of exception can emerge from the method call.

@deprecated

This is new in Java 1.1. It is used to tag features that were superseded by an improved feature. The deprecated tag is a suggestion that you no longer use this particular feature, since sometime in the future it is likely

---

to be removed. Methods that are marked **@deprecated** cause the compiler to issue warnings if it is used.

Documentation example

Here is the first Java program again, this time with documentation comments added:

```
//: Property.java
import java.util.*;

/** The first Thinking in Java example program.
  * Lists system information on current machine.
  * @author Bruce Eckel
  * @author http://www.BruceEckel.com
  * @version 1.0
  */
public class Property {
  /** Sole entry point to class & application
    * @param args array of string arguments
    * @return No return value
    * @exception exceptions No exceptions thrown
    */
  public static void main(String[] args) {
    System.out.println(new Date());
    Properties p = System.getProperties();
    p.list(System.out);
    System.out.println("--- Memory Usage:");
    Runtime rt = Runtime.getRuntime();
    System.out.println("Total Memory = "
                        + rt.totalMemory()
                        + " Free Memory = "
                        + rt.freeMemory());
  }
} ///:~
```

The first line:

```
//: Property.java
```

uses my own technique of putting a ':' as a special marker for the comment line containing the source file name. The last line also finishes with a comment, and this one indicates the end of the source code listing, which allows it to be automatically extracted from the text of the book and checked with a compiler. This is described in detail in Chapter 17.

Coding style

The unofficial standard in Java is to capitalize the first letter of a class name. If the class name consists of several words, they are run together (that is, you don't use underscores to separate the names) and the first letter of each embedded word is capitalized, such as:

```
class AllTheColorsOfTheRainbow { // ...
```

For almost everything else: methods, fields (member variables) and object handle names, the accepted style is just as it is for classes *except* that the first letter of the identifier is lower case. For example:

```
class AllTheColorsOfTheRainbow {
    int anIntegerRepresentingColors;
    void changeTheHueOfTheColor(int newHue) {
        // ...
    }
    // ...
}
```

Of course, you should remember that the user must also type all these long names, and be merciful.

Summary

In this chapter you have seen enough of Java programming to understand how to write a simple program, and you have gotten an overview of the language and some of its basic ideas. However, the examples so far have all been of the form "do this, then do that, then do something else." What if you want the program to make choices, such as "if the result of doing this is red, do that, if not, then do something else"? The support in Java for this fundamental programming activity will be covered in the next chapter.

Exercises

I. Following the first example in this chapter, create a "Hello, World" program that simply prints out that statement. You need only a single method in your class (the "main" one that gets executed when the program starts). Remember to make it **static** and to put the argument

---

list in, even though you don't use the argument list. Compile the program with **javac** and run it using **java**.

2. Write a program that prints three arguments taken from the command line.

3. Find the code for the second version of **Property.java**, which is the simple comment documentation example. Execute **javadoc** on the file and view the results with your Web browser.

4. Take the program in Exercise 1 and add comment documentation to it. Extract this comment documentation into an HTML file using **javadoc** and view it with your Web browser.

3: Controlling program flow

Like a sentient creature, a program must manipulate its
world and make choices during execution.

In Java you manipulate objects and data using operators, and you make
choices with execution control statements. Java was inherited from C++,
so most of these statements and operators will be familiar to C and C++
programmers. Java has also added some improvements and
simplifications.

Using Java operators

An operator takes one or more arguments and produces a new value. The
arguments are in a different form than ordinary method calls, but the
effect is the same. You should be reasonably comfortable with the general
concept of operators from your previous programming experience.

Addition (+), subtraction and unary minus (-), multiplication (*), division (/) and assignment (=) all work much the same in any programming language.

All operators produce a value from their operands. In addition, an operator can change the value of an operand. This is called a *side effect*. The most common use for operators that modify their operands is to generate the side effect, but you should keep in mind that the value produced is available for your use just as in operators without side effects.

Almost all operators work only with primitives. The exceptions are '=', '==' and '!=', which work with all objects (and are a point of confusion for objects). In addition, the **String** class supports '+' and '+='.

Precedence

Operator precedence defines how an expression evaluates when several operators are present. Java has specific rules that determine the order of evaluation. The easiest one to remember is that multiplication and division happen before addition and subtraction. Programmers often forget the other precedence rules, so you should use parentheses to make the order of evaluation explicit. For example:

```
A = X + Y - 2/2 + Z;
```

has a very different meaning from the same statement with a particular grouping of parentheses:

```
A = X + (Y - 2)/(2 + Z);
```

Assignment

Assignment is performed with the operator =. It means "take the value of the right-hand side (often called the *rvalue*) and copy it into the left-hand side (often called the *lvalue*). An rvalue is any constant, variable or expression that can produce a value, but an lvalue must be a distinct, named variable. (That is, there must be a physical space to store a value.) For instance, you can assign a constant value to a variable (**A = 4;**), but you cannot assign anything to constant value – it cannot be an lvalue. (You can't say **4 = A;**.)

Assignment of primitives is quite straightforward. Since the primitive holds the actual value and not a handle to an object, when you assign primitives you copy the contents from one place to another. For example,

---

if you say **A** = **B** for primitives, then the contents of **B** is copied into **A**. If you then go on to modify **A**, **B** is naturally unaffected by this modification. This is what you've come to expect as a programmer for most situations.

When you assign objects, however, things change. Whenever you manipulate an object, what you're manipulating is the handle, so when you assign "from one object to another" you're actually copying a handle from one place to another. This means that if you say **C** = **D** for objects you end up with both **C** and **D** pointing to the object that, originally, only **D** pointed to. The following example will demonstrate this.

As an aside, the first thing you see is a **package** statement for **package c03**, indicating this book's Chapter 3. The first code listing of each chapter will contain a package statement like this to establish the chapter number for the remaining code listings in that chapter. In Chapter 17, you'll see that as a result, all the listings in chapter 3 (except those that have different package names) will be automatically placed in a subdirectory called **c03**, Chapter 4's listings will be in **c04** and so on. All this will happen via the **CodePackager.java** program shown in Chapter 17, and in Chapter 5 the concept of packages will be fully explained. What you need to recognize at this point is that, for this book, lines of code of the form **package c03** are used just to establish the chapter subdirectory for the listings in the chapter.

In order to run the program, you must ensure that the classpath contains the root directory where you installed the source code for this book. (From this directory, you'll see the subdirectories **c02**, **c03**, **c04**, etc.)

For later versions of Java (1.1.4 and on), when your **main( )** is inside a file with a **package** statement, you must give the full package name before the program name in order to run the program. In this case, the command line is:

```
java c03.Assignment
```

Keep this in mind any time you're running a program that's in a **package**.

Here's the example:

```
//: Assignment.java
// Assignment with objects is a bit tricky
package c03;

class Number {
```

```
      int i;
}

public class Assignment {
  public static void main(String[] args) {
    Number n1 = new Number();
    Number n2 = new Number();
    n1.i = 9;
    n2.i = 47;
    System.out.println("1: n1.i: " + n1.i +
      ", n2.i: " + n2.i);
    n1 = n2;
    System.out.println("2: n1.i: " + n1.i +
      ", n2.i: " + n2.i);
    n1.i = 27;
    System.out.println("3: n1.i: " + n1.i +
      ", n2.i: " + n2.i);
  }
} ///:~
```

The **Number** class is simple, and two instances of it (**n1** and **n2**) are created within **main( )**. The **i** value within each **Number** is given a different value, and then **n2** is assigned to **n1**, and **n1** is changed. In many programming languages you would expect **n1** and **n2** to be independent at all times, but because you've assigned a handle here's the output you'll see:

```
1: n1.i: 9, n2.i: 47
2: n1.i: 47, n2.i: 47
3: n1.i: 27, n2.i: 27
```

Changing the **n1** object appears to change the **n2** object as well! This is because both **n1** and **n2** contain the same handle, which is pointing to the same object. (The original handle that was in **n1** that pointed to the object holding a value of 9 was overwritten during the assignment and effectively lost; its object will be cleaned up by the garbage collector.)

This phenomenon is often called *aliasing* and it's a fundamental way that Java works with objects. But what if you don't want aliasing to occur in this case? You could forego the assignment and say:

```
n1.i = n2.i;
```

This retains the two separate objects instead of tossing one and tying **n1** and **n2** to the same object, but you'll soon realize that manipulating the fields within objects is messy and goes against good object–oriented design principles. This is a non–trivial topic, so it is left for Chapter 12, which is devoted to aliasing. In the meantime, you should keep in mind that assignment for objects can add surprises.

Aliasing during method calls

Aliasing will also occur when you pass an object into a method:

```
//: PassObject.java
// Passing objects to methods can be a bit tricky

class Letter {
  char c;
}

public class PassObject {
  static void f(Letter y) {
    y.c = 'z';
  }
  public static void main(String[] args) {
    Letter x = new Letter();
    x.c = 'a';
    System.out.println("1: x.c: " + x.c);
    f(x);
    System.out.println("2: x.c: " + x.c);
  }
} ///:~
```

In many programming languages, the method **f( )** would appear to be making a copy of its argument **Letter y** inside the scope of the method. But once again a handle is being passed so the line

```
y.c = 'z';
```

is actually changing the object outside of **f( )**. The output shows this:

```
1: x.c: a
2: x.c: z
```

Aliasing and its solution is a complex issue and, although you must wait until Chapter 12 for all the answers, you should be aware of it at this point so you can watch for pitfalls.

Mathematical operators

The basic mathematical operators are the same as the ones available in most programming languages: addition (**+**), subtraction (**-**), division (**/**), multiplication (*****) and modulus (**%**, produces the remainder from integer division). Integer division truncates, rather than rounds, the result.

Java also uses a shorthand notation to perform an operation and an assignment at the same time. This is denoted by an operator followed by an equal sign, and is consistent with all the operators in the language (whenever it makes sense). For example, to add 4 to the variable **x** and assign the result to **x**, use: **x += 4;**.

This example shows the use of the mathematical operators:

```
//: MathOps.java
// Demonstrates the mathematical operators
import java.util.*;

public class MathOps {
  // Create a shorthand to save typing:
  static void prt(String s) {
    System.out.println(s);
  }
  // shorthand to print a string and an int:
  static void pInt(String s, int i) {
    prt(s + " = " + i);
  }
  // shorthand to print a string and a float:
  static void pFlt(String s, float f) {
    prt(s + " = " + f);
  }
  public static void main(String[] args) {
    // Create a random number generator,
    // seeds with current time by default:
    Random rand = new Random();
    int i, j, k;
    // '%' limits maximum value to 99:
    j = rand.nextInt() % 100;
    k = rand.nextInt() % 100;
    pInt("j",j);   pInt("k",k);
    i = j + k; pInt("j + k", i);
    i = j - k; pInt("j - k", i);
    i = k / j; pInt("k / j", i);
    i = k * j; pInt("k * j", i);
```

```
        i = k % j; pInt("k % j", i);
        j %= k; pInt("j %= k", j);
        // Floating-point number tests:
        float u,v,w;   // applies to doubles, too
        v = rand.nextFloat();
        w = rand.nextFloat();
        pFlt("v", v); pFlt("w", w);
        u = v + w; pFlt("v + w", u);
        u = v - w; pFlt("v - w", u);
        u = v * w; pFlt("v * w", u);
        u = v / w; pFlt("v / w", u);
        // the following also works for
        // char, byte, short, int, long,
        // and double:
        u += v; pFlt("u += v", u);
        u -= v; pFlt("u -= v", u);
        u *= v; pFlt("u *= v", u);
        u /= v; pFlt("u /= v", u);
    }
} ///:~
```

The first thing you will see are some shorthand methods for printing: the **prt( )** method prints a **String**, the **pInt( )** prints a **String** followed by an **int** and the **pFlt( )** prints a **String** followed by a **float**. Of course, they all ultimately end up using **System.out.println( )**.

To generate numbers, the program first creates a **Random** object. Because no arguments are passed during creation, Java uses the current time as a seed for the random number generator. The program generates a number of different types of random numbers with the **Random** object simply by calling different methods: **nextInt( )**, **nextLong( )**, **nextFloat( )** or **nextDouble( )**.

The modulus operator, when used with the result of the random number generator, limits the result to an upper bound of the operand minus one (99 in this case).

Unary minus and plus operators

The unary minus (–) and unary plus (+) are the same operators as binary minus and plus. The compiler figures out which use is intended by the way you write the expression. For instance, the statement

```
x = -a;
```

has an obvious meaning. The compiler is able to figure out:

```
x = a * -b;
```

but the reader might get confused, so it is more clear to say:

```
x = a * (-b);
```

The unary minus produces the negative of the value. Unary plus provides symmetry with unary minus, although it doesn't do much.

Auto increment and decrement

Java, like C, is full of shortcuts. Shortcuts can make code much easier to type, and either easier or harder to read.

Two of the nicer shortcuts are the increment and decrement operators (often referred to as the auto-increment and auto-decrement operators). The decrement operator is -- and means "decrease by one unit." The increment operator is ++ and means "increase by one unit." If **A** is an **int**, for example, the expression **++A** is equivalent to (**A = A + 1**). Increment and decrement operators produce the value of the variable as a result.

There are two versions of each type of operator, often called the prefix and postfix versions. Pre-increment means the ++ operator appears before the variable or expression, and post-increment means the ++ operator appears after the variable or expression. Similarly, pre-decrement means the -- operator appears before the variable or expression, and post-decrement means the -- operator appears after the variable or expression. For pre-increment and pre-decrement, (i.e., **++A** or **--A**), the operation is performed and the value is produced. For post-increment and post-decrement (i.e. **A++** or **A--**), the value is produced, then the operation is performed. As an example:

```
//: AutoInc.java
// Demonstrates the ++ and -- operators

public class AutoInc {
  public static void main(String[] args) {
    int i = 1;
    prt("i : " + i);
    prt("++i : " + ++i); // Pre-increment
    prt("i++ : " + i++); // Post-increment
    prt("i : " + i);
    prt("--i : " + --i); // Pre-decrement
    prt("i-- : " + i--); // Post-decrement
```

```
        prt("i : " + i);
    }
    static void prt(String s) {
        System.out.println(s);
    }
} ///:~
```

The output for this program is:

```
i : 1
++i : 2
i++ : 2
i : 3
--i : 2
i-- : 2
i : 1
```

You can see that for the prefix form you get the value after the operation has been performed, but with the postfix form you get the value before the operation is performed. These are the only operators (other than those involving assignment) that have side effects. (That is, they change the operand rather than using just its value.)

The increment operator is one explanation for the name C++, implying "one step beyond C." In an early Java speech, Bill Joy (one of the creators), said that "Java=C++--" (C plus plus minus minus), suggesting that Java is C++ with the unnecessary hard parts removed and therefore a much simpler language. As you progress in this book you'll see that many parts are simpler, and yet Java isn't *that* much easier than C++.

Relational operators

Relational operators generate a **boolean** result. They evaluate the relationship between the values of the operands. A relational expression produces **true** if the relationship is true, and **false** if the relationship is untrue. The relational operators are less than (<), greater than (>), less than or equal to (<=), greater than or equal to (>=), equivalent (==) and not equivalent (!=). Equivalence and nonequivalence works with all built-in data types, but the other comparisons won't work with type **boolean**.

Testing object equivalence

The relational operators **==** and **!=** also work with all objects, but their meaning often confuses the first-time Java programmer. Here's an example:

```
//: Equivalence.java

public class Equivalence {
  public static void main(String[] args) {
    Integer n1 = new Integer(47);
    Integer n2 = new Integer(47);
    System.out.println(n1 == n2);
    System.out.println(n1 != n2);
  }
} ///:~
```

The expression **System.out.println(n1 == n2)** will print out the result of the **boolean** comparison within it. Surely the output should be **true** and then **false**, since both **Integer** objects are the same. But while the *contents* of the objects are the same, the handles are not the same and the operators **==** and **!=** compare object handles. So the output is actually **false** and then **true**. Naturally, this surprises people at first.

What if you want to compare the actual contents of an object for equivalence? You must use the special method **equals( )** that exists for all objects (not primitives, which work fine with **==** and **!=**). Here's how it's used:

```
//: EqualsMethod.java

public class EqualsMethod {
  public static void main(String[] args) {
    Integer n1 = new Integer(47);
    Integer n2 = new Integer(47);
    System.out.println(n1.equals(n2));
  }
} ///:~
```

The result will be **true**, as you would expect. Ah, but it's not as simple as that. If you create your own class, like this:

```
//: EqualsMethod2.java

class Value {
  int i;
```

```
        }

public class EqualsMethod2 {
  public static void main(String[] args) {
    Value v1 = new Value();
    Value v2 = new Value();
    v1.i = v2.i = 100;
    System.out.println(v1.equals(v2));
  }
} ///:~
```

you're back to square one: the result is **false**. This is because the default
behavior of **equals( )** is to compare handles. So unless you *override*
equals( ) in your new class you won't get the desired behavior.
Unfortunately, you won't learn about overriding until Chapter 7, but
being aware of the way **equals( )** behaves might save you some grief in
the meantime.

Most of the Java library classes implement **equals( )** so that it compares
the contents of objects instead of their handles.

Logical operators

The logical operators AND (&&), OR (||) and NOT (!) produce a **boolean**
value of **true** or **false** based on the logical relationship of its arguments.
This example uses the relational and logical operators:

```
//: Bool.java
// Relational and logical operators
import java.util.*;

public class Bool {
  public static void main(String[] args) {
    Random rand = new Random();
    int i = rand.nextInt() % 100;
    int j = rand.nextInt() % 100;
    prt("i = " + i);
    prt("j = " + j);
    prt("i > j is " + (i > j));
    prt("i < j is " + (i < j));
    prt("i >= j is " + (i >= j));
    prt("i <= j is " + (i <= j));
    prt("i == j is " + (i == j));
    prt("i != j is " + (i != j));
```

```
      // Treating an int as a boolean is
      // not legal Java
//! prt("i && j is " + (i && j));
//! prt("i || j is " + (i || j));
//! prt("!i is " + !i);

    prt("(i < 10) && (j < 10) is "
        + ((i < 10) && (j < 10)) );
    prt("(i < 10) || (j < 10) is "
        + ((i < 10) || (j < 10)) );
  }
  static void prt(String s) {
    System.out.println(s);
  }
} ///:~
```

You can apply AND, OR, or NOT to **boolean** values only. You can't use a non-**boolean** as if it were a **boolean** in a logical expression as you can in C and C++. You can see the failed attempts at doing this commented out with a //! comment marker. The subsequent expressions, however, produce **boolean** values using relational comparisons, then use logical operations on the results.

One output listing looked like this:

```
i = 85
j = 4
i > j is true
i < j is false
i >= j is true
i <= j is false
i == j is false
i != j is true
(i < 10) && (j < 10) is false
(i < 10) || (j < 10) is true
```

Note that a **boolean** value is automatically converted to an appropriate text form if it's used where a **String** is expected.

You can replace the definition for **int** in the above program with any other primitive data type except **boolean**. Be aware, however, that the comparison of floating-point numbers is very strict. A number that is the tiniest fraction different from another number is still "not equal." A number that is the tiniest bit above zero is still nonzero.

Short-circuiting

When dealing with logical operators you run into a phenomenon called "short circuiting." This means that the expression will be evaluated only until the truth or falsehood of the entire expression can be unambiguously determined. As a result, all the parts of a logical expression might not be evaluated. Here's an example that demonstrates short-circuiting:

```
//: ShortCircuit.java
// Demonstrates short-circuiting behavior
// with logical operators.

public class ShortCircuit {
  static boolean test1(int val) {
    System.out.println("test1(" + val + ")");
    System.out.println("result: " + (val < 1));
    return val < 1;
  }
  static boolean test2(int val) {
    System.out.println("test2(" + val + ")");
    System.out.println("result: " + (val < 2));
    return val < 2;
  }
  static boolean test3(int val) {
    System.out.println("test3(" + val + ")");
    System.out.println("result: " + (val < 3));
    return val < 3;
  }
  public static void main(String[] args) {
    if(test1(0) && test2(2) && test3(2))
      System.out.println("expression is true");
    else
      System.out.println("expression is false");
  }
} ///:~
```

Each test performs a comparison against the argument and returns true or false. It also prints information to show you that it's being called. The tests are used in the expression:

```
if(test1(0) && test2(2) && test3(2))
```

You might naturally think that all three tests would be executed, but the output shows otherwise:

```
test1(0)
result: true
test2(2)
result: false
expression is false
```

The first test produced a **true** result, so the expression evaluation continues. However, the second test produced a **false** result. Since this means that the whole expression must be **false**, why continue evaluating the rest of the expression? It could be expensive. The reason for short-circuiting, in fact, is precisely that; you can get a potential performance increase if all the parts of a logical expression do not need to be evaluated.

Bitwise operators

The bitwise operators allow you to manipulate individual bits in an integral primitive data type. Bitwise operators perform boolean algebra on the corresponding bits in the two arguments to produce the result.

The bitwise operators come from C's low-level orientation; you were often manipulating hardware directly and had to set the bits in hardware registers. Java was originally designed to be embedded in TV set-top boxes, so this low-level orientation still made sense. However, you probably won't use the bitwise operators much.

The bitwise AND operator (&) produces a one in the output bit if both input bits are one; otherwise it produces a zero. The bitwise OR operator (|) produces a one in the output bit if either input bit is a one and produces a zero only if both input bits are zero. The bitwise, EXCLUSIVE OR, or XOR (^), produces a one in the output bit if one or the other input bit is a one, but not both. The bitwise NOT (~, also called the ones complement operator) is a unary operator; it takes only one argument. (All other bitwise operators are binary operators.) Bitwise NOT produces the opposite of the input bit – a one if the input bit is zero, a zero if the input bit is one.

The bitwise operators and logical operators use the same characters, so it is helpful to have a mnemonic device to help you remember the meanings: since bits are "small," there is only one character in the bitwise operators.

Bitwise operators can be combined with the = sign to unite the operation and assignment: &=, |= and ^= are all legitimate. (Since ~ is a unary operator it cannot be combined with the = sign.)

The **boolean** type is treated as a one-bit value so it is somewhat different. You can perform a bitwise AND, OR and XOR, but you can't perform a bitwise NOT (presumably to prevent confusion with the logical NOT). For **boolean**s the bitwise operators have the same effect as the logical operators except that they do not short circuit. Also, the bitwise operators on **boolean**s gives you a XOR logical operator that is not included under the list of "logical" operators. You're prevented from using **boolean**s in shift expressions, which is described next.

Shift operators

The shift operators also manipulate bits. They can be used solely with primitive, integral types. The left-shift operator (**<<**) produces the operand to the left of the operator shifted to the left by the number of bits specified after the operator (inserting zeroes at the lower-order bits). The signed right-shift operator (**>>**) produces the operand to the left of the operator shifted to the right by the number of bits specified after the operator. The signed right shift **>>** uses *sign extension*: if the value is positive, zeroes are inserted at the higher-order bits; if the value is negative, ones are inserted at the higher-order bits. Java has also added the unsigned right shift **>>>**, which uses *zero extension*: regardless of the sign, zeroes are inserted at the higher-order bits. This operator does not exist in C or C++.

If you shift a **char**, **byte**, or **short**, it will be promoted to **int** before the shift takes place, and the result will be an **int**. Only the five low-order bits of the right-hand side will be used. This prevents you from shifting more than the number of bits in an **int**. If you're operating on a **long**, **long** will be the result. Only the six low-order bits of the right-hand side will be used so you can't shift more than the number of bits in a **long**. There is a problem, however, with the unsigned right shift. If you use it with **byte** or **short** you might not get the correct results. (It's broken in Java 1.0 and Java 1.1.) These are promoted to **int** and right shifted, but the zero extension does *not* occur, so you get **-1** in those cases. The following example can be used to test your implementation:

```
//: URShift.java
// Test of unsigned right shift

public class URShift {
  public static void main(String[] args) {
    int i = -1;
    i >>>= 10;
    System.out.println(i);
```

```
      long l = -1;
      l >>>= 10;
      System.out.println(l);
      short s = -1;
      s >>>= 10;
      System.out.println(s);
      byte b = -1;
      b >>>= 10;
      System.out.println(b);
  }
} ///:~
```

Shifts can be combined with the equal sign (**<<=** or **>>=** or **>>>=**). The lvalue is replaced by the lvalue shifted by the rvalue.

Here's an example that demonstrates the use of all the operators involving bits:

```
//: BitManipulation.java
// Using the bitwise operators
import java.util.*;

public class BitManipulation {
  public static void main(String[] args) {
    Random rand = new Random();
    int i = rand.nextInt();
    int j = rand.nextInt();
    pBinInt("-1", -1);
    pBinInt("+1", +1);
    int maxpos = 2147483647;
    pBinInt("maxpos", maxpos);
    int maxneg = -2147483648;
    pBinInt("maxneg", maxneg);
    pBinInt("i", i);
    pBinInt("~i", ~i);
    pBinInt("-i", -i);
    pBinInt("j", j);
    pBinInt("i & j", i & j);
    pBinInt("i | j", i | j);
    pBinInt("i ^ j", i ^ j);
    pBinInt("i << 5", i << 5);
    pBinInt("i >> 5", i >> 5);
    pBinInt("(~i) >> 5", (~i) >> 5);
    pBinInt("i >>> 5", i >>> 5);
    pBinInt("(~i) >>> 5", (~i) >>> 5);
```

```
      long l = rand.nextLong();
      long m = rand.nextLong();
      pBinLong("-1L", -1L);
      pBinLong("+1L", +1L);
      long ll = 9223372036854775807L;
      pBinLong("maxpos", ll);
      long lln = -9223372036854775808L;
      pBinLong("maxneg", lln);
      pBinLong("l", l);
      pBinLong("~l", ~l);
      pBinLong("-l", -l);
      pBinLong("m", m);
      pBinLong("l & m", l & m);
      pBinLong("l | m", l | m);
      pBinLong("l ^ m", l ^ m);
      pBinLong("l << 5", l << 5);
      pBinLong("l >> 5", l >> 5);
      pBinLong("(~l) >> 5", (~l) >> 5);
      pBinLong("l >>> 5", l >>> 5);
      pBinLong("(~l) >>> 5", (~l) >>> 5);
    }
    static void pBinInt(String s, int i) {
      System.out.println(
        s + ", int: " + i + ", binary: ");
      System.out.print("   ");
      for(int j = 31; j >=0; j--)
        if(((1 << j) &  i) != 0)
          System.out.print("1");
        else
          System.out.print("0");
      System.out.println();
    }
    static void pBinLong(String s, long l) {
      System.out.println(
        s + ", long: " + l + ", binary: ");
      System.out.print("   ");
      for(int i = 63; i >=0; i--)
        if(((1L << i) & l) != 0)
          System.out.print("1");
        else
          System.out.print("0");
      System.out.println();
    }
```

```
} ///:~
```

The two methods at the end, **pBinInt( )** and **pBinLong( )** take an **int** or a **long**, respectively, and print it out in binary format along with a descriptive string. You can ignore the implementation of these for now.

You'll note the use of **System.out.print( )** instead of **System.out.println( )**. The **print( )** method does not put out a new line, so it allows you to output a line in pieces.

As well as demonstrating the effect of all the bitwise operators for **int** and **long**, this example also shows the minimum, maximum, +1 and -1 values for **int** and **long** so you can see what they look like. Note that the high bit represents the sign: 0 means positive and 1 means negative. The output for the **int** portion looks like this:

```
-1, int: -1, binary:
   11111111111111111111111111111111
+1, int: 1, binary:
   00000000000000000000000000000001
maxpos, int: 2147483647, binary:
   01111111111111111111111111111111
maxneg, int: -2147483648, binary:
   10000000000000000000000000000000
i, int: 59081716, binary:
   00000011100001011000001111110100
~i, int: -59081717, binary:
   11111100011110100111110000001011
-i, int: -59081716, binary:
   11111100011110100111110000001100
j, int: 198850956, binary:
   00001011110110100011100110001100
i & j, int: 58720644, binary:
   00000011100000000000000110000100
i | j, int: 199212028, binary:
   00001011110111111011101111111100
i ^ j, int: 140491384, binary:
   00001000010111111011101001111000
i << 5, int: 1890614912, binary:
   01110001011000001111101000000000
i >> 5, int: 1846303, binary:
   00000000000111000010110000011111
(~i) >> 5, int: -1846304, binary:
   11111111111000111101001111100000
i >>> 5, int: 1846303, binary:
```

```
             000000000001110000010110000011111
     (~i) >>> 5, int: 132371424, binary:
             00000111111000111101001111100000
```

The binary representation of the numbers is referred to as *signed two's complement*.

Ternary if-else operator

This operator is unusual because it has three operands. It is truly an operator because it produces a value, unlike the ordinary if-else statement that you'll see in the next section of this chapter. The expression is of the form
boolean-exp ? value0 : value1
If *boolean-exp* evaluates to **true**, *value0* is evaluated and its result becomes the value produced by the operator. If *boolean-exp* is **false**, *value1* is evaluated and its result becomes the value produced by the operator.

Of course, you could use an ordinary **if-else** statement (described later), but the ternary operator is much terser. Although C prides itself on being a terse language, and the ternary operator might have been introduced partly for efficiency, you should be somewhat wary of using it on an everyday basis – it's easy to produce unreadable code.

The conditional operator can be used for its side effects or for the value it produces, but in general you want the value since that's what makes the operator distinct from the **if-else**. Here's an example:

```
static int ternary(int i) {
  return i < 10 ? i * 100 : i * 10;
}
```

You can see that this code is more compact than what you'd need to write without the ternary operator:

```
static int alternative(int i) {
  if (i < 10)
    return i * 100;
  return i * 10;
}
```

The second form is easier to understand, and doesn't require a lot more typing. So be sure to ponder your reasons when choosing the ternary operator.

The comma operator

The comma is used in C and C++ not only as a separator in function argument lists, but also as an operator for sequential evaluation. The sole place that the comma *operator* is used in Java is in **for** loops, which will be described later in this chapter.

String operator +

There's one special usage of an operator in Java: the **+** operator can be used to concatenate strings, as you've already seen. It seems a natural use of the **+** even though it doesn't fit with the traditional way that **+** is used. This capability seemed like a good idea in C++, so *operator overloading* was added to C++ to allow the C++ programmer to add meanings to almost any operator. Unfortunately, operator overloading combined with some of the other restrictions in C++ turns out to be a fairly complicated feature for programmers to design into their classes. Although operator overloading would have been much simpler to implement in Java than it was in C++, this feature was still considered too complex, so Java programmers cannot implement their own overloaded operators as C++ programmers can.

The use of the **String +** has some interesting behavior. If an expression begins with a **String**, then all operands that follow must be **String**s:

```
int x = 0, y = 1, z = 2;
String sString = "x, y, z ";
System.out.println(sString + x + y + z);
```

Here, the Java compiler will convert **x**, **y**, and **z** into their **String** representations instead of adding them together first. However, if you say:

```
System.out.println(x + sString);
```

earlier versions of Java will signal an error. (Later versions, however, will turn **x** into a **String**.) So if you're putting together a **String** (using an earlier version of Java) with addition, make sure the first element is a **String** (or a quoted sequence of characters, which the compiler recognizes as a **String**).

Thinking in Java

Common pitfalls when using operators

One of the pitfalls when using operators is trying to get away without parentheses when you are even the least bit uncertain about how an expression will evaluate. This is still true in Java.

An extremely common error in C and C++ looks like this:

```
while(x = y) {
   // ....
}
```

The programmer was trying to test for equivalence (==) rather than do an assignment. In C and C++ the result of this assignment will always be **true** if **y** is nonzero, and you'll probably get an infinite loop. In Java, the result of this expression is not a **boolean**, and the compiler expects a **boolean** and won't convert from an **int**, so it will conveniently give you a compile-time error and catch the problem before you ever try to run the program. So the pitfall never happens in Java. (The only time you won't get a compile-time error is when **x** and **y** are **boolean**, in which case **x = y** is a legal expression, and in the above case, probably an error.)

A similar problem in C and C++ is using bitwise AND and OR instead of logical. Bitwise AND and OR use one of the characters (**&** or **|**) while logical AND and OR use two (**&&** and **||**). Just as with **=** and **==**, it's easy to type just one character instead of two. In Java, the compiler again prevents this because it won't let you cavalierly use one type where it doesn't belong.

Casting operators

The word *cast* is used in the sense of "casting into a mold." Java will automatically change one type of data into another when appropriate. For instance, if you assign an integral value to a floating-point variable, the compiler will automatically convert the **int** to a **float**. Casting allows you to make this type conversion explicit, or to force it when it wouldn't normally happen.

To perform a cast, put the desired data type (including all modifiers) inside parentheses to the left of any value. Here's an example:

```
void casts() {
   int i = 200;
   long l = (long)i;
   long 12 = (long)200;
```

}

As you can see, it's possible to perform a cast on a numeric value as well as on a variable. In both casts shown here, however, the cast is superfluous, since the compiler will automatically promote an **int** value to a **long** when necessary. You can still put a cast in to make a point or to make your code more clear. In other situations, a cast is essential just to get the code to compile.

In C and C++, casting can cause some headaches. In Java, casting is safe, with the exception that when you perform a so-called *narrowing conversion* (that is, when you go from a data type that can hold more information to one that doesn't hold as much) you run the risk of losing information. Here the compiler forces you to do a cast, in effect saying "this can be a dangerous thing to do – if you want me to do it anyway you must make the cast explicit." With a *widening conversion* an explicit cast is not needed because the new type will more than hold the information from the old type so that no information is ever lost.

Java allows you to cast any primitive type to any other primitive type, except for **boolean**, which doesn't allow any casting at all. Class types do not allow casting. To convert one to the other there must be special methods. (**String** is a special case, and you'll find out later in the book that objects can be cast within a *family* of types; an **Oak** can be cast to a **Tree** and vice-versa, but not to a foreign type such as a **Rock**.)

Literals

Ordinarily when you insert a literal value into a program the compiler knows exactly what type to make it. Sometimes, however, the type is ambiguous. When this happens you must guide the compiler by adding some extra information in the form of characters associated with the literal value. The following code shows these characters:

```
//: Literals.java

class Literals {
  char c = 0xffff; // max char hex value
  byte b = 0x7f; // max byte hex value
  short s = 0x7fff; // max short hex value
  int i1 = 0x2f; // Hexadecimal (lowercase)
  int i2 = 0X2F; // Hexadecimal (uppercase)
  int i3 = 0177; // Octal (leading zero)
  // Hex and Oct also work with long.
  long n1 = 200L; // long suffix
```

```
    long n2 = 2001; // long suffix
    long n3 = 200;
    //! long 16(200); // not allowed
    float f1 = 1;
    float f2 = 1F; // float suffix
    float f3 = 1f; // float suffix
    float f4 = 1e-45f; // 10 to the power
    float f5 = 1e+9f; // float suffix
    double d1 = 1d; // double suffix
    double d2 = 1D; // double suffix
    double d3 = 47e47d; // 10 to the power
} ///:~
```

Hexadecimal (base 16), which works with all the integral data types, is denoted by a leading **0x** or **0X** followed by 0–9 and a–f either in upper or lower case. If you try to initialize a variable with a value bigger than it can hold (regardless of the numerical form of the value), the compiler will give you an error message. Notice in the above code the maximum possible hexadecimal values for **char**, **byte**, and **short**. If you exceed these, the compiler will automatically make the value an **int** and tell you that you need a narrowing cast for the assignment. You'll know you've stepped over the line.

Octal (base 8) is denoted by a leading zero in the number and digits from 0-7. There is no literal representation for binary numbers in C, C++ or Java.

A trailing character after a literal value establishes its type. Upper or lowercase **L** means **long**, upper or lowercase **F** means **float** and upper or lowercase **D** means **double**.

Exponents use a notation that I've always found rather dismaying: **1.39 e-47f**. In science and engineering, 'e' refers to the base of natural logarithms, approximately 2.718. (A more precise **double** value is available in Java as **Math.E**.) This is used in exponentiation expressions such as $1.39 \times e^{-47}$, which means 1.39×2.718^{-47}. However, when FORTRAN was invented they decided that **e** would naturally mean "ten to the power," which is an odd decision because FORTRAN was designed for science and engineering and one would think its designers would be sensitive about introducing such an ambiguity.[1] At any rate, this custom

---

[1] John Kirkham writes, "I started computing in 1962 using FORTRAN II on an IBM 1620. At that time, and throughout the 1960s and into the 1970s, FORTRAN was an all uppercase language. This probably started because many of the early

was followed in C, C++ and now Java. So if you're used to thinking in terms of **e** as the base of natural logarithms, you must do a mental translation when you see an expression such as **1.39 e-47f** in Java; it means 1.39×10^{-47}.

Note that you don't need to use the trailing character when the compiler can figure out the appropriate type. With

```
long n3 = 200;
```

there's no ambiguity, so an **L** after the 200 would be superfluous. However, with

```
float f4 = 1e-47f; // 10 to the power
```

the compiler normally takes exponential numbers as doubles, so without the trailing **f** it will give you an error telling you that you must use a cast to convert **double** to **float**.

Promotion

You'll discover that if you perform any mathematical or bitwise operations on primitive data types that are smaller than an **int** (that is, **char**, **byte**, or **short**), those values will be promoted to **int** before performing the operations, and the resulting value will be of type **int**. So if you want to assign back into the smaller type, you must use a cast. (And, since you're assigning back into a smaller type, you might be losing information.) In general, the largest data type in an expression is the one that determines the size of the result of that expression; if you multiply a **float** and a **double**, the result will be **double**; if you add an **int** and a **long**, the result will be **long**.

---

input devices were old teletype units that used 5 bit Baudot code, which had no lowercase capability. The 'E' in the exponential notation was also always upper case and was never confused with the natural logarithm base 'e', which is always lower case. The 'E' simply stood for exponential, which was for the base of the number system used – usually 10. At the time octal was also widely used by programmers. Although I never saw it used, if I had seen an octal number in exponential notation I would have considered it to be base 8. The first time I remember seeing an exponential using a lower case 'e' was in the late 1970s and I also found it confusing. The problem arose as lowercase crept into FORTRAN, not at its beginning. We actually had functions to use if you really wanted to use the natural logarithm base, but they were all uppercase."

Java has no "sizeof"

In C and C++, the **sizeof( )** operator satisfies a specific need: it tells you the number of bytes allocated for data items. The most compelling need for **sizeof( )** in C and C++ is portability. Different data types might be different sizes on different machines, so the programmer must find out how big those types are when performing operations that are sensitive to size. For example, one computer might store integers in 32 bits, whereas another might store integers as 16 bits. Programs could store larger values in integers on the first machine. As you might imagine, portability is a huge headache for C and C++ programmers.

Java does not need a **sizeof( )** operator for this purpose because all the data types are the same size on all machines. You do not need to think about portability on this level – it is designed into the language.

Precedence revisited

Upon hearing me complain about the complexity of remembering operator precedence during one of my seminars, a student suggested a mnemonic that is simultaneously a commentary: "Ulcer Addicts Really Like C A lot."

Mnemonic	Operator type	Operators
Ulcer	Unary	+ - ++ – [[rest...]]
Addicts	Arithmetic (and shift)	* / % + - << >>
Really	Relational	> < >= <= == !=
Like	Logical (and bitwise)	&& || & | ^
C	Conditional (ternary)	A > B ? X : Y
A Lot	Assignment	= (and compound assignment like *=)

Of course, with the shift and bitwise operators distributed around the table it is not a perfect mnemonic, but for non–bit operations it works.

A compendium of operators

The following example shows which primitive data types can be used with particular operators. Basically, it is the same example repeated over and over, but using different primitive data types. The file will compile without error because the lines that would cause errors are commented out with a //!.

```
//: AllOps.java
// Tests all the operators on all the
// primitive data types to show which
// ones are accepted by the Java compiler.

class AllOps {
  // To accept the results of a boolean test:
  void f(boolean b) {}
  void boolTest(boolean x, boolean y) {
    // Arithmetic operators:
    //! x = x * y;
    //! x = x / y;
    //! x = x % y;
    //! x = x + y;
    //! x = x - y;
    //! x++;
    //! x--;
    //! x = +y;
    //! x = -y;
    // Relational and logical:
    //! f(x > y);
    //! f(x >= y);
    //! f(x < y);
    //! f(x <= y);
    f(x == y);
    f(x != y);
    f(!y);
    x = x && y;
    x = x || y;
    // Bitwise operators:
    //! x = ~y;
    x = x & y;
    x = x | y;
    x = x ^ y;
    //! x = x << 1;
    //! x = x >> 1;
    //! x = x >>> 1;
    // Compound assignment:
    //! x += y;
    //! x -= y;
    //! x *= y;
    //! x /= y;
    //! x %= y;
    //! x <<= 1;
```

```
//! x >>= 1;
//! x >>>= 1;
x &= y;
x ^= y;
x |= y;
// Casting:
//! char c = (char)x;
//! byte B = (byte)x;
//! short s = (short)x;
//! int i = (int)x;
//! long l = (long)x;
//! float f = (float)x;
//! double d = (double)x;
}
void charTest(char x, char y) {
  // Arithmetic operators:
  x = (char)(x * y);
  x = (char)(x / y);
  x = (char)(x % y);
  x = (char)(x + y);
  x = (char)(x - y);
  x++;
  x--;
  x = (char)+y;
  x = (char)-y;
  // Relational and logical:
  f(x > y);
  f(x >= y);
  f(x < y);
  f(x <= y);
  f(x == y);
  f(x != y);
  //! f(!x);
  //! f(x && y);
  //! f(x || y);
  // Bitwise operators:
  x= (char)~y;
  x = (char)(x & y);
  x  = (char)(x | y);
  x = (char)(x ^ y);
  x = (char)(x << 1);
  x = (char)(x >> 1);
  x = (char)(x >>> 1);
  // Compound assignment:
```

```
        x += y;
        x -= y;
        x *= y;
        x /= y;
        x %= y;
        x <<= 1;
        x >>= 1;
        x >>>= 1;
        x &= y;
        x ^= y;
        x |= y;
        // Casting:
        //! boolean b = (boolean)x;
        byte B = (byte)x;
        short s = (short)x;
        int i = (int)x;
        long l = (long)x;
        float f = (float)x;
        double d = (double)x;
    }
    void byteTest(byte x, byte y) {
        // Arithmetic operators:
        x = (byte)(x* y);
        x = (byte)(x / y);
        x = (byte)(x % y);
        x = (byte)(x + y);
        x = (byte)(x - y);
        x++;
        x--;
        x = (byte)+ y;
        x = (byte)- y;
        // Relational and logical:
        f(x > y);
        f(x >= y);
        f(x < y);
        f(x <= y);
        f(x == y);
        f(x != y);
        //! f(!x);
        //! f(x && y);
        //! f(x || y);
        // Bitwise operators:
        x = (byte)~y;
        x = (byte)(x & y);
```

```
x = (byte)(x | y);
x = (byte)(x ^ y);
x = (byte)(x << 1);
x = (byte)(x >> 1);
x = (byte)(x >>> 1);
// Compound assignment:
x += y;
x -= y;
x *= y;
x /= y;
x %= y;
x <<= 1;
x >>= 1;
x >>>= 1;
x &= y;
x ^= y;
x |= y;
// Casting:
//! boolean b = (boolean)x;
char c = (char)x;
short s = (short)x;
int i = (int)x;
long l = (long)x;
float f = (float)x;
double d = (double)x;
}
void shortTest(short x, short y) {
// Arithmetic operators:
x = (short)(x * y);
x = (short)(x / y);
x = (short)(x % y);
x = (short)(x + y);
x = (short)(x - y);
x++;
x--;
x = (short)+y;
x = (short)-y;
// Relational and logical:
f(x > y);
f(x >= y);
f(x < y);
f(x <= y);
f(x == y);
f(x != y);
```

```
    //! f(!x);
    //! f(x && y);
    //! f(x || y);
    // Bitwise operators:
    x = (short)~y;
    x = (short)(x & y);
    x = (short)(x | y);
    x = (short)(x ^ y);
    x = (short)(x << 1);
    x = (short)(x >> 1);
    x = (short)(x >>> 1);
    // Compound assignment:
    x += y;
    x -= y;
    x *= y;
    x /= y;
    x %= y;
    x <<= 1;
    x >>= 1;
    x >>>= 1;
    x &= y;
    x ^= y;
    x |= y;
    // Casting:
    //! boolean b = (boolean)x;
    char c = (char)x;
    byte B = (byte)x;
    int i = (int)x;
    long l = (long)x;
    float f = (float)x;
    double d = (double)x;
  }
  void intTest(int x, int y) {
    // Arithmetic operators:
    x = x * y;
    x = x / y;
    x = x % y;
    x = x + y;
    x = x - y;
    x++;
    x--;
    x = +y;
    x = -y;
    // Relational and logical:
```

```
      f(x > y);
      f(x >= y);
      f(x < y);
      f(x <= y);
      f(x == y);
      f(x != y);
      //! f(!x);
      //! f(x && y);
      //! f(x || y);
      // Bitwise operators:
      x = ~y;
      x = x & y;
      x = x | y;
      x = x ^ y;
      x = x << 1;
      x = x >> 1;
      x = x >>> 1;
      // Compound assignment:
      x += y;
      x -= y;
      x *= y;
      x /= y;
      x %= y;
      x <<= 1;
      x >>= 1;
      x >>>= 1;
      x &= y;
      x ^= y;
      x |= y;
      // Casting:
      //! boolean b = (boolean)x;
      char c = (char)x;
      byte B = (byte)x;
      short s = (short)x;
      long l = (long)x;
      float f = (float)x;
      double d = (double)x;
    }
    void longTest(long x, long y) {
      // Arithmetic operators:
      x = x * y;
      x = x / y;
      x = x % y;
      x = x + y;
```

```
    x = x - y;
    x++;
    x--;
    x = +y;
    x = -y;
    // Relational and logical:
    f(x > y);
    f(x >= y);
    f(x < y);
    f(x <= y);
    f(x == y);
    f(x != y);
    //! f(!x);
    //! f(x && y);
    //! f(x || y);
    // Bitwise operators:
    x = ~y;
    x = x & y;
    x = x | y;
    x = x ^ y;
    x = x << 1;
    x = x >> 1;
    x = x >>> 1;
    // Compound assignment:
    x += y;
    x -= y;
    x *= y;
    x /= y;
    x %= y;
    x <<= 1;
    x >>= 1;
    x >>>= 1;
    x &= y;
    x ^= y;
    x |= y;
    // Casting:
    //! boolean b = (boolean)x;
    char c = (char)x;
    byte B = (byte)x;
    short s = (short)x;
    int i = (int)x;
    float f = (float)x;
    double d = (double)x;
}
```

```java
void floatTest(float x, float y) {
    // Arithmetic operators:
    x = x * y;
    x = x / y;
    x = x % y;
    x = x + y;
    x = x - y;
    x++;
    x--;
    x = +y;
    x = -y;
    // Relational and logical:
    f(x > y);
    f(x >= y);
    f(x < y);
    f(x <= y);
    f(x == y);
    f(x != y);
    //! f(!x);
    //! f(x && y);
    //! f(x || y);
    // Bitwise operators:
    //! x = ~y;
    //! x = x & y;
    //! x = x | y;
    //! x = x ^ y;
    //! x = x << 1;
    //! x = x >> 1;
    //! x = x >>> 1;
    // Compound assignment:
    x += y;
    x -= y;
    x *= y;
    x /= y;
    x %= y;
    //! x <<= 1;
    //! x >>= 1;
    //! x >>>= 1;
    //! x &= y;
    //! x ^= y;
    //! x |= y;
    // Casting:
    //! boolean b = (boolean)x;
    char c = (char)x;
```

```java
    byte B = (byte)x;
    short s = (short)x;
    int i = (int)x;
    long l = (long)x;
    double d = (double)x;
  }
  void doubleTest(double x, double y) {
    // Arithmetic operators:
    x = x * y;
    x = x / y;
    x = x % y;
    x = x + y;
    x = x - y;
    x++;
    x--;
    x = +y;
    x = -y;
    // Relational and logical:
    f(x > y);
    f(x >= y);
    f(x < y);
    f(x <= y);
    f(x == y);
    f(x != y);
    //! f(!x);
    //! f(x && y);
    //! f(x || y);
    // Bitwise operators:
    //! x = ~y;
    //! x = x & y;
    //! x = x | y;
    //! x = x ^ y;
    //! x = x << 1;
    //! x = x >> 1;
    //! x = x >>> 1;
    // Compound assignment:
    x += y;
    x -= y;
    x *= y;
    x /= y;
    x %= y;
    //! x <<= 1;
    //! x >>= 1;
    //! x >>>= 1;
```

```
//! x &= y;
//! x ^= y;
//! x |= y;
// Casting:
//! boolean b = (boolean)x;
char c = (char)x;
byte B = (byte)x;
short s = (short)x;
int i = (int)x;
long l = (long)x;
float f = (float)x;
  }
} ///:~
```

Note that **boolean** is quite limited. You can assign to it the values **true** and **false**, and you can test it for truth or falsehood, but you cannot add booleans or perform any other type of operation on them.

In **char**, **byte**, and **short** you can see the effect of promotion with the arithmetic operators. Each arithmetic operation on any of those types results in an **int** result, which must be explicitly cast back to the original type (a narrowing conversion that might lose information) to assign back to that type. With **int** values, however, you do not need to cast, because everything is already an **int**. Don't be lulled into thinking everything is safe, though. If you multiply two **ints** that are big enough, you'll overflow the result. The following example demonstrates this:

```
//: Overflow.java
// Surprise! Java lets you overflow.

public class Overflow {
  public static void main(String[] args) {
    int big = 0x7fffffff; // max int value
    prt("big = " + big);
    int bigger = big * 4;
    prt("bigger = " + bigger);
  }
  static void prt(String s) {
    System.out.println(s);
  }
} ///:~
```

The output of this is:

```
big = 2147483647
bigger = -4
```

and you get no errors or warnings from the compiler, and no exceptions at run-time. Java is good, but it's not *that* good.

Compound assignments do *not* require casts for **char**, **byte**, or **short**, even though they are performing promotions that have the same results as the direct arithmetic operations. On the other hand, the lack of the cast certainly simplifies the code.

You can see that, with the exception of **boolean**, any primitive type can be cast to any other primitive type. Again, you must be aware of the effect of a narrowing conversion when casting to a smaller type, otherwise you might unknowingly lose information during the cast.

Execution control

Java uses all of C's execution control statements, so if you've programmed with C or C++ then most of what you see will be familiar. Most procedural programming languages have some kind of control statements, and there is often overlap among languages. In Java, the keywords include **if-else**, **while**, **do-while**, **for**, and a selection statement called **switch**. Java does not, however, support the much-maligned **goto** (which can still be the most expedient way to solve certain types of problems). You can still do a goto-like jump, but it is much more constrained than a typical **goto**.

true and false

All conditional statements use the truth or falsehood of a conditional expression to determine the execution path. An example of a conditional expression is **A == B**. This uses the conditional operator **==** to see if the value of **A** is equivalent to the value of **B.** The expression returns **true** or **false**. Any of the relational operators you've seen earlier in this chapter can be used to produce a conditional statement. Note that Java doesn't allow you to use a number as a **boolean**, even though it's allowed in C and C++ (where truth is nonzero and falsehood is zero). If you want to use a non-**boolean** in a **boolean** test, such as **if(a)**, you must first convert it to a **boolean** value using a conditional expression, such as **if(a != 0)**.

if-else

The **if-else** statement is probably the most basic way to control program flow. The **else** is optional, so you can use **if** in two forms:

if(*Boolean-expression*)
  statement

or

if(*Boolean-expression*)
  statement
else
  statement

The conditional must produce a Boolean result. The *statement* means either a simple statement terminated by a semicolon or a compound statement, which is a group of simple statements enclosed in braces. Anytime the word "*statement*" is used, it always implies that the statement can be simple or compound.

As an example of **if-else**, here is a **test( )** method that will tell you whether a guess is above, below, or equivalent to a target number:

```
static int test(int testval) {
    int result = 0;
    if(testval > target)
        result = -1;
    else if(testval < target)
        result = +1;
    else
        result = 0; // match
    return result;
}
```

It is conventional to indent the body of a control flow statement so the reader might easily determine where it begins and ends.

return

The **return** keyword has two purposes: it specifies what value a method will return (if it doesn't have a **void** return value) and it causes that value to be returned immediately. The **test( )** method above can be rewritten to take advantage of this:

```
static int test2(int testval) {
```

```
      if(testval > target)
        return -1;
      if(testval < target)
        return +1;
      return 0; // match
    }
```

There's no need for **else** because the method will not continue after executing a **return**.

Iteration

while, **do-while** and **for** control looping and are sometimes classified as *iteration statements*. A *statement* repeats until the controlling *Boolean-expression* evaluates to false. The form for a **while** loop is

while(*Boolean-expression*)
  statement

The *Boolean-expression* is evaluated once at the beginning of the loop and again before each further iteration of the *statement*.

Here's a simple example that generates random numbers until a particular condition is met:

```
//: WhileTest.java
// Demonstrates the while loop

public class WhileTest {
  public static void main(String[] args) {
    double r = 0;
    while(r < 0.99d) {
      r = Math.random();
      System.out.println(r);
    }
  }
} ///:~
```

This uses the **static** method **random( )** in the **Math** library, which generates a **double** value between 0 and 1. (It includes 0, but not 1.) The conditional expression for the **while** says "keep doing this loop until the number is 0.99 or greater." Each time you run this program you'll get a different-sized list of numbers.

do-while

The form for **do-while** is

do
  statement
while(*Boolean-expression*);

The sole difference between **while** and **do-while** is that the statement of
the **do-while** always executes at least once, even if the expression
evaluates to false the first time. In a **while**, if the conditional is false the
first time the statement never executes. In practice, **do-while** is less
common than **while**.

for

A **for** loop performs initialization before the first iteration. Then it
performs conditional testing and, at the end of each iteration, some form
of "stepping." The form of the **for** loop is:

for(*initialization*; *Boolean-expression*; *step*)
  statement

Any of the expressions *initialization*, *Boolean-expression* or *step* can be
empty. The expression is tested before each iteration, and as soon as it
evaluates to **false** execution will continue at the line following the **for**
statement. At the end of each loop, the *step* executes.

for loops are usually used for "counting" tasks:

```
//: ListCharacters.java
// Demonstrates "for" loop by listing
// all the ASCII characters.

public class ListCharacters {
  public static void main(String[] args) {
  for( char c = 0; c < 128; c++)
    if (c != 26 )   // ANSI Clear screen
      System.out.println(
        "value: " + (int)c +
        " character: " + c);
  }
} ///:~
```

Note that the variable **c** is defined at the point where it is used, inside the control expression of the **for** loop, rather than at the beginning of the block denoted by the open curly brace. The scope of **c** is the expression controlled by the **for**.

Traditional procedural languages like C require that all variables be defined at the beginning of a block so when the compiler creates a block it can allocate space for those variables. In Java and C++ you can spread your variable declarations throughout the block, defining them at the point that you need them. This allows a more natural coding style and makes code easier to understand.

You can define multiple variables within a **for** statement, but they must be of the same type:

```
for(int i = 0, j = 1;
    i < 10 && j != 11;
    i++, j++)
  /* body of for loop */;
```

The **int** definition in the **for** statement covers both **i** and **j**. The ability to define variables in the control expression is limited to the **for** loop. You cannot use this approach with any of the other selection or iteration statements.

The comma operator

Earlier in this chapter I stated that the comma *operator* (not the comma *separator*, which is used to separate function arguments) has only one use in Java: in the control expression of a **for** loop. In both the initialization and step portions of the control expression you can have a number of statements separated by commas, and those statements will be evaluated sequentially. The previous bit of code uses this ability. Here's another example:

```
//: CommaOperator.java

public class CommaOperator {
  public static void main(String[] args) {
    for(int i = 1, j = i + 10; i < 5;
        i++, j = i * 2) {
      System.out.println("i= " + i + " j= " + j);
    }
  }
} ///:~
```

Here's the output:

```
i= 1 j= 11
i= 2 j= 4
i= 3 j= 6
i= 4 j= 8
```

You can see that in both the initialization and step portions the statements are evaluated in sequential order. Also, the initialization portion can have any number of definitions *of one type*.

break and continue

Inside the body of any of the iteration statements you can also control the flow of the loop by using **break** and **continue**. **break** quits the loop without executing the rest of the statements in the loop. **continue** stops the execution of the current iteration and goes back to the beginning of the loop to begin a new iteration.

This program shows examples of **break** and **continue** within **for** and **while** loops:

```java
//: BreakAndContinue.java
// Demonstrates break and continue keywords

public class BreakAndContinue {
  public static void main(String[] args) {
    for(int i = 0; i < 100; i++) {
      if(i == 74) break; // Out of for loop
      if(i % 9 != 0) continue; // Next iteration
      System.out.println(i);
    }
    int i = 0;
    // An "infinite loop":
    while(true) {
      i++;
      int j = i * 27;
      if(j == 1269) break; // Out of loop
      if(i % 10 != 0) continue; // Top of loop
      System.out.println(i);
    }
  }
} ///:~
```

In the **for** loop the value of **i** never gets to 100 because the **break** statement breaks out of the loop when **i** is 74. Normally, you'd use a **break** like this only if you didn't know when the terminating condition was going to occur. The **continue** statement causes execution to go back to the top of the iteration loop (thus incrementing **i**) whenever **i** is not evenly divisible by 9. When it is, the value is printed.

The second portion shows an "infinite loop" that would, in theory, continue forever. However, inside the loop there is a **break** statement that will break out of the loop. In addition, you'll see that the **continue** moves back to the top of the loop without completing the remainder. (Thus printing happens only when the value of **i** is divisible by 9.) The output is:

```
0
9
18
27
36
45
54
63
72
10
20
30
40
```

The value 0 is printed because 0 % 9 produces 0.

A second form of the infinite loop is **for(;;)**. The compiler treats both **while(true)** and **for(;;)** in the same way so whichever one you use is a matter of programming taste.

The infamous "goto"

The **goto** keyword has been present in programming languages from the beginning. Indeed, **goto** was the genesis of program control in assembly language: "if condition A, then jump here, otherwise jump there." If you read the assembly code that is ultimately generated by virtually any compiler, you'll see that program control contains many jumps. However, **goto** jumps at the source-code level, and that's what brought it into disrepute. If a program will always jump from one point to another, isn't there some way to reorganize the code so the flow of control is not so jumpy? **goto** fell into true disfavor with the publication of the famous

"Goto considered harmful" paper by Edsger Dijkstra, and since then goto-bashing has been a popular sport, with advocates of the cast-out keyword scurrying for cover.

As is typical in situations like this, the middle ground is the most fruitful. The problem is not the use of **goto** but the overuse of **goto**, and in rare situations **goto** is the best way to structure control flow.

Although **goto** is a reserved word in Java, it is not used in the language; Java has no **goto**. However, it does have something that looks a bit like a jump tied in with the **break** and **continue** keywords. It's not a jump but rather a way to break out of an iteration statement. The reason it's often thrown in with discussions of **goto** is because it uses the same mechanism: a label.

A label is an identifier followed by a colon, like this:

```
label1:
```

The *only* place a label is useful in Java is right before an iteration statement. And that means *right* before – it does no good to put any other statement between the label and the iteration. And the sole reason to put a label before an iteration is if you're going to nest another iteration or a switch inside it. That's because the **break** and **continue** keywords will normally interrupt only the current loop, but when used with a label they'll interrupt the loops up to where the label exists:

```
label1:
outer-iteration {
  inner-iteration {
    //...
    break; // 1
    //...
    continue;  // 2
    //...
    continue label1; // 3
    //...
    break label1;  // 4
  }
}
```

In case 1, the **break** breaks out of the inner iteration and you end up in the outer iteration. In case 2, the **continue** moves back to the beginning of the inner iteration. But in case 3, the **continue label1** breaks out of the inner iteration *and* the outer iteration, all the way back to **label1**. Then it does in fact continue the iteration, but starting at the outer

---

iteration. In case 4, the **break label1** also breaks all the way out to **label1**, but it does not re-enter the iteration. It actually does break out of both iterations.

Here is an example using **for** loops:

```java
//: LabeledFor.java
// Java's "labeled for loop"

public class LabeledFor {
  public static void main(String[] args) {
    int i = 0;
    outer: // Can't have statements here
    for(; true ;) { // infinite loop
      inner: // Can't have statements here
      for(; i < 10; i++) {
        prt("i = " + i);
        if(i == 2) {
          prt("continue");
          continue;
        }
        if(i == 3) {
          prt("break");
          i++; // Otherwise i never
               // gets incremented.
          break;
        }
        if(i == 7) {
          prt("continue outer");
          i++; // Otherwise i never
               // gets incremented.
          continue outer;
        }
        if(i == 8) {
          prt("break outer");
          break outer;
        }
        for(int k = 0; k < 5; k++) {
          if(k == 3) {
            prt("continue inner");
            continue inner;
          }
        }
      }
    }
  }
```

```
        // Can't break or continue
        // to labels here
    }
    static void prt(String s) {
        System.out.println(s);
    }
} ///:~
```

This uses the **prt( )** method that has been defined in the other examples.

Note that **break** breaks out of the **for** loop, and that the increment-expression doesn't occur until the end of the pass through the **for** loop. Since **break** skips the increment expression, the increment is performed directly in the case of **i == 3**. The **continue outer** statement in the case of **I == 7** also goes to the top of the loop and also skips the increment, so it too is incremented directly.

Here is the output:

```
i = 0
continue inner
i = 1
continue inner
i = 2
continue
i = 3
break
i = 4
continue inner
i = 5
continue inner
i = 6
continue inner
i = 7
continue outer
i = 8
break outer
```

If not for the **break outer** statement, there would be no way to get out of the outer loop from within an inner loop, since **break** by itself can break out of only the innermost loop. (The same is true for **continue**.)

Of course, in the cases where breaking out of a loop will also exit the method, you can simply use a **return**.

Here is a demonstration of labeled **break** and **continue** statements with **while** loops:

```
//: LabeledWhile.java
// Java's "labeled while" loop

public class LabeledWhile {
  public static void main(String[] args) {
    int i = 0;
    outer:
    while(true) {
      prt("Outer while loop");
      while(true) {
        i++;
        prt("i = " + i);
        if(i == 1) {
          prt("continue");
          continue;
        }
        if(i == 3) {
          prt("continue outer");
          continue outer;
        }
        if(i == 5) {
          prt("break");
          break;
        }
        if(i == 7) {
          prt("break outer");
          break outer;
        }
      }
    }
  }
  static void prt(String s) {
    System.out.println(s);
  }
} ///:~
```

The same rules hold true for **while**:

1. A plain **continue** goes to the top of the innermost loop and continues.

2. A labeled **continue** goes to the label and re-enters the loop right after that label.

3. A **break** "drops out of the bottom" of the loop.

4. A labeled **break** drops out of the bottom of the end of the loop denoted by the label.

The output of this method makes it clear:

```
Outer while loop
i = 1
continue
i = 2
i = 3
continue outer
Outer while loop
i = 4
i = 5
break
Outer while loop
i = 6
i = 7
break outer
```

It's important to remember that the *only* reason to use labels in Java is when you have nested loops and you want to **break** or **continue** through more than one nested level.

In Dijkstra's "goto considered harmful" paper, what he specifically objected to was the labels, not the goto. He observed that the number of bugs seems to increase with the number of labels in a program. Labels and gotos make programs difficult to analyze statically, since it introduces cycles in the program execution graph. Note that Java labels don't suffer from this problem, since they are constrained in their placement and can't be used to transfer control in an ad hoc manner. It's also interesting to note that this is a case where a language feature is made more useful by restricting the power of the statement.

switch

The **switch** is sometimes classified as a *selection statement*. The **switch** statement selects from among pieces of code based on the value of an integral expression. Its form is:

```
switch(integral-selector) {
  case integral-value1 : statement; break;
  case integral-value2 : statement; break;
  case integral-value3 : statement; break;
  case integral-value4 : statement; break;
  case integral-value5 : statement; break;
      // ...
  default: statement;
}
```

Integral-selector is an expression that produces an integral value. The **switch** compares the result of *integral-selector* to each *integral-value*. If it finds a match, the corresponding *statement* (simple or compound) executes. If no match occurs, the **default** *statement* executes.

You will notice in the above definition that each **case** ends with a **break**, which causes execution to jump to the end of the **switch** body. This is the conventional way to build a **switch** statement, but the **break** is optional. If it is missing, the code for the following case statements execute until a **break** is encountered. Although you don't usually want this kind of behavior, it can be useful to an experienced programmer. Note the last statement, for the **default**, doesn't have a **break** because the execution just falls through to where the **break** would have taken it anyway. You could put a **break** at the end of the **default** statement with no harm if you considered it important for style's sake.

The **switch** statement is a clean way to implement multi-way selection (i.e., selecting from among a number of different execution paths), but it requires a selector that evaluates to an integral value such as **int** or **char**. If you want to use, for example, a string or a floating-point number as a selector, it won't work in a **switch** statement. For non-integral types, you must use a series of **if** statements.

Here's an example that creates letters randomly and determines whether they're vowels or consonants:

```
//: VowelsAndConsonants.java
// Demonstrates the switch statement

public class VowelsAndConsonants {
  public static void main(String[] args) {
    for(int i = 0; i < 100; i++) {
      char c = (char)(Math.random() * 26 + 'a');
      System.out.print(c + ": ");
      switch(c) {
```

```
            case 'a':
            case 'e':
            case 'i':
            case 'o':
            case 'u':
                    System.out.println("vowel");
                    break;
            case 'y':
            case 'w':
                    System.out.println(
                      "Sometimes a vowel");
                    break;
            default:
                    System.out.println("consonant");
            }
        }
    }
} ///:~
```

Since **Math.random( )** generates a value between 0 and 1, you need only multiply it by the upper bound of the range of numbers you want to produce (26 for the letters in the alphabet) and add an offset to establish the lower bound.

Although it appears you're switching on a character here, the **switch** statement is actually using the integral value of the character. The singly-quoted characters in the **case** statements also produce integral values that are used for comparison.

Notice how the **case**s can be "stacked" on top of each other to provide multiple matches for a particular piece of code. You should also be aware that it's essential to put the **break** statement at the end of a particular case, otherwise control will simply drop through and continue processing on the next case.

Calculation details

The statement:

```
    char c = (char)(Math.random() * 26 + 'a');
```

deserves a closer look. **Math.random( )** produces a **double**, so the value 26 is converted to a **double** to perform the multiplication, which also produces a **double**. This means that 'a' must be converted to a **double** to perform the addition. The **double** result is turned back into a **char** with a cast.

First, what does the cast to **char** do? That is, if you have the value 29.7 and you cast it to a **char**, is the resulting value 30 or 29? The answer to this can be seen in this example:

```
//: CastingNumbers.java
// What happens when you cast a float or double
// to an integral value?

public class CastingNumbers {
  public static void main(String[] args) {
    double
      above = 0.7,
      below = 0.4;
    System.out.println("above: " + above);
    System.out.println("below: " + below);
    System.out.println(
      "(int)above: " + (int)above);
    System.out.println(
      "(int)below: " + (int)below);
    System.out.println(
      "(char)('a' + above): " +
      (char)('a' + above));
    System.out.println(
      "(char)('a' + below): " +
      (char)('a' + below));
  }
} ///:~
```

The output is:

```
above: 0.7
below: 0.4
(int)above: 0
(int)below: 0
(char)('a' + above): a
(char)('a' + below): a
```

So the answer is that casting from a **float** or **double** to an integral value always truncates.

The second question has to do with **Math.random( )**. Does it produce a value from zero to one, inclusive or exclusive of the value '1'? In math lingo, is it (0,1), or [0,1], or (0,1] or [0,1)? (The square bracket means "includes" whereas the parenthesis means "doesn't include.") Again, a test program provides the answer:

Thinking in Java *www.BruceEckel.com*

```
//: RandomBounds.java
// Does Math.random() produce 0.0 and 1.0?

public class RandomBounds {
  static void usage() {
    System.err.println("Usage: \n\t" +
      "RandomBounds lower\n\t" +
      "RandomBounds upper");
    System.exit(1);
  }
  public static void main(String[] args) {
    if(args.length != 1) usage();
    if(args[0].equals("lower")) {
      while(Math.random() != 0.0)
        ; // Keep trying
      System.out.println("Produced 0.0!");
    }
    else if(args[0].equals("upper")) {
      while(Math.random() != 1.0)
        ; // Keep trying
      System.out.println("Produced 1.0!");
    }
    else
      usage();
  }
} ///:~
```

To run the program, you type a command line of either:

```
java RandomBounds lower
```

or

```
java RandomBounds upper
```

In both cases you are forced to break out of the program manually, so it would *appear* that **Math.random( )** never produces either 0.0 or 1.0. But this is where such an experiment can be deceiving. If you consider that there are 2^{128} different double fractions between 0 and 1, the likelihood of reaching any one value experimentally might exceed the lifetime of one computer, or even one experimenter. It turns out that 0.0 *is* included in the output of **Math.random( )**. Or, in math lingo, it is [0,1).

Summary

This chapter concludes the study of fundamental features that appear in most programming languages: calculation, operator precedence, type casting, and selection and iteration. Now you're ready to begin taking steps that move you closer to the world of object-oriented programming. The next chapter will cover the important issues of initialization and cleanup of objects, followed in the subsequent chapter by the essential concept of implementation hiding.

Exercises

1. Write a program that prints values from one to 100.

2. Modify Exercise 1 so that the program exits by using the **break** keyword at value 47. Try using **return** instead.

3. Create a **switch** statement that prints a message for each **case**, and put the **switch** inside a **for** loop that tries each **case**. Put a **break** after each **case** and test it, then remove the **breaks** and see what happens.

4: Initialization and cleanup

As the computer revolution progresses, "unsafe" programming has become one of the major culprits that makes programming expensive.

Two of these safety issues are *initialization* and *cleanup*. Many C bugs occur when the programmer forgets to initialize a variable. This is especially true with libraries when users don't know how to initialize a library component, or even that they must. Cleanup is a special problem because it's easy to forget about an element when you're done with it, since it no longer concerns you. Thus, the resources used by that element are retained and you can easily end up running out of resources (most notably memory).

C++ introduced the concept of a *constructor*, a special method automatically called when an object is created. Java also adopted the constructor, and in addition has a garbage collector that automatically releases memory resources when they're no longer being used. This chapter examines the issues of initialization and cleanup and their support in Java.

Guaranteed initialization with the constructor

You can imagine creating a method called **initialize( )** for every class you write. The name is a hint that it should be called before using the object. Unfortunately, this means the user must remember to call the method. In Java, the class designer can guarantee initialization of every object by providing a special method called a *constructor*. If a class has a constructor, Java automatically calls that constructor when an object is created, before users can even get their hands on it. So initialization is guaranteed.

The next challenge is what to name this method. There are two issues. The first is that any name you use could clash with a name you might like to use as a member in the class. The second is that because the compiler is responsible for calling the constructor, it must always know which method to call. The C++ solution seems the easiest and most logical, so it's also used in Java: The name of the constructor is the same as the name of the class. It makes sense that such a method will be called automatically on initialization.

Here's a simple class with a constructor: (See page 97 if you have trouble executing this program.)

```
//: SimpleConstructor.java
// Demonstration of a simple constructor
package c04;

class Rock {
  Rock() { // This is the constructor
    System.out.println("Creating Rock");
  }
}

public class SimpleConstructor {
  public static void main(String[] args) {
    for(int i = 0; i < 10; i++)
      new Rock();
```

```
    }
  } ///:~
```

Now, when an object is created:

```
  new Rock();
```

storage is allocated and the constructor is called. It is guaranteed that the object will be properly initialized before you can get your hands on it.

Note that the coding style of making the first letter of all methods lower case does not apply to constructors, since the name of the constructor must match the name of the class *exactly*.

Like any method, the constructor can have arguments to allow you to specify *how* an object is created. The above example can easily be changed so the constructor takes an argument:

```
class Rock {
  Rock(int i) {
    System.out.println(
      "Creating Rock number " + i);
  }
}

public class SimpleConstructor {
  public static void main(String[] args) {
    for(int i = 0; i < 10; i++)
      new Rock(i);
  }
}
```

Constructor arguments provide you with a way to provide parameters for the initialization of an object. For example, if the class **Tree** has a constructor that takes a single integer argument denoting the height of the tree, you would create a **Tree** object like this:

```
  Tree t = new Tree(12);   // 12-foot tree
```

If **Tree(int)** is your only constructor, then the compiler won't let you create a **Tree** object any other way.

Constructors eliminate a large class of problems and make the code easier to read. In the preceding code fragment, for example, you don't see an explicit call to some **initialize( )** method that is conceptually separate from definition. In Java, definition and initialization are unified concepts – you can't have one without the other.

The constructor is an unusual type of method because it has no return value. This is distinctly different from a **void** return value, in which the method returns nothing but you still have the option to make it return something else. Constructors return nothing and you don't have an option. If there were a return value, and if you could select your own, the compiler would somehow need to know what to do with that return value.

Method overloading

One of the important features in any programming language is the use of names. When you create an object, you give a name to a region of storage. A method is a name for an action. By using names to describe your system, you create a program that is easier for people to understand and change. It's a lot like writing prose – the goal is to communicate with your readers.

You refer to all objects and methods by using names. Well-chosen names make it easier for you and others to understand your code.

A problem arises when mapping the concept of nuance in human language onto a programming language. Often, the same word expresses a number of different meanings – it's *overloaded*. This is useful, especially when it comes to trivial differences. You say "wash the shirt," "wash the car," and "wash the dog." It would be silly to be forced to say, "shirtWash the shirt," "carWash the car," and "dogWash the dog" just so the listener doesn't need to make any distinction about the action performed. Most human languages are redundant, so even if you miss a few words, you can still determine the meaning. We don't need unique identifiers – we can deduce meaning from context.

Most programming languages (C in particular) require you to have a unique identifier for each function. So you could not have one function called **print( )** for printing integers and another called **print( )** for printing floats – each function requires a unique name.

In Java, another factor forces the overloading of method names: the constructor. Because the constructor's name is predetermined by the name of the class, there can be only one constructor name. But what if you want to create an object in more than one way? For example, suppose you build a class that can initialize itself in a standard way and by reading information from a file. You need two constructors, one that takes no arguments (the *default* constructor), and one that takes a **String** as an argument, which is the name of the file from which to initialize the object. Both are constructors, so they must have the same name – the name of the class. Thus *method overloading* is essential to allow the same method name to be used with different argument types. And although method overloading is a must for constructors, it's a general convenience and can be used with any method.

Here's an example that shows both overloaded constructors and overloaded ordinary methods:

```
//: Overloading.java
// Demonstration of both constructor
// and ordinary method overloading.
import java.util.*;

class Tree {
  int height;
  Tree() {
    prt("Planting a seedling");
    height = 0;
  }
  Tree(int i) {
    prt("Creating new Tree that is "
        + i + " feet tall");
    height = i;
  }
  void info() {
    prt("Tree is " + height
        + " feet tall");
  }
  void info(String s) {
    prt(s + ": Tree is "
        + height + " feet tall");
  }
  static void prt(String s) {
    System.out.println(s);
  }
}

public class Overloading {
  public static void main(String[] args) {
    for(int i = 0; i < 5; i++) {
      Tree t = new Tree(i);
      t.info();
      t.info("overloaded method");
    }
```

```
      // Overloaded constructor:
      new Tree();
  }
} ///:~
```

A **Tree** object can be created either as a seedling, with no argument, or as a plant grown in a nursery, with an existing height. To support this, there are two constructors, one that takes no arguments (we call constructors that take no arguments *default constructors*[1]) and one that takes the existing height.

You might also want to call the **info( )** method in more than one way. For example, with a **String** argument if you have an extra message you want printed, and without if you have nothing more to say. It would seem strange to give two separate names to what is obviously the same concept. Fortunately, method overloading allows you to use the same name for both.

Distinguishing overloaded methods

If the methods have the same name, how can Java know which method you mean? There's a simple rule: Each overloaded method must take a unique list of argument types.

If you think about this for a second, it makes sense: how else could a programmer tell the difference between two methods that have the same name, other than by the types of their arguments?

Even differences in the ordering of arguments is sufficient to distinguish two methods: (Although you don't normally want to take this approach, as it produces difficult-to-maintain code.)

```
//: OverloadingOrder.java
// Overloading based on the order of
// the arguments.

public class OverloadingOrder {
  static void print(String s, int i) {
    System.out.println(
```

---

[1] In some of the Java literature from Sun they instead refer to these with the clumsy but descriptive name "no-arg constructors." The term "default constructor" has been in use for many years and so I will use that.

```
        "String: " + s +
        ", int: " + i);
    }
    static void print(int i, String s) {
      System.out.println(
        "int: " + i +
        ", String: " + s);
    }
    public static void main(String[] args) {
      print("String first", 11);
      print(99, "Int first");
    }
  } ///:~
```

The two **print( )** methods have identical arguments, but the order is different, and that's what makes them distinct.

Overloading with primitives

Primitives can be automatically promoted from a smaller type to a larger one and this can be slightly confusing in combination with overloading. The following example demonstrates what happens when a primitive is handed to an overloaded method:

```
//: PrimitiveOverloading.java
// Promotion of primitives and overloading

public class PrimitiveOverloading {
  // boolean can't be automatically converted
  static void prt(String s) {
    System.out.println(s);
  }

  void f1(char x) { prt("f1(char)"); }
  void f1(byte x) { prt("f1(byte)"); }
  void f1(short x) { prt("f1(short)"); }
  void f1(int x) { prt("f1(int)"); }
  void f1(long x) { prt("f1(long)"); }
  void f1(float x) { prt("f1(float)"); }
  void f1(double x) { prt("f1(double)"); }

  void f2(byte x) { prt("f2(byte)"); }
  void f2(short x) { prt("f2(short)"); }
  void f2(int x) { prt("f2(int)"); }
```

```java
void f2(long x) { prt("f2(long)"); }
void f2(float x) { prt("f2(float)"); }
void f2(double x) { prt("f2(double)"); }

void f3(short x) { prt("f3(short)"); }
void f3(int x) { prt("f3(int)"); }
void f3(long x) { prt("f3(long)"); }
void f3(float x) { prt("f3(float)"); }
void f3(double x) { prt("f3(double)"); }

void f4(int x) { prt("f4(int)"); }
void f4(long x) { prt("f4(long)"); }
void f4(float x) { prt("f4(float)"); }
void f4(double x) { prt("f4(double)"); }

void f5(long x) { prt("f5(long)"); }
void f5(float x) { prt("f5(float)"); }
void f5(double x) { prt("f5(double)"); }

void f6(float x) { prt("f6(float)"); }
void f6(double x) { prt("f6(double)"); }

void f7(double x) { prt("f7(double)"); }

void testConstVal() {
  prt("Testing with 5");
  f1(5);f2(5);f3(5);f4(5);f5(5);f6(5);f7(5);
}
void testChar() {
  char x = 'x';
  prt("char argument:");
  f1(x);f2(x);f3(x);f4(x);f5(x);f6(x);f7(x);
}
void testByte() {
  byte x = 0;
  prt("byte argument:");
  f1(x);f2(x);f3(x);f4(x);f5(x);f6(x);f7(x);
}
void testShort() {
  short x = 0;
  prt("short argument:");
  f1(x);f2(x);f3(x);f4(x);f5(x);f6(x);f7(x);
}
void testInt() {
```

```
    int x = 0;
    prt("int argument:");
    f1(x);f2(x);f3(x);f4(x);f5(x);f6(x);f7(x);
  }
  void testLong() {
    long x = 0;
    prt("long argument:");
    f1(x);f2(x);f3(x);f4(x);f5(x);f6(x);f7(x);
  }
  void testFloat() {
    float x = 0;
    prt("float argument:");
    f1(x);f2(x);f3(x);f4(x);f5(x);f6(x);f7(x);
  }
  void testDouble() {
    double x = 0;
    prt("double argument:");
    f1(x);f2(x);f3(x);f4(x);f5(x);f6(x);f7(x);
  }
  public static void main(String[] args) {
    PrimitiveOverloading p =
      new PrimitiveOverloading();
    p.testConstVal();
    p.testChar();
    p.testByte();
    p.testShort();
    p.testInt();
    p.testLong();
    p.testFloat();
    p.testDouble();
  }
} ///:~
```

If you view the output of this program, you'll see that the constant value 5 is treated as an **int**, so if an overloaded method is available that takes an **int** it is used. In all other cases, if you have a data type that is smaller than the argument in the method, that data type is promoted. **char** produces a slightly different effect, since if it doesn't find an exact **char** match, it is promoted to **int**.

What happens if your argument is *bigger* than the argument expected by the overloaded method? A modification of the above program gives the answer:

```
//: Demotion.java
```

```
// Demotion of primitives and overloading

public class Demotion {
  static void prt(String s) {
    System.out.println(s);
  }

  void f1(char x) { prt("f1(char)"); }
  void f1(byte x) { prt("f1(byte)"); }
  void f1(short x) { prt("f1(short)"); }
  void f1(int x) { prt("f1(int)"); }
  void f1(long x) { prt("f1(long)"); }
  void f1(float x) { prt("f1(float)"); }
  void f1(double x) { prt("f1(double)"); }

  void f2(char x) { prt("f2(char)"); }
  void f2(byte x) { prt("f2(byte)"); }
  void f2(short x) { prt("f2(short)"); }
  void f2(int x) { prt("f2(int)"); }
  void f2(long x) { prt("f2(long)"); }
  void f2(float x) { prt("f2(float)"); }

  void f3(char x) { prt("f3(char)"); }
  void f3(byte x) { prt("f3(byte)"); }
  void f3(short x) { prt("f3(short)"); }
  void f3(int x) { prt("f3(int)"); }
  void f3(long x) { prt("f3(long)"); }

  void f4(char x) { prt("f4(char)"); }
  void f4(byte x) { prt("f4(byte)"); }
  void f4(short x) { prt("f4(short)"); }
  void f4(int x) { prt("f4(int)"); }

  void f5(char x) { prt("f5(char)"); }
  void f5(byte x) { prt("f5(byte)"); }
  void f5(short x) { prt("f5(short)"); }

  void f6(char x) { prt("f6(char)"); }
  void f6(byte x) { prt("f6(byte)"); }

  void f7(char x) { prt("f7(char)"); }

  void testDouble() {
    double x = 0;
```

```
      prt("double argument:");
      f1(x);f2((float)x);f3((long)x);f4((int)x);
      f5((short)x);f6((byte)x);f7((char)x);
  }
  public static void main(String[] args) {
      Demotion p = new Demotion();
      p.testDouble();
  }
} ///:~
```

Here, the methods take narrower primitive values. If your argument is wider then you must *cast* to the necessary type using the type name in parentheses. If you don't do this, the compiler will issue an error message.

You should be aware that this is a *narrowing conversion*, which means you might lose information during the cast. This is why the compiler forces you to do it – to flag the narrowing conversion.

Overloading on return values

It is common to wonder "Why only class names and method argument lists? Why not distinguish between methods based on their return values?" For example, these two methods, which have the same name and arguments, are easily distinguished from each other:

```
void f() {}
int f() {}
```

This works fine when the compiler can unequivocally determine the meaning from the context, as in **int x = f( )**. However, you can call a method and ignore the return value; this is often referred to as *calling a method for its side effect* since you don't care about the return value but instead want the other effects of the method call. So if you call the method this way:

```
f();
```

how can Java determine which **f( )** should be called? And how could someone reading the code see it? Because of this sort of problem, you cannot use return value types to distinguish overloaded methods.

Default constructors

As mentioned previously, a default constructor is one without arguments, used to create a "vanilla object." If you create a class that has no constructors, the compiler will automatically create a default constructor for you. For example:

```
//: DefaultConstructor.java

class Bird {
  int i;
}

public class DefaultConstructor {
  public static void main(String[] args) {
    Bird nc = new Bird(); // default!
  }
} ///:~
```

The line

```
new Bird();
```

creates a new object and calls the default constructor, even though one was not explicitly defined. Without it we would have no method to call to build our object. However, if you define any constructors (with or without arguments), the compiler will *not* synthesize one for you:

```
class Bush {
  Bush(int i) {}
  Bush(double d) {}
}
```

Now if you say:

```
new Bush();
```

the compiler will complain that it cannot find a constructor that matches. It's as if when you don't put in any constructors, the compiler says "You are bound to need *some* constructor, so let me make one for you." But if you write a constructor, the compiler says "You've written a constructor so you know what you're doing; if you didn't put in a default it's because you meant to leave it out."

The **this** keyword

If you have two objects of the same type called **a** and **b**, you might wonder how it is that you can call a method **f( )** for both those objects:

```
class Banana { void f(int i) { /* ... */ } }
Banana a = new Banana(), b = new Banana();
a.f(1);
b.f(2);
```

If there's only one method called **f( )**, how can that method know whether it's being called for the object **a** or **b**?

To allow you to write the code in a convenient object-oriented syntax in which you "send a message to an object," the compiler does some undercover work for you. There's a secret first argument passed to the method **f( )**, and that argument is the handle to the object that's being manipulated. So the two method calls above become something like:

```
Banana.f(a,1);
Banana.f(b,2);
```

This is internal and you can't write these expressions and get the compiler to accept them, but it gives you an idea of what's happening.

Suppose you're inside a method and you'd like to get the handle to the current object. Since that handle is passed *secretly* by the compiler, there's no identifier for it. However, for this purpose there's a keyword: **this**. The **this** keyword – which can be used only inside a method – produces the handle to the object the method has been called for. You can treat this handle just like any other object handle. Keep in mind that if you're calling a method of your class from within another method of your class, you don't need to use **this**; you simply call the method. The current **this** handle is automatically used for the other method. Thus you can say:

```
class Apricot {
  void pick() { /* ... */ }
  void pit() { pick(); /* ... */ }
}
```

Inside **pit( )**, you *could* say **this.pick( )** but there's no need to. The compiler does it for you automatically. The **this** keyword is used only for those special cases in which you need to explicitly use the handle to the current object. For example, it's often used in **return** statements when you want to return the handle to the current object:

```
//: Leaf.java
// Simple use of the "this" keyword

public class Leaf {
  private int i = 0;
  Leaf increment() {
    i++;
    return this;
  }
  void print() {
    System.out.println("i = " + i);
  }
  public static void main(String[] args) {
    Leaf x = new Leaf();
    x.increment().increment().increment().print();
  }
} ///:~
```

Because **increment( )** returns the handle to the current object via the **this** keyword, multiple operations can easily be performed on the same object.

Calling constructors from constructors

When you write several constructors for a class, there are times when you'd like to call one constructor from another to avoid duplicating code. You can do this using the **this** keyword.

Normally, when you say **this**, it is in the sense of "this object" or "the current object," and by itself it produces the handle to the current object. In a constructor, the **this** keyword takes on a different meaning when you give it an argument list: it makes an explicit call to the constructor that matches that argument list. Thus you have a straightforward way to call other constructors:

```
//: Flower.java
// Calling constructors with "this"

public class Flower {
  private int petalCount = 0;
  private String s = new String("null");
  Flower(int petals) {
    petalCount = petals;
    System.out.println(
      "Constructor w/ int arg only, petalCount= "
      + petalCount);
```

```
        }
        Flower(String ss) {
          System.out.println(
            "Constructor w/ String arg only, s=" + ss);
          s = ss;
        }
        Flower(String s, int petals) {
          this(petals);
//!       this(s); // Can't call two!
          this.s = s; // Another use of "this"
          System.out.println("String & int args");
        }
        Flower() {
          this("hi", 47);
          System.out.println(
            "default constructor (no args)");
        }
        void print() {
//!       this(11); // Not inside non-constructor!
          System.out.println(
            "petalCount = " + petalCount + " s = "+ s);
        }
        public static void main(String[] args) {
          Flower x = new Flower();
          x.print();
        }
      } ///:~
```

The constructor **Flower(String s, int petals)** shows that, while you can call one constructor using **this**, you cannot call two. In addition, the constructor call must be the first thing you do or you'll get a compiler error message.

This example also shows another way you'll see **this** used. Since the name of the argument **s** and the name of the member data **s** are the same, there's an ambiguity. You can resolve it by saying **this.s** to refer to the member data. You'll often see this form used in Java code, and it's used in numerous places in this book.

In **print( )** you can see that the compiler won't let you call a constructor from inside any method other than a constructor.

The meaning of **static**

With the **this** keyword in mind, you can more fully understand what it means to make a method **static**. It means that there is no **this** for that particular method. You cannot call non-**static** methods from inside **static** methods[2] (although the reverse is possible), and you can call a **static** method for the class itself, without any object. In fact, that's primarily what a **static** method is for. It's as if you're creating the equivalent of a global function (from C). Except global functions are not permitted in Java, and putting the **static** method inside a class allows it access to other **static** methods and to **static** fields.

Some people argue that **static** methods are not object-oriented since they do have the semantics of a global function; with a **static** method you don't send a message to an object, since there's no **this**. This is probably a fair argument, and if you find yourself using a *lot* of static methods you should probably rethink your strategy. However, **static**s are pragmatic and there are times when you genuinely need them, so whether or not they are "proper OOP" should be left to the theoreticians. Indeed, even Smalltalk has the equivalent in its "class methods."

Cleanup: finalization and garbage collection

Programmers know about the importance of initialization, but often forget the importance of cleanup. After all, who needs to clean up an **int**? But with libraries, simply "letting go" of an object once you're done with it is not always safe. Of course, Java has the garbage collector to reclaim the memory of objects that are no longer used. Now consider a very special and unusual case. Suppose your object allocates "special" memory without using **new**. The garbage collector knows only how to release memory allocated *with* **new**, so it won't know how to release the object's "special" memory. To handle this case, Java provides a method called **finalize( )** that you can define for your class. Here's how it's *supposed* to work. When the garbage collector is ready to release the storage used for

---

[2] The one case in which this is possible occurs if you pass a handle to an object into the **static** method. Then, via the handle (which is now effectively **this**), you can call non-**static** methods and access non-**static** fields. But typically if you want to do something like this you'll just make an ordinary, non-**static** method.

your object, it will first call **finalize( )**, and only on the next garbage-collection pass will it reclaim the object's memory. So if you choose to use **finalize( )**, it gives you the ability to perform some important cleanup *at the time of garbage collection*.

This is a potential programming pitfall because some programmers, especially C++ programmers, might initially mistake **finalize( )** for the *destructor* in C++, which is a function that is always called when an object is destroyed. But it is important to distinguish between C++ and Java here, because in C++ *objects always get destroyed* (in a bug-free program), whereas in Java objects do not always get garbage-collected. Or, put another way:

Garbage collection is not destruction.

If you remember this, you will stay out of trouble. What it means is that if there is some activity that must be performed before you no longer need an object, you must perform that activity yourself. Java has no destructor or similar concept, so you must create an ordinary method to perform this cleanup. For example, suppose in the process of creating your object it draws itself on the screen. If you don't explicitly erase its image from the screen, it might never get cleaned up. If you put some kind of erasing functionality inside **finalize( )**, then if an object is garbage-collected, the image will first be removed from the screen, but if it isn't, the image will remain. So a second point to remember is:

Your objects might not get garbage collected.

You might find that the storage for an object never gets released because your program never nears the point of running out of storage. If your program completes and the garbage collector never gets around to releasing the storage for any of your objects, that storage will be returned to the operating system *en masse* as the program exits. This is a good thing, because garbage collection has some overhead, and if you never do it you never incur that expense.

What is **finalize( )** for?

You might believe at this point that you should not use **finalize( )** as a general-purpose cleanup method. What good is it?

A third point to remember is:

Garbage collection is only about memory.

That is, the sole reason for the existence of the garbage collector is to recover memory that your program is no longer using. So any activity that is associated with garbage collection, most notably your **finalize( )** method, must also be only about memory and its deallocation.

Does this mean that if your object contains other objects **finalize( )** should explicitly release those objects? Well, no – the garbage collector takes care of the release of all object memory regardless of how the object is created. It turns out that the need for **finalize( )** is limited to special cases, in which your object can allocate some storage in some way other than creating an object. But, you might observe, everything in Java is an object so how can this be?

It would seem that **finalize( )** is in place because of the possibility that you'll do something C-like by allocating memory using a mechanism other than the normal one in Java. This can happen primarily through *native methods*, which are a way to call non-Java code from Java. (Native methods are discussed in Appendix A.) C and C++ are the only languages currently supported by native methods, but since they can call subprograms in other languages, you can effectively call anything. Inside the non-Java code, C's **malloc( )** family of functions might be called to allocate storage, and unless you call **free( )** that storage will not be released, causing a memory leak. Of course, **free( )** is a C and C++ function, so you'd need call it in a native method inside your **finalize( )**.

After reading this, you probably get the idea that you won't use **finalize( )** much. You're correct; it is not the appropriate place for normal cleanup to occur. So where should normal cleanup be performed?

You must perform cleanup

To clean up an object, the user of that object must call a cleanup method at the point the cleanup is desired. This sounds pretty straightforward, but it collides a bit with the C++ concept of the destructor. In C++, all objects are destroyed. Or rather, all objects *should be* destroyed. If the C++ object is created as a local, i.e. on the stack (not possible in Java), then the destruction happens at the closing curly brace of the scope in which the object was created. If the object was created using **new** (like in Java) the destructor is called when the programmer calls the C++ operator **delete** (which doesn't exist in Java). If the programmer forgets, the destructor is never called and you have a memory leak, plus the other parts of the object never get cleaned up.

In contrast, Java doesn't allow you to create local objects – you must always use **new**. But in Java, there's no "delete" to call for releasing the object since the garbage collector releases the storage for you. So from a simplistic standpoint you could say that because of garbage collection, Java has no destructor. You'll see as this book progresses, however, that the presence of a garbage collector does not remove the need or utility of destructors. (And you should never call **finalize( )** directly, so that's not an appropriate avenue for a solution.) If you want some kind of cleanup performed other than storage release you must *still* call a method in Java, which is the equivalent of a C++ destructor without the convenience.

One of the things **finalize( )** can be useful for is observing the process of garbage collection. The following example shows you what's going on and summarizes the previous descriptions of garbage collection:

```
//: Garbage.java
// Demonstration of the garbage
// collector and finalization

class Chair {
  static boolean gcrun = false;
  static boolean f = false;
  static int created = 0;
  static int finalized = 0;
  int i;
  Chair() {
    i = ++created;
    if(created == 47)
      System.out.println("Created 47");
  }
  protected void finalize() {
    if(!gcrun) {
      gcrun = true;
      System.out.println(
        "Beginning to finalize after " +
        created + " Chairs have been created");
    }
    if(i == 47) {
      System.out.println(
        "Finalizing Chair #47, " +
        "Setting flag to stop Chair creation");
      f = true;
    }
    finalized++;
    if(finalized >= created)
      System.out.println(
```

```
              "All " + finalized + " finalized");
    }
  }

  public class Garbage {
    public static void main(String[] args) {
      if(args.length == 0) {
        System.err.println("Usage: \n" +
          "java Garbage before\n  or:\n" +
          "java Garbage after");
        return;
      }
      while(!Chair.f) {
        new Chair();
        new String("To take up space");
      }
      System.out.println(
        "After all Chairs have been created:\n" +
        "total created = " + Chair.created +
        ", total finalized = " + Chair.finalized);
      if(args[0].equals("before")) {
        System.out.println("gc():");
        System.gc();
        System.out.println("runFinalization():");
        System.runFinalization();
      }
      System.out.println("bye!");
      if(args[0].equals("after"))
        System.runFinalizersOnExit(true);
    }
  } ///:~
```

The above program creates many **Chair** objects, and at some point after the garbage collector begins running, the program stops creating **Chair**s. Since the garbage collector can run at any time, you don't know exactly when it will start up, so there's a flag called **gcrun** to indicate whether the garbage collector has started running yet. A second flag **f** is a way for **Chair** to tell the **main( )** loop that it should stop making objects. Both of these flags are set within **finalize( )**, which is called during garbage collection.

Two other **static** variables, **created** and **finalized**, keep track of the number of **objs** created versus the number that get finalized by the garbage collector. Finally, each **Chair** has its own (non-**static**) **int i** so it can keep track of what number it is. When **Chair** number 47 is finalized, the flag is set to **true** to bring the process of **Chair** creation to a stop.

All this happens in **main( )**, in the loop

```
while(!Chair.f) {
  new Chair();
  new String("To take up space");
}
```

You might wonder how this loop could ever finish, since there's nothing inside that changes the value of **Chair.f**. However, the **finalize( )** process will, eventually, when it finalizes number 47.

 The creation of a **String** object during each iteration is simply extra garbage being created to encourage the garbage collector to kick in, which it will do when it starts to get nervous about the amount of memory available.

When you run the program, you provide a command-line argument of "before" or "after." The "before" argument will call the **System.gc( )** method (to force execution of the garbage collector) along with the **System.runFinalization( )** method to run the finalizers. These methods were available in Java 1.0, but the **runFinalizersOnExit( )** method that is invoked by using the "after" argument is available only in Java 1.1[3] and beyond. (Note you can call this method any time during program execution, and the execution of the finalizers is independent of whether the garbage collector runs).

The preceding program shows that, in Java 1.1, the promise that finalizers will always be run holds true, but only if you explicitly force it to happen yourself. If you use an argument that isn't "before" or "after" (such as "none"), then neither finalization process will occur, and you'll get an output like this:

```
Created 47
```

---

[3] Unfortunately, the implementations of the garbage collector in Java 1.0 would never call **finalize( )** correctly. As a result, **finalize( )** methods that were essential (such as those to close a file) often didn't get called. The documentation claimed that all finalizers would be called at the exit of a program, even if the garbage collector hadn't been run on those objects by the time the program terminated. This wasn't true, so as a result you couldn't reliably expect **finalize( )** to be called for all objects. Effectively, **finalize( )** was useless in Java 1.0.

```
Beginning to finalize after 8694 Chairs have been
created
Finalizing Chair #47, Setting flag to stop Chair
creation
After all Chairs have been created:
total created = 9834, total finalized = 108
bye!
```

Thus, not all finalizers get called by the time the program completes.[4] To force finalization to happen, you can call **System.gc( )** followed by **System.runFinalization( )**. This will destroy all the objects that are no longer in use up to that point. The odd thing about this is that you call **gc( )** *before* you call **runFinalization( )**, which seems to contradict the Sun documentation, which claims that finalizers are run first, and then the storage is released. However, if you call **runFinalization( )** first, and then **gc( )**, the finalizers will not be executed.

One reason that Java 1.1 might default to skipping finalization for all objects is because it seems to be expensive. When you use either of the approaches that force garbage collection you might notice longer delays than you would without the extra finalization.

Member initialization

Java goes out of its way to guarantee that any variable is properly initialized before it is used. In the case of variables that are defined locally to a method, this guarantee comes in the form of a compile-time error. So if you say:

```
void f() {
   int i;
   i++;
}
```

You'll get an error message that says that **i** might not have been initialized. Of course, the compiler could have given **i** a default value, but it's more likely that this is a programmer error and a default value would have covered that up. Forcing the programmer to provide an initialization value is more likely to catch a bug.

---

[4] By the time you read this, some Java Virtual Machines may show different behavior.

If a primitive is a data member of a class, however, things are a bit different. Since any method can initialize or use that data, it might not be practical to force the user to initialize it to its appropriate value before the data is used. However, it's unsafe to leave it with a garbage value, so each primitive data member of a class is guaranteed to get an initial value. Those values can be seen here:

```
//: InitialValues.java
// Shows default initial values

class Measurement {
  boolean t;
  char c;
  byte b;
  short s;
  int i;
  long l;
  float f;
  double d;
  void print() {
    System.out.println(
       "Data type        Inital value\n" +
       "boolean          " + t + "\n" +
       "char             " + c + "\n" +
       "byte             " + b + "\n" +
       "short            " + s + "\n" +
       "int              " + i + "\n" +
       "long             " + l + "\n" +
       "float            " + f + "\n" +
       "double           " + d);
  }
}

public class InitialValues {
  public static void main(String[] args) {
    Measurement d = new Measurement();
    d.print();
    /* In this case you could also say:
    new Measurement().print();
    */
  }
} ///:~
```

The output of this program is:

```
Data type          Inital value
boolean            false
char
byte               0
short              0
int                0
long               0
float              0.0
double             0.0
```

The **char** value is a null, which doesn't print.

You'll see later that when you define an object handle inside a class without initializing it to a new object, that handle is given a value of null.

You can see that even though the values are not specified, they automatically get initialized. So at least there's no threat of working with uninitialized variables.

Specifying initialization

What happens if you want to give a variable an initial value? One direct way to do this is simply to assign the value at the point you define the variable in the class. (Notice you cannot do this in C++, although C++ novices always try.) Here the field definitions in class **Measurement** are changed to provide initial values:

```
class Measurement {
  boolean b = true;
  char c = 'x';
  byte B = 47;
  short s = 0xff;
  int i = 999;
  long l = 1;
  float f = 3.14f;
  double d = 3.14159;
  //. . .
```

You can also initialize non-primitive objects in this same way. If **Depth** is a class, you can insert a variable and initialize it like so:

```
class Measurement {
  Depth o = new Depth();
```

```
    boolean b = true;
    // . . .
```

If you haven't given **o** an initial value and you go ahead and try to use it anyway, you'll get a run-time error called an *exception* (covered in Chapter 9).

You can even call a method to provide an initialization value:

```
class CInit {
    int i = f();
    //...
}
```

This method can have arguments, of course, but those arguments cannot be other class members that haven't been initialized yet. Thus, you can do this:

```
class CInit {
    int i = f();
    int j = g(i);
    //...
}
```

But you cannot do this:

```
class CInit {
    int j = g(i);
    int i = f();
    //...
}
```

This is one place in which the compiler, appropriately, *does* complain about forward referencing, since this has to do with the order of initialization and not the way the program is compiled.

This approach to initialization is simple and straightforward. It has the limitation that *every* object of type **Measurement** will get these same initialization values. Sometimes this is exactly what you need, but at other times you need more flexibility.

Constructor initialization

The constructor can be used to perform initialization, and this gives you greater flexibility in your programming since you can call methods and perform actions at run time to determine the initial values. There's one thing to keep in mind, however: you aren't precluding the automatic initialization, which happens before the constructor is entered. So, for example, if you say:

```
class Counter {
    int i;
    Counter() { i = 7; }
    // . . .
```

then **i** will first be initialized to zero, then to 7. This is true with all the primitive types and with object handles, including those that are given explicit initialization at the point of definition. For this reason, the compiler doesn't try to force you to initialize elements in the constructor at any particular place, or before they are used – initialization is already guaranteed.[5]

Order of initialization

Within a class, the order of initialization is determined by the order that the variables are defined within the class. Even if the variable definitions are scattered throughout in between method definitions, the variables are initialized before any methods can be called – even the constructor. For example:

```
//: OrderOfInitialization.java
// Demonstrates initialization order.

// When the constructor is called, to create a
// Tag object, you'll see a message:
class Tag {
    Tag(int marker) {
        System.out.println("Tag(" + marker + ")");
    }
}

class Card {
    Tag t1 = new Tag(1); // Before constructor
    Card() {
        // Indicate we're in the constructor:
```

---

[5] In contrast, C++ has the *constructor initializer list* that causes initialization to occur before entering the constructor body, and is enforced for objects. See *Thinking in C++*.

```
      System.out.println("Card()");
      t3 = new Tag(33); // Re-initialize t3
  }
  Tag t2 = new Tag(2); // After constructor
  void f() {
      System.out.println("f()");
  }
  Tag t3 = new Tag(3); // At end
}

public class OrderOfInitialization {
  public static void main(String[] args) {
      Card t = new Card();
      t.f(); // Shows that construction is done
  }
} ///:~
```

In **Card**, the definitions of the **Tag** objects are intentionally scattered about to prove that they'll all get initialized before the constructor is entered or anything else can happen. In addition, **t3** is re-initialized inside the constructor. The output is:

```
Tag(1)
Tag(2)
Tag(3)
Card()
Tag(33)
f()
```

Thus, the **t3** handle gets initialized twice, once before and once during the constructor call. (The first object is dropped, so it can be garbage-collected later.) This might not seem efficient at first, but it guarantees proper initialization – what would happen if an overloaded constructor were defined that did *not* initialize **t3** and there wasn't a "default" initialization for **t3** in its definition?

Static data initialization

When the data is **static** the same thing happens; if it's a primitive and you don't initialize it, it gets the standard primitive initial values. If it's a handle to an object, it's null unless you create a new object and attach your handle to it.

If you want to place initialization at the point of definition, it looks the same as for non-statics. But since there's only a single piece of storage for a **static**, regardless of how many objects are created the question of when that storage gets initialized arises. An example makes this question clear:

```java
//: StaticInitialization.java
// Specifying initial values in a
// class definition.

class Bowl {
  Bowl(int marker) {
    System.out.println("Bowl(" + marker + ")");
  }
  void f(int marker) {
    System.out.println("f(" + marker + ")");
  }
}

class Table {
  static Bowl b1 = new Bowl(1);
  Table() {
    System.out.println("Table()");
    b2.f(1);
  }
  void f2(int marker) {
    System.out.println("f2(" + marker + ")");
  }
  static Bowl b2 = new Bowl(2);
}

class Cupboard {
  Bowl b3 = new Bowl(3);
  static Bowl b4 = new Bowl(4);
  Cupboard() {
    System.out.println("Cupboard()");
    b4.f(2);
  }
  void f3(int marker) {
    System.out.println("f3(" + marker + ")");
  }
  static Bowl b5 = new Bowl(5);
}

public class StaticInitialization {
  public static void main(String[] args) {
    System.out.println(
      "Creating new Cupboard() in main");
```

```
    new Cupboard();
    System.out.println(
      "Creating new Cupboard() in main");
    new Cupboard();
    t2.f2(1);
    t3.f3(1);
  }
  static Table t2 = new Table();
  static Cupboard t3 = new Cupboard();
} ///:~
```

Bowl allows you to view the creation of a class, and **Table** and **Cupboard** create **static** members of **Bowl** scattered through their class definitions. Note that **Cupboard** creates a non-**static Bowl b3** prior to the **static** definitions. The output shows what happens:

```
Bowl(1)
Bowl(2)
Table()
f(1)
Bowl(4)
Bowl(5)
Bowl(3)
Cupboard()
f(2)
Creating new Cupboard() in main
Bowl(3)
Cupboard()
f(2)
Creating new Cupboard() in main
Bowl(3)
Cupboard()
f(2)
f2(1)
f3(1)
```

The **static** initialization occurs only if it's necessary. If you don't create a **Table** object and you never refer to **Table.b1** or **Table.b2**, the **static Bowl b1** and **b2** will never be created. However, they are created only when the *first* **Table** object is created (or the first **static** access occurs). After that, the **static** object is not re-initialized.

The order of initialization is **statics** first, if they haven't already been initialized by a previous object creation, and then the non-**static** objects. You can see the evidence of this in the output.

It's helpful to summarize the process of creating an object. Consider a class called **Dog**:

1. The first time an object of type **Dog** is created, *or* the first time a **static** method or **static** field of class **Dog** is accessed, the Java interpreter must locate **Dog.class**, which it does by searching through the classpath.

2. As **Dog.class** is loaded (which creates a **Class** object, which you'll learn about later), all of its **static** initializers are run. Thus, **static** initialization takes place only once, as the **Class** object is loaded for the first time.

3. When you create a **new Dog( )**, the construction process for a **Dog** object first allocates enough storage for a **Dog** object on the heap.

4. This storage is wiped to zero, automatically setting all the primitives in **Dog** to their default values (zero for numbers and the equivalent for **boolean** and **char**).

5. Any initializations that occur at the point of field definition are executed.

6. Constructors are executed. As you shall see in Chapter 6, this might actually involve a fair amount of activity, especially when inheritance is involved.

Explicit static initialization

Java allows you to group other **static** initializations inside a special "**static** construction clause" (sometimes called a *static block*) in a class. It looks like this:

```
class Spoon {
   static int i;
   static {
      i = 47;
   }
   // . . .
```

So it looks like a method, but it's just the **static** keyword followed by a method body. This code, like the other **static** initialization, is executed only once, the first time you make an object of that class *or* you access a **static** member of that class (even if you never make an object of that class). For example:

```
//: ExplicitStatic.java
```

```
// Explicit static initialization
// with the "static" clause.

class Cup {
  Cup(int marker) {
    System.out.println("Cup(" + marker + ")");
  }
  void f(int marker) {
    System.out.println("f(" + marker + ")");
  }
}

class Cups {
  static Cup c1;
  static Cup c2;
  static {
    c1 = new Cup(1);
    c2 = new Cup(2);
  }
  Cups() {
    System.out.println("Cups()");
  }
}

public class ExplicitStatic {
  public static void main(String[] args) {
    System.out.println("Inside main()");
    Cups.c1.f(99);   // (1)
  }
  static Cups x = new Cups();   // (2)
  static Cups y = new Cups();   // (2)
} ///:~
```

The **static** initializers for **Cups** will be run when either the access of the **static** object **c1** occurs on the line marked (1), or if line (1) is commented out and the lines marked (2) are uncommented. If both (1) and (2) are commented out, the **static** initialization for **Cups** never occurs.

Non-static instance initialization

Java 1.1 provides a similar syntax for initializing non-static variables for each object. Here's an example:

```
//: Mugs.java
// Java 1.1 "Instance Initialization"
```

```
class Mug {
  Mug(int marker) {
    System.out.println("Mug(" + marker + ")");
  }
  void f(int marker) {
    System.out.println("f(" + marker + ")");
  }
}

public class Mugs {
  Mug c1;
  Mug c2;
  {
    c1 = new Mug(1);
    c2 = new Mug(2);
    System.out.println("c1 & c2 initialized");
  }
  Mugs() {
    System.out.println("Mugs()");
  }
  public static void main(String[] args) {
    System.out.println("Inside main()");
    Mugs x = new Mugs();
  }
} ///:~
```

You can see that the instance initialization clause:

```
{
  c1 = new Mug(1);
  c2 = new Mug(2);
  System.out.println("c1 & c2 initialized");
}
```

looks exactly like the static initialization clause except for the missing **static** keyword. This syntax is necessary to support the initialization of *anonymous inner classes* (see Chapter 7).

Array initialization

Initializing arrays in C is error-prone and tedious. C++ uses *aggregate initialization* to make it much safer.[6] Java has no "aggregates" like C++, since everything is an object in Java. It does have arrays, and these are supported with array initialization.

An array is simply a sequence of either objects or primitives, all the same type and packaged together under one identifier name. Arrays are defined and used with the square-brackets *indexing operator* [ ]. To define an array you simply follow your type name with empty square brackets:

```
int[] a1;
```

You can also put the square brackets after the identifier to produce exactly the same meaning:

```
int a1[];
```

This conforms to expectations from C and C++ programmers. The former style, however, is probably a more sensible syntax, since it says that the type is "an **int** array." That style will be used in this book.

The compiler doesn't allow you to tell it how big the array is. This brings us back to that issue of "handles." All that you have at this point is a handle to an array, and there's been no space allocated for the array. To create storage for the array you must write an initialization expression. For arrays, initialization can appear anywhere in your code, but you can also use a special kind of initialization expression that must occur at the point where the array is created. This special initialization is a set of values surrounded by curly braces. The storage allocation (the equivalent of using **new**) is taken care of by the compiler in this case. For example:

```
int[] a1 = { 1, 2, 3, 4, 5 };
```

So why would you ever define an array handle without an array?

```
int[] a2;
```

Well, it's possible to assign one array to another in Java, so you can say:

```
a2 = a1;
```

---

[6] See *Thinking in C++* for a complete description of aggregate initialization.

What you're really doing is copying a handle, as demonstrated here:

```
//: Arrays.java
// Arrays of primitives.

public class Arrays {
  public static void main(String[] args) {
    int[] a1 = { 1, 2, 3, 4, 5 };
    int[] a2;
    a2 = a1;
    for(int i = 0; i < a2.length; i++)
      a2[i]++;
    for(int i = 0; i < a1.length; i++)
      prt("a1[" + i + "] = " + a1[i]);
  }
  static void prt(String s) {
    System.out.println(s);
  }
} ///:~
```

You can see that **a1** is given an initialization value while **a2** is not; **a2** is assigned later – in this case, to another array.

There's something new here: all arrays have an intrinsic member (whether they're arrays of objects or arrays of primitives) that you can query – but not change – to tell you how many elements there are in the array. This member is **length**. Since arrays in Java, like C and C++, start counting from element zero, the largest element you can index is **length - 1**. If you go out of bounds, C and C++ quietly accept this and allow you to stomp all over your memory, which is the source of many infamous bugs. However, Java protects you against such problems by causing a run-time error (an *exception*, the subject of Chapter 9) if you step out of bounds. Of course, checking every array access costs time and code and there's no way to turn it off, which means that array accesses might be a source of inefficiency in your program if they occur at a critical juncture. For Internet security and programmer productivity, the Java designers thought that this was a worthwhile tradeoff.

What if you don't know how many elements you're going to need in your array while you're writing the program? You simply use **new** to create the elements in the array. Here, **new** works even though it's creating an array of primitives (**new** won't create a non-array primitive):

```
//: ArrayNew.java
// Creating arrays with new.
```

```
import java.util.*;

public class ArrayNew {
  static Random rand = new Random();
  static int pRand(int mod) {
    return Math.abs(rand.nextInt()) % mod;
  }
  public static void main(String[] args) {
    int[] a;
    a = new int[pRand(20)];
    prt("length of a = " + a.length);
    for(int i = 0; i < a.length; i++)
      prt("a[" + i + "] = " + a[i]);
  }
  static void prt(String s) {
    System.out.println(s);
  }
} ///:~
```

Since the size of the array is chosen at random (using the **pRand( )** method defined earlier), it's clear that array creation is actually happening at run-time. In addition, you'll see from the output of this program that array elements of primitive types are automatically initialized to "empty" values. (For numerics, this is zero, for **char**, it's **null**, and for **boolean**, it's **false**.)

Of course, the array could also have been defined and initialized in the same statement:

```
int[] a = new int[pRand(20)];
```

If you're dealing with an array of non-primitive objects, you must always use **new**. Here, the handle issue comes up again because what you create is an array of handles. Consider the wrapper type **Integer,** which is a class and not a primitive:

```
//: ArrayClassObj.java
// Creating an array of non-primitive objects.
import java.util.*;

public class ArrayClassObj {
  static Random rand = new Random();
  static int pRand(int mod) {
    return Math.abs(rand.nextInt()) % mod;
  }
  public static void main(String[] args) {
```

```
      Integer[] a = new Integer[pRand(20)];
      prt("length of a = " + a.length);
      for(int i = 0; i < a.length; i++) {
        a[i] = new Integer(pRand(500));
        prt("a[" + i + "] = " + a[i]);
      }
    }
    static void prt(String s) {
      System.out.println(s);
    }
  } ///:~
```

Here, even after **new** is called to create the array:

```
  Integer[] a = new Integer[pRand(20)];
```

it's only an array of handles, and not until the handle itself is initialized by creating a new **Integer** object is the initialization complete:

```
  a[i] = new Integer(pRand(500));
```

If you forget to create the object, however, you'll get an exception at run-time when you try to read the empty array location.

Take a look at the formation of the **String** object inside the print statements. You can see that the handle to the **Integer** object is automatically converted to produce a **String** representing the value inside the object.

It's also possible to initialize arrays of objects using the curly-brace-enclosed list. There are two forms, the first of which is the only one allowed in Java 1.0. The second (equivalent) form is allowed starting with Java 1.1:

```
//: ArrayInit.java
// Array initialization

public class ArrayInit {
  public static void main(String[] args) {
    Integer[] a = {
      new Integer(1),
      new Integer(2),
      new Integer(3),
    };

    // Java 1.1 only:
```

Thinking in Java   *www.BruceEckel.com*

```
        Integer[] b = new Integer[] {
          new Integer(1),
          new Integer(2),
          new Integer(3),
        };
    }
} ///:~
```

This is useful at times, but it's more limited since the size of the array is determined at compile time. The final comma in the list of initializers is optional. (This feature makes for easier maintenance of long lists.)

The second form of array initialization, added in Java 1.1, provides a convenient syntax to create and call methods that can produce the same effect as C's *variable argument lists* (known as "varargs" in C). These included, if you choose, unknown quantity of arguments as well as unknown type. Since all classes are ultimately inherited from the common root class **Object**, you can create a method that takes an array of **Object** and call it like this:

```
//: VarArgs.java
// Using the Java 1.1 array syntax to create
// variable argument lists

class A { int i; }

public class VarArgs {
  static void f(Object[] x) {
    for(int i = 0; i < x.length; i++)
      System.out.println(x[i]);
  }
  public static void main(String[] args) {
    f(new Object[] {
        new Integer(47), new VarArgs(),
        new Float(3.14), new Double(11.11) });
    f(new Object[] {"one", "two", "three" });
    f(new Object[] {new A(), new A(), new A()});
  }
} ///:~
```

At this point, there's not much you can do with these unknown objects, and this program uses the automatic **String** conversion to do something useful with each **Object**. In Chapter 11 (run-time type identification or RTTI) you'll learn how to discover the exact type of such objects so that you can do something more interesting with them.

Multidimensional arrays

Java allows you to easily create multidimensional arrays:

```
//: MultiDimArray.java
// Creating multidimensional arrays.
import java.util.*;

public class MultiDimArray {
  static Random rand = new Random();
  static int pRand(int mod) {
    return Math.abs(rand.nextInt()) % mod;
  }
  public static void main(String[] args) {
    int[][] a1 = {
      { 1, 2, 3, },
      { 4, 5, 6, },
    };
    for(int i = 0; i < a1.length; i++)
      for(int j = 0; j < a1[i].length; j++)
        prt("a1[" + i + "][" + j +
            "] = " + a1[i][j]);
    // 3-D array with fixed length:
    int[][][] a2 = new int[2][2][4];
    for(int i = 0; i < a2.length; i++)
      for(int j = 0; j < a2[i].length; j++)
        for(int k = 0; k < a2[i][j].length;
            k++)
          prt("a2[" + i + "][" +
              j + "][" + k +
              "] = " + a2[i][j][k]);
    // 3-D array with varied-length vectors:
    int[][][] a3 = new int[pRand(7)][][];
    for(int i = 0; i < a3.length; i++) {
      a3[i] = new int[pRand(5)][];
      for(int j = 0; j < a3[i].length; j++)
        a3[i][j] = new int[pRand(5)];
    }
    for(int i = 0; i < a3.length; i++)
      for(int j = 0; j < a3[i].length; j++)
        for(int k = 0; k < a3[i][j].length;
            k++)
          prt("a3[" + i + "][" +
              j + "][" + k +
```

```
          "] = " + a3[i][j][k]);
     // Array of non-primitive objects:
     Integer[][] a4 = {
       { new Integer(1), new Integer(2)},
       { new Integer(3), new Integer(4)},
       { new Integer(5), new Integer(6)},
     };
     for(int i = 0; i < a4.length; i++)
       for(int j = 0; j < a4[i].length; j++)
         prt("a4[" + i + "][" + j +
             "] = " + a4[i][j]);
     Integer[][] a5;
     a5 = new Integer[3][];
     for(int i = 0; i < a5.length; i++) {
       a5[i] = new Integer[3];
       for(int j = 0; j < a5[i].length; j++)
         a5[i][j] = new Integer(i*j);
     }
     for(int i = 0; i < a5.length; i++)
       for(int j = 0; j < a5[i].length; j++)
         prt("a5[" + i + "][" + j +
             "] = " + a5[i][j]);
   }
   static void prt(String s) {
     System.out.println(s);
   }
} ///:~
```

The code used for printing uses **length** so that it doesn't depend on fixed array sizes.

The first example shows a multidimensional array of primitives. You delimit each vector in the array with curly braces:

```
int[][] a1 = {
  { 1, 2, 3, },
  { 4, 5, 6, },
};
```

Each set of square brackets moves you into the next level of the array.

The second example shows a three-dimensional array allocated with **new**. Here, the whole array is allocated at once:

```
int[][][] a2 = new int[2][2][4];
```

But the third example shows that each vector in the arrays that make up the matrix can be of any length:

```
int[][][] a3 = new int[pRand(7)][][];
for(int i = 0; i < a3.length; i++) {
  a3[i] = new int[pRand(5)][];
  for(int j = 0; j < a3[i].length; j++)
    a3[i][j] = new int[pRand(5)];
}
```

The first **new** creates an array with a random-length first element and the rest undetermined. The second **new** inside the for loop fills out the elements but leaves the third index undetermined until you hit the third **new**.

You will see from the output that array values are automatically initialized to zero if you don't give them an explicit initialization value.

You can deal with arrays of non-primitive objects in a similar fashion, which is shown in the fourth example, demonstrating the ability to collect many **new** expressions with curly braces:

```
Integer[][] a4 = {
  { new Integer(1), new Integer(2) },
  { new Integer(3), new Integer(4) },
  { new Integer(5), new Integer(6) },
};
```

The fifth example shows how an array of non-primitive objects can be built up piece by piece:

```
Integer[][] a5;
a5 = new Integer[3][];
for(int i = 0; i < a5.length; i++) {
  a5[i] = new Integer[3];
  for(int j = 0; j < a5[i].length; j++)
    a5[i][j] = new Integer(i*j);
}
```

The **i*j** is just to put an interesting value into the **Integer**.

Summary

The seemingly elaborate mechanism for initialization, the constructor, should give you a strong hint about the critical importance placed on initialization in the language. As Stroustrup was designing C++, one of the first observations he made about productivity in C was that improper initialization of variables causes a significant portion of programming problems. These kinds of bugs are hard to find, and similar issues apply to improper cleanup. Because constructors allow you to *guarantee* proper initialization and cleanup (the compiler will not allow an object to be created without the proper constructor calls), you get complete control and safety.

In C++, destruction is quite important because objects created with **new** must be explicitly destroyed. In Java, the garbage collector automatically releases the memory for all objects, so the equivalent cleanup method in Java isn't necessary much of the time. In cases where you don't need destructor-like behavior, Java's garbage collector greatly simplifies programming, and adds much-needed safety in managing memory. Some garbage collectors are even cleaning up other resources like graphics and file handles. However, the garbage collector does add a run-time cost, the expense of which is difficult to put into perspective because of the overall slowness of Java interpreters at this writing. As this changes, we'll be able to discover if the overhead of the garbage collector will preclude the use of Java for certain types of programs. (One of the issues is the unpredictability of the garbage collector.)

Because of the guarantee that all objects will be constructed, there's actually more to the constructor than what is shown here. In particular, when you create new classes using either *composition* or *inheritance* the guarantee of construction also holds, and some additional syntax is necessary to support this. You'll learn about composition, inheritance and how they affect constructors in future chapters.

Exercises

I.   Create a class with a default constructor (one that takes no arguments) that prints a message. Create an object of this class.

2.   Add an overloaded constructor to Exercise 1 that takes a **String** argument and prints it along with your message.

3.   Create an array of object handles of the class you created in Exercise 2, but don't actually create objects to assign into the array. When you run the program, notice whether the initialization messages from the constructor calls are printed.

4. Complete Exercise 3 by creating objects to attach to the array of handles.

5. Experiment with **Garbage.java** by running the program using the arguments "before," "after" and "none." Repeat the process and see if you detect any patterns in the output. Change the code so that **System.runFinalization( )** is called before **System.gc( )** and observe the results.

5: Hiding the implementation

A primary consideration in object-oriented design is "separating the things that change from the things that stay the same."

This is particularly important for libraries. The user (*client programmer*) of that library must be able to rely on the part they use, and know that they won't need to rewrite code if a new version of the library comes out. On the flip side, the library creator must have the freedom to make modifications and improvements with the certainty that the client programmer's code won't be affected by those changes.

This can be achieved through convention. For example, the library programmer must agree to not remove existing methods when modifying a class in the library, since that would break the client programmer's code. The reverse situation is thornier, however. In the case of a data member, how can the library creator know which data members have been accessed by client programmers? This is also true with methods that are only part of the implementation of a class, and not meant to be used directly by the client programmer. But what if the library creator wants to rip out an old implementation and put in a new one? Changing any of those members might break a client programmer's code. Thus the library creator is in a strait jacket and can't change anything.

To solve this problem, Java provides *access specifiers* to allow the library creator to say what is available to the client programmer and what is not. The levels of access control from "most access" to "least access" are **public**, "friendly" (which has no keyword), **protected**, and **private**. From the previous paragraph you might think that, as a library designer, you'll want to keep everything as "private" as possible, and expose only the methods that you want the client programmer to use. This is exactly right, even though it's often counterintuitive for people who program in other languages (especially C) and are used to accessing everything without restriction. By the end of this chapter you should be convinced of the value of access control in Java.

The concept of a library of components and the control over who can access the components of that library is not complete, however. There's still the question of how the components are bundled together into a cohesive library unit. This is controlled with the **package** keyword in Java, and the access specifiers are affected by whether a class is in the same package or in a separate package. So to begin this chapter, you'll learn how library components are placed into packages. Then you'll be able to understand the complete meaning of the access specifiers.

package: the library unit

A package is what you get when you use the **import** keyword to bring in an entire library, such as

```
import java.util.*;
```

This brings in the entire utility library that's part of the standard Java distribution. Since **Vector** is in **java.util**, you can now either specify the full name **java.util.Vector** (which you can do without the **import** statement), or you can simply say **Vector** (because of the **import**).

If you want to bring in a single class, you can name that class in the **import** statement

```
import java.util.Vector;
```

Now you can use **Vector** with no qualification. However, none of the other classes in **java.util** are available.

The reason for all this importing is to provide a mechanism to manage "name spaces." The names of all your class members are insulated from each other. A method **f( )** inside a class **A** will not clash with an **f( )** that has the same signature (argument list) in class **B**. But what about the class names? Suppose you create a **stack** class that is installed on a machine that already has a **stack** class that's written by someone else? With Java on the Internet, this can happen without the user knowing it since classes can get downloaded automatically in the process of running a Java program.

This potential clashing of names is why it's important to have complete control over the name spaces in Java, and to be able to create a completely unique name regardless of the constraints of the Internet.

So far, most of the examples in this book have existed in a single file and have been designed for local use, and haven't bothered with package names. (In this case the class name is placed in the "default package.") This is certainly an option, and for simplicity's sake this approach will be used whenever possible throughout the rest of the book. If you're planning to create a program that is "Internet friendly," however, you must think about preventing class name clashes.

When you create a source-code file for Java, it's commonly called a *compilation unit* (sometimes a *translation unit*). Each compilation unit must have a name ending in **.java**, and inside the compilation unit there can be a public class that must have the same name as the file (including capitalization, but excluding the **.java** filename extension). If you don't do this, the compiler will complain. There can be only *one* **public** class in each compilation unit (again, the compiler will complain). The rest of the classes in that compilation unit, if there are any, are hidden from the world outside that package because they're *not* **public**, and they comprise "support" classes for the main **public** class.

When you compile a **.java** file you get an output file with exactly the same name but an extension of **.class** *for each class in the* **.java** file. Thus you can end up with quite a few **.class** files from a small number of **.java** files. If you've programmed with a compiled language, you might be used to the compiler spitting out an intermediate form (usually an "obj" file) that is then packaged together with others of its kind using a linker (to create an executable file) or a librarian (to create a library). That's not how Java works. A working program is a bunch of **.class** files, which can be packaged and compressed into a JAR file (using the **jar** utility in Java 1.1). The Java interpreter is responsible for finding, loading and interpreting these files.[1]

A library is also a bunch of these class files. Each file has one class that is **public** (you're not forced to have a **public** class, but it's typical), so there's one component for each file. If you want to say that all these components (that are in their own separate **.java** and **.class** files) belong together, that's where the **package** keyword comes in.

When you say:

```
package mypackage;
```

at the beginning of a file, where the **package** statement *must* appear as the first non-comment in the file, you're stating that this compilation unit is part of a library named **mypackage**. Or, put another way, you're saying that the **public** class name within this compilation unit is under the umbrella of the name **mypackage**, and if anyone wants to use the name they must either fully specify the name or use the **import** keyword in combination with **mypackage** (using the choices given previously). Note that the convention for Java packages is to use all lowercase letters, even for intermediate words.

For example, suppose the name of the file is **MyClass.java**. This means there can be one and only one **public** class in that file, and the name of that class must be **MyClass** (including the capitalization):

```
package mypackage;
public class MyClass {
  // . . .
```

Now, if someone wants to use **MyClass** or, for that matter, any of the other **public** classes in **mypackage**, they must use the **import** keyword to make the name or names in **mypackage** available. The alternative is to give the fully-qualified name:

```
mypackage.MyClass m = new mypackage.MyClass();
```

The **import** keyword can make this much cleaner:

---

[1] There's nothing in Java that forces the use of an interpreter. There exist native-code Java compilers that generate a single executable file.

```
import mypackage.*;
// . . .
MyClass m = new MyClass();
```

It's worth keeping in mind that what the **package** and **import** keywords allow you to do, as a library designer, is to divide up the single global name space so you won't have clashing names, no matter how many people get on the Internet and start writing classes in Java.

Creating unique package names

You might observe that, since a package never really gets "packaged" into a single file, a package could be made up of many **.class** files, and things could get a bit cluttered. To prevent this, a logical thing to do is to place all the **.class** files for a particular package into a single directory; that is, use the hierarchical file structure of the operating system to your advantage. This is how Java handles the problem of clutter.

It also solves two other problems: creating unique package names and finding those classes that might be buried in a directory structure someplace. This is accomplished, as was introduced in Chapter 2, by encoding the path of the location of the **.class** file into the name of the **package**. The compiler enforces this, but by convention, the first part of the **package** name is the Internet domain name of the creator of the class, reversed. Since Internet domain names are guaranteed to be unique (by InterNIC,[2] who controls their assignment) *if* you follow this convention it's guaranteed that your **package** name will be unique and thus you'll never have a name clash. (That is, until you lose the domain name to someone else who starts writing Java code with the same path names as you did.) Of course, if you don't have your own domain name then you must fabricate an unlikely combination (such as your first and last name) to create unique package names. If you've decided to start publishing Java code it's worth the relatively small effort to get a domain name.

The second part of this trick is resolving the **package** name into a directory on your machine, so when the Java program runs and it needs to load the **.class** file (which it does dynamically, at the point in the program where it needs to create an object of that particular class, or the first time you access a **static** member of the class), it can locate the directory where the **.class** file resides.

---

[2] ftp://ftp.internic.net

The Java interpreter proceeds as follows. First, it finds the environment variable CLASSPATH (set via the operating system when Java, or a tool like a Java-enabled browser, is installed on a machine). CLASSPATH contains one or more directories that are used as roots for a search for **.class** files. Starting at that root, the interpreter will take the package name and replace each dot with a slash to generate a path name from the CLASSPATH root (so **package foo.bar.baz** becomes **foo\bar\baz** or **foo/bar/baz** depending on your operating system). This is then concatenated to the various entries in the CLASSPATH. That's where it looks for the **.class** file with the name corresponding to the class you're trying to create. (It also searches some standard directories relative to where the Java interpreter resides).

To understand this, consider my domain name, which is **bruceeckel.com**. By reversing this, **com.bruceeckel** establishes my unique global name for my classes. (The com, edu, org, etc. extension was formerly capitalized in Java packages, but this was changed in Java 1.2 so the entire package name is lowercase.) I can further subdivide this by deciding that I want to create a library named **util**, so I'll end up with a package name:

```
package com.bruceeckel.util;
```

Now this package name can be used as an umbrella name space for the following two files:

```
//: Vector.java
// Creating a package
package com.bruceeckel.util;

public class Vector {
  public Vector() {
    System.out.println(
      "com.bruceeckel.util.Vector");
  }
} ///:~
```

When you create your own packages, you'll discover that the **package** statement must be the first non-comment code in the file. The second file looks much the same:

```
//: List.java
// Creating a package
package com.bruceeckel.util;

public class List {
```

```
    public List() {
       System.out.println(
         "com.bruceeckel.util.List");
    }
} ///:~
```

Both of these files are placed in the subdirectory on my system:

```
C:\DOC\JavaT\com\bruceeckel\util
```

If you walk back through this, you can see the package name **com.bruceeckel.util**, but what about the first portion of the path? That's taken care of in the CLASSPATH environment variable, which is, on my machine:

```
CLASSPATH=.;D:\JAVA\LIB;C:\DOC\JavaT
```

You can see that the CLASSPATH can contain a number of alternative search paths. There's a variation when using JAR files, however. You must put the name of the JAR file in the classpath, not just the path where it's located. So for a JAR named **grape.jar** your classpath would include:

```
CLASSPATH=.;D:\JAVA\LIB;C:\flavors\grape.jar
```

Once the classpath is set up properly, the following file can be placed in any directory: (See page 97 if you have trouble executing this program.):

```
//: LibTest.java
// Uses the library
package c05;
import com.bruceeckel.util.*;

public class LibTest {
  public static void main(String[] args) {
    Vector v = new Vector();
    List l = new List();
  }
} ///:~
```

When the compiler encounters the **import** statement, it begins searching at the directories specified by CLASSPATH, looking for subdirectory com\bruceeckel\util, then seeking the compiled files of the appropriate names (**Vector.class** for **Vector** and **List.class** for **List**). Note that both the classes and the desired methods in **Vector** and **List** must be **public**.

Automatic compilation

The first time you create an object of an imported class (or you access a **static** member of a class), the compiler will hunt for the **.class** file of the same name (so if you're creating an object of class **X**, it looks for **X.class**) in the appropriate directory. If it finds only **X.class**, that's what it must use. However, if it also finds an **X.java** in the same directory, the compiler will compare the date stamp on the two files, and if **X.java** is more recent than **X.class**, it will *automatically recompile* **X.java** to generate an up-to-date **X.class**.

If a class is not in a **.java** file of the same name as that class, this behavior will not occur for that class.

Collisions

What happens if two libraries are imported via * and they include the same names? For example, suppose a program does this:

```
import com.bruceeckel.util.*;
import java.util.*;
```

Since **java.util.*** also contains a **Vector** class, this causes a potential collision. However, as long as the collision doesn't actually occur, everything is OK – this is good because otherwise you might end up doing a lot of typing to prevent collisions that would never happen.

The collision *does* occur if you now try to make a **Vector**:

```
Vector v = new Vector();
```

Which **Vector** class does this refer to? The compiler can't know, and the reader can't know either. So the compiler complains and forces you to be explicit. If I want the standard Java **Vector**, for example, I must say:

```
java.util.Vector v = new java.util.Vector();
```

Since this (along with the CLASSPATH) completely specifies the location of that **Vector**, there's no need for the **import java.util.*** statement unless I'm using something else from **java.util**.

A custom tool library

With this knowledge, you can now create your own libraries of tools to reduce or eliminate duplicate code. Consider, for example, creating an alias for **System.out.println( )** to reduce typing. This can be part of a package called **tools**:

```
//: P.java
// The P.rint & P.rintln shorthand
package com.bruceeckel.tools;

public class P {
  public static void rint(Object obj) {
    System.out.print(obj);
  }
  public static void rint(String s) {
    System.out.print(s);
  }
  public static void rint(char[] s) {
    System.out.print(s);
  }
  public static void rint(char c) {
    System.out.print(c);
  }
  public static void rint(int i) {
    System.out.print(i);
  }
  public static void rint(long l) {
    System.out.print(l);
  }
  public static void rint(float f) {
    System.out.print(f);
  }
  public static void rint(double d) {
    System.out.print(d);
  }
  public static void rint(boolean b) {
    System.out.print(b);
  }
  public static void rintln() {
    System.out.println();
  }
  public static void rintln(Object obj) {
    System.out.println(obj);
  }
  public static void rintln(String s) {
    System.out.println(s);
  }
  public static void rintln(char[] s) {
```

```
      System.out.println(s);
  }
  public static void rintln(char c) {
      System.out.println(c);
  }
  public static void rintln(int i) {
      System.out.println(i);
  }
  public static void rintln(long l) {
      System.out.println(l);
  }
  public static void rintln(float f) {
      System.out.println(f);
  }
  public static void rintln(double d) {
      System.out.println(d);
  }
  public static void rintln(boolean b) {
      System.out.println(b);
  }
} ///:~
```

All the different data types can now be printed out either with a newline
(**P.println( )**) or without a newline (**P.print( )**).

You can guess that the location of this file must be in a directory that
starts at one of the CLASSPATH locations, then continues
com/bruceeckel/tools. After compiling, the **P.class** file can be used
anywhere on your system with an **import** statement:

```
//: ToolTest.java
// Uses the tools library
import com.bruceeckel.tools.*;

public class ToolTest {
  public static void main(String[] args) {
    P.rintln("Available from now on!");
  }
} ///:~
```

So from now on, whenever you come up with a useful new utility, you
can add it to the **tools** directory. (Or to your own personal **util** or **tools**
directory.)

Classpath pitfall

The **P.java** file brought up an interesting pitfall. Especially with early implementations of Java, setting the classpath correctly is generally quite a headache. During the development of this book, the **P.java** file was introduced and seemed to work fine, but at some point it began breaking. For a long time I was certain that this was the fault of one implementation of Java or another, but finally I discovered that at one point I had introduced a program (**CodePackager.java**, shown in Chapter 17) that used a different class **P**. Because it was used as a tool, it was *sometimes* placed in the classpath, and other times it wasn't. When it was, the **P** in **CodePackager.java** was found first by Java when executing a program in which it was looking for the class in **com.bruceeckel.tools**, and the compiler would say that a particular method couldn't be found. This was frustrating because you can see the method in the above class **P** and no further diagnostics were reported to give you a clue that it was finding a completely different class. (That wasn't even **public**.)

At first this could seem like a compiler bug, but if you look at the **import** statement it says only "here's where you *might* find **P**." However, the compiler is supposed to look anywhere in its classpath, so if it finds a **P** there it will use it, and if it finds the "wrong" one *first* during a search then it will stop looking. This is slightly different from the case described on page 196 because there the offending classes were both in packages, and here there was a **P** that was not in a package, but could still be found during a normal classpath search.

If you're having an experience like this, check to make sure that there's only one class of each name anywhere in your classpath.

Using imports to change behavior

A feature that is missing from Java is C's *conditional compilation*, which allows you to change a switch and get different behavior without changing any other code. The reason such a feature was left out of Java is probably because it is most often used in C to solve cross-platform issues: different portions of the code are compiled depending on the platform that the code is being compiled for. Since Java is intended to be automatically cross-platform, such a feature should not be necessary.

However, there are other valuable uses for conditional compilation. A very common use is for debugging code. The debugging features are enabled during development, and disabled for a shipping product. Allen

---

Holub (www.holub.com) came up with the idea of using packages to mimic conditional compilation. He used this to create a Java version of C's very useful *assertion mechanism*, whereby you can say "this should be true" or "this should be false" and if the statement doesn't agree with your assertion you'll find out about it. Such a tool is quite helpful during debugging.

Here is the class that you'll use for debugging:

```
//: Assert.java
// Assertion tool for debugging
package com.bruceeckel.tools.debug;

public class Assert {
  private static void perr(String msg) {
    System.err.println(msg);
  }
  public final static void is_true(boolean exp) {
    if(!exp) perr("Assertion failed");
  }
  public final static void is_false(boolean exp){
    if(exp) perr("Assertion failed");
  }
  public final static void
  is_true(boolean exp, String msg) {
    if(!exp) perr("Assertion failed: " + msg);
  }
  public final static void
  is_false(boolean exp, String msg) {
    if(exp) perr("Assertion failed: " + msg);
  }
} ///:~
```

This class simply encapsulates boolean tests, which print error messages if they fail. In Chapter 9, you'll learn about a more sophisticated tool for dealing with errors called *exception handling*, but the **perr( )** method will work fine in the meantime.

When you want to use this class, you add a line in your program:

```
import com.bruceeckel.tools.debug.*;
```

To remove the assertions so you can ship the code, a second **Assert** class is created, but in a different package:

```
//: Assert.java
```

```
// Turning off the assertion output
// so you can ship the program.
package com.bruceeckel.tools;

public class Assert {
  public final static void is_true(boolean exp){}
  public final static void is_false(boolean exp){}
  public final static void
  is_true(boolean exp, String msg) {}
  public final static void
  is_false(boolean exp, String msg) {}
} ///:~
```

Now if you change the previous **import** statement to:

```
import com.bruceeckel.tools.*;
```

The program will no longer print out assertions. Here's an example:

```
//: TestAssert.java
// Demonstrating the assertion tool
package c05;
// Comment the following, and uncomment the
// subsequent line to change assertion behavior:
import com.bruceeckel.tools.debug.*;
// import com.bruceeckel.tools.*;

public class TestAssert {
  public static void main(String[] args) {
    Assert.is_true((2 + 2) == 5);
    Assert.is_false((1 + 1) == 2);
    Assert.is_true((2 + 2) == 5, "2 + 2 == 5");
    Assert.is_false((1 + 1) == 2, "1 +1 != 2");
  }
} ///:~
```

By changing the **package** that's imported, you change your code from the debug version to the production version. This technique can be used for any kind of conditional code.

Package caveat

It's worth remembering that anytime you create a package, you implicitly specify a directory structure when you give the package a name. The package *must* live in the directory indicated by its name, which must be a directory that is searchable starting from the CLASSPATH. Experimenting with the **package** keyword can be a bit frustrating at first, because unless you adhere to the package-name to directory-path rule, you'll get a lot of mysterious run-time messages about not being able to find a particular class, even if that class is sitting there in the same directory. If you get a message like this, try commenting out the **package** statement, and if it runs you'll know where the problem lies.

Java access specifiers

The Java access specifiers **public**, **protected** and **private** are placed in front of each definition for each member in your class, whether it's a data member or a method. Each access specifier controls the access for only that particular definition. This is a distinct contrast to C++, in which the access specifier controls all the definitions following it until another access specifier comes along.

One way or another, everything has some kind of access specified for it. In the following sections, you'll learn all about the various types of access, starting with the default access.

"Friendly"

What if you give no access specifier at all, as in all the examples before this chapter? The default access has no keyword, but it is commonly referred to as "friendly." It means that all the other classes in the current package have access to the friendly member, but to all the classes outside of this package the member appears to be private. Since a compilation unit – a file – can belong only to a single package, all the classes within a single compilation unit are automatically friendly with each other. Thus, friendly elements are also said to have *package access*.

Friendly access allows you to group related classes together in a package so that they can easily interact with each other. When you put classes together in a package (thus granting mutual access to their friendly members; e.g. making them "friends") you "own" the code in that package. It makes sense that only code that you own should have friendly access to other code that you own. You could say that friendly access gives a meaning or a reason for grouping classes together in a package. In many languages the way you organize your definitions in files can be willy-nilly, but in Java you're compelled to organize them in a sensible fashion. In addition, you'll probably want to exclude classes that shouldn't have access to the classes being defined in the current package.

An important question in any relationship is "Who can access my **private** implementation?" The class controls which code has access to its members. There's no magic way to "break in;" someone in another package can't declare a new class and say, "Hi, I'm a friend of **Bob**'s!" and expect to see the **protected**, friendly, and **private** members of **Bob**. The only way to grant access to a member is to:

1. Make the member **public**. Then everybody, everywhere, can access it.

2. Make the member friendly by leaving off any access specifier, and put the other classes in the same package. Then the other classes can access the member.

3. As you'll see in a later chapter where inheritance is introduced, an inherited class can access a **protected** member as well as a **public** member (but not **private** members). It can access friendly members only if the two classes are in the same package. But don't worry about that now.

4. Provide "accessor/mutator" methods (also known as "get/set" methods) that read and change the value. This is the most civilized approach in terms of OOP, and it is fundamental to Java Beans, as you'll see in Chapter 13.

public: interface access

When you use the **public** keyword, it means that the member declaration that immediately follows **public** is available to everyone, in particular to the client programmer who uses the library. Suppose you define a package **dessert** containing the following compilation unit: (See page 97 if you have trouble executing this program.)

```
//: Cookie.java
// Creates a library
package c05.dessert;

public class Cookie {
  public Cookie() {
    System.out.println("Cookie constructor");
  }
  void foo() { System.out.println("foo"); }
} ///:~
```

Remember, **Cookie.java** must reside in a subdirectory called **dessert**, in a directory under **C05** (indicating Chapter 5 of this book) that must be under one of the CLASSPATH directories. Don't make the mistake of thinking that Java will always look at the current directory as one of the starting points for searching. If you don't have a '.' as one of the paths in your CLASSPATH, Java won't look there.

Now if you create a program that uses **Cookie**:

```
//: Dinner.java
// Uses the library
import c05.dessert.*;

public class Dinner {
  public Dinner() {
    System.out.println("Dinner constructor");
  }
  public static void main(String[] args) {
    Cookie x = new Cookie();
    //! x.foo(); // Can't access
  }
} ///:~
```

You can create a **Cookie** object, since its constructor is **public** and the class is **public**. (We'll look more at the concept of a public class later.) However, the **foo( )** member is inaccessible inside **Dinner.java** since **foo( )** is friendly only within package **dessert**.

The default package

You might be surprised to discover that the following code compiles, even though it would appear that it breaks the rules:

```
//: Cake.java
// Accesses a class in a separate
// compilation unit.

class Cake {
  public static void main(String[] args) {
    Pie x = new Pie();
    x.f();
  }
} ///:~
```

In a second file, in the same directory:

```
//: Pie.java
// The other class

class Pie {
  void f() { System.out.println("Pie.f()"); }
} ///:~
```

You might initially view these as completely foreign files, and yet **Cake** is able to create a **Pie** object and call its **f( )** method! You'd typically think that **Pie** and **f( )** are friendly and therefore not available to **Cake**. They *are* friendly – that part is correct. The reason that they are available in **Cake.java** is because they are in the same directory and have no explicit package name. Java treats files like this as implicitly part of the "default package" for that directory, and therefore friendly to all the other files in that directory.

private: you can't touch that!

The **private** keyword that means no one can access that member except that particular class, inside methods of that class. Other classes in the same package cannot access **private** members, so it's as if you're even insulating the class against yourself. On the other hand, it's not unlikely that a package might be created by several people collaborating together, so **private** allows you to freely change that member without concern that it will affect another class in the same package. The default "friendly" package access is often an adequate amount of hiding; remember, a "friendly" member is inaccessible to the user of the package. This is nice, since the default access is the one that you normally use. Thus, you'll typically think about access for the members that you explicitly want to make **public** for the client programmer, and as a result, you might not initially think you'll use the **private** keyword often since it's tolerable to get away without it. (This is a distinct contrast with C++.) However, it turns out that the consistent use of **private** is very important, especially where multithreading is concerned. (As you'll see in Chapter 14.)

Here's an example of the use of **private**:

```
//: IceCream.java
// Demonstrates "private" keyword

class Sundae {
  private Sundae() {}
  static Sundae makeASundae() {
    return new Sundae();
```

```
        }
    }

    public class IceCream {
        public static void main(String[] args) {
            //! Sundae x = new Sundae();
            Sundae x = Sundae.makeASundae();
        }
    } ///:~
```

This shows an example in which **private** comes in handy: you might want to control how an object is created and prevent someone from directly accessing a particular constructor (or all of them). In the example above, you cannot create a **Sundae** object via its constructor; instead you must call the **makeASundae( )** method to do it for you.[3]

Any method that you're certain is only a "helper" method for that class can be made **private** to ensure that you don't accidentally use it elsewhere in the package and thus prohibit you from changing or removing the method. Making a method **private** guarantees that you retain this option. (However, just because the handle is **private** doesn't mean that some other object can't have a **public** handle to the same object. See Chapter 12 for issues about aliasing.)

protected: "sort of friendly"

The **protected** access specifier requires a jump ahead to understand. First, you should be aware that you don't need to understand this section to continue through the book up through the inheritance chapter. But for completeness, here is a brief description and example using **protected**.

The **protected** keyword deals with a concept called *inheritance*, which takes an existing class and adds new members to that class without touching the existing class, which we refer to as the *base class*. You can also change the behavior of existing members of the class. To inherit from an existing class, you say that your new class **extends** an existing class, like this:

```
class Foo extends Bar {
```

---

[3] There's another effect in this case: Since the default constructor is the only one defined, and it's **private**, it will prevent inheritance of this class. (A subject that will be introduced in Chapter 6.)

The rest of the class definition looks the same.

If you create a new package and you inherit from a class in another package, the only members you have access to are the **public** members of the original package. (Of course, if you perform the inheritance in the *same* package, you have the normal package access to all the "friendly" members.) Sometimes the creator of the base class would like to take a particular member and grant access to derived classes but not the world in general. That's what **protected** does. If you refer back to the file **Cookie.java** on page 203, the following class *cannot* access the "friendly" member:

```
//: ChocolateChip.java
// Can't access friendly member
// in another class
import c05.dessert.*;

public class ChocolateChip extends Cookie {
  public ChocolateChip() {
    System.out.println(
      "ChocolateChip constructor");
  }
  public static void main(String[] args) {
    ChocolateChip x = new ChocolateChip();
    //! x.foo(); // Can't access foo
  }
} ///:~
```

One of the interesting things about inheritance is that if a method **foo( )** exists in class **Cookie**, then it also exists in any class inherited from **Cookie**. But since **foo( )** is "friendly" in a foreign package, it's unavailable to us in this one. Of course, you could make it **public**, but then everyone would have access and maybe that's not what you want. If we change the class **Cookie** as follows:

```
public class Cookie {
  public Cookie() {
    System.out.println("Cookie constructor");
  }
  protected void foo() {
    System.out.println("foo");
  }
}
```

then **foo( )** still has "friendly" access within package **dessert**, but it is also accessible to anyone inheriting from **Cookie**. However, it is *not* **public**.

Interface and implementation

Access control is often referred to as *implementation hiding*. Wrapping data and methods within classes (combined with implementation hiding this is often called *encapsulation*) produces a data type with characteristics and behaviors, but access control puts boundaries within that data type for two important reasons. The first is to establish what the client programmers can and can't use. You can build your internal mechanisms into the structure without worrying that the client programmers will think it's part of the interface that they should be using.

This feeds directly into the second reason, which is to separate the interface from the implementation. If the structure is used in a set of programs, but users can't do anything but send messages to the **public** interface, then you can change anything that's *not* **public** (e.g. "friendly," **protected**, or **private**) without requiring modifications to their code.

We're now in the world of object-oriented programming, where a **class** is actually describing "a class of objects," as you would describe a class of fishes or a class of birds. Any object belonging to this class will share these characteristics and behaviors. The class is a description of the way all objects of this type will look and act.

In the original OOP language, Simula-67, the keyword **class** was used to describe a new data type. The same keyword has been used for most object-oriented languages. This is the focal point of the whole language: the creation of new data types that are more than just boxes containing data and methods.

The class is the fundamental OOP concept in Java. It is one of the keywords that will *not* be set in bold in this book – it becomes annoying with a word repeated as often as "class."

For clarity, you might prefer a style of creating classes that puts the **public** members at the beginning, followed by the **protected**, friendly and **private** members. The advantage is that the user of the class can then read down from the top and see first what's important to them (the **public** members, because they can be accessed outside the file) and stop reading when they encounter the non-public members, which are part of the internal implementation. However, with the comment documentation supported by javadoc (described in Chapter 2) the issue of code readability by the client programmer becomes less important.

```
public class X {
    public void pub1( ) { /* . . . */ }
    public void pub2( ) { /* . . . */ }
    public void pub3( ) { /* . . . */ }
    private void priv1( ) { /*        */ }
    private void priv2( ) { /* . . . */ }
    private void priv3( ) { /* . . . */ }
    private int i;
    // . . .
}
```

This will make it only partially easier to read because the interface and implementation are still mixed together. That is, you still see the source code – the implementation – because it's right there in the class. Displaying the interface to the consumer of a class is really the job of the *class browser*, a tool whose job is to look at all the available classes and show you what you can do with them (i.e. what members are available) in a useful fashion. By the time you read this, good browsers should be an expected part of any good Java development tool.

Class access

In Java, the access specifiers can also be used to determine which classes *within* a library will be available to the users of that library. If you want a class to be available to a client programmer, you place the **public** keyword somewhere before the opening brace of the class body. This controls whether the client programmer can even create an object of the class.

To control the access of a class, the specifier must appear before the keyword **class**. Thus you can say:

```
public class Widget {
```

That is, if the name of your library is **mylib** any client programmer can access **Widget** by saying

```
import mylib.Widget;
```

or

```
import mylib.*;
```

However, there's an extra pair of constraints:

1. There can be only one **public** class per compilation unit (file). The idea is that each compilation unit has a single public interface represented by that public class. It can have as many supporting "friendly" classes as you want. If you have more than one **public** class inside a compilation unit, the compiler will give you an error message.

2. The name of the **public** class must exactly match the name of the file containing the compilation unit, including capitalization. So for **Widget**, the name of the file must be **Widget.java**, not **widget.java** or **WIDGET.java**. Again, you'll get a compile-time error if they don't agree.

3. It is possible, though not typical, to have a compilation unit with no public class at all. In this case, you can name the file whatever you like.

What if you've got a class inside **mylib** that you're just using to accomplish the tasks performed by **Widget** or some other **public** class in **mylib**? You don't want to go to the bother of creating documentation for the client programmer, and you think that sometime later you might want to completely change things and rip out your class altogether, substituting a different one. To give you this flexibility, you need to ensure that no client programmers become dependent on your particular implementation details hidden inside **mylib**. To accomplish this, you just leave the **public** keyword off the class, in which case it becomes friendly. (That class can be used only within that package.)

Note that a class cannot be **private** (that would make it accessible to no one but the class), or **protected**.[4] So you have only two choices for class access: "friendly" or **public**. If you don't want anyone else to have access to that class, you can make all the constructors **private**, thereby preventing anyone but you, inside a **static** member of the class, from creating an object of that class.[5] Here's an example:

---

[4] Actually, a Java 1.1 *inner class* can be private or protected, but that's a special case. These will be introduced in Chapter 7.

[5] You can also do it by inheriting (Chapter 6) from that class.

```
//: Lunch.java
// Demonstrates class access specifiers.
// Make a class effectively private
// with private constructors:

class Soup {
  private Soup() {}
  // (1) Allow creation via static method:
  public static Soup makeSoup() {
    return new Soup();
  }
  // (2) Create a static object and
  // return a reference upon request.
  // (The "Singleton" pattern):
  private static Soup ps1 = new Soup();
  public static Soup access() {
    return ps1;
  }
  public void f() {}
}

class Sandwich { // Uses Lunch
  void f() { new Lunch(); }
}

// Only one public class allowed per file:
public class Lunch {
  void test() {
    // Can't do this! Private constructor:
    //! Soup priv1 = new Soup();
    Soup priv2 = Soup.makeSoup();
    Sandwich f1 = new Sandwich();
    Soup.access().f();
  }
} ///:~
```

Up to now, most of the methods have been returning either **void** or a
primitive type so the definition:

```
public static Soup access() {
  return ps1;
}
```

might look a little confusing at first. The word before the method name
(**access**) tells what the method returns. So far this has most often been

void, which means it returns nothing. But you can also return a handle to an object, which is what happens here. This method returns a handle to an object of class **Soup**.

The **class Soup** shows how to prevent direct creation of a class by making all the constructors **private**. Remember that if you don't explicitly create at least one constructor, the default constructor (a constructor with no arguments) will be created for you. By writing the default constructor, it won't be created automatically. By making it **private**, no one can create an object of that class. But now how does anyone use this class? The above example shows two options. First, a **static** method is created that creates a new **Soup** and returns a handle to it. This could be useful if you want to do some extra operations on the **Soup** before returning it, or if you want to keep count of how many **Soup** objects to create (perhaps to restrict their population).

The second option uses what's called a *design pattern*, which will be discussed later in this book. This particular pattern is called a "singleton" because it allows only a single object to ever be created. The object of class **Soup** is created as a **static private** member of **Soup**, so there's one and only one, and you can't get at it except through the **public** method **access( )**.

As previously mentioned, if you don't put an access specifier for class access it defaults to "friendly." This means that an object of that class can be created by any other class in the package, but not outside the package. (Remember, all the files within the same directory that don't have explicit **package** declarations are implicitly part of the default package for that directory.) However, if a **static** member of that class is **public**, the client programmer can still access that **static** member even though they cannot create an object of that class.

Summary

In any relationship it's important to have boundaries that are respected by all parties involved. When you create a library, you establish a relationship with the user of that library – the client programmer – who is another programmer, but one putting together an application or using your library to build a bigger library.

Without rules, client programmers can do anything they want with all the members of a class, even if you might prefer they don't directly manipulate some of the members. Everything's naked to the world.

This chapter looked at how classes are built to form libraries; first, the way a group of classes is packaged within a library, and second, the way the class controls access to its members.

It is estimated that a C programming project begins to break down somewhere between 50K and 100K lines of code because C has a single "name space" so names begin to collide, causing an extra management overhead. In Java, the **package** keyword, the package naming scheme and the **import** keyword give you complete control over names, so the issue of name collision is easily avoided.

There are two reasons for controlling access to members. The first is to keep users' hands off tools that they shouldn't touch; tools that are necessary for the internal machinations of the data type, but not part of the interface that users need to solve their particular problems. So making methods and fields private is a service to users because they can easily see what's important to them and what they can ignore. It simplifies their understanding of the class.

The second and most important reason for access control is to allow the library designer to change the internal workings of the class without worrying about how it will affect the client programmer. You might build a class one way at first, and then discover that restructuring your code will provide much greater speed. If the interface and implementation are clearly separated and protected, you can accomplish this without forcing the user to rewrite their code.

Access specifiers in Java give valuable control to the creator of a class. The users of the class can clearly see exactly what they can use and what to ignore. More important, though, is the ability to ensure that no user becomes dependent on any part of the underlying implementation of a class. If you know this as the creator of the class, you can change the underlying implementation with the knowledge that no client programmer will be affected by the changes because they can't access that part of the class.

When you have the ability to change the underlying implementation, you can not only improve your design later, but you also have the freedom to make mistakes. No matter how carefully you plan and design you'll make mistakes. Knowing that it's relatively safe to make these mistakes means you'll be more experimental, you'll learn faster and you'll finish your project sooner.

The public interface to a class is what the user *does* see, so that is the most important part of the class to get "right" during analysis and design. Even that allows you some leeway for change. If you don't get the interface right the first time, you can *add* more methods, as long as you don't remove any that client programmers have already used in their code.

Exercises

I. Create a class with **public**, **private**, **protected**, and "friendly" data members and method members. Create an object of this class and see what kind of compiler messages you get when you try to access all the class members. Be aware that classes in the same directory are part of the "default" package.

2. Create a class with **protected** data. Create a second class in the same file with a method that manipulates the **protected** data in the first class.

3. Create a new directory and edit your CLASSPATH to include that new directory. Copy the **P.class** file to your new directory and then change the names of the file, the **P** class inside and the method names. (You might also want to add additional output to watch how it works.) Create another program in a different directory that uses your new class.

4. Create the following file in the c05 directory (presumably in your CLASSPATH):

```
//: PackagedClass.java
package c05;
class PackagedClass {
  public PackagedClass() {
    System.out.println(
      "Creating a packaged class");
  }
} ///:~
```

Then create the following file in a directory other than c05:

```
//: Foreign.java
package c05.foreign;
import c05.*;
public class Foreign {
    public static void main (String[] args) {
```

```
            PackagedClass pc = new PackagedClass();
    }
} ///:~
```

Explain why the compiler generates an error. Would making the **Foreign** class part of the c05 package change anything?

6: Reusing classes

One of the most compelling features about Java is code reuse. But to be revolutionary, you've got to be able to do a lot more than copy code and change it.

That's the approach used in procedural languages like C, and it hasn't worked very well. Like everything in Java, the solution revolves around the class. You reuse code by creating new classes, but instead of creating them from scratch, you use existing classes that someone has already built and debugged.

The trick is to use the classes without soiling the existing code. In this chapter you'll see two ways to accomplish this. The first is quite straightforward: You simply create objects of your existing class inside the new class. This is called *composition* because the new class is composed of objects of existing classes. You're simply reusing the functionality of the code, not its form.

The second approach is more subtle. It creates a new class as a *type of* an existing class. You literally take the form of the existing class and add code to it without modifying the existing class. This magical act is called *inheritance*, and the compiler does most of the work. Inheritance is one of the cornerstones of object-oriented programming and has additional implications that will be explored in the next chapter.

It turns out that much of the syntax and behavior are similar for both composition and inheritance (which makes sense because they are both ways of making new types from existing types). In this chapter, you'll learn about these code reuse mechanisms.

Composition syntax

Until now, composition has been used quite frequently. You simply place object handles inside new classes. For example, suppose you'd like an object that holds several **String** objects, a couple of primitives and an object of another class. For the non-primitive objects, just put handles inside your new class, and for the primitives just define them inside your class: (See page 97 if you have trouble executing this program.)

```
//: SprinklerSystem.java
// Composition for code reuse
package c06;

class WaterSource {
  private String s;
  WaterSource() {
    System.out.println("WaterSource()");
    s = new String("Constructed");
  }
  public String toString() { return s; }
}

public class SprinklerSystem {
  private String valve1, valve2, valve3, valve4;
  WaterSource source;
  int i;
  float f;
  void print() {
    System.out.println("valve1 = " + valve1);
    System.out.println("valve2 = " + valve2);
    System.out.println("valve3 = " + valve3);
    System.out.println("valve4 = " + valve4);
    System.out.println("i = " + i);
    System.out.println("f = " + f);
    System.out.println("source = " + source);
```

```
      }
      public static void main(String[] args) {
         SprinklerSystem x = new SprinklerSystem();
         x.print();
      }
   } ///:~
```

One of the methods defined in **WaterSource** is special: **toString( )**. You will learn later that every non-primitive object has a **toString( )** method, and it's called in special situations when the compiler wants a **String** but it's got one of these objects. So in the expression:

```
   System.out.println("source = " + source);
```

the compiler sees you trying to add a **String** object (**"source = "**) to a **WaterSource**. This doesn't make sense to it, because you can only "add" a **String** to another **String**, so it says "I'll turn **source** into a **String** by calling **toString( )**!" After doing this it can combine the two **String**s and pass the resulting **String** to **System.out.println( )**. Any time you want to allow this behavior with a class you create you need only write a **toString( )** method.

At first glance, you might assume – Java being as safe and careful as it is – that the compiler would automatically construct objects for each of the handles in the above code, for example calling the default constructor for **WaterSource** to initialize **source**. The output of the print statement is in fact:

```
      valve1 = null
      valve2 = null
      valve3 = null
      valve4 = null
      i = 0
      f = 0.0
      source = null
```

Primitives that are fields in a class are automatically initialized to zero, as noted in Chapter 2. But the object handles are initialized to **null**, and if you try to call methods for any of them you'll get an exception. It's actually pretty good (and useful) that you can still print them out without throwing an exception.

It makes sense that the compiler doesn't just create a default object for every handle because that would incur unnecessary overhead in many cases. If you want the handles initialized, you can do it:

1. At the point the objects are defined. This means that they'll always be initialized before the constructor is called.

2. In the constructor for that class

3. Right before you actually need to use the object. This can reduce overhead, if there are situations where the object doesn't need to be created.

All three approaches are shown here:

```
//: Bath.java
// Constructor initialization with composition

class Soap {
  private String s;
  Soap() {
    System.out.println("Soap()");
    s = new String("Constructed");
  }
  public String toString() { return s; }
}

public class Bath {
  private String
    // Initializing at point of definition:
    s1 = new String("Happy"),
    s2 = "Happy",
    s3, s4;
  Soap castille;
  int i;
  float toy;
  Bath() {
    System.out.println("Inside Bath()");
    s3 = new String("Joy");
    i = 47;
    toy = 3.14f;
    castille = new Soap();
  }
  void print() {
    // Delayed initialization:
    if(s4 == null)
      s4 = new String("Joy");
    System.out.println("s1 = " + s1);
    System.out.println("s2 = " + s2);
```

Thinking in Java   *www.BruceEckel.com*

```
        System.out.println("s3 = " + s3);
        System.out.println("s4 = " + s4);
        System.out.println("i = " + i);
        System.out.println("toy = " + toy);
        System.out.println("castille = " + castille);
    }
    public static void main(String[] args) {
        Bath b = new Bath();
        b.print();
    }
} ///:~
```

Note that in the **Bath** constructor a statement is executed before any of
the initializations take place. When you don't initialize at the point of
definition, there's still no guarantee that you'll perform any initialization
before you send a message to an object handle – except for the inevitable
run-time exception.

Here's the output for the program:

```
Inside Bath()
Soap()
s1 = Happy
s2 = Happy
s3 = Joy
s4 = Joy
i = 47
toy = 3.14
castille = Constructed
```

When **print( )** is called it fills in **s4** so that all the fields are properly
initialized by the time they are used.

Inheritance syntax

Inheritance is such an integral part of Java (and OOP languages in
general) that it was introduced in Chapter 1 and has been used
occasionally in chapters before this one because certain situations
required it. In addition, you're always doing inheritance when you create
a class, because if you don't say otherwise you inherit from Java's
standard root class **Object**.

The syntax for composition is obvious, but to perform inheritance there's
a distinctly different form. When you inherit, you say "This new class is

---

like that old class." You state this in code by giving the name of the class as usual, but before the opening brace of the class body, put the keyword **extends** followed by the name of the *base class*. When you do this, you automatically get all the data members and methods in the base class. Here's an example:

```
//: Detergent.java
// Inheritance syntax & properties

class Cleanser {
  private String s = new String("Cleanser");
  public void append(String a) { s += a; }
  public void dilute() { append(" dilute()"); }
  public void apply() { append(" apply()"); }
  public void scrub() { append(" scrub()"); }
  public void print() { System.out.println(s); }
  public static void main(String[] args) {
    Cleanser x = new Cleanser();
    x.dilute(); x.apply(); x.scrub();
    x.print();
  }
}

public class Detergent extends Cleanser {
  // Change a method:
  public void scrub() {
    append(" Detergent.scrub()");
    super.scrub(); // Call base-class version
  }
  // Add methods to the interface:
  public void foam() { append(" foam()"); }
  // Test the new class:
  public static void main(String[] args) {
    Detergent x = new Detergent();
    x.dilute();
    x.apply();
    x.scrub();
    x.foam();
    x.print();
    System.out.println("Testing base class:");
    Cleanser.main(args);
  }
} ///:~
```

This demonstrates a number of features. First, in the **Cleanser append( )** method, **String**s are concatenated to **s** using the **+=** operator, which is one of the operators (along with '**+**') that the Java designers "overloaded" to work with **String**s.

Second, both **Cleanser** and **Detergent** contain a **main( )** method. You can create a **main( )** for each one of your classes, and it's often recommended to code this way so that your test code is wrapped in with the class. Even if you have a lot of classes in a program only the **main( )** for the **public** class invoked on the command line will be called. (And you can have only one **public** class per file.) So in this case, when you say **java Detergent**, **Detergent.main( )** will be called. But you can also say **java Cleanser** to invoke **Cleanser.main( )**, even though **Cleanser** is not a **public** class. This technique of putting a **main( )** in each class allows easy unit testing for each class. And you don't need to remove the **main( )** when you're finished testing; you can leave it in for later testing.

Here, you can see that **Detergent.main( )** calls **Cleanser.main( )** explicitly.

It's important that all of the methods in **Cleanser** are **public**. Remember that if you leave off any access specifier the member defaults to "friendly," which allows access only to package members. Thus, within this package, anyone could use those methods if there were no access specifier. **Detergent** would have no trouble, for example. However, if a class from some other package were to inherit **Cleanser** it could access only **public** members. So to plan for inheritance, as a general rule make all fields **private** and all methods **public**. (**protected** members also allow access by derived classes; you'll learn about this later.) Of course, in particular cases you must make adjustments, but this is a useful guideline.

Note that **Cleanser** has a set of methods in its interface: **append( )**, **dilute( )**, **apply( )**, **scrub( )** and **print( )**. Because **Detergent** is *derived from* **Cleanser** (via the **extends** keyword) it automatically gets all these methods in its interface, even though you don't see them all explicitly defined in **Detergent**. You can think of inheritance, then, as *reusing the interface*. (The implementation comes along for free, but that part isn't the primary point.)

As seen in **scrub( )**, it's possible to take a method that's been defined in the base class and modify it. In this case, you might want to call the method from the base class inside the new version. But inside **scrub( )** you cannot simply call **scrub( )**, since that would produce a recursive call, which isn't what you want. To solve this problem Java has the keyword **super** that refers to the "superclass" that the current class has been inherited from. Thus the expression **super.scrub( )** calls the base-class version of the method **scrub( )**.

When inheriting you're not restricted to using the methods of the base class. You can also add new methods to the derived class exactly the way you put any method in a class: just define it. The **extends** keyword suggests that you are going to add new methods to the base-class interface, and the method **foam( )** is an example of this.

In **Detergent.main( )** you can see that for a **Detergent** object you can call all the methods that are available in **Cleanser** as well as in **Detergent** (i.e. **foam( )**).

Initializing the base class

Since there are now two classes involved – the base class and the derived class – instead of just one, it can be a bit confusing to try to imagine the resulting object produced by a derived class. From the outside, it looks like the new class has the same interface as the base class and maybe some additional methods and fields. But inheritance doesn't just copy the interface of the base class. When you create an object of the derived class, it contains within it a *subobject* of the base class. This subobject is the same as if you had created an object of the base class by itself. It's just that, from the outside, the subobject of the base class is wrapped within the derived-class object.

Of course, it's essential that the base-class subobject be initialized correctly and there's only one way to guarantee that: perform the initialization in the constructor, by calling the base-class constructor, which has all the appropriate knowledge and privileges to perform the base-class initialization. Java automatically inserts calls to the base-class constructor in the derived-class constructor. The following example shows this working with three levels of inheritance:

```
//: Cartoon.java
// Constructor calls during inheritance

class Art {
  Art() {
    System.out.println("Art constructor");
  }
}

class Drawing extends Art {
  Drawing() {
```

```
      System.out.println("Drawing constructor");
    }
}

public class Cartoon extends Drawing {
  Cartoon() {
    System.out.println("Cartoon constructor");
  }
  public static void main(String[] args) {
    Cartoon x = new Cartoon();
  }
} ///:~
```

The output for this program shows the automatic calls:

```
Art constructor
Drawing constructor
Cartoon constructor
```

You can see that the construction happens from the base "outward," so the base class is initialized before the derived-class constructors can access it.

Even if you don't create a constructor for **Cartoon( )**, the compiler will synthesize a default constructor for you that calls the base class constructor.

Constructors with arguments

The above example has default constructors; that is, they don't have any arguments. It's easy for the compiler to call these because there's no question about what arguments to pass. If your class doesn't have default arguments or if you want to call a base-class constructor that has an argument you must explicitly write the calls to the base-class constructor using the **super** keyword and the appropriate argument list:

```
//: Chess.java
// Inheritance, constructors and arguments

class Game {
  Game(int i) {
    System.out.println("Game constructor");
  }
}

class BoardGame extends Game {
```

```
      BoardGame(int i) {
        super(i);
        System.out.println("BoardGame constructor");
      }
    }

    public class Chess extends BoardGame {
      Chess() {
        super(11);
        System.out.println("Chess constructor");
      }
      public static void main(String[] args) {
        Chess x = new Chess();
      }
    } ///:~
```

If you don't call the base-class constructor in **BoardGame( )**, the
compiler will complain that it can't find a constructor of the form
Game( ). In addition, the call to the base-class constructor *must* be the
first thing you do in the derived-class constructor. (The compiler will
remind you if you get it wrong.)

Catching base constructor exceptions

As just noted, the compiler forces you to place the base-class constructor
call first in the body of the derived-class constructor. This means nothing
else can appear before it. As you'll see in Chapter 9, this also prevents a
derived-class constructor from catching any exceptions that come from a
base class. This can be inconvenient at times.

Combining composition and inheritance

It is very common to use composition and inheritance together. The
following example shows the creation of a more complex class, using
both inheritance and composition, along with the necessary constructor
initialization:

```
//: PlaceSetting.java
// Combining composition & inheritance

class Plate {
```

```
    Plate(int i) {
      System.out.println("Plate constructor");
    }
  }

  class DinnerPlate extends Plate {
    DinnerPlate(int i) {
      super(i);
      System.out.println(
        "DinnerPlate constructor");
    }
  }

  class Utensil {
    Utensil(int i) {
      System.out.println("Utensil constructor");
    }
  }

  class Spoon extends Utensil {
    Spoon(int i) {
      super(i);
      System.out.println("Spoon constructor");
    }
  }

  class Fork extends Utensil {
    Fork(int i) {
      super(i);
      System.out.println("Fork constructor");
    }
  }

  class Knife extends Utensil {
    Knife(int i) {
      super(i);
      System.out.println("Knife constructor");
    }
  }

  // A cultural way of doing something:
  class Custom {
    Custom(int i) {
      System.out.println("Custom constructor");
```

```
      }
    }

    public class PlaceSetting extends Custom {
      Spoon sp;
      Fork frk;
      Knife kn;
      DinnerPlate pl;
      PlaceSetting(int i) {
        super(i + 1);
        sp = new Spoon(i + 2);
        frk = new Fork(i + 3);
        kn = new Knife(i + 4);
        pl = new DinnerPlate(i + 5);
        System.out.println(
          "PlaceSetting constructor");
      }
      public static void main(String[] args) {
        PlaceSetting x = new PlaceSetting(9);
      }
    } ///:~
```

While the compiler forces you to initialize the base classes, and requires that you do it right at the beginning of the constructor, it doesn't watch over you to make sure that you initialize the member objects, so you must remember to pay attention to that.

Guaranteeing proper cleanup

Java doesn't have the C++ concept of a *destructor*, a method that is automatically called when an object is destroyed. The reason is probably that in Java the practice is simply to forget about objects rather than to destroy them, allowing the garbage collector to reclaim the memory as necessary.

Often this is fine, but there are times when your class might perform some activities during its lifetime that require cleanup. As mentioned in Chapter 4, you can't know when the garbage collector will be called, or if it will be called. So if you want something cleaned up for a class, you must write a special method to do it explicitly, and make sure that the client programmer knows that they must call this method. On top of this, as described in Chapter 9 (exception handling), you must guard against an exception by putting such cleanup in a **finally** clause.

Consider an example of a computer-aided design system that draws pictures on the screen:

```java
//: CADSystem.java
// Ensuring proper cleanup
import java.util.*;

class Shape {
  Shape(int i) {
    System.out.println("Shape constructor");
  }
  void cleanup() {
    System.out.println("Shape cleanup");
  }
}

class Circle extends Shape {
  Circle(int i) {
    super(i);
    System.out.println("Drawing a Circle");
  }
  void cleanup() {
    System.out.println("Erasing a Circle");
    super.cleanup();
  }
}

class Triangle extends Shape {
  Triangle(int i) {
    super(i);
    System.out.println("Drawing a Triangle");
  }
  void cleanup() {
    System.out.println("Erasing a Triangle");
    super.cleanup();
  }
}

class Line extends Shape {
  private int start, end;
  Line(int start, int end) {
    super(start);
    this.start = start;
    this.end = end;
    System.out.println("Drawing a Line: " +
```

```
              start + ", " + end);
  }
  void cleanup() {
    System.out.println("Erasing a Line: " +
            start + ", " + end);
    super.cleanup();
  }
}

public class CADSystem extends Shape {
  private Circle c;
  private Triangle t;
  private Line[] lines = new Line[10];
  CADSystem(int i) {
    super(i + 1);
    for(int j = 0; j < 10; j++)
      lines[j] = new Line(j, j*j);
    c = new Circle(1);
    t = new Triangle(1);
    System.out.println("Combined constructor");
  }
  void cleanup() {
    System.out.println("CADSystem.cleanup()");
    t.cleanup();
    c.cleanup();
    for(int i = 0; i < lines.length; i++)
      lines[i].cleanup();
    super.cleanup();
  }
  public static void main(String[] args) {
    CADSystem x = new CADSystem(47);
    try {
      // Code and exception handling...
    } finally {
      x.cleanup();
    }
  }
} ///:~
```

Everything in this system is some kind of **Shape** (which is itself a kind of **Object** since it's implicitly inherited from the root class). Each class redefines **Shape**'s **cleanup( )** method in addition to calling the base-class version of that method using **super**. The specific **Shape** classes **Circle**, **Triangle** and **Line** all have constructors that "draw," although any method called during the lifetime of the object could be responsible for doing something that needs cleanup. Each class has its own **cleanup( )** method to restore non-memory things back to the way they were before the object existed.

In **main( )**, you can see two keywords that are new, and won't officially be introduced until Chapter 9: **try** and **finally**. The **try** keyword indicates that the block that follows (delimited by curly braces) is a *guarded region*, which means that it is given special treatment. One of these special treatments is that the code in the **finally** clause following this guarded region is *always* executed, no matter how the **try** block exits. (With exception handling, it's possible to leave a **try** block in a number of non-ordinary ways.) Here, the **finally** clause is saying "always call **cleanup( )** for **x**, no matter what happens." These keywords will be explained thoroughly in Chapter 9.

Note that in your cleanup method you must also pay attention to the calling order for the base-class and member-object cleanup methods in case one subobject depends on another. In general, you should follow the same form that is imposed by a C++ compiler on its destructors: First perform all of the work specific to your class (which might require that base-class elements still be viable) then call the base-class cleanup method, as demonstrated here.

There can be many cases in which the cleanup issue is not a problem; you just let the garbage collector do the work. But when you must do it explicitly, diligence and attention is required.

Order of garbage collection

There's not much you can rely on when it comes to garbage collection. The garbage collector might never be called. If it is, it can reclaim objects in any order it wants. In addition, implementations of the garbage collector in Java 1.0 often don't call the **finalize( )** methods. It's best to not rely on garbage collection for anything but memory reclamation. If you want cleanup to take place, make your own cleanup methods and don't rely on **finalize( )**. (As mentioned earlier, Java 1.1 can be forced to call all the finalizers.)

Name hiding

Only C++ programmers might be surprised by name hiding, since it works differently in that language. If a Java base class has a method name that's overloaded several times, redefining that method name in the derived class will *not* hide any of the base-class versions. Thus

---

overloading works regardless of whether the method was defined at this level or in a base class:

```
//: Hide.java
// Overloading a base-class method name
// in a derived class does not hide the
// base-class versions

class Homer {
  char doh(char c) {
    System.out.println("doh(char)");
    return 'd';
  }
  float doh(float f) {
    System.out.println("doh(float)");
    return 1.0f;
  }
}

class Milhouse {}

class Bart extends Homer {
  void doh(Milhouse m) {}
}

class Hide {
  public static void main(String[] args) {
    Bart b = new Bart();
    b.doh(1); // doh(float) used
    b.doh('x');
    b.doh(1.0f);
    b.doh(new Milhouse());
  }
} ///:~
```

As you'll see in the next chapter, it's far more common to override methods of the same name using exactly the same signature and return type as in the base class. It can be confusing otherwise (which is why C++ disallows it, to prevent you from making what is probably a mistake).

Choosing composition vs. inheritance

Both composition and inheritance allow you to place subobjects inside your new class. You might wonder about the difference between the two, and when to choose one over the other.

Composition is generally used when you want the features of an existing class inside your new class, but not its interface. That is, you embed an object so that you can use it to implement features of your new class, but the user of your new class sees the interface you've defined rather than the interface from the embedded object. For this effect, you embed **private** objects of existing classes inside your new class.

Sometimes it makes sense to allow the class user to directly access the composition of your new class; that is, to make the member objects **public**. The member objects use implementation hiding themselves, so this is a safe thing to do and when the user knows you're assembling a bunch of parts, it makes the interface easier to understand. A **car** object is a good example:

```
//: Car.java
// Composition with public objects

class Engine {
  public void start() {}
  public void rev() {}
  public void stop() {}
}

class Wheel {
  public void inflate(int psi) {}
}

class Window {
  public void rollup() {}
  public void rolldown() {}
}

class Door {
  public Window window = new Window();
  public void open() {}
```

```
    public void close() {}
}

public class Car {
  public Engine engine = new Engine();
  public Wheel[] wheel = new Wheel[4];
  public Door left = new Door(),
      right = new Door(); // 2-door
  Car() {
    for(int i = 0; i < 4; i++)
      wheel[i] = new Wheel();
  }
  public static void main(String[] args) {
    Car car = new Car();
    car.left.window.rollup();
    car.wheel[0].inflate(72);
  }
} ///:~
```

Because the composition of a car is part of the analysis of the problem (and not simply part of the underlying design), making the members public assists the client programmer's understanding of how to use the class and requires less code complexity for the creator of the class.

When you inherit, you take an existing class and make a special version of it. In general, this means that you're taking a general-purpose class and specializing it for a particular need. With a little thought, you'll see that it would make no sense to compose a car using a vehicle object – a car doesn't contain a vehicle, it *is* a vehicle. The *is-a* relationship is expressed with inheritance, and the *has-a* relationship is expressed with composition.

protected

Now that you've been introduced to inheritance, the keyword **protected** finally has meaning. In an ideal world, **private** members would always be hard-and-fast **private**, but in real projects there are times when you want to make something hidden from the world at large and yet allow access for members of derived classes. The **protected** keyword is a nod to pragmatism. It says "This is **private** as far as the class user is concerned, but available to anyone who inherits from this class or anyone else in the same **package**." That is, **protected** in Java is automatically "friendly."

The best tack to take is to leave the data members **private** – you should always preserve your right to change the underlying implementation. You can then allow controlled access to inheritors of your class through **protected** methods:

```
//: Orc.java
// The protected keyword
import java.util.*;

class Villain {
  private int i;
  protected int read() { return i; }
  protected void set(int ii) { i = ii; }
  public Villain(int ii) { i = ii; }
  public int value(int m) { return m*i; }
}

public class Orc extends Villain {
  private int j;
  public Orc(int jj) { super(jj); j = jj; }
  public void change(int x) { set(x); }
} ///:~
```

You can see that **change( )** has access to **set( )** because it's **protected**.

Incremental development

One of the advantages of inheritance is that it supports *incremental development* by allowing you to introduce new code without causing bugs in existing code. This also isolates new bugs to the new code. By inheriting from an existing, functional class and adding data members and methods (and redefining existing methods), you leave the existing code – that someone else might still be using – untouched and unbugged. If a bug happens, you know that it's in your new code, which is much shorter and easier to read than if you had modified the body of existing code.

It's rather amazing how cleanly the classes are separated. You don't even need the source code for the methods in order to reuse the code. At most, you just import a package. (This is true for both inheritance and composition.)

It's important to realize that program development is an incremental process, just like human learning. You can do as much analysis as you want, but you still won't know all the answers when you set out on a project. You'll have much more success – and more immediate feedback – if you start out to "grow" your project as an organic, evolutionary creature, rather than constructing it all at once like a glass-box skyscraper.

Although inheritance for experimentation can be a useful technique, at some point after things stabilize you need to take a new look at your class hierarchy with an eye to collapsing it into a sensible structure. Remember that underneath it all, inheritance is meant to express a relationship that says "This new class is a *type of* that old class." Your program should not be concerned with pushing bits around, but instead with creating and manipulating objects of various types to express a model in the terms that come from the problem space.

Upcasting

The most important aspect of inheritance is not that it provides methods for the new class. It's the relationship expressed between the new class and the base class. This relationship can be summarized by saying "The new class *is a type of* the existing class."

This description is not just a fanciful way of explaining inheritance – it's supported directly by the language. As an example, consider a base class called **Instrument** that represents musical instruments and a derived class called **Wind**. Because inheritance means that all of the methods in the base class are also available in the derived class, any message you can send to the base class can also be sent to the derived class. If the **Instrument** class has a **play( )** method, so will **Wind** instruments. This means we can accurately say that a **Wind** object is also a type of **Instrument**. The following example shows how the compiler supports this notion:

```
//: Wind.java
// Inheritance & upcasting
import java.util.*;

class Instrument {
  public void play() {}
  static void tune(Instrument i) {
    // ...
    i.play();
  }
}
```

```
// Wind objects are instruments
// because they have the same interface:
class Wind extends Instrument {
  public static void main(String[] args) {
    Wind flute = new Wind();
    Instrument.tune(flute); // Upcasting
  }
} ///:~
```

What's interesting in this example is the **tune( )** method, which accepts an **Instrument** handle. However, in **Wind**.main( ) the **tune( )** method is called by giving it a **Wind** handle. Given that Java is particular about type checking, it seems strange that a method that accepts one type will readily accept another type, until you realize that a **Wind** object is also an **Instrument** object, and there's no method that **tune( )** could call for an **Instrument** that isn't also in **Wind**. Inside **tune( )**, the code works for **Instrument** and anything derived from **Instrument**, and the act of converting a **Wind** handle into an **Instrument** handle is called *upcasting*.

Why "upcasting"?

The reason for the term is historical and is based on the way class inheritance diagrams have traditionally been drawn with the root at the top of the page, growing downward. (Of course, you can draw your diagrams any way you find helpful.) The inheritance diagram for **Wind.java** is then:

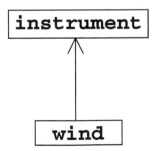

Casting from derived to base moves *up* on the inheritance diagram, so it's commonly referred to as upcasting. Upcasting is always safe because you're going from a more specific type to a more general type. That is, the derived class is a superset of the base class. It might contain more methods than the base class, but it must contain *at least* the methods in the base class. The only thing that can occur to the class interface during the upcast is that it can lose methods, not gain them. This is why the compiler allows upcasting without any explicit casts or other special notation.

You can also perform the reverse of upcasting, called *downcasting*, but this involves a dilemma that is the subject of Chapter 11.

Composition vs. inheritance revisited

In object-oriented programming, the most likely way that you'll create and use code is by simply packaging data and methods together into a class, and using objects of that class. Occasionally, you'll use existing classes to build new classes with composition. Even less frequently than that you'll use inheritance. So although inheritance gets a lot of emphasis while learning OOP, it doesn't mean that you should use it everywhere you possibly can. On the contrary, you should use it sparingly, only when it's clear that inheritance is useful. One of the clearest ways to determine whether you should use composition or inheritance is to ask whether you'll ever need to upcast from your new class to the base class. If you must upcast, then inheritance is necessary, but if you don't need to upcast, then you should look closely at whether you need inheritance. The next chapter (polymorphism) provides one of the most compelling reasons for upcasting, but if you remember to ask "Do I need to upcast?", you'll have a good tool for deciding between composition and inheritance.

The **final** keyword

The **final** keyword has slightly different meanings depending on the context, but in general it says "This cannot be changed." You might want to prevent changes for two reasons: design or efficiency. Because these two reasons are quite different, it's possible to misuse the **final** keyword.

The following sections discuss the three places where **final** can be used: for data, methods and for a class.

Final data

Many programming languages have a way to tell the compiler that a piece of data is "constant." A constant is useful for two reasons:

1. It can be a *compile-time constant* that won't ever change.

2. It can be a value initialized at run-time that you don't want changed.

In the case of a compile-time constant the compiler is allowed to "fold" the constant value into any calculations in which it's used; that is, the calculation can be performed at compile time, eliminating some run-time overhead. In Java, these sorts of constants must be primitives and are expressed using the **final** keyword. A value must be given at the time of definition of such a constant.

A field that is both **static** and **final** has only one piece of storage that cannot be changed.

When using **final** with object handles rather than primitives the meaning gets a bit confusing. With a primitive, **final** makes the *value* a constant, but with an object handle, **final** makes the handle a constant. The handle must be initialized to an object at the point of declaration, and the handle can never be changed to point to another object. However, the object can be modified; Java does not provide a way to make any arbitrary object a constant. (You can, however, write your class so that objects have the effect of being constant.) This restriction includes arrays, which are also objects.

Here's an example that demonstrates **final** fields:

```
//: FinalData.java
// The effect of final on fields

class Value {
   int i = 1;
}

public class FinalData {
   // Can be compile-time constants
   final int i1 = 9;
   static final int I2 = 99;
   // Typical public constant:
   public static final int I3 = 39;
   // Cannot be compile-time constants:
   final int i4 = (int)(Math.random()*20);
   static final int i5 = (int)(Math.random()*20);

   Value v1 = new Value();
   final Value v2 = new Value();
   static final Value v3 = new Value();
   //! final Value v4; // Pre-Java 1.1 Error:
                       // no initializer
   // Arrays:
```

```
    final int[] a = { 1, 2, 3, 4, 5, 6 };

  public void print(String id) {
    System.out.println(
      id + ": " + "i4 = " + i4 +
      ", i5 = " + i5);
  }
  public static void main(String[] args) {
    FinalData fd1 = new FinalData();
    //! fd1.i1++; // Error: can't change value
    fd1.v2.i++; // Object isn't constant!
    fd1.v1 = new Value(); // OK -- not final
    for(int i = 0; i < fd1.a.length; i++)
      fd1.a[i]++; // Object isn't constant!
    //! fd1.v2 = new Value(); // Error: Can't
    //! fd1.v3 = new Value(); // change handle
    //! fd1.a = new int[3];

    fd1.print("fd1");
    System.out.println("Creating new FinalData");
    FinalData fd2 = new FinalData();
    fd1.print("fd1");
    fd2.print("fd2");
  }
} ///:~
```

Since **i1** and **I2** are **final** primitives with compile-time values, they can both be used as compile-time constants and are not different in any important way. **I3** is the more typical way you'll see such constants defined: **public** so they're usable outside the package, **static** to emphasize that there's only one, and **final** to say that it's a constant. Note that **final static** primitives with constant initial values (that is, compile-time constants) are named with all capitals by convention. Also note that **i5** cannot be known at compile time, so it is not capitalized.

Just because something is **final** doesn't mean that its value is known at compile-time. This is demonstrated by initializing **i4** and **i5** at run-time using randomly generated numbers. This portion of the example also shows the difference between making a **final** value **static** or non-**static**. This difference shows up only when the values are initialized at run-time, since the compile-time values are treated the same by the compiler. (And presumably optimized out of existence.) The difference is shown in the output from one run:

```
fd1: i4 = 15, i5 = 9
```

```
    Creating new FinalData
    fd1: i4 = 15, i5 = 9
    fd2: i4 = 10, i5 = 9
```

Note that the values of **i4** for **fd1** and **fd2** are unique, but the value for **i5** is not changed by creating the second **FinalData** object. That's because it's **static** and is initialized once upon loading and not each time a new object is created.

The variables **v1** through **v4** demonstrate the meaning of a **final** handle. As you can see in **main( )**, just because **v2** is **final** doesn't mean that you can't change its value. However, you cannot re-bind **v2** to a new object, precisely because it's **final**. That's what **final** means for a handle. You can also see the same meaning holds true for an array, which is just another kind of handle. (There is know way that I know of to make the array handles themselves **final**.) Making handles **final** seems less useful than making primitives **final**.

Blank finals

Java 1.1 allows the creation of *blank finals*, which are fields that are declared as **final** but are not given an initialization value. In all cases, the blank final *must* be initialized before it is used, and the compiler ensures this. However, blank finals provide much more flexibility in the use of the **final** keyword since, for example, a **final** field inside a class can now be different for each object and yet it retains its immutable quality. Here's an example:

```
//: BlankFinal.java
// "Blank" final data members

class Poppet { }

class BlankFinal {
   final int i = 0; // Initialized final
   final int j; // Blank final
   final Poppet p; // Blank final handle
   // Blank finals MUST be initialized
   // in the constructor:
   BlankFinal() {
      j = 1; // Initialize blank final
      p = new Poppet();
   }
   BlankFinal(int x) {
      j = x; // Initialize blank final
```

```
      p = new Poppet();
  }
  public static void main(String[] args) {
    BlankFinal bf = new BlankFinal();
  }
} ///:~
```

You're forced to perform assignments to finals either with an expression at the point of definition of the field or in every constructor. This way it's guaranteed that the final field is always initialized before use.

Final arguments

Java 1.1 allows you to make arguments **final** by declaring them as such in the argument list. This means that inside the method you cannot change what the argument handle points to:

```
//: FinalArguments.java
// Using "final" with method arguments

class Gizmo {
  public void spin() {}
}

public class FinalArguments {
  void with(final Gizmo g) {
    //! g = new Gizmo(); // Illegal -- g is final
    g.spin();
  }
  void without(Gizmo g) {
    g = new Gizmo(); // OK -- g not final
    g.spin();
  }
  // void f(final int i) { i++; } // Can't change
  // You can only read from a final primitive:
  int g(final int i) { return i + 1; }
  public static void main(String[] args) {
    FinalArguments bf = new FinalArguments();
    bf.without(null);
    bf.with(null);
  }
} ///:~
```

Note that you can still assign a **null** handle to an argument that's final without the compiler catching it, just like you can with a non-final argument.

The methods **f( )** and **g( )** show what happens when primitive arguments are **final**: you can only read the argument, but you can't change it.

Final methods

There are two reasons for **final** methods. The first is to put a "lock" on the method to prevent any inheriting class from changing its meaning. This is done for design reasons when you want to make sure that a method's behavior is retained during inheritance and cannot be overridden.

The second reason for **final** methods is efficiency. If you make a method **final**, you are allowing the compiler to turn any calls to that method into *inline* calls. When the compiler sees a **final** method call it can (at its discretion) skip the normal approach of inserting code to perform the method call mechanism (push arguments on the stack, hop over to the method code and execute it, hop back and clean off the stack arguments, and deal with the return value) and instead replace the method call with a copy of the actual code in the method body. This eliminates the overhead of the method call. Of course, if a method is big, then your code begins to bloat and you probably won't see any performance gains from inlining since any improvements will be dwarfed by the amount of time spent inside the method. It is implied that the Java compiler is able to detect these situations and choose wisely whether to inline a **final** method. However, it's better to not trust that the compiler is able to do this and make a method **final** only if it's quite small or if you want to explicitly prevent overriding.

Any **private** methods in a class are implicitly **final**. Because you can't access a **private** method, you can't override it (the compiler gives an error message if you try). You can add the **final** specifier to a **private** method but it doesn't give that method any extra meaning.

Final classes

When you say that an entire class is **final** (by preceding its definition with the **final** keyword), you state that you don't want to inherit from this class or allow anyone else to do so. In other words, for some reason the design of your class is such that there is never a need to make any changes, or for safety or security reasons you don't want subclassing.

Alternatively, you might be dealing with an efficiency issue and you want to make sure that any activity involved with objects of this class is as efficient as possible.

```
//: Jurassic.java
// Making an entire class final

class SmallBrain {}

final class Dinosaur {
   int i = 7;
   int j = 1;
   SmallBrain x = new SmallBrain();
   void f() {}
}

//! class Further extends Dinosaur {}
// error: Cannot extend final class 'Dinosaur'

public class Jurassic {
   public static void main(String[] args) {
      Dinosaur n = new Dinosaur();
      n.f();
      n.i = 40;
      n.j++;
   }
} ///:~
```

Note that the data members can be **final** or not, as you choose. The same rules apply to **final** for data members regardless of whether the class is defined as **final**. Defining the class as **final** simply prevents inheritance – nothing more. However, because it prevents inheritance all methods in a **final** class are implicitly **final**, since there's no way to override them. So the compiler has the same efficiency options as it does if you explicitly declare a method **final**.

You can add the **final** specifier to a method in a **final** class, but it doesn't add any meaning.

Final caution

It can seem to be sensible to make a method **final** while you're designing a class. You might feel that efficiency is very important when using your class and that no one could possibly want to override your methods anyway. Sometimes this is true.

But be careful with your assumptions. In general, it's difficult to anticipate how a class can be reused, especially a general-purpose class. If you define a method as **final** you might prevent the possibility of reusing your class through inheritance in some other programmer's project simply because you couldn't imagine it being used that way.

The standard Java library is a good example of this. In particular, the **Vector** class is commonly used and might be even more useful if, in the name of efficiency, all the methods hadn't been made **final**. It's easily conceivable that you might want to inherit and override with such a fundamentally useful class, but the designers somehow decided this wasn't appropriate. This is ironic for two reasons. First, **Stack** is inherited from **Vector**, which says that a **Stack** *is* a **Vector**, which isn't really true. Second, many of the most important methods of **Vector**, such as **addElement( )** and **elementAt( )** are **synchronized**, which as you will see in Chapter 14 incurs a significant performance overhead that probably wipes out any gains provided by **final**. This lends credence to the theory that programmers are consistently bad at guessing where optimizations should occur. It's just too bad that such a clumsy design made it into the standard library where we must all cope with it.

It's also interesting to note that **Hashtable**, another important standard library class, does *not* have any **final** methods. As mentioned elsewhere in this book, it's quite obvious that some classes were designed by completely different people than others. (Notice the brevity of the method names in **Hashtable** compared to those in **Vector**.) This is precisely the sort of thing that should *not* be obvious to consumers of a class library. When things are inconsistent it just makes more work for the user. Yet another paean to the value of design and code walkthroughs.

Initialization and class loading

In many more traditional languages, programs are loaded all at once as part of the startup process. This is followed by initialization, and then the program begins. The process of initialization in these languages must be carefully controlled so that the order of initialization of **statics** doesn't cause trouble. C++, for example, has problems if one **static** expects another **static** to be valid before the second one has been initialized.

Java doesn't have this problem because it takes a different approach to loading. Because everything in Java is an object, many activities become easier, and this is one of them. As you will learn in the next chapter, the code for each object exists in a separate file. That file isn't loaded until the code is needed. In general, you can say that until an object of that class is constructed, the class code doesn't get loaded. Since there can be some subtleties with **static** methods, you can also say, "Class code is loaded at the point of first use."

The point of first use is also where the **static** initialization takes place. All the **static** objects and the **static** code block will be initialized in textual order (that is, the order that you write them down in the class definition) at the point of loading. The **static**s, of course, are initialized only once.

Initialization with inheritance

It's helpful to look at the whole initialization process, including inheritance, to get a full picture of what happens. Consider the following code:

```
//: Beetle.java
// The full process of initialization.

class Insect {
  int i = 9;
  int j;
  Insect() {
    prt("i = " + i + ", j = " + j);
    j = 39;
  }
  static int x1 =
    prt("static Insect.x1 initialized");
  static int prt(String s) {
    System.out.println(s);
    return 47;
  }
}

public class Beetle extends Insect {
  int k = prt("Beetle.k initialized");
  Beetle() {
    prt("k = " + k);
    prt("j = " + j);
  }
  static int x2 =
    prt("static Beetle.x2 initialized");
```

```
      static int prt(String s) {
         System.out.println(s);
         return 63;
      }
      public static void main(String[] args) {
         prt("Beetle constructor");
         Beetle b = new Beetle();
      }
    } ///:~
```

The output for this program is:

```
static Insect.x initialized
static Beetle.x initialized
Beetle constructor
i = 9, j = 0
Beetle.k initialized
k = 63
j = 39
```

The first thing that happens when you run Java on **Beetle** is that the loader goes out and finds that class. In the process of loading it, the loader notices that it has a base class (that's what the **extends** keyword says), which it then loads. This will happen whether or not you're going to make an object of that base class. (Try commenting out the object creation to prove it to yourself.)

If the base class has a base class, that second base class would then be loaded, and so on. Next, the **static** initialization in the root base class (in this case, **Insect**) is performed, and then the next derived class, and so on. This is important because the derived-class static initialization might depend on the base class member being initialized properly.

At this point, the necessary classes have all been loaded so the object can be created. First, all the primitives in this object are set to their default values and the object handles are set to **null**. Then the base-class constructor will be called. In this case the call is automatic, but you can also specify the constructor call (as the first operation in the **Beetle( )** constructor) using **super**. The base class construction goes through the same process in the same order as the derived-class constructor. After the base-class constructor completes, the instance variables are initialized in textual order. Finally, the rest of the body of the constructor is executed.

Summary

Both inheritance and composition allow you to create a new type from existing types. Typically, however, you use composition to reuse existing types as part of the underlying implementation of the new type and inheritance when you want to reuse the interface. Since the derived class has the base-class interface, it can be *upcast* to the base, which is critical for polymorphism, as you'll see in the next chapter.

Despite the strong emphasis on inheritance in object–oriented programming, when you start a design you should generally prefer composition during the first cut and use inheritance only when it is clearly necessary. (As you'll see in the next chapter.) Composition tends to be more flexible. In addition, by using the added artifice of inheritance with your member type, you can change the exact type, and thus the behavior, of those member objects at run-time. Therefore, you can change the behavior of the composed object at run-time.

Although code reuse through composition and inheritance is helpful for rapid project development, you'll generally want to redesign your class hierarchy before allowing other programmers to become dependent on it. Your goal is a hierarchy in which each class has a specific use and is neither too big (encompassing so much functionality that it's unwieldy to reuse) nor annoyingly small (you can't use it by itself or without adding functionality). Your finished classes should be easily reused.

Exercises

I.   Create two classes, **A** and **B**, with default constructors (empty argument lists) that announce themselves. Inherit a new class called **C** from **A**, and create a member **B** inside **C**. Do not create a constructor for **C**. Create an object of class **C** and observe the results.

2.   Modify Exercise 1 so that **A** and **B** have constructors with arguments instead of default constructors. Write a constructor for **C** and perform all initialization within **C**'s constructor.

3.   Take the file **Cartoon.java** and comment out the constructor for the **Cartoon** class. Explain what happens.

4. Take the file **Chess.java** and comment out the constructor for the **Chess** class. Explain what happens.

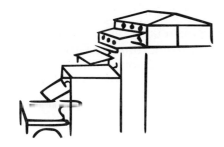

7: Polymorphism

Polymorphism is the third essential feature of an object-oriented programming language, after data abstraction and inheritance.

It provides another dimension of separation of interface from implementation, to decouple *what* from *how*. Polymorphism allows improved code organization and readability as well as the creation of *extensible* programs that can be "grown" not only during the original creation of the project but also when new features are desired.

Encapsulation creates new data types by combining characteristics and behaviors. Implementation hiding separates the interface from the implementation by making the details **private**. This sort of mechanical organization makes ready sense to someone with a procedural programming background. But polymorphism deals with decoupling in terms of *types*. In the last chapter, you saw how inheritance allows the treatment of an object as its own type *or* its base type. This ability is critical because it allows many types (derived from the same base type) to be treated as if they were one type, and a single piece of code to work on all those different types equally. The polymorphic method call allows one type to express its distinction from another, similar type, as long as they're both derived from the same base type. This distinction is expressed through differences in behavior of the methods you can call through the base class.

In this chapter, you'll learn about polymorphism (also called *dynamic binding* or *late binding* or *run-time binding*) starting from the basics, with simple examples that strip away everything but the polymorphic behavior of the program.

Upcasting

In Chapter 6 you saw how an object can be used as its own type or as an object of its base type. Taking an object handle and treating it as the handle of the base type is called *upcasting* because of the way inheritance trees are drawn with the base class at the top.

You also saw a problem arise, which is embodied in the following: (See page 97 if you have trouble executing this program.)

```
//: Music.java
// Inheritance & upcasting
package c07;

class Note {
  private int value;
  private Note(int val) { value = val; }
  public static final Note
    middleC = new Note(0),
    cSharp = new Note(1),
    cFlat = new Note(2);
} // Etc.

class Instrument {
  public void play(Note n) {
    System.out.println("Instrument.play()");
  }
}

// Wind objects are instruments
// because they have the same interface:
class Wind extends Instrument {
  // Redefine interface method:
  public void play(Note n) {
    System.out.println("Wind.play()");
```

```
    }
  }

public class Music {
  public static void tune(Instrument i) {
    // ...
    i.play(Note.middleC);
  }
  public static void main(String[] args) {
    Wind flute = new Wind();
    tune(flute); // Upcasting
  }
} ///:~
```

The method **Music.tune( )** accepts an **Instrument** handle, but also anything derived from **Instrument**. In **main( )**, you can see this happening as a **Wind** handle is passed to **tune( )**, with no cast necessary. This is acceptable; the interface in **Instrument** must exist in **Wind**, because **Wind** is inherited from **Instrument**. Upcasting from **Wind** to **Instrument** may "narrow" that interface, but it cannot make it anything less than the full interface to **Instrument**.

Why upcast?

This program might seem strange to you. Why should anyone intentionally *forget* the type of an object? This is what happens when you upcast, and it seems like it could be much more straightforward if **tune( )** simply takes a **Wind** handle as its argument. This brings up an essential point: If you did that, you'd need to write a new **tune( )** for every type of **Instrument** in your system. Suppose we follow this reasoning and add **Stringed** and **Brass** instruments:

```
//: Music2.java
// Overloading instead of upcasting

class Note2 {
  private int value;
  private Note2(int val) { value = val; }
  public static final Note2
    middleC = new Note2(0),
    cSharp = new Note2(1),
    cFlat = new Note2(2);
} // Etc.
```

```
class Instrument2 {
  public void play(Note2 n) {
    System.out.println("Instrument2.play()");
  }
}

class Wind2 extends Instrument2 {
  public void play(Note2 n) {
    System.out.println("Wind2.play()");
  }
}

class Stringed2 extends Instrument2 {
  public void play(Note2 n) {
    System.out.println("Stringed2.play()");
  }
}

class Brass2 extends Instrument2 {
  public void play(Note2 n) {
    System.out.println("Brass2.play()");
  }
}

public class Music2 {
  public static void tune(Wind2 i) {
    i.play(Note2.middleC);
  }
  public static void tune(Stringed2 i) {
    i.play(Note2.middleC);
  }
  public static void tune(Brass2 i) {
    i.play(Note2.middleC);
  }
  public static void main(String[] args) {
    Wind2 flute = new Wind2();
    Stringed2 violin = new Stringed2();
    Brass2 frenchHorn = new Brass2();
    tune(flute); // No upcasting
    tune(violin);
    tune(frenchHorn);
  }
} ///:~
```

This works, but there's a major drawback: You must write type-specific methods for each new **Instrument2** class you add. This means more programming in the first place, but it also means that if you want to add a new method like **tune( )** or a new type of **Instrument**, you've got a lot of work to do. Add the fact that the compiler won't give you any error messages if you forget to overload one of your methods and the whole process of working with types becomes unmanageable.

Wouldn't it be much nicer if you could just write a single method that takes the base class as its argument, and not any of the specific derived classes? That is, wouldn't it be nice if you could forget that there are derived classes, and write your code to talk only to the base class?

That's exactly what polymorphism allows you to do. However, most programmers (who come from a procedural programming background) have a bit of trouble with the way polymorphism works.

The twist

The difficulty with **Music.java** can be seen by running the program. The output is **Wind.play( )**. This is clearly the desired output, but it doesn't seem to make sense that it would work that way. Look at the **tune( )** method:

```
public static void tune(Instrument i) {
  // ...
  i.play(Note.middleC);
}
```

It receives an **Instrument** handle. So how can the compiler possibly know that this **Instrument** handle points to a **Wind** in this case and not a **Brass** or **Stringed**? The compiler can't. To get a deeper understanding of the issue, it's useful to examine the subject of *binding*.

Method call binding

Connecting a method call to a method body is called *binding*. When binding is performed before the program is run (by the compiler and linker, if there is one), it's called *early binding*. You might not have heard the term before because it has never been an option with procedural languages. C compilers have only one kind of method call, and that's early binding.

The confusing part of the above program revolves around early binding because the compiler cannot know the correct method to call when it has only an **Instrument** handle.

The solution is called *late binding*, which means that the binding occurs at run-time based on the type of object. Late binding is also called *dynamic binding* or *run-time binding*. When a language implements late binding, there must be some mechanism to determine the type of the object at run-time and to call the appropriate method. That is, the compiler still doesn't know the object type, but the method-call mechanism finds out and calls the correct method body. The late-binding mechanism varies from language to language, but you can imagine that some sort of type information must be installed in the objects.

All method binding in Java uses late binding unless a method has been declared **final**. This means that you ordinarily don't need to make any decisions about whether late binding will occur – it happens automatically.

Why would you declare a method **final**? As noted in the last chapter, it prevents anyone from overriding that method. Perhaps more importantly, it effectively "turns off" dynamic binding, or rather it tells the compiler that dynamic binding isn't necessary. This allows the compiler to generate more efficient code for **final** method calls.

Producing the right behavior

Once you know that all method binding in Java happens polymorphically via late binding, you can write your code to talk to the base-class and know that all the derived-class cases will work correctly using the same code. Or to put it another way, you "send a message to an object and let the object figure out the right thing to do."

The classic example in OOP is the "shape" example. This is commonly used because it is easy to visualize, but unfortunately it can confuse novice programmers into thinking that OOP is just for graphics programming, which is of course not the case.

The shape example has a base class called **Shape** and various derived types: **Circle**, **Square**, **Triangle**, etc. The reason the example works so well is that it's easy to say "a circle is a type of shape" and be understood. The inheritance diagram shows the relationships:

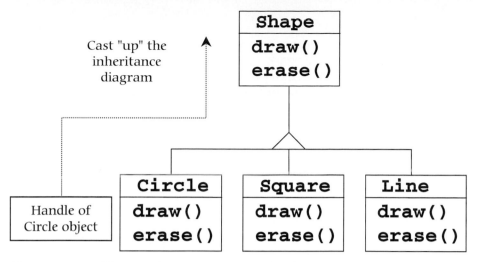

Cast "up" the inheritance diagram

The upcast could occur in a statement as simple as:

```
Shape s = new Circle();
```

Here, a **Circle** object is created and the resulting handle is immediately assigned to a **Shape**, which would seem to be an error (assigning one type to another) and yet it's fine because a **Circle** *is* a **Shape** by inheritance. So the compiler agrees with the statement and doesn't issue an error message.

When you call one of the base class methods (that have been overridden in the derived classes):

```
s.draw();
```

Again, you might expect that **Shape**'s **draw( )** is called because this is, after all, a **Shape** handle, so how could the compiler know to do anything else? And yet the proper **Circle.draw( )** is called because of late binding (polymorphism).

The following example puts it a slightly different way:

```
//: Shapes.java
// Polymorphism in Java

class Shape {
  void draw() {}
  void erase() {}
}

class Circle extends Shape {
  void draw() {
```

```java
      System.out.println("Circle.draw()");
    }
    void erase() {
      System.out.println("Circle.erase()");
    }
}

class Square extends Shape {
    void draw() {
      System.out.println("Square.draw()");
    }
    void erase() {
      System.out.println("Square.erase()");
    }
}

class Triangle extends Shape {
    void draw() {
      System.out.println("Triangle.draw()");
    }
    void erase() {
      System.out.println("Triangle.erase()");
    }
}

public class Shapes {
    public static Shape randShape() {
      switch((int)(Math.random() * 3)) {
        default: // To quiet the compiler
        case 0: return new Circle();
        case 1: return new Square();
        case 2: return new Triangle();
      }
    }
    public static void main(String[] args) {
      Shape[] s = new Shape[9];
      // Fill up the array with shapes:
      for(int i = 0; i < s.length; i++)
        s[i] = randShape();
      // Make polymorphic method calls:
      for(int i = 0; i < s.length; i++)
        s[i].draw();
    }
} ///:~
```

The base class **Shape** establishes the common interface to anything inherited from **Shape** – that is, all shapes can be drawn and erased. The derived classes override these definitions to provide unique behavior for each specific type of shape.

The main class **Shapes** contains a **static** method **randShape( )** that produces a handle to a randomly-selected **Shape** object each time you call it. Note that the upcasting happens in each of the **return** statements, which take a handle to a **Circle**, **Square**, or **Triangle** and send it out of the method as the return type, **Shape**. So whenever you call this method you never get a chance to see what specific type it is, since you always get back a plain **Shape** handle.

main( ) contains an array of **Shape** handles filled through calls to **randShape( )**. At this point you know you have **Shapes**, but you don't know anything more specific than that (and neither does the compiler). However, when you step through this array and call **draw( )** for each one, the correct type-specific behavior magically occurs, as you can see from one output example:

```
Circle.draw()
Triangle.draw()
Circle.draw()
Circle.draw()
Circle.draw()
Square.draw()
Triangle.draw()
Square.draw()
Square.draw()
```

Of course, since the shapes are all chosen randomly each time, your runs will have different results. The point of choosing the shapes randomly is to drive home the understanding that the compiler can have no special knowledge that allows it to make the correct calls at compile time. All the calls to **draw( )** are made through dynamic binding.

Extensibility

Now let's return to the musical instrument example. Because of polymorphism, you can add as many new types as you want to the system without changing the **tune( )** method. In a well-designed OOP program, most or all of your methods will follow the model of **tune( )** and communicate only with the base-class interface. Such a program is *extensible* because you can add new functionality by inheriting new data types from the common base class. The methods that manipulate the

---

base-class interface will not need to be changed at all to accommodate the new classes.

Consider what happens if you take the instrument example and add more methods in the base class and a number of new classes. Here's the diagram:

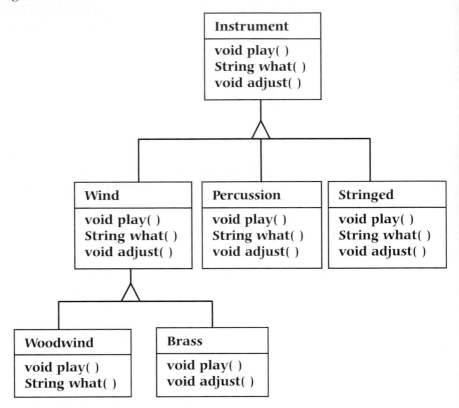

All these new classes work correctly with the old, unchanged **tune( )** method. Even if **tune( )** is in a separate file and new methods are added to the interface of **Instrument**, **tune( )** works correctly without recompilation. Here is the implementation of the above diagram:

```
//: Music3.java
// An extensible program
import java.util.*;

class Instrument3 {
  public void play() {
    System.out.println("Instrument3.play()");
  }
```

```java
    public String what() {
      return "Instrument3";
    }
    public void adjust() {}
}

class Wind3 extends Instrument3 {
  public void play() {
    System.out.println("Wind3.play()");
  }
  public String what() { return "Wind3"; }
  public void adjust() {}
}

class Percussion3 extends Instrument3 {
  public void play() {
    System.out.println("Percussion3.play()");
  }
  public String what() { return "Percussion3"; }
  public void adjust() {}
}

class Stringed3 extends Instrument3 {
  public void play() {
    System.out.println("Stringed3.play()");
  }
  public String what() { return "Stringed3"; }
  public void adjust() {}
}

class Brass3 extends Wind3 {
  public void play() {
    System.out.println("Brass3.play()");
  }
  public void adjust() {
    System.out.println("Brass3.adjust()");
  }
}

class Woodwind3 extends Wind3 {
  public void play() {
    System.out.println("Woodwind3.play()");
  }
  public String what() { return "Woodwind3"; }
```

```
    }

public class Music3 {
  // Doesn't care about type, so new types
  // added to the system still work right:
  static void tune(Instrument3 i) {
    // ...
    i.play();
  }
  static void tuneAll(Instrument3[] e) {
    for(int i = 0; i < e.length; i++)
      tune(e[i]);
  }
  public static void main(String[] args) {
    Instrument3[] orchestra = new Instrument3[5];
    int i = 0;
    // Upcasting during addition to the array:
    orchestra[i++] = new Wind3();
    orchestra[i++] = new Percussion3();
    orchestra[i++] = new Stringed3();
    orchestra[i++] = new Brass3();
    orchestra[i++] = new Woodwind3();
    tuneAll(orchestra);
  }
} ///:~
```

The new methods are **what( )**, which returns a **String** handle with a description of the class, and **adjust( )**, which provides some way to adjust each instrument.

In **main( )**, when you place something inside the **Instrument3** array you automatically upcast to **Instrument3**.

You can see that the **tune( )** method is blissfully ignorant of all the code changes that have happened around it, and yet it works correctly. This is exactly what polymorphism is supposed to provide. Your code changes don't cause damage to parts of the program that should not be affected. Put another way, polymorphism is one of the most important techniques that allow the programmer to "separate the things that change from the things that stay the same."

Overriding vs. overloading

Let's take a different look at the first example in this chapter. In the following program, the interface of the method **play( )** is changed in the process of overriding it, which means that you haven't *overridden* the method, but instead *overloaded* it. The compiler allows you to overload methods so it gives no complaint. But the behavior is probably not what you want. Here's the example:

```
//: WindError.java
// Accidentally changing the interface

class NoteX {
  public static final int
    MIDDLE_C = 0, C_SHARP = 1, C_FLAT = 2;
}

class InstrumentX {
  public void play(int NoteX) {
    System.out.println("InstrumentX.play()");
  }
}

class WindX extends InstrumentX {
  // OOPS! Changes the method interface:
  public void play(NoteX n) {
    System.out.println("WindX.play(NoteX n)");
  }
}

public class WindError {
  public static void tune(InstrumentX i) {
    // ...
    i.play(NoteX.MIDDLE_C);
  }
  public static void main(String[] args) {
    WindX flute = new WindX();
    tune(flute); // Not the desired behavior!
  }
} ///:~
```

There's another confusing aspect thrown in here. In **InstrumentX**, the **play( )** method takes an **int** that has the identifier **NoteX**. That is, even though **NoteX** is a class name, it can also be used as an identifier without

---

complaint. But in **WindX**, **play( )** takes a **NoteX** handle that has an identifier **n**. (Although you could even say **play(NoteX NoteX)** without an error.) Thus it appears that the programmer intended to override **play( )** but mistyped the method a bit. The compiler, however, assumed that an overload and not an override was intended. Note that if you follow the standard Java naming convention, the argument identifier would be **noteX**, which would distinguish it from the class name.

In **tune**, the **InstrumentX i** is sent the **play( )** message, with one of **NoteX**'s members (**MIDDLE_C**) as an argument. Since **NoteX** contains **int** definitions, this means that the **int** version of the now-overloaded **play( )** method is called, and since that has *not* been overridden the base-class version is used.

The output is:

```
InstrumentX.play()
```

This certainly doesn't appear to be a polymorphic method call. Once you understand what's happening, you can fix the problem fairly easily, but imagine how difficult it might be to find the bug if it's buried in a program of significant size.

Abstract classes and methods

In all the instrument examples, the methods in the base class **Instrument** were always "dummy" methods. If these methods are ever called, you've done something wrong. That's because the intent of **Instrument** is to create a *common interface* for all the classes derived from it.

The only reason to establish this common interface is so it can be expressed differently for each different subtype. It establishes a basic form, so you can say what's in common with all the derived classes. Another way of saying this is to call **Instrument** an *abstract base class* (or simply an *abstract class*). You create an abstract class when you want to manipulate a set of classes through this common interface. All derived-class methods that match the signature of the base-class declaration will be called using the dynamic binding mechanism. (However, as seen in the last section, if the method's name is the same as the base class but the arguments are different, you've got overloading, which probably isn't what you want.)

If you have an abstract class like **Instrument**, objects of that class almost always have no meaning. That is, **Instrument** is meant to express only the interface, and not a particular implementation, so creating an **Instrument** object makes no sense, and you'll probably want to prevent the user from doing it. This can be accomplished by making all the methods in **Instrument** print error messages, but this delays the information until run-time and requires reliable exhaustive testing on the user's part. It's always better to catch problems at compile time.

Java provides a mechanism for doing this called the *abstract method*. This is a method that is incomplete; it has only a declaration and no method body. Here is the syntax for an abstract method declaration:

```
abstract void X();
```

A class containing abstract methods is called an *abstract class*. If a class contains one or more abstract methods, the class must be qualified as **abstract.** (Otherwise, the compiler gives you an error message.)

If an abstract class is incomplete, what is the compiler supposed to do when someone tries to make an object of that class? It cannot safely create an object of an abstract class, so you get an error message from the compiler. This way the compiler ensures the purity of the abstract class, and you don't need to worry about misusing it.

If you inherit from an abstract class and you want to make objects of the new type, you must provide method definitions for all the abstract methods in the base class. If you don't (and you may choose not to), then the derived class is also abstract and the compiler will force you to qualify *that* class with the **abstract** keyword.

It's possible to declare a class as **abstract** *without* including any **abstract** methods. This is useful when you've got a class in which it doesn't make sense to have any **abstract** methods, and yet you want to prevent any instances of that class.

The **Instrument** class can easily be turned into an abstract class. Only some of the methods will be abstract, since making a class abstract doesn't force you to make all the methods abstract. Here's what it looks like:

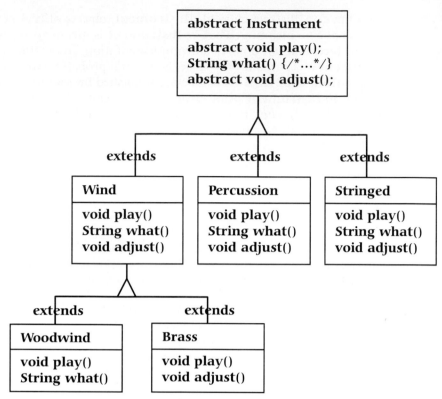

Here's the orchestra example modified to use **abstract** classes and methods:

```
//: Music4.java
// Abstract classes and methods
import java.util.*;

abstract class Instrument4 {
  int i; // storage allocated for each
  public abstract void play();
  public String what() {
    return "Instrument4";
  }
  public abstract void adjust();
}

class Wind4 extends Instrument4 {
  public void play() {
    System.out.println("Wind4.play()");
  }
```

```
    public String what() { return "Wind4"; }
    public void adjust() {}
}

class Percussion4 extends Instrument4 {
  public void play() {
    System.out.println("Percussion4.play()");
  }
  public String what() { return "Percussion4"; }
  public void adjust() {}
}

class Stringed4 extends Instrument4 {
  public void play() {
    System.out.println("Stringed4.play()");
  }
  public String what() { return "Stringed4"; }
  public void adjust() {}
}

class Brass4 extends Wind4 {
  public void play() {
    System.out.println("Brass4.play()");
  }
  public void adjust() {
    System.out.println("Brass4.adjust()");
  }
}

class Woodwind4 extends Wind4 {
  public void play() {
    System.out.println("Woodwind4.play()");
  }
  public String what() { return "Woodwind4"; }
}

public class Music4 {
  // Doesn't care about type, so new types
  // added to the system still work right:
  static void tune(Instrument4 i) {
    // ...
    i.play();
  }
  static void tuneAll(Instrument4[] e) {
```

```
      for(int i = 0; i < e.length; i++)
        tune(e[i]);
    }
    public static void main(String[] args) {
      Instrument4[] orchestra = new Instrument4[5];
      int i = 0;
      // Upcasting during addition to the array:
      orchestra[i++] = new Wind4();
      orchestra[i++] = new Percussion4();
      orchestra[i++] = new Stringed4();
      orchestra[i++] = new Brass4();
      orchestra[i++] = new Woodwind4();
      tuneAll(orchestra);
    }
} ///:~
```

You can see that there's really no change except in the base class.

It's helpful to create **abstract** classes and methods because they make the abstractness of a class explicit and tell both the user and the compiler how it was intended to be used.

Interfaces

The **interface** keyword takes the abstract concept one step further. You could think of it as a "pure" abstract class. It allows the creator to establish the form for a class: method names, argument lists and return types, but no method bodies. An **interface** can also contain data members of primitive types, but these are implicitly **static** and **final**. An **interface** provides only a form, but no implementation.

An **interface** says: "This is what all classes that *implement* this particular interface will look like." Thus, any code that uses a particular **interface** knows what methods might be called for that **interface**, and that's all. So the **interface** is used to establish a "protocol" between classes. (Some object-oriented programming languages have a keyword called *protocol* to do the same thing.)

To create an **interface**, use the **interface** keyword instead of the **class** keyword. Like a class, you can add the **public** keyword before the **interface** keyword (but only if that **interface** is defined in a file of the same name) or leave it off to give "friendly" status.

To make a class that conforms to a particular **interface** (or group of **interface**s) use the **implements** keyword. You're saying "The **interface** is what it looks like and here's how it *works*." Other than that, it bears a strong resemblance to inheritance. The diagram for the instrument example shows this:

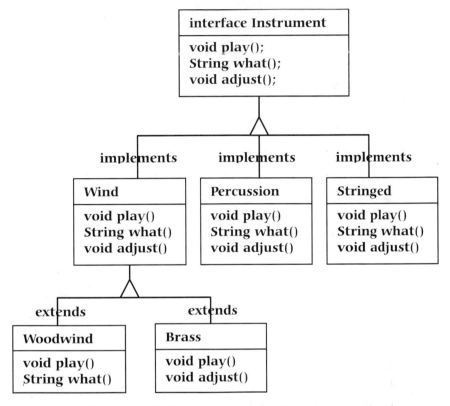

Once you've implemented an **interface**, that implementation becomes an ordinary class that can be extended in the regular way.

You can choose to explicitly declare the method declarations in an **interface** as **public**. But they are **public** even if you don't say it. So when you **implement** an **interface**, the methods from the **interface** must be defined as **public**. Otherwise they would default to "friendly" and you'd be restricting the accessibility of a method during inheritance, which is not allowed by the Java compiler.

You can see this in the modified version of the **Instrument** example. Note that every method in the **interface** is strictly a declaration, which is the only thing the compiler allows. In addition, none of the methods in **Instrument5** are declared as **public**, but they're automatically **public** anyway:

```
//: Music5.java
// Interfaces
import java.util.*;

interface Instrument5 {
  // Compile-time constant:
  int i = 5; // static & final
  // Cannot have method definitions:
  void play(); // Automatically public
  String what();
  void adjust();
}

class Wind5 implements Instrument5 {
  public void play() {
    System.out.println("Wind5.play()");
  }
  public String what() { return "Wind5"; }
  public void adjust() {}
}

class Percussion5 implements Instrument5 {
  public void play() {
    System.out.println("Percussion5.play()");
  }
  public String what() { return "Percussion5"; }
  public void adjust() {}
}

class Stringed5 implements Instrument5 {
  public void play() {
    System.out.println("Stringed5.play()");
  }
  public String what() { return "Stringed5"; }
  public void adjust() {}
}

class Brass5 extends Wind5 {
  public void play() {
    System.out.println("Brass5.play()");
  }
  public void adjust() {
    System.out.println("Brass5.adjust()");
  }
```

```
    }

class Woodwind5 extends Wind5 {
  public void play() {
    System.out.println("Woodwind5.play()");
  }
  public String what() { return "Woodwind5"; }
}

public class Music5 {
  // Doesn't care about type, so new types
  // added to the system still work right:
  static void tune(Instrument5 i) {
    // ...
    i.play();
  }
  static void tuneAll(Instrument5[] e) {
    for(int i = 0; i < e.length; i++)
      tune(e[i]);
  }
  public static void main(String[] args) {
    Instrument5[] orchestra = new Instrument5[5];
    int i = 0;
    // Upcasting during addition to the array:
    orchestra[i++] = new Wind5();
    orchestra[i++] = new Percussion5();
    orchestra[i++] = new Stringed5();
    orchestra[i++] = new Brass5();
    orchestra[i++] = new Woodwind5();
    tuneAll(orchestra);
  }
} ///:~
```

The rest of the code works the same. It doesn't matter if you are
upcasting to a "regular" class called **Instrument5**, an **abstract** class
called **Instrument5**, or to an **interface** called **Instrument5**. The
behavior is the same. In fact, you can see in the **tune( )** method that
there isn't any evidence about whether **Instrument5** is a "regular" class,
an **abstract** class or an **interface**. This is the intent: Each approach gives
the programmer different control over the way objects are created and
used.

"Multiple inheritance" in Java

The **interface** isn't simply a "more pure" form of **abstract** class. It has a higher purpose than that. Because an **interface** has no implementation at all – that is, there is no storage associated with an **interface** – there's nothing to prevent many **interfaces** from being combined. This is valuable because there are times when you need to say "An **x** is an **a** *and* a **b** *and* a **c**." In C++, this act of combining multiple class interfaces is called *multiple inheritance,* and it carries some rather sticky baggage because each class can have an implementation. In Java, you can perform the same act, but only one of the classes can have an implementation, so the problems seen in C++ do not occur with Java when combining multiple interfaces:

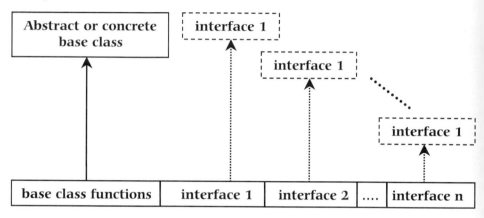

In a derived class, you aren't forced to have a base class that is either an **abstract** or "concrete" (one with no **abstract** methods). If you *do* inherit from a non-**interface**, you can inherit from only one. All the rest of the base elements must be **interfaces**. You place all the interface names after the **implements** keyword and separate them with commas. You can have as many **interfaces** as you want and each one becomes an independent type that you can upcast to. The following example shows a concrete class combined with several **interfaces** to produce a new class:

```
//: Adventure.java
// Multiple interfaces
import java.util.*;

interface CanFight {
  void fight();
}

interface CanSwim {
```

Thinking in Java *www.BruceEckel.com*

```
    void swim();
}

interface CanFly {
  void fly();
}

class ActionCharacter {
  public void fight() {}
}

class Hero extends ActionCharacter
    implements CanFight, CanSwim, CanFly {
  public void swim() {}
  public void fly() {}
}

public class Adventure {
  static void t(CanFight x) { x.fight(); }
  static void u(CanSwim x) { x.swim(); }
  static void v(CanFly x) { x.fly(); }
  static void w(ActionCharacter x) { x.fight(); }
  public static void main(String[] args) {
    Hero i = new Hero();
    t(i); // Treat it as a CanFight
    u(i); // Treat it as a CanSwim
    v(i); // Treat it as a CanFly
    w(i); // Treat it as an ActionCharacter
  }
} ///:~
```

You can see that **Hero** combines the concrete class **ActionCharacter** with
the interfaces **CanFight**, **CanSwim**, and **CanFly**. When you combine a
concrete class with interfaces this way, the concrete class must come first,
then the interfaces. (The compiler gives an error otherwise.)

Note that the signature for **fight( )** is the same in the **interface CanFight**
and the class **ActionCharacter**, and that **fight( )** is *not* provided with a
definition in **Hero**. The rule for an **interface** is that you can inherit from
it (as you will see shortly), but then you've got another **interface**. If you
want to create an object of the new type, it must be a class with all
definitions provided. Even though **Hero** does not explicitly provide a
definition for **fight( )**, the definition comes along with **ActionCharacter**
so it is automatically provided and it's possible to create objects of **Hero**.

In class **Adventure**, you can see that there are four methods that take as arguments the various interfaces and the concrete class. When a **Hero** object is created, it can be passed to any of these methods, which means it is being upcast to each **interface** in turn. Because of the way interfaces are designed in Java, this works without a hitch and without any particular effort on the part of the programmer.

Keep in mind that the core reason for interfaces is shown in the above example: to be able to upcast to more than one base type. However, a second reason for using interfaces is the same as using an **abstract** base class: to prevent the client programmer from making an object of this class and to establish that it is only an interface. This brings up a question: Should you use an **interface** or an **abstract** class? An **interface** gives you the benefits of an **abstract** class *and* the benefits of an **interface**, so if it's possible to create your base class without any method definitions or member variables you should always prefer **interface**s to **abstract** classes. In fact, if you know something is going to be a base class, your first choice should be to make it an **interface**, and only if you're forced to have method definitions or member variables should you change to an **abstract** class.

Extending an interface
with inheritance

You can easily add new method declarations to an **interface** using inheritance, and you can also combine several **interface**s into a new **interface** with inheritance. In both cases you get a new **interface**, as seen in this example:

```
//: HorrorShow.java
// Extending an interface with inheritance

interface Monster {
  void menace();
}

interface DangerousMonster extends Monster {
  void destroy();
}

interface Lethal {
  void kill();
}
```

```
class DragonZilla implements DangerousMonster {
  public void menace() {}
  public void destroy() {}
}

interface Vampire
    extends DangerousMonster, Lethal {
  void drinkBlood();
}

class HorrorShow {
  static void u(Monster b) { b.menace(); }
  static void v(DangerousMonster d) {
    d.menace();
    d.destroy();
  }
  public static void main(String[] args) {
    DragonZilla if2 = new DragonZilla();
    u(if2);
    v(if2);
  }
} ///:~
```

DangerousMonster is a simple extension to **Monster** that produces a new **interface**. This is implemented in **DragonZilla**.

The syntax used in **Vampire** works *only* when inheriting interfaces. Normally, you can use **extends** with only a single class, but since an **interface** can be made from multiple other interfaces, **extends** can refer to multiple base interfaces when building a new **interface**. As you can see, the **interface** names are simply separated with commas.

Grouping constants

Because any fields you put into an **interface** are automatically **static** and **final**, the **interface** is a convenient tool for creating groups of constant values, much as you would with an **enum** in C or C++. For example:

```
//: Months.java
// Using interfaces to create groups of constants
package c07;

public interface Months {
  int
```

```
          JANUARY = 1, FEBRUARY = 2, MARCH = 3,
          APRIL = 4, MAY = 5, JUNE = 6, JULY = 7,
          AUGUST = 8, SEPTEMBER = 9, OCTOBER = 10,
          NOVEMBER = 11, DECEMBER = 12;
} ///:~
```

Notice the Java style of using all uppercase letters (with underscores to separate multiple words in a single identifier) for **static final** primitives that have constant initializers – that is, for compile-time constants.

The fields in an **interface** are automatically **public**, so it's unnecessary to specify that.

Now you can use the constants from outside the package by importing **c07.*** or **c07.Months** just as you would with any other package, and referencing the values with expressions like **Months.JANUARY**. Of course, what you get is just an **int** so there isn't the extra type safety that C++'s **enum** has, but this (commonly-used) technique is certainly an improvement over hard-coding numbers into your programs. (This is often referred to as using "magic numbers" and it produces very difficult-to-maintain code.)

If you do want extra type safety, you can build a class like this:[1]

```
//: Month2.java
// A more robust enumeration system
package c07;

public final class Month2 {
  private String name;
  private Month2(String nm) { name = nm; }
  public String toString() { return name; }
  public final static Month2
    JAN = new Month2("January"),
    FEB = new Month2("February"),
    MAR = new Month2("March"),
    APR = new Month2("April"),
    MAY = new Month2("May"),
    JUN = new Month2("June"),
    JUL = new Month2("July"),
    AUG = new Month2("August"),
    SEP = new Month2("September"),
```

---

[1] This approach was inspired by an e-mail from Rich Hoffarth.

```
      OCT = new Month2("October"),
      NOV = new Month2("November"),
      DEC = new Month2("December");
  public final static Month2[] month =   {
     JAN, JAN, FEB, MAR, APR, MAY, JUN,
     JUL, AUG, SEP, OCT, NOV, DEC
  };
  public static void main(String[] args) {
     Month2 m = Month2.JAN;
     System.out.println(m);
     m = Month2.month[12];
     System.out.println(m);
     System.out.println(m == Month2.DEC);
     System.out.println(m.equals(Month2.DEC));
  }
} ///:~
```

The class is called **Month2** since there's already a **Month** in the standard
Java library. It's a **final** class with a **private** constructor so no one can
inherit from it or make any instances of it. The only instances are the
final static ones created in the class itself: **JAN, FEB, MAR**, etc. These
objects are also used in the array **month**, which lets you choose months
by number instead of by name. (Notice the extra **JAN** in the array to
provide an offset by one, so that December is month 12.) In **main( )** you
can see the type safety: **m** is a **Month2** object so it can be assigned only
to a **Month2**. The previous example **Months.java** provided only **int**
values, so an **int** variable intended to represent a month could actually be
given any integer value, which wasn't too safe.

This approach also allows you to use **==** or **equals( )** interchangeably, as
shown at the end of **main( )**.

Initializing fields in interfaces

Fields defined in interfaces are automatically **static** and **final**. These
cannot be "blank finals," but they can be initialized with non-constant
expressions. For example:

```
//: RandVals.java
// Initializing interface fields with
// non-constant initializers
import java.util.*;

public interface RandVals {
   int rint = (int)(Math.random() * 10);
```

```
  long rlong = (long)(Math.random() * 10);
  float rfloat = (float)(Math.random() * 10);
  double rdouble = Math.random() * 10;
} ///:~
```

Since the fields are **static**, they are initialized when the class is first loaded, upon first access of any of the fields. Here's a simple test:

```
//: TestRandVals.java

public class TestRandVals {
  public static void main(String[] args) {
    System.out.println(RandVals.rint);
    System.out.println(RandVals.rlong);
    System.out.println(RandVals.rfloat);
    System.out.println(RandVals.rdouble);
  }
} ///:~
```

The fields, of course, are not part of the interface but instead are stored in the **static** storage area for that interface.

Inner classes

In Java 1.1 it's possible to place a class definition within another class definition. This is called an *inner class*. The inner class is a useful feature because it allows you to group classes that logically belong together and to control the visibility of one within the other. However, it's important to understand that inner classes are distinctly different from composition.

Often, while you're learning about them, the need for inner classes isn't immediately obvious. At the end of this section, after all of the syntax and semantics of inner classes have been described, you'll find an example that should make clear the benefits of inner classes.

You create an inner class just as you'd expect: by placing the class definition inside a surrounding class: (See page 97 if you have trouble executing this program.)

```
//: Parcel1.java
// Creating inner classes
package c07.parcel1;

public class Parcel1 {
```

```
class Contents {
  private int i = 11;
  public int value() { return i; }
}
class Destination {
  private String label;
  Destination(String whereTo) {
    label = whereTo;
  }
  String readLabel() { return label; }
}
// Using inner classes looks just like
// using any other class, within Parcel1:
public void ship(String dest) {
  Contents c = new Contents();
  Destination d = new Destination(dest);
}
public static void main(String[] args) {
  Parcel1 p = new Parcel1();
  p.ship("Tanzania");
}
} ///:~
```

The inner classes, when used inside **ship( )**, look just like the use of any other classes. Here, the only practical difference is that the names are nested within **Parcel1**. You'll see in a while that this isn't the only difference.

More typically, an outer class will have a method that returns a handle to an inner class, like this:

```
//: Parcel2.java
// Returning a handle to an inner class
package c07.parcel2;

public class Parcel2 {
  class Contents {
    private int i = 11;
    public int value() { return i; }
  }
  class Destination {
    private String label;
    Destination(String whereTo) {
      label = whereTo;
    }
```

```
        String readLabel() { return label; }
      }
      public Destination to(String s) {
        return new Destination(s);
      }
      public Contents cont() {
        return new Contents();
      }
      public void ship(String dest) {
        Contents c = cont();
        Destination d = to(dest);
      }
      public static void main(String[] args) {
        Parcel2 p = new Parcel2();
        p.ship("Tanzania");
        Parcel2 q = new Parcel2();
        // Defining handles to inner classes:
        Parcel2.Contents c = q.cont();
        Parcel2.Destination d = q.to("Borneo");
      }
} ///:~
```

If you want to make an object of the inner class anywhere except from within a non-**static** method of the outer class, you must specify the type of that object as *OuterClassName.InnerClassName*, as seen in **main( )**.

Inner classes and upcasting

So far, inner classes don't seem that dramatic. After all, if it's hiding you're after, Java already has a perfectly good hiding mechanism – just allow the class to be "friendly" (visible only within a package) rather than creating it as an inner class.

However, inner classes really come into their own when you start upcasting to a base class, and in particular to an **interface.** (The effect of producing an interface handle from an object that implements it is essentially the same as upcasting to a base class.) That's because the inner class can then be completely unseen and unavailable to anyone, which is convenient for hiding the implementation. All you get back is a handle to the base class or the **interface,** and it's possible that you can't even find out the exact type, as shown here:

```
//: Parcel3.java
// Returning a handle to an inner class
package c07.parcel3;
```

```
abstract class Contents {
  abstract public int value();
}

interface Destination {
  String readLabel();
}

public class Parcel3 {
  private class PContents extends Contents {
    private int i = 11;
    public int value() { return i; }
  }
  protected class PDestination
      implements Destination {
    private String label;
    private PDestination(String whereTo) {
      label = whereTo;
    }
    public String readLabel() { return label; }
  }
  public Destination dest(String s) {
    return new PDestination(s);
  }
  public Contents cont() {
    return new PContents();
  }
}

class Test {
  public static void main(String[] args) {
    Parcel3 p = new Parcel3();
    Contents c = p.cont();
    Destination d = p.dest("Tanzania");
    // Illegal -- can't access private class:
    //! Parcel3.PContents c = p.new PContents();
  }
} ///:~
```

Now **Contents** and **Destination** represent interfaces available to the client programmer. (The **interface**, remember, automatically makes all of its members **public**.) For convenience, these are placed inside a single file, but ordinarily **Contents** and **Destination** would each be **public** in their own files.

In **Parcel3**, something new has been added: the inner class **PContents** is **private** so no one but **Parcel3** can access it. **PDestination** is **protected**, so no one but **Parcel3**, classes in the **Parcel3** package (since **protected** also gives package access; that is, **protected** is also "friendly"), and the inheritors of **Parcel3** can access **PDestination**. This means that the client programmer has restricted knowledge and access to these members. In fact, you can't even downcast to a **private** inner class (or a **protected** inner class unless you're an inheritor), because you can't access the name, as you can see in **class Test**. Thus, the **private** inner class provides a way for the class designer to completely prevent any type-coding dependencies and to completely hide details about implementation. In addition, extension of an **interface** is useless from the client programmer's perspective since the client programmer cannot access any additional methods that aren't part of the public **interface** class. This also provides an opportunity for the Java compiler to generate more efficient code.

Normal (non-inner) classes cannot be made **private** or **protected** – only **public** or "friendly."

Note that **Contents** doesn't need to be an **abstract** class. You could use an ordinary class here as well, but the most typical starting point for such a design is an **interface**.

Inner classes in methods and scopes

What you've seen so far encompasses the typical use for inner classes. In general, the code that you'll write and read involving inner classes will be "plain" inner classes that are simple and easy to understand. However, the design for inner classes is quite complete and there are a number of other, more obscure, ways that you can use them if you choose: inner classes can be created within a method or even an arbitrary scope. There are two reasons for doing this:

1. As shown previously, you're implementing an interface of some kind so that you can create and return a handle.

2. You're solving a complicated problem and you want to create a class to aid in your solution, but you don't want it publicly available.

In the following examples, the previous code will be modified to use:

1. A class defined within a method

2. A class defined within a scope inside a method

Thinking in Java

3. An anonymous class implementing an **interface**

4. An anonymous class extending a class that has a non-default constructor

5. An anonymous class that performs field initialization

6. An anonymous class that performs construction using instance initialization (anonymous inner classes cannot have constructors)

This will all take place within the package **innerscopes**. First, the common interfaces from the previous code will be defined in their own files so they can be used in all the examples:

```
//: Destination.java
package c07.innerscopes;

interface Destination {
   String readLabel();
} ///:~
```

The point has been made that **Contents** could be an **abstract** class, so here it will be in a more natural form, as an **interface**:

```
//: Contents.java
package c07.innerscopes;

interface Contents {
   int value();
} ///:~
```

Although it's an ordinary class with an implementation, **Wrapping** is also being used as a common "interface" to its derived classes:

```
//: Wrapping.java
package c07.innerscopes;

public class Wrapping {
   private int i;
   public Wrapping(int x) { i = x; }
   public int value() { return i; }
} ///:~
```

You'll notice above that **Wrapping** has a constructor that requires an argument, to make things a bit more interesting.

The first example shows the creation of an entire class within the scope of a method (instead of the scope of another class):

```
//: Parcel4.java
// Nesting a class within a method
package c07.innerscopes;

public class Parcel4 {
  public Destination dest(String s) {
    class PDestination
        implements Destination {
      private String label;
      private PDestination(String whereTo) {
        label = whereTo;
      }
      public String readLabel() { return label; }
    }
    return new PDestination(s);
  }
  public static void main(String[] args) {
    Parcel4 p = new Parcel4();
    Destination d = p.dest("Tanzania");
  }
} ///:~
```

The class **PDestination** is part of **dest( )** rather than being part of **Parcel4**. (Also notice that you could use the class identifier **PDestination** for an inner class inside each class in the same subdirectory without a name clash.) Therefore, **PDestination** cannot be accessed outside of **dest( )**. Notice the upcasting that occurs in the return statement – nothing comes out of **dest( )** except a handle to the base class **Destination**. Of course, the fact that the name of the class **PDestination** is placed inside **dest( )** doesn't mean that **PDestination** is not a valid object once **dest( )** returns.

The next example shows how you can nest an inner class within any arbitrary scope:

```
//: Parcel5.java
// Nesting a class within a scope
package c07.innerscopes;

public class Parcel5 {
  private void internalTracking(boolean b) {
    if(b) {
```

```
            class TrackingSlip {
              private String id;
              TrackingSlip(String s) {
                id = s;
              }
              String getSlip() { return id; }
            }
            TrackingSlip ts = new TrackingSlip("slip");
            String s = ts.getSlip();
          }
          // Can't use it here! Out of scope:
          //! TrackingSlip ts = new TrackingSlip("x");
        }
      public void track() { internalTracking(true); }
      public static void main(String[] args) {
        Parcel5 p = new Parcel5();
        p.track();
      }
    } ///:~
```

The class **TrackingSlip** is nested inside the scope of an **if** statement. This does not mean that the class is conditionally created – it gets compiled along with everything else. However, it's not available outside the scope in which it is defined. Other than that, it looks just like an ordinary class.

The next example looks a little strange:

```
//: Parcel6.java
// A method that returns an anonymous inner class
package c07.innerscopes;

public class Parcel6 {
  public Contents cont() {
    return new Contents() {
      private int i = 11;
      public int value() { return i; }
    }; // Semicolon required in this case
  }
  public static void main(String[] args) {
    Parcel6 p = new Parcel6();
    Contents c = p.cont();
  }
} ///:~
```

The **cont( )** method combines the creation of the return value with the definition of the class that represents that return value! In addition, the class is anonymous – it has no name. To make matters a bit worse, it looks like you're starting out to create a **Contents** object:

```
return new Contents()
```

but then, before you get to the semicolon, you say, "But wait, I think I'll slip in a class definition":

```
return new Contents() {
  private int i = 11;
  public int value() { return i; }
};
```

What this strange syntax means is "create an object of an anonymous class that's inherited from **Contents**." The handle returned by the **new** expression is automatically upcast to a **Contents** handle. The anonymous inner class syntax is a shorthand for:

```
class MyContents extends Contents {
  private int i = 11;
  public int value() { return i; }
}
return new MyContents();
```

In the anonymous inner class, **Contents** is created using a default constructor. The following code shows what to do if your base class needs a constructor with an argument:

```
//: Parcel7.java
// An anonymous inner class that calls the
// base-class constructor
package c07.innerscopes;

public class Parcel7 {
  public Wrapping wrap(int x) {
    // Base constructor call:
    return new Wrapping(x) {
      public int value() {
        return super.value() * 47;
      }
    }; // Semicolon required
  }
  public static void main(String[] args) {
    Parcel7 p = new Parcel7();
```

```
    Wrapping w = p.wrap(10);
  }
} ///:~
```

That is, you simply pass the appropriate argument to the base-class constructor, seen here as the **x** passed in **new Wrapping(x)**. An anonymous class cannot have a constructor where you would normally call **super( )**.

In both of the previous examples, the semicolon doesn't mark the end of the class body (as it does in C++). Instead, it marks the end of the expression that happens to contain the anonymous class. Thus, it's identical to the use of the semicolon everywhere else.

What happens if you need to perform some kind of initialization for an object of an anonymous inner class? Since it's anonymous, there's no name to give the constructor so you can't have a constructor. You can, however, perform initialization at the point of definition of your fields:

```
//: Parcel8.java
// An anonymous inner class that performs
// initialization. A briefer version
// of Parcel5.java.
package c07.innerscopes;

public class Parcel8 {
  // Argument must be final to use inside
  // anonymous inner class:
  public Destination dest(final String dest) {
    return new Destination() {
      private String label = dest;
      public String readLabel() { return label; }
    };
  }
  public static void main(String[] args) {
    Parcel8 p = new Parcel8();
    Destination d = p.dest("Tanzania");
  }
} ///:~
```

If you're defining an anonymous inner class and want to use an object that's defined outside the anonymous inner class, the compiler requires that the outside object be **final**. This is why the argument to **dest( )** is **final**. If you forget, you'll get a compile-time error message.

As long as you're simply assigning a field, the above approach is fine. But what if you need to perform some constructor-like activity? With Java 1.1 *instance initialization*, you can, in effect, create a constructor for an anonymous inner class:

```
//: Parcel9.java
// Using "instance initialization" to perform
// construction on an anonymous inner class
package c07.innerscopes;

public class Parcel9 {
  public Destination
  dest(final String dest, final float price) {
    return new Destination() {
      private int cost;
      // Instance initialization for each object:
      {
        cost = Math.round(price);
        if(cost > 100)
          System.out.println("Over budget!");
      }
      private String label = dest;
      public String readLabel() { return label; }
    };
  }
  public static void main(String[] args) {
    Parcel9 p = new Parcel9();
    Destination d = p.dest("Tanzania", 101.395F);
  }
} ///:~
```

Inside the instance initializer you can see code that couldn't be executed as part of a field initializer (that is, the **if** statement). So in effect, an instance initializer is the constructor for an anonymous inner class. Of course, it's limited; you can't overload instance initializers so you can have only one of these constructors.

The link to the outer class

So far, it appears that inner classes are just a name-hiding and code-organization scheme, which is helpful but not totally compelling. However, there's another twist. When you create an inner class, objects of that inner class have a link to the enclosing object that made them, and so they can access the members of that enclosing object – *without* any special qualifications. In addition, inner classes have access rights to all the elements in the enclosing class.[2] The following example demonstrates this:

```
//: Sequence.java
// Holds a sequence of Objects

interface Selector {
  boolean end();
  Object current();
  void next();
}

public class Sequence {
  private Object[] o;
  private int next = 0;
  public Sequence(int size) {
    o = new Object[size];
  }
  public void add(Object x) {
    if(next < o.length) {
      o[next] = x;
      next++;
    }
  }
  private class SSelector implements Selector {
    int i = 0;
    public boolean end() {
      return i == o.length;
    }
    public Object current() {
      return o[i];
    }
    public void next() {
      if(i < o.length) i++;
    }
  }
  public Selector getSelector() {
    return new SSelector();
```

---

[2] This is very different from the design of *nested classes* in C++, which is simply a name-hiding mechanism. There is no link to an enclosing object and no implied permissions in C++.

```
    }
    public static void main(String[] args) {
      Sequence s = new Sequence(10);
      for(int i = 0; i < 10; i++)
        s.add(Integer.toString(i));
      Selector sl = s.getSelector();
      while(!sl.end()) {
        System.out.println((String)sl.current());
        sl.next();
      }
    }
  } ///:~
```

The **Sequence** is simply a fixed-sized array of **Object** with a class wrapped around it. You call **add( )** to add a new **Object** to the end of the sequence (if there's room left). To fetch each of the objects in a **Sequence**, there's an interface called **Selector**, which allows you to see if you're at the **end( )**, to look at the **current( ) Object**, and to move to the **next( ) Object** in the **Sequence**. Because **Selector** is an **interface**, many other classes can implement the **interface** in their own ways, and many methods can take the **interface** as an argument, in order to create generic code.

Here, the **SSelector** is a private class that provides **Selector** functionality. In **main( )**, you can see the creation of a **Sequence**, followed by the addition of a number of **String** objects. Then, a **Selector** is produced with a call to **getSelector( )** and this is used to move through the **Sequence** and select each item.

At first, the creation of **SSelector** looks like just another inner class. But examine it closely. Note that each of the methods **end( )**, **current( )**, and **next( )** refer to **o**, which is a handle that isn't part of **SSelector**, but is instead a **private** field in the enclosing class. However, the inner class can access methods and fields from the enclosing class as if they owned them. This turns out to be very convenient, as you can see in the above example.

So an inner class has access to the members of the enclosing class. How can this happen? The inner class must keep a reference to the particular object of the enclosing class that was responsible for creating it. Then when you refer to a member of the enclosing class, that (hidden) reference is used to select that member. Fortunately, the compiler takes care of all these details for you, but you can also understand now that an object of an inner class can be created only in association with an object of the enclosing class. The process of construction requires the initialization of the handle to the object of the enclosing class, and the compiler will complain if it cannot access the handle. Most of the time this occurs without any intervention on the part of the programmer.

static inner classes

To understand the meaning of **static** when applied to inner classes, you must remember that the object of the inner class implicitly keeps a handle to the object of the enclosing class that created it. This is not true, however, when you say an inner class is **static**. A **static** inner class means:

1. You don't need an outer-class object in order to create an object of a **static** inner class.

2. You can't access an outer-class object from an object of a **static** inner class.

There are some restrictions: **static** members can be at only the outer level of a class, so inner classes cannot have **static** data or **static** inner classes.

If you don't need to create an object of the outer class in order to create an object of the inner class, you can make everything **static**. For this to work, you must also make the inner classes **static**:

```
//: Parcel10.java
// Static inner classes
package c07.parcel10;

abstract class Contents {
  abstract public int value();
}

interface Destination {
  String readLabel();
}

public class Parcel10 {
  private static class PContents
  extends Contents {
    private int i = 11;
    public int value() { return i; }
  }
  protected static class PDestination
      implements Destination {
```

```
      private String label;
      private PDestination(String whereTo) {
        label = whereTo;
      }
      public String readLabel() { return label; }
    }
    public static Destination dest(String s) {
      return new PDestination(s);
    }
    public static Contents cont() {
      return new PContents();
    }
    public static void main(String[] args) {
      Contents c = cont();
      Destination d = dest("Tanzania");
    }
} ///:~
```

In **main( )**, no object of **Parcel10** is necessary; instead you use the normal syntax for selecting a **static** member to call the methods that return handles to **Contents** and **Destination**.

Normally you can't put any code inside an **interface**, but a **static** inner class can be part of an **interface**. Since the class is **static** it doesn't violate the rules for interfaces – the **static** inner class is only placed inside the namespace of the interface:

```
//: IInterface.java
// Static inner classes inside interfaces

class IInterface {
  static class Inner {
    int i, j, k;
    public Inner() {}
    void f() {}
  }
} ///:~
```

Earlier in the book I suggested putting a **main( )** in every class to act as a test bed for that class. One drawback to this is the amount of extra code you must carry around. If this is a problem, you can use a **static** inner class to hold your test code:

```
//: TestBed.java
// Putting test code in a static inner class
```

```
class TestBed {
  TestBed() {}
  void f() { System.out.println("f()"); }
  public static class Tester {
    public static void main(String[] args) {
      TestBed t = new TestBed();
      t.f();
    }
  }
} ///:~
```

This generates a separate class called **TestBed$Tester** (to run the program you say **java TestBed$Tester**). You can use this class for testing, but you don't need to include it in your shipping product.

Referring to the outer class object

If you need to produce the handle to the outer class object, you name the outer class followed by a dot and **this**. For example, in the class **Sequence.SSelector**, any of its methods can produce the stored handle to the outer class **Sequence** by saying **Sequence.this**. The resulting handle is automatically the correct type. (This is known and checked at compile time, so there is no run-time overhead.)

Sometimes you want to tell some other object to create an object of one of its inner classes. To do this you must provide a handle to the other outer class object in the **new** expression, like this:

```
//: Parcel11.java
// Creating inner classes
package c07.parcel11;

public class Parcel11 {
  class Contents {
    private int i = 11;
    public int value() { return i; }
  }
  class Destination {
    private String label;
    Destination(String whereTo) {
      label = whereTo;
    }
    String readLabel() { return label; }
  }
  public static void main(String[] args) {
```

```
        Parcel11 p = new Parcel11();
        // Must use instance of outer class
        // to create an instances of the inner class:
        Parcel11.Contents c = p.new Contents();
        Parcel11.Destination d =
          p.new Destination("Tanzania");
      }
    } ///:~
```

To create an object of the inner class directly, you don't follow the same form and refer to the outer class name **Parcel11** as you might expect, but instead you must use an *object* of the outer class to make an object of the inner class:

```
    Parcel11.Contents c = p.new Contents();
```

Thus, it's not possible to create an object of the inner class unless you already have an object of the outer class. This is because the object of the inner class is quietly connected to the object of the outer class that it was made from. However, if you make a **static** inner class, then it doesn't need a handle to the outer class object.

Inheriting from inner classes

Because the inner class constructor must attach to a handle of the enclosing class object, things are slightly complicated when you inherit from an inner class. The problem is that the "secret" handle to the enclosing class object *must* be initialized, and yet in the derived class there's no longer a default object to attach to. The answer is to use a syntax provided to make the association explicit:

```
//: InheritInner.java
// Inheriting an inner class

class WithInner {
  class Inner {}
}

public class InheritInner
    extends WithInner.Inner {
  //! InheritInner() {} // Won't compile
  InheritInner(WithInner wi) {
    wi.super();
  }
  public static void main(String[] args) {
```

```
        WithInner wi = new WithInner();
        InheritInner ii = new InheritInner(wi);
    }
} ///:~
```

You can see that **InheritInner** is extending only the inner class, not the outer one. But when it comes time to create a constructor, the default one is no good and you can't just pass a handle to an enclosing object. In addition, you must use the syntax

```
    enclosingClassHandle.super();
```

inside the constructor. This provides the necessary handle and the program will then compile.

Can inner classes be overridden?

What happens when you create an inner class, then inherit from the enclosing class and redefine the inner class? That is, is it possible to override an inner class? This seems like it would be a powerful concept, but "overriding" an inner class as if it were another method of the outer class doesn't really do anything:

```
//: BigEgg.java
// An inner class cannot be overriden
// like a method

class Egg {
  protected class Yolk {
    public Yolk() {
      System.out.println("Egg.Yolk()");
    }
  }
  private Yolk y;
  public Egg() {
    System.out.println("New Egg()");
    y = new Yolk();
  }
}

public class BigEgg extends Egg {
  public class Yolk {
    public Yolk() {
      System.out.println("BigEgg.Yolk()");
    }
```

```
    }
    public static void main(String[] args) {
        new BigEgg();
    }
} ///:~
```

The default constructor is synthesized automatically by the compiler, and this calls the base-class default constructor. You might think that since a **BigEgg** is being created, the "overridden" version of **Yolk** would be used, but this is not the case. The output is:

```
New Egg()
Egg.Yolk()
```

This example simply shows that there isn't any extra inner class magic going on when you inherit from the outer class. However, it's still possible to explicitly inherit from the inner class:

```
//: BigEgg2.java
// Proper inheritance of an inner class

class Egg2 {
    protected class Yolk {
        public Yolk() {
            System.out.println("Egg2.Yolk()");
        }
        public void f() {
            System.out.println("Egg2.Yolk.f()");
        }
    }
    private Yolk y = new Yolk();
    public Egg2() {
        System.out.println("New Egg2()");
    }
    public void insertYolk(Yolk yy) { y = yy; }
    public void g() { y.f(); }
}

public class BigEgg2 extends Egg2 {
    public class Yolk extends Egg2.Yolk {
        public Yolk() {
            System.out.println("BigEgg2.Yolk()");
        }
        public void f() {
            System.out.println("BigEgg2.Yolk.f()");
```

```
      }
    }
    public BigEgg2() { insertYolk(new Yolk()); }
    public static void main(String[] args) {
      Egg2 e2 = new BigEgg2();
      e2.g();
    }
} ///:~
```

Now **BiggEgg2.Yolk** explicitly **extends Egg2.Yolk** and overrides its methods. The method **insertYolk( )** allows **BigEgg2** to upcast one of its own **Yolk** objects into the **y** handle in **Egg2**, so when **g( )** calls **y.f( )** the overridden version of **f( )** is used. The output is:

```
Egg2.Yolk()
New Egg2()
Egg2.Yolk()
BigEgg2.Yolk()
BigEgg2.Yolk.f()
```

The second call to **Egg2.Yolk( )** is the base-class constructor call of the **BigEgg2.Yolk** constructor. You can see that the overridden version of **f( )** is used when **g( )** is called.

Inner class identifiers

Since every class produces a **.class** file that holds all the information about how to create objects of this type (this information produces a meta-class called the **Class** object), you might guess that inner classes must also produce **.class** files to contain the information for *their* **Class** objects. The names of these files/classes have a strict formula: the name of the enclosing class, followed by a '**$**', followed by the name of the inner class. For example, the **.class** files created by **InheritInner.java** include:

```
InheritInner.class
WithInner$Inner.class
WithInner.class
```

If inner classes are anonymous, the compiler simply starts generating numbers as inner class identifiers. If inner classes are nested within inner classes, their names are simply appended after a '**$**' and the outer class identifier(s).

Although this scheme of generating internal names is simple and straightforward, it's also robust and handles most situations.[3] Since it is the standard naming scheme for Java, the generated files are automatically platform-independent. (Note that the Java compiler is changing your inner classes in all sorts of other ways in order to make them work.)

Why inner classes: control frameworks

At this point you've seen a lot of syntax and semantics describing the way inner classes work, but this doesn't answer the question of why they exist. Why did Sun go to so much trouble to add such a fundamental language feature in Java 1.1? The answer is something that I will refer to here as a *control framework*.

An *application framework* is a class or a set of classes that's designed to solve a particular type of problem. To apply an application framework, you inherit from one or more classes and override some of the methods. The code you write in the overridden methods customizes the general solution provided by that application framework to solve your specific problem. The control framework is a particular type of application framework dominated by the need to respond to events; a system that primarily responds to events is called an *event-driven system*. One of the most important problems in application programming is the graphical user interface (GUI), which is almost entirely event-driven. As you will see in Chapter 13, the Java 1.1 AWT is a control framework that elegantly solves the GUI problem using inner classes.

To see how inner classes allow the simple creation and use of control frameworks, consider a control framework whose job is to execute events whenever those events are "ready." Although "ready" could mean anything, in this case the default will be based on clock time. What follows is a control framework that contains no specific information about what it's controlling. First, here is the interface that describes any control event. It's an **abstract** class instead of an actual **interface** because the default behavior is control based on time, so some of the implementation can be included here:

---

[3] On the other hand, '$' is a meta-character to the Unix shell and so you'll sometimes have trouble when listing the **.class** files. This is a bit strange coming from Sun, a Unix-based company. My guess is that they weren't considering this issue, but instead thought you'd naturally focus on the source-code files.

```
//: Event.java
// The common methods for any control event
package c07.controller;

abstract public class Event {
  private long evtTime;
  public Event(long eventTime) {
    evtTime = eventTime;
  }
  public boolean ready() {
    return System.currentTimeMillis() >= evtTime;
  }
  abstract public void action();
  abstract public String description();
} ///:~
```

The constructor simply captures the time when you want the **Event** to run, while **ready( )** tells you when it's time to run it. Of course, **ready( )** could be overridden in a derived class to base the **Event** on something other than time.

action( ) is the method that's called when the **Event** is **ready( )**, and **description( )** gives textual information about the **Event**.

The next file contains the actual control framework that manages and fires events. The first class is really just a "helper" class whose job is to hold **Event** objects. You could replace it with any appropriate collection, and in Chapter 8 you'll discover other collections that will do the trick without requiring you to write this extra code:

```
//: Controller.java
// Along with Event, the generic
// framework for all control systems:
package c07.controller;

// This is just a way to hold Event objects.
class EventSet {
  private Event[] events = new Event[100];
  private int index = 0;
  private int next = 0;
  public void add(Event e) {
    if(index >= events.length)
      return; // (In real life, throw exception)
    events[index++] = e;
  }
```

```
    public Event getNext() {
      boolean looped = false;
      int start = next;
      do {
        next = (next + 1) % events.length;
        // See if it has looped to the beginning:
        if(start == next) looped = true;
        // If it loops past start, the list
        // is empty:
        if((next == (start + 1) % events.length)
           && looped)
          return null;
      } while(events[next] == null);
      return events[next];
    }
    public void removeCurrent() {
      events[next] = null;
    }
  }
}

public class Controller {
  private EventSet es = new EventSet();
  public void addEvent(Event c) { es.add(c); }
  public void run() {
    Event e;
    while((e = es.getNext()) != null) {
      if(e.ready()) {
        e.action();
        System.out.println(e.description());
        es.removeCurrent();
      }
    }
  }
} ///:~
```

EventSet arbitrarily holds 100 **Event**s. (If a "real" collection from
Chapter 8 is used here you don't need to worry about its maximum size,
since it will resize itself). The **index** is used to keep track of the next
available space, and **next** is used when you're looking for the next **Event**
in the list, to see whether you've looped around. This is important during
a call to **getNext( )**, because **Event** objects are removed from the list
(using **removeCurrent( )**) once they're run, so **getNext( )** will encounter
holes in the list as it moves through it.

Note that **removeCurrent( )** doesn't just set some flag indicating that the object is no longer in use. Instead, it sets the handle to **null**. This is important because if the garbage collector sees a handle that's still in use then it can't clean up the object. If you think your handles might hang around (as they would here), then it's a good idea to set them to **null** to give the garbage collector permission to clean them up.

Controller is where the actual work goes on. It uses an **EventSet** to hold its **Event** objects, and **addEvent( )** allows you to add new events to this list. But the important method is **run( )**. This method loops through the **EventSet**, hunting for an **Event** object that's **ready( )** to run. For each one it finds **ready( )**, it calls the **action( )** method, prints out the **description( )**, and then removes the **Event** from the list.

Note that so far in this design you know nothing about exactly *what* an **Event** does. And this is the crux of the design; how it "separates the things that change from the things that stay the same." Or, to use my term, the "vector of change" is the different actions of the various kinds of **Event** objects, and you express different actions by creating different **Event** subclasses.

This is where inner classes come into play. They allow two things:

1. To express the entire implementation of a control-framework application in a single class, thereby encapsulating everything that's unique about that implementation. Inner classes are used to express the many different kinds of **action( )** necessary to solve the problem. In addition, the following example uses **private** inner classes so the implementation is completely hidden and can be changed with impunity.

2. Inner classes keep this implementation from becoming awkward, since you're able to easily access any of the members in the outer class. Without this ability the code might become unpleasant enough that you'd end up seeking an alternative.

Consider a particular implementation of the control framework designed to control greenhouse functions.[4] Each action is entirely different: turning lights, water, and thermostats on and off, ringing bells, and restarting the system. But the control framework is designed to easily

---

[4] For some reason this has always been a pleasing problem for me to solve; it came from *C++ Inside & Out*, but Java allows a much more elegant solution.

isolate this different code. For each type of action you inherit a new
Event inner class, and write the control code inside of **action( )**.

As is typical with an application framework, the class
GreenhouseControls is inherited from **Controller**:

```
//: GreenhouseControls.java
// This produces a specific application of the
// control system, all in a single class. Inner
// classes allow you to encapsulate different
// functionality for each type of event.
package c07.controller;

public class GreenhouseControls
      extends Controller {
  private boolean light = false;
  private boolean water = false;
  private String thermostat = "Day";
  private class LightOn extends Event {
    public LightOn(long eventTime) {
      super(eventTime);
    }
    public void action() {
      // Put hardware control code here to
      // physically turn on the light.
      light = true;
    }
    public String description() {
      return "Light is on";
    }
  }
  private class LightOff extends Event {
    public LightOff(long eventTime) {
      super(eventTime);
    }
    public void action() {
      // Put hardware control code here to
      // physically turn off the light.
      light = false;
    }
    public String description() {
      return "Light is off";
    }
  }
  private class WaterOn extends Event {
```

```
        public WaterOn(long eventTime) {
          super(eventTime);
        }
        public void action() {
          // Put hardware control code here
          water = true;
        }
        public String description() {
          return "Greenhouse water is on";
        }
      }
      private class WaterOff extends Event {
        public WaterOff(long eventTime) {
          super(eventTime);
        }
        public void action() {
          // Put hardware control code here
          water = false;
        }
        public String description() {
          return "Greenhouse water is off";
        }
      }
      private class ThermostatNight extends Event {
        public ThermostatNight(long eventTime) {
          super(eventTime);
        }
        public void action() {
          // Put hardware control code here
          thermostat = "Night";
        }
        public String description() {
          return "Thermostat on night setting";
        }
      }
      private class ThermostatDay extends Event {
        public ThermostatDay(long eventTime) {
          super(eventTime);
        }
        public void action() {
          // Put hardware control code here
          thermostat = "Day";
        }
        public String description() {
```

```
      return "Thermostat on day setting";
    }
  }
  // An example of an action() that inserts a
  // new one of itself into the event list:
  private int rings;
  private class Bell extends Event {
    public Bell(long eventTime) {
      super(eventTime);
    }
    public void action() {
      // Ring bell every 2 seconds, rings times:
      System.out.println("Bing!");
      if(--rings > 0)
        addEvent(new Bell(
          System.currentTimeMillis() + 2000));
    }
    public String description() {
      return "Ring bell";
    }
  }
  private class Restart extends Event {
    public Restart(long eventTime) {
      super(eventTime);
    }
    public void action() {
      long tm = System.currentTimeMillis();
      // Instead of hard-wiring, you could parse
      // configuration information from a text
      // file here:
      rings = 5;
      addEvent(new ThermostatNight(tm));
      addEvent(new LightOn(tm + 1000));
      addEvent(new LightOff(tm + 2000));
      addEvent(new WaterOn(tm + 3000));
      addEvent(new WaterOff(tm + 8000));
      addEvent(new Bell(tm + 9000));
      addEvent(new ThermostatDay(tm + 10000));
      // Can even add a Restart object!
      addEvent(new Restart(tm + 20000));
    }
    public String description() {
      return "Restarting system";
    }
```

```
      }
    public static void main(String[] args) {
        GreenhouseControls gc =
          new GreenhouseControls();
        long tm = System.currentTimeMillis();
        gc.addEvent(gc.new Restart(tm));
        gc.run();
    }
} ///:~
```

Note that **light, water, thermostat,** and **rings** all belong to the outer class **GreenhouseControls,** and yet the inner classes have no problem accessing those fields. Also, most of the **action( )** methods also involve some sort of hardware control, which would most likely involve calls to non–Java code.

Most of the **Event** classes look similar, but **Bell** and **Restart** are special. **Bell** rings, and if it hasn't yet rung enough times it adds a new **Bell** object to the event list, so it will ring again later. Notice how inner classes *almost* look like multiple inheritance: **Bell** has all the methods of **Event** and it also appears to have all the methods of the outer class **GreenhouseControls**.

Restart is responsible for initializing the system, so it adds all the appropriate events. Of course, a more flexible way to accomplish this is to avoid hard-coding the events and instead read them from a file. (An exercise in Chapter 10 asks you to modify this example to do just that.) Since **Restart( )** is just another **Event** object, you can also add a **Restart** object within **Restart.action( )** so that the system regularly restarts itself. And all you need to do in **main( )** is create a **GreenhouseControls** object and add a **Restart** object to get it going.

This example should move you a long way toward appreciating the value of inner classes, especially when used within a control framework. However, in the latter half of Chapter 13 you'll see how elegantly inner classes are used to describe the actions of a graphical user interface. By the time you finish that section you should be fully convinced.

Constructors and polymorphism

As usual, constructors are different from other kinds of methods. This is also true when polymorphism is involved. Even though constructors are not polymorphic (although you can have a kind of "virtual constructor," as you will see in Chapter 11), it's important to understand the way constructors work in complex hierarchies and with polymorphism. This understanding will help you avoid unpleasant entanglements.

Order of constructor calls

The order of constructor calls was briefly discussed in Chapter 4, but that was before inheritance and polymorphism were introduced.

A constructor for the base class is always called in the constructor for a derived class, chaining upward so that a constructor for every base class is called. This makes sense because the constructor has a special job: to see that the object is built properly. A derived class has access to its own members only, and not to those of the base class (whose members are typically **private**). Only the base-class constructor has the proper knowledge and access to initialize its own elements. Therefore, it's essential that all constructors get called, otherwise the entire object wouldn't be constructed properly. That's why the compiler enforces a constructor call for every portion of a derived class. It will silently call the default constructor if you don't explicitly call a base-class constructor in the derived-class constructor body. If there is no default constructor, the compiler will complain. (In the case where a class has no constructors, the compiler will automatically synthesize a default constructor.)

Let's take a look at an example that shows the effects of composition, inheritance, and polymorphism on the order of construction:

```
//: Sandwich.java
// Order of constructor calls

class Meal {
  Meal() { System.out.println("Meal()"); }
}

class Bread {
```

```
      Bread() { System.out.println("Bread()"); }
    }

    class Cheese {
      Cheese() { System.out.println("Cheese()"); }
    }

    class Lettuce {
      Lettuce() { System.out.println("Lettuce()"); }
    }

    class Lunch extends Meal {
      Lunch() { System.out.println("Lunch()");}
    }

    class PortableLunch extends Lunch {
      PortableLunch() {
        System.out.println("PortableLunch()");
      }
    }

    class Sandwich extends PortableLunch {
      Bread b = new Bread();
      Cheese c = new Cheese();
      Lettuce l = new Lettuce();
      Sandwich() {
        System.out.println("Sandwich()");
      }
      public static void main(String[] args) {
        new Sandwich();
      }
    } ///:~
```

This example creates a complex class out of other classes, and each class has a constructor that announces itself. The important class is **Sandwich**, which reflects three levels of inheritance (four, if you count the implicit inheritance from **Object**) and three member objects. When a **Sandwich** object is created in **main( )**, the output is:

```
    Meal()
    Lunch()
    PortableLunch()
    Bread()
    Cheese()
    Lettuce()
```

```
Sandwich()
```

This means that the order of constructor calls for a complex object is as follows:

1. The base-class constructor is called. This step is repeated recursively such that the root of the hierarchy is constructed first, followed by the next-derived class, etc., until the most-derived class is reached.

2. Member initializers are called in the order of declaration.

3. The body of the derived-class constructor is called.

The order of the constructor calls is important. When you inherit, you know all about the base class and can access any **public** and **protected** members of the base class. This means that you must be able to assume that all the members of the base class are valid when you're in the derived class. In a normal method, construction has already taken place, so all the members of all parts of the object have been built. Inside the constructor, however, you must be able to assume that all members that you use have been built. The only way to guarantee this is for the base-class constructor to be called first. Then when you're in the derived-class constructor, all the members you can access in the base class have been initialized. "Knowing that all members are valid" inside the constructor is also the reason that, whenever possible, you should initialize all member objects (that is, objects placed in the class using composition) at their point of definition in the class (e.g.: **b**, **c**, and **l** in the example above). If you follow this practice, you will help ensure that all base class members *and* member objects of the current object have been initialized. Unfortunately, this doesn't handle every case, as you will see in the next section.

Inheritance and **finalize( )**

When you use composition to create a new class, you never worry about finalizing the member objects of that class. Each member is an independent object and thus is garbage collected and finalized regardless of whether it happens to be a member of your class. With inheritance, however, you must override **finalize( )** in the derived class if you have any special cleanup that must happen as part of garbage collection. When you override **finalize( )** in an inherited class, it's important to remember to call the base-class version of **finalize( )**, since otherwise the base-class finalization will not happen. The following example proves this:

```
//: Frog.java
// Testing finalize with inheritance

class DoBaseFinalization {
  public static boolean flag = false;
}

class Characteristic {
  String s;
  Characteristic(String c) {
    s = c;
    System.out.println(
      "Creating Characteristic " + s);
  }
  protected void finalize() {
    System.out.println(
      "finalizing Characteristic " + s);
  }
}

class LivingCreature {
  Characteristic p =
    new Characteristic("is alive");
  LivingCreature() {
    System.out.println("LivingCreature()");
  }
  protected void finalize() {
    System.out.println(
      "LivingCreature finalize");
    // Call base-class version LAST!
    if(DoBaseFinalization.flag)
      try {
        super.finalize();
      } catch(Throwable t) {}
  }
}

class Animal extends LivingCreature {
  Characteristic p =
    new Characteristic("has heart");
  Animal() {
    System.out.println("Animal()");
  }
  protected void finalize() {
```

```
      System.out.println("Animal finalize");
      if(DoBaseFinalization.flag)
        try {
          super.finalize();
        } catch(Throwable t) {}
  }
}

class Amphibian extends Animal {
  Characteristic p =
    new Characteristic("can live in water");
  Amphibian() {
    System.out.println("Amphibian()");
  }
  protected void finalize() {
    System.out.println("Amphibian finalize");
    if(DoBaseFinalization.flag)
      try {
        super.finalize();
      } catch(Throwable t) {}
  }
}

public class Frog extends Amphibian {
  Frog() {
    System.out.println("Frog()");
  }
  protected void finalize() {
    System.out.println("Frog finalize");
    if(DoBaseFinalization.flag)
      try {
        super.finalize();
      } catch(Throwable t) {}
  }
  public static void main(String[] args) {
    if(args.length != 0 &&
      args[0].equals("finalize"))
      DoBaseFinalization.flag = true;
    else
      System.out.println("not finalizing bases");
    new Frog(); // Instantly becomes garbage
    System.out.println("bye!");
    // Must do this to guarantee that all
    // finalizers will be called:
```

```
      System.runFinalizersOnExit(true);
  }
} ///:~
```

The class **DoBaseFinalization** simply holds a flag that indicates to each class in the hierarchy whether to call **super.finalize( )**. This flag is set based on a command-line argument, so you can view the behavior with and without base-class finalization.

Each class in the hierarchy also contains a member object of class **Characteristic**. You will see that regardless of whether the base class finalizers are called, the **Characteristic** member objects are always finalized.

Each overridden **finalize( )** must have access to at least **protected** members since the **finalize( )** method in class **Object** is **protected** and the compiler will not allow you to reduce the access during inheritance. ("Friendly" is less accessible than **protected**.)

In **Frog.main( )**, the **DoBaseFinalization** flag is configured and a single **Frog** object is created. Remember that garbage collection and in particular finalization might not happen for any particular object so to enforce this, **System.runFinalizersOnExit(true)** adds the extra overhead to guarantee that finalization takes place. Without base-class finalization, the output is:

```
not finalizing bases
Creating Characteristic is alive
LivingCreature()
Creating Characteristic has heart
Animal()
Creating Characteristic can live in water
Amphibian()
Frog()
bye!
Frog finalize
finalizing Characteristic is alive
finalizing Characteristic has heart
finalizing Characteristic can live in water
```

You can see that, indeed, no finalizers are called for the base classes of **Frog**. But if you add the "finalize" argument on the command line, you get:

```
Creating Characteristic is alive
LivingCreature()
```

```
Creating Characteristic has heart
Animal()
Creating Characteristic can live in water
Amphibian()
Frog()
bye!
Frog finalize
Amphibian finalize
Animal finalize
LivingCreature finalize
finalizing Characteristic is alive
finalizing Characteristic has heart
finalizing Characteristic can live in water
```

Although the order the member objects are finalized is the same order that they are created, technically the order of finalization of objects is unspecified. With base classes, however, you have control over the order of finalization. The best order to use is the one that's shown here, which is the reverse of the order of initialization. Following the form that's used in C++ for destructors, you should perform the derived-class finalization first, then the base-class finalization. That's because the derived-class finalization could call some methods in the base class that require that the base-class components are still alive, so you must not destroy them prematurely.

Behavior of polymorphic methods inside constructors

The hierarchy of constructor calls brings up an interesting dilemma. What happens if you're inside a constructor and you call a dynamically-bound method of the object being constructed? Inside an ordinary method you can imagine what will happen – the dynamically-bound call is resolved at run-time because the object cannot know whether it belongs to the class the method is in or some class derived from it. For consistency, you might think this is what should happen inside constructors.

This is not exactly the case. If you call a dynamically-bound method inside a constructor, the overridden definition for that method is used. However, the *effect* can be rather unexpected, and can conceal some difficult-to-find bugs.

Conceptually, the constructor's job is to bring the object into existence (which is hardly an ordinary feat). Inside any constructor, the entire object might be only partially formed – you can know only that the base-class objects have been initialized, but you cannot know which classes are inherited from you. A dynamically-bound method call, however, reaches "forward" or "outward" into the inheritance hierarchy. It calls a method in a derived class. If you do this inside a constructor, you call a method that might manipulate members that haven't been initialized yet – a sure recipe for disaster.

You can see the problem in the following example:

```
//: PolyConstructors.java
// Constructors and polymorphism
// don't produce what you might expect.

abstract class Glyph {
  abstract void draw();
  Glyph() {
    System.out.println("Glyph() before draw()");
    draw();
    System.out.println("Glyph() after draw()");
  }
}

class RoundGlyph extends Glyph {
  int radius = 1;
  RoundGlyph(int r) {
    radius = r;
    System.out.println(
      "RoundGlyph.RoundGlyph(), radius = "
      + radius);
  }
  void draw() {
    System.out.println(
      "RoundGlyph.draw(), radius = " + radius);
  }
}

public class PolyConstructors {
  public static void main(String[] args) {
    new RoundGlyph(5);
  }
} ///:~
```

In **Glyph**, the **draw( )** method is **abstract**, so it is designed to be overridden. Indeed, you are forced to override it in **RoundGlyph**. But the

Glyph constructor calls this method, and the call ends up in **RoundGlyph.draw( )**, which would seem to be the intent. But look at the output:

```
Glyph() before draw()
RoundGlyph.draw(), radius = 0
Glyph() after draw()
RoundGlyph.RoundGlyph(), radius = 5
```

When **Glyph**'s constructor calls **draw( )**, the value of **radius** isn't even the default initial value 1. It's zero. This would probably result in either a dot or nothing at all being drawn on the screen, and you'd be staring, trying to figure out why the program won't work.

The order of initialization described in the previous section isn't quite complete, and that's the key to solving the mystery. The actual process of initialization is:

1. The storage allocated for the object is initialized to binary zero before anything else happens.

2. The base-class constructors are called as described previously. At this point, the overridden **draw( )** method is called, (yes, *before* the **RoundGlyph** constructor is called), which discovers a **radius** value of zero, due to step 1.

3. Member initializers are called in the order of declaration.

4. The body of the derived-class constructor is called.

There's an upside to this, which is that everything is at least initialized to zero (or whatever zero means for that particular data type) and not just left as garbage. This includes object handles that are embedded inside a class via composition. So if you forget to initialize that handle you'll get an exception at run time. Everything else gets zero, which is usually a telltale value when looking at output.

On the other hand, you should be pretty horrified at the outcome of this program. You've done a perfectly logical thing and yet the behavior is mysteriously wrong, with no complaints from the compiler. (C++ produces more rational behavior in this situation.) Bugs like this could easily be buried and take a long time to discover.

As a result, a good guideline for constructors is, "Do as little as possible to set the object into a good state, and if you can possibly avoid it, don't call any methods." The only safe methods to call inside a constructor are those that are **final** in the base class. (This also applies to **private**

---

methods, which are automatically **final**.) These cannot be overridden and thus cannot produce this kind of surprise.

Designing with inheritance

Once you learn about polymorphism, it can seem that everything ought to be inherited because polymorphism is such a clever tool. This can burden your designs; in fact if you choose inheritance first when you're using an existing class to make a new class things can become needlessly complicated.

A better approach is to choose composition first, when it's not obvious which one you should use. Composition does not force a design into an inheritance hierarchy. But composition is also more flexible since it's possible to dynamically choose a type (and thus behavior) when using composition, whereas inheritance requires an exact type to be known at compile time. The following example illustrates this:

```
//: Transmogrify.java
// Dynamically changing the behavior of
// an object via composition.

interface Actor {
  void act();
}

class HappyActor implements Actor {
  public void act() {
    System.out.println("HappyActor");
  }
}

class SadActor implements Actor {
  public void act() {
    System.out.println("SadActor");
  }
}

class Stage {
  Actor a = new HappyActor();
  void change() { a = new SadActor(); }
  void go() { a.act(); }
}
```

```
public class Transmogrify {
  public static void main(String[] args) {
    Stage s = new Stage();
    s.go(); // Prints "HappyActor"
    s.change();
    s.go(); // Prints "SadActor"
  }
} ///:~
```

A **Stage** object contains a handle to an **Actor**, which is initialized to a **HappyActor** object. This means **go( )** produces a particular behavior. But since a handle can be re-bound to a different object at run time, a handle for a **SadActor** object can be substituted in **a** and then the behavior produced by **go( )** changes. Thus you gain dynamic flexibility at run time. In contrast, you can't decide to inherit differently at run time; that must be completely determined at compile time.

A general guideline is "Use inheritance to express differences in behavior, and member variables to express variations in state." In the above example, both are used: two different classes are inherited to express the difference in the **act( )** method, and **Stage** uses composition to allow its state to be changed. In this case, that change in state happens to produce a change in behavior.

Pure inheritance vs. extension

When studying inheritance, it would seem that the cleanest way to create an inheritance hierarchy is to take the "pure" approach. That is, only methods that have been established in the base class or **interface** are to be overridden in the derived class, as seen in this diagram:

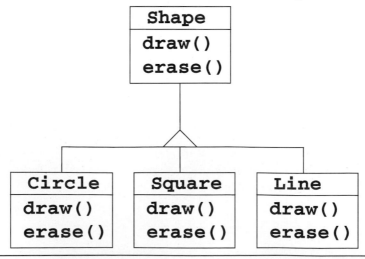

Thinking in Java   *www.BruceEckel.com*

This can be termed a pure "is-a" relationship because the interface of a class establishes what it is. Inheritance guarantees that any derived class will have the interface of the base class and nothing less. If you follow the above diagram, derived classes will also have *no more* than the base class interface.

This can be thought of as *pure substitution*, because derived class objects can be perfectly substituted for the base class, and you never need to know any extra information about the subclasses when you're using them:

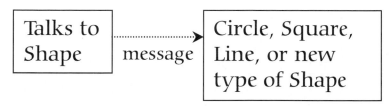

"Is a"

That is, the base class can receive any message you can send to the derived class because the two have exactly the same interface. All you need to do is upcast from the derived class and never look back to see what exact type of object you're dealing with. Everything is handled through polymorphism.

When you see it this way, it seems like a pure "is-a" relationship is the only sensible way to do things, and any other design indicates muddled thinking and is by definition broken. This too is a trap. As soon as you start thinking this way, you'll turn around and discover that extending the interface (which, unfortunately, the keyword **extends** seems to promote) is the perfect solution to a particular problem. This could be termed an "is-like-a" relationship because the derived class is *like* the base class – it has the same fundamental interface – but it has other features that require additional methods to implement:

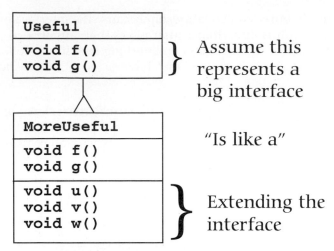

Assume this
represents a
big interface

"Is like a"

Extending the
interface

While this is also a useful and sensible approach (depending on the situation) it has a drawback. The extended part of the interface in the derived class is not available from the base class, so once you upcast you can't call the new methods:

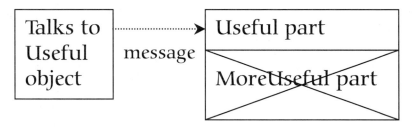

If you're not upcasting in this case, it won't bother you, but often you'll get into a situation in which you need to rediscover the exact type of the object so you can access the extended methods of that type. The following sections show how this is done.

Downcasting and run-time type identification

Since you lose the specific type information via an *upcast* (moving up the inheritance hierarchy), it makes sense that to retrieve the type information – that is, to move back down the inheritance hierarchy – you use a *downcast*. However, you know an upcast is always safe; the base class cannot have a bigger interface than the derived class, therefore every message you send through the base class interface is guaranteed to be accepted. But with a downcast, you don't really know that a shape (for example) is actually a circle. It could instead be a triangle or square or some other type.

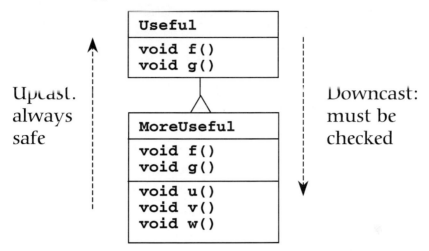

Upcast:
always
safe

Downcast:
must be
checked

To solve this problem there must be some way to guarantee that a downcast is correct, so you won't accidentally cast to the wrong type and then send a message that the object can't accept. This would be quite unsafe.

In some languages (like C++) you must perform a special operation in order to get a type-safe downcast, but in Java *every cast* is checked! So even though it looks like you're just performing an ordinary parenthesized cast, at run time this cast is checked to ensure that it is in fact the type you think it is. If it isn't, you get a **ClassCastException**. This act of checking types at run time is called *run-time type identification* (RTTI). The following example demonstrates the behavior of RTTI:

```
//: RTTI.java
// Downcasting & Run-Time Type
// Identification (RTTI)
import java.util.*;

class Useful {
  public void f() {}
  public void g() {}
}

class MoreUseful extends Useful {
  public void f() {}
  public void g() {}
```

```
      public void u() {}
      public void v() {}
      public void w() {}
}

public class RTTI {
   public static void main(String[] args) {
     Useful[] x = {
       new Useful(),
       new MoreUseful()
     };
     x[0].f();
     x[1].g();
     // Compile-time: method not found in Useful:
     //! x[1].u();
     ((MoreUseful)x[1]).u(); // Downcast/RTTI
     ((MoreUseful)x[0]).u(); // Exception thrown
   }
} ///:~
```

As in the diagram, **MoreUseful** extends the interface of **Useful**. But since it's inherited, it can also be upcast to a **Useful**. You can see this happening in the initialization of the array **x** in **main( )**. Since both objects in the array are of class **Useful**, you can send the **f( )** and **g( )** methods to both, and if you try to call **u( )** (which exists only in **MoreUseful**) you'll get a compile-time error message.

If you want to access the extended interface of a **MoreUseful** object, you can try to downcast. If it's the correct type, it will be successful. Otherwise, you'll get a **ClassCastException**. You don't need to write any special code for this exception, since it indicates a programmer error that could happen anywhere in a program.

There's more to RTTI than a simple cast. For example, there's a way to see what type you're dealing with *before* you try to downcast it. All of Chapter 11 is devoted to the study of different aspects of Java run-time type identification.

Summary

Polymorphism means "different forms." In object-oriented programming, you have the same face (the common interface in the base class) and different forms using that face: the different versions of the dynamically-bound methods.

You've seen in this chapter that it's impossible to understand, or even create, an example of polymorphism without using data abstraction and inheritance. Polymorphism is a feature that cannot be viewed in isolation (like a **switch** statement, for example), but instead works only in concert, as part of a "big picture" of class relationships. People are often confused by other, non-object-oriented features of Java, like method overloading, which are sometimes presented as object-oriented. Don't be fooled: If it isn't late binding, it isn't polymorphism.

To use polymorphism, and thus object-oriented techniques, effectively in your programs you must expand your view of programming to include not just members and messages of an individual class, but also the commonality among classes and their relationships with each other. Although this requires significant effort, it's a worthy struggle, because the results are faster program development, better code organization, extensible programs, and easier code maintenance.

Exercises

1. Create an inheritance hierarchy of **Rodent**: **Mouse**, **Gerbil**, **Hamster**, etc. In the base class, provide methods that are common to all **Rodent**s, and override these in the derived classes to perform different behaviors depending on the specific type of **Rodent**. Create an array of **Rodent**, fill it with different specific types of **Rodent**s, and call your base-class methods to see what happens.

2. Change Exercise 1 so that **Rodent** is an **interface**.

3. Repair the problem in **WindError.java**.

4. In **GreenhouseControls.java**, add **Event** inner classes that turn fans on and off.

8: Holding
your objects

It's a fairly simple program that has only a fixed quantity of objects with known lifetimes.

In general, your programs will always be creating new objects based on some criteria that will be known only at the time the program is running. You won't know until run-time the quantity or even the exact type of the objects you need. To solve the general programming problem, you need to create any number of objects, anytime, anywhere. So you can't rely on creating a named handle to hold each one of your objects:

```
MyObject myHandle;
```

since you'll never know how many of these things you'll actually need.

To solve this rather essential problem, Java has several ways to hold objects (or rather, handles to objects). The built-in type is the array, which has been discussed before and will get additional coverage in this chapter. Also, the Java utilities library has some *collection classes* (also known as *container classes*, but that term is used by the AWT so "collection" will be used here) that provide more sophisticated ways to hold and even manipulate your objects. This will comprise the remainder of this chapter.

Arrays

Most of the necessary introduction to arrays is in the last section of Chapter 4, which shows how you define and initialize an array. Holding objects is the focus of this chapter, and an array is just one way to hold objects. But there are a number of other ways to hold objects, so what makes an array special?

There are two issues that distinguish arrays from other types of collections: efficiency and type. The array is the most efficient way that Java provides to store and access a sequence of objects (actually, object handles). The array is a simple linear sequence, which makes element access fast, but you pay for this speed: when you create an array object, its size is fixed and cannot be changed for the lifetime of that array object. You might suggest creating an array of a particular size and then, if you run out of space, creating a new one and moving all the handles from the old one to the new one. This is the behavior of the **Vector** class, which will be studied later in the chapter. However, because of the overhead of this size flexibility, a **Vector** is measurably less efficient than an array.

The **vector** class in C++ *does* know the type of objects it holds, but it has a different drawback when compared with arrays in Java: the C++ **vector**'s **operator**[] doesn't do bounds checking, so you can run past the end. (It's possible, however, to ask how big the **vector** is, and the **at( )** method *does* perform bounds checking.) In Java, you get bounds checking regardless of whether you're using an array or a collection – you'll get a **RuntimeException** if you exceed the bounds. As you'll learn in Chapter 9, this type of exception indicates a programmer error and thus you don't need to check for it in your code. As an aside, the reason the C++ **vector** doesn't check bounds with every access is speed – in Java you have the constant performance overhead of bounds checking all the time for both arrays and collections.

The other generic collection classes that will be studied in this chapter, **Vector**, **Stack**, and **Hashtable**, all deal with objects as if they had no specific type. That is, they treat them as type **Object**, the root class of all classes in Java. This works fine from one standpoint: you need to build only one collection, and any Java object will go into that collection. (Except for primitives – these can be placed in collections as constants using the Java primitive wrapper classes, or as changeable values by wrapping in your own class.) This is the second place where an array is superior to the generic collections: when you create an array, you create it to hold a specific type. This means that you get compile-time type checking to prevent you from putting the wrong type in, or mistaking the type that you're extracting. Of course, Java will prevent you from sending an inappropriate message to an object, either at compile-time or at run-time. So it's not as if it's riskier one way or the other, it's just nicer if the compiler points it out to you, faster at run-time, and there's less likelihood that the end user will get surprised by an exception.

For efficiency and type checking it's always worth trying to use an array if you can. However, when you're trying to solve a more general problem arrays can be too restrictive. After looking at arrays, the rest of this chapter will be devoted to the collection classes provided by Java.

Arrays are first-class objects

Regardless of what type of array you're working with, the array identifier is actually a handle to a true object that's created on the heap. The heap object can be created either implicitly, as part of the array initialization syntax, or explicitly with a **new** expression. Part of the heap object (in fact, the only field or method you can access) is the read-only **length** member that tells you how many elements can be stored in that array object. The '[]' syntax is the only other access that you have to the array object.

The following example shows the various ways that an array can be initialized, and how the array handles can be assigned to different array objects. It also shows that arrays of objects and arrays of primitives are almost identical in their use. The only difference is that arrays of objects hold handles while arrays of primitives hold the primitive values directly. (See page 97 if you have trouble executing this program.)

```
//: ArraySize.java
// Initialization & re-assignment of arrays
package c08;

class Weeble {} // A small mythical creature

public class ArraySize {
  public static void main(String[] args) {
    // Arrays of objects:
```

```
Weeble[] a; // Null handle
Weeble[] b = new Weeble[5]; // Null handles
Weeble[] c = new Weeble[4];
for(int i = 0; i < c.length; i++)
  c[i] = new Weeble();
Weeble[] d = {
  new Weeble(), new Weeble(), new Weeble()
};
// Compile error: variable a not initialized:
//!System.out.println("a.length=" + a.length);
System.out.println("b.length = " + b.length);
// The handles inside the array are
// automatically initialized to null:
for(int i = 0; i < b.length; i++)
  System.out.println("b[" + i + "]=" + b[i]);
System.out.println("c.length = " + c.length);
System.out.println("d.length = " + d.length);
a = d;
System.out.println("a.length = " + a.length);
// Java 1.1 initialization syntax:
a = new Weeble[] {
  new Weeble(), new Weeble()
};
System.out.println("a.length = " + a.length);

// Arrays of primitives:
int[] e; // Null handle
int[] f = new int[5];
int[] g = new int[4];
for(int i = 0; i < g.length; i++)
  g[i] = i*i;
int[] h = { 11, 47, 93 };
// Compile error: variable e not initialized:
//!System.out.println("e.length=" + e.length);
System.out.println("f.length = " + f.length);
// The primitives inside the array are
// automatically initialized to zero:
for(int i = 0; i < f.length; i++)
  System.out.println("f[" + i + "]=" + f[i]);
System.out.println("g.length = " + g.length);
System.out.println("h.length = " + h.length);
e = h;
System.out.println("e.length = " + e.length);
// Java 1.1 initialization syntax:
```

```
        e = new int[] { 1, 2 };
        System.out.println("e.length = " + e.length);
    }
} ///:~
```

Here's the output from the program:

```
b.length = 5
b[0]=null
b[1]=null
b[2]=null
b[3]=null
b[4]=null
c.length = 4
d.length = 3
a.length = 3
a.length = 2
f.length = 5
f[0]=0
f[1]=0
f[2]=0
f[3]=0
f[4]=0
g.length = 4
h.length = 3
e.length = 3
e.length = 2
```

The array **a** is initially just a **null** handle, and the compiler prevents you from doing anything with this handle until you've properly initialized it. The array **b** is initialized to point to an array of **Weeble** handles, but no actual **Weeble** objects are ever placed in that array. However, you can still ask what the size of the array is, since **b** is pointing to a legitimate object. This brings up a slight drawback: you can't find out how many elements are actually *in* the array, since **length** tells you only how many elements *can* be placed in the array; that is, the size of the array object, not the number of elements it actually holds. However, when an array object is created its handles are automatically initialized to **null** so you can see whether a particular array slot has an object in it by checking to see whether it's **null**. Similarly, an array of primitives is automatically initialized to zero for numeric types, **null** for **char**, and **false** for **boolean**.

Array **c** shows the creation of the array object followed by the assignment of **Weeble** objects to all the slots in the array. Array **d** shows the "aggregate initialization" syntax that causes the array object to be created (implicitly with **new** on the heap, just like for array **c**) *and* initialized with **Weeble** objects, all in one statement.

The expression

```
a = d;
```

shows how you can take a handle that's attached to one array object and assign it to another array object, just as you can do with any other type of object handle. Now both **a** and **d** are pointing to the same array object on the heap.

Java 1.1 adds a new array initialization syntax, which could be thought of as a "dynamic aggregate initialization." The Java 1.0 aggregate initialization used by **d** must be used at the point of **d**'s definition, but with the Java 1.1 syntax you can create and initialize an array object anywhere. For example, suppose **hide( )** is a method that takes an array of **Weeble** objects. You could call it by saying:

```
hide(d);
```

but in Java 1.1 you can also dynamically create the array you want to pass as the argument:

```
hide(new Weeble[] { new Weeble(), new Weeble() });
```

This new syntax provides a more convenient way to write code in some situations.

The second part of the above example shows that primitive arrays work just like object arrays *except* that primitive arrays hold the primitive values directly.

Collections of primitives

Collection classes can hold only handles to objects. An array, however, can be created to hold primitives directly, as well as handles to objects. It *is* possible to use the "wrapper" classes such as **Integer**, **Double**, etc. to place primitive values inside a collection, but as you'll see later in this chapter in the **WordCount.java** example, the wrapper classes for primitives are only somewhat useful anyway. Whether you put primitives in arrays or wrap them in a class that's placed in a collection is a question of efficiency. It's much more efficient to create and access an array of primitives than a collection of wrapped primitives.

Of course, if you're using a primitive type and you need the flexibility of a collection that automatically expands when more space is needed, the array won't work and you're forced to use a collection of wrapped primitives. You might think that there should be a specialized type of **Vector** for each of the primitive data types, but Java doesn't provide this for you. Some sort of templatizing mechanism might someday provide a better way for Java to handle this problem.[1]

Returning an array

Suppose you're writing a method and you don't just want to return one thing, but a whole bunch of things. Languages like C and C++ make this difficult because you can't just return an array, only a pointer to an array. This introduces problems because it becomes messy to control the lifetime of the array, which easily leads to memory leaks.

Java takes a similar approach, but you just "return an array." Actually, of course, you're returning a handle to an array, but with Java you never worry about responsibility for that array – it will be around as long as you need it, and the garbage collector will clean it up when you're done.

As an example, consider returning an array of **String**:

```
//: IceCream.java
// Returning arrays from methods

public class IceCream {
  static String[] flav = {
    "Chocolate", "Strawberry",
    "Vanilla Fudge Swirl", "Mint Chip",
    "Mocha Almond Fudge", "Rum Raisin",
    "Praline Cream", "Mud Pie"
  };
  static String[] flavorSet(int n) {
    // Force it to be positive & within bounds:
    n = Math.abs(n) % (flav.length + 1);
    String[] results = new String[n];
    int[] picks = new int[n];
    for(int i = 0; i < picks.length; i++)
      picks[i] = -1;
```

---

[1] This is one of the places where C++ is distinctly superior to Java, since C++ supports *parameterized types* with the **template** keyword.

```
      for(int i = 0; i < picks.length; i++) {
        retry:
        while(true) {
          int t =
            (int)(Math.random() * flav.length);
          for(int j = 0; j < i; j++)
            if(picks[j] == t) continue retry;
          picks[i] = t;
          results[i] = flav[t];
          break;
        }
      }
      return results;
    }
    public static void main(String[] args) {
      for(int i = 0; i < 20; i++) {
        System.out.println(
          "flavorSet(" + i + ") = ");
        String[] fl = flavorSet(flav.length);
        for(int j = 0; j < fl.length; j++)
          System.out.println("\t" + fl[j]);
      }
    }
} ///:~
```

The method **flavorSet( )** creates an array of **String** called **results**. The
size of this array is **n**, determined by the argument you pass into the
method. Then it proceeds to choose flavors randomly from the array **flav**
and place them into **results**, which it finally returns. Returning an array
is just like returning any other object – it's a handle. It's not important
that the array was created within **flavorSet( )**, or that the array was
created anyplace else, for that matter. The garbage collector takes care of
cleaning up the array when you're done with it, and the array will
persist for as long as you need it.

As an aside, notice that when **flavorSet( )** chooses flavors randomly, it
ensures that a random choice hasn't been picked before. This is
performed in a seemingly infinite **while** loop that keeps making random
choices until it finds one that's not already in the **picks** array. (Of course,
a **String** comparison could also have been performed to see if the random
choice was already in the **results** array, but **String** comparisons are
inefficient.) If it's successful it adds the entry and **breaks** out to go find
the next one (**i** gets incremented). But if **t** is a number that's already in
picks, then a labeled **continue** is used to jump back two levels, which

forces a new **t** to be selected. It's particularly convincing to watch this happen with a debugger.

main( ) prints out 20 full sets of flavors, so you can see that **flavorSet( )** chooses the flavors in a random order each time. It's easiest to see this if you redirect the output into a file. And while you're looking at the file, remember, you're not really hungry. (You just *want* the ice cream, you don't *need* it.)

Collections

To summarize what we've seen so far, your first, most efficient choice to hold a group of objects should be an array, and you're forced into this choice if you want to hold a group of primitives. In the remainder of the chapter we'll look at the more general case, when you don't know at the time you're writing the program how many objects you're going to need, or if you need a more sophisticated way to store your objects. Java provides four types of *collection classes* to solve this problem: **Vector**, **BitSet**, **Stack**, and **Hashtable**. Although compared to other languages that provide collections this is a fairly meager supply, you can nonetheless solve a surprising number of problems using these tools.

Among their other characteristics – **Stack**, for example, implements a LIFO (last-in, first-out) sequence, and **Hashtable** is an *associative array* that lets you associate any object with any other object – the Java collection classes will automatically resize themselves. Thus, you can put in any number of objects and you don't need to worry about how big to make the collection while you're writing the program.

Disadvantage: unknown type

The "disadvantage" to using the Java collections is that you lose type information when you put an object into a collection. This happens because, when the collection was written, the programmer of that collection had no idea what specific type you wanted to put in the collection, and making the collection hold only your type would prevent it from being a general-purpose tool. So instead, the collection holds handles to objects of type **Object**, which is of course every object in Java, since it's the root of all the classes. (Of course, this doesn't include primitive types, since they aren't inherited from anything.) This is a great solution, except for these reasons:

1. Since the type information is thrown away when you put an object handle into a collection, *any* type of object can be put into your collection, even if you mean it to hold only, say, cats. Someone could just as easily put a dog into the collection.

2. Since the type information is lost, the only thing the collection knows it holds is a handle to an **Object**. You must perform a cast to the correct type before you use it.

On the up side, Java won't let you *misuse* the objects that you put into a collection. If you throw a dog into a collection of cats, then go through and try to treat everything in the collection as a cat, you'll get an exception when you get to the dog. In the same vein, if you try to cast the dog handle that you pull out of the cat collection into a cat, you'll get an exception at run-time.

Here's an example:

```java
//: CatsAndDogs.java
// Simple collection example (Vector)
import java.util.*;

class Cat {
  private int catNumber;
  Cat(int i) {
    catNumber = i;
  }
  void print() {
    System.out.println("Cat #" + catNumber);
  }
}

class Dog {
  private int dogNumber;
  Dog(int i) {
    dogNumber = i;
  }
  void print() {
    System.out.println("Dog #" + dogNumber);
  }
}

public class CatsAndDogs {
  public static void main(String[] args) {
    Vector cats = new Vector();
```

Thinking in Java

```
      for(int i = 0; i < 7; i++)
        cats.addElement(new Cat(i));
      // Not a problem to add a dog to cats:
      cats.addElement(new Dog(7));
      for(int i = 0; i < cats.size(); i++)
        ((Cat)cats.elementAt(i)).print();
      // Dog is detected only at run-time
    }
  } ///:~
```

You can see that using a **Vector** is straightforward: create one, put objects in using **addElement( )**, and later get them out with **elementAt( )**. (Note that **Vector** has a method **size( )** to let you know how many elements have been added so you don't inadvertently run off the end and cause an exception.)

The classes **Cat** and **Dog** are distinct – they have nothing in common except that they are **Object**s. (If you don't explicitly say what class you're inheriting from, you automatically inherit from **Object**.) The **Vector** class, which comes from **java.util**, holds **Object**s, so not only can you put **Cat** objects into this collection using the **Vector** method **addElement( )**, but you can also add **Dog** objects without complaint at either compile-time or run-time. When you go to fetch out what you think are **Cat** objects using the **Vector** method **elementAt( )**, you get back a handle to an **Object** that you must cast to a **Cat**. Then you need to surround the entire expression with parentheses to force the evaluation of the cast before calling the **print( )** method for **Cat**, otherwise you'll get a syntax error. Then, at run-time, when you try to cast the **Dog** object to a **Cat**, you'll get an exception.

This is more than just an annoyance. It's something that can create some difficult-to-find bugs. If one part (or several parts) of a program inserts objects into a collection, and you discover only in a separate part of the program through an exception that a bad object was placed in the collection, then you must find out where the bad insert occurred. You do this by code inspection, which is about the worst debugging tool you have. On the upside, it's convenient to start with some standardized collection classes for programming, despite the scarcity and awkwardness.

Sometimes it works right anyway

It turns out that in some cases things seem to work correctly without casting back to your original type. The first case is quite special: the **String** class has some extra help from the compiler to make it work smoothly. Whenever the compiler expects a **String** object and it hasn't got one, it will automatically call the **toString( )** method that's defined in **Object** and can be overridden by any Java class. This method produces the desired **String** object, which is then used wherever it was wanted.

Thus, all you need to do to make objects of your class print out is to override the **toString( )** method, as shown in the following example:

```
//: WorksAnyway.java
// In special cases, things just seem
// to work correctly.
import java.util.*;

class Mouse {
  private int mouseNumber;
  Mouse(int i) {
    mouseNumber = i;
  }
  // Magic method:
  public String toString() {
    return "This is Mouse #" + mouseNumber;
  }
  void print(String msg) {
    if(msg != null) System.out.println(msg);
    System.out.println(
      "Mouse number " + mouseNumber);
  }
}

class MouseTrap {
  static void caughtYa(Object m) {
    Mouse mouse = (Mouse)m; // Cast from Object
    mouse.print("Caught one!");
  }
}

public class WorksAnyway {
  public static void main(String[] args) {
    Vector mice = new Vector();
    for(int i = 0; i < 3; i++)
      mice.addElement(new Mouse(i));
    for(int i = 0; i < mice.size(); i++) {
      // No cast necessary, automatic call
      // to Object.toString():
      System.out.println(
```

```
          "Free mouse: " + mice.elementAt(i));
       MouseTrap.caughtYa(mice.elementAt(i));
    }
  }
} ///:~
```

You can see the redefinition of **toString( )** in **Mouse**. In the second **for**
loop in **main( )** you find the statement:

```
System.out.println("Free mouse: " +
mice.elementAt(i));
```

After the '**+**' sign the compiler expects to see a **String** object.
elementAt( ) produces an **Object**, so to get the desired **String** the
compiler implicitly calls **toString( )**. Unfortunately, you can work this
kind of magic only with **String**; it isn't available for any other type.

A second approach to hiding the cast has been placed inside **Mousetrap**.
The **caughtYa( )** method accepts not a **Mouse**, but an **Object,** which it
then casts to a **Mouse**. This is quite presumptuous, of course, since by
accepting an **Object** anything could be passed to the method. However, if
the cast is incorrect – if you passed the wrong type – you'll get an
exception at run-time. This is not as good as compile-time checking but
it's still robust. Note that in the use of this method:

```
MouseTrap.caughtYa(mice.elementAt(i));
```

no cast is necessary.

Making a type-conscious **Vector**

You might not want to give up on this issue just yet. A more ironclad
solution is to create a new class using the **Vector**, such that it will accept
only your type and produce only your type:

```
//: GopherVector.java
// A type-conscious Vector
import java.util.*;

class Gopher {
  private int gopherNumber;
  Gopher(int i) {
    gopherNumber = i;
  }
  void print(String msg) {
    if(msg != null) System.out.println(msg);
```

```
      System.out.println(
         "Gopher number " + gopherNumber);
    }
  }

  class GopherTrap {
    static void caughtYa(Gopher g) {
      g.print("Caught one!");
    }
  }

  class GopherVector {
    private Vector v = new Vector();
    public void addElement(Gopher m) {
      v.addElement(m);
    }
    public Gopher elementAt(int index) {
      return (Gopher)v.elementAt(index);
    }
    public int size() { return v.size(); }
    public static void main(String[] args) {
      GopherVector gophers = new GopherVector();
      for(int i = 0; i < 3; i++)
        gophers.addElement(new Gopher(i));
      for(int i = 0; i < gophers.size(); i++)
        GopherTrap.caughtYa(gophers.elementAt(i));
    }
  } ///:~
```

This is similar to the previous example, except that the new
GopherVector class has a **private** member of type **Vector** (inheriting
from **Vector** tends to be frustrating, for reasons you'll see later), and
methods just like **Vector**. However, it doesn't accept and produce generic
Objects, only **Gopher** objects.

Because a **GopherVector** will accept only a **Gopher**, if you were to say:

```
gophers.addElement(new Pigeon());
```

you would get an error message *at compile time*. This approach, while
more tedious from a coding standpoint, will tell you immediately if
you're using a type improperly.

Note that no cast is necessary when using **elementAt( )** – it's always a
Gopher.

Parameterized types

This kind of problem isn't isolated – there are numerous cases in which you need to create new types based on other types, and in which it is useful to have specific type information at compile-time. This is the concept of a *parameterized type*. In C++, this is directly supported by the language in *templates*. At one point, Java had reserved the keyword **generic** to someday support parameterized types, but it's uncertain if this will ever occur.

Enumerators (iterators)

In any collection class, you must have a way to put things in and a way to get things out. After all, that's the primary job of a collection – to hold things. In the **Vector**, **addElement( )** is the way that you insert objects, and **elementAt( )** is *one* way to get things out. **Vector** is quite flexible – you can select anything at any time, and select multiple elements at once using different indexes.

If you want to start thinking at a higher level, there's a drawback: you need to know the exact type of the collection in order to use it. This might not seem bad at first, but what if you start out using a **Vector**, and later on in your program you decide, for efficiency, that you want to change to a **List** (which is part of the Java 1.2 collections library)? Or you'd like to write a piece of code that doesn't know or care what type of collection it's working with.

The concept of an *iterator* can be used to achieve this next level of abstraction. This is an object whose job is to move through a sequence of objects and select each object in that sequence without the client programmer knowing or caring about the underlying structure of that sequence. In addition, an iterator is usually what's called a "light-weight" object; that is, one that's cheap to create. For that reason, you'll often find seemingly strange constraints for iterators; for example, some iterators can move in only one direction.

The Java **Enumeration**[2] is an example of an iterator with these kinds of constraints. There's not much you can do with one except:

---

[2] The term *iterator* is common in C++ and elsewhere in OOP, so it's difficult to know why the Java team used a strange name. The collections library in Java 1.2 fixes this as well as many other problems.

1. Ask a collection to hand you an **Enumeration** using a method called **elements( )**. This **Enumeration** will be ready to return the first element in the sequence on your first call to its **nextElement( )** method.

2. Get the next object in the sequence with **nextElement( )**.

3. See if there *are* any more objects in the sequence with **hasMoreElements( )**.

That's all. It's a simple implementation of an iterator, but still powerful. To see how it works, let's revisit the **CatsAndDogs.java** program from earlier in the chapter. In the original version, the method **elementAt( )** was used to select each element, but in the following modified version an enumeration is used:

```
//: CatsAndDogs2.java
// Simple collection with Enumeration
import java.util.*;

class Cat2 {
  private int catNumber;
  Cat2(int i) {
    catNumber = i;
  }
  void print() {
    System.out.println("Cat number " +catNumber);
  }
}

class Dog2 {
  private int dogNumber;
  Dog2(int i) {
    dogNumber = i;
  }
  void print() {
    System.out.println("Dog number " +dogNumber);
  }
}

public class CatsAndDogs2 {
  public static void main(String[] args) {
    Vector cats = new Vector();
    for(int i = 0; i < 7; i++)
      cats.addElement(new Cat2(i));
```

```
        // Not a problem to add a dog to cats:
        cats.addElement(new Dog2(7));
        Enumeration e = cats.elements();
        while(e.hasMoreElements())
           ((Cat2)e.nextElement()).print();
        // Dog is detected only at run-time
    }
} ///:~
```

You can see that the only change is in the last few lines. Instead of:

```
        for(int i = 0; i < cats.size(); i++)
           ((Cat)cats.elementAt(i)).print();
```

an **Enumeration** is used to step through the sequence:

```
    while(e.hasMoreElements())
           ((Cat2)e.nextElement()).print();
```

With the **Enumeration**, you don't need to worry about the number of elements in the collection. That's taken care of for you by **hasMoreElements( )** and **nextElement( )**.

As another example, consider the creation of a general-purpose printing method:

```
//: HamsterMaze.java
// Using an Enumeration
import java.util.*;

class Hamster {
  private int hamsterNumber;
  Hamster(int i) {
    hamsterNumber = i;
  }
  public String toString() {
    return "This is Hamster #" + hamsterNumber;
  }
}

class Printer {
  static void printAll(Enumeration e) {
    while(e.hasMoreElements())
      System.out.println(
        e.nextElement().toString());
  }
```

```
    }

public class HamsterMaze {
  public static void main(String[] args) {
    Vector v = new Vector();
    for(int i = 0; i < 3; i++)
      v.addElement(new Hamster(i));
    Printer.printAll(v.elements());
  }
} ///:~
```

Look closely at the printing method:

```
static void printAll(Enumeration e) {
  while(e.hasMoreElements())
    System.out.println(
      e.nextElement().toString());
}
```

Note that there's no information about the type of sequence. All you have is an **Enumeration**, and that's all you need to know about the sequence: that you can get the next object, and that you can know when you're at the end. This idea of taking a collection of objects and passing through it to perform an operation on each one is powerful and will be seen throughout this book.

This particular example is even more generic, since it uses the ubiquitous **toString( )** method (ubiquitous only because it's part of the **Object** class). An alternative way to call print (although probably slightly less efficient, if you could even notice the difference) is:

```
System.out.println("" + e.nextElement());
```

which uses the "automatic conversion to **String**" that's wired into Java. When the compiler sees a **String**, followed by a '**+**', it expects another **String** to follow and calls **toString( )** automatically. (In Java 1.1, the first **String** is unnecessary; any object will be converted to a **String**.) You can also perform a cast, which has the effect of calling **toString( )**:

```
System.out.println((String)e.nextElement());
```

In general, however, you'll want to do something more than call **Object** methods, so you'll run up against the type-casting issue again. You must assume you've gotten an **Enumeration** to a sequence of the particular type you're interested in, and cast the resulting objects to that type (getting a run-time exception if you're wrong).

Types of collections

The standard Java 1.0 and 1.1 library comes with a bare minimum set of collection classes, but they're probably enough to get by with for many of your programming projects. (As you'll see at the end of this chapter, Java 1.2 provides a radically redesigned and filled-out library of collections.)

Vector

The **Vector** is quite simple to use, as you've seen so far. Although most of the time you'll just use **addElement( )** to insert objects, **elementAt( )** to get them out one at a time, and **elements( )** to get an **Enumeration** to the sequence, there's also a set of other methods that can be useful. As usual with the Java libraries, we won't use or talk about them all here, but be sure to look them up in the electronic documentation to get a feel for what they can do.

Crashing Java

The Java standard collections contain a **toString( )** method so they can produce a **String** representation of themselves, including the objects they hold. Inside of **Vector**, for example, the **toString( )** steps through the elements of the **Vector** and calls **toString( )** for each one. Suppose you'd like to print out the address of your class. It seems to make sense to simply refer to **this** (in particular, C++ programmers are prone to this approach):

```
//: CrashJava.java
// One way to crash Java
import java.util.*;

public class CrashJava {
  public String toString() {
    return "CrashJava address: " + this + "\n";
  }
  public static void main(String[] args) {
    Vector v = new Vector();
    for(int i = 0; i < 10; i++)
      v.addElement(new CrashJava());
    System.out.println(v);
  }
} ///:~
```

It turns out that if you simply create a **CrashJava** object and print it out, you'll get an endless sequence of exceptions. However, if you place the **CrashJava** objects in a **Vector** and print out that **Vector** as shown here, it can't handle it and you don't even get an exception; Java just crashes. (But at least it didn't bring down my operating system.) This was tested with Java 1.1.

What's happening is automatic type conversion for **Strings**. When you say:

```
"CrashJava address: " + this
```

The compiler sees a **String** followed by a '**+**' and something that's not a **String**, so it tries to convert **this** to a **String**. It does this conversion by calling **toString( )**, which produces a recursive call. When this occurs inside a **Vector,** it appears that the stack overflows without the exception-handling mechanism getting a chance to respond.

If you really do want to print the address of the object in this case, the solution is to call the **Object toString( )** method, which does just that. So instead of saying **this**, you'd say **super.toString( )**. (This only works if you're directly inheriting from **Object** or if none of your parent classes have overridden the **toString( )** method).

BitSet

A **BitSet** is really a **Vector** of bits, and it is used if you want to efficiently store a lot of on–off information. It's efficient only from the standpoint of size; if you're looking for efficient access, it is slightly slower than using an array of some native type.

In addition, the minimum size of the **BitSet** is that of a long: 64 bits. This implies that if you're storing anything smaller, like 8 bits, a **BitSet** will be wasteful, so you're better off creating your own class to hold your flags.

In a normal **Vector**, the collection will expand as you add more elements. The **BitSet** does this as well – sort of. That is, sometimes it works and sometimes it doesn't, which makes it appear that the Java version 1.0 implementation of **BitSet** is just badly done. (It is fixed in Java 1.1.) The following example shows how the **BitSet** works and demonstrates the version 1.0 bug:

```
//: Bits.java
// Demonstration of BitSet
```

```
import java.util.*;

public class Bits {
  public static void main(String[] args) {
    Random rand = new Random();
    // Take the LSB of nextInt():
    byte bt = (byte)rand.nextInt();
    BitSet bb = new BitSet();
    for(int i = 7, i >=0, i  )
      if(((1 << i) &  bt) != 0)
        bb.set(i);
      else
        bb.clear(i);
    System.out.println("byte value: " + bt);
    printBitSet(bb);

    short st = (short)rand.nextInt();
    BitSet bs = new BitSet();
    for(int i = 15; i >=0; i--)
      if(((1 << i) &  st) != 0)
        bs.set(i);
      else
        bs.clear(i);
    System.out.println("short value: " + st);
    printBitSet(bs);

    int it = rand.nextInt();
    BitSet bi = new BitSet();
    for(int i = 31; i >=0; i--)
      if(((1 << i) &  it) != 0)
        bi.set(i);
      else
        bi.clear(i);
    System.out.println("int value: " + it);
    printBitSet(bi);

    // Test bitsets >= 64 bits:
    BitSet b127 = new BitSet();
    b127.set(127);
    System.out.println("set bit 127: " + b127);
    BitSet b255 = new BitSet(65);
    b255.set(255);
    System.out.println("set bit 255: " + b255);
    BitSet b1023 = new BitSet(512);
```

```
// Without the following, an exception is thrown
// in the Java 1.0 implementation of BitSet:
//      b1023.set(1023);
    b1023.set(1024);
    System.out.println("set bit 1023: " + b1023);
  }
  static void printBitSet(BitSet b) {
    System.out.println("bits: " + b);
    String bbits = new String();
    for(int j = 0; j < b.size() ; j++)
      bbits += (b.get(j) ? "1" : "0");
    System.out.println("bit pattern: " + bbits);
  }
} ///:~
```

The random number generator is used to create a random **byte**, **short**, and **int**, and each one is transformed into a corresponding bit pattern in a **BitSet**. This works fine because a **BitSet** is 64 bits, so none of these cause it to increase in size. But in Java 1.0, when the **BitSet** is greater than 64 bits, some strange behavior occurs. If you set a bit that's just one greater than the **BitSet**'s currently-allocated storage, it will expand nicely. But if you try to set bits at higher locations than that without first just touching the boundary, you'll get an exception, since the **BitSet** won't expand properly in Java 1.0. The example shows a **BitSet** of 512 bits being created. The constructor allocates storage for twice that number of bits. Then if you try to set bit 1024 or greater without first setting bit 1023, you'll throw an exception in Java 1.0. Fortunately, this is fixed in Java 1.1, but avoid using the **BitSet** if you write code for Java 1.0.

Stack

A **Stack** is sometimes referred to as a "last-in, first-out" (LIFO) collection. That is, whatever you "push" on the **Stack** last is the first item you can "pop" out. Like all of the other collections in Java, what you push and pop are **Object**s, so you must cast what you pop.

What's rather odd is that instead of using a **Vector** as a building block to create a **Stack**, **Stack** is inherited from **Vector**. So it has all of the characteristics and behaviors of a **Vector** *plus* some extra **Stack** behaviors. It's difficult to know whether the designers explicitly decided that this was an especially useful way to do things, or whether it was just a naïve design.

Here's a simple demonstration of **Stack** that reads each line from an array and pushes it as a **String**:

```
//: Stacks.java
// Demonstration of Stack Class
import java.util.*;

public class Stacks {
  static String[] months = {
    "January", "February", "March", "April",
    "May", "June", "July", "August", "September",
    "October", "November", "December" };
  public static void main(String[] args) {
    Stack stk = new Stack();
    for(int i = 0; i < months.length; i++)
      stk.push(months[i] + " ");
    System.out.println("stk = " + stk);
    // Treating a stack as a Vector:
    stk.addElement("The last line");
    System.out.println(
      "element 5 = " + stk.elementAt(5));
    System.out.println("popping elements:");
    while(!stk.empty())
      System.out.println(stk.pop());
  }
} ///:~
```

Each line in the **months** array is inserted into the **Stack** with **push( )**, and later fetched from the top of the stack with a **pop( )**. To make a point, **Vector** operations are also performed on the **Stack** object. This is possible because, by virtue of inheritance, a **Stack** *is* a **Vector**. Thus, all operations that can be performed on a **Vector** can also be performed on a **Stack**, such as **elementAt( )**.

Hashtable

A **Vector** allows you to select from a sequence of objects using a number, so in a sense it associates numbers to objects. But what if you'd like to select from a sequence of objects using some other criterion? A **Stack** is an example: its selection criterion is "the last thing pushed on the stack." A powerful twist on this idea of "selecting from a sequence" is alternately termed a *map*, a *dictionary*, or an *associative array*. Conceptually, it seems like a vector, but instead of looking up objects using a number, you look them up using *another object*! This is often a key process in a program.

The concept shows up in Java as the **abstract** class **Dictionary**. The interface for this class is straightforward: **size( )** tells you how many elements are within, **isEmpty( )** is **true** if there are no elements, **put(Object key, Object value)** adds a value (the thing you want), and associates it with a key (the thing you look it up with). **get(Object key)** produces the value given the corresponding key, and **remove(Object key)** removes the key-value pair from the list. There are enumerations: **keys( )** produces an **Enumeration** of the keys, and **elements( )** produces an **Enumeration** of all the values. That's all there is to a **Dictionary**.

A **Dictionary** isn't terribly difficult to implement. Here's a simple approach, which uses two **Vectors**, one for keys and one for values:

```
//: AssocArray.java
// Simple version of a Dictionary
import java.util.*;

public class AssocArray extends Dictionary {
  private Vector keys = new Vector();
  private Vector values = new Vector();
  public int size() { return keys.size(); }
  public boolean isEmpty() {
    return keys.isEmpty();
  }
  public Object put(Object key, Object value) {
    keys.addElement(key);
    values.addElement(value);
    return key;
  }
  public Object get(Object key) {
    int index = keys.indexOf(key);
    // indexOf() Returns -1 if key not found:
    if(index == -1) return null;
    return values.elementAt(index);
  }
  public Object remove(Object key) {
    int index = keys.indexOf(key);
    if(index == -1) return null;
    keys.removeElementAt(index);
    Object returnval = values.elementAt(index);
    values.removeElementAt(index);
    return returnval;
  }
  public Enumeration keys() {
    return keys.elements();
```

```
      }
      public Enumeration elements() {
        return values.elements();
      }
      // Test it:
      public static void main(String[] args) {
        AssocArray aa = new AssocArray();
        for(char c = 'a'; c <= 'z'; c++)
          aa.put(String.valueOf(c),
                 String.valueOf(c)
                 .toUpperCase());
        char[] ca = { 'a', 'e', 'i', 'o', 'u' };
        for(int i = 0; i < ca.length; i++)
          System.out.println("Uppercase: " +
                 aa.get(String.valueOf(ca[i])));
      }
    } ///:~
```

The first thing you see in the definition of **AssocArray** is that it **extends Dictionary**. This means that **AssocArray** *is a type of* **Dictionary**, so you can make the same requests of it that you can a **Dictionary**. If you make your own **Dictionary**, as is done here, all you need to do is fill in all the methods that are in **Dictionary**. (And you *must* override all the methods because all of them – with the exception of the constructor – are abstract.)

The **Vector**s **keys** and **values** are linked by a common index number. That is, if you call **put( )** with a key of "roof" and a value of "blue" (assuming you're associating the various parts of a house with the colors they are to be painted) and there are already 100 elements in the **AssocArray**, then "roof" will be the 101 element of **keys** and "blue" will be the 101 element of **values**. And if you look at **get( )**, when you pass "roof" in as the key, it produces the index number with **keys.indexOf( )**, and then uses that index number to produce the value in the associated **values** vector.

The test in **main( )** is simple; it's just a map of lowercase characters to uppercase characters, which could obviously be done in a number of more efficient ways. But it shows that **AssocArray** is functional.

The standard Java library contains only one embodiment of a **Dictionary**, called **Hashtable**.[3] Java's **Hashtable** has the same basic interface as **AssocArray** (since they both inherit **Dictionary**), but it differs in one distinct way: efficiency. If you look at what must be done for a **get( )**, it seems pretty slow to search through a **Vector** for the key. This is where **Hashtable** speeds things up. Instead of the tedious linear search for the key, it uses a special value called a *hash code*. The hash code is a way to take some information in the object in question and turn it into a "relatively unique" **int** for that object. All objects have a hash code, and **hashCode( )** is a method in the root class **Object**. A **Hashtable** takes the **hashCode( )** of the object and uses it to quickly hunt for the key. This results in a dramatic performance improvement.[4] The *way* that a **Hashtable** works is beyond the scope of this book[5] – all you need to know is that **Hashtable** is a fast **Dictionary**, and that a **Dictionary** is a useful tool.

As an example of the use of a **Hashtable**, consider a program to check the randomness of Java's **Math.random( )** method. Ideally, it would produce a perfect distribution of random numbers, but to test this you need to generate a bunch of random numbers and count the ones that fall in the various ranges. A **Hashtable** is perfect for this, since it associates objects with objects (in this case, the values produced by **Math.random( )** with the number of times those values appear):

```
//: Statistics.java
// Simple demonstration of Hashtable
```

[3] If you plan to use RMI (described in Chapter 15), you should be aware that there's a problem when putting remote objects into a **Hashtable**. (See *Core Java*, by Cornell & Horstmann, Prentice-Hall 1997).

[4] If these speedups still don't meet your performance needs, you can further accelerate table lookup by writing your own hash table routine. This avoids delays due to casting to and from **Object**s and synchronization built into the Java Class Library hash table routine. To reach even higher levels of performance, speed enthusiasts can use Donald Knuth's *The Art of Computer Programming, Volume 3: Sorting and Searching, Second Edition* to replace overflow bucket lists with arrays that have two additional benefits: they can be optimized for disk storage characteristics and they can save most of the time of creating and garbage collecting individual records.

[5] The best reference I know of is *Practical Algorithms for Programmers*, by Andrew Binstock and John Rex, Addison-Wesley 1995.

```
import java.util.*;

class Counter {
  int i = 1;
  public String toString() {
    return Integer.toString(i);
  }
}

class Statistics {
  public static void main(String[] args) {
    Hashtable ht = new Hashtable();
    for(int i = 0; i < 10000; i++) {
      // Produce a number between 0 and 20:
      Integer r =
        new Integer((int)(Math.random() * 20));
      if(ht.containsKey(r))
        ((Counter)ht.get(r)).i++;
      else
        ht.put(r, new Counter());
    }
    System.out.println(ht);
  }
} ///:~
```

In **main( )**, each time a random number is generated it is wrapped inside an **Integer** object so that handle can be used with the **Hashtable**. (You can't use a primitive with a collection, only an object handle.) The **containsKey( )** method checks to see if this key is already in the collection. (That is, has the number been found already?) If so, the **get( )** methods gets the associated value for the key, which in this case is a **Counter** object. The value **i** inside the counter is then incremented to indicate that one more of this particular random number has been found.

If the key has not been found yet, the method **put( )** will place a new key-value pair into the **Hashtable**. Since **Counter** automatically initializes its variable **i** to one when it's created, it indicates the first occurrence of this particular random number.

To display the **Hashtable**, it is simply printed out. The **Hashtable toString( )** method moves through all the key-value pairs and calls the **toString( )** for each one. The **Integer toString( )** is pre-defined, and you can see the **toString( )** for **Counter**. The output from one run (with some line breaks added) is:

```
{19=526, 18=533, 17=460, 16=513, 15=521, 14=495,
 13=512, 12=483, 11=488, 10=487, 9=514, 8=523,
 7=497, 6=487, 5=480, 4=489, 3=509, 2=503, 1=475,
 0=505}
```

You might wonder at the necessity of the class **Counter**, which seems like it doesn't even have the functionality of the wrapper class **Integer**. Why not use **int** or **Integer**? Well, you can't use an **int** because all of the collections can hold only **Object** handles. After seeing collections the wrapper classes might begin to make a little more sense to you, since you can't put any of the primitive types in collections. However, the only thing you *can* do with the Java wrappers is to initialize them to a particular value and read that value. That is, there's no way to change a value once a wrapper object has been created. This makes the **Integer** wrapper immediately useless to solve our problem, so we're forced to create a new class that does satisfy the need.

Creating "key" classes

In the previous example, a standard library class (**Integer**) was used as a key for the **Hashtable**. It worked fine as a key, because it has all the necessary wiring to make it work correctly as a key. But a common pitfall occurs when using **Hashtables** when you create your own classes to be used as keys. For example, consider a weather predicting system that matches **Groundhog** objects to **Prediction** objects. It seems fairly straightforward: you create the two classes and use **Groundhog** as the key and **Prediction** as the value:

```
//: SpringDetector.java
// Looks plausible, but doesn't work right.
import java.util.*;

class Groundhog {
  int ghNumber;
  Groundhog(int n) { ghNumber = n; }
}

class Prediction {
  boolean shadow = Math.random() > 0.5;
  public String toString() {
    if(shadow)
      return "Six more weeks of Winter!";
    else
      return "Early Spring!";
  }
```

```
    }

public class SpringDetector {
  public static void main(String[] args) {
    Hashtable ht = new Hashtable();
    for(int i = 0; i < 10; i++)
      ht.put(new Groundhog(i), new Prediction());
    System.out.println("ht = " + ht + "\n");
    System.out.println(
      "Looking up prediction for groundhog #3:");
    Groundhog gh = new Groundhog(3);
    if(ht.containsKey(gh))
      System.out.println((Prediction)ht.get(gh));
  }
} ///:~
```

Each **Groundhog** is given an identity number, so you can look up a
Prediction in the **Hashtable** by saying "Give me the **Prediction**
associated with **Groundhog** number 3." The **Prediction** class contains a
boolean that is initialized using **Math.random( )**, and a **toString( )** that
interprets the result for you. In **main( )**, a **Hashtable** is filled with
Groundhogs and their associated **Prediction**s. The **Hashtable** is printed
so you can see that it has been filled. Then a **Groundhog** with an identity
number of 3 is used to look up the prediction for **Groundhog #3**.

It seems simple enough, but it doesn't work. The problem is that
Groundhog is inherited from the common root class **Object** (which is
what happens if you don't specify a base class, thus all classes are
ultimately inherited from **Object**). It is **Object**'s **hashCode( )** method that
is used to generate the hash code for each object, and by default it just
uses the address of its object. Thus, the first instance of **Groundhog(3)**
does *not* produce a hash code equal to the hash code for the second
instance of **Groundhog(3)** that we tried to use as a lookup.

You might think that all you need to do is write an appropriate override
for **hashCode( )**. But it still won't work until you've done one more
thing: override the **equals( )** that is also part of **Object**. This method is
used by the **Hashtable** when trying to determine if your key is equal to
any of the keys in the table. Again, the default **Object.equals( )** simply
compares object addresses, so one **Groundhog(3)** is not equal to another
Groundhog(3).

Thus, to use your own classes as keys in a **Hashtable**, you must override
both **hashCode( )** and **equals( )**, as shown in the following solution to
the problem above:

```
//: SpringDetector2.java
// If you create a class that's used as a key in
// a Hashtable, you must override hashCode()
// and equals().
import java.util.*;

class Groundhog2 {
  int ghNumber;
  Groundhog2(int n) { ghNumber = n; }
  public int hashCode() { return ghNumber; }
  public boolean equals(Object o) {
    if ((o != null) && (o instanceof Groundhog2))
      return
        ghNumber == ((Groundhog2)o).ghNumber;
    else return false;
  }
}

public class SpringDetector2 {
  public static void main(String[] args) {
    Hashtable ht = new Hashtable();
    for(int i = 0; i < 10; i++)
      ht.put(new Groundhog2(i),new Prediction());
    System.out.println("ht = " + ht + "\n");
    System.out.println(
      "Looking up prediction for groundhog #3:");
    Groundhog2 gh = new Groundhog2(3);
    if(ht.containsKey(gh))
      System.out.println((Prediction)ht.get(gh));
  }
} ///:~
```

Note that this uses the **Prediction** class from the previous example, so
SpringDetector.java must be compiled first or you'll get a compile-time
error when you try to compile **SpringDetector2.java**.

Groundhog2.hashCode( ) returns the ground hog number as an
identifier. (In this example, the programmer is responsible for ensuring
that no two ground hogs exist with the same ID number.) The
hashCode( ) is not required to return a unique identifier, but the
equals( ) method must be able to strictly determine whether two objects
are equivalent.

The **equals( )** method does two sanity checks: to see if the object is **null**,
and if not, whether it is an instance of **Groundhog2** (using the

instanceof keyword, which is fully explained in Chapter 11). It should be a **Groundhog2** to even continue executing **equals( )**. The comparison, as you can see, is based on the actual **ghNumber**s. This time, when you run the program, you'll see it produces the correct output. (Many of the Java library classes override the **hashcode( )** and **equals( )** methods to be based upon their contents.)

Properties: a type of **Hashtable**

In the first example in this book, a type of **Hashtable** was used called **Properties**. In that example, the lines:

```
Properties p = System.getProperties();
p.list(System.out);
```

called the **static** method **getProperties( )** to get a special **Properties** object that described the system characteristics. The method **list( )** is a method of **Properties** that sends the contents to any stream output that you choose. There's also a **save( )** method to allow you to write your property list to a file in a way that it can be retrieved later with the **load( )** method.

Although the **Properties** class is inherited from **Hashtable**, it also *contains* a second **Hashtable** that acts to hold the list of "default" properties. So if a property isn't found in the primary list, the defaults will be searched.

The **Properties** class is also available for use in your programs (an example is **ClassScanner.java** in Chapter 17). You can find more complete details in the Java library documentation.

Enumerators revisited

We can now demonstrate the true power of the **Enumeration**: the ability to separate the operation of traversing a sequence from the underlying structure of that sequence. In the following example, the class **PrintData** uses an **Enumeration** to move through a sequence and call the **toString( )** method for every object. Two different types of collections are created, a **Vector** and a **Hashtable**, and they are each filled with, respectively, **Mouse** and **Hamster** objects. (These classes are defined earlier in the chapter; notice you must have compiled **HamsterMaze.java** and **WorksAnyway.java** for the following program to compile.) Because an **Enumeration** hides the structure of the underlying collection, **PrintData** doesn't know or care what kind of collection the **Enumeration** comes from:

```
//: Enumerators2.java
// Revisiting Enumerations
import java.util.*;

class PrintData {
  static void print(Enumeration e) {
    while(e.hasMoreElements())
      System.out.println(
        e.nextElement().toString());
  }
}

class Enumerators2 {
  public static void main(String[] args) {
    Vector v = new Vector();
    for(int i = 0; i < 5; i++)
      v.addElement(new Mouse(i));

    Hashtable h = new Hashtable();
    for(int i = 0; i < 5; i++)
      h.put(new Integer(i), new Hamster(i));

    System.out.println("Vector");
    PrintData.print(v.elements());
    System.out.println("Hashtable");
    PrintData.print(h.elements());
  }
} ///:~
```

Note that **PrintData.print( )** takes advantage of the fact that the objects in these collections are of class **Object** so it can call **toString( )**. It's more likely that in your problem, you must make the assumption that your **Enumeration** is walking through a collection of some specific type. For example, you might assume that everything in the collection is a **Shape** with a **draw( )** method. Then you must downcast from the **Object** that **Enumeration.nextElement()** returns to produce a **Shape**.

Sorting

One of the things missing in the Java 1.0 and 1.1 libraries is algorithmic operations, even simple sorting. So it makes sense to create a **Vector** that sorts itself using the classic Quicksort.

A problem with writing generic sorting code is that sorting must perform comparisons based on the actual type of the object. Of course, one approach is to write a different sorting method for every different type, but you should be able to recognize that this does not produce code that is easily re-used for new types.

A primary goal of programming design is to "separate things that change from things that stay the same," and here, the code that stays the same is the general sort algorithm, but the thing that changes from one use to the next is the way objects are compared. So instead of hard-wiring the comparison code into many different sort routines, the technique of the *callback* will be used. With a callback, the part of the code that varies from case to case is encapsulated inside its own class, and the part of the code that's always the same will call back to the code that changes. That way you can make different objects to express different ways of comparison and feed them to the same sorting code.

The following **interface** describes how to compare two objects, and thus encapsulates "the things that change" for this particular problem:

```
//: Compare.java
// Interface for sorting callback:
package c08;

interface Compare {
  boolean lessThan(Object lhs, Object rhs);
  boolean lessThanOrEqual(Object lhs, Object rhs);
} ///:~
```

For both methods, the **lhs** represents the "left hand" object and the **rhs** represents the "right hand" object in the comparison.

A subclass of **Vector** can be created that implements the Quicksort using **Compare**. The algorithm, which is known for its speed, will not be explained here. For details, see *Practical Algorithms for Programmers*, by Binstock & Rex, Addison-Wesley 1995.

```
//: SortVector.java
// A generic sorting vector
package c08;
import java.util.*;

public class SortVector extends Vector {
  private Compare compare; // To hold the callback
  public SortVector(Compare comp) {
    compare = comp;
```

```
    }
    public void sort() {
      quickSort(0, size() - 1);
    }
    private void quickSort(int left, int right) {
      if(right > left) {
        Object o1 = elementAt(right);
        int i = left - 1;
        int j = right;
        while(true) {
          while(compare.lessThan(
                elementAt(++i), o1))
            ;
          while(j > 0)
            if(compare.lessThanOrEqual(
                elementAt(--j), o1))
              break; // out of while
          if(i >= j) break;
          swap(i, j);
        }
        swap(i , right);
        quickSort(left, i-1);
        quickSort(i+1, right);
      }
    }
    private void swap(int loc1, int loc2) {
      Object tmp = elementAt(loc1);
      setElementAt(elementAt(loc2), loc1);
      setElementAt(tmp, loc2);
    }
} ///:~
```

You can now see the reason for the term "callback," since the
quickSort( ) method "calls back" to the methods in **Compare**. You can
also see how this technique has produced generic, reusable code.

To use the **SortVector**, you must create a class that implements **Compare**
for the kind of objects that you're sorting. This is a place where an inner
class is not essential, but it can make sense for code organization. Here's
an example for **String** objects:

```
//: StringSortTest.java
// Testing the generic sorting Vector
package c08;
import java.util.*;
```

```
public class StringSortTest {
  static class StringCompare implements Compare {
    public boolean lessThan(Object l, Object r) {
      return ((String)l).toLowerCase().compareTo(
        ((String)r).toLowerCase()) < 0;
    }
    public boolean
    lessThanOrEqual(Object l, Object r) {
      return ((String)l).toLowerCase().compareTo(
        ((String)r).toLowerCase()) <= 0;
    }
  }
  public static void main(String[] args) {
    SortVector sv =
      new SortVector(new StringCompare());
    sv.addElement("d");
    sv.addElement("A");
    sv.addElement("C");
    sv.addElement("c");
    sv.addElement("b");
    sv.addElement("B");
    sv.addElement("D");
    sv.addElement("a");
    sv.sort();
    Enumeration e = sv.elements();
    while(e.hasMoreElements())
      System.out.println(e.nextElement());
  }
} ///:~
```

The inner class is **static** because it does not need a link to an outer class in order for it to function.

You can see how, once the framework is set up, it's easy to reuse a design like this – you simply write the class that encapsulates "the things that change" and hand an object to the **SortVector**.

The comparison forces the strings to lower case, so that the capital **A**'s end up next to the small **a**'s and not in some entirely different place. This example shows, however, a slight deficiency in this approach, since the test code above puts the uppercase and lowercase single letters of the same letter in the order that they appear: A a b B c C d D. This is not usually much of a problem, because you're usually working with longer strings and in that situation the effect doesn't show up. (The Java 1.2 collections provide sorting functionality that solves this problem.)

Inheritance (**extends**) is used here to create a new type of **Vector** – that is, **SortVector** *is a* **Vector** with some added functionality. The use of inheritance here is powerful but it presents problems. It turns out that some methods are **final** (described in Chapter 7), so you cannot override them. If you want to create a sorted **Vector** that accepts and produces only **String** objects you run into a wall, since **addElement( )** and **elementAt( )** are **final**, and these are precisely the methods you'd need to override so they accept and produce only **String** objects. No luck there.

On the other hand, consider composition: the placing of an object *inside* a new class. Rather than rewrite the above code to accomplish this, we can simply use a **SortVector** inside the new class. In this case, the inner class to implement the interface **Compare** will be created anonymously:

```
//: StrSortVector.java
// Automatically sorted Vector that
// accepts and produces only Strings
package c08;
import java.util.*;

public class StrSortVector {
  private SortVector v = new SortVector(
    // Anonymous inner class:
    new Compare() {
      public boolean
      lessThan(Object l, Object r) {
        return
          ((String)l).toLowerCase().compareTo(
          ((String)r).toLowerCase()) < 0;
      }
      public boolean
      lessThanOrEqual(Object l, Object r) {
        return
          ((String)l).toLowerCase().compareTo(
          ((String)r).toLowerCase()) <= 0;
      }
    }
  );
  private boolean sorted = false;
  public void addElement(String s) {
    v.addElement(s);
    sorted = false;
```

```
      }
      public String elementAt(int index) {
        if(!sorted) {
          v.sort();
          sorted = true;
        }
        return (String)v.elementAt(index);
      }
      public Enumeration elements() {
        if(!sorted) {
          v.sort();
          sorted = true;
        }
        return v.elements();
      }
      // Test it:
      public static void main(String[] args) {
        StrSortVector sv = new StrSortVector();
        sv.addElement("d");
        sv.addElement("A");
        sv.addElement("C");
        sv.addElement("c");
        sv.addElement("b");
        sv.addElement("B");
        sv.addElement("D");
        sv.addElement("a");
        Enumeration e = sv.elements();
        while(e.hasMoreElements())
          System.out.println(e.nextElement());
      }
    } ///:~
```

This quickly reuses the code from **SortVector** to create the desired
functionality. However, not all of the **public** methods from **SortVector**
and **Vector** appear in **StrSortVector**. When reusing code this way, you
can make a definition in the new class for each one in the contained class,
or you can start with just a few and periodically go back and add more
when you need them. Eventually the new class design will settle down.

The advantage to this approach is that it will take only **String** objects
and produce only **String** objects, and the checking happens at compile
time instead of run time. Of course, that's only true for **addElement( )**
and **elementAt( )**; **elements( )** still produces an **Enumeration** that is
untyped at compile time. Type checking for the **Enumeration** and in
StrSortVector still happens, of course, it just happens at run-time by

throwing exceptions if you do something wrong. It's a trade-off: do you find out about something *for sure* at compile time or *probably* at run-time? (That is, "probably not while you're testing the code" and "probably when the program user tries something you didn't test for.") Given the choices and the hassle, it's easier to use inheritance and just grit your teeth while casting – again, if parameterized types are ever added to Java, they will solve this problem.

You can see there's a flag called **sorted** in this class. You could sort the vector every time **addElement( )** is called, and constantly keep it in a sorted state. But usually people add a lot of elements to a **Vector** before beginning to read it. So sorting after every **addElement( )** would be less efficient than waiting until someone wants to read the vector and then sorting it, which is what is done here. The technique of delaying a process until it is absolutely necessary is called *lazy evaluation*. (There is an analogous technique called *lazy initialization* which waits until a field value is necessary before initializing it.)

The generic collection library

You've seen in this chapter that the standard Java library has some fairly useful collections, but far from a complete set. In addition, algorithms like sorting are not supported at all. One of the strengths of C++ is its libraries, in particular the *Standard Template Library* (STL) that provides a fairly full set of collections as well as many algorithms like sorting and searching that work with those collections. Based on this model, the ObjectSpace company was inspired to create the *Generic Collection Library for Java* (formerly called the *Java Generic Library*, but the abbreviation JGL is still used – the old name infringed on Sun's copyright), which follows the design of the STL as much as possible (given the differences between the two languages). The JGL seems to fulfill many, if not all, of the needs for a collection library, or as far as one could go in this direction without C++'s template mechanism. The JGL includes linked lists, sets, queues, maps, stacks, sequences, and iterators that are far more functional than **Enumeration**, as well as a full set of algorithms such as searching and sorting. ObjectSpace also made, in some cases, more intelligent design decisions than the Sun library designers. For example, the methods in the JGL collections are *not* final so it's easy to inherit and override those methods.

The JGL has been included in some vendors' Java distributions and ObjectSpace has made the JGL freely available for all uses, including commercial use, at *http://www.ObjectSpace.com*. The online documentation that comes in the JGL package is quite good and should be adequate to get you started.

The new collections

To me, collection classes are one of the most powerful tools for raw programming. You might have gathered that I'm somewhat disappointed in the collections provided in Java through version 1.1. As a result, it's a tremendous pleasure to see that collections were given proper attention in Java 1.2, and thoroughly redesigned (by Joshua Bloch at Sun). I consider the new collections to be one of the two major features in Java 1.2 (the other is the Swing library, covered in Chapter 13) because they significantly increase your programming muscle and help bring Java in line with more mature programming systems.

Some of the redesign makes things tighter and more sensible. For example, many names are shorter, cleaner, and easier to understand, as well as to type. Some names are changed to conform to accepted terminology: a particular favorite of mine is "iterator" instead of "enumeration."

The redesign also fills out the functionality of the collections library. You can now have the behavior of linked lists, queues, and dequeues (double-ended queues, pronounced "decks").

The design of a collections library is difficult (true of most library design problems). In C++, the STL covered the bases with many different classes. This was better than what was available prior to the STL (nothing), but it didn't translate well into Java. The result was a rather confusing morass of classes. On the other extreme, I've seen a collections library that consists of a single class, "collection," which acts like a **Vector** and a **Hashtable** at the same time. The designers of the new collections library wanted to strike a balance: the full functionality that you expect from a mature collections library, but easier to learn and use than the STL and other similar collections libraries. The result can seem a bit odd in places. Unlike some of the decisions made in the early Java libraries, these oddities were not accidents, but carefully considered decisions based on tradeoffs in complexity. It might take you a little while to get comfortable with some aspects of the library, but I think you'll find yourself rapidly acquiring and using these new tools.

The new collections library takes the issue of "holding your objects" and divides it into two distinct concepts:

---

1. **Collection**: a group of individual elements, often with some rule applied to them. A **List** must hold the elements in a particular sequence, and a **Set** cannot have any duplicate elements. (A *bag*, which is not implemented in the new collections library since **List**s provide you with that functionality, has no such rules.)

2. **Map**: a group of key-value object pairs (what you've seen up until now as a **Hashtable**). At first glance, this might seem like it ought to be a **Collection** of pairs, but when you try to implement it that way the design gets awkward, so it's clearer to make it a separate concept. On the other hand, it's convenient to look at portions of a **Map** by creating a **Collection** to represent that portion. Thus, a **Map** can return a **Set** of its keys, a **List** of its values, or a **List** of its pairs. **Map**s, like arrays, can easily be expanded to multiple dimensions without adding new concepts: you simply make a **Map** whose values are **Map**s (and the values of *those* **Map**s can be **Map**s, etc.).

Collections and **Map**s may be implemented in many different ways, according to your programming needs. It's helpful to look at a diagram of the new collections:

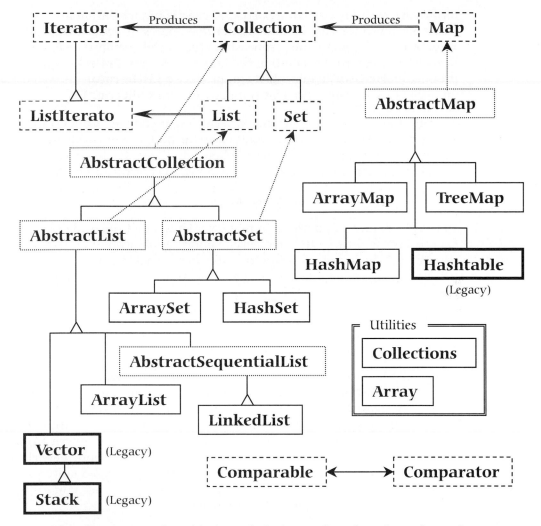

This diagram can be a bit overwhelming at first, but throughout the rest of this chapter you'll see that there are really only three collection components: **Map**, **List**, and **Set**, and only two or three implementations of each one[6] (with, typically, a preferred version). When you see this, the new collections should not seem so daunting.

The dashed boxes represent **interface**s, the dotted boxes represent **abstract** classes, and the solid boxes are regular (concrete) classes. The

---

[6] This chapter was written while Java 1.2 was still in beta, so the diagram does not show the **TreeSet** class that was added later.

---

dashed arrows indicate that a particular class is implementing an **interface** (or in the case of an **abstract** class, partially implementing that **interface**). The double-line arrows show that a class can produce objects of the class the arrow is pointing to. For example, any **Collection** can produce an **Iterator**, while a **List** can produce a **ListIterator** (as well as an ordinary **Iterator**, since **List** is inherited from **Collection**).

The interfaces that are concerned with holding objects are **Collection**, **List**, **Set**, and **Map**. Typically, you'll write the bulk of your code to talk to these interfaces, and the only place where you'll specify the precise type you're using is at the point of creation. So you can create a **List** like this:

```
List x = new LinkedList();
```

Of course, you can also decide to make **x** a **LinkedList** (instead of a generic **List**) and carry the precise type information around with **x**. The beauty (and the intent) of using the **interface** is that if you decide you want to change your implementation, all you need to do is change it at the point of creation, like this:

```
List x = new ArrayList();
```

The rest of your code can remain untouched.

In the class hierarchy, you can see a number of classes whose names begin with "**Abstract**," and these can seem a bit confusing at first. They are simply tools that partially implement a particular interface. If you were making your own **Set**, for example, you wouldn't start with the **Set** interface and implement all the methods, instead you'd inherit from **AbstractSet** and do the minimal necessary work to make your new class. However, the new collections library contains enough functionality to satisfy your needs virtually all the time. So for our purposes, you can ignore any class that begins with "**Abstract**."

Therefore, when you look at the diagram, you're really concerned with only those **interface**s at the top of the diagram and the concrete classes (those with solid boxes around them). You'll typically make an object of a concrete class, upcast it to the corresponding **interface**, and then use the **interface** throughout the rest of your code. Here's a simple example, which fills a **Collection** with **String** objects and then prints each element in the **Collection**:

```
//: SimpleCollection.java
// A simple example using the new Collections
package c08.newcollections;
import java.util.*;
```

```
public class SimpleCollection {
  public static void main(String[] args) {
    Collection c = new ArrayList();
    for(int i = 0; i < 10; i++)
      c.add(Integer.toString(i));
    Iterator it = c.iterator();
    while(it.hasNext())
      System.out.println(it.next());
  }
} ///:~
```

All the code examples for the new collections libraries will be placed in the subdirectory **newcollections**, so you'll be reminded that these work only with Java 1.2. As a result, you must invoke the program by saying:

```
java c08.newcollections.SimpleCollection
```

with a similar syntax for the rest of the programs in the package.

You can see that the new collections are part of the **java.util** library, so you don't need to add any extra **import** statements to use them.

The first line in **main( )** creates an **ArrayList** object and then upcasts it to a **Collection**. Since this example uses only the **Collection** methods, any object of a class inherited from **Collection** would work, but **ArrayList** is the typical workhorse **Collection** and takes the place of **Vector**.

The **add( )** method, as its name suggests, puts a new element in the **Collection**. However, the documentation carefully states that **add( )** "ensures that this Collection contains the specified element." This is to allow for the meaning of **Set**, which adds the element only if it isn't already there. With an **ArrayList**, or any sort of **List**, **add( )** always means "put it in."

All **Collection**s can produce an **Iterator** via their **iterator( )** method. An **Iterator** is just like an **Enumeration**, which it replaces, except:

1. It uses a name (iterator) that is historically understood and accepted in the OOP community.

2. It uses shorter method names than **Enumeration**: **hasNext( )** instead of **hasMoreElements( )**, and **next( )** instead of **nextElement( )**.

3. It adds a new method, **remove( )**, which removes the last element produced by the **Iterator**. So you can call **remove( )** only once for every time you call **next( )**.

In **SimpleCollection.java**, you can see that an **Iterator** is created and used to traverse the **Collection**, printing each element.

Using Collections

The following table shows everything you can do with a **Collection**, and thus, everything you can do with a **Set** or a **List**. (**List** also has additional functionality.) **Maps** are not inherited from **Collection**, and will be treated separately.

boolean add(Object)	*Ensures that the Collection contains the argument. Returns false if it doesn't add the argument.
boolean addAll(Collection)	*Adds all the elements in the argument. Returns true if any elements were added.
void clear( )	*Removes all the elements in the Collection.
boolean contains(Object)	True if the Collection contains the argument.
boolean containsAll(Collection)	True if the Collection contains all the elements in the argument.
boolean isEmpty( )	True if the Collection has no elements.
Iterator iterator( )	Returns an Iterator that you can use to move through the elements in the Collection.
boolean remove(Object)	*If the argument is in the Collection, one instance of that element is removed. Returns true if a removal occurred.
boolean removeAll(Collection)	*Removes all the elements that are contained in the argument. Returns true if any removals occurred.
boolean retainAll(Collection)	*Retains only elements that are contained in the argument (an "intersection" from set theory). Returns true if any changes occurred.

int size( )	Returns the number of elements in the Collection.
Object[] toArray( )	Returns an array containing all the elements in the Collection.
	*This is an "optional" method, which means it might not be implemented by a particular Collection. If not, that method throws an UnsupportedOperationException. Exceptions will be covered in Chapter 9.

The following example demonstrates all of these methods. Again, these work with anything that inherits from **Collection**; an **ArrayList** is used as a kind of "least-common denominator":

```
//: Collection1.java
// Things you can do with all Collections
package c08.newcollections;
import java.util.*;

public class Collection1 {
  // Fill with 'size' elements, start
  // counting at 'start':
  public static Collection
  fill(Collection c, int start, int size) {
    for(int i = start; i < start + size; i++)
      c.add(Integer.toString(i));
    return c;
  }
  // Default to a "start" of 0:
  public static Collection
  fill(Collection c, int size) {
    return fill(c, 0, size);
  }
  // Default to 10 elements:
  public static Collection fill(Collection c) {
    return fill(c, 0, 10);
  }
  // Create & upcast to Collection:
  public static Collection newCollection() {
    return fill(new ArrayList());
    // ArrayList is used for simplicity, but it's
    // only seen as a generic Collection
    // everywhere else in the program.
```

```
    }
    // Fill a Collection with a range of values:
    public static Collection
    newCollection(int start, int size) {
      return fill(new ArrayList(), start, size);
    }
    // Moving through a List with an iterator:
    public static void print(Collection c) {
      for(Iterator x = c.iterator(); x.hasNext();)
        System.out.print(x.next() + " ");
      System.out.println();
    }
    public static void main(String[] args) {
      Collection c = newCollection();
      c.add("ten");
      c.add("eleven");
      print(c);
      // Find max and min elements; this means
      // different things depending on the way
      // the Comparable interface is implemented:
      System.out.println("Collections.max(c) = " +
        Collections.max(c));
      System.out.println("Collections.min(c) = " +
        Collections.min(c));
      // Add a Collection to another Collection
      c.addAll(newCollection());
      print(c);
      c.remove("3"); // Removes the first one
      print(c);
      c.remove("3"); // Removes the second one
      print(c);
      // Remove all components that are in the
      // argument collection:
      c.removeAll(newCollection());
      print(c);
      c.addAll(newCollection());
      print(c);
      // Is an element in this Collection?
      System.out.println(
        "c.contains(\"4\") = " + c.contains("4"));
      // Is a Collection in this Collection?
      System.out.println(
        "c.containsAll(newCollection()) = " +
        c.containsAll(newCollection()));
```

```
Collection c2 = newCollection(5, 3);
// Keep all the elements that are in both
// c and c2 (an intersection of sets):
c.retainAll(c2);
print(c);
// Throw away all the elements in c that
// also appear in c2:
c.removeAll(c2);
System.out.println("c.isEmpty()    " +
  c.isEmpty());
c = newCollection();
print(c);
c.clear(); // Remove all elements
System.out.println("after c.clear():");
print(c);
  }
} ///:~
```

The first methods provide a way to fill any **Collection** with test data, in this case just **int**s converted to **String**s. The second method will be used frequently throughout the rest of this chapter.

The two versions of **newCollection( )** create **ArrayList**s containing different sets of data and return them as **Collection** objects, so it's clear that nothing other than the **Collection** interface is being used.

The **print( )** method will also be used throughout the rest of this section. Since it moves through a **Collection** using an **Iterator**, which any **Collection** can produce, it will work with **List**s and **Set**s and any **Collection** that a **Map** produces.

main( ) uses simple exercises to show all of the methods in **Collection**.

The following sections compare the various implementations of **List**, **Set**, and **Map** and indicate in each case (with an asterisk) which one should be your default choice. You'll notice that the legacy classes **Vector**, **Stack**, and **Hashtable** are *not* included because in all cases there are preferred classes within the new collections.

Using Lists

List (interface)	Order is the most important feature of a **List**; it promises to maintain elements in a particular sequence. **List** adds a number of methods to **Collection** that allow insertion and removal of

	elements in the middle of a **List**. (This is recommended only for a **LinkedList**.) A **List** will produce a **ListIterator**, and using this you can traverse the **List** in both directions, as well as insert and remove elements in the middle of the list (again, recommended only for a **LinkedList**).
ArrayList*	A **List** backed by an array. Use instead of **Vector** as a general-purpose object holder. Allows rapid random access to elements, but is slow when inserting and removing elements from the middle of a list. **ListIterator** should be used only for back-and-forth traversal of an **ArrayList**, but not for inserting and removing elements, which is expensive compared to **LinkedList**.
LinkedList	Provides optimal sequential access, with inexpensive insertions and deletions from the middle of the list. Relatively slow for random access. (Use **ArrayList** instead.) Also has **addFirst( )**, **addLast( )**, **getFirst( )**, **getLast( )**, **removeFirst( )**, and **removeLast( )** (which are not defined in any interfaces or base classes) to allow it to be used as a stack, a queue, and a dequeue.

The methods in the following example each cover a different group of activities: things that every list can do (**basicTest( )**), moving around with an **Iterator** (**iterMotion( )**) versus changing things with an **Iterator** (**iterManipulation( )**), seeing the effects of **List** manipulation (**testVisual( )**), and operations available only to **LinkedList**s.

```
//: List1.java
// Things you can do with Lists
package c08.newcollections;
import java.util.*;

public class List1 {
  // Wrap Collection1.fill() for convenience:
  public static List fill(List a) {
    return (List)Collection1.fill(a);
  }
  // You can use an Iterator, just as with a
  // Collection, but you can also use random
  // access with get():
  public static void print(List a) {
    for(int i = 0; i < a.size(); i++)
      System.out.print(a.get(i) + " ");
```

```
      System.out.println();
    }
    static boolean b;
    static Object o;
    static int i;
    static Iterator it;
    static ListIterator lit;
    public static void basicTest(List a) {
      a.add(1, "1"); // Add at location 1
      a.add("x"); // Add at end
      // Add a collection:
      a.addAll(fill(new ArrayList()));
      // Add a collection starting at location 3:
      a.addAll(3, fill(new ArrayList()));
      b = a.contains("1"); // Is it in there?
      // Is the entire collection in there?
      b = a.containsAll(fill(new ArrayList()));
      // Lists allow random access, which is cheap
      // for ArrayList, expensive for LinkedList:
      o = a.get(1); // Get object at location 1
      i = a.indexOf("1"); // Tell index of object
      // indexOf, starting search at location 2:
      i = a.indexOf("1", 2);
      b = a.isEmpty(); // Any elements inside?
      it = a.iterator(); // Ordinary Iterator
      lit = a.listIterator(); // ListIterator
      lit = a.listIterator(3); // Start at loc 3
      i = a.lastIndexOf("1"); // Last match
      i = a.lastIndexOf("1", 2); // ...after loc 2
      a.remove(1); // Remove location 1
      a.remove("3"); // Remove this object
      a.set(1, "y"); // Set location 1 to "y"
      // Make an array from the List:
      Object[] array = a.toArray();
      // Keep everything that's in the argument
      // (the intersection of the two sets):
      a.retainAll(fill(new ArrayList()));
      // Remove elements in this range:
      a.removeRange(0, 2);
      // Remove everything that's in the argument:
      a.removeAll(fill(new ArrayList()));
      i = a.size(); // How big is it?
      a.clear(); // Remove all elements
    }
```

```
public static void iterMotion(List a) {
  ListIterator it = a.listIterator();
  b = it.hasNext();
  b = it.hasPrevious();
  o = it.next();
  i = it.nextIndex();
  o = it.previous();
  i = it.previousIndex();
}
public static void iterManipulation(List a) {
  ListIterator it = a.listIterator();
  it.add("47");
  // Must move to an element after add():
  it.next();
  // Remove the element that was just produced:
  it.remove();
  // Must move to an element after remove():
  it.next();
  // Change the element that was just produced:
  it.set("47");
}
public static void testVisual(List a) {
  print(a);
  List b = new ArrayList();
  fill(b);
  System.out.print("b = ");
  print(b);
  a.addAll(b);
  a.addAll(fill(new ArrayList()));
  print(a);
  // Shrink the list by removing all the
  // elements beyond the first 1/2 of the list
  System.out.println(a.size());
  System.out.println(a.size()/2);
  a.removeRange(a.size()/2, a.size()/2 + 2);
  print(a);
  // Insert, remove, and replace elements
  // using a ListIterator:
  ListIterator x = a.listIterator(a.size()/2);
  x.add("one");
  print(a);
  System.out.println(x.next());
  x.remove();
  System.out.println(x.next());
```

```
      x.set("47");
      print(a);
      // Traverse the list backwards:
      x = a.listIterator(a.size());
      while(x.hasPrevious())
        System.out.print(x.previous() + " ");
      System.out.println();
      System.out.println("testVisual finished");
    }
    // There are some things that only
    // LinkedLists can do:
    public static void testLinkedList() {
      LinkedList ll = new LinkedList();
      Collection1.fill(ll, 5);
      print(ll);
      // Treat it like a stack, pushing:
      ll.addFirst("one");
      ll.addFirst("two");
      print(ll);
      // Like "peeking" at the top of a stack:
      System.out.println(ll.getFirst());
      // Like popping a stack:
      System.out.println(ll.removeFirst());
      System.out.println(ll.removeFirst());
      // Treat it like a queue, pulling elements
      // off the tail end:
      System.out.println(ll.removeLast());
      // With the above operations, it's a dequeue!
      print(ll);
    }
    public static void main(String args[]) {
      // Make and fill a new list each time:
      basicTest(fill(new LinkedList()));
      basicTest(fill(new ArrayList()));
      iterMotion(fill(new LinkedList()));
      iterMotion(fill(new ArrayList()));
      iterManipulation(fill(new LinkedList()));
      iterManipulation(fill(new ArrayList()));
      testVisual(fill(new LinkedList()));
      testLinkedList();
    }
} ///:~
```

In **basicTest( )** and **iterMotion( )** the calls are simply made to show the proper syntax, and while the return value is captured, it is not used. In

---

some cases, the return value isn't captured since it isn't typically used. You should look up the full usage of each of these methods in your online documentation before you use them.

Using Sets

Set has exactly the same interface as **Collection**, so there isn't any extra functionality as there is with the two different **List**s. Instead, the **Set** is exactly a **Collection**, it just has different behavior. (This is the ideal use of inheritance and polymorphism: to express different behavior.) A **Set** allows only one instance of each object value to exist (what constitutes the "value" of an object is more complex, as you shall see).

Set (interface)	Each element that you add to the **Set** must be unique; otherwise the **Set** doesn't add the duplicate element. Objects added to a **Set** must define **equals( )** to establish object uniqueness. **Set** has exactly the same interface as **Collection**. A **Set** does not guarantee it will maintain its elements in any particular order.
HashSet*	For all **Set**s except very small ones. Objects must also define **hashCode( )**.
ArraySet	A **Set** backed by an array. Designed for very small **Set**s, especially those that are frequently created and destroyed. For small **Set**s, creation and iteration is substantially cheaper than for **HashSet**. Performance gets quite bad when the **Set** is large. **HashCode( )** is not required.
TreeSet	An ordered **Set** backed by a red-black tree.[7] This way, you can extract an ordered sequence from a **Set**.

The following example does *not* show everything you can do with a **Set**, since the interface is the same as **Collection** and so was exercised in the previous example. Instead, this demonstrates the behavior that makes a **Set** unique:

```
//: Set1.java
// Things you can do with Sets
package c08.newcollections;
import java.util.*;
```

---

[7] At the time of this writing, **TreeSet** had only been announced and was not yet implemented, so there are no examples here that use **TreeSet**.

```
public class Set1 {
  public static void testVisual(Set a) {
    Collection1.fill(a);
    Collection1.fill(a);
    Collection1.fill(a);
    Collection1.print(a); // No duplicates!
    // Add another set to this one:
    a.addAll(a);
    a.add("one");
    a.add("one");
    a.add("one");
    Collection1.print(a);
    // Look something up:
    System.out.println("a.contains(\"one\"): " +
      a.contains("one"));
  }
  public static void main(String[] args) {
    testVisual(new HashSet());
    testVisual(new ArraySet());
  }
} ///:~
```

Duplicate values are added to the **Set**, but when it is printed you'll see the **Set** has accepted only one instance of each value.

When you run this program you'll notice that the order maintained by the **HashSet** is different from **ArraySet**, since each has a different way of storing elements so they can be located later. (**ArraySet** keeps them sorted, while **HashSet** uses a hashing function, which is designed specifically for rapid lookups.) When creating your own types, be aware that a **Set** needs a way to maintain a storage order, just as with the "groundhog" examples shown earlier in this chapter. Here's an example:

```
//: Set2.java
// Putting your own type in a Set
package c08.newcollections;
import java.util.*;

class MyType {
  private int i;
  public MyType(int n) { i = n; }
  public boolean equals(Object o) {
    if ((o != null) && (o instanceof MyType))
      return
```

```
          i == ((MyType)o).i;
       else return false;
    }
    // Required for HashSet, not for ArraySet:
    public int hashCode() { return i; }
    public String toString() { return i + " "; }
}

public class Set2 {
  public static Set fill(Set a, int size) {
    for(int i = 0; i < size; i++)
      a.add(new MyType(i));
    return a;
  }
  public static Set fill(Set a) {
    return fill(a, 10);
  }
  public static void test(Set a) {
    fill(a);
    fill(a); // Try to add duplicates
    fill(a);
    a.addAll(fill(new ArraySet()));
    Collection1.print(a);
  }
  public static void main(String[] args) {
    test(new HashSet());
    test(new ArraySet());
  }
} ///:~
```

The definitions for **equals( )** and **hashCode( )** follow the form given in the "groundhog" examples. You must define an **equals( )** in both cases, but the **hashCode( )** is necessary only if the class will be placed in a **HashSet** (which is likely, since that should generally be your first choice as a **Set** implementation).

Using Maps

Map (interface)	Maintains key-value associations (pairs), so you can look up a value using a key.
HashMap*	Implementation based on a hash table. (Use this instead of **Hashtable**.) Provides constant-time performance for inserting and locating pairs. Performance can be adjusted via constructors that allow you to set the

	capacity and *load factor* of the hash table.
ArrayMap	**Map** backed by an **ArrayList**. Gives precise control over the order of iteration. Designed for very small **Maps**, especially those that are frequently created and destroyed. For very small **Maps**, creation and iteration is substantially cheaper than for **HashMap**. Performance gets very bad when the **Map** is large.
TreeMap	Implementation based on a red-black tree. When you view the keys or the pairs, they will be in sorted order (determined by **Comparable** or **Comparator**, discussed later). The point of a **TreeMap** is that you get the results in sorted order. **TreeMap** is the only **Map** with the **subMap( )** method, which allows you to return a portion of the tree.

The following example contains two sets of test data and a **fill( )** method that allows you to fill any map with any two-dimensional array of **Objects**. These tools will be used in other **Map** examples, as well.

```
//: Map1.java
// Things you can do with Maps
package c08.newcollections;
import java.util.*;

public class Map1 {
  public final static String[][] testData1 = {
      { "Happy", "Cheerful disposition" },
      { "Sleepy", "Prefers dark, quiet places" },
      { "Grumpy", "Needs to work on attitude" },
      { "Doc", "Fantasizes about advanced degree"},
      { "Dopey", "'A' for effort" },
      { "Sneezy", "Struggles with allergies" },
      { "Bashful", "Needs self-esteem workshop"},
  };
  public final static String[][] testData2 = {
      { "Belligerent", "Disruptive influence" },
      { "Lazy", "Motivational problems" },
      { "Comatose", "Excellent behavior" }
  };
  public static Map fill(Map m, Object[][] o) {
    for(int i = 0; i < o.length; i++)
      m.put(o[i][0], o[i][1]);
    return m;
  }
  // Producing a Set of the keys:
```

```java
public static void printKeys(Map m) {
  System.out.print("Size = " + m.size() +", ");
  System.out.print("Keys: ");
  Collection1.print(m.keySet());
}
// Producing a Collection of the values:
public static void printValues(Map m) {
  System.out.print("Values: ");
  Collection1.print(m.values());
}
// Iterating through Map.Entry objects (pairs):
public static void print(Map m) {
  Collection entries = m.entries();
  Iterator it = entries.iterator();
  while(it.hasNext()) {
    Map.Entry e = (Map.Entry)it.next();
    System.out.println("Key = " + e.getKey() +
      ", Value = " + e.getValue());
  }
}
public static void test(Map m) {
  fill(m, testData1);
  // Map has 'Set' behavior for keys:
  fill(m, testData1);
  printKeys(m);
  printValues(m);
  print(m);
  String key = testData1[4][0];
  String value = testData1[4][1];
  System.out.println("m.containsKey(\"" + key +
    "\"): " + m.containsKey(key));
  System.out.println("m.get(\"" + key + "\"): "
    + m.get(key));
  System.out.println("m.containsValue(\""
    + value + "\"): " +
    m.containsValue(value));
  Map m2 = fill(new ArrayMap(), testData2);
  m.putAll(m2);
  printKeys(m);
  m.remove(testData2[0][0]);
  printKeys(m);
  m.clear();
  System.out.println("m.isEmpty(): "
    + m.isEmpty());
```

```
      fill(m, testData1);
      // Operations on the Set change the Map:
      m.keySet().removeAll(m.keySet());
      System.out.println("m.isEmpty(): "
        + m.isEmpty());
  }
  public static void main(String args[]) {
    System.out.println("Testing ArrayMap");
    test(new ArrayMap());
    System.out.println("Testing HashMap");
    test(new HashMap());
    System.out.println("Testing TreeMap");
    test(new TreeMap());
  }
} ///:~
```

The **printKeys( )**, **printValues( )**, and **print( )** methods are not only
useful utilities, they also demonstrate the production of **Collection** views
of a **Map**. The **keySet( )** method produces a **Set** backed by the keys in the
Map; here, it is treated as only a **Collection**. Similar treatment is given to
values( ), which produces a **List** containing all the values in the **Map**.
(Note that keys must be unique, while values can contain duplicates.)
Since these **Collection**s are backed by the **Map**, any changes in a
Collection will be reflected in the associated **Map**.

The **print( )** method grabs the **Iterator** produced by **entries** and uses it
to print both the key and value for each pair. The rest of the program
provides simple examples of each **Map** operation, and tests each type of
Map.

When creating your own class to use as a key in a **Map**, you must deal
with the same issues discussed previously for **Set**s.

Choosing an implementation

From the diagram on page 363 you can see that there are really only
three collection components: **Map**, **List**, and **Set**, and only two or three
implementations of each interface. If you need to use the functionality
offered by a particular **interface**, how do you decide which particular
implementation to use?

To understand the answer, you must be aware that each different
implementation has its own features, strengths, and weaknesses. For
example, you can see in the diagram that the "feature" of **Hashtable**,
Vector, and **Stack** is that they are legacy classes, so that existing code

doesn't break. On the other hand, it's best if you don't use those for new (Java 1.2) code.

The distinction between the other collections often comes down to what they are "backed by;" that is, the data structures that physically implement your desired **interface**. This means that, for example, **ArrayList**, **LinkedList**, and **Vector** (which is roughly equivalent to **ArrayList**) all implement the **List** interface so your program will produce the same results regardless of the one you use. However, **ArrayList** (and **Vector**) is backed by an array, while the **LinkedList** is implemented in the usual way for a doubly-linked list, as individual objects each containing data along with handles to the previous and next elements in the list. Because of this, if you want to do many insertions and removals in the middle of a list a **LinkedList** is the appropriate choice. (**LinkedList** also has additional functionality that is established in **AbstractSequentialList**.) If not, an **ArrayList** is probably faster.

As another example, a **Set** can be implemented as either an **ArraySet** or a **HashSet**. An **ArraySet** is backed by an **ArrayList** and is designed to support only small numbers of elements, especially in situations in which you're creating and destroying a lot of **Set** objects. However, if you're going to have larger quantities in your **Set**, the performance of **ArraySet** will get very bad, very quickly. When you're writing a program that needs a **Set**, you should choose **HashSet** by default, and change to **ArraySet** only in special cases where performance improvements are indicated and necessary.

Choosing between Lists

The most convincing way to see the differences between the implementations of **List** is with a performance test. The following code establishes an inner base class to use as a test framework, then creates an anonymous inner class for each different test. Each of these inner classes is called by the **test( )** method. This approach allows you to easily add and remove new kinds of tests.

```
//: ListPerformance.java
// Demonstrates performance differences in Lists
package c08.newcollections;
import java.util.*;

public class ListPerformance {
  private static final int REPS = 100;
  private abstract static class Tester {
    String name;
```

```
      int size; // Test quantity
      Tester(String name, int size) {
        this.name = name;
        this.size = size;
      }
      abstract void test(List a);
    }
    private static Tester[] tests = {
      new Tester("get", 300) {
        void test(List a) {
          for(int i = 0; i < REPS; i++) {
            for(int j = 0; j < a.size(); j++)
              a.get(j);
          }
        }
      },
      new Tester("iteration", 300) {
        void test(List a) {
          for(int i = 0; i < REPS; i++) {
            Iterator it = a.iterator();
            while(it.hasNext())
              it.next();
          }
        }
      },
      new Tester("insert", 1000) {
        void test(List a) {
          int half = a.size()/2;
          String s = "test";
          ListIterator it = a.listIterator(half);
          for(int i = 0; i < size * 10; i++)
            it.add(s);
        }
      },
      new Tester("remove", 5000) {
        void test(List a) {
          ListIterator it = a.listIterator(3);
          while(it.hasNext()) {
            it.next();
            it.remove();
          }
        }
      },
    };
```

```
public static void test(List a) {
  // A trick to print out the class name:
  System.out.println("Testing " +
    a.getClass().getName());
  for(int i = 0; i < tests.length; i++) {
    Collection1.fill(a, tests[i].size);
    System.out.print(tests[i].name);
    long t1 = System.currentTimeMillis();
    tests[i].test(a);
    long t2 = System.currentTimeMillis();
    System.out.println(": " + (t2 - t1));
  }
}
public static void main(String[] args) {
  test(new ArrayList());
  test(new LinkedList());
}
} ///:~
```

The inner class **Tester** is **abstract**, to provide a base class for the specific tests. It contains a **String** to be printed when the test starts, a **size** parameter to be used by the test for quantity of elements or repetitions of tests, a constructor to initialize the fields, and an **abstract** method **test( )** that does the work. All the different types of tests are collected in one place, the array **tests**, which is initialized with different anonymous inner classes that inherit from **Tester**. To add or remove tests, simply add or remove an inner class definition from the array, and everything else happens automatically.

The **List** that's handed to **test( )** is first filled with elements, then each test in the **tests** array is timed. The results will vary from machine to machine; they are intended to give only an order of magnitude comparison between the performance of the different collections. Here is a summary of one run:

Type	Get	Iteration	Insert	Remove
ArrayList	110	270	1920	4780
LinkedList	1870	7580	170	110

You can see that random accesses (**get( )**) and iterations are cheap for **ArrayList**s and expensive for **LinkedList**s. On the other hand, insertions and removals from the middle of a list are significantly cheaper for a **LinkedList** than for an **ArrayList**. The best approach is probably to choose an **ArrayList** as your default and to change to a **LinkedList** if you discover performance problems because of many insertions and removals from the middle of the list.

Choosing between Sets

You can choose between an **ArraySet** and a **HashSet**, depending on the size of the **Set** (if you need to produce an ordered sequence from a **Set**, use **TreeSet**[8]). The following test program gives an indication of this tradeoff:

```
//: SetPerformance.java
// Demonstrates performance differences in Sets
package c08.newcollections;
import java.util.*;

public class SetPerformance {
  private static final int REPS = 100;
  private abstract static class Tester {
    String name;
    Tester(String name) { this.name = name; }
    abstract void test(Set s, int size);
  }
  private static Tester[] tests = {
    new Tester("add") {
      void test(Set s, int size) {
        for(int i = 0; i < REPS; i++) {
          s.clear();
          Collection1.fill(s, size);
        }
      }
    },
    new Tester("contains") {
      void test(Set s, int size) {
        for(int i = 0; i < REPS; i++)
          for(int j = 0; j < size; j++)
            s.contains(Integer.toString(j));
      }
    },
    new Tester("iteration") {
      void test(Set s, int size) {
```

---

[8] **TreeSet** was not available at the time of this writing, but you can easily add a test for it into this example.

```
        for(int i = 0; i < REPS * 10; i++) {
          Iterator it = s.iterator();
          while(it.hasNext())
            it.next();
        }
      }
    },
  };
  public static void test(Set s, int size) {
    // A trick to print out the class name:
    System.out.println("Testing " +
      s.getClass().getName() + " size " + size);
    Collection1.fill(s, size);
    for(int i = 0; i < tests.length; i++) {
      System.out.print(tests[i].name);
      long t1 = System.currentTimeMillis();
      tests[i].test(s, size);
      long t2 = System.currentTimeMillis();
      System.out.println(": " +
        ((double)(t2 - t1)/(double)size));
    }
  }
  public static void main(String[] args) {
    // Small:
    test(new ArraySet(), 10);
    test(new HashSet(), 10);
    // Medium:
    test(new ArraySet(), 100);
    test(new HashSet(), 100);
    // Large:
    test(new HashSet(), 1000);
    test(new ArraySet(), 500);
  }
} ///:~
```

The last test of **ArraySet** is only 500 elements instead of 1000 because it is so slow.

Type	Test size	Add	Contains	Iteration
ArraySet	10	5.0	6.0	11.0
	100	24.2	23.1	4.9
	500	100.18	97.12	4.5

	10	5.0	6.0	16.0
HashSet	100	5.5	5.0	6.0
	1000	6.1	6.09	5.77

HashSet is clearly superior to **ArraySet** for **add( )** and **contains( )**, and the performance is effectively independent of size. You'll virtually never want to use an **ArraySet** for regular programming.

Choosing between Maps

When choosing between implementations of **Map**, the size of the **Map** is what most strongly affects performance, and the following test program gives an indication of this tradeoff:

```
//: MapPerformance.java
// Demonstrates performance differences in Maps
package c08.newcollections;
import java.util.*;

public class MapPerformance {
  private static final int REPS = 100;
  public static Map fill(Map m, int size) {
    for(int i = 0; i < size; i++) {
      String x = Integer.toString(i);
      m.put(x, x);
    }
    return m;
  }
  private abstract static class Tester {
    String name;
    Tester(String name) { this.name = name; }
    abstract void test(Map m, int size);
  }
  private static Tester[] tests = {
    new Tester("put") {
      void test(Map m, int size) {
        for(int i = 0; i < REPS; i++) {
          m.clear();
          fill(m, size);
        }
      }
    },
    new Tester("get") {
```

```java
        void test(Map m, int size) {
          for(int i = 0; i < REPS; i++)
            for(int j = 0; j < size; j++)
              m.get(Integer.toString(j));
        }
      },
      new Tester("iteration") {
        void test(Map m, int size) {
          for(int i = 0; i < REPS * 10; i++) {
            Iterator it = m.entries().iterator();
            while(it.hasNext())
              it.next();
          }
        }
      },
    };
  public static void test(Map m, int size) {
    // A trick to print out the class name:
    System.out.println("Testing " +
      m.getClass().getName() + " size " + size);
    fill(m, size);
    for(int i = 0; i < tests.length; i++) {
      System.out.print(tests[i].name);
      long t1 = System.currentTimeMillis();
      tests[i].test(m, size);
      long t2 = System.currentTimeMillis();
      System.out.println(": " +
        ((double)(t2 - t1)/(double)size));
    }
  }
  public static void main(String[] args) {
    // Small:
    test(new ArrayMap(), 10);
    test(new HashMap(), 10);
    test(new TreeMap(), 10);
    // Medium:
    test(new ArrayMap(), 100);
    test(new HashMap(), 100);
    test(new TreeMap(), 100);
    // Large:
    test(new HashMap(), 1000);
    // You might want to comment these out since
    // they can take a while to run:
    test(new ArrayMap(), 500);
```

```
        test(new TreeMap(), 500);
    }
} ///:~
```

Because the size of the map is the issue, you'll see that the timing tests divide the time by the size to normalize each measurement. Here is one set of results. (Yours will probably be different.)

Type	Test size	Put	Get	Iteration
ArrayMap	10	22.0	44.0	17.0
	100	68.7	118.6	8.8
	500	155.22	259.36	4.84
TreeMap	10	17.0	16.0	11.0
	100	18.1	70.3	8.3
	500	11.22	148.4	4.62
HashMap	10	11.0	11.0	33.0
	100	9.9	10.4	12.1
	1000	13.18	10.65	5.77

Even for size 10, the **ArrayMap** performance is worse than **HashMap** – except for iteration, which is not usually what you're concerned about when using a **Map**. (**get( )** is generally the place where you'll spend most of your time.) The **TreeMap** has respectable **put( )** and iteration times, but the **get( )** is not so good. Why would you use a **TreeMap** if it has good **put( )** and iteration times? So you could use it not as a **Map**, but as a way to create an ordered list. The behavior of a tree is such that it's always in order and doesn't have to be specially sorted. (The *way* it is ordered will be discussed later.) Once you fill a **TreeMap**, you can call **keySet( )** to get a **Set** view of the keys, then **toArray( )** to produce an array of those keys. You can then use the **static** method **Array.binarySearch( )** (discussed later) to rapidly find objects in your sorted array. Of course, you would probably only do this if, for some reason, the behavior of a **HashMap** was unacceptable, since **HashMap** is designed to rapidly find things. In the end, when you're using a **Map** your first choice should be **HashMap**, and only rarely will you need to investigate the alternatives.

There is another performance issue that the above table does not address, and that is speed of creation. The following program tests creation speed for different types of **Map**:

```
//: MapCreation.java
// Demonstrates time differences in Map creation
package c08.newcollections;
import java.util.*;
```

```
public class MapCreation {
  public static void main(String[] args) {
    final long REPS = 100000;
    long t1 = System.currentTimeMillis();
    System.out.print("ArrayMap");
    for(long i = 0; i < REPS; i++)
      new ArrayMap();
    long t2 = System.currentTimeMillis();
    System.out.println(": " + (t2 - t1));
    t1 = System.currentTimeMillis();
    System.out.print("TreeMap");
    for(long i = 0; i < REPS; i++)
      new TreeMap();
    t2 = System.currentTimeMillis();
    System.out.println(": " + (t2 - t1));
    t1 = System.currentTimeMillis();
    System.out.print("HashMap");
    for(long i = 0; i < REPS; i++)
      new HashMap();
    t2 = System.currentTimeMillis();
    System.out.println(": " + (t2 - t1));
  }
} ///:~
```

At the time this program was written, the creation speed of **TreeMap** was dramatically faster than the other two types. (Although you should try it, since there was talk of performance improvements to **ArrayMap**.) This, along with the acceptable and consistent **put( )** performance of **TreeMap**, suggests a possible strategy if you're creating many **Map**s, and only later in your program doing many lookups: Create and fill **TreeMap**s, and when you start looking things up, convert the important **TreeMap**s into **HashMap**s using the **HashMap(Map)** constructor. Again, you should only worry about this sort of thing after it's been proven that you have a performance bottleneck. ("First make it work, then make it fast – if you must.")

Unsupported operations

It's possible to turn an array into a **List** with the **static Arrays.toList( )** method:

```
//: Unsupported.java
// Sometimes methods defined in the Collection
```

```
// interfaces don't work!
package c08.newcollections;
import java.util.*;

public class Unsupported {
  private static String[] s = {
    "one", "two", "three", "four", "five",
    "six", "seven", "eight", "nine", "ten",
  };
  static List a = Arrays.toList(s);
  static List a2 = Arrays.toList(
    new String[] { s[3], s[4], s[5] });
  public static void main(String[] args) {
    Collection1.print(a); // Iteration
    System.out.println(
      "a.contains(" + s[0] + ") = " +
      a.contains(s[0]));
    System.out.println(
      "a.containsAll(a2) = " +
      a.containsAll(a2));
    System.out.println("a.isEmpty() = " +
      a.isEmpty());
    System.out.println(
      "a.indexOf(" + s[5] + ") = " +
      a.indexOf(s[5]));
    // Traverse backwards:
    ListIterator lit = a.listIterator(a.size());
    while(lit.hasPrevious())
      System.out.print(lit.previous());
    System.out.println();
    // Set the elements to different values:
    for(int i = 0; i < a.size(); i++)
      a.set(i, "47");
    Collection1.print(a);
    // Compiles, but won't run:
    lit.add("X"); // Unsupported operation
    a.clear(); // Unsupported
    a.add("eleven"); // Unsupported
    a.addAll(a2); // Unsupported
    a.retainAll(a2); // Unsupported
    a.remove(s[0]); // Unsupported
    a.removeAll(a2); // Unsupported
  }
} ///:~
```

You'll discover that only a portion of the **Collection** and **List** interfaces are actually implemented. The rest of the methods cause the unwelcome appearance of something called an **UnsupportedOperationException**. You'll learn all about exceptions in the next chapter, but the short story is that the **Collection interface**, as well as some of the other **interface**s in the new collections library, contain "optional" methods, which might or might not be "supported" in the concrete class that **implements** that **interface**. Calling an unsupported method causes an **UnsupportedOperationException** to indicate a programming error.

"What?!?" you say, incredulous. "The whole point of **interface**s and base classes is that they promise these methods will do something meaningful! This breaks that promise – it says that not only will calling some methods *not* perform a meaningful behavior, they will stop the program! Type safety was just thrown out the window!" It's not quite that bad. With a **Collection**, **List**, **Set**, or **Map**, the compiler still restricts you to calling only the methods in that **interface**, so it's not like Smalltalk (in which you can call any method for any object, and find out only when you run the program whether your call does anything). In addition, most methods that take a **Collection** as an argument only read from that **Collection** –all the "read" methods of **Collection** are *not* optional.

This approach prevents an explosion of interfaces in the design. Other designs for collection libraries always seem to end up with a confusing plethora of interfaces to describe each of the variations on the main theme and are thus difficult to learn. It's not even possible to capture all of the special cases in **interface**s, because someone can always invent a new **interface**. The "unsupported operation" approach achieves an important goal of the new collections library: it is simple to learn and use. For this approach to work, however:

1. The **UnsupportedOperationException** must be a rare event. That is, for most classes all operations should work, and only in special cases should an operation be unsupported. This is true in the new collections library, since the classes you'll use 99 percent of the time – **ArrayList**, **LinkedList**, **HashSet**, and **HashMap**, as well as the other concrete implementations – support all of the operations. The design does provide a "back door" if you want to create a new **Collection** without providing meaningful definitions for all the methods in the **Collection interface**, and yet still fit it into the existing library.

2. When an operation *is* unsupported, there should be reasonable likelihood that an **UnsupportedOperationException** will appear at implementation time, rather than after you've shipped the product to the customer. After all, it indicates a programming error: you've used

a class incorrectly. This point is less certain, and is where the experimental nature of this design comes into play. Only over time will we find out how well it works.

In the example above, **Arrays.toList( )** produces a **List** that is backed by a fixed-size array. Therefore it makes sense that the only supported operations are the ones that don't change the size of the array. If, on the other hand, a new **interface** were required to express this different kind of behavior (called, perhaps, "**FixedSizeList**"), it would throw open the door to complexity and soon you wouldn't know where to start when trying to use the library.

The documentation for a method that takes a **Collection**, **List**, **Set**, or **Map** as an argument should specify which of the optional methods must be implemented. For example, sorting requires the **set( )** and **Iterator.set( )** methods but not **add( )** and **remove( )**.

Sorting and searching

Java 1.2 adds utilities to perform sorting and searching for arrays or **List**s. These utilities are **static** methods of two new classes: **Arrays** for sorting and searching arrays, and **Collections** for sorting and searching **List**s.

Arrays

The **Arrays** class has an overloaded **sort( )** and **binarySearch( )** for arrays of all the primitive types, as well as for **String** and **Object**. Here's an example that shows sorting and searching an array of **byte** (all the other primitives look the same) and an array of **String**:

```
//: Array1.java
// Testing the sorting & searching in Arrays
package c08.newcollections;
import java.util.*;

public class Array1 {
  static Random r = new Random();
  static String ssource =
    "ABCDEFGHIJKLMNOPQRSTUVWXYZ" +
    "abcdefghijklmnopqrstuvwxyz";
  static char[] src = ssource.toCharArray();
  // Create a random String
  public static String randString(int length) {
    char[] buf = new char[length];
```

```java
    int rnd;
    for(int i = 0; i < length; i++) {
      rnd = Math.abs(r.nextInt()) % src.length;
      buf[i] = src[rnd];
    }
    return new String(buf);
  }
  // Create a random array of Strings:
  public static
  String[] randStrings(int length, int size) {
    String[] s = new String[size];
    for(int i = 0; i < size; i++)
      s[i] = randString(length);
    return s;
  }
  public static void print(byte[] b) {
    for(int i = 0; i < b.length; i++)
      System.out.print(b[i] + " ");
    System.out.println();
  }
  public static void print(String[] s) {
    for(int i = 0; i < s.length; i++)
      System.out.print(s[i] + " ");
    System.out.println();
  }
  public static void main(String[] args) {
    byte[] b = new byte[15];
    r.nextBytes(b); // Fill with random bytes
    print(b);
    Arrays.sort(b);
    print(b);
    int loc = Arrays.binarySearch(b, b[10]);
    System.out.println("Location of " + b[10] +
      " = " + loc);
    // Test String sort & search:
    String[] s = randStrings(4, 10);
    print(s);
    Arrays.sort(s);
    print(s);
    loc = Arrays.binarySearch(s, s[4]);
    System.out.println("Location of " + s[4] +
      " = " + loc);
  }
} ///:~
```

The first part of the class contains utilities to generate random **String** objects using an array of characters from which random letters can be selected. **randString( )** returns a string of any length, and **randStrings( )** creates an array of random **String**s, given the length of each **String** and the desired size of the array. The two **print( )** methods simplify the display of the sample arrays. In **main( )**, **Random.nextBytes( )** fills the array argument with randomly-selected **byte**s. (There are no corresponding **Random** methods to create arrays of the other primitive data types.) Once you have an array, you can see that it's only a single method call to perform a **sort( )** or **binarySearch( )**. There's an important warning concerning **binarySearch( )**: If you do not call **sort( )** before you perform a **binarySearch( )**, unpredictable behavior can occur, including infinite loops.

Sorting and searching with **String**s looks the same, but when you run the program you'll notice something interesting: the sorting is lexicographic, so uppercase letters precede lowercase letters in the character set. Thus, all the capital letters are at the beginning of the list, followed by the lowercase letters, so 'Z' precedes 'a'. It turns out that even telephone books are typically sorted this way.

Comparable and Comparator

What if this isn't what you want? For example, the index in this book would not be too useful if you had to look in two places for everything that begins with 'A' or 'a'.

When you want to sort an array of **Object**, there's a problem. What determines the ordering of two **Object**s? Unfortunately, the original Java designers didn't consider this an important problem, or it would have been defined in the root class **Object**. As a result, ordering must be imposed on **Object**s from the outside, and the new collections library provides a standard way to do this (which is almost as good as defining it in **Object**).

There is a **sort( )** for arrays of **Object** (and **String**, of course, is an **Object**) that takes a second argument: an object that implements the **Comparator** interface (part of the new collections library) and performs comparisons with its single **compare( )** method. This method takes the two objects to be compared as its arguments and returns a negative integer if the first argument is less than the second, zero if they're equal, and a positive integer if the first argument is greater than the second. With this knowledge, the **String** portion of the example above can be re-implemented to perform an alphabetic sort:

```
//: AlphaComp.java
// Using Comparator to perform an alphabetic sort
package c08.newcollections;
import java.util.*;

public class AlphaComp implements Comparator {
  public int compare(Object o1, Object o2) {
    // Assume it's used only for Strings...
    String s1 = ((String)o1).toLowerCase();
    String s2 = ((String)o2).toLowerCase();
    return s1.compareTo(s2);
  }
  public static void main(String[] args) {
    String[] s = Array1.randStrings(4, 10);
    Array1.print(s);
    AlphaComp ac = new AlphaComp();
    Arrays.sort(s, ac);
    Array1.print(s);
    // Must use the Comparator to search, also:
    int loc = Arrays.binarySearch(s, s[3], ac);
    System.out.println("Location of " + s[3] +
      " = " + loc);
  }
} ///:~
```

By casting to **String**, the **compare( )** method implicitly tests to ensure
that it is used only with **String** objects – the run-time system will catch
any discrepancies. After forcing both **String**s to lower case, the
String.compareTo( ) method produces the desired results.

When you use your own **Comparator** to perform a **sort( )**, you must
use that same **Comparator** when using **binarySearch( )**.

The **Arrays** class has another **sort( )** method that takes a single
argument: an array of **Object**, but with no **Comparator**. This **sort( )**
method must also have some way to compare two **Objects**. It uses the
natural comparison method that is imparted to a class by implementing
the **Comparable interface**. This **interface** has a single method,
compareTo( ), which compares the object to its argument and returns
negative, zero, or positive depending on whether it is less than, equal to,
or greater than the argument. A simple example demonstrates this:

```
//: CompClass.java
// A class that implements Comparable
package c08.newcollections;
```

```
import java.util.*;

public class CompClass implements Comparable {
  private int i;
  public CompClass(int ii) { i = ii; }
  public int compareTo(Object o) {
    // Implicitly tests for correct type:
    int argi = ((CompClass)o).i;
    if(i == argi) return 0;
    if(i < argi) return -1;
    return 1;
  }
  public static void print(Object[] a) {
    for(int i = 0; i < a.length; i++)
      System.out.print(a[i] + " ");
    System.out.println();
  }
  public String toString() { return i + ""; }
  public static void main(String[] args) {
    CompClass[] a = new CompClass[20];
    for(int i = 0; i < a.length; i++)
      a[i] = new CompClass(
          (int)(Math.random() *100));
    print(a);
    Arrays.sort(a);
    print(a);
    int loc = Arrays.binarySearch(a, a[3]);
    System.out.println("Location of " + a[3] +
      " = " + loc);
  }
} ///:~
```

Of course, your **compareTo( )** method can be as complex as necessary.

Lists

A **List** can be sorted and searched in the same fashion as an array. The **static** methods to sort and search a **List** are contained in the class **Collections**, but they have similar signatures as the ones in **Arrays**: **sort(List)** to sort a **List** of objects that implement **Comparable**, **binarySearch(List, Object)** to find an object in the list, **sort(List, Comparator)** to sort a **List** using a **Comparator**, and

---

binarySearch(List, Object, Comparator) to find an object in that list.[9]
This example uses the previously-defined **CompClass** and **AlphaComp** to
demonstrate the sorting tools in **Collections**:

```
//: ListSort.java
// Sorting and searching Lists with 'Collections'
package c08.newcollections;
import java.util.*;

public class ListSort {
  public static void main(String[] args) {
    final int SZ = 20;
    // Using "natural comparison method":
    List a = new ArrayList();
    for(int i = 0; i < SZ; i++)
      a.add(new CompClass(
          (int)(Math.random() *100)));
    Collection1.print(a);
    Collections.sort(a);
    Collection1.print(a);
    Object find = a.get(SZ/2);
    int loc = Collections.binarySearch(a, find);
    System.out.println("Location of " + find +
      " = " + loc);
    // Using a Comparator:
    List b = new ArrayList();
    for(int i = 0; i < SZ; i++)
      b.add(Array1.randString(4));
    Collection1.print(b);
    AlphaComp ac = new AlphaComp();
    Collections.sort(b, ac);
    Collection1.print(b);
    find = b.get(SZ/2);
    // Must use the Comparator to search, also:
    loc = Collections.binarySearch(b, find, ac);
    System.out.println("Location of " + find +
      " = " + loc);
  }
} ///:~
```

---

[9] At the time of this writing, a **Collections.stableSort( )** had been announced, to
perform a merge sort, but it was unavailable for testing.

The use of these methods is identical to the ones in **Arrays**, but you're using a **List** instead of an array.

The **TreeMap** must also order its objects according to **Comparable** or **Comparator**.

Utilities

There are a number of other useful utilities in the **Collections** class:

enumeration(Collection)	Produces an old-style **Enumeration** for the argument.
max(Collection) **min(Collection)**	Produces the maximum or minimum element in the argument using the natural comparison method of the objects in the **Collection**.
max(Collection, Comparator) **min(Collection, Comparator)**	Produces the maximum or minimum element in the **Collection** using the **Comparator**.
nCopies(int n, Object o)	Returns an immutable **List** of size **n** whose handles all point to **o**.
subList(List, int min, int max)	Returns a new **List** backed by the specified argument **List** that is a window into that argument with indexes starting at **min** and stopping just before **max**.

Note that **min( )** and **max( )** work with **Collection** objects, not with **List**s, so you don't need to worry about whether the **Collection** should be sorted or not. (As mentioned earlier, you *do* need to **sort( )** a **List** or an array before performing a **binarySearch( )**.)

Making a **Collection** or **Map** unmodifiable

Often it is convenient to create a read-only version of a **Collection** or **Map**. The **Collections** class allows you to do this by passing the original container into a method that hands back a read-only version. There are four variations on this method, one each for **Collection** (if you don't want to treat a **Collection** as a more specific type), **List**, **Set**, and **Map**. This example shows the proper way to build read-only versions of each:

```
//: ReadOnly.java
// Using the Collections.unmodifiable methods
package c08.newcollections;
```

```java
import java.util.*;

public class ReadOnly {
  public static void main(String[] args) {
    Collection c = new ArrayList();
    Collection1.fill(c); // Insert useful data
    c = Collections.unmodifiableCollection(c);
    Collection1.print(c); // Reading is OK
    //! c.add("one"); // Can't change it

    List a = new ArrayList();
    Collection1.fill(a);
    a = Collections.unmodifiableList(a);
    ListIterator lit = a.listIterator();
    System.out.println(lit.next()); // Reading OK
    //! lit.add("one"); // Can't change it

    Set s = new HashSet();
    Collection1.fill(s);
    s = Collections.unmodifiableSet(s);
    Collection1.print(s); // Reading OK
    //! s.add("one"); // Can't change it

    Map m = new HashMap();
    Map1.fill(m, Map1.testData1);
    m = Collections.unmodifiableMap(m);
    Map1.print(m); // Reading OK
    //! m.put("Ralph", "Howdy!");
  }
} ///:~
```

In each case, you must fill the container with meaningful data *before* you make it read-only. Once it is loaded, the best approach is to replace the existing handle with the handle that is produced by the "unmodifiable" call. That way, you don't run the risk of accidentally changing the contents once you've made it unmodifiable. On the other hand, this tool also allows you to keep a modifiable container as **private** within a class and to return a read-only handle to that container from a method call. So you can change it from within the class but everyone else can only read it.

Calling the "unmodifiable" method for a particular type does not cause compile-time checking, but once the transformation has occurred, any calls to methods that modify the contents of a particular container will produce an **UnsupportedOperationException**.

Synchronizing a **Collection** or **Map**

The **synchronized** keyword is an important part of the subject of *multithreading*, a more complicated topic that will not be introduced until Chapter 14. Here, I shall note only that the **Collections** class contains a way to automatically synchronize an entire container. The syntax is similar to the "unmodifiable" methods:

```
//: synchronization.java
// Using the Collections.synchronized methods
package c08.newcollections;
import java.util.*;

public class Synchronization {
  public static void main(String[] args) {
    Collection c =
      Collections.synchronizedCollection(
        new ArrayList());
    List list = Collections.synchronizedList(
      new ArrayList());
    Set s = Collections.synchronizedSet(
      new HashSet());
    Map m = Collections.synchronizedMap(
      new HashMap());
  }
} ///:~
```

In this case, you immediately pass the new container through the appropriate "synchronized" method; that way there's no chance of accidentally exposing the unsynchronized version.

The new collections also have a mechanism to prevent more than one process from modifying the contents of a container. The problem occurs if you're iterating through a container and some other process steps in and inserts, removes, or changes an object in that container. Maybe you've already passed that object, maybe it's ahead of you, maybe the size of the container shrinks after you call **size( )** – there are many scenarios for disaster. The new collections library incorporates a *fail fast* mechanism that looks for any changes to the container other than the ones your process is personally responsible for. If it detects that someone else is modifying the container, it immediately produces a **ConcurrentModificationException**. This is the "fail-fast" aspect – it doesn't try to detect a problem later on using a more complex algorithm.

Chapter 8: Holding Your Objects   399

Summary

To review the collections provided in the standard Java (1.0 and 1.1) library (**BitSet** is not included here since it's more of a special-purpose class):

1. An array associates numerical indices to objects. It holds objects of a known type so you don't have to cast the result when you're looking up an object. It can be multidimensional, and it can hold primitives. However, its size cannot be changed once you create it.

2. A **Vector** also associates numerical indices to objects – you can think of arrays and **Vector**s as random-access collections. The **Vector** automatically resizes itself as you add more elements. But a **Vector** can hold only **Object** handles, so it won't hold primitives and you must always cast the result when you pull an **Object** handle out of a collection.

3. A **Hashtable** is a type of **Dictionary**, which is a way to associate, not numbers, but *objects* with other objects. A **Hashtable** also supports random access to objects, in fact, its whole design is focused around rapid access.

4. A **Stack** is a last-in, first-out (LIFO) queue.

If you're familiar with data structures, you might wonder why there's not a larger set of collections. From a functionality standpoint, do you really *need* a larger set of collections? With a **Hashtable**, you can put things in and find them quickly, and with an **Enumeration**, you can iterate through the sequence and perform an operation on every element in the sequence. That's a powerful tool, and maybe it should be enough.

But a **Hashtable** has no concept of order. **Vector**s and arrays give you a linear order, but it's expensive to insert an element into the middle of either one. In addition, queues, dequeues, priority queues, and trees are about *ordering* the elements, not just putting them in and later finding them or moving through them linearly. These data structures are also useful, and that's why they were included in Standard C++. For this reason, you should consider the collections in the standard Java library only as a starting point, and, if you must use Java 1.0 or 1.1, use the JGL when your needs go beyond that.

If you can use Java 1.2 you should use only the new collections, which are likely to satisfy all your needs. Note that the bulk of this book was created using Java 1.1, so you'll see that the collections used through the

---

rest of the book are the ones that are available only in Java 1.1: **Vector** and **Hashtable**. This is a somewhat painful restriction at times, but it provides better backward compatibility with older Java code. If you're writing new code in Java 1.2, the new collections will serve you much better.

Exercises

1. Create a new class called **Gerbil** with an **int gerbilNumber** that's initialized in the constructor (similar to the **Mouse** example in this chapter). Give it a method called **hop( )** that prints out which gerbil number this is and that it's hopping. Create a **Vector** and add a bunch of **Gerbil** objects to the **Vector**. Now use the **elementAt( )** method to move through the **Vector** and call **hop( )** for each **Gerbil**.

2. Modify Exercise 1 so you use an **Enumeration** to move through the **Vector** while calling **hop( )**.

3. In **AssocArray.java**, change the example so it uses a **Hashtable** instead of an **AssocArray**.

4. Take the **Gerbil** class in Exercise 1 and put it into a **Hashtable** instead, associating the name of the **Gerbil** as a **String** (the key) for each **Gerbil** (the value) you put in the table. Get an **Enumeration** for the **keys( )** and use it to move through the **Hashtable**, looking up the **Gerbil** for each key and printing out the key and telling the **gerbil** to **hop( )**.

5. Change Exercise 1 in Chapter 7 to use a **Vector** to hold the **Rodent**s and an **Enumeration** to move through the sequence of **Rodent**s. Remember that a **Vector** holds only **Object**s so you must use a cast (i.e.: RTTI) when accessing individual **Rodent**s.

6. (Intermediate) In Chapter 7, locate the **GreenhouseControls.java** example, which consists of three files. In **Controller.java**, the class **EventSet** is just a collection. Change the code to use a **Stack** instead of an **EventSet**. This will require more than just replacing **EventSet** with **Stack**; you'll also need to use an **Enumeration** to cycle through the set of events. You'll probably find it easier if at times you treat the collection as a **Stack** and at other times as a **Vector**.

7.   (Challenging). Find the source code for **Vector** in the Java source code library that comes with all Java distributions. Copy this code and make a special version called **intVector** that holds only **int**s. Consider what it would take to make a special version of **Vector** for all the primitive types. Now consider what happens if you want to make a linked list class that works with all the primitive types. If parameterized types are ever implemented in Java, they will provide a way to do this work for you automatically (as well as many other benefits).

9: Error handling
with exceptions

The basic philosophy of Java is that "badly-formed code
will not be run."

As with C++, the ideal time to catch the error is at compile time, before
you even try to run the program. However, not all errors can be detected
at compile time. The rest of the problems must be handled at run-time
through some formality that allows the originator of the error to pass
appropriate information to a recipient who will know how to handle the
difficulty properly.

In C and other earlier languages, there could be several of these
formalities, and they were generally established by convention and not as
part of the programming language. Typically, you returned a special
value or set a flag, and the recipient was supposed to look at the value or
the flag and determine that something was amiss. However, as the years
passed, it was discovered that programmers who use a library tend to
think of themselves as invincible, as in, "Yes, errors might happen to

others but not in *my* code." So, not too surprisingly, they wouldn't check for the error conditions (and sometimes the error conditions were too silly to check for[1]). If you *were* thorough enough to check for an error every time you called a method, your code could turn into an unreadable nightmare. Because programmers could still coax systems out of these languages they were resistant to admitting the truth: This approach to handling errors was a major limitation to creating large, robust, maintainable programs.

The solution is to take the casual nature out of error handling and to enforce formality. This actually has a long history, since implementations of *exception handling* go back to operating systems in the 1960s and even to BASIC's **on error goto**. But C++ exception handling was based on Ada, and Java's is based primarily on C++ (although it looks even more like Object Pascal).

The word "exception" is meant in the sense of "I take exception to that." At the point where the problem occurs you might not know what to do with it, but you do know that you can't just continue on merrily; you must stop and somebody, somewhere, must figure out what to do. But you don't have enough information in the current context to fix the problem. So you hand the problem out to a higher context where someone is qualified to make the proper decision (much like a chain of command).

The other rather significant benefit of exceptions is that they clean up error handling code. Instead of checking for a particular error and dealing with it at multiple places in your program, you no longer need to check at the point of the method call (since the exception will guarantee that someone catches it). And, you need to handle the problem in only one place, the so-called *exception handler*. This saves you code and it separates the code that describes what you want to do from the code that is executed when things go awry. In general, reading, writing, and debugging code becomes much clearer with exceptions than when using the old way.

Because exception handling is enforced by the Java compiler, there are only so many examples that can be written in this book without learning about exception handling. This chapter introduces you to the code you need to write to properly handle the exceptions, and the way you can generate your own exceptions if one of your methods gets into trouble.

---

[1] The C programmer can look up the return value of **printf( )** for an example of this.

Basic exceptions

An *exceptional condition* is a problem that prevents the continuation of the method or scope that you're in. It's important to distinguish an exceptional condition from a normal problem, in which you have enough information in the current context to somehow cope with the difficulty. With an exceptional condition, you cannot continue processing because *you don't have the information necessary to deal with the problem in the current context*. All you can do is jump out of the current context and relegate that problem to a higher context. This is what happens when you throw an exception.

A simple example is a divide. If you're about to divide by zero, it's worth checking to make sure you don't go ahead and perform the divide. But what does it mean that the denominator is zero? Maybe you know, in the context of the problem you're trying to solve in that particular method, how to deal with a zero denominator. But if it's an unexpected value, you can't deal with it and so must throw an exception rather than continuing along that path.

When you throw an exception, several things happen. First, the exception object is created in the same way that any Java object is created: on the heap, with **new**. Then the current path of execution (the one you couldn't continue, remember) is stopped and the handle for the exception object is ejected from the current context. At this point the exception-handling mechanism takes over and begins to look for an appropriate place to continue executing the program. This appropriate place is the *exception handler*, whose job is to recover from the problem so the program can either try another tack or simply continue.

As a simple example of throwing an exception, consider an object handle called **t**. It's possible that you might be passed a handle that hasn't been initialized, so you might want to check before trying to call a method using that object handle. You can send information about the error into a larger context by creating an object representing your information and "throwing" it out of your current context. This is called *throwing an exception*. Here's what it looks like:

```
if(t == null)
    throw new NullPointerException();
```

This throws the exception, which allows you – in the current context – to abdicate responsibility for thinking about the issue further. It's just magically handled somewhere else. Precisely *where* will be shown shortly.

Exception arguments

Like any object in Java, you always create exceptions on the heap using **new** and a constructor gets called. There are two constructors in all the standard exceptions; the first is the default constructor, and the second takes a string argument so you can place pertinent information in the exception:

```
if(t == null)
    throw new NullPointerException("t = null");
```

This string can later be extracted using various methods, as will be shown later.

The keyword **throw** causes a number of relatively magical things to happen. First it executes the **new**-expression to create an object that isn't there under normal program execution, and of course, the constructor is called for that object. Then the object is, in effect, "returned" from the method, even though that object type isn't normally what the method is designed to return. A simplistic way to think about exception handling is as an alternate return mechanism, although you get into trouble if you take that analogy too far. You can also exit from ordinary scopes by throwing an exception. But a value is returned, and the method or scope exits.

Any similarity to an ordinary return from a method ends here, because *where* you return is someplace completely different from where you return for a normal method call. (You end up in an appropriate exception handler that might be miles away – many levels lower on the call stack – from where the exception was thrown.)

In addition, you can throw any type of **Throwable** object that you want. Typically, you'll throw a different class of exception for each different type of error. The idea is to store the information in the exception object *and* in the type of exception object chosen, so someone in the bigger context can figure out what to do with your exception. (Often, the only information is the type of exception object, and nothing meaningful is stored within the exception object.)

Catching an exception

If a method throws an exception, it must assume that exception is caught and dealt with. One of the advantages of Java exception handling is that it allows you to concentrate on the problem you're trying to solve in one place, and then deal with the errors from that code in another place.

To see how an exception is caught, you must first understand the concept of a *guarded region*, which is a section of code that might produce exceptions, and is followed by the code to handle those exceptions.

The **try** block

If you're inside a method and you throw an exception (or another method you call within this method throws an exception), that method will exit in the process of throwing. If you don't want a **throw** to leave a method, you can set up a special block within that method to capture the exception. This is called the *try block* because you "try" your various method calls there. The try block is an ordinary scope, preceded by the keyword **try**:

```
try {
    // Code that might generate exceptions
}
```

If you were checking for errors carefully in a programming language that didn't support exception handling, you'd have to surround every method call with setup and error testing code, even if you call the same method several times. With exception handling, you put everything in a try block and capture all the exceptions in one place. This means your code is a lot easier to write and easier to read because the goal of the code is not confused with the error checking.

Exception handlers

Of course, the thrown exception must end up someplace. This "place" is the *exception handler*, and there's one for every exception type you want to catch. Exception handlers immediately follow the try block and are denoted by the keyword **catch**:

```
try {
    // Code that might generate exceptions
} catch(Type1 id1) {
    // Handle exceptions of Type1
} catch(Type2 id2) {
    // Handle exceptions of Type2
} catch(Type3 id3) {
    // Handle exceptions of Type3
```

```
    }
    // etc...
```

Each catch clause (exception handler) is like a little method that takes one and only one argument of a particular type. The identifier (**id1**, **id2**, and so on) can be used inside the handler, just like a method argument. Sometimes you never use the identifier because the type of the exception gives you enough information to deal with the exception, but the identifier must still be there.

The handlers must appear directly after the try block. If an exception is thrown, the exception-handling mechanism goes hunting for the first handler with an argument that matches the type of the exception. Then it enters that catch clause, and the exception is considered handled. (The search for handlers stops once the catch clause is finished.) Only the matching catch clause executes; it's not like a **switch** statement in which you need a **break** after each **case** to prevent the remaining ones from executing.

Note that, within the try block, a number of different method calls might generate the same exception, but you need only one handler.

Termination vs. resumption

There are two basic models in exception-handling theory. In *termination* (which is what Java and C++ support), you assume the error is so critical there's no way to get back to where the exception occurred. Whoever threw the exception decided that there was no way to salvage the situation, and they don't *want* to come back.

The alternative is called *resumption*. It means that the exception handler is expected to do something to rectify the situation, and then the faulting method is retried, presuming success the second time. If you want resumption, it means you still hope to continue execution after the exception is handled. In this case, your exception is more like a method call – which is how you should set up situations in Java in which you want resumption-like behavior. (That is, don't throw an exception; call a method that fixes the problem.) Alternatively, place your **try** block inside a **while** loop that keeps reentering the **try** block until the result is satisfactory.

Historically, programmers using operating systems that supported resumptive exception handling eventually ended up using termination-like code and skipping resumption. So although resumption sounds attractive at first, it seems it isn't quite so useful in practice. The dominant reason is probably the *coupling* that results: your handler must often be aware of where the exception is thrown from and contain non-generic code specific to the throwing location. This makes the code difficult to write and maintain, especially for large systems where the exception can be generated from many points.

The exception specification

In Java, you're required to inform the client programmer, who calls your method, of the exceptions that might be thrown from your method. This is civilized because the caller can know exactly what code to write to catch all potential exceptions. Of course, if source code is available, the client programmer could hunt through and look for **throw** statements, but often a library doesn't come with sources. To prevent this from being a problem, Java provides syntax (and *forces* you to use that syntax) to allow you to politely tell the client programmer what exceptions this method throws, so the client programmer can handle them. This is the *exception specification* and it's part of the method declaration, appearing after the argument list.

The exception specification uses an additional keyword, **throws**, followed by a list of all the potential exception types. So your method definition might look like this:

```
void f() throws tooBig, tooSmall, divZero { //...
```

If you say

```
void f() { // ...
```

it means that no exceptions are thrown from the method. (*Except* for the exceptions of type **RuntimeException**, which can reasonably be thrown anywhere – this will be described later.)

You can't lie about an exception specification – if your method causes exceptions and doesn't handle them, the compiler will detect this and tell you that you must either handle the exception or indicate with an exception specification that it may be thrown from your method. By enforcing exception specifications from top to bottom, Java guarantees that exception correctness can be ensured *at compile time*.[2]

---

[2] This is a significant improvement over C++ exception handling, which doesn't catch violations of exception specifications until run time, when it's not very useful.

There is one place you can lie: you can claim to throw an exception that you don't. The compiler takes your word for it and forces the users of your method to treat it as if it really does throw that exception. This has the beneficial effect of being a placeholder for that exception, so you can actually start throwing the exception later without requiring changes to existing code.

Catching any exception

It is possible to create a handler that catches any type of exception. You do this by catching the base-class exception type **Exception** (there are other types of base exceptions, but **Exception** is the base that's pertinent to virtually all programming activities):

```
catch(Exception e) {
   System.out.println("caught an exception");
}
```

This will catch any exception, so if you use it you'll want to put it at the *end* of your list of handlers to avoid pre-empting any exception handlers that might otherwise follow it.

Since the **Exception** class is the base of all the exception classes that are important to the programmer, you don't get much specific information about the exception, but you can call the methods that come from *its* base type **Throwable**:

String getMessage( )
Gets the detail message.

String toString( )
Returns a short description of the Throwable, including the detail message if there is one.

void printStackTrace( )
void printStackTrace(PrintStream)
Prints the Throwable and the Throwable's call stack trace. The call stack shows the sequence of method calls that brought you to the point at which the exception was thrown.

The first version prints to standard error, the second prints to a stream of your choice. If you're working under Windows, you can't redirect standard error so you might want to use the second version and send the results to **System.out**; that way the output can be redirected any way you want.

In addition, you get some other methods from **Throwable**'s base type **Object** (everybody's base type). The one that might come in handy for exceptions is **getClass( )**, which returns an object representing the class of this object. You can in turn query this **Class** object for its name with **getName( )** or **toString( )**. You can also do more sophisticated things with **Class** objects that aren't necessary in exception handling. **Class** objects will be studied later in the book.

Here's an example that shows the use of the **Exception** methods: (See page 97 if you have trouble executing this program.)

```
//: ExceptionMethods.java
// Demonstrating the Exception Methods
package c09;

public class ExceptionMethods {
  public static void main(String[] args) {
    try {
      throw new Exception("Here's my Exception");
    } catch(Exception e) {
      System.out.println("Caught Exception");
      System.out.println(
        "e.getMessage(): " + e.getMessage());
      System.out.println(
        "e.toString(): " + e.toString());
      System.out.println("e.printStackTrace():");
      e.printStackTrace();
    }
  }
} ///:~
```

The output for this program is:

```
Caught Exception
e.getMessage(): Here's my Exception
e.toString(): java.lang.Exception: Here's my
Exception
e.printStackTrace():
java.lang.Exception: Here's my Exception
        at ExceptionMethods.main
```

You can see that the methods provide successively more information – each is effectively a superset of the previous one.

Rethrowing an exception

Sometimes you'll want to rethrow the exception that you just caught, particularly when you use **Exception** to catch any exception. Since you already have the handle to the current exception, you can simply re-throw that handle:

```
catch(Exception e) {
  System.out.println("An exception was thrown");
  throw e;
}
```

Rethrowing an exception causes the exception to go to the exception handlers in the next-higher context. Any further **catch** clauses for the same **try** block are still ignored. In addition, everything about the exception object is preserved, so the handler at the higher context that catches the specific exception type can extract all the information from that object.

If you simply re-throw the current exception, the information that you print about that exception in **printStackTrace( )** will pertain to the exception's origin, not the place where you re-throw it. If you want to install new stack trace information, you can do so by calling **fillInStackTrace( )**, which returns an exception object that it creates by stuffing the current stack information into the old exception object. Here's what it looks like:

```
//: Rethrowing.java
// Demonstrating fillInStackTrace()

public class Rethrowing {
  public static void f() throws Exception {
    System.out.println(
      "originating the exception in f()");
    throw new Exception("thrown from f()");
  }
  public static void g() throws Throwable {
    try {
      f();
    } catch(Exception e) {
      System.out.println(
        "Inside g(), e.printStackTrace()");
      e.printStackTrace();
      throw e; // 17
      // throw e.fillInStackTrace(); // 18
```

```
      }
    }
    public static void
    main(String[] args) throws Throwable {
      try {
        g();
      } catch(Exception e) {
        System.out.println(
          "Caught in main, e.printStackTrace()");
        e.printStackTrace();
      }
    }
} ///:~
```

The important line numbers are marked inside of comments. With line 17 un-commented (as shown), the output is:

```
originating the exception in f()
Inside g(), e.printStackTrace()
java.lang.Exception: thrown from f()
        at Rethrowing.f(Rethrowing.java:8)
        at Rethrowing.g(Rethrowing.java:12)
        at Rethrowing.main(Rethrowing.java:24)
Caught in main, e.printStackTrace()
java.lang.Exception: thrown from f()
        at Rethrowing.f(Rethrowing.java:8)
        at Rethrowing.g(Rethrowing.java:12)
        at Rethrowing.main(Rethrowing.java:24)
```

So the exception stack trace always remembers its true point of origin, no matter how many times it gets rethrown.

With line 17 commented and line 18 un-commented, **fillInStackTrace( )** is used instead, and the result is:

```
originating the exception in f()
Inside g(), e.printStackTrace()
java.lang.Exception: thrown from f()
        at Rethrowing.f(Rethrowing.java:8)
        at Rethrowing.g(Rethrowing.java:12)
        at Rethrowing.main(Rethrowing.java:24)
Caught in main, e.printStackTrace()
java.lang.Exception: thrown from f()
        at Rethrowing.g(Rethrowing.java:18)
        at Rethrowing.main(Rethrowing.java:24)
```

Because of **fillInStackTrace( )**, line 18 becomes the new point of origin of the exception.

The class **Throwable** must appear in the exception specification for **g( )** and **main( )** because **fillInStackTrace( )** produces a handle to a **Throwable** object. Since **Throwable** is a base class of **Exception**, it's possible to get an object that's a **Throwable** but *not* an **Exception**, so the handler for **Exception** in **main( )** might miss it. To make sure everything is in order, the compiler forces an exception specification for **Throwable**. For example, the exception in the following program is *not* caught in **main( )**:

```
//: ThrowOut.java
public class ThrowOut {
  public static void
  main(String[] args) throws Throwable {
    try {
      throw new Throwable();
    } catch(Exception e) {
      System.out.println("Caught in main()");
    }
  }
} ///:~
```

It's also possible to rethrow a different exception from the one you caught. If you do this, you get a similar effect as when you use **fillInStackTrace( )**: the information about the original site of the exception is lost, and what you're left with is the information pertaining to the new **throw**:

```
//: RethrowNew.java
// Rethrow a different object from the one that
// was caught

public class RethrowNew {
  public static void f() throws Exception {
    System.out.println(
      "originating the exception in f()");
    throw new Exception("thrown from f()");
  }
  public static void main(String[] args) {
    try {
      f();
    } catch(Exception e) {
      System.out.println(
```

```
                "Caught in main, e.printStackTrace()");
            e.printStackTrace();
            throw new NullPointerException("from main");
        }
    }
} ///:~
```

The output is:

```
Originating the exception in f()
Caught in main, e.printStackTrace()
java.lang.Exception: thrown from f()
        at RethrowNew.f(RethrowNew.java:8)
        at RethrowNew.main(RethrowNew.java:13)
java.lang.NullPointerException: from main
        at RethrowNew.main(RethrowNew.java:18)
```

The final exception knows only that it came from **main( )**, and not from
f( ). Note that **Throwable** isn't necessary in any of the exception
specifications.

You never have to worry about cleaning up the previous exception, or
any exceptions for that matter. They're all heap-based objects created
with **new**, so the garbage collector automatically cleans them all up.

Standard Java exceptions

Java contains a class called **Throwable** that describes anything that can
be thrown as an exception. There are two general types of **Throwable**
objects ("types of" = "inherited from"). **Error** represents compile-time
and system errors that you don't worry about catching (except in special
cases). **Exception** is the basic type that can be thrown from any of the
standard Java library class methods and from your methods and run-
time accidents.

The best way to get an overview of the exceptions is to browse online
Java documentation from *http://java.sun.com*. (Of course, it's easier to
download it first.) It's worth doing this once just to get a feel for the
various exceptions, but you'll soon see that there isn't anything special
between one exception and the next except for the name. Also, the
number of exceptions in Java keeps expanding; basically it's pointless to
print them in a book. Any new library you get from a third-party vendor
will probably have its own exceptions as well. The important thing to
understand is the concept and what you should do with the exceptions.

```
java.lang.Exception
```

This is the basic exception class your program can catch. Other exceptions are derived from this. The basic idea is that the name of the exception represents the problem that occurred and the exception name is intended to be relatively self-explanatory. The exceptions are not all defined in **java.lang**; some are created to support other libraries such as **util**, **net**, and **io**, which you can see from their full class names or what they are inherited from. For example, all IO exceptions are inherited from **java.io.IOException**.

The special case of RuntimeException

The first example in this chapter was

```
if(t == null)
    throw new NullPointerException();
```

It can be a bit horrifying to think that you must check for **null** on every handle that is passed into a method (since you can't know if the caller has passed you a valid handle). Fortunately, you don't – this is part of the standard run-time checking that Java performs for you, and if any call is made to a null handle, Java will automatically throw a **NullPointerException**. So the above bit of code is always superfluous.

There's a whole group of exception types that are in this category. They're always thrown automatically by Java and you don't need to include them in your exception specifications. Conveniently enough, they're all grouped together by putting them under a single base class called **RuntimeException**, which is a perfect example of inheritance: it establishes a family of types that have some characteristics and behaviors in common. Also, you never need to write an exception specification saying that a method might throw a **RuntimeException**, since that's just assumed. Because they indicate bugs, you virtually never catch a **RuntimeException** – it's dealt with automatically. If you were forced to check for **RuntimeException**s your code could get messy. Even though you don't typically catch **RuntimeExceptions**, in your own packages you might choose to throw some of the **RuntimeException**s.

What happens when you don't catch such exceptions? Since the compiler doesn't enforce exception specifications for these, it's quite plausible that a **RuntimeException** could percolate all the way out to your **main( )** method without being caught. To see what happens in this case, try the following example:

```
//: NeverCaught.java
// Ignoring RuntimeExceptions

public class NeverCaught {
  static void f() {
    throw new RuntimeException("From f()");
  }
  static void g() {
    f();
  }
  public static void main(String[] args) {
    g();
  }
} ///:~
```

You can already see that a **RuntimeException** (or anything inherited from it) is a special case, since the compiler doesn't require an exception specification for these types.

The output is:

```
java.lang.RuntimeException: From f()
        at NeverCaught.f(NeverCaught.java:9)
        at NeverCaught.g(NeverCaught.java:12)
        at NeverCaught.main(NeverCaught.java:15)
```

So the answer is: If a RuntimeException gets all the way out to **main( )** without being caught, **printStackTrace( )** is called for that exception as the program exits.

Keep in mind that it's possible to ignore only **RuntimeException**s in your coding, since all other handling is carefully enforced by the compiler. The reasoning is that a **RuntimeException** represents a programming error:

1. An error you cannot catch (receiving a null handle handed to your method by a client programmer, for example)

2. An error that you, as a programmer, should have checked for in your code (such as **ArrayIndexOutOfBoundsException** where you should have paid attention to the size of the array).

You can see what a tremendous benefit it is to have exceptions in this case, since they help in the debugging process.

It's interesting to notice that you cannot classify Java exception handling as a single-purpose tool. Yes, it is designed to handle those pesky run-time errors that will occur because of forces outside your code's control,

---

but it's also essential for certain types of programming bugs that the compiler cannot detect.

Creating your own exceptions

You're not stuck using the Java exceptions. This is important because you'll often need to create your own exceptions to denote a special error that your library is capable of creating, but which was not foreseen when the Java hierarchy was created.

To create your own exception class, you're forced to inherit from an existing type of exception, preferably one that is close in meaning to your new exception. Inheriting an exception is quite simple:

```
//: Inheriting.java
// Inheriting your own exceptions

class MyException extends Exception {
  public MyException() {}
  public MyException(String msg) {
    super(msg);
  }
}

public class Inheriting {
  public static void f() throws MyException {
    System.out.println(
      "Throwing MyException from f()");
    throw new MyException();
  }
  public static void g() throws MyException {
    System.out.println(
      "Throwing MyException from g()");
    throw new MyException("Originated in g()");
  }
  public static void main(String[] args) {
    try {
      f();
    } catch(MyException e) {
      e.printStackTrace();
    }
    try {
      g();
```

```
      } catch(MyException e) {
        e.printStackTrace();
      }
    }
  } ///:~
```

The inheritance occurs in the creation of the new class:

```
class MyException extends Exception {
  public MyException() {}
  public MyException(String msg) {
    super(msg);
  }
}
```

The key phrase here is **extends Exception**, which says "it's everything an **Exception** is and more." The added code is small – the addition of two constructors that define the way **MyException** is created. Remember that the compiler automatically calls the base-class default constructor if you don't explicitly call a base-class constructor, as in the **MyException( )** default constructor. In the second constructor, the base-class constructor with a **String** argument is explicitly invoked by using the **super** keyword.

The output of the program is:

```
Throwing MyException from f()
MyException
        at Inheriting.f(Inheriting.java:16)
        at Inheriting.main(Inheriting.java:24)
Throwing MyException from g()
MyException: Originated in g()
        at Inheriting.g(Inheriting.java:20)
        at Inheriting.main(Inheriting.java:29)
```

You can see the absence of the detail message in the **MyException** thrown from **f( )**.

The process of creating your own exceptions can be taken further. You can add extra constructors and members:

```
//: Inheriting2.java
// Inheriting your own exceptions

class MyException2 extends Exception {
  public MyException2() {}
```

```java
    public MyException2(String msg) {
      super(msg);
    }
    public MyException2(String msg, int x) {
      super(msg);
      i = x;
    }
    public int val() { return i; }
    private int i;
}

public class Inheriting2 {
  public static void f() throws MyException2 {
    System.out.println(
      "Throwing MyException2 from f()");
    throw new MyException2();
  }
  public static void g() throws MyException2 {
    System.out.println(
      "Throwing MyException2 from g()");
    throw new MyException2("Originated in g()");
  }
  public static void h() throws MyException2 {
    System.out.println(
      "Throwing MyException2 from h()");
    throw new MyException2(
      "Originated in h()", 47);
  }
  public static void main(String[] args) {
    try {
      f();
    } catch(MyException2 e) {
      e.printStackTrace();
    }
    try {
      g();
    } catch(MyException2 e) {
      e.printStackTrace();
    }
    try {
      h();
    } catch(MyException2 e) {
      e.printStackTrace();
      System.out.println("e.val() = " + e.val());
```

```
        }
      }
    } ///:~
```

A data member **i** has been added, along with a method that reads that value and an additional constructor that sets it. The output is:

```
Throwing MyException2 from f()
MyException2
        at Inheriting2.f(Inheriting2.java:22)
        at Inheriting2.main(Inheriting2.java:34)
Throwing MyException2 from g()
MyException2: Originated in g()
        at Inheriting2.g(Inheriting2.java:26)
        at Inheriting2.main(Inheriting2.java:39)
Throwing MyException2 from h()
MyException2: Originated in h()
        at Inheriting2.h(Inheriting2.java:30)
        at Inheriting2.main(Inheriting2.java:44)
e.val() = 47
```

Since an exception is just another kind of object, you can continue this process of embellishing the power of your exception classes. Keep in mind, however, that all this dressing up might be lost on the client programmers using your packages, since they might simply look for the exception to be thrown and nothing more. (That's the way most of the Java library exceptions are used.) If this is the case, it's possible to create a new exception type with almost no code at all:

```
//: SimpleException.java
class SimpleException extends Exception {
} ///:~
```

This relies on the compiler to create the default constructor (which automatically calls the base-class default constructor). Of course, in this case you don't get a **SimpleException(String)** constructor, but in practice that isn't used much.

Exception restrictions

When you override a method, you can throw only the exceptions that have been specified in the base-class version of the method. This is a useful restriction, since it means that code that works with the base class will automatically work with any object derived from the base class (a fundamental OOP concept, of course), including exceptions.

This example demonstrates the kinds of restrictions imposed (at compile time) for exceptions:

```
//: StormyInning.java
// Overridden methods may throw only the
// exceptions specified in their base-class
// versions, or exceptions derived from the
// base-class exceptions.

class BaseballException extends Exception {}
class Foul extends BaseballException {}
class Strike extends BaseballException {}

abstract class Inning {
  Inning() throws BaseballException {}
  void event () throws BaseballException {
   // Doesn't actually have to throw anything
  }
  abstract void atBat() throws Strike, Foul;
  void walk() {} // Throws nothing
}

class StormException extends Exception {}
class RainedOut extends StormException {}
class PopFoul extends Foul {}

interface Storm {
  void event() throws RainedOut;
  void rainHard() throws RainedOut;
}

public class StormyInning extends Inning
     implements Storm {
  // OK to add new exceptions for constructors,
  // but you must deal with the base constructor
  // exceptions:
  StormyInning() throws RainedOut,
    BaseballException {}
  StormyInning(String s) throws Foul,
    BaseballException {}
  // Regular methods must conform to base class:
//! void walk() throws PopFoul {} //Compile error
```

```
     // Interface CANNOT add exceptions to existing
     // methods from the base class:
//! public void event() throws RainedOut {}
     // If the method doesn't already exist in the
     // base class, the exception is OK:
     public void rainHard() throws RainedOut {}
     // You can choose to not throw any exceptions,
     // even if base version does:
     public void event() {}
     // Overridden methods can throw
     // inherited exceptions:
     void atBat() throws PopFoul {}
     public static void main(String[] args) {
       try {
         StormyInning si = new StormyInning();
         si.atBat();
       } catch(PopFoul e) {
       } catch(RainedOut e) {
       } catch(BaseballException e) {}
       // Strike not thrown in derived version.
       try {
         // What happens if you upcast?
         Inning i = new StormyInning();
         i.atBat();
         // You must catch the exceptions from the
         // base-class version of the method:
       } catch(Strike e) {
       } catch(Foul e) {
       } catch(RainedOut e) {
       } catch(BaseballException e) {}
     }
   } ///:~
```

In **Inning**, you can see that both the constructor and the **event( )** method say they will throw an exception, but they never do. This is legal because it allows you to force the user to catch any exceptions that you might add in overridden versions of **event( )**. The same idea holds for **abstract** methods, as seen in **atBat( )**.

The **interface Storm** is interesting because it contains one method (**event( )**)that is defined in **Inning**, and one method that isn't. Both methods throw a new type of exception, **RainedOut**. When **StormyInning extends Inning** and **implements Storm**, you'll see that the **event( )** method in **Storm** *cannot* change the exception interface of **event( )** in **Inning**. Again, this makes sense because otherwise you'd never know if you were catching the correct thing when working with the base class. Of course, if a method described in an **interface** is not in the base class, such as **rainHard( )**, then there's no problem if it throws exceptions.

The restriction on exceptions does not apply to constructors. You can see in **StormyInning** that a constructor can throw anything it wants, regardless of what the base-class constructor throws. However, since a base-class constructor must always be called one way or another (here, the default constructor is called automatically), the derived-class constructor must declare any base-class constructor exceptions in its exception specification.

The reason **StormyInning.walk( )** will not compile is that it throws an exception, while **Inning.walk( )** does not. If this was allowed, then you could write code that called **Inning.walk( )** and that didn't have to handle any exceptions, but then when you substituted an object of a class derived from **Inning**, exceptions would be thrown so your code would break. By forcing the derived-class methods to conform to the exception specifications of the base-class methods, substitutability of objects is maintained.

The overridden **event( )** method shows that a derived-class version of a method may choose to not throw any exceptions, even if the base-class version does. Again, this is fine since it doesn't break any code that is written assuming the base-class version throws exceptions. Similar logic applies to **atBat( )**, which throws **PopFoul**, an exception that is derived from **Foul** thrown by the base-class version of **atBat( )**. This way, if someone writes code that works with **Inning** and calls **atBat( )**, they must catch the **Foul** exception. Since **PopFoul** is derived from **Foul**, the exception handler will also catch **PopFoul**.

The last point of interest is in **main( )**. Here you can see that if you're dealing with exactly a **StormyInning** object, the compiler forces you to catch only the exceptions that are specific to that class, but if you upcast to the base type then the compiler (correctly) forces you to catch the exceptions for the base type. All these constraints produce much more robust exception-handling code.[3]

---

[3] ANSI/ISO C++ added similar constraints that require derived-method exceptions to be the same as, or derived from, the exceptions thrown by the base-class method. This is one case in which C++ is actually able to check exception specifications at compile time.

It's useful to realize that although exception specifications are enforced by the compiler during inheritance, the exception specifications are not part of the type of a method, which is comprised of only the method name and argument types. Therefore, you cannot overload methods based on exception specifications. In addition, because an exception specification exists in a base-class version of a method doesn't mean that it must exist in the derived-class version of the method, and this is quite different from inheriting the methods (that is, a method in the base class must also exist in the derived class). Put another way, the "exception specification interface" for a particular method may narrow during inheritance and overriding, but it may not widen – this is precisely the opposite of the rule for the class interface during inheritance.

Performing cleanup with finally

There's often some piece of code that you want to execute whether or not an exception occurs in a **try** block. This usually pertains to some operation other than memory recovery (since that's taken care of by the garbage collector). To achieve this effect, you use a **finally** clause[4] at the end of all the exception handlers. The full picture of an exception-handling section is thus:

```
try {
  // The guarded region:
  // Dangerous stuff that might throw A, B, or C
} catch (A a1) {
  // Handle A
} catch (B b1) {
  // Handle B
} catch (C c1) {
  // Handle C
} finally {
  // Stuff that happens every time
}
```

To demonstrate that the **finally** clause always runs, try this program:

---

[4] C++ exception handling does not have the **finally** clause because it relies on destructors to accomplish this sort of cleanup.

```
//: FinallyWorks.java
// The finally clause is always executed

public class FinallyWorks {
  static int count = 0;
  public static void main(String[] args) {
    while(true) {
      try {
        // post-increment is zero first time:
        if(count++ == 0)
          throw new Exception();
        System.out.println("No exception");
      } catch(Exception e) {
        System.out.println("Exception thrown");
      } finally {
        System.out.println("in finally clause");
        if(count == 2) break; // out of "while"
      }
    }
  }
} ///:~
```

This program also gives a hint for how you can deal with the fact that exceptions in Java (like exceptions in C++) do not allow you to resume back to where the exception was thrown, as discussed earlier. If you place your **try** block in a loop, you can establish a condition that must be met before you continue the program. You can also add a **static** counter or some other device to allow the loop to try several different approaches before giving up. This way you can build a greater level of robustness into your programs.

The output is:

```
Exception thrown
in finally clause
No exception
in finally clause
```

Whether an exception is thrown or not, the **finally** clause is always executed.

What's **finally** for?

In a language without garbage collection *and* without automatic destructor calls,[5] **finally** is important because it allows the programmer to guarantee the release of memory regardless of what happens in the **try** block. But Java has garbage collection, so releasing memory is virtually never a problem. Also, it has no destructors to call. So when do you need to use **finally** in Java?

finally is necessary when you need to set something *other* than memory back to its original state. This is usually something like an open file or network connection, something you've drawn on the screen or even a switch in the outside world, as modeled in the following example:

```
//: OnOffSwitch.java
// Why use finally?

class Switch {
  boolean state = false;
  boolean read() { return state; }
  void on() { state = true; }
  void off() { state = false; }
}

public class OnOffSwitch {
  static Switch sw = new Switch();
  public static void main(String[] args) {
    try {
      sw.on();
      // Code that can throw exceptions...
      sw.off();
    } catch(NullPointerException e) {
      System.out.println("NullPointerException");
      sw.off();
    } catch(IllegalArgumentException e) {
      System.out.println("IOException");
      sw.off();
```

---

[5] A destructor is a function that's always called when an object becomes unused. You always know exactly where and when the destructor gets called. C++ has automatic destructor calls, but Delphi's Object Pascal versions 1 and 2 do not (which changes the meaning and use of the concept of a destructor for that language).

```
      }
    }
  } ///:~
```

The goal here is to make sure that the switch is off when **main( )** is completed, so **sw.off( )** is placed at the end of the try block and at the end of each exception handler. But it's possible that an exception could be thrown that isn't caught here, so **sw.off( )** would be missed. However, with **finally** you can place the closure code from a try block in just one place:

```
//: WithFinally.java
// Finally Guarantees cleanup

class Switch2 {
  boolean state = false;
  boolean read() { return state; }
  void on() { state = true; }
  void off() { state = false; }
}

public class WithFinally {
  static Switch2 sw = new Switch2();
  public static void main(String[] args) {
    try {
      sw.on();
      // Code that can throw exceptions...
    } catch(NullPointerException e) {
      System.out.println("NullPointerException");
    } catch(IllegalArgumentException e) {
      System.out.println("IOException");
    } finally {
      sw.off();
    }
  }
} ///:~
```

Here the **sw.off( )** has been moved to just one place, where it's guaranteed to run no matter what happens.

Even in cases in which the exception is not caught in the current set of **catch** clauses, **finally** will be executed before the exception-handling mechanism continues its search for a handler at the next higher level:

```
//: AlwaysFinally.java
// Finally is always executed
```

```
class Ex extends Exception {}

public class AlwaysFinally {
  public static void main(String[] args) {
    System.out.println(
      "Entering first try block");
    try {
      System.out.println(
        "Entering second try block");
      try {
        throw new Ex();
      } finally {
        System.out.println(
          "finally in 2nd try block");
      }
    } catch(Ex e) {
      System.out.println(
        "Caught Ex in first try block");
    } finally {
      System.out.println(
        "finally in 1st try block");
    }
  }
} ///:~
```

The output for this program shows you what happens:

```
Entering first try block
Entering second try block
finally in 2nd try block
Caught Ex in first try block
finally in 1st try block
```

The **finally** statement will also be executed in situations in which **break** and **continue** statements are involved. Note that, along with the labeled **break** and labeled **continue**, **finally** eliminates the need for a **goto** statement in Java.

Pitfall: the lost exception

In general, Java's exception implementation is quite outstanding, but unfortunately there's a flaw. Although exceptions are an indication of a crisis in your program and should never be ignored, it's possible for an exception to simply be lost. This happens with a particular configuration using a **finally** clause:

```java
//: LostMessage.java
// How an exception can be lost

class VeryImportantException extends Exception {
  public String toString() {
    return "A very important exception!";
  }
}

class HoHumException extends Exception {
  public String toString() {
    return "A trivial exception";
  }
}

public class LostMessage {
  void f() throws VeryImportantException {
    throw new VeryImportantException();
  }
  void dispose() throws HoHumException {
    throw new HoHumException();
  }
  public static void main(String[] args)
      throws Exception {
    LostMessage lm = new LostMessage();
    try {
      lm.f();
    } finally {
      lm.dispose();
    }
  }
} ///:~
```

The output is:

```
A trivial exception
        at
LostMessage.dispose(LostMessage.java:21)
        at LostMessage.main(LostMessage.java:29)
```

You can see that there's no evidence of the **VeryImportantException**, which is simply replaced by the **HoHumException** in the **finally** clause.

This is a rather serious pitfall, since it means that an exception can be completely lost, and in a far more subtle and difficult-to-detect fashion than the example above. In contrast, C++ treats the situation in which a second exception is thrown before the first one is handled as a dire programming error. Perhaps a future version of Java will repair the problem. (The above results were produced with Java 1.1.)

Constructors

When writing code with exceptions, it's particularly important that you always ask, "If an exception occurs, will this be properly cleaned up?" Most of the time you're fairly safe, but in constructors there's a problem. The constructor puts the object into a safe starting state, but it might perform some operation – such as opening a file – that doesn't get cleaned up until the user is finished with the object and calls a special cleanup method. If you throw an exception from inside a constructor, these cleanup behaviors might not occur properly. This means that you must be especially diligent while you write your constructor.

Since you've just learned about **finally**, you might think that it is the correct solution. But it's not quite that simple, because **finally** performs the cleanup code *every time*, even in the situations in which you don't want the cleanup code executed until the cleanup method runs. Thus, if you do perform cleanup in **finally**, you must set some kind of flag when the constructor finishes normally and don't do anything in the finally block if the flag is set. Because this isn't particularly elegant (you are coupling your code from one place to another), it's best if you try to avoid performing this kind of cleanup in **finally** unless you are forced to.

In the following example, a class called **InputFile** is created that opens a file and allows you to read it one line (converted into a **String**) at a time. It uses the classes **FileReader** and **BufferedReader** from the Java standard IO library that will be discussed in Chapter 10, but which are simple enough that you probably won't have any trouble understanding their basic use:

```
//: Cleanup.java
// Paying attention to exceptions
// in constructors
import java.io.*;

class InputFile {
  private BufferedReader in;
  InputFile(String fname) throws Exception {
```

```
      try {
        in =
          new BufferedReader(
            new FileReader(fname));
        // Other code that might throw exceptions
      } catch(FileNotFoundException e) {
        System.out.println(
          "Could not open " + fname);
        // Wasn't open, so don't close it
        throw e;
      } catch(Exception e) {
        // All other exceptions must close it
        try {
          in.close();
        } catch(IOException e2) {
          System.out.println(
            "in.close() unsuccessful");
        }
        throw e;
      } finally {
        // Don't close it here!!!
      }
    }
    String getLine() {
      String s;
      try {
        s = in.readLine();
      } catch(IOException e) {
        System.out.println(
          "readLine() unsuccessful");
        s = "failed";
      }
      return s;
    }
    void cleanup() {
      try {
        in.close();
      } catch(IOException e2) {
        System.out.println(
          "in.close() unsuccessful");
      }
    }
  }
```

```
public class Cleanup {
  public static void main(String[] args) {
    try {
      InputFile in =
        new InputFile("Cleanup.java");
      String s;
      int i = 1;
      while((s = in.getLine()) != null)
        System.out.println(""+ i++ + ": " + s);
      in.cleanup();
    } catch(Exception e) {
      System.out.println(
        "Caught in main, e.printStackTrace()");
      e.printStackTrace();
    }
  }
} ///:~
```

This example uses Java 1.1 IO classes.

The constructor for **InputFile** takes a **String** argument, which is the
name of the file you want to open. Inside a **try** block, it creates a
FileReader using the file name. A **FileReader** isn't particularly useful
until you turn around and use it to create a **BufferedReader** that you
can actually talk to – notice that one of the benefits of **InputFile** is that it
combines these two actions.

If the **FileReader** constructor is unsuccessful, it throws a
FileNotFoundException, which must be caught separately because that's
the one case in which you don't want to close the file since it wasn't
successfully opened. Any *other* catch clauses must close the file because it
was opened by the time those catch clauses are entered. (Of course, this is
trickier if more than one method can throw a **FileNotFoundException**.
In that case, you might want to break things into several **try** blocks.) The
close( ) method throws an exception that is tried and caught even though
it's within the block of another **catch** clause – it's just another pair of
curly braces to the Java compiler. After performing local operations, the
exception is re-thrown, which is appropriate because this constructor
failed, and you wouldn't want the calling method to assume that the
object had been properly created and was valid.

In this example, which doesn't use the aforementioned flagging
technique, the **finally** clause is definitely *not* the place to **close( )** the file,
since that would close it every time the constructor completed. Since we

want the file to be open for the useful lifetime of the **InputFile** object this would not be appropriate.

The **getLine( )** method returns a **String** containing the next line in the file. It calls **readLine( )**, which can throw an exception, but that exception is caught so **getLine( )** doesn't throw any exceptions. One of the design issues with exceptions is whether to handle an exception completely at this level, to handle it partially and pass the same exception (or a different one) on, or whether to simply pass it on. Passing it on, when appropriate, can certainly simplify coding. The **getLine( )** method becomes:

```
String getLine() throws IOException {
    return in.readLine();
}
```

But of course, the caller is now responsible for handling any **IOException** that might arise.

The **cleanup( )** method must be called by the user when they are finished using the **InputFile** object to release the system resources (such as file handles) that are used by the **BufferedReader** and/or **FileReader** objects.[6] You don't want to do this until you're finished with the **InputFile** object, at the point you're going to let it go. You might think of putting such functionality into a **finalize( )** method, but as mentioned in Chapter 4 you can't always be sure that **finalize( )** will be called (even if you *can* be sure that it will be called, you don't know *when*). This is one of the downsides to Java – all cleanup other than memory cleanup doesn't happen automatically, so you must inform the client programmer that they are responsible, and possibly guarantee that cleanup occurs using **finalize( )**.

In **Cleanup.java** an **InputFile** is created to open the same source file that creates the program, and this file is read in a line at a time, and line numbers are added. All exceptions are caught generically in **main( )**, although you could choose greater granularity.

One of the benefits of this example is to show you why exceptions are introduced at this point in the book. Exceptions are so integral to programming in Java, especially because the compiler enforces them, that you can accomplish only so much without knowing how to work with them.

---

[6] In C++, a *destructor* would handle this for you.

Exception matching

When an exception is thrown, the exception-handling system looks through the "nearest" handlers in the order they are written. When it finds a match, the exception is considered handled, and no further searching occurs.

Matching an exception doesn't require a perfect match between the exception and its handler. A derived-class object will match a handler for the base class, as shown in this example:

```
//: Human.java
// Catching Exception Hierarchies

class Annoyance extends Exception {}
class Sneeze extends Annoyance {}

public class Human {
  public static void main(String[] args) {
    try {
      throw new Sneeze();
    } catch(Sneeze s) {
      System.out.println("Caught Sneeze");
    } catch(Annoyance a) {
      System.out.println("Caught Annoyance");
    }
  }
} ///:~
```

The **Sneeze** exception will be caught by the first **catch** clause that it matches, which is the first one, of course. However, if you remove the first catch clause:

```
try {
  throw new Sneeze();
} catch(Annoyance a) {
  System.out.println("Caught Annoyance");
}
```

The remaining catch clause will still work because it's catching the base class of **Sneeze**. Put another way, **catch(Annoyance e)** will catch a **Annoyance** *or any class derived from it*. This is useful because if you decide to add more exceptions to a method, if they're all inherited from

---

the same base class then the client programmer's code will not need changing, assuming they catch the base class, at the very least.

If you try to "mask" the derived-class exceptions by putting the base-class catch clause first, like this:

```
try {
    throw new Sneeze();
} catch(Annoyance a) {
    System.out.println("Caught Annoyance");
} catch(Sneeze s) {
    System.out.println("Caught Sneeze");
}
```

the compiler will give you an error message, since it sees that the **Sneeze** catch-clause can never be reached.

Exception guidelines

Use exceptions to:

1. Fix the problem and call the method (which caused the exception) again.

2. Patch things up and continue without retrying the method.

3. Calculate some alternative result instead of what the method was supposed to produce.

4. Do whatever you can in the current context and rethrow the *same* exception to a higher context.

5. Do whatever you can in the current context and throw a *different* exception to a higher context.

6. Terminate the program.

7. Simplify. If your exception scheme makes things more complicated, then it is painful and annoying to use.

8. Make your library and program safer. This is a short-term investment (for debugging) and a long-term investment (for application robustness).

Summary

Improved error recovery is one of the most powerful ways that you can increase the robustness of your code. Error recovery is a fundamental concern for every program you write, and it's especially important in Java, in which one of the primary goals is to create program components for others to use. To create a robust system, each component must be robust.

The goals for exception handling in Java are to simplify the creation of large, reliable programs using less code than currently possible, with more confidence that your application doesn't have an unhandled error.

Exceptions are not terribly difficult to learn, and are one of those features that provide immediate and significant benefits to your project. Fortunately, Java enforces all aspects of exceptions so it's guaranteed that they will be used consistently by both library designer and client programmer.

Exercises

1. Create a class with a **main( )** that throws an object of class **Exception** inside a **try** block. Give the constructor for **Exception** a string argument. Catch the exception inside a **catch** clause and print out the string argument. Add a **finally** clause and print a message to prove you were there.

2. Create your own exception class using the **extends** keyword. Write a constructor for this class that takes a **String** argument and stores it inside the object with a **String** handle. Write a method that prints out the stored **String**. Create a try-catch clause to exercise your new exception.

3. Write a class with a method that throws an exception of the type created in Exercise 2. Try compiling it without an exception specification to see what the compiler says. Add the appropriate

---

exception specification. Try out your class and its exception inside a try–catch clause.

4. In chapter 5, find the two programs called **Assert.java** and modify these to throw their own type of exception instead of printing to **System.err**. This exception should be an inner class that extends RuntimeException.

10: The Java IO system

Creating a good input/output (IO) system is one of the more difficult tasks for the language designer.

This is evidenced by the number of different approaches. The challenge seems to be in covering all eventualities. Not only are there different kinds of IO that you want to communicate with (files, the console, network connections), but you need to talk to them in a wide variety of ways (sequential, random-access, binary, character, by lines, by words, etc.).

The Java library designers attacked the problem by creating lots of classes. In fact, there are so many classes for Java's IO system that it can be intimidating at first (ironically, the Java IO design actually prevents an explosion of classes). There has also been a significant change in the IO library between Java 1.0 and Java 1.1. Instead of simply replacing the old library with a new one, the designers at Sun extended the old library and added the new one alongside it. As a result you can sometimes end up mixing the old and new libraries and creating even more intimidating code.

This chapter will help you understand the variety of IO classes in the standard Java library and how to use them. The first portion of the chapter will introduce the "old" Java 1.0 IO stream library, since there is a significant amount of existing code that uses that library. The remainder of the chapter will introduce the new features in the Java 1.1 IO library. Note that when you compile some of the code in the first part of the chapter with a Java 1.1 compiler you can get a "deprecated feature" warning message at compile time. The code still works; the compiler is just suggesting that you use certain new features that are described in the latter part of this chapter. It is valuable, however, to see the difference between the old and new way of doing things and that's why it was left in – to increase your understanding (and to allow you to read code written for Java 1.0).

Input and output

The Java library classes for IO are divided by input and output, as you can see by looking at the online Java class hierarchy with your Web browser. By inheritance, all classes derived from **InputStream** have basic methods called **read( )** for reading a single byte or array of bytes. Likewise, all classes derived from **OutputStream** have basic methods called **write( )** for writing a single byte or array of bytes. However, you won't generally use these methods; they exist so more sophisticated classes can use them as they provide a more useful interface. Thus, you'll rarely create your stream object by using a single class, but instead will layer multiple objects together to provide your desired functionality. The fact that you create more than one object to create a single resulting stream is the primary reason that Java's stream library is confusing.

It's helpful to categorize the classes by their functionality. The library designers started by deciding that all classes that had anything to do with input would be inherited from **InputStream** and all classes that were associated with output would be inherited from **OutputStream**.

Types of **InputStream**

InputStream's job is to represent classes that produce input from different sources. These sources can be (and each has an associated subclass of **InputStream**):

1. An array of bytes

2. A **String** object

3. A file

4. A "pipe," which works like a physical pipe: you put things in one end and they come out the other

5. A sequence of other streams, so you can collect them together into a single stream

6. Other sources, such as an Internet connection. (This will be discussed in a later chapter.)

In addition, the **FilterInputStream** is also a type of **InputStream**, to provide a base class for "decorator" classes that attach attributes or useful interfaces to input streams. This is discussed later.

Table 10-1. Types of InputStream

Class	Function	Constructor Arguments
		How to use it
ByteArray-InputStream	Allows a buffer in memory to be used as an **InputStream**.	The buffer from which to extract the bytes.
		As a source of data. Connect it to a **FilterInputStream** object to provide a useful interface.
StringBuffer-InputStream	Converts a **String** into an **InputStream**.	A **String**. The underlying implementation actually uses a **StringBuffer**.
		As a source of data. Connect it to a **FilterInputStream** object to provide a useful interface.
File-InputStream	For reading information from a file.	A **String** representing the file name, or a **File** or **FileDescriptor** object.
		As a source of data. Connect it to a **FilterInputStream** object to provide a useful interface.

Piped- InputStream	Produces the data that's being written to the associated **PipedOutput-Stream**. Implements the "piping" concept.	**PipedOutputStream**
		As a source of data in multithreading. Connect it to a **FilterInputStream** object to provide a useful interface.
Sequence- InputStream	Coverts two or more **InputStream** objects into a single **InputStream**.	Two **InputStream** objects or an **Enumeration** for a container of **InputStream** objects.
		As a source of data. Connect it to a **FilterInputStream** object to provide a useful interface.
Filter- InputStream	Abstract class which is an interface for decorators that provide useful functionality to the other **InputStream** classes. See Table 10-3.	See Table 10-3.
		See Table 10-3.

Types of **OutputStream**

This category includes the classes that decide where your output will go: an array of bytes (no **String**, however; presumably you can create one using the array of bytes), a file, or a "pipe."

In addition, the **FilterOutputStream** provides a base class for "decorator" classes that attach attributes or useful interfaces to output streams. This is discussed later.

Table 10-2. Types of OutputStream

Class	Function	Constructor Arguments
		How to use it
ByteArray-OutputStream	Creates a buffer in memory. All the data that you send to the stream is placed in this buffer.	Optional initial size of the buffer.
		To designate the destination of your data. Connect it to a **FilterOutputStream** object to provide a useful interface.
File-OutputStream	For sending information to a file.	A **String** representing the file name, or a **File** or **FileDescriptor** object.
		To designate the destination of your data. Connect it to a **FilterOutputStream** object to provide a useful interface.
Piped-OutputStream	Any information you write to this automatically ends up as input for the associated **PipedInput-Stream.** Implements the "piping" concept.	**PipedInputStream**
		To designate the destination of your data for multithreading. Connect it to a **FilterOutputStream** object to provide a useful interface.
Filter-OutputStream	Abstract class which is an interface for decorators that provide useful functionality to the other **OutputStream** classes. See Table 10-4.	See Table 10-4.
		See Table 10-4.

Adding attributes
and useful interfaces

The use of layered objects to dynamically and transparently add responsibilities to individual objects is referred to as the *decorator* pattern. (Patterns[1] are the subject of Chapter 16.) The decorator pattern specifies that all objects that wrap around your initial object have the same interface, to make the use of the decorators transparent – you send the same message to an object whether it's been decorated or not. This is the reason for the existence of the "filter" classes in the Java IO library: the abstract "filter" class is the base class for all the decorators. (A decorator must have the same interface as the object it decorates, but the decorator can also extend the interface, which occurs in several of the "filter" classes).

Decorators are often used when subclassing requires a large number of subclasses to support every possible combination needed – so many that subclassing becomes impractical. The Java IO library requires many different combinations of features which is why the decorator pattern is a good approach. There is a drawback to the decorator pattern, however. Decorators give you much more flexibility while you're writing a program (since you can easily mix and match attributes), but they add complexity to your code. The reason that the Java IO library is awkward to use is that you must create many classes – the "core" IO type plus all the decorators – in order to get the single IO object that you want.

The classes that provide the decorator interface to control a particular **InputStream** or **OutputStream** are the **FilterInputStream** and **FilterOutputStream** – which don't have very intuitive names. They are derived, respectively, from **InputStream** and **OutputStream**, and they are abstract classes, in theory to provide a common interface for all the different ways you want to talk to a stream. In fact, **FilterInputStream** and **FilterOutputStream** simply mimic their base classes, which is the key requirement of the decorator.

---

[1] In *Design Patterns*, Erich Gamma *et al.*, Addison-Wesley 1995. Described later in this book.

Reading from an **InputStream**
with **FilterInputStream**

The **FilterInputStream** classes accomplish two significantly different things. **DataInputStream** allows you to read different types of primitive data as well as **String** objects. (All the methods start with "read," such as **readByte( )**, **readFloat( )**, etc.) This, along with its companion **DataOutputStream**, allows you to move primitive data from one place to another via a stream. These "places" are determined by the classes in Table 10-1. If you're reading data in blocks and parsing it yourself, you won't need **DataInputStream**, but in most other cases you will want to use it to automatically format the data you read.

The remaining classes modify the way an **InputStream** behaves internally: whether it's buffered or unbuffered, if it keeps track of the lines it's reading (allowing you to ask for line numbers or set the line number), and whether you can push back a single character. The last two classes look a lot like support for building a compiler (that is, they were added to support the construction of the Java compiler), so you probably won't use them in general programming.

You'll probably need to buffer your input almost every time, regardless of the IO device you're connecting to, so it would have made more sense for the IO library to make a special case for unbuffered input rather than buffered input.

Table 10-3. Types of FilterInputStream

Class	Function	Constructor Arguments
		How to use it
Data-InputStream	Used in concert with **DataOutputStream**, so you can read primitives (int, char, long, etc.) from a stream in a portable fashion.	**InputStream**
		Contains a full interface to allow you to read primitive types.

Buffered-InputStream	Use this to prevent a physical read every time you want more data. You're saying "Use a buffer."	InputStream, with optional buffer size.
		This doesn't provide an interface *per se*, just a requirement that a buffer be used. Attach an interface object.
LineNumber-InputStream	Keeps track of line numbers in the input stream; you can call **getLineNumber( )** and **setLineNumber(int)**.	InputStream
		This just adds line numbering, so you'll probably attach an interface object.
Pushback-InputStream	Has a one byte push-back buffer so that you can push back the last character read.	InputStream
		Generally used in the scanner for a compiler and probably included because the Java compiler needed it. You probably won't use this.

Writing to an **OutputStream** with **FilterOutputStream**

The complement to **DataInputStream** is **DataOutputStream**, which formats each of the primitive types and **String** objects onto a stream in such a way that any **DataInputStream**, on any machine, can read them. All the methods start with "write," such as **writeByte( )**, **writeFloat( )**, etc.

If you want to do true formatted output, for example, to the console, use a **PrintStream**. This is the endpoint that allows you to print all of the primitive data types and **String** objects in a viewable format as opposed to **DataOutputStream**, whose goal is to put them on a stream in a way that **DataInputStream** can portably reconstruct them. The **System.out** static object is a **PrintStream**.

The two important methods in **PrintStream** are **print( )** and **println( )**, which are overloaded to print out all the various types. The difference between **print( )** and **println( )** is that the latter adds a newline when it's done.

BufferedOutputStream is a modifier and tells the stream to use buffering so you don't get a physical write every time you write to the stream. You'll probably always want to use this with files, and possibly console IO.

Table 10-4. Types of FilterOutputStream

Class	Function	Constructor Arguments
		How to use it
Data-OutputStream	Used in concert with **DataInputStream** so you can write primitives (int, char, long, etc.) to a stream in a portable fashion.	**OutputStream**
		Contains full interface to allow you to write primitive types.
PrintStream	For producing formatted output. While **DataOutputStream** handles the *storage* of data, **PrintStream** handles *display*.	**OutputStream**, with optional boolean indicating that the buffer is flushed with every newline.
		Should be the "final" wrapping for your **OutputStream** object. You'll probably use this a lot.
Buffered-OutputStream	Use this to prevent a physical write every time you send a piece of data. You're saying "Use a buffer." You can call **flush( )** to flush the buffer.	**OutputStream**, with optional buffer size.
		This doesn't provide an interface *per se*, just a requirement that a buffer is used. Attach an interface object.

Off by itself: RandomAccessFile

RandomAccessFile is used for files containing records of known size so that you can move from one record to another using **seek( )**, then read or change the records. The records don't have to be the same size; you just have to be able to determine how big they are and where they are placed in the file.

At first it's a little bit hard to believe that **RandomAccessFile** is not part of the **InputStream** or **OutputStream** hierarchy. It has no association with those hierarchies other than that it happens to implement the **DataInput** and **DataOutput** interfaces (which are also implemented by **DataInputStream** and **DataOutputStream**). It doesn't even use any of the functionality of the existing **InputStream** or **OutputStream** classes – it's a completely separate class, written from scratch, with all of its own (mostly native) methods. The reason for this may be that **RandomAccessFile** has essentially different behavior than the other IO types, since you can move forward and backward within a file. In any event, it stands alone, as a direct descendant of **Object**.

Essentially, a **RandomAccessFile** works like a **DataInputStream** pasted together with a **DataOutputStream** and the methods **getFilePointer( )** to find out where you are in the file, **seek( )** to move to a new point in the file, and **length( )** to determine the maximum size of the file. In addition, the constructors require a second argument (identical to **fopen( )** in C) indicating whether you are just randomly reading (**"r"**) or reading and writing (**"rw"**). There's no support for write-only files, which could suggest that **RandomAccessFile** might have worked well if it were inherited from **DataInputStream**.

What's even more frustrating is that you could easily imagine wanting to seek within other types of streams, such as a **ByteArrayInputStream**, but the seeking methods are available only in **RandomAccessFile**, which works for files only. **BufferedInputStream** does allow you to **mark( )** a position (whose value is held in a single internal variable) and **reset( )** to that position, but this is limited and not too useful.

The **File** class

The **File** class has a deceiving name – you might think it refers to a file, but it doesn't. It can represent either the *name* of a particular file or the *names* of a set of files in a directory. If it's a set of files, you can ask for the set with the **list( )** method, and this returns an array of **String**. It makes sense to return an array rather than one of the flexible collection classes because the number of elements is fixed, and if you want a different directory listing you just create a different **File** object. In fact, "FilePath" would have been a better name. This section shows a complete example of the use of this class, including the associated **FilenameFilter** interface.

A directory lister

Suppose you'd like to see a directory listing. The **File** object can be listed in two ways. If you call **list( )** with no arguments, you'll get the full list that the **File** object contains. However, if you want a restricted list, for example, all of the files with an extension of **.java**, then you use a "directory filter," which is a class that tells how to select the **File** objects for display.

Here's the code for the example: (See page 97 if you have trouble executing this program.)

```
//: DirList.java
// Displays directory listing
package c10;
import java.io.*;

public class DirList {
  public static void main(String[] args) {
    try {
      File path = new File(".");
      String[] list;
      if(args.length == 0)
        list = path.list();
      else
        list = path.list(new DirFilter(args[0]));
      for(int i = 0; i < list.length; i++)
        System.out.println(list[i]);
    } catch(Exception e) {
      e.printStackTrace();
```

```
      }
    }
  }

  class DirFilter implements FilenameFilter {
    String afn;
    DirFilter(String afn) { this.afn = afn; }
    public boolean accept(File dir, String name) {
      // Strip path information:
      String f = new File(name).getName();
      return f.indexOf(afn) != -1;
    }
  } ///:~
```

The **DirFilter** class "implements" the **interface FilenameFilter**.
(Interfaces were covered in Chapter 7.) It's useful to see how simple the
FilenameFilter interface is:

```
  public interface FilenameFilter {
    boolean accept(File dir, String name);
  }
```

It says that all that this type of object does is provide a method called
accept( ). The whole reason behind the creation of this class is to provide
the **accept( )** method to the **list( )** method so that **list( )** can *call back*
accept( ) to determine which file names should be included in the list.
Thus, this technique is often referred to as a *callback* or sometimes a
functor (that is, **DirFilter** is a functor because its only job is to hold a
method). Because **list( )** takes a **FilenameFilter** object as its argument, it
means that you can pass an object of any class that implements
FilenameFilter to choose (even at run-time) how the **list( )** method will
behave. The purpose of a callback is to provide flexibility in the behavior
of code.

DirFilter shows that just because an **interface** contains only a set of
methods, you're not restricted to writing only those methods. (You must
at least provide definitions for all the methods in an interface, however.)
In this case, the **DirFilter** constructor is also created.

The **accept( )** method must accept a **File** object representing the directory
that a particular file is found in, and a **String** containing the name of
that file. You might choose to use or ignore either of these arguments,
but you will probably at least use the file name. Remember that the **list( )**
method is calling **accept( )** for each of the file names in the directory
object to see which one should be included – this is indicated by the
boolean result returned by **accept( )**.

To make sure that what you're working with is only the name and contains no path information, all you have to do is take the **String** object and create a **File** object out of it, then call **getName( )** which strips away all the path information (in a platform-independent way). Then **accept( )** uses the **String** class **indexOf( )** method to see if the search string **afn** appears anywhere in the name of the file. If **afn** is found within the string, the return value is the starting index of **afn**, but if it's not found the return value is –1. Keep in mind that this is a simple string search and does not have regular expression "wildcard" matching such as "fo? h?r*" which is much more difficult to implement.

The **list( )** method returns an array. You can query this array for its length and then move through it selecting the array elements. This ability to easily pass an array in and out of a method is a tremendous improvement over the behavior of C and C++.

Anonymous inner classes

This example is ideal for rewriting using an anonymous inner class (described in Chapter 7). As a first cut, a method **filter( )** is created that returns a handle to a **FilenameFilter**:

```
//: DirList2.java
// Uses Java 1.1 anonymous inner classes
import java.io.*;

public class DirList2 {
  public static FilenameFilter
  filter(final String afn) {
    // Creation of anonymous inner class:
    return new FilenameFilter() {
      String fn = afn;
      public boolean accept(File dir, String n) {
        // Strip path information:
        String f = new File(n).getName();
        return f.indexOf(fn) != -1;
      }
    }; // End of anonymous inner class
  }
  public static void main(String[] args) {
    try {
      File path = new File(".");
      String[] list;
      if(args.length == 0)
        list = path.list();
```

```
       else
         list = path.list(filter(args[0]));
       for(int i = 0; i < list.length; i++)
         System.out.println(list[i]);
     } catch(Exception e) {
       e.printStackTrace();
     }
   }
 } ///:~
```

Note that the argument to **filter( )** must be **final**. This is required by the anonymous inner class so that it can use an object from outside its scope.

This design is an improvement because the **FilenameFilter** class is now tightly bound to **DirList2**. However, you can take this approach one step further and define the anonymous inner class as an argument to **list( )**, in which case it's even smaller:

```
//: DirList3.java
// Building the anonymous inner class "in-place"
import java.io.*;

public class DirList3 {
  public static void main(final String[] args) {
    try {
      File path = new File(".");
      String[] list;
      if(args.length == 0)
        list = path.list();
      else
        list = path.list(
          new FilenameFilter() {
            public boolean
            accept(File dir, String n) {
              String f = new File(n).getName();
              return f.indexOf(args[0]) != -1;
            }
          });
      for(int i = 0; i < list.length; i++)
        System.out.println(list[i]);
    } catch(Exception e) {
      e.printStackTrace();
    }
  }
} ///:~
```

The argument to **main( )** is now **final**, since the anonymous inner class uses **args[0]** directly.

This shows you how anonymous inner classes allow the creation of quick-and-dirty classes to solve problems. Since everything in Java revolves around classes, this can be a useful coding technique. One benefit is that it keeps the code that solves a particular problem isolated together in one spot. On the other hand, it is not always as easy to read, so you must use it judiciously.

A sorted directory listing

Ah, you say that you want the file names *sorted*? Since there's no support for sorting in Java 1.0 or Java 1.1 (although sorting *is* included in Java 1.2), it will have to be added into the program directly using the **SortVector** created in Chapter 8:

```
//: SortedDirList.java
// Displays sorted directory listing
import java.io.*;
import c08.*;

public class SortedDirList {
   private File path;
   private String[] list;
   public SortedDirList(final String afn) {
      path = new File(".");
      if(afn == null)
         list = path.list();
      else
         list = path.list(
             new FilenameFilter() {
                public boolean
                accept(File dir, String n) {
                   String f = new File(n).getName();
                   return f.indexOf(afn) != -1;
                }
             });
      sort();
   }
   void print() {
      for(int i = 0; i < list.length; i++)
         System.out.println(list[i]);
   }
```

```
      private void sort() {
        StrSortVector sv = new StrSortVector();
        for(int i = 0; i < list.length; i++)
          sv.addElement(list[i]);
        // The first time an element is pulled from
        // the StrSortVector the list is sorted:
        for(int i = 0; i < list.length; i++)
          list[i] = sv.elementAt(i);
      }
      // Test it:
      public static void main(String[] args) {
        SortedDirList sd;
        if(args.length == 0)
          sd = new SortedDirList(null);
        else
          sd = new SortedDirList(args[0]);
        sd.print();
      }
    } ///:~
```

A few other improvements have been made. Instead of creating **path** and **list** as local variables to **main( )**, they are members of the class so their values can be accessible for the lifetime of the object. In fact, **main( )** is now just a way to test the class. You can see that the constructor of the class automatically sorts the list once that list has been created.

The sort is case-insensitive so you don't end up with a list of all the words starting with capital letters, followed by the rest of the words starting with all the lowercase letters. However, you'll notice that within a group of file names that begin with the same letter the capitalized words are listed first, which is still not quite the desired behavior for the sort. This problem will be fixed in Java 1.2.

Checking for and creating directories

The **File** class is more than just a representation for an existing directory path, file, or group of files. You can also use a **File** object to create a new directory or an entire directory path if it doesn't exist. You can also look at the characteristics of files (size, last modification date, read/write), see whether a **File** object represents a file or a directory, and delete a file. This program shows the remaining methods available with the **File** class:

```
//: MakeDirectories.java
// Demonstrates the use of the File class to
// create directories and manipulate files.
```

```
import java.io.*;

public class MakeDirectories {
  private final static String usage =
    "Usage:MakeDirectories path1 ...\n" +
    "Creates each path\n" +
    "Usage:MakeDirectories -d path1 ...\n" +
    "Deletes each path\n" +
    "Usage:MakeDirectories -r path1 path2\n" +
    "Renames from path1 to path2\n";
  private static void usage() {
    System.err.println(usage);
    System.exit(1);
  }
  private static void fileData(File f) {
    System.out.println(
      "Absolute path: " + f.getAbsolutePath() +
      "\n Can read: " + f.canRead() +
      "\n Can write: " + f.canWrite() +
      "\n getName: " + f.getName() +
      "\n getParent: " + f.getParent() +
      "\n getPath: " + f.getPath() +
      "\n length: " + f.length() +
      "\n lastModified: " + f.lastModified());
    if(f.isFile())
      System.out.println("it's a file");
    else if(f.isDirectory())
      System.out.println("it's a directory");
  }
  public static void main(String[] args) {
    if(args.length < 1) usage();
    if(args[0].equals("-r")) {
      if(args.length != 3) usage();
      File
        old = new File(args[1]),
        rname = new File(args[2]);
      old.renameTo(rname);
      fileData(old);
      fileData(rname);
      return; // Exit main
    }
    int count = 0;
    boolean del = false;
    if(args[0].equals("-d")) {
```

```
            count++;
            del = true;
        }
      for( ; count < args.length; count++) {
        File f = new File(args[count]);
        if(f.exists()) {
           System.out.println(f + " exists");
           if(del) {
              System.out.println("deleting..." + f);
              f.delete();
           }
        }
        else { // Doesn't exist
           if(!del) {
              f.mkdirs();
              System.out.println("created " + f);
           }
        }
        fileData(f);
      }
    }
} ///:~
```

In **fileData( )** you can see the various file investigation methods put to use to display information about the file or directory path.

The first method that's exercised by **main( )** is **renameTo( )**, which allows you to rename (or move) a file to an entirely new path represented by the argument, which is another **File** object. This also works with directories of any length.

If you experiment with the above program, you'll find that you can make a directory path of any complexity because **mkdirs( )** will do all the work for you. In Java 1.0, the **-d** flag reports that the directory is deleted but it's still there; in Java 1.1 the directory is actually deleted.

Typical uses of IO streams

Although there are a lot of IO stream classes in the library that can be combined in many different ways, there are just a few ways that you'll probably end up using them. However, they require attention to get the correct combinations. The following rather long example shows the creation and use of typical IO configurations so you can use it as a reference when writing your own code. Note that each configuration begins with a commented number and title that corresponds to the heading for the appropriate explanation that follows in the text.

```
//: IOStreamDemo.java
// Typical IO Stream Configurations
import java.io.*;
import com.bruceeckel.tools.*;

public class IOStreamDemo {
  public static void main(String[] args) {
    try {
      // 1. Buffered input file
      DataInputStream in =
        new DataInputStream(
          new BufferedInputStream(
            new FileInputStream(args[0])));
      String s, s2 = new String();
      while((s = in.readLine()) != null)
        s2 += s + "\n";
      in.close();

      // 2. Input from memory
      StringBufferInputStream in2 =
          new StringBufferInputStream(s2);
      int c;
      while((c = in2.read()) != -1)
        System.out.print((char)c);

      // 3. Formatted memory input
      try {
        DataInputStream in3 =
          new DataInputStream(
            new StringBufferInputStream(s2));
        while(true)
          System.out.print((char)in3.readByte());
      } catch(EOFException e) {
        System.out.println(
          "End of stream encountered");
      }

      // 4. Line numbering & file output
      try {
        LineNumberInputStream li =
          new LineNumberInputStream(
            new StringBufferInputStream(s2));
```

```java
      DataInputStream in4 =
        new DataInputStream(li);
      PrintStream out1 =
        new PrintStream(
          new BufferedOutputStream(
            new FileOutputStream(
              "IODemo.out")));
      while((s = in4.readLine()) != null )
        out1.println(
          "Line " + li.getLineNumber() + s);
      out1.close(); // finalize() not reliable!
    } catch(EOFException e) {
      System.out.println(
        "End of stream encountered");
    }

    // 5. Storing & recovering data
    try {
      DataOutputStream out2 =
        new DataOutputStream(
          new BufferedOutputStream(
            new FileOutputStream("Data.txt")));
      out2.writeBytes(
        "Here's the value of pi: \n");
      out2.writeDouble(3.14159);
      out2.close();
      DataInputStream in5 =
        new DataInputStream(
          new BufferedInputStream(
            new FileInputStream("Data.txt")));
      System.out.println(in5.readLine());
      System.out.println(in5.readDouble());
    } catch(EOFException e) {
      System.out.println(
        "End of stream encountered");
    }

    // 6. Reading/writing random access files
    RandomAccessFile rf =
      new RandomAccessFile("rtest.dat", "rw");
    for(int i = 0; i < 10; i++)
      rf.writeDouble(i*1.414);
    rf.close();
```

```
          rf =
            new RandomAccessFile("rtest.dat", "rw");
          rf.seek(5*8);
          rf.writeDouble(47.0001);
          rf.close();

          rf =
            new RandomAccessFile("rtest.dat", "r");
          for(int i = 0; i < 10; i++)
            System.out.println(
              "Value " + i + ": " +
              rf.readDouble());
          rf.close();

          // 7. File input shorthand
          InFile in6 = new InFile(args[0]);
          String s3 = new String();
          System.out.println(
            "First line in file: " +
            in6.readLine());
            in6.close();

          // 8. Formatted file output shorthand
          PrintFile out3 = new PrintFile("Data2.txt");
          out3.print("Test of PrintFile");
          out3.close();

          // 9. Data file output shorthand
          OutFile out4 = new OutFile("Data3.txt");
          out4.writeBytes("Test of outDataFile\n\r");
          out4.writeChars("Test of outDataFile\n\r");
          out4.close();

        } catch(FileNotFoundException e) {
          System.out.println(
            "File Not Found:" + args[0]);
        } catch(IOException e) {
          System.out.println("IO Exception");
        }
      }
    } ///:~
```

Input streams

Of course, one common thing you'll want to do is print formatted output to the console, but that's already been simplified in the package **com.bruceeckel.tools** created in Chapter 5.

Parts 1 through 4 demonstrate the creation and use of input streams (although part 4 also shows the simple use of an output stream as a testing tool).

1. Buffered input file

To open a file for input, you use a **FileInputStream** with a **String** or a **File** object as the file name. For speed, you'll want that file to be buffered so you give the resulting handle to the constructor for a **BufferedInputStream**. To read input in a formatted fashion, you give that resulting handle to the constructor for a **DataInputStream**, which is your final object and the interface you read from.

In this example, only the **readLine( )** method is used, but of course any of the **DataInputStream** methods are available. When you reach the end of the file, **readLine( )** returns **null** so that is used to break out of the **while** loop.

The **String s2** is used to accumulate the entire contents of the file (including newlines that must be added since **readLine( )** strips them off). **s2** is then used in the later portions of this program. Finally, **close( )** is called to close the file. Technically, **close( )** will be called when **finalize( )** is run, and this is supposed to happen (whether or not garbage collection occurs) as the program exits. However, Java 1.0 has a rather important bug, so this doesn't happen. In Java 1.1 you must explicitly call **System.runFinalizersOnExit(true)** to guarantee that **finalize( )** will be called for every object in the system. The safest approach is to explicitly call **close( )** for files.

2. Input from memory

This piece takes the **String s2** that now contains the entire contents of the file and uses it to create a **StringBufferInputStream.** (A **String**, not a **StringBuffer**, is required as the constructor argument.) Then **read( )** is used to read each character one at a time and send it out to the console. Note that **read( )** returns the next byte as an **int** and thus it must be cast to a **char** to print properly.

3. Formatted memory input

The interface for **StringBufferInputStream** is limited, so you usually enhance it by wrapping it inside a **DataInputStream**. However, if you choose to read the characters out a byte at a time using **readByte( )**, any value is valid so the return value cannot be used to detect the end of input. Instead, you can use the **available( )** method to find out how many more characters are available. Here's an example that shows how to read a file one byte at a time:

```
//: TestEOF.java
// Testing for the end of file while reading
// a byte at a time.
import java.io.*;

public class TestEOF {
  public static void main(String[] args) {
    try {
      DataInputStream in =
        new DataInputStream(
         new BufferedInputStream(
          new FileInputStream("TestEof.java")));
      while(in.available() != 0)
        System.out.print((char)in.readByte());
    } catch (IOException e) {
      System.err.println("IOException");
    }
  }
} ///:~
```

Note that **available( )** works differently depending on what sort of medium you're reading from – it's literally "the number of bytes that can be read *without blocking*." With a file this means the whole file, but with a different kind of stream this might not be true, so use it thoughtfully.

You could also detect the end of input in cases like these by catching an exception. However, the use of exceptions for control flow is considered a misuse of that feature.

4. Line numbering and file output

This example shows the use of the **LineNumberInputStream** to keep track of the input line numbers. Here, you cannot simply gang all the constructors together, since you have to keep a handle to the **LineNumberInputStream**. (Note that this is *not* an inheritance situation,

---

so you cannot simply cast **in4** to a **LineNumberInputStream.**) Thus, **li** holds the handle to the **LineNumberInputStream,** which is then used to create a **DataInputStream** for easy reading.

This example also shows how to write formatted data to a file. First, a **FileOutputStream** is created to connect to the file. For efficiency, this is made a **BufferedOutputStream,** which is what you'll virtually always want to do, but you're forced to do it explicitly. Then for the formatting it's turned into a **PrintStream.** The data file created this way is readable as an ordinary text file.

One of the methods that indicates when a **DataInputStream** is exhausted is **readLine( ),** which returns **null** when there are no more strings to read. Each line is printed to the file along with its line number, which is acquired through **li.**

You'll see an explicit **close( )** for **out1,** which would make sense *if* the program were to turn around and read the same file again. However, this program ends without ever looking at the file **IODemo.out.** As mentioned before, if you don't call **close( )** for all your output files, you might discover that the buffers don't get flushed so they're incomplete.

Output streams

The two primary kinds of output streams are separated by the way they write data: one writes it for human consumption, and the other writes it to be re-acquired by a **DataInputStream.** The **RandomAccessFile** stands alone, although its data format is compatible with the **DataInputStream** and **DataOutputStream.**

5. Storing and recovering data

A **PrintStream** formats data so it's readable by a human. To output data so that it can be recovered by another stream, you use a **DataOutputStream** to write the data and a **DataInputStream** to recover the data. Of course, these streams could be anything, but here a file is used, buffered for both reading and writing.

Note that the character string is written using **writeBytes( )** and not **writeChars( ).** If you use the latter, you'll be writing the 16-bit Unicode characters. Since there is no complementary "readChars" method in **DataInputStream,** you're stuck pulling these characters off one at a time with **readChar( ).** So for ASCII, it's easier to write the characters as bytes followed by a newline; then use **readLine( )** to read back the bytes as a regular ASCII line.

The **writeDouble( )** stores the **double** number to the stream and the complementary **readDouble( )** recovers it. But for any of the reading methods to work correctly, you must know the exact placement of the data item in the stream, since it would be equally possible to read the stored **double** as a simple sequence of bytes, or as a **char**, etc. So you must either have a fixed format for the data in the file or extra information must be stored in the file that you parse to determine where the data is located.

6. Reading and writing random access files

As previously noted, the **RandomAccessFile** is almost totally isolated from the rest of the IO hierarchy, save for the fact that it implements the **DataInput** and **DataOutput** interfaces. So you cannot combine it with any of the aspects of the **InputStream** and **OutputStream** subclasses. Even though it might make sense to treat a **ByteArrayInputStream** as a random access element, you can use **RandomAccessFile** to only open a file. You must assume a **RandomAccessFile** is properly buffered since you cannot add that.

The one option you have is in the second constructor argument: you can open a **RandomAccessFile** to read (**"r"**) or read and write (**"rw"**).

Using a **RandomAccessFile** is like using a combined **DataInputStream** and **DataOutputStream** (because it implements the equivalent interfaces). In addition, you can see that **seek( )** is used to move about in the file and change one of the values.

Shorthand for file manipulation

Since there are certain canonical forms that you'll be using regularly with files, you may wonder why you have to do all of that typing – this is one of the drawbacks of the decorator pattern. This portion shows the creation and use of shorthand versions of typical file reading and writing configurations. These shorthands are placed in the **package com.bruceeckel.tools** that was begun in Chapter 5 (See page 196). To add each class to the library, simply place it in the appropriate directory and add the **package** statement.

7. File input shorthand

The creation of an object that reads a file from a buffered **DataInputStream** can be encapsulated into a class called **InFile**:

```
//: InFile.java
```

```
// Shorthand class for opening an input file
package com.bruceeckel.tools;
import java.io.*;

public class InFile extends DataInputStream {
  public InFile(String filename)
    throws FileNotFoundException {
    super(
      new BufferedInputStream(
        new FileInputStream(filename)));
  }
  public InFile(File file)
    throws FileNotFoundException {
    this(file.getPath());
  }
} ///:~
```

Both the **String** versions of the constructor and the **File** versions are included, to parallel the creation of a **FileInputStream**.

Now you can reduce your chances of repetitive stress syndrome while creating files, as seen in the example.

8. Formatted file output shorthand

The same kind of approach can be taken to create a **PrintStream** that writes to a buffered file. Here's the extension to **com.bruceeckel.tools**:

```
//: PrintFile.java
// Shorthand class for opening an output file
// for human-readable output.
package com.bruceeckel.tools;
import java.io.*;

public class PrintFile extends PrintStream {
  public PrintFile(String filename)
    throws IOException {
    super(
      new BufferedOutputStream(
        new FileOutputStream(filename)));
  }
  public PrintFile(File file)
    throws IOException {
    this(file.getPath());
  }
```

```
    } ///:~
```

Note that it is not possible for a constructor to catch an exception that's thrown by a base-class constructor.

9. Data file output shorthand

Finally, the same kind of shorthand can create a buffered output file for data storage (as opposed to human-readable storage):

```
//: OutFile.java
// Shorthand class for opening an output file
// for data storage.
package com.bruceeckel.tools;
import java.io.*;

public class OutFile extends DataOutputStream {
  public OutFile(String filename)
    throws IOException {
    super(
      new BufferedOutputStream(
        new FileOutputStream(filename)));
  }
  public OutFile(File file)
    throws IOException {
    this(file.getPath());
  }
} ///:~
```

It is curious (and unfortunate) that the Java library designers didn't think to provide these conveniences as part of their standard.

Reading from standard input

Following the approach pioneered in Unix of "standard input," "standard output," and "standard error output," Java has **System.in**, **System.out**, and **System.err**. Throughout the book you've seen how to write to standard output using **System.out**, which is already pre-wrapped as a **PrintStream** object. **System.err** is likewise a **PrintStream**, but **System.in** is a raw **InputStream**, with no wrapping. This means that while you can use **System.out** and **System.err** right away, **System.in** must be wrapped before you can read from it.

Typically, you'll want to read input a line at a time using **readLine( )**, so you'll want to wrap **System.in** in a **DataInputStream**. This is the "old"

Java 1.0 way to do line input. A bit later in the chapter you'll see the Java 1.1 solution. Here's an example that simply echoes each line that you type in:

```
//: Echo.java
// How to read from standard input
import java.io.*;

public class Echo {
  public static void main(String[] args) {
    DataInputStream in =
      new DataInputStream(
        new BufferedInputStream(System.in));
    String s;
    try {
      while((s = in.readLine()).length() != 0)
        System.out.println(s);
      // An empty line terminates the program
    } catch(IOException e) {
      e.printStackTrace();
    }
  }
} ///:~
```

The reason for the **try** block is that **readLine( )** can throw an **IOException**. Note that **System.in** should also be buffered, as with most streams

It's a bit inconvenient that you're forced to wrap **System.in** in a **DataInputStream** in each program, but perhaps it was designed this way to allow maximum flexibility.

Piped streams

The **PipedInputStream** and **PipedOutputStream** have been mentioned only briefly in this chapter. This is not to suggest that they aren't useful, but their value is not apparent until you begin to understand multithreading, since the piped streams are used to communicate between threads. This is covered along with an example in Chapter 14.

StreamTokenizer

Although **StreamTokenizer** is not derived from **InputStream** or
OutputStream, it works only with **InputStream** objects, so it rightfully
belongs in the IO portion of the library.

The **StreamTokenizer** class is used to break any **InputStream** into a
sequence of "tokens," which are bits of text delimited by whatever you
choose. For example, your tokens could be words, and then they would
be delimited by white space and punctuation.

Consider a program to count the occurrence of words in a text file:

```java
//: SortedWordCount.java
// Counts words in a file, outputs
// results in sorted form.
import java.io.*;
import java.util.*;
import c08.*; // Contains StrSortVector

class Counter {
  private int i = 1;
  int read() { return i; }
  void increment() { i++; }
}

public class SortedWordCount {
  private FileInputStream file;
  private StreamTokenizer st;
  private Hashtable counts = new Hashtable();
  SortedWordCount(String filename)
    throws FileNotFoundException {
    try {
      file = new FileInputStream(filename);
      st = new StreamTokenizer(file);
      st.ordinaryChar('.');
      st.ordinaryChar('-');
    } catch(FileNotFoundException e) {
      System.out.println(
        "Could not open " + filename);
      throw e;
    }
  }
  void cleanup() {
```

```java
        try {
          file.close();
        } catch(IOException e) {
          System.out.println(
            "file.close() unsuccessful");
        }
      }
      void countWords() {
        try {
          while(st.nextToken() !=
            StreamTokenizer.TT_EOF) {
            String s;
            switch(st.ttype) {
              case StreamTokenizer.TT_EOL:
                s = new String("EOL");
                break;
              case StreamTokenizer.TT_NUMBER:
                s = Double.toString(st.nval);
                break;
              case StreamTokenizer.TT_WORD:
                s = st.sval; // Already a String
                break;
              default: // single character in ttype
                s = String.valueOf((char)st.ttype);
            }
            if(counts.containsKey(s))
              ((Counter)counts.get(s)).increment();
            else
              counts.put(s, new Counter());
          }
        } catch(IOException e) {
          System.out.println(
            "st.nextToken() unsuccessful");
        }
      }
      Enumeration values() {
        return counts.elements();
      }
      Enumeration keys() { return counts.keys(); }
      Counter getCounter(String s) {
        return (Counter)counts.get(s);
      }
      Enumeration sortedKeys() {
        Enumeration e = counts.keys();
```

```
        StrSortVector sv = new StrSortVector();
        while(e.hasMoreElements())
          sv.addElement((String)e.nextElement());
        // This call forces a sort:
        return sv.elements();
      }
    public static void main(String[] args) {
      try {
        SortedWordCount wc =
          new SortedWordCount(args[0]);
        wc.countWords();
        Enumeration keys = wc.sortedKeys();
        while(keys.hasMoreElements()) {
          String key = (String)keys.nextElement();
          System.out.println(key + ": "
                    + wc.getCounter(key).read());
        }
        wc.cleanup();
      } catch(Exception e) {
        e.printStackTrace();
      }
    }
  } ///:~
```

It makes sense to present these in a sorted form, but since Java 1.0 and
Java 1.1 don't have any sorting methods, that will have to be mixed in.
This is easy enough to do with a **StrSortVector**. (This was created in
Chapter 8, and is part of the package created in that chapter. Remember
that the starting directory for all the subdirectories in this book must be
in your class path for the program to compile successfully.)

To open the file, a **FileInputStream** is used, and to turn the file into
words a **StreamTokenizer** is created from the **FileInputStream**. In
StreamTokenizer, there is a default list of separators, and you can add
more with a set of methods. Here, **ordinaryChar( )** is used to say "This
character has no significance that I'm interested in," so the parser doesn't
include it as part of any of the words that it creates. For example, saying
st.ordinaryChar('.') means that periods will not be included as parts of
the words that are parsed. You can find more information in the online
documentation that comes with Java.

In **countWords( )**, the tokens are pulled one at a time from the stream,
and the **ttype** information is used to determine what to do with each
token, since a token can be an end–of–line, a number, a string, or a single
character.

Once a token is found, the **Hashtable counts** is queried to see if it already contains the token as a key. If it does, the corresponding **Counter** object is incremented to indicate that another instance of this word has been found. If not, a new **Counter** is created – since the **Counter** constructor initializes its value to one, this also acts to count the word.

SortedWordCount is not a type of **Hashtable**, so it wasn't inherited. It performs a specific type of functionality, so even though the **keys( )** and **values( )** methods must be re-exposed, that still doesn't mean that inheritance should be used since a number of **Hashtable** methods are inappropriate here. In addition, other methods like **getCounter( )**, which get the **Counter** for a particular **String**, and **sortedKeys( )**, which produces an **Enumeration**, finish the change in the shape of **SortedWordCount**'s interface.

In **main( )** you can see the use of a **SortedWordCount** to open and count the words in a file – it just takes two lines of code. Then an enumeration to a sorted list of keys (words) is extracted, and this is used to pull out each key and associated **Count**. Note that the call to **cleanup( )** is necessary to ensure that the file is closed.

A second example using **StreamTokenizer** can be found in Chapter 17.

StringTokenizer

Although it isn't part of the IO library, the **StringTokenizer** has sufficiently similar functionality to **StreamTokenizer** that it will be described here.

The **StringTokenizer** returns the tokens within a string one at a time. These tokens are consecutive characters delimited by tabs, spaces, and newlines. Thus, the tokens of the string "Where is my cat?" are "Where", "is", "my", and "cat?" Like the **StreamTokenizer**, you can tell the **StringTokenizer** to break up the input in any way that you want, but with **StringTokenizer** you do this by passing a second argument to the constructor, which is a **String** of the delimiters you wish to use. In general, if you need more sophistication, use a **StreamTokenizer**.

You ask a **StringTokenizer** object for the next token in the string using the **nextToken( )** method, which either returns the token or an empty string to indicate that no tokens remain.

As an example, the following program performs a limited analysis of a sentence, looking for key phrase sequences to indicate whether happiness or sadness is implied.

```
//: AnalyzeSentence.java
// Look for particular sequences
// within sentences.
import java.util.*;

public class AnalyzeSentence {
  public static void main(String[] args) {
    analyze("I am happy about this");
    analyze("I am not happy about this");
    analyze("I am not! I am happy");
    analyze("I am sad about this");
    analyze("I am not sad about this");
    analyze("I am not! I am sad");
    analyze("Are you happy about this?");
    analyze("Are you sad about this?");
    analyze("It's you! I am happy");
    analyze("It's you! I am sad");
  }
  static StringTokenizer st;
  static void analyze(String s) {
    prt("\nnew sentence >> " + s);
    boolean sad = false;
    st = new StringTokenizer(s);
    while (st.hasMoreTokens()) {
      String token = next();
      // Look until you find one of the
      // two starting tokens:
      if(!token.equals("I") &&
         !token.equals("Are"))
        continue; // Top of while loop
      if(token.equals("I")) {
        String tk2 = next();
        if(!tk2.equals("am")) // Must be after I
          break; // Out of while loop
        else {
          String tk3 = next();
          if(tk3.equals("sad")) {
            sad = true;
            break; // Out of while loop
          }
          if (tk3.equals("not")) {
            String tk4 = next();
            if(tk4.equals("sad"))
              break; // Leave sad false
```

```
                if(tk4.equals("happy")) {
                  sad = true;
                  break;
                }
              }
            }
          }
        }
        if(token.equals("Are")) {
          String tk2 = next();
          if(!tk2.equals("you"))
            break; // Must be after Are
          String tk3 = next();
          if(tk3.equals("sad"))
            sad = true;
          break; // Out of while loop
        }
      }
      if(sad) prt("Sad detected");
    }
    static String next() {
      if(st.hasMoreTokens()) {
        String s = st.nextToken();
        prt(s);
        return s;
      }
      else
        return "";
    }
    static void prt(String s) {
      System.out.println(s);
    }
  } ///:~
```

For each string being analyzed, a **while** loop is entered and tokens are pulled off the string. Notice the first **if** statement, which says to **continue** (go back to the beginning of the loop and start again) if the token is neither an "I" nor an "Are." This means that it will get tokens until an "I" or an "Are" is found. You might think to use the == instead of the **equals( )** method, but that won't work correctly, since == compares handle values while **equals( )** compares contents.

The logic of the rest of the **analyze( )** method is that the pattern that's being searched for is "I am sad," "I am not happy," or "Are you sad?" Without the **break** statement, the code for this would be even messier than it is. You should be aware that a typical parser (this is a primitive example of one) normally has a table of these tokens and a piece of code that moves through the states in the table as new tokens are read.

You should think of the **StringTokenizer** only as shorthand for a simple and specific kind of **StreamTokenizer**. However, if you have a **String** that you want to tokenize and **StringTokenizer** is too limited, all you have to do is turn it into a stream with **StringBufferInputStream** and then use that to create a much more powerful **StreamTokenizer**.

Java 1.1 IO streams

At this point you might be scratching your head, wondering if there is another design for IO streams that could require *more* typing. Could someone have come up with an odder design?" Prepare yourself: Java 1.1 makes some significant modifications to the IO stream library. When you see the **Reader** and **Writer** classes your first thought (like mine) might be that these were meant to replace the **InputStream** and **OutputStream** classes. But that's not the case. Although some aspects of the original streams library are deprecated (if you use them you will receive a warning from the compiler), the old streams have been left in for backwards compatibility and:

1. New classes have been put into the old hierarchy, so it's obvious that Sun is not abandoning the old streams.

2. There are times when you're supposed to use classes in the old hierarchy *in combination* with classes in the new hierarchy and to accomplish this there are "bridge" classes: **InputStreamReader** converts an **InputStream** to a **Reader** and **OutputStreamWriter** converts an **OutputStream** to a **Writer**.

As a result there are situations in which you have *more* layers of wrapping with the new IO stream library than with the old. Again, this is a drawback of the decorator pattern – the price you pay for added flexibility.

The most important reason for adding the **Reader** and **Writer** hierarchies in Java 1.1 is for internationalization. The old IO stream hierarchy supports only 8-bit byte streams and doesn't handle the 16-bit Unicode characters well. Since Unicode is used for internationalization (and Java's native **char** is 16-bit Unicode), the **Reader** and **Writer** hierarchies were added to support Unicode in all IO operations. In addition, the new libraries are designed for faster operations than the old.

As is the practice in this book, I will attempt to provide an overview of the classes but assume that you will use online documentation to determine all the details, such as the exhaustive list of methods.

Sources and sinks of data

Almost all of the Java 1.0 IO stream classes have corresponding Java 1.1 classes to provide native Unicode manipulation. It would be easiest to say "Always use the new classes, never use the old ones," but things are not that simple. Sometimes you are forced into using the Java 1.0 IO stream classes because of the library design; in particular, the **java.util.zip** libraries are new additions to the old stream library and they rely on old stream components. So the most sensible approach to take is to *try* to use the **Reader** and **Writer** classes whenever you can, and you'll discover the situations when you have to drop back into the old libraries because your code won't compile.

Here is a table that shows the correspondence between the sources and sinks of information (that is, where the data physically comes from or goes to) in the old and new libraries.

Sources & Sinks: Java 1.0 class	Corresponding Java 1.1 class
InputStream	**Reader** converter: **InputStreamReader**
OutputStream	**Writer** converter: **OutputStreamWriter**
FileInputStream	**FileReader**
FileOutputStream	**FileWriter**
StringBufferInputStream	**StringReader**
(no corresponding class)	**StringWriter**
ByteArrayInputStream	**CharArrayReader**
ByteArrayOutputStream	**CharArrayWriter**
PipedInputStream	**PipedReader**
PipedOutputStream	**PipedWriter**

In general, you'll find that the interfaces in the old library components and the new ones are similar if not identical.

Modifying stream behavior

In Java 1.0, streams were adapted for particular needs using "decorator" subclasses of **FilterInputStream** and **FilterOutputStream**. Java 1.1 IO streams continues the use of this idea, but the model of deriving all of the decorators from the same "filter" base class is not followed. This can make it a bit confusing if you're trying to understand it by looking at the class hierarchy.

In the following table, the correspondence is a rougher approximation than in the previous table. The difference is because of the class organization: while **BufferedOutputStream** is a subclass of **FilterOutputStream**, **BufferedWriter** is *not* a subclass of **FilterWriter** (which, even though it is **abstract**, has no subclasses and so appears to have been put in either as a placeholder or simply so you wouldn't wonder where it was). However, the interfaces to the classes are quite a close match and it's apparent that you're supposed to use the new versions instead of the old whenever possible (that is, except in cases where you're forced to produce a **Stream** instead of a **Reader** or **Writer**).

Filters: Java 1.0 class	Corresponding Java 1.1 class
FilterInputStream	**FilterReader**
FilterOutputStream	**FilterWriter** (**abstract** class with no subclasses)
BufferedInputStream	**BufferedReader** (also has **readLine( )**)
BufferedOutputStream	**BufferedWriter**
DataInputStream	use **DataInputStream** (Except when you need to use **readLine( )**, when you should use a **BufferedReader**)
PrintStream	**PrintWriter**
LineNumberInputStream	**LineNumberReader**
StreamTokenizer	**StreamTokenizer** (use constructor that takes a **Reader** instead)
PushBackInputStream	**PushBackReader**

There's one direction that's quite clear: Whenever you want to use **readLine( )**, you shouldn't do it with a **DataInputStream** any more (this is met with a deprecation message at compile time), but instead use a **BufferedReader**. Other than this, **DataInputStream** is still a "preferred" member of the Java 1.1 IO library.

To make the transition to using a **PrintWriter** easier, it has constructors that take any **OutputStream** object. However, **PrintWriter** has no more

---

support for formatting than **PrintStream** does; the interfaces are
virtually the same.

Unchanged Classes

Apparently, the Java library designers felt that they got some of the
classes right the first time so there were no changes to these and you can
go on using them as they are:

Java 1.0 classes without corresponding Java 1.1 classes
DataOutputStream
File
RandomAccessFile
SequenceInputStream

The **DataOutputStream**, in particular, is used without change, so for
storing and retrieving data in a transportable format you're forced to
stay in the **InputStream** and **OutputStream** hierarchies.

An example

To see the effect of the new classes, let's look at the appropriate portion of
the **IOStreamDemo.java** example modified to use the **Reader** and
Writer classes:

```
//: NewIODemo.java
// Java 1.1 IO typical usage
import java.io.*;

public class NewIODemo {
  public static void main(String[] args) {
    try {
      // 1. Reading input by lines:
      BufferedReader in =
        new BufferedReader(
          new FileReader(args[0]));
      String s, s2 = new String();
      while((s = in.readLine()) != null)
        s2 += s + "\n";
      in.close();

      // 1b. Reading standard input:
      BufferedReader stdin =
```

```java
      new BufferedReader(
        new InputStreamReader(System.in));
    System.out.print("Enter a line:");
    System.out.println(stdin.readLine());

    // 2. Input from memory
    StringReader in2 = new StringReader(s2);
    int c;
    while((c = in2.read()) != 1)
      System.out.print((char)c);

    // 3. Formatted memory input
    try {
      DataInputStream in3 =
        new DataInputStream(
          // Oops: must use deprecated class:
          new StringBufferInputStream(s2));
      while(true)
        System.out.print((char)in3.readByte());
    } catch(EOFException e) {
      System.out.println("End of stream");
    }

    // 4. Line numbering & file output
    try {
      LineNumberReader li =
        new LineNumberReader(
          new StringReader(s2));
      BufferedReader in4 =
        new BufferedReader(li);
      PrintWriter out1 =
        new PrintWriter(
          new BufferedWriter(
            new FileWriter("IODemo.out")));
      while((s = in4.readLine()) != null )
        out1.println(
          "Line " + li.getLineNumber() + s);
      out1.close();
    } catch(EOFException e) {
      System.out.println("End of stream");
    }

    // 5. Storing & recovering data
    try {
```

```
DataOutputStream out2 =
  new DataOutputStream(
    new BufferedOutputStream(
      new FileOutputStream("Data.txt")));
out2.writeDouble(3.14159);
out2.writeBytes("That was pi");
out2.close();
DataInputStream in5 =
  new DataInputStream(
    new BufferedInputStream(
      new FileInputStream("Data.txt")));
BufferedReader in5br =
  new BufferedReader(
    new InputStreamReader(in5));
// Must use DataInputStream for data:
System.out.println(in5.readDouble());
// Can now use the "proper" readLine():
System.out.println(in5br.readLine());
} catch(EOFException e) {
System.out.println("End of stream");
}

// 6. Reading and writing random access
// files is the same as before.
// (not repeated here)

} catch(FileNotFoundException e) {
System.out.println(
  "File Not Found:" + args[1]);
} catch(IOException e) {
System.out.println("IO Exception");
}
}
} ///:~
```

In general, you'll see that the conversion is fairly straightforward and the code looks quite similar. There are some important differences, though. First of all, since random access files have not changed, section 6 is not repeated.

Section 1 shrinks a bit because if all you're doing is reading line input you need only to wrap a **BufferedReader** around a **FileReader**. Section 1b shows the new way to wrap **System.in** for reading console input, and this expands because **System.in** is a **DataInputStream** and

BufferedReader needs a **Reader** argument, so **InputStreamReader** is brought in to perform the translation.

In section 2 you can see that if you have a **String** and want to read from it you just use a **StringReader** instead of a **StringBufferInputStream** and the rest of the code is identical.

Section 3 shows a bug in the design of the new IO stream library. If you have a **String** and you want to read from it, you're *not* supposed to use a **StringBufferInputStream** any more. When you compile code involving a **StringBufferInputStream** constructor, you get a deprecation message telling you to not use it. Instead, you're supposed to use a **StringReader**. However, if you want to do formatted memory input as in section 3, you're forced to use a **DataInputStream** – there is no "DataReader" to replace it – and a **DataInputStream** constructor requires an **InputStream** argument. So you have no choice but to use the deprecated **StringBufferInputStream** class. The compiler will give you a deprecation message but there's nothing you can do about it.[2]

Section 4 is a reasonably straightforward translation from the old streams to the new, with no surprises. In section 5, you're forced to use all the old streams classes because **DataOutputStream** and **DataInputStream** require them and there are no alternatives. However, you don't get any deprecation messages at compile time. If a stream is deprecated, typically its constructor produces a deprecation message to prevent you from using the entire class, but in the case of **DataInputStream** only the **readLine( )** method is deprecated since you're supposed to use a **BufferedReader** for **readLine( )** (but a **DataInputStream** for all other formatted input).

If you compare section 5 with that section in **IOStreamDemo.java**, you'll notice that in *this* version, the data is written *before* the text. That's because a bug was introduced in Java 1.1, which is shown in the following code:

```
//: IOBug.java
// Java 1.1 (and higher?) IO Bug
import java.io.*;

public class IOBug {
  public static void main(String[] args)
  throws Exception {
```

---

[2] Perhaps by the time you read this, the bug will be fixed.

```
DataOutputStream out =
  new DataOutputStream(
    new BufferedOutputStream(
      new FileOutputStream("Data.txt")));
out.writeDouble(3.14159);
out.writeBytes("That was the value of pi\n");
out.writeBytes("This is pi/2:\n");
out.writeDouble(3.14159/2);
out.close();

DataInputStream in =
  new DataInputStream(
    new BufferedInputStream(
      new FileInputStream("Data.txt")));
BufferedReader inbr =
  new BufferedReader(
    new InputStreamReader(in));
// The doubles written BEFORE the line of text
// read back correctly:
System.out.println(in.readDouble());
// Read the lines of text:
System.out.println(inbr.readLine());
System.out.println(inbr.readLine());
// Trying to read the doubles after the line
// produces an end-of-file exception:
System.out.println(in.readDouble());
  }
} ///:~
```

It appears that anything you write after a call to **writeBytes( )** is not recoverable. This is a rather limiting bug, and we can hope that it will be fixed by the time you read this. You should run the above program to test it; if you don't get an exception and the values print correctly then you're out of the woods.

Redirecting standard IO

Java 1.1 has added methods in class **System** that allow you to redirect the standard input, output, and error IO streams using simple static method calls:

setIn(InputStream)
setOut(PrintStream)
setErr(PrintStream)

Redirecting output is especially useful if you suddenly start creating a large amount of output on your screen and it's scrolling past faster than you can read it. Redirecting input is valuable for a command-line program in which you want to test a particular user-input sequence repeatedly. Here's a simple example that shows the use of these methods:

```java
//: Redirecting.java
// Demonstrates the use of redirection for
// standard IO in Java 1.1
import java.io.*;

class Redirecting {
  public static void main(String[] args) {
    try {
      BufferedInputStream in =
        new BufferedInputStream(
          new FileInputStream(
            "Redirecting.java"));
      // Produces deprecation message:
      PrintStream out =
        new PrintStream(
          new BufferedOutputStream(
            new FileOutputStream("test.out")));
      System.setIn(in);
      System.setOut(out);
      System.setErr(out);

      BufferedReader br =
        new BufferedReader(
          new InputStreamReader(System.in));
      String s;
      while((s = br.readLine()) != null)
        System.out.println(s);
      out.close(); // Remember this!
    } catch(IOException e) {
      e.printStackTrace();
    }
  }
} ///:~
```

This program attaches standard input to a file, and redirects standard output and standard error to another file.

This is another example in which a deprecation message is inevitable. The message you can get when compiling with the -**deprecation** flag is:

Note: *The constructor java.io.PrintStream(java.io.OutputStream) has been deprecated.*

However, both **System.setOut( )** and **System.setErr( )** require a **PrintStream** object as an argument, so you are forced to call the **PrintStream** constructor. You might wonder, if Java 1.1 deprecates the entire **PrintStream** class by deprecating the constructor, why the library designers, at the same time as they added this deprecation, also add new methods to **System** that required a **PrintStream** rather than a **PrintWriter**, which is the new and preferred replacement. It's a mystery.

Compression

Java 1.1 has also added some classes to support reading and writing streams in a compressed format. These are wrapped around existing IO classes to provide compression functionality.

One aspect of these Java 1.1 classes stands out: They are not derived from the new **Reader** and **Writer** classes, but instead are part of the **InputStream** and **OutputStream** hierarchies. So you might be forced to mix the two types of streams. (Remember that you can use **InputStreamReader** and **OutputStreamWriter** to provide easy conversion between one type and another.)

Java 1.1 Compression class	Function
CheckedInputStream	**GetCheckSum( )** produces checksum for any **InputStream** (not just decompression)
CheckedOutputStream	**GetCheckSum( )** produces checksum for any **OutputStream** (not just compression)
DeflaterOutputStream	Base class for compression classes
ZipOutputStream	A **DeflaterOutputStream** that compresses data into the Zip file format
GZIPOutputStream	A **DeflaterOutputStream** that compresses data into the GZIP file format
InflaterInputStream	Base class for decompression classes
ZipInputStream	A **DeflaterInputStream** that Decompresses data that has been stored in the Zip file format
GZIPInputStream	A **DeflaterInputStream** that decompresses data that has been stored in the GZIP file format

Although there are many compression algorithms, Zip and GZIP are possibly the most commonly used. Thus you can easily manipulate your compressed data with the many tools available for reading and writing these formats.

Simple compression with GZIP

The GZIP interface is simple and thus is probably more appropriate when you have a single stream of data that you want to compress (rather than a collection of dissimilar pieces of data). Here's an example that compresses a single file:

```
//: GZIPcompress.java
// Uses Java 1.1 GZIP compression to compress
// a file whose name is passed on the command
// line.
import java.io.*;
import java.util.zip.*;

public class GZIPcompress {
  public static void main(String[] args) {
    try {
      BufferedReader in =
        new BufferedReader(
          new FileReader(args[0]));
      BufferedOutputStream out =
        new BufferedOutputStream(
          new GZIPOutputStream(
            new FileOutputStream("test.gz")));
      System.out.println("Writing file");
      int c;
      while((c = in.read()) != -1)
        out.write(c);
      in.close();
      out.close();
      System.out.println("Reading file");
      BufferedReader in2 =
        new BufferedReader(
          new InputStreamReader(
            new GZIPInputStream(
              new FileInputStream("test.gz"))));
      String s;
      while((s = in2.readLine()) != null)
        System.out.println(s);
```

```
      } catch(Exception e) {
        e.printStackTrace();
      }
    }
  } ///:~
```

The use of the compression classes is straightforward – you simply wrap your output stream in a **GZIPOutputStream** or **ZipOutputStream** and your input stream in a **GZIPInputStream** or **ZipInputStream**. All else is ordinary IO reading and writing. This is, however, a good example of when you're forced to mix the old IO streams with the new: **in** uses the **Reader** classes, whereas **GZIPOutputStream**'s constructor can accept only an **OutputStream** object, not a **Writer** object.

Multi-file storage with Zip

The Java 1.1 library that supports the Zip format is much more extensive. With it you can easily store multiple files, and there's even a separate class to make the process of reading a Zip file easy. The library uses the standard Zip format so that it works seamlessly with all the tools currently downloadable on the Internet. The following example has the same form as the previous example, but it handles as many command-line arguments as you want. In addition, it shows the use of the **Checksum** classes to calculate and verify the checksum for the file. There are two **Checksum** types: **Adler32** (which is faster) and **CRC32** (which is slower but slightly more accurate).

```
//: ZipCompress.java
// Uses Java 1.1 Zip compression to compress
// any number of files whose names are passed
// on the command line.
import java.io.*;
import java.util.*;
import java.util.zip.*;

public class ZipCompress {
  public static void main(String[] args) {
    try {
      FileOutputStream f =
        new FileOutputStream("test.zip");
      CheckedOutputStream csum =
        new CheckedOutputStream(
          f, new Adler32());
      ZipOutputStream out =
```

```java
    new ZipOutputStream(
      new BufferedOutputStream(csum));
out.setComment("A test of Java Zipping");
// Can't read the above comment, though
for(int i = 0; i < args.length; i++) {
  System.out.println(
    "Writing file " + args[i]);
  BufferedReader in =
    new BufferedReader(
      new FileReader(args[i]));
  out.putNextEntry(new ZipEntry(args[i]));
  int c;
  while((c = in.read()) != -1)
    out.write(c);
  in.close();
}
out.close();
// Checksum valid only after the file
// has been closed!
System.out.println("Checksum: " +
  csum.getChecksum().getValue());
// Now extract the files:
System.out.println("Reading file");
FileInputStream fi =
    new FileInputStream("test.zip");
CheckedInputStream csumi =
  new CheckedInputStream(
    fi, new Adler32());
ZipInputStream in2 =
  new ZipInputStream(
    new BufferedInputStream(csumi));
ZipEntry ze;
System.out.println("Checksum: " +
  csumi.getChecksum().getValue());
while((ze = in2.getNextEntry()) != null) {
  System.out.println("Reading file " + ze);
  int x;
  while((x = in2.read()) != -1)
    System.out.write(x);
}
in2.close();
// Alternative way to open and read
// zip files:
ZipFile zf = new ZipFile("test.zip");
```

```
        Enumeration e = zf.entries();
        while(e.hasMoreElements()) {
          ZipEntry ze2 = (ZipEntry)e.nextElement();
          System.out.println("File: " + ze2);
          // ... and extract the data as before
        }
      } catch(Exception e) {
        e.printStackTrace();
      }
    }
  } ///:~
```

For each file to add to the archive, you must call **putNextEntry( )** and pass it a **ZipEntry** object. The **ZipEntry** object contains an extensive interface that allows you to get and set all the data available on that particular entry in your Zip file: name, compressed and uncompressed sizes, date, CRC checksum, extra field data, comment, compression method, and whether it's a directory entry. However, even though the Zip format has a way to set a password, this is not supported in Java's Zip library. And although **CheckedInputStream** and **CheckedOutputStream** support both **Adler32** and **CRC32** checksums, the **ZipEntry** class supports only an interface for CRC. This is a restriction of the underlying Zip format, but it might limit you from using the faster **Adler32**.

To extract files, **ZipInputStream** has a **getNextEntry( )** method that returns the next **ZipEntry** if there is one. As a more succinct alternative, you can read the file using a **ZipFile** object, which has a method **entries( )** to return an **Enumeration** to the **ZipEntries**.

In order to read the checksum you must somehow have access to the associated **Checksum** object. Here, a handle to the **CheckedOutputStream** and **CheckedInputStream** objects is retained, but you could also just hold onto a handle to the **Checksum** object.

A baffling method in Zip streams is **setComment( )**. As shown above, you can set a comment when you're writing a file, but there's no way to recover the comment in the **ZipInputStream**. Comments appear to be supported fully on an entry-by-entry basis only via **ZipEntry**.

Of course, you are not limited to files when using the **GZIP** or **Zip** libraries – you can compress anything, including data to be sent through a network connection.

The Java archive (jar) utility

The Zip format is also used in the Java 1.1 JAR (Java ARchive) file format, which is a way to collect a group of files into a single compressed file, just like Zip. However, like everything else in Java, JAR files are cross-platform so you don't need to worry about platform issues. You can also include audio and image files as well as class files.

JAR files are particularly helpful when you deal with the Internet. Before JAR files, your Web browser would have to make repeated requests of a Web server in order to download all of the files that make up an applet. In addition, each of these files was uncompressed. By combining all of the files for a particular applet into a single JAR file, only one server request is necessary and the transfer is faster because of compression. And each entry in a JAR file can be digitally signed for security (refer to the Java documentation for details).

A JAR file consists of a single file containing a collection of zipped files along with a "manifest" that describes them. (You can create your own manifest file; otherwise the **jar** program will do it for you.) You can find out more about JAR manifests in the online documentation.

The **jar** utility that comes with Sun's JDK automatically compresses the files of your choice. You invoke it on the command line:

```
jar [options] destination [manifest] inputfile(s)
```

The options are simply a collection of letters (no hyphen or any other indicator is necessary). These are:

c	Creates a new or empty archive.
t	Lists the table of contents.
x	Extracts all files
x file	Extracts the named file
f	Says: "I'm going to give you the name of the file." If you don't use this, **jar** assumes that its input will come from standard input, or, if it is creating a file, its output will go to standard output.
m	Says that the first argument will be the name of the user-created manifest file
v	Generates verbose output describing what **jar** is doing
O	Only store the files; doesn't compress the files (use to create a JAR file that you can put in your classpath)
M	Don't automatically create a manifest file

If a subdirectory is included in the files to be put into the JAR file, that subdirectory is automatically added, including all of its subdirectories, etc. Path information is also preserved.

Here are some typical ways to invoke **jar**:

```
jar cf myJarFile.jar *.class
```

This creates a JAR file called **myJarFile.jar** that contains all of the class files in the current directory, along with an automatically-generated manifest file.

```
jar cmf myJarFile.jar myManifestFile.mf *.class
```

Like the previous example, but adding a user-created manifest file called **myManifestFile.mf**.

```
jar tf myJarFile.jar
```

Produces a table of contents of the files in **myJarFile.jar**.

```
jar tvf myJarFile.jar
```

Adds the "verbose" flag to give more detailed information about the files in **myJarFile.jar**.

```
jar cvf myApp.jar audio classes image
```

Assuming **audio**, **classes**, and **image** are subdirectories, this combines all of the subdirectories into the file **myApp.jar**. The "verbose" flag is also included to give extra feedback while the **jar** program is working.

If you create a JAR file using the **O** option, that file can be placed in your CLASSPATH:

```
CLASSPATH="lib1.jar;lib2.jar;"
```

Then Java can search **lib1.jar** and **lib2.jar** for class files.

The **jar** tool isn't as useful as a **zip** utility. For example, you can't add or update files to an existing JAR file; you can create JAR files only from scratch. Also, you can't move files into a JAR file, erasing them as they are moved. However, a JAR file created on one platform will be transparently readable by the **jar** tool on any other platform (a problem that sometimes plagues **zip** utilities).

As you will see in Chapter 13, JAR files are also used to package Java Beans.

Object serialization

Java 1.1 has added an interesting feature called *object serialization* that allows you to take any object that implements the **Serializable** interface and turn it into a sequence of bytes that can later be restored fully into the original object. This is even true across a network, which means that the serialization mechanism automatically compensates for differences in operating systems. That is, you can create an object on a Windows machine, serialize it, and send it across the network to a Unix machine where it will be correctly reconstructed. You don't have to worry about the data representations on the different machines, the byte ordering, or any other details.

By itself, object serialization is interesting because it allows you to implement *lightweight persistence*. Remember that persistence means an object's lifetime is not determined by whether a program is executing – the object lives *in between* invocations of the program. By taking a serializable object and writing it to disk, then restoring that object when the program is re-invoked, you're able to produce the effect of persistence. The reason it's called "lightweight" is that you can't simply define an object using some kind of "persistent" keyword and let the system take care of the details (although this might happen in the future). Instead, you must explicitly serialize and de-serialize the objects in your program.

Object serialization was added to the language to support two major features. Java 1.1's *remote method invocation* (RMI) allows objects that live on other machines to behave as if they live on your machine. When sending messages to remote objects, object serialization is necessary to transport the arguments and return values. RMI is discussed in Chapter 15.

Object serialization is also necessary for Java Beans, introduced in Java 1.1. When a Bean is used, its state information is generally configured at design time. This state information must be stored and later recovered when the program is started; object serialization performs this task.

Serializing an object is quite simple, as long as the object implements the **Serializable** interface (this interface is just a flag and has no methods). In Java 1.1, many standard library classes have been changed so they're serializable, including all of the wrappers for the primitive types, all of the collection classes, and many others. Even **Class** objects can be serialized. (See Chapter 11 for the implications of this.)

To serialize an object, you create some sort of **OutputStream** object and then wrap it inside an **ObjectOutputStream** object. At this point you need only call **writeObject( )** and your object is serialized and sent to the **OutputStream**. To reverse the process, you wrap an **InputStream** inside an **ObjectInputStream** and call **readObject( )**. What comes back is, as usual, a handle to an upcast **Object**, so you must downcast to set things straight.

A particularly clever aspect of object serialization is that it not only saves an image of your object but it also follows all the handles contained in your object and saves *those* objects, and follows all the handles in each of those objects, etc. This is sometimes referred to as the "web of objects" that a single object can be connected to, and it includes arrays of handles to objects as well as member objects. If you had to maintain your own object serialization scheme, maintaining the code to follow all these links would be a bit mind–boggling. However, Java object serialization seems to pull it off flawlessly, no doubt using an optimized algorithm that traverses the web of objects. The following example tests the serialization mechanism by making a "worm" of linked objects, each of which has a link to the next segment in the worm as well as an array of handles to objects of a different class, **Data**:

```
//: Worm.java
// Demonstrates object serialization in Java 1.1
import java.io.*;

class Data implements Serializable {
  private int i;
  Data(int x) { i = x; }
  public String toString() {
    return Integer.toString(i);
  }
}

public class Worm implements Serializable {
  // Generate a random int value:
  private static int r() {
    return (int)(Math.random() * 10);
  }
  private Data[] d = {
    new Data(r()), new Data(r()), new Data(r())
  };
  private Worm next;
  private char c;
  // Value of i == number of segments
```

```
Worm(int i, char x) {
  System.out.println(" Worm constructor: " + i);
  c = x;
  if(--i > 0)
    next = new Worm(i, (char)(x + 1));
}
Worm() {
  System.out.println("Default constructor");
}
public String toString() {
  String s = ":" + c + "(";
  for(int i = 0; i < d.length; i++)
    s += d[i].toString();
  s += ")";
  if(next != null)
    s += next.toString();
  return s;
}
public static void main(String[] args) {
  Worm w = new Worm(6, 'a');
  System.out.println("w = " + w);
  try {
    ObjectOutputStream out =
      new ObjectOutputStream(
        new FileOutputStream("worm.out"));
    out.writeObject("Worm storage");
    out.writeObject(w);
    out.close(); // Also flushes output
    ObjectInputStream in =
      new ObjectInputStream(
        new FileInputStream("worm.out"));
    String s = (String)in.readObject();
    Worm w2 = (Worm)in.readObject();
    System.out.println(s + ", w2 = " + w2);
  } catch(Exception e) {
    e.printStackTrace();
  }
  try {
    ByteArrayOutputStream bout =
      new ByteArrayOutputStream();
    ObjectOutputStream out =
      new ObjectOutputStream(bout);
    out.writeObject("Worm storage");
    out.writeObject(w);
```

```
                    out.flush();
                    ObjectInputStream in =
                      new ObjectInputStream(
                        new ByteArrayInputStream(
                          bout.toByteArray())));
                    String s = (String)in.readObject();
                    Worm w3 = (Worm)in.readObject();
                    System.out.println(s + ", w3 = " + w3);
                  } catch(Exception e) {
                    e.printStackTrace();
                  }
                }
              } ///:~
```

To make things interesting, the array of **Data** objects inside **Worm** are initialized with random numbers. (This way you don't suspect the compiler of keeping some kind of meta-information.) Each **Worm** segment is labeled with a **char** that's automatically generated in the process of recursively generating the linked list of **Worm**s. When you create a **Worm**, you tell the constructor how long you want it to be. To make the **next** handle it calls the **Worm** constructor with a length of one less, etc. The final **next** handle is left as **null**, indicating the end of the **Worm**.

The point of all this was to make something reasonably complex that couldn't easily be serialized. The act of serializing, however, is quite simple. Once the **ObjectOutputStream** is created from some other stream, **writeObject( )** serializes the object. Notice the call to **writeObject( )** for a **String**, as well. You can also write all the primitive data types using the same methods as **DataOutputStream** (they share the same interface).

There are two separate **try** blocks that look similar. The first writes and reads a file and the second, for variety, writes and reads a **ByteArray**. You can read and write an object using serialization to any **DataInputStream** or **DataOutputStream** including, as you will see in the networking chapter, a network. The output from one run was:

```
Worm constructor: 6
Worm constructor: 5
Worm constructor: 4
Worm constructor: 3
Worm constructor: 2
Worm constructor: 1
w = :a(262):b(100):c(396):d(480):e(316):f(398)
```

```
Worm storage, w2 =
:a(262):b(100):c(396):d(480):e(316):f(398)
Worm storage, w3 =
:a(262):b(100):c(396):d(480):e(316):f(398)
```

You can see that the deserialized object really does contain all of the links that were in the original object.

Note that no constructor, not even the default constructor, is called in the process of deserializing a **Serializable** object. The entire object is restored by recovering data from the **InputStream**.

Object serialization is another Java 1.1 feature that is not part of the new **Reader** and **Writer** hierarchies, but instead uses the old **InputStream** and **OutputStream** hierarchies. Thus you might encounter situations in which you're forced to mix the two hierarchies.

Finding the class

You might wonder what's necessary for an object to be recovered from its serialized state. For example, suppose you serialize an object and send it as a file or through a network to another machine. Could a program on the other machine reconstruct the object using only the contents of the file?

The best way to answer this question is (as usual) by performing an experiment. The following file goes in the subdirectory for this chapter:

```
//: Alien.java
// A serializable class
import java.io.*;

public class Alien implements Serializable {
} ///:~
```

The file that creates and serializes an **Alien** object goes in the same directory:

```
//: FreezeAlien.java
// Create a serialized output file
import java.io.*;

public class FreezeAlien {
  public static void main(String[] args)
      throws Exception {
    ObjectOutput out =
```

```
      new ObjectOutputStream(
        new FileOutputStream("file.x"));
      Alien zorcon = new Alien();
      out.writeObject(zorcon);
    }
  } ///:~
```

Rather than catching and handling exceptions, this program takes the quick and dirty approach of passing the exceptions out of **main( )**, so they'll be reported on the command line.

Once the program is compiled and run, copy the resulting **file.x** to a subdirectory called **xfiles**, where the following code goes:

```
//: ThawAlien.java
// Try to recover a serialized file without the
// class of object that's stored in that file.
package c10.xfiles;
import java.io.*;

public class ThawAlien {
  public static void main(String[] args)
      throws Exception {
    ObjectInputStream in =
      new ObjectInputStream(
        new FileInputStream("file.x"));
    Object mystery = in.readObject();
    System.out.println(
      mystery.getClass().toString());
  }
} ///:~
```

This program opens the file and reads in the object **mystery** successfully. However, as soon as you try to find out anything about the object – which requires the **Class** object for **Alien** – the Java Virtual Machine (JVM) cannot find **Alien.class** (unless it happens to be in the Classpath, which it shouldn't be in this example). You'll get a **ClassNotFoundException.** (Once again, all evidence of alien life vanishes before proof of its existence can be verified!)

If you expect to do much after you've recovered an object that has been serialized, you must make sure that the JVM can find the associated **.class** file either in the local class path or somewhere on the Internet.

Controlling serialization

As you can see, the default serialization mechanism is trivial to use. But what if you have special needs? Perhaps you have special security issues and you don't want to serialize portions of your object, or perhaps it just doesn't make sense for one sub-object to be serialized if that part needs to be created anew when the object is recovered.

You can control the process of serialization by implementing the **Externalizable** interface instead of the **Serializable** interface. The **Externalizable** interface extends the **Serializable** interface and adds two methods, **writeExternal( )** and **readExternal( )**, that are automatically called for your object during serialization and deserialization so that you can perform your special operations.

The following example shows simple implementations of the **Externalizable** interface methods. Note that **Blip1** and **Blip2** are nearly identical except for a subtle difference (see if you can discover it by looking at the code):

```
//: Blips.java
// Simple use of Externalizable & a pitfall
import java.io.*;
import java.util.*;

class Blip1 implements Externalizable {
  public Blip1() {
    System.out.println("Blip1 Constructor");
  }
  public void writeExternal(ObjectOutput out)
      throws IOException {
    System.out.println("Blip1.writeExternal");
  }
  public void readExternal(ObjectInput in)
      throws IOException, ClassNotFoundException {
    System.out.println("Blip1.readExternal");
  }
}

class Blip2 implements Externalizable {
  Blip2() {
    System.out.println("Blip2 Constructor");
  }
  public void writeExternal(ObjectOutput out)
      throws IOException {
```

```
        System.out.println("Blip2.writeExternal");
      }
    public void readExternal(ObjectInput in)
        throws IOException, ClassNotFoundException {
      System.out.println("Blip2.readExternal");
    }
}

public class Blips {
  public static void main(String[] args) {
    System.out.println("Constructing objects:");
    Blip1 b1 = new Blip1();
    Blip2 b2 = new Blip2();
    try {
      ObjectOutputStream o =
        new ObjectOutputStream(
          new FileOutputStream("Blips.out"));
      System.out.println("Saving objects:");
      o.writeObject(b1);
      o.writeObject(b2);
      o.close();
      // Now get them back:
      ObjectInputStream in =
        new ObjectInputStream(
          new FileInputStream("Blips.out"));
      System.out.println("Recovering b1:");
      b1 = (Blip1)in.readObject();
      // OOPS! Throws an exception:
//!   System.out.println("Recovering b2:");
//!   b2 = (Blip2)in.readObject();
    } catch(Exception e) {
      e.printStackTrace();
    }
  }
} ///:~
```

The output for this program is:

```
Constructing objects:
Blip1 Constructor
Blip2 Constructor
Saving objects:
Blip1.writeExternal
Blip2.writeExternal
Recovering b1:
```

```
    Blip1 Constructor
    Blip1.readExternal
```

The reason that the **Blip2** object is not recovered is that trying to do so causes an exception. Can you see the difference between **Blip1** and **Blip2**? The constructor for **Blip1** is **public**, while the constructor for **Blip2** is not, and that causes the exception upon recovery. Try making **Blip2**'s constructor **public** and removing the //! comments to see the correct results.

When **b1** is recovered, the **Blip1** default constructor is called. This is different from recovering a **Serializable** object, in which the object is constructed entirely from its stored bits, with no constructor calls. With an **Externalizable** object, all the normal default construction behavior occurs (including the initializations at the point of field definition), and *then* **readExternal( )** is called. You need to be aware of this – in particular the fact that all the default construction always takes place – to produce the correct behavior in your **Externalizable** objects.

Here's an example that shows what you must do to fully store and retrieve an **Externalizable** object:

```
//: Blip3.java
// Reconstructing an externalizable object
import java.io.*;
import java.util.*;

class Blip3 implements Externalizable {
  int i;
  String s; // No initialization
  public Blip3() {
    System.out.println("Blip3 Constructor");
    // s, i not initialized
  }
  public Blip3(String x, int a) {
    System.out.println("Blip3(String x, int a)");
    s = x;
    i = a;
    // s & i initialized only in non-default
    // constructor.
  }
  public String toString() { return s + i; }
  public void writeExternal(ObjectOutput out)
      throws IOException {
    System.out.println("Blip3.writeExternal");
```

```
    // You must do this:
    out.writeObject(s); out.writeInt(i);
  }
  public void readExternal(ObjectInput in)
    throws IOException, ClassNotFoundException {
    System.out.println("Blip3.readExternal");
    // You must do this:
    s = (String)in.readObject();
    i =in.readInt();
  }
  public static void main(String[] args) {
    System.out.println("Constructing objects:");
    Blip3 b3 = new Blip3("A String ", 47);
    System.out.println(b3.toString());
    try {
      ObjectOutputStream o =
        new ObjectOutputStream(
          new FileOutputStream("Blip3.out"));
      System.out.println("Saving object:");
      o.writeObject(b3);
      o.close();
      // Now get it back:
      ObjectInputStream in =
        new ObjectInputStream(
          new FileInputStream("Blip3.out"));
      System.out.println("Recovering b3:");
      b3 = (Blip3)in.readObject();
      System.out.println(b3.toString());
    } catch(Exception e) {
      e.printStackTrace();
    }
  }
} ///:~
```

The fields **s** and **i** are initialized only in the second constructor, but not in
the default constructor. This means that if you don't initialize **s** and **i** in
readExternal, it will be **null** (since the storage for the object gets wiped
to zero in the first step of object creation). If you comment out the two
lines of code following the phrases "You must do this" and run the
program, you'll see that when the object is recovered, **s** is **null** and **i** is
zero.

If you are inheriting from an **Externalizable** object, you'll typically call
the base-class versions of **writeExternal( )** and **readExternal( )** to
provide proper storage and retrieval of the base-class components.

So to make things work correctly you must not only write the important data from the object during the **writeExternal( )** method (there is no default behavior that writes any of the member objects for an **Externalizable** object), but you must also recover that data in the **readExternal( )** method. This can be a bit confusing at first because the default construction behavior for an **Externalizable** object can make it seem like some kind of storage and retrieval takes place automatically. It does not.

The transient keyword

When you're controlling serialization, there might be a particular subobject that you don't want Java's serialization mechanism to automatically save and restore. This is commonly the case if that subobject represents sensitive information that you don't want to serialize, such as a password. Even if that information is **private** in the object, once it's serialized it's possible for someone to access it by reading a file or intercepting a network transmission.

One way to prevent sensitive parts of your object from being serialized is to implement your class as **Externalizable**, as shown previously. Then nothing is automatically serialized and you can explicitly serialize only the necessary parts inside **writeExternal( )**.

If you're working with a **Serializable** object, however, all serialization happens automatically. To control this, you can turn off serialization on a field-by-field basis using the **transient** keyword, which says "Don't bother saving or restoring this – I'll take care of it."

For example, consider a **Login** object that keeps information about a particular login session. Suppose that, once you verify the login, you want to store the data, but without the password. The easiest way to do this is by implementing **Serializable** and marking the **password** field as **transient**. Here's what it looks like:

```
//: Logon.java
// Demonstrates the "transient" keyword
import java.io.*;
import java.util.*;

class Logon implements Serializable {
  private Date date = new Date();
  private String username;
  private transient String password;
  Logon(String name, String pwd) {
```

```java
      username = name;
      password = pwd;
  }
  public String toString() {
    String pwd =
      (password == null) ? "(n/a)" : password;
    return "logon info: \n    " +
      "username: " + username +
      "\n    date: " + date.toString() +
      "\n    password: " + pwd;
  }
  public static void main(String[] args) {
    Logon a = new Logon("Hulk", "myLittlePony");
    System.out.println( "logon a = " + a);
    try {
      ObjectOutputStream o =
        new ObjectOutputStream(
          new FileOutputStream("Logon.out"));
      o.writeObject(a);
      o.close();
      // Delay:
      int seconds = 5;
      long t = System.currentTimeMillis()
             + seconds * 1000;
      while(System.currentTimeMillis() < t)
        ;
      // Now get them back:
      ObjectInputStream in =
        new ObjectInputStream(
          new FileInputStream("Logon.out"));
      System.out.println(
        "Recovering object at " + new Date());
      a = (Logon)in.readObject();
      System.out.println( "logon a = " + a);
    } catch(Exception e) {
      e.printStackTrace();
    }
  }
} ///:~
```

You can see that the **date** and **username** fields are ordinary (not **transient**), and thus are automatically serialized. However, the **password** is **transient**, and so is not stored to disk; also the serialization mechanism makes no attempt to recover it. The output is:

```
logon a = logon info:
   username: Hulk
   date: Sun Mar 23 18:25:53 PST 1997
   password: myLittlePony
Recovering object at Sun Mar 23 18:25:59 PST 1997
logon a = logon info:
   username: Hulk
   date: Sun Mar 23 18:25:53 PST 1997
   password: (n/a)
```

When the object is recovered, the **password** field is **null**. Note that **toString( )** must check for a **null** value of **password** because if you try to assemble a **String** object using the overloaded '**+**' operator, and that operator encounters a **null** handle, you'll get a **NullPointerException**. (Newer versions of Java might contain code to avoid this problem.)

You can also see that the **date** field is stored to and recovered from disk and not generated anew.

Since **Externalizable** objects do not store any of their fields by default, the **transient** keyword is for use with **Serializable** objects only.

An alternative to **Externalizable**

If you're not keen on implementing the **Externalizable** interface, there's another approach. You can implement the **Serializable** interface and *add* (notice I say "add" and not "override" or "implement") methods called **writeObject( )** and **readObject( )** that will automatically be called when the object is serialized and deserialized, respectively. That is, if you provide these two methods they will be used instead of the default serialization.

The methods must have these exact signatures:

```
private void
  writeObject(ObjectOutputStream stream)
    throws IOException;

private void
  readObject(ObjectInputStream stream)
    throws IOException, ClassNotFoundException
```

From a design standpoint, things get really weird here. First of all, you might think that because these methods are not part of a base class or the **Serializable** interface, they ought to be defined in their own interface(s). But notice that they are defined as **private**, which means they are to be called only by other members of this class. However, you don't actually call them from other members of this class, but instead the **writeObject( )** and **readObject( )** methods of the **ObjectOutputStream** and **ObjectInputStream** objects call your object's **writeObject( )** and **readObject( )** methods. (Notice my tremendous restraint in not launching into a long diatribe about using the same method names here. In a word: confusing.) You might wonder how the **ObjectOutputStream** and **ObjectInputStream** objects have access to **private** methods of your class. We can only assume that this is part of the serialization magic.

In any event, anything defined in an **interface** is automatically **public** so if **writeObject( )** and **readObject( )** must be **private**, then they can't be part of an **interface**. Since you must follow the signatures exactly, the effect is the same as if you're implementing an **interface**.

It would appear that when you call **ObjectOutputStream.writeObject( )**, the **Serializable** object that you pass it to is interrogated (using reflection, no doubt) to see if it implements its own **writeObject( )**. If so, the normal serialization process is skipped and the **writeObject( )** is called. The same sort of situation exists for **readObject( )**.

There's one other twist. Inside your **writeObject( )**, you can choose to perform the default **writeObject( )** action by calling **defaultWriteObject( )**. Likewise, inside **readObject( )** you can call **defaultReadObject( )**. Here is a simple example that demonstrates how you can control the storage and retrieval of a **Serializable** object:

```
//: SerialCtl.java
// Controlling serialization by adding your own
// writeObject() and readObject() methods.
import java.io.*;

public class SerialCtl implements Serializable {
  String a;
  transient String b;
  public SerialCtl(String aa, String bb) {
    a = "Not Transient: " + aa;
    b = "Transient: " + bb;
  }
  public String toString() {
    return a + "\n" + b;
  }
  private void
    writeObject(ObjectOutputStream stream)
```

```
      throws IOException {
    stream.defaultWriteObject();
    stream.writeObject(b);
  }
  private void
    readObject(ObjectInputStream stream)
      throws IOException, ClassNotFoundException {
    stream.defaultReadObject();
    b = (String)stream.readObject();
  }
  public static void main(String[] args) {
    SerialCtl sc =
      new SerialCtl("Test1", "Test2");
    System.out.println("Before:\n" + sc);
    ByteArrayOutputStream buf =
      new ByteArrayOutputStream();
    try {
      ObjectOutputStream o =
        new ObjectOutputStream(buf);
      o.writeObject(sc);
      // Now get it back:
      ObjectInputStream in =
        new ObjectInputStream(
          new ByteArrayInputStream(
            buf.toByteArray()));
      SerialCtl sc2 = (SerialCtl)in.readObject();
      System.out.println("After:\n" + sc2);
    } catch(Exception e) {
      e.printStackTrace();
    }
  }
} ///:~
```

In this example, one **String** field is ordinary and the other is **transient**, to prove that the non-**transient** field is saved by the **defaultWriteObject( )** method and the **transient** field is saved and restored explicitly. The fields are initialized inside the constructor rather than at the point of definition to prove that they are not being initialized by some automatic mechanism during deserialization.

If you are going to use the default mechanism to write the non-**transient** parts of your object, you must call **defaultWriteObject( )** as the first operation in **writeObject( )** and **defaultReadObject( )** as the first operation in **readObject( )**. These are strange method calls. It would appear, for example, that you are calling **defaultWriteObject( )** for an

ObjectOutputStream and passing it no arguments, and yet it somehow turns around and knows the handle to your object and how to write all the non-**transient** parts. Spooky.

The storage and retrieval of the **transient** objects uses more familiar code. And yet, think about what happens here. In **main( )**, a **SerialCtl** object is created, and then it's serialized to an **ObjectOutputStream**. (Notice in this case that a buffer is used instead of a file – it's all the same to the **ObjectOutputStream**.) The serialization occurs in the line:

```
o.writeObject(sc);
```

The **writeObject( )** method must be examining **sc** to see if it has its own **writeObject( )** method. (Not by checking the interface – there isn't one – or the class type, but by actually hunting for the method using reflection.) If it does, it uses that. A similar approach holds true for **readObject( )**. Perhaps this was the only practical way that they could solve the problem, but it's certainly strange.

Versioning

It's possible that you might want to change the version of a serializable class (objects of the original class might be stored in a database, for example). This is supported but you'll probably do it only in special cases, and it requires an extra depth of understanding that we will not attempt to achieve here. The JDK1.1 HTML documents downloadable from Sun (which might be part of your Java package's online documents) cover this topic quite thoroughly.

Using persistence

It's quite appealing to use serialization technology to store some of the state of your program so that you can easily restore the program to the current state later. But before you can do this, some questions must be answered. What happens if you serialize two objects that both have a handle to a third object? When you restore those two objects from their serialized state, do you get only one occurrence of the third object? What if you serialize your two objects to separate files and deserialize them in different parts of your code?

Here's an example that shows the problem:

```
//: MyWorld.java
import java.io.*;
import java.util.*;
```

```
class House implements Serializable {}

class Animal implements Serializable {
  String name;
  House preferredHouse;
  Animal(String nm, House h) {
    name = nm;
    preferredHouse = h;
  }
  public String toString() {
    return name + "[" + super.toString() +
      "], " + preferredHouse + "\n";
  }
}

public class MyWorld {
  public static void main(String[] args) {
    House house = new House();
    Vector   animals = new Vector();
    animals.addElement(
      new Animal("Bosco the dog", house));
    animals.addElement(
      new Animal("Ralph the hamster", house));
    animals.addElement(
      new Animal("Fronk the cat", house));
    System.out.println("animals: " + animals);

    try {
      ByteArrayOutputStream buf1 =
        new ByteArrayOutputStream();
      ObjectOutputStream o1 =
        new ObjectOutputStream(buf1);
      o1.writeObject(animals);
      o1.writeObject(animals); // Write a 2nd set
      // Write to a different stream:
      ByteArrayOutputStream buf2 =
        new ByteArrayOutputStream();
      ObjectOutputStream o2 =
        new ObjectOutputStream(buf2);
      o2.writeObject(animals);
      // Now get them back:
      ObjectInputStream in1 =
        new ObjectInputStream(
```

```
          new ByteArrayInputStream(
            buf1.toByteArray()));
        ObjectInputStream in2 =
          new ObjectInputStream(
            new ByteArrayInputStream(
              buf2.toByteArray()));
        Vector animals1 = (Vector)in1.readObject();
        Vector animals2 = (Vector)in1.readObject();
        Vector animals3 = (Vector)in2.readObject();
        System.out.println("animals1: " + animals1);
        System.out.println("animals2: " + animals2);
        System.out.println("animals3: " + animals3);
      } catch(Exception e) {
        e.printStackTrace();
      }
    }
} ///:~
```

One thing that's interesting here is that it's possible to use object serialization to and from a byte array as a way of doing a "deep copy" of any object that's **Serializable**. (A deep copy means that you're duplicating the entire web of objects, rather than just the basic object and its handles.) Copying is covered in depth in Chapter 12.

Animal objects contain fields of type **House**. In **main( )**, a **Vector** of these **Animal**s is created and it is serialized twice to one stream and then again to a separate stream. When these are deserialized and printed, you see the following results for one run (the objects will be in different memory locations each run):

```
animals: [Bosco the dog[Animal@1cc76c],
House@1cc769
, Ralph the hamster[Animal@1cc76d], House@1cc769
, Fronk the cat[Animal@1cc76e], House@1cc769
]
animals1: [Bosco the dog[Animal@1cca0c],
House@1cca16
, Ralph the hamster[Animal@1cca17], House@1cca16
, Fronk the cat[Animal@1cca1b], House@1cca16
]
animals2: [Bosco the dog[Animal@1cca0c],
House@1cca16
, Ralph the hamster[Animal@1cca17], House@1cca16
, Fronk the cat[Animal@1cca1b], House@1cca16
]
```

```
animals3: [Bosco the dog[Animal@1cca52],
House@1cca5c
, Ralph the hamster[Animal@1cca5d], House@1cca5c
, Fronk the cat[Animal@1cca61], House@1cca5c
]
```

Of course you expect that the deserialized objects have different addresses
from their originals. But notice that in **animals1** and **animals2** the same
addresses appear, including the references to the **House** object that both
share. On the other hand, when **animals3** is recovered the system has no
way of knowing that the objects in this other stream are aliases of the
objects in the first stream, so it makes a completely different web of
objects.

As long as you're serializing everything to a single stream, you'll be able
to recover the same web of objects that you wrote, with no accidental
duplication of objects. Of course, you can change the state of your objects
in between the time you write the first and the last, but that's your
responsibility – the objects will be written in whatever state they are in
(and with whatever connections they have to other objects) at the time
you serialize them.

The safest thing to do if you want to save the state of a system is to
serialize as an "atomic" operation. If you serialize some things, do some
other work, and serialize some more, etc., then you will not be storing
the system safely. Instead, put all the objects that comprise the state of
your system in a single collection and simply write that collection out in
one operation. Then you can restore it with a single method call as well.

The following example is an imaginary computer-aided design (CAD)
system that demonstrates the approach. In addition, it throws in the
issue of **static** fields – if you look at the documentation you'll see that
Class is **Serializable**, so it should be easy to store the **static** fields by
simply serializing the **Class** object. That seems like a sensible approach,
anyway.

```
//: CADState.java
// Saving and restoring the state of a
// pretend CAD system.
import java.io.*;
import java.util.*;

abstract class Shape implements Serializable {
  public static final int
    RED = 1, BLUE = 2, GREEN = 3;
  private int xPos, yPos, dimension;
```

```java
  private static Random r = new Random();
  private static int counter = 0;
  abstract public void setColor(int newColor);
  abstract public int getColor();
  public Shape(int xVal, int yVal, int dim) {
    xPos = xVal;
    yPos = yVal;
    dimension = dim;
  }
  public String toString() {
    return getClass().toString() +
      " color[" + getColor() +
      "] xPos[" + xPos +
      "] yPos[" + yPos +
      "] dim[" + dimension + "]\n";
  }
  public static Shape randomFactory() {
    int xVal = r.nextInt() % 100;
    int yVal = r.nextInt() % 100;
    int dim = r.nextInt() % 100;
    switch(counter++ % 3) {
      default:
      case 0: return new Circle(xVal, yVal, dim);
      case 1: return new Square(xVal, yVal, dim);
      case 2: return new Line(xVal, yVal, dim);
    }
  }
}

class Circle extends Shape {
  private static int color = RED;
  public Circle(int xVal, int yVal, int dim) {
    super(xVal, yVal, dim);
  }
  public void setColor(int newColor) {
    color = newColor;
  }
  public int getColor() {
    return color;
  }
}

class Square extends Shape {
  private static int color;
```

```
    public Square(int xVal, int yVal, int dim) {
      super(xVal, yVal, dim);
      color = RED;
    }
    public void setColor(int newColor) {
      color = newColor;
    }
    public int getColor() {
      return color;
    }
}

class Line extends Shape {
  private static int color = RED;
  public static void
  serializeStaticState(ObjectOutputStream os)
      throws IOException {
    os.writeInt(color);
  }
  public static void
  deserializeStaticState(ObjectInputStream os)
      throws IOException {
    color = os.readInt();
  }
  public Line(int xVal, int yVal, int dim) {
    super(xVal, yVal, dim);
  }
  public void setColor(int newColor) {
    color = newColor;
  }
  public int getColor() {
    return color;
  }
}

public class CADState {
  public static void main(String[] args)
      throws Exception {
    Vector shapeTypes, shapes;
    if(args.length == 0) {
      shapeTypes = new Vector();
      shapes = new Vector();
      // Add handles to the class objects:
      shapeTypes.addElement(Circle.class);
```

```
        shapeTypes.addElement(Square.class);
        shapeTypes.addElement(Line.class);
        // Make some shapes:
        for(int i = 0; i < 10; i++)
          shapes.addElement(Shape.randomFactory());
        // Set all the static colors to GREEN:
        for(int i = 0; i < 10; i++)
          ((Shape)shapes.elementAt(i))
            .setColor(Shape.GREEN);
        // Save the state vector:
        ObjectOutputStream out =
          new ObjectOutputStream(
            new FileOutputStream("CADState.out"));
        out.writeObject(shapeTypes);
        Line.serializeStaticState(out);
        out.writeObject(shapes);
      } else { // There's a command-line argument
        ObjectInputStream in =
          new ObjectInputStream(
            new FileInputStream(args[0]));
        // Read in the same order they were written:
        shapeTypes = (Vector)in.readObject();
        Line.deserializeStaticState(in);
        shapes = (Vector)in.readObject();
      }
      // Display the shapes:
      System.out.println(shapes);
    }
} ///:~
```

The **Shape** class **implements Serializable**, so anything that is inherited from **Shape** is automatically **Serializable** as well. Each **Shape** contains data, and each derived **Shape** class contains a **static** field that determines the color of all of those types of **Shape**s. (Placing a **static** field in the base class would result in only one field, since **static** fields are not duplicated in derived classes.) Methods in the base class can be overridden to set the color for the various types (**static** methods are not dynamically bound, so these are normal methods). The **randomFactory( )** method creates a different **Shape** each time you call it, using random values for the **Shape** data.

Circle and **Square** are straightforward extensions of **Shape**; the only difference is that **Circle** initializes **color** at the point of definition and **Square** initializes it in the constructor. We'll leave the discussion of **Line** for later.

In **main( )**, one **Vector** is used to hold the **Class** objects and the other to hold the shapes. If you don't provide a command line argument the **shapeTypes Vector** is created and the **Class** objects are added, and then the **shapes Vector** is created and **Shape** objects are added. Next, all the **static color** values are set to **GREEN**, and everything is serialized to the file **CADState.out**.

If you provide a command line argument (presumably **CADState.out**), that file is opened and used to restore the state of the program. In both situations, the resulting **Vector** of **Shapes** is printed out. The results from one run are:

```
>java CADState
[class Circle color[3] xPos[-51] yPos[-99] dim[38]
, class Square color[3] xPos[2] yPos[61] dim[-46]
, class Line color[3] xPos[51] yPos[73] dim[64]
, class Circle color[3] xPos[-70] yPos[1] dim[16]
, class Square color[3] xPos[3] yPos[94] dim[-36]
, class Line color[3] xPos[-84] yPos[-21] dim[-35]
, class Circle color[3] xPos[-75] yPos[-43]
dim[22]
, class Square color[3] xPos[81] yPos[30] dim[-45]
, class Line color[3] xPos[-29] yPos[92] dim[17]
, class Circle color[3] xPos[17] yPos[90] dim[-76]
]

>java CADState CADState.out
[class Circle color[1] xPos[-51] yPos[-99] dim[38]
, class Square color[0] xPos[2] yPos[61] dim[-46]
, class Line color[3] xPos[51] yPos[73] dim[64]
, class Circle color[1] xPos[-70] yPos[1] dim[16]
, class Square color[0] xPos[3] yPos[94] dim[-36]
, class Line color[3] xPos[-84] yPos[-21] dim[-35]
, class Circle color[1] xPos[-75] yPos[-43]
dim[22]
, class Square color[0] xPos[81] yPos[30] dim[-45]
, class Line color[3] xPos[-29] yPos[92] dim[17]
, class Circle color[1] xPos[17] yPos[90] dim[-76]
]
```

You can see that the values of **xPos**, **yPos**, and **dim** were all stored and recovered successfully, but there's something wrong with the retrieval of the **static** information. It's all '3' going in, but it doesn't come out that way. **Circles** have a value of 1 (**RED**, which is the definition), and **Squares** have a value of 0 (remember, they are initialized in the constructor). It's as if the **static**s didn't get serialized at all! That's right – even though class **Class** is **Serializable**, it doesn't do what you expect. So if you want to serialize **static**s, you must do it yourself.

This is what the **serializeStaticState( )** and **deserializeStaticState( )** **static** methods in **Line** are for. You can see that they are explicitly called as part of the storage and retrieval process. (Note that the order of writing to the serialize file and reading back from it must be maintained.) Thus to make **CADState.java** run correctly you must (1) Add a **serializeStaticState( )** and **deserializeStaticState( )** to the shapes, (2) Remove the **Vector shapeTypes** and all code related to it, and (3) Add calls to the new serialize and deserialize static methods in the shapes.

Another issue you might have to think about is security, since serialization also saves **private** data. If you have a security issue, those fields should be marked as **transient**. But then you have to design a secure way to store that information so that when you do a restore you can reset those **private** variables.

Summary

The Java IO stream library does seem to satisfy the basic requirements: you can perform reading and writing with the console, a file, a block of memory, or even across the Internet (as you will see in Chapter 15). It's possible (by inheriting from **InputStream** and **OutputStream**) to create new types of input and output objects. And you can even add a simple extensibility to the kinds of objects a stream will accept by redefining the **toString( )** method that's automatically called when you pass an object to a method that's expecting a **String** (Java's limited "automatic type conversion").

There are questions left unanswered by the documentation and design of the IO stream library. For example, it would have been nice if you could say that you want an exception thrown if you try to overwrite a file when opening it for output – some programming systems allow you to specify that you want to open an output file, but only if it doesn't already exist. In Java, it appears that you are supposed to use a **File** object to determine whether a file exists, because if you open it as an **FileOutputStream** or **FileWriter** it will always get overwritten. By representing both files and directory paths, the **File** class also suggests poor design by violating the maxim "Don't try to do too much in a single class."

The IO stream library brings up mixed feelings. It does much of the job and it's portable. But if you don't already understand the decorator pattern, the design is non-intuitive, so there's extra overhead in learning and teaching it. It's also incomplete: there's no support for the kind of output formatting that almost every other language's IO package supports. (This was not remedied in Java 1.1, which missed the opportunity to change the library design completely, and instead added even more special cases and complexity.) The Java 1.1 changes to the IO library haven't been replacements, but rather additions, and it seems that the library designers couldn't quite get straight which features are deprecated and which are preferred, resulting in annoying deprecation messages that show up the contradictions in the library design.

However, once you *do* understand the decorator pattern and begin using the library in situations that require its flexibility, you can begin to benefit from this design, at which point its cost in extra lines of code may not bother you as much.

Exercises

1. Open a text file so that you can read the file one line at a time. Read each line as a **String** and place that **String** object into a **Vector**. Print out all of the lines in the **Vector** in reverse order.

2. Modify Exercise 1 so that the name of the file you read is provided as a command-line argument.

3. Modify Exercise 2 to also open a text file so you can write text into it. Write the lines in the **Vector**, along with line numbers, out to the file.

4. Modify Exercise 2 to force all the lines in the **Vector** to upper case and send the results to **System.out**.

5. Modify Exercise 2 to take additional arguments of words to find in the file. Print out any lines in which the words match.

6. In **Blips.java**, copy the file and rename it to **BlipCheck.java** and rename the class **Blip2** to **BlipCheck** (making it **public** in the process). Remove the //! marks in the file and execute the program including the offending lines. Next, comment out the default constructor for **BlipCheck**. Run it and explain why it works.

7.   In **Blip3.java**, comment out the two lines after the phrases "You must do this:" and run the program. Explain the result and why it differs from when the two lines are in the program.

8.   Convert the **SortedWordCount.java** program to use the Java 1.1 IO Streams.

9.   Repair the program **CADState.java** as described in the text.

10. (Intermediate) In Chapter 7, locate the **GreenhouseControls.java** example, which consists of three files. In **GreenhouseControls.java**, the **Restart( )** inner class has a hard-coded set of events. Change the program so that it reads the events and their relative times from a text file. (Challenging: Use a factory method from Chapter 16 to build the events.)

11: Run-time type identification

The idea of run-time type identification (RTTI) seems fairly simple at first: it lets you find the exact type of an object when you have a handle to only the base type.

However, the *need* for RTTI uncovers a whole plethora of interesting (and often perplexing) OO design issues and raises fundamental questions of how you should structure your programs.

This chapter looks at the ways that Java allows you to discover information about objects and classes at run-time. This takes two forms: "traditional" RTTI, which assumes that you have all the types available at compile-time and run-time, and the "reflection" mechanism in Java 1.1, which allows you to discover class information solely at run-time. The "traditional" RTTI will be covered first, followed by a discussion of reflection.

The need for RTTI

Consider the now familiar example of a class hierarchy that uses polymorphism. The generic type is the base class **Shape**, and the specific derived types are **Circle**, **Square**, and **Triangle**:

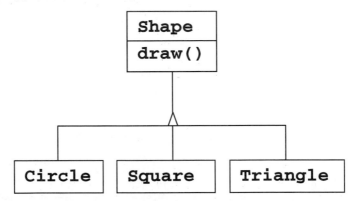

This is a typical class hierarchy diagram, with the base class at the top and the derived classes growing downward. The normal goal in object-oriented programming is for the bulk of your code to manipulate handles to the base type (**Shape**, in this case), so if you decide to extend the program by adding a new class (**Rhomboid**, derived from **Shape**, for example), the bulk of the code is not affected. In this example, the dynamically bound method in the **Shape** interface is **draw( )**, so the intent is for the client programmer to call **draw( )** through a generic **Shape** handle. **draw( )** is overridden in all of the derived classes, and because it is a dynamically bound method, the proper behavior will occur even though it is called through a generic **Shape** handle. That's polymorphism.

Thus, you generally create a specific object (**Circle**, **Square**, or **Triangle**), upcast it to a **Shape** (forgetting the specific type of the object), and use that anonymous **Shape** handle in the rest of the program.

As a brief review of polymorphism and upcasting, you might code the above example as follows: (See page 97 if you have trouble executing this program.)

```
//: Shapes.java
package c11;
import java.util.*;

interface Shape {
```

```
    void draw();
}

class Circle implements Shape {
  public void draw() {
    System.out.println("Circle.draw()");
  }
}

class Square implements Shape {
  public void draw() {
    System.out.println("Square.draw()");
  }
}

class Triangle implements Shape {
  public void draw() {
    System.out.println("Triangle.draw()");
  }
}

public class Shapes {
  public static void main(String[] args) {
    Vector s = new Vector();
    s.addElement(new Circle());
    s.addElement(new Square());
    s.addElement(new Triangle());
    Enumeration e = s.elements();
    while(e.hasMoreElements())
      ((Shape)e.nextElement()).draw();
  }
} ///:~
```

The base class could be coded as an **interface**, an **abstract** class, or an ordinary class. Since **Shape** has no concrete members (that is, members with definitions), and it's not intended that you ever create a plain **Shape** object, the most appropriate and flexible representation is an **interface**. It's also cleaner because you don't have all those **abstract** keywords lying about.

Each of the derived classes overrides the base-class **draw** method so it behaves differently. In **main( )**, specific types of **Shape** are created and then added to a **Vector**. This is the point at which the upcast occurs because the **Vector** holds only **Object**s. Since everything in Java (with the exception of primitives) is an **Object**, a **Vector** can also hold **Shape** objects. But during an upcast to **Object**, it also loses any specific information, including the fact that the objects are **shape**s. To the **Vector**, they are just **Object**s.

At the point you fetch an element out of the **Vector** with **nextElement( )**, things get a little busy. Since **Vector** holds only **Object**s, **nextElement( )** naturally produces an **Object** handle. But we know it's really a **Shape** handle, and we want to send **Shape** messages to that object. So a cast to **Shape** is necessary using the traditional "(**Shape**)" cast. This is the most basic form of RTTI, since in Java all casts are checked at run-time for correctness. That's exactly what RTTI means: at run-time, the type of an object is identified.

In this case, the RTTI cast is only partial: the **Object** is cast to a **Shape**, and not all the way to a **Circle**, **Square**, or **Triangle**. That's because the only thing we *know* at this point is that the **Vector** is full of **Shape**s. At compile-time, this is enforced only by your own self-imposed rules, but at run-time the cast ensures it.

Now polymorphism takes over and the exact method that's called for the **Shape** is determined by whether the handle is for a **Circle**, **Square**, or **Triangle**. And in general, this is how it should be; you want the bulk of your code to know as little as possible about *specific* types of objects, and to just deal with the general representation of a family of objects (in this case, **Shape**). As a result, your code will be easier to write, read, and maintain, and your designs will be easier to implement, understand, and change. So polymorphism is the general goal in object-oriented programming.

But what if you have a special programming problem that's easiest to solve if you know the exact type of a generic handle? For example, suppose you want to allow your users to highlight all the shapes of any particular type by turning them purple. This way, they can find all the triangles on the screen by highlighting them. This is what RTTI accomplishes: you can ask a handle to a **Shape** exactly what type it's referring to.

The **Class** object

To understand how RTTI works in Java, you must first know how type information is represented at run time. This is accomplished through a special kind of object called the *Class object*, which contains information about the class. (This is sometimes called a *meta-class*.) In fact, the **Class** object is used to create all of the "regular" objects of your class.

There's a **Class** object for each class that is part of your program. That is, each time you write a new class, a single **Class** object is also created (and stored, appropriately enough, in an identically named **.class** file). At run time, when you want to make an object of that class, the Java Virtual Machine (JVM) that's executing your program first checks to see if the **Class** object for that type is loaded. If not, the JVM loads it by finding the **.class** file with that name. Thus, a Java program isn't completely loaded before it begins, which is different from many traditional languages.

Once the **Class** object for that type is in memory, it is used to create all objects of that type.

If this seems shadowy or if you don't really believe it, here's a demonstration program to prove it:

```
//: SweetShop.java
// Examination of the way the class loader works

class Candy {
  static {
    System.out.println("Loading Candy");
  }
}

class Gum {
  static {
    System.out.println("Loading Gum");
  }
}

class Cookie {
  static {
    System.out.println("Loading Cookie");
  }
}

public class SweetShop {
  public static void main(String[] args) {
    System.out.println("inside main");
    new Candy();
    System.out.println("After creating Candy");
    try {
      Class.forName("Gum");
    } catch(ClassNotFoundException e) {
      e.printStackTrace();
```

```
      }
      System.out.println(
        "After Class.forName(\"Gum\")");
      new Cookie();
      System.out.println("After creating Cookie");
    }
  } ///:~
```

Each of the classes **Candy**, **Gum**, and **Cookie** has a **static** clause that is executed as the class is loaded for the first time. Information will be printed out to tell you when loading occurs for that class. In **main( )**, the object creations are spread out between print statements to help detect the time of loading.

A particularly interesting line is:

```
Class.forName("Gum");
```

This method is a **static** member of **Class** (to which all **Class** objects belong). A **Class** object is like any other object and so you can get and manipulate a handle to it. (That's what the loader does.) One of the ways to get a handle to the **Class** object is **forName( )**, which takes a **String** containing the textual name (watch the spelling and capitalization!) of the particular class you want a handle for. It returns a **Class** handle.

The output of this program for one JVM is:

```
inside main
Loading Candy
After creating Candy
Loading Gum
After Class.forName("Gum")
Loading Cookie
After creating Cookie
```

You can see that each **Class** object is loaded only when it's needed, and the **static** initialization is performed upon class loading.

Interestingly enough, a different JVM yielded:

```
Loading Candy
Loading Cookie
inside main
After creating Candy
Loading Gum
After Class.forName("Gum")
After creating Cookie
```

It appears that this JVM anticipated the need for **Candy** and **Cookie** by examining the code in **main( )**, but could not see **Gum** because it was created by a call to **forName( )** and not through a more typical call to **new**. While this JVM produces the desired effect because it does get the classes loaded before they're needed, it's uncertain whether the behavior shown is precisely correct.

Class literals

In Java 1.1 you have a second way to produce the handle to the **Class** object: use the *class literal*. In the above program this would look like:

```
Gum.class;
```

which is not only simpler, but also safer since it's checked at compile time. Because it eliminates the method call, it's also more efficient.

Class literals work with regular classes as well as interfaces, arrays, and primitive types. In addition, there's a standard field called **TYPE** that exists for each of the primitive wrapper classes. The **TYPE** field produces a handle to the **Class** object for the associated primitive type, such that:

... is equivalent to ...	
boolean.class	Boolean.TYPE
char.class	Character.TYPE
byte.class	Byte.TYPE
short.class	Short.TYPE
int.class	Integer.TYPE
long.class	Long.TYPE
float.class	Float.TYPE
double.class	Double.TYPE
void.class	Void.TYPE

Checking before a cast

So far, you've seen RTTI forms including:

1. The classic cast, e.g. "**(Shape)**," which uses RTTI to make sure the cast is correct and throws a **ClassCastException** if you've performed a bad cast.

2. The **Class** object representing the type of your object. The **Class** object can be queried for useful runtime information.

In C++, the classic cast "**(Shape)**" does *not* perform RTTI. It simply tells the compiler to treat the object as the new type. In Java, which does perform the type check, this cast is often called a "type safe downcast." The reason for the term "downcast" is the historical arrangement of the class hierarchy diagram. If casting a **Circle** to a **Shape** is an upcast, then casting a **Shape** to a **Circle** is a downcast. However, you know a **Circle** is also a **Shape**, and the compiler freely allows an upcast assignment, but you *don't* know that a **Shape** is necessarily a **Circle**, so the compiler doesn't allow you to perform a downcast assignment without using an explicit cast.

There's a third form of RTTI in Java. This is the keyword **instanceof** that tells you if an object is an instance of a particular type. It returns a **boolean** so you use it in the form of a question, like this:

```
if(x instanceof Dog)
   ((Dog)x).bark();
```

The above **if** statement checks to see if the object **x** belongs to the class **Dog** *before* casting **x** to a **Dog**. It's important to use **instanceof** before a downcast when you don't have other information that tells you the type of the object; otherwise you'll end up with a **ClassCastException**.

Ordinarily, you might be hunting for one type (triangles to turn purple, for example), but the following program shows how to tally *all* of the objects using **instanceof**.

```
//: PetCount.java
// Using instanceof
package c11.petcount;
import java.util.*;

class Pet {}
class Dog extends Pet {}
class Pug extends Dog {}
class Cat extends Pet {}
class Rodent extends Pet {}
class Gerbil extends Rodent {}
class Hamster extends Rodent {}

class Counter { int i; }

public class PetCount {
  static String[] typenames = {
    "Pet", "Dog", "Pug", "Cat",
    "Rodent", "Gerbil", "Hamster",
```

```
      };
      public static void main(String[] args) {
        Vector pets = new Vector();
        try {
          Class[] petTypes = {
            Class.forName("c11.petcount.Dog"),
            Class.forName("c11.petcount.Pug"),
            Class.forName("c11.petcount.Cat"),
            Class.forName("c11.petcount.Rodent"),
            Class.forName("c11.petcount.Gerbil"),
            Class.forName("c11.petcount.Hamster"),
          };
          for(int i = 0; i < 15; i++)
            pets.addElement(
              petTypes[
                (int)(Math.random()*petTypes.length)]
                .newInstance());
        } catch(InstantiationException e) {}
          catch(IllegalAccessException e) {}
          catch(ClassNotFoundException e) {}
        Hashtable h = new Hashtable();
        for(int i = 0; i < typenames.length; i++)
          h.put(typenames[i], new Counter());
        for(int i = 0; i < pets.size(); i++) {
          Object o = pets.elementAt(i);
          if(o instanceof Pet)
            ((Counter)h.get("Pet")).i++;
          if(o instanceof Dog)
            ((Counter)h.get("Dog")).i++;
          if(o instanceof Pug)
            ((Counter)h.get("Pug")).i++;
          if(o instanceof Cat)
            ((Counter)h.get("Cat")).i++;
          if(o instanceof Rodent)
            ((Counter)h.get("Rodent")).i++;
          if(o instanceof Gerbil)
            ((Counter)h.get("Gerbil")).i++;
          if(o instanceof Hamster)
            ((Counter)h.get("Hamster")).i++;
        }
        for(int i = 0; i < pets.size(); i++)
          System.out.println(
            pets.elementAt(i).getClass().toString());
        for(int i = 0; i < typenames.length; i++)
```

```
        System.out.println(
            typenames[i] + " quantity: " +
            ((Counter)h.get(typenames[i])).i);
    }
} ///:~
```

There's a rather narrow restriction on **instanceof** in Java 1.0: You can compare it to a named type only, and not to a **Class** object. In the example above you might feel that it's tedious to write out all of those **instanceof** expressions, and you're right. But in Java 1.0 there is no way to cleverly automate it by creating a **Vector** of **Class** objects and comparing it to those instead. This isn't as great a restriction as you might think, because you'll eventually understand that your design is probably flawed if you end up writing a lot of **instanceof** expressions.

Of course this example is contrived – you'd probably put a **static** data member in each type and increment it in the constructor to keep track of the counts. You would do something like that *if* you had control of the source code for the class and could change it. Since this is not always the case, RTTI can come in handy.

Using class literals

It's interesting to see how the **PetCount.java** example can be rewritten using Java 1.1 class literals. The result is cleaner in many ways:

```
//: PetCount2.java
// Using Java 1.1 class literals
package c11.petcount2;
import java.util.*;

class Pet {}
class Dog extends Pet {}
class Pug extends Dog {}
class Cat extends Pet {}
class Rodent extends Pet {}
class Gerbil extends Rodent {}
class Hamster extends Rodent {}

class Counter { int i; }

public class PetCount2 {
  public static void main(String[] args) {
    Vector pets = new Vector();
    Class[] petTypes = {
```

```
          // Class literals work in Java 1.1+ only:
          Pet.class,
          Dog.class,
          Pug.class,
          Cat.class,
          Rodent.class,
          Gerbil.class,
          Hamster.class,
        };
        try {
          for(int i = 0; i < 15; i++) {
            // Offset by one to eliminate Pet.class:
            int rnd = 1 + (int)(
              Math.random() * (petTypes.length - 1));
            pets.addElement(
              petTypes[rnd].newInstance());
          }
        } catch(InstantiationException e) {}
          catch(IllegalAccessException e) {}
        Hashtable h = new Hashtable();
        for(int i = 0; i < petTypes.length; i++)
          h.put(petTypes[i].toString(),
            new Counter());
        for(int i = 0; i < pets.size(); i++) {
          Object o = pets.elementAt(i);
          if(o instanceof Pet)
            ((Counter)h.get(
              "class c11.petcount2.Pet")).i++;
          if(o instanceof Dog)
            ((Counter)h.get(
              "class c11.petcount2.Dog")).i++;
          if(o instanceof Pug)
            ((Counter)h.get(
              "class c11.petcount2.Pug")).i++;
          if(o instanceof Cat)
            ((Counter)h.get(
              "class c11.petcount2.Cat")).i++;
          if(o instanceof Rodent)
            ((Counter)h.get(
              "class c11.petcount2.Rodent")).i++;
          if(o instanceof Gerbil)
            ((Counter)h.get(
              "class c11.petcount2.Gerbil")).i++;
          if(o instanceof Hamster)
```

```
        ((Counter)h.get(
          "class c11.petcount2.Hamster")).i++;
      }
      for(int i = 0; i < pets.size(); i++)
        System.out.println(
          pets.elementAt(i).getClass().toString());
      Enumeration keys = h.keys();
      while(keys.hasMoreElements()) {
        String nm = (String)keys.nextElement();
        Counter cnt = (Counter)h.get(nm);
        System.out.println(
          nm.substring(nm.lastIndexOf('.') + 1) +
          " quantity: " + cnt.i);
      }
    }
  } ///:~
```

Here, the **typenames** array has been removed in favor of getting the type name strings from the **Class** object. Notice the extra work for this: the class name is not, for example, **Gerbil**, but instead **c11.petcount2.Gerbil** since the package name is included. Notice also that the system can distinguish between classes and interfaces.

You can also see that the creation of **petTypes** does not need to be surrounded by a **try** block since it's evaluated at compile time and thus won't throw any exceptions, unlike **Class.forName( )**.

When the **Pet** objects are dynamically created, you can see that the random number is restricted so it is between 1 and **petTypes.length** and does not include zero. That's because zero refers to **Pet.class**, and presumably a generic **Pet** object is not interesting. However, since **Pet.class** is part of **petTypes** the result is that all of the pets get counted.

A dynamic *instanceof*

Java 1.1 has added the **isInstance** method to the class **Class**. This allows you to dynamically call the **instanceof** operator, which you could do only statically in Java 1.0 (as previously shown). Thus, all those tedious **instanceof** statements can be removed in the **PetCount** example:

```
//: PetCount3.java
// Using Java 1.1 isInstance()
package c11.petcount3;
import java.util.*;
```

```
class Pet {}
class Dog extends Pet {}
class Pug extends Dog {}
class Cat extends Pet {}
class Rodent extends Pet {}
class Gerbil extends Rodent {}
class Hamster extends Rodent {}

class Counter { int i; }

public class PetCount3 {
  public static void main(String[] args) {
    Vector pets = new Vector();
    Class[] petTypes = {
      Pet.class,
      Dog.class,
      Pug.class,
      Cat.class,
      Rodent.class,
      Gerbil.class,
      Hamster.class,
    };
    try {
      for(int i = 0; i < 15; i++) {
        // Offset by one to eliminate Pet.class:
        int rnd = 1 + (int)(
          Math.random() * (petTypes.length - 1));
        pets.addElement(
          petTypes[rnd].newInstance());
      }
    } catch(InstantiationException e) {}
      catch(IllegalAccessException e) {}
    Hashtable h = new Hashtable();
    for(int i = 0; i < petTypes.length; i++)
      h.put(petTypes[i].toString(),
        new Counter());
    for(int i = 0; i < pets.size(); i++) {
      Object o = pets.elementAt(i);
      // Using isInstance to eliminate individual
      // instanceof expressions:
      for (int j = 0; j < petTypes.length; ++j)
        if (petTypes[j].isInstance(o)) {
          String key = petTypes[j].toString();
          ((Counter)h.get(key)).i++;
```

```
          }
        }
      for(int i = 0; i < pets.size(); i++)
        System.out.println(
          pets.elementAt(i).getClass().toString());
      Enumeration keys = h.keys();
      while(keys.hasMoreElements()) {
        String nm = (String)keys.nextElement();
        Counter cnt = (Counter)h.get(nm);
        System.out.println(
          nm.substring(nm.lastIndexOf('.') + 1) +
          " quantity: " + cnt.i);
      }
    }
} ///:~
```

You can see that the Java 1.1 **isInstance( )** method has eliminated the need for the **instanceof** expressions. In addition, this means that you can add new types of pets simply by changing the **petTypes** array; the rest of the program does not need modification (as it did when using the **instanceof** expressions).

RTTI syntax

Java performs its RTTI using the **Class** object, even if you're doing something like a cast. The class **Class** also has a number of other ways you can use RTTI.

First, you must get a handle to the appropriate **Class** object. One way to do this, as shown in the previous example, is to use a string and the **Class.forName( )** method. This is convenient because you don't need an object of that type in order to get the **Class** handle. However, if you do already have an object of the type you're interested in, you can fetch the **Class** handle by calling a method that's part of the **Object** root class: **getClass( )**. This returns the **Class** handle representing the actual type of the object. **Class** has several interesting and sometimes useful methods, demonstrated in the following example:

```
//: ToyTest.java
// Testing class Class

interface HasBatteries {}
interface Waterproof {}
interface ShootsThings {}
```

```
class Toy {
  // Comment out the following default
  // constructor to see
  // NoSuchMethodError from (*1*)
  Toy() {}
  Toy(int i) {}
}

class FancyToy extends Toy
    implements HasBatteries,
      Waterproof, ShootsThings {
  FancyToy() { super(1); }
}

public class ToyTest {
  public static void main(String[] args) {
    Class c = null;
    try {
      c = Class.forName("FancyToy");
    } catch(ClassNotFoundException e) {}
    printInfo(c);
    Class[] faces = c.getInterfaces();
    for(int i = 0; i < faces.length; i++)
      printInfo(faces[i]);
    Class cy = c.getSuperclass();
    Object o = null;
    try {
      // Requires default constructor:
      o = cy.newInstance(); // (*1*)
    } catch(InstantiationException e) {}
      catch(IllegalAccessException e) {}
    printInfo(o.getClass());
  }
  static void printInfo(Class cc) {
    System.out.println(
      "Class name: " + cc.getName() +
      " is interface? [" +
      cc.isInterface() + "]");
  }
} ///:~
```

You can see that **class FancyToy** is quite complicated, since it inherits from **Toy** and **implements** the **interface**s of **HasBatteries**, **Waterproof**, and **ShootsThings**. In **main( )**, a **Class** handle is created and initialized to the **FancyToy Class** using **forName( )** inside an appropriate **try** block.

The **Class.getInterfaces( )** method returns an array of **Class** objects representing the interfaces that are contained in the **Class** object of interest.

If you have a **Class** object you can also ask it for its direct base class using **getSuperclass( )**. This, of course, returns a **Class** handle that you can further query. This means that, at run time, you can discover an object's entire class hierarchy.

The **newInstance( )** method of **Class** can, at first, seem like just another way to **clone( )** an object. However, you can create a new object with **newInstance( )** *without* an existing object, as seen here, because there is no **Toy** object, only **cy**, which is a handle to **y**'s **Class** object. This is a way to implement a "virtual constructor," which allows you to say "I don't know exactly what type you are, but create yourself properly anyway." In the example above, **cy** is just a **Class** handle with no further type information known at compile time. And when you create a new instance, you get back an **Object** handle. But that handle is pointing to a **Toy** object. Of course, before you can send any messages other than those accepted by **Object**, you have to investigate it a bit and do some casting. In addition, the class that's being created with **newInstance( )** must have a default constructor. There's no way to use **newInstance( )** to create objects that have non-default constructors, so this can be a bit limiting in Java 1. However, the *reflection* API in Java 1.1 (discussed in the next section) allows you to dynamically use any constructor in a class.

The final method in the listing is **printInfo( )**, which takes a **Class** handle and gets its name with **getName( )**, and finds out whether it's an interface with **isInterface( )**.

The output from this program is:

```
Class name: FancyToy is interface? [false]
Class name: HasBatteries is interface? [true]
Class name: Waterproof is interface? [true]
Class name: ShootsThings is interface? [true]
Class name: Toy is interface? [false]
```

Thus, with the **Class** object you can find out just about everything you want to know about an object.

Reflection: run-time class information

If you don't know the precise type of an object, RTTI will tell you. However, there's a limitation: the type must be known at compile time in order for you to be able to detect it using RTTI and do something useful with the information. Put another way, the compiler must know about all the classes you're working with for RTTI.

This doesn't seem like that much of a limitation at first, but suppose you're given a handle to an object that's not in your program space. In fact, the class of the object isn't even available to your program at compile time. For example, suppose you get a bunch of bytes from a disk file or from a network connection and you're told that those bytes represent a class. Since the compiler can't know about the class while it's compiling the code, how can you possibly use such a class?

In a traditional programming environment this seems like a far-fetched scenario. But as we move into a larger programming world there are important cases in which this happens. The first is component-based programming in which you build projects using *Rapid Application Development* (RAD) in an application builder tool. This is a visual approach to creating a program (which you see on the screen as a *form*) by moving icons that represent components onto the form. These components are then configured by setting some of their values at program time. This design-time configuration requires that any component be instantiable and that it expose some part of itself and allow its values to be read and set. In addition, components that handle GUI events must expose information about appropriate methods so that the RAD environment can assist the programmer in overriding these event-handling methods. Reflection provides the mechanism to detect the available methods and produce the method names. Java 1.1 provides a structure for component-based programming through Java Beans (described in Chapter 13).

Another compelling motivation for discovering class information at run-time is to provide the ability to create and execute objects on remote platforms across a network. This is called *Remote Method Invocation* (RMI) and it allows a Java program (version 1.1 and higher) to have objects distributed across many machines. This distribution can happen for a number of reasons: perhaps you're doing a computation-intensive task and you want to break it up and put pieces on machines that are idle in

---

order to speed things up. In some situations you might want to place code that handles particular types of tasks (e.g. "Business Rules" in a multi-tier client/server architecture) on a particular machine so that machine becomes a common repository describing those actions and it can be easily changed to affect everyone in the system. (This is an interesting development since the machine exists solely to make software changes easy!) Along these lines, distributed computing also supports specialized hardware that might be good at a particular task – matrix inversions, for example – but inappropriate or too expensive for general purpose programming.

In Java 1.1, the class **Class** (described previously in this chapter) is extended to support the concept of *reflection*, and there's an additional library, **java.lang.reflect,** with classes **Field**, **Method**, and **Constructor** (each of which implement the **Member interface**). Objects of these types are created by the JVM at run-time to represent the corresponding member in the unknown class. You can then use the **Constructor**s to create new objects, the **get( )** and **set( )** methods to read and modify the fields associated with **Field** objects, and the **invoke( )** method to call a method associated with a **Method** object. In addition, you can call the convenience methods **getFields( )**, **getMethods( )**, **getConstructors( )**, etc., to return arrays of the objects representing the fields, methods, and constructors. (You can find out more by looking up the class **Class** in your online documentation.) Thus, the class information for anonymous objects can be completely determined at run time, and nothing need be known at compile time.

It's important to realize that there's nothing magic about reflection. When you're using reflection to interact with an object of an unknown type, the JVM will simply look at the object and see that it belongs to a particular class (just like ordinary RTTI) but then, before it can do anything else, the **Class** object must be loaded. Thus, the **.class** file for that particular type must still be available to the JVM, either on the local machine or across the network. So the true difference between RTTI and reflection is that with RTTI, the compiler opens and examines the **.class** file at compile time. Put another way, you can call all the methods of an object in the "normal" way. With reflection, the **.class** file is unavailable at compile time; it is opened and examined by the run-time environment.

A class method extractor

You'll rarely need to use the reflection tools directly; they're in the language to support the other Java features such as object serialization (described in Chapter 10), Java Beans, and RMI (described later in the

```
   public boolean
     java.lang.String.endsWith(java.lang.String)
```

It would be even nicer if the qualifiers like **java.lang** could be stripped
off. The **StreamTokenizer** class introduced in the previous chapter can
help solve this problem:

```
//: ShowMethodsClean.java
// ShowMethods with the qualifiers stripped
// to make the results easier to read
import java.lang.reflect.*;
import java.io.*;

public class ShowMethodsClean {
  static final String usage =
    "usage: \n" +
    "ShowMethodsClean qualified.class.name\n" +
    "To show all methods in class or: \n" +
    "ShowMethodsClean qualif.class.name word\n" +
    "To search for methods involving 'word'";
  public static void main(String[] args) {
    if(args.length < 1) {
      System.out.println(usage);
      System.exit(0);
    }
    try {
      Class c = Class.forName(args[0]);
      Method[] m = c.getMethods();
      Constructor[] ctor = c.getConstructors();
      // Convert to an array of cleaned Strings:
      String[] n =
        new String[m.length + ctor.length];
      for(int i = 0; i < m.length; i++) {
        String s = m[i].toString();
        n[i] = StripQualifiers.strip(s);
      }
      for(int i = 0; i < ctor.length; i++) {
        String s = ctor[i].toString();
        n[i + m.length] =
          StripQualifiers.strip(s);
      }
      if(args.length == 1)
        for (int i = 0; i < n.length; i++)
          System.out.println(n[i]);
      else
```

```
            for (int i = 0; i < n.length; i++)
               if(n[i].indexOf(args[1]) != -1)
                  System.out.println(n[i]);
         } catch (ClassNotFoundException e) {
            System.out.println("No such class: " + e);
         }
      }
   }
}

class StripQualifiers {
   private StreamTokenizer st;
   public StripQualifiers(String qualified) {
      st = new StreamTokenizer(
         new StringReader(qualified));
      st.ordinaryChar(' '); // Keep the spaces
   }
   public String getNext() {
      String s = null;
      try {
         if(st.nextToken() !=
               StreamTokenizer.TT_EOF) {
            switch(st.ttype) {
               case StreamTokenizer.TT_EOL:
                  s = null;
                  break;
               case StreamTokenizer.TT_NUMBER:
                  s = Double.toString(st.nval);
                  break;
               case StreamTokenizer.TT_WORD:
                  s = new String(st.sval);
                  break;
               default: // single character in ttype
                  s = String.valueOf((char)st.ttype);
            }
         }
      } catch(IOException e) {
         System.out.println(e);
      }
      return s;
   }
   public static String strip(String qualified) {
      StripQualifiers sq =
         new StripQualifiers(qualified);
      String s = "", si;
```

```
        while((si = sq.getNext()) != null) {
          int lastDot = si.lastIndexOf('.');
          if(lastDot != -1)
            si = si.substring(lastDot + 1);
          s += si;
        }
        return s;
    }
} ///:~
```

The class **ShowMethodsClean** is quite similar to the previous **ShowMethods**, except that it takes the arrays of **Method** and **Constructor** and converts them into a single array of **String**. Each of these **String** objects is then passed through **StripQualifiers.Strip( )** to remove all the method qualification. As you can see, this uses the **StreamTokenizer** and **String** manipulation to do its work.

This tool can be a real time-saver while you're programming, when you can't remember if a class has a particular method and you don't want to go walking through the class hierarchy in the online documentation, or if you don't know whether that class can do anything with, for example, **Color** objects.

Chapter 17 contains a GUI version of this program so you can leave it running while you're writing code, to allow quick lookups.

Summary

RTTI allows you to discover type information from an anonymous base-class handle. Thus, it's ripe for misuse by the novice since it might make sense before polymorphic method calls do. For many people coming from a procedural background, it's difficult not to organize their programs into sets of **switch** statements. They could accomplish this with RTTI and thus lose the important value of polymorphism in code development and maintenance. The intent of Java is that you use polymorphic method calls throughout your code, and you use RTTI only when you must.

However, using polymorphic method calls as they are intended requires that you have control of the base-class definition because at some point in the extension of your program you might discover that the base class doesn't include the method you need. If the base class comes from a library or is otherwise controlled by someone else, a solution to the problem is RTTI: You can inherit a new type and add your extra method. Elsewhere in the code you can detect your particular type and call that special method. This doesn't destroy the polymorphism and extensibility of the program because adding a new type will not require you to hunt for switch statements in your program. However, when you add new code in your main body that requires your new feature, you must use RTTI to detect your particular type.

Putting a feature in a base class might mean that, for the benefit of one particular class, all of the other classes derived from that base require some meaningless stub of a method. This makes the interface less clear and annoys those who must override abstract methods when they derive from that base class. For example, consider a class hierarchy representing musical instruments. Suppose you wanted to clear the spit valves of all the appropriate instruments in your orchestra. One option is to put a **ClearSpitValve( )** method in the base class **Instrument**, but this is confusing because it implies that **Percussion** and **Electronic** instruments also have spit valves. RTTI provides a much more reasonable solution in this case because you can place the method in the specific class (**Wind** in this case), where it's appropriate. However, a more appropriate solution is to put a **prepareInstrument( )** method in the base class, but you might not see this when you're first solving the problem and could mistakenly assume that you must use RTTI.

Finally, RTTI will sometimes solve efficiency problems. If your code nicely uses polymorphism, but it turns out that one of your objects reacts to this general purpose code in a horribly inefficient way, you can pick out that type using RTTI and write case-specific code to improve the efficiency.

Exercises

1. Write a method that takes an object and recursively prints all the classes in that object's hierarchy.

2. In **ToyTest.java**, comment out **Toy**'s default constructor and explain what happens.

3. Create a new type of collection that uses a **Vector**. Capture the type of the first object you put in it, and then allow the user to insert objects of only that type from then on.

4. Write a program to determine whether an array of **char** is a primitive type or a true object.

538   *Thinking in Java*   *www.BruceEckel.com*

5. Implement **clearSpitValve( )** as described in this chapter.

6. Implement the **rotate(Shape)** method described in this chapter, such that it checks to see if it is rotating a **Circle** (and, if so, doesn't perform the operation).

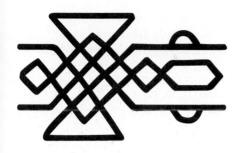

12: Passing and returning objects

By this time you should be reasonably comfortable with the idea that when you're "passing" an object, you're actually passing a handle.

In many programming languages, if not all of them, you can use that language's "regular" way to pass objects around and most of the time everything works fine. But it always seems that there comes a point at which you must do something irregular and suddenly things get a bit more complicated (or in the case of C++, quite complicated). Java is no exception, and it's important that you understand exactly what's happening with them as you pass them around and assign to them. This chapter will provide that insight.

Another way to pose the question of this chapter, if you're coming from a programming language so equipped, is "Does Java have pointers?" Some have claimed that pointers are hard and dangerous and therefore bad, and since Java is all goodness and light and will lift your earthly programming burdens, it cannot possibly contain such things. However, it's more accurate to say that Java has pointers; indeed, every object identifier in Java (except for primitives) is one of these pointers, but their use is restricted and guarded not only by the compiler but by the run-time system. Or to put in another way, Java has pointers, but no pointer arithmetic. These are what I've been calling "handles," and you can think of them as "safety pointers," not unlike the safety scissors of elementary school- they aren't sharp so you cannot hurt yourself without great effort, but they can sometimes be slow and tedious.

Passing handles around

When you pass a handle into a method, you're still pointing to the same object. A simple experiment demonstrates this: (See page 97 if you have trouble executing this program.)

```
//: PassHandles.java
// Passing handles around
package c12;

public class PassHandles {
  static void f(PassHandles h) {
    System.out.println("h inside f(): " + h);
  }
  public static void main(String[] args) {
    PassHandles p = new PassHandles();
    System.out.println("p inside main(): " + p);
    f(p);
  }
} ///:~
```

The method **toString( )** is automatically invoked in the print statements, and **PassHandles** inherits directly from **Object** with no redefinition of **toString( )**. Thus, **Object**'s version of **toString( )** is used, which prints out the class of the object followed by the address where that object is located (not the handle, but the actual object storage). The output looks like this:

```
   p inside main(): PassHandles@1653748
   h inside f(): PassHandles@1653748
```

You can see that both **p** and **h** refer to the same object. This is far more efficient than duplicating a new **PassHandles** object just so that you can send an argument to a method. But it brings up an important issue.

Aliasing

Aliasing means that more than one handle is tied to the same object, as in the above example. The problem with aliasing occurs when someone *writes* to that object. If the owners of the other handles aren't expecting that object to change, they'll be surprised. This can be demonstrated with a simple example:

```
//: Alias1.java
// Aliasing two handles to one object

public class Alias1 {
  int i;
  Alias1(int ii) { i = ii; }
  public static void main(String[] args) {
    Alias1 x = new Alias1(7);
    Alias1 y = x; // Assign the handle
    System.out.println("x: " + x.i);
    System.out.println("y: " + y.i);
    System.out.println("Incrementing x");
    x.i++;
    System.out.println("x: " + x.i);
    System.out.println("y: " + y.i);
  }
} ///:~
```

In the line:

```
Alias1 y = x; // Assign the handle
```

a new **Alias1** handle is created, but instead of being assigned to a fresh object created with **new**, it's assigned to an existing handle. So the contents of handle **x**, which is the address of the object **x** is pointing to, is assigned to **y**, and thus both **x** and **y** are attached to the same object. So when **x**'s **i** is incremented in the statement:

```
x.i++;
```

y's **i** will be affected as well. This can be seen in the output:

```
x:  7
y:  7
Incrementing x
x:  8
y:  8
```

One good solution in this case is to simply not do it: don't consciously alias more than one handle to an object at the same scope. Your code will be much easier to understand and debug. However, when you're passing a handle in as an argument – which is the way Java is supposed to work – you automatically alias because the local handle that's created can modify the "outside object" (the object that was created outside the scope of the method). Here's an example:

```
//: Alias2.java
// Method calls implicitly alias their
// arguments.

public class Alias2 {
  int i;
  Alias2(int ii) { i = ii; }
  static void f(Alias2 handle) {
    handle.i++;
  }
  public static void main(String[] args) {
    Alias2 x = new Alias2(7);
    System.out.println("x: " + x.i);
    System.out.println("Calling f(x)");
    f(x);
    System.out.println("x: " + x.i);
  }
} ///:~
```

The output is:

```
x:  7
Calling f(x)
x:  8
```

The method is changing its argument, the outside object. When this kind of situation arises, you must decide whether it makes sense, whether the user expects it, and whether it's going to cause problems.

In general, you call a method in order to produce a return value and/or a change of state in the object *that the method is called for*. (A method is how you "send a message" to that object.) It's much less common to call a method in order to manipulate its arguments; this is referred to as "calling a method for its *side effects*." Thus, when you create a method that modifies its arguments the user must be clearly instructed and warned about the use of that method and its potential surprises. Because of the confusion and pitfalls, it's much better to avoid changing the argument.

If you need to modify an argument during a method call and you don't intend to modify the outside argument, then you should protect that argument by making a copy inside your method. That's the subject of much of this chapter.

Making local copies

To review: all argument passing in Java is performed by passing handles. That is, when you pass "an object," you're really passing only a handle to an object that lives outside the method, so if you perform any modifications with that handle, you modify the outside object. In addition:

♦   Aliasing happens automatically during argument passing.

♦   There are no local objects, only local handles.

♦   Handles have scopes, objects do not.

♦   Object lifetime is never an issue in Java.

♦   There is no language support (e.g. const) to prevent objects from being modified (to prevent negative effects of aliasing).

If you're only reading information from an object and not modifying it, passing a handle is the most efficient form of argument passing. This is nice; the default way of doing things is also the most efficient. However, sometimes it's necessary to be able to treat the object as if it were "local" so that changes you make affect only a local copy and do not modify the outside object. Many programming languages support the ability to automatically make a local copy of the outside object, inside the method.[1] Java does not, but it allows you to produce this effect.

---

[1] In C, which generally handles small bits of data, the default is pass-by-value. C++ had to follow this form, but with objects pass-by-value isn't usually the

Pass by value

This brings up the terminology issue, which always seems good for an argument. The term is "pass by value," and the meaning depends on how you perceive the operation of the program. The general meaning is that you get a local copy of whatever you're passing, but the real question is how you think about what you're passing. When it comes to the meaning of "pass by value," there are two fairly distinct camps:

1. Java passes everything by value. When you're passing primitives into a method, you get a distinct copy of the primitive. When you're passing a handle into a method, you get a copy of the handle. Ergo, everything is pass by value. Of course, the assumption is that you're always thinking (and caring) that handles are being passed, but it seems like the Java design has gone a long way toward allowing you to ignore (most of the time) that you're working with a handle. That is, it seems to allow you to think of the handle as "the object," since it implicitly dereferences it whenever you make a method call.

2. Java passes primitives by value (no argument there), but objects are passed by reference. This is the world view that the handle is an alias for the object, so you *don't* think about passing handles, but instead say "I'm passing the object." Since you don't get a local copy of the object when you pass it into a method, objects are clearly not passed by value. There appears to be some support for this view within Sun, since one of the "reserved but not implemented" keywords is **byvalue**. (There's no knowing, however, whether that keyword will ever see the light of day.)

Having given both camps a good airing and after saying "It depends on how you think of a handle," I will attempt to sidestep the issue for the rest of the book. In the end, it isn't *that* important – what is important is that you understand that passing a handle allows the caller's object to be changed unexpectedly.

Cloning objects

The most likely reason for making a local copy of an object is if you're going to modify that object and you don't want to modify the caller's object. If you decide that you want to make a local copy, you simply use

---

most efficient way. In addition, coding classes to support pass-by-value in C++ is a big headache.

the **clone( )** method to perform the operation. This is a method that's
defined as **protected** in the base class **Object** and which you must
override as **public** in any derived classes that you want to clone. For
example, the standard library class **Vector** overrides **clone( )**, so we can
call **clone( )** for **Vector**:

```
//: Cloning.java
// The clone() operation works for only a few
// items in the standard Java library.
import java.util.*;

class Int {
  private int i;
  public Int(int ii) { i = ii; }
  public void increment() { i++; }
  public String toString() {
    return Integer.toString(i);
  }
}

public class Cloning {
  public static void main(String[] args) {
    Vector v = new Vector();
    for(int i = 0; i < 10; i++ )
      v.addElement(new Int(i));
    System.out.println("v: " + v);
    Vector v2 = (Vector)v.clone();
    // Increment all v2's elements:
    for(Enumeration e = v2.elements();
        e.hasMoreElements();  )
      ((Int)e.nextElement()).increment();
    // See if it changed v's elements:
    System.out.println("v: " + v);
  }
} ///:~
```

The **clone( )** method produces an **Object**, which must then be recast to
the proper type. This example shows how **Vector**'s **clone( )** method *does
not* automatically try to clone each of the objects that the **Vector** contains
– the old **Vector** and the cloned **Vector** are aliased to the same objects.
This is often called a *shallow copy*, since it's copying only the "surface"
portion of an object. The actual object consists of this "surface" plus all
the objects that the handles are pointing to, plus all the objects *those*
objects are pointing to, etc. This is often referred to as the "web of
objects." Copying the entire mess is called a *deep copy*.

You can see the effect of the shallow copy in the output, where the actions performed on **v2** affect **v**:

```
v: [0, 1, 2, 3, 4, 5, 6, 7, 8, 9]
v: [1, 2, 3, 4, 5, 6, 7, 8, 9, 10]
```

Not trying to **clone( )** the objects contained in the **Vector** is probably a fair assumption because there's no guarantee that those objects *are* cloneable.[2]

Adding cloneability to a class

Even though the clone method is defined in the base-of-all-classes **Object**, cloning is *not* automatically available in every class.[3] This would seem to be counterintuitive to the idea that base-class methods are always available in derived classes. Cloning in Java goes against this idea; if you want it to exist for a class, you must specifically add code to make cloning work.

Using a trick with **protected**

To prevent default clonability in every class you create, the **clone( )** method is **protected** in the base class **Object**. Not only does this mean that it's not available by default to the client programmer who is simply using the class (not subclassing it), but it also means that you cannot call **clone( )** via a handle to the base class. (Although that might seem to be useful in some situations, such as to polymorphically clone a bunch of **Object**s.) It is in effect a way to give you, at compile time, the

---

[2] This is not the dictionary spelling of the word, but it's what is used in the Java library, so I've used it here, too, in some hopes of reducing confusion.

[3] You can apparently create a simple counter-example to this statement, like this:
```
public class Cloneit implements Cloneable {
  public static void main (String[] args)
  throws CloneNotSupportedException {
    Cloneit a = new Cloneit();
    Cloneit b = (Cloneit)a.clone();
  }
}
```
However, this only works because **main( )** is a method of **Cloneit** and thus has permission to call the **protected** base-class method **clone( )**. If you call it from a different class, it won't compile.

---

information that your object is not cloneable – and oddly enough most classes in the standard Java library are not cloneable. Thus, if you say:

```
Integer x = new Integer(1);
x = x.clone();
```

You will get, at compile time, an error message that says **clone( )** is not accessible (since **Integer** doesn't override it and it defaults to the **protected** version).

If, however, you're in a class derived from **Object** (as all classes are), then you have permission to call **Object.clone( )** because it's **protected** and you're an inheritor. The base class **clone( )** has useful functionality – it performs the actual bitwise duplication *of the derived-class object*, thus acting as the common cloning operation. However, you then need to make *your* clone operation **public** for it to be accessible. So two key issues when you clone are: virtually always call **super.clone( )** and make your clone **public**.

You'll probably want to override **clone( )** in any further derived classes, otherwise your (now **public**) **clone( )** will be used, and that might not do the right thing (although, since **Object.clone( )** makes a copy of the actual object, it might). The **protected** trick works only once, the first time you inherit from a class that has no clonability and you want to make a class that's cloneable. In any classes inherited from your class the **clone( )** method is available since it's not possible in Java to reduce the access of a method during derivation. That is, once a class is cloneable, everything derived from it is cloneable unless you use provided mechanisms (described later) to "turn off" cloning.

Implementing the **Cloneable** interface

There's one more thing you need to do to complete the clonability of an object: implement the **Cloneable interface**. This **interface** is a bit strange because it's empty!

```
interface Cloneable {}
```

The reason for implementing this empty **interface** is obviously not because you are going to upcast to **Cloneable** and call one of its methods. The use of **interface** here is considered by some to be a "hack" because it's using a feature for something other than its original intent. Implementing the **Cloneable interface** acts as a kind of a flag, wired into the type of the class.

There are two reasons for the existence of the **Cloneable interface**. First, you might have an upcast handle to a base type and not know whether it's possible to clone that object. In this case, you can use the **instanceof** keyword (described in Chapter 11) to find out whether the handle is connected to an object that can be cloned:

```
if(myHandle instanceof Cloneable) // ...
```

The second reason is that mixed into this design for clonability was the thought that maybe you didn't want all types of objects to be cloneable. So **Object.clone( )** verifies that a class implements the **Cloneable** interface. If not, it throws a **CloneNotSupportedException** exception. So in general, you're forced to **implement Cloneable** as part of support for cloning.

Successful cloning

Once you understand the details of implementing the **clone( )** method, you're able to create classes that can be easily duplicated to provide a local copy:

```java
//: LocalCopy.java
// Creating local copies with clone()
import java.util.*;

class MyObject implements Cloneable {
  int i;
  MyObject(int ii) { i = ii; }
  public Object clone() {
    Object o = null;
    try {
      o = super.clone();
    } catch (CloneNotSupportedException e) {
      System.out.println("MyObject can't clone");
    }
    return o;
  }
  public String toString() {
    return Integer.toString(i);
  }
}

public class LocalCopy {
  static MyObject g(MyObject v) {
    // Passing a handle, modifies outside object:
```

```
      v.i++;
      return v;
    }
    static MyObject f(MyObject v) {
      v = (MyObject)v.clone(); // Local copy
      v.i++;
      return v;
    }
    public static void main(String[] args) {
      MyObject a = new MyObject(11);
      MyObject b = g(a);
      // Testing handle equivalence,
      // not object equivalence:
      if(a == b)
        System.out.println("a == b");
      else
        System.out.println("a != b");
      System.out.println("a = " + a);
      System.out.println("b = " + b);
      MyObject c = new MyObject(47);
      MyObject d = f(c);
      if(c == d)
        System.out.println("c == d");
      else
        System.out.println("c != d");
      System.out.println("c = " + c);
      System.out.println("d = " + d);
    }
} ///:~
```

First of all, **clone( )** must be accessible so you must make it **public**.
Second, for the initial part of your **clone( )** operation you should call the
base-class version of **clone( )**. The **clone( )** that's being called here is the
one that's predefined inside **Object**, and you can call it because it's
protected and thereby accessible in derived classes.

Object.clone( ) figures out how big the object is, creates enough memory
for a new one, and copies all the bits from the old to the new. This is
called a *bitwise copy*, and is typically what you'd expect a **clone( )** method
to do. But before **Object.clone( )** performs its operations, it first checks
to see if a class is **Cloneable**, that is, whether it implements the
Cloneable interface. If it doesn't, **Object.clone( )** throws a
CloneNotSupportedException to indicate that you can't clone it. Thus,
you've got to surround your call to **super.clone( )** with a try-catch

---

block, to catch an exception that should never happen (because you've implemented the **Cloneable** interface).

In **LocalCopy**, the two methods **g( )** and **f( )** demonstrate the difference between the two approaches for argument passing. **g( )** shows passing by reference in which it modifies the outside object and returns a reference to that outside object, while **f( )** clones the argument, thereby decoupling it and leaving the original object alone. It can then proceed to do whatever it wants, and even to return a handle to this new object without any ill effects to the original. Notice the somewhat curious-looking statement:

```
v = (MyObject)v.clone();
```

This is where the local copy is created. To prevent confusion by such a statement, remember that this rather strange coding idiom is perfectly feasible in Java because everything that has a name is actually a handle. So the handle **v** is used to **clone( )** a copy of what it refers to, and this returns a handle to the base type **Object** (because it's defined that way in **Object.clone( )**) that must then be cast to the proper type.

In **main( )**, the difference between the effects of the two different argument-passing approaches in the two different methods is tested. The output is:

```
a == b
a = 12
b = 12
c != d
c = 47
d = 48
```

It's important to notice that the equivalence tests in Java do not look inside the objects being compared to see if their values are the same. The **==** and **!=** operators are simply comparing the contents of the *handles*. If the addresses inside the handles are the same, the handles are pointing to the same object and are therefore "equal." So what the operators are really testing is whether the handles are aliased to the same object!

The effect of Object.clone( )

What actually happens when **Object.clone( )** is called that makes it so essential to call **super.clone( )** when you override **clone( )** in your class? The **clone( )** method in the root class is responsible for creating the correct amount of storage and making the bitwise copy of the bits from the original object into the new object's storage. That is, it doesn't just make storage and copy an **Object** – it actually figures out the size of the precise object that's being copied and duplicates that. Since all this is happening from the code in the **clone( )** method defined in the root class (that has no idea what's being inherited from it), you can guess that the process involves RTTI to determine the actual object that's being cloned. This way, the **clone( )** method can create the proper amount of storage and do the correct bitcopy for that type.

Whatever you do, the first part of the cloning process should normally be a call to **super.clone( )**. This establishes the groundwork for the cloning operation by making an exact duplicate. At this point you can perform other operations necessary to complete the cloning.

To know for sure what those other operations are, you need to understand exactly what **Object.clone( )** buys you. In particular, does it automatically clone the destination of all the handles? The following example tests this:

```java
//: Snake.java
// Tests cloning to see if destination of
// handles are also cloned.

public class Snake implements Cloneable {
  private Snake next;
  private char c;
  // Value of i == number of segments
  Snake(int i, char x) {
    c = x;
    if(--i > 0)
      next = new Snake(i, (char)(x + 1));
  }
  void increment() {
    c++;
    if(next != null)
      next.increment();
  }
  public String toString() {
    String s = ":" + c;
    if(next != null)
      s += next.toString();
    return s;
  }
  public Object clone() {
    Object o = null;
```

```
          try {
            o = super.clone();
          } catch (CloneNotSupportedException e) {}
          return o;
        }
        public static void main(String[] args) {
          Snake s = new Snake(5, 'a');
          System.out.println("s = " + s);
          Snake s2 = (Snake)s.clone();
          System.out.println("s2 = " + s2);
          s.increment();
          System.out.println(
            "after s.increment, s2 = " + s2);
        }
      } ///:~
```

A **Snake** is made up of a bunch of segments, each of type **Snake**. Thus, it's a singly-linked list. The segments are created recursively, decrementing the first constructor argument for each segment until zero is reached. To give each segment a unique tag, the second argument, a **char**, is incremented for each recursive constructor call.

The **increment( )** method recursively increments each tag so you can see the change, and the **toString( )** recursively prints each tag. The output is:

```
s = :a:b:c:d:e
s2 = :a:b:c:d:e
after s.increment, s2 = :a:c:d:e:f
```

This means that only the first segment is duplicated by **Object.clone( )**, so it does a shallow copy. If you want the whole snake to be duplicated – a deep copy – you must perform the additional operations inside your overridden **clone( )**.

You'll typically call **super.clone( )** in any class derived from a cloneable class to make sure that all of the base-class operations (including **Object.clone( )**) take place. This is followed by an explicit call to **clone( )** for every handle in your object; otherwise those handles will be aliased to those of the original object. It's analogous to the way constructors are called – base-class constructor first, then the next-derived constructor, and so on to the most-derived constructor. The difference is that **clone( )** is not a constructor so there's nothing to make it happen automatically. You must make sure to do it yourself.

Cloning a composed object

There's a problem you'll encounter when trying to deep copy a composed object. You must assume that the **clone( )** method in the member objects will in turn perform a deep copy on *their* handles, and so on. This is quite a commitment. It effectively means that for a deep copy to work you must either control all of the code in all of the classes, or at least have enough knowledge about all of the classes involved in the deep copy to know that they are performing their own deep copy correctly.

This example shows what you must do to accomplish a deep copy when dealing with a composed object:

```
//: DeepCopy.java
// Cloning a composed object

class DepthReading implements Cloneable {
  private double depth;
  public DepthReading(double depth) {
    this.depth = depth;
  }
  public Object clone() {
    Object o = null;
    try {
      o = super.clone();
    } catch (CloneNotSupportedException e) {
      e.printStackTrace();
    }
    return o;
  }
}

class TemperatureReading implements Cloneable {
  private long time;
  private double temperature;
  public TemperatureReading(double temperature) {
    time = System.currentTimeMillis();
    this.temperature = temperature;
  }
  public Object clone() {
    Object o = null;
    try {
      o = super.clone();
    } catch (CloneNotSupportedException e) {
      e.printStackTrace();
```

```
      }
      return o;
    }
  }

class OceanReading implements Cloneable {
  private DepthReading depth;
  private TemperatureReading temperature;
  public OceanReading(double tdata, double ddata){
    temperature = new TemperatureReading(tdata);
    depth = new DepthReading(ddata);
  }
  public Object clone() {
    OceanReading o = null;
    try {
      o = (OceanReading)super.clone();
    } catch (CloneNotSupportedException e) {
      e.printStackTrace();
    }
    // Must clone handles:
    o.depth = (DepthReading)o.depth.clone();
    o.temperature =
      (TemperatureReading)o.temperature.clone();
    return o; // Upcasts back to Object
  }
}

public class DeepCopy {
  public static void main(String[] args) {
    OceanReading reading =
      new OceanReading(33.9, 100.5);
    // Now clone it:
    OceanReading r =
      (OceanReading)reading.clone();
  }
} ///:~
```

DepthReading and **TemperatureReading** are quite similar; they both
contain only primitives. Therefore, the **clone( )** method can be quite
simple: it calls **super.clone( )** and returns the result. Note that the
clone( ) code for both classes is identical.

OceanReading is composed of **DepthReading** and **TemperatureReading**
objects and so, to produce a deep copy, its **clone( )** must clone the handles
inside **OceanReading**. To accomplish this, the result of **super.clone( )**

must be cast to an **OceanReading** object (so you can access the **depth** and **temperature** handles).

A deep copy with **Vector**

Let's revisit the **Vector** example from earlier in this chapter. This time the **Int2** class is cloneable so the **Vector** can be deep copied:

```
//: AddingClone.java
// You must go through a few gyrations to
// add cloning to your own class.
import java.util.*;

class Int2 implements Cloneable {
  private int i;
  public Int2(int ii) { i = ii; }
  public void increment() { i++; }
  public String toString() {
    return Integer.toString(i);
  }
  public Object clone() {
    Object o = null;
    try {
      o = super.clone();
    } catch (CloneNotSupportedException e) {
      System.out.println("Int2 can't clone");
    }
    return o;
  }
}

// Once it's cloneable, inheritance
// doesn't remove cloneability:
class Int3 extends Int2 {
  private int j; // Automatically duplicated
  public Int3(int i) { super(i); }
}

public class AddingClone {
  public static void main(String[] args) {
    Int2 x = new Int2(10);
    Int2 x2 = (Int2)x.clone();
    x2.increment();
    System.out.println(
```

```
        "x = " + x + ", x2 = " + x2);
    // Anything inherited is also cloneable:
    Int3 x3 = new Int3(7);
    x3 = (Int3)x3.clone();

    Vector v = new Vector();
    for(int i = 0; i < 10; i++ )
      v.addElement(new Int2(i));
    System.out.println("v: " + v);
    Vector v2 = (Vector)v.clone();
    // Now clone each element:
    for(int i = 0; i < v.size(); i++)
      v2.setElementAt(
        ((Int2)v2.elementAt(i)).clone(), i);
    // Increment all v2's elements:
    for(Enumeration e = v2.elements();
        e.hasMoreElements(); )
      ((Int2)e.nextElement()).increment();
    // See if it changed v's elements:
    System.out.println("v: " + v);
    System.out.println("v2: " + v2);
  }
} ///:~
```

Int3 is inherited from **Int2** and a new primitive member **int j** is added. You might think that you'd need to override **clone( )** again to make sure **j** is copied, but that's not the case. When **Int2**'s **clone( )** is called as **Int3**'s **clone( )**, it calls **Object.clone( )**, which determines that it's working with an **Int3** and duplicates all the bits in the **Int3**. As long as you don't add handles that need to be cloned, the one call to **Object.clone( )** performs all of the necessary duplication, regardless of how far down in the hierarchy **clone( )** is defined.

You can see what's necessary in order to do a deep copy of a **Vector**: after the **Vector** is cloned, you have to step through and clone each one of the objects pointed to by the **Vector**. You'd have to do something similar to this to do a deep copy of a **Hashtable**.

The remainder of the example shows that the cloning did happen by showing that, once an object is cloned, you can change it and the original object is left untouched.

Deep copy via serialization

When you consider Java 1.1 object serialization (introduced in Chapter 10), you might observe that an object that's serialized and then deserialized is, in effect, cloned.

So why not use serialization to perform deep copying? Here's an example that compares the two approaches by timing them:

```
//: Compete.java
import java.io.*;

class Thing1 implements Serializable {}
class Thing2 implements Serializable {
  Thing1 o1 = new Thing1();
}

class Thing3 implements Cloneable {
  public Object clone() {
    Object o = null;
    try {
      o = super.clone();
    } catch (CloneNotSupportedException e) {
      System.out.println("Thing3 can't clone");
    }
    return o;
  }
}

class Thing4 implements Cloneable {
  Thing3 o3 = new Thing3();
  public Object clone() {
    Thing4 o = null;
    try {
      o = (Thing4)super.clone();
    } catch (CloneNotSupportedException e) {
      System.out.println("Thing4 can't clone");
    }
    // Clone the field, too:
    o.o3 = (Thing3)o3.clone();
    return o;
  }
}

public class Compete {
```

```
    static final int SIZE = 5000;
    public static void main(String[] args) {
      Thing2[] a = new Thing2[SIZE];
      for(int i = 0; i < a.length; i++)
        a[i] = new Thing2();
      Thing4[] b = new Thing4[SIZE];
      for(int i = 0; i < b.length; i++)
        b[i] = new Thing4();
      try {
        long t1 = System.currentTimeMillis();
        ByteArrayOutputStream buf =
          new ByteArrayOutputStream();
        ObjectOutputStream o =
          new ObjectOutputStream(buf);
        for(int i = 0; i < a.length; i++)
          o.writeObject(a[i]);
        // Now get copies:
        ObjectInputStream in =
          new ObjectInputStream(
            new ByteArrayInputStream(
              buf.toByteArray()));
        Thing2[] c = new Thing2[SIZE];
        for(int i = 0; i < c.length; i++)
          c[i] = (Thing2)in.readObject();
        long t2 = System.currentTimeMillis();
        System.out.println(
          "Duplication via serialization: " +
          (t2 - t1) + " Milliseconds");
        // Now try cloning:
        t1 = System.currentTimeMillis();
        Thing4[] d = new Thing4[SIZE];
        for(int i = 0; i < d.length; i++)
          d[i] = (Thing4)b[i].clone();
        t2 = System.currentTimeMillis();
        System.out.println(
          "Duplication via cloning: " +
          (t2 - t1) + " Milliseconds");
      } catch(Exception e) {
        e.printStackTrace();
      }
    }
} ///:~
```

Thing2 and **Thing4** contain member objects so that there's some deep copying going on. It's interesting to notice that while **Serializable** classes are easy to set up, there's much more work going on to duplicate them. Cloning involves a lot of work to set up the class, but the actual duplication of objects is relatively simple. The results really tell the tale. Here is the output from three different runs:

```
Duplication via serialization: 3400 Milliseconds
Duplication via cloning: 110 Milliseconds

Duplication via serialization: 3410 Milliseconds
Duplication via cloning: 110 Milliseconds

Duplication via serialization: 3520 Milliseconds
Duplication via cloning: 110 Milliseconds
```

Despite the obviously huge time difference between serialization and cloning, you'll also notice that the serialization technique seems to vary significantly in its duration, while cloning takes the same amount of time every time.

Adding cloneability further down a hierarchy

If you create a new class, its base class defaults to **Object**, which defaults to non-clonability (as you'll see in the next section). As long as you don't explicitly add clonability, you won't get it. But you can add it in at any layer and it will then be cloneable from that layer downward, like this:

```
//: HorrorFlick.java
// You can insert Cloneability at any
// level of inheritance.
import java.util.*;

class Person {}
class Hero extends Person {}
class Scientist extends Person
    implements Cloneable {
  public Object clone() {
    try {
      return super.clone();
    } catch (CloneNotSupportedException e) {
      // this should never happen:
      // It's Cloneable already!
      throw new InternalError();
    }
```

```
      }
    }
    class MadScientist extends Scientist {}

    public class HorrorFlick {
      public static void main(String[] args) {
        Person p = new Person();
        Hero h = new Hero();
        Scientist s = new Scientist();
        MadScientist m = new MadScientist();

        // p = (Person)p.clone(); // Compile error
        // h = (Hero)h.clone(); // Compile error
        s = (Scientist)s.clone();
        m = (MadScientist)m.clone();
      }
    } ///:~
```

Before clonability was added, the compiler stopped you from trying to clone things. When clonability is added in **Scientist**, then **Scientist** and all its descendants are cloneable.

Why this strange design?

If all this seems to be a strange scheme, that's because it is. You might wonder why it worked out this way. What is the meaning behind this design? What follows is not a substantiated story – probably because much of the marketing around Java makes it out to be a perfectly-designed language – but it does go a long way toward explaining how things ended up the way they did.

Originally, Java was designed as a language to control hardware boxes, and definitely not with the Internet in mind. In a general-purpose language like this, it makes sense that the programmer be able to clone any object. Thus, **clone( )** was placed in the root class **Object**, *but* it was a **public** method so you could always clone any object. This seemed to be the most flexible approach, and after all, what could it hurt?

Well, when Java was seen as the ultimate Internet programming language, things changed. Suddenly, there are security issues, and of course, these issues are dealt with using objects, and you don't necessarily want anyone to be able to clone your security objects. So what you're seeing is a lot of patches applied on the original simple and straightforward scheme: **clone( )** is now **protected** in **Object**. You must override it *and* **implement Cloneable** *and* deal with the exceptions.

It's worth noting that you must use the **Cloneable** interface *only* if you're going to call **Object**'s **clone( )**, method, since that method checks at run-time to make sure that your class implements **Cloneable**. But for consistency (and since **Cloneable** is empty anyway) you should implement it.

Controlling cloneability

You might suggest that, to remove clonability, the **clone( )** method simply be made **private**, but this won't work since you cannot take a base-class method and make it more **private** in a derived class. So it's not that simple. And yet, it's necessary to be able to control whether an object can be cloned. There are actually a number of attitudes you can take to this in a class that you design:

1. Indifference. You don't do anything about cloning, which means that your class can't be cloned but a class that inherits from you can add cloning if it wants. This works only if the default **Object.clone( )** will do something reasonable with all the fields in your class.

2. Support **clone( )**. Follow the standard practice of implementing **Cloneable** and overriding **clone( )**. In the overridden **clone( )**, you call **super.clone( )** and catch all exceptions (so your overridden **clone( )** doesn't throw any exceptions).

3. Support cloning conditionally. If your class holds handles to other objects that might or might not be cloneable (an example of this is a collection class), you can try to clone all of the objects that you have handles to as part of your cloning, and if they throw exceptions just pass them through. For example, consider a special sort of **Vector** that tries to clone all the objects it holds. When you write such a **Vector**, you don't know what sort of objects the client programmer might put into your **Vector**, so you don't know whether they can be cloned.

4. Don't implement **Cloneable** but override **clone( )** as **protected**, producing the correct copying behavior for any fields. This way, anyone inheriting from this class can override **clone( )** and call **super.clone( )** to produce the correct copying behavior. Note that your implementation can and should invoke **super.clone( )** even though that method expects a **Cloneable** object (it will throw an exception otherwise), because no one will directly invoke it on an object of your type. It will get invoked only through a derived class, which, if it is to work successfully, implements **Cloneable**.

5. Try to prevent cloning by not implementing **Cloneable** and overriding **clone( )** to throw an exception. This is successful only if any class derived from this calls **super.clone( )** in its redefinition of **clone( )**. Otherwise, a programmer may be able to get around it.

6. Prevent cloning by making your class **final**. If **clone( )** has not been overridden by any of your ancestor classes, then it can't be. If it has, then override it again and throw **CloneNotSupportedException**. Making the class **final** is the only way to guarantee that cloning is prevented. In addition, when dealing with security objects or other situations in which you want to control the number of objects created you should make all constructors **private** and provide one or more special methods for creating objects. That way, these methods can restrict the number of objects created and the conditions in which they're created. (A particular case of this is the *singleton* pattern shown in Chapter 16.)

Here's an example that shows the various ways cloning can be implemented and then, later in the hierarchy, "turned off:"

```
//: CheckCloneable.java
// Checking to see if a handle can be cloned

// Can't clone this because it doesn't
// override clone():
class Ordinary {}

// Overrides clone, but doesn't implement
// Cloneable:
class WrongClone extends Ordinary {
  public Object clone()
      throws CloneNotSupportedException {
    return super.clone(); // Throws exception
  }
}

// Does all the right things for cloning:
class IsCloneable extends Ordinary
    implements Cloneable {
  public Object clone()
      throws CloneNotSupportedException {
    return super.clone();
  }
}
```

```
// Turn off cloning by throwing the exception:
class NoMore extends IsCloneable {
  public Object clone()
      throws CloneNotSupportedException {
    throw new CloneNotSupportedException();
  }
}

class TryMore extends NoMore {
  public Object clone()
      throws CloneNotSupportedException {
    // Calls NoMore.clone(), throws exception:
    return super.clone();
  }
}

class BackOn extends NoMore {
  private BackOn duplicate(BackOn b) {
    // Somehow make a copy of b
    // and return that copy. This is a dummy
    // copy, just to make the point:
    return new BackOn();
  }
  public Object clone() {
    // Doesn't call NoMore.clone():
    return duplicate(this);
  }
}

// Can't inherit from this, so can't override
// the clone method like in BackOn:
final class ReallyNoMore extends NoMore {}

public class CheckCloneable {
  static Ordinary tryToClone(Ordinary ord) {
    String id = ord.getClass().getName();
    Ordinary x = null;
    if(ord instanceof Cloneable) {
      try {
        System.out.println("Attempting " + id);
        x = (Ordinary)((IsCloneable)ord).clone();
        System.out.println("Cloned " + id);
      } catch(CloneNotSupportedException e) {
        System.out.println(
```

```
                 "Could not clone " + id);
      }
    }
    return x;
  }
  public static void main(String[] args) {
    // Upcasting:
    Ordinary[] ord = {
      new IsCloneable(),
      new WrongClone(),
      new NoMore(),
      new TryMore(),
      new BackOn(),
      new ReallyNoMore(),
    };
    Ordinary x = new Ordinary();
    // This won't compile, since clone() is
    // protected in Object:
    //! x = (Ordinary)x.clone();
    // tryToClone() checks first to see if
    // a class implements Cloneable:
    for(int i = 0; i < ord.length; i++)
      tryToClone(ord[i]);
  }
} ///:~
```

The first class, **Ordinary**, represents the kinds of classes we've seen throughout the book: no support for cloning, but as it turns out, no prevention of cloning either. But if you have a handle to an **Ordinary** object that might have been upcast from a more derived class, you can't tell if it can be cloned or not.

The class **WrongClone** shows an incorrect way to implement cloning. It does override **Object.clone( )** and makes that method **public**, but it doesn't implement **Cloneable**, so when **super.clone( )** is called (which results in a call to **Object.clone( )**), **CloneNotSupportedException** is thrown so the cloning doesn't work.

In **IsCloneable** you can see all the right actions performed for cloning: **clone( )** is overridden and **Cloneable** is implemented. However, this **clone( )** method and several others that follow in this example *do not* catch **CloneNotSupportedException**, but instead pass it through to the caller, who must then put a try-catch block around it. In your own **clone( )** methods you will typically catch **CloneNotSupportedException** *inside* **clone( )** rather than passing it through. As you'll see, in this example it's more informative to pass the exceptions through.

Class **NoMore** attempts to "turn off" cloning in the way that the Java designers intended: in the derived class **clone( )**, you throw **CloneNotSupportedException**. The **clone( )** method in class **TryMore** properly calls **super.clone( )**, and this resolves to **NoMore.clone( )**, which throws an exception and prevents cloning.

But what if the programmer doesn't follow the "proper" path of calling **super.clone( )** inside the overridden **clone( )** method? In **BackOn**, you can see how this can happen. This class uses a separate method **duplicate( )** to make a copy of the current object and calls this method inside **clone( )** *instead* of calling **super.clone( )**. The exception is never thrown and the new class is cloneable. You can't rely on throwing an exception to prevent making a cloneable class. The only sure-fire solution is shown in **ReallyNoMore**, which is **final** and thus cannot be inherited. That means if **clone( )** throws an exception in the **final** class, it cannot be modified with inheritance and the prevention of cloning is assured. (You cannot explicitly call **Object.clone( )** from a class that has an arbitrary level of inheritance; you are limited to calling **super.clone( )**, which has access to only the direct base class.) Thus, if you make any objects that involve security issues, you'll want to make those classes **final**.

The first method you see in class **CheckCloneable** is **tryToClone( )**, which takes any **Ordinary** object and checks to see whether it's cloneable with **instanceof**. If so, it casts the object to an **IsCloneable**, calls **clone( )** and casts the result back to **Ordinary**, catching any exceptions that are thrown. Notice the use of run-time type identification (see Chapter 11) to print out the class name so you can see what's happening.

In **main( )**, different types of **Ordinary** objects are created and upcast to **Ordinary** in the array definition. The first two lines of code after that create a plain **Ordinary** object and try to clone it. However, this code will not compile because **clone( )** is a **protected** method in **Object**. The remainder of the code steps through the array and tries to clone each object, reporting the success or failure of each. The output is:

```
Attempting IsCloneable
Cloned IsCloneable
Attempting NoMore
Could not clone NoMore
Attempting TryMore
Could not clone TryMore
Attempting BackOn
Cloned BackOn
```

```
Attempting ReallyNoMore
Could not clone ReallyNoMore
```

So to summarize, if you want a class to be cloneable:

1. Implement the **Cloneable** interface.

2. Override **clone( )**.

3. Call **super.clone( )** inside your **clone( )**.

4. Capture exceptions inside your **clone( )**.

This will produce the most convenient effects.

The copy-constructor

Cloning can seem to be a complicated process to set up. It might seem like there should be an alternative. One approach that might occur to you (especially if you're a C++ programmer) is to make a special constructor whose job it is to duplicate an object. In C++, this is called the *copy constructor*. At first, this seems like the obvious solution. Here's an example:

```
//: CopyConstructor.java
// A constructor for copying an object
// of the same type, as an attempt to create
// a local copy.

class FruitQualities {
  private int weight;
  private int color;
  private int firmness;
  private int ripeness;
  private int smell;
  // etc.
  FruitQualities() { // Default constructor
    // do something meaningful...
  }
  // Other constructors:
  // ...
  // Copy constructor:
  FruitQualities(FruitQualities f) {
    weight = f.weight;
    color = f.color;
    firmness = f.firmness;
```

```
      ripeness = f.ripeness;
      smell = f.smell;
      // etc.
  }
}

class Seed {
  // Members...
  Seed() { /* Default constructor */ }
  Seed(Seed s) { /* Copy constructor */ }
}

class Fruit {
  private FruitQualities fq;
  private int seeds;
  private Seed[] s;
  Fruit(FruitQualities q, int seedCount) {
    fq = q;
    seeds = seedCount;
    s = new Seed[seeds];
    for(int i = 0; i < seeds; i++)
      s[i] = new Seed();
  }
  // Other constructors:
  // ...
  // Copy constructor:
  Fruit(Fruit f) {
    fq = new FruitQualities(f.fq);
    seeds = f.seeds;
    // Call all Seed copy-constructors:
    for(int i = 0; i < seeds; i++)
      s[i] = new Seed(f.s[i]);
    // Other copy-construction activities...
  }
  // To allow derived constructors (or other
  // methods) to put in different qualities:
  protected void addQualities(FruitQualities q) {
    fq = q;
  }
  protected FruitQualities getQualities() {
    return fq;
  }
}
```

```
class Tomato extends Fruit {
  Tomato() {
    super(new FruitQualities(), 100);
  }
  Tomato(Tomato t) { // Copy-constructor
    super(t); // Upcast for base copy-constructor
    // Other copy-construction activities...
  }
}

class ZebraQualities extends FruitQualities {
  private int stripedness;
  ZebraQualities() { // Default constructor
    // do something meaningful...
  }
  ZebraQualities(ZebraQualities z) {
    super(z);
    stripedness = z.stripedness;
  }
}

class GreenZebra extends Tomato {
  GreenZebra() {
    addQualities(new ZebraQualities());
  }
  GreenZebra(GreenZebra g) {
    super(g); // Calls Tomato(Tomato)
    // Restore the right qualities:
    addQualities(new ZebraQualities());
  }
  void evaluate() {
    ZebraQualities zq =
      (ZebraQualities)getQualities();
    // Do something with the qualities
    // ...
  }
}

public class CopyConstructor {
  public static void ripen(Tomato t) {
    // Use the "copy constructor":
    t = new Tomato(t);
    System.out.println("In ripen, t is a " +
      t.getClass().getName());
```

```
      }
      public static void slice(Fruit f) {
         f = new Fruit(f); // Hmmm... will this work?
         System.out.println("In slice, f is a " +
            f.getClass().getName());
      }
      public static void main(String[] args) {
         Tomato tomato = new Tomato();
         ripcn(tomato); // OK
         slice(tomato); // OOPS!
         GreenZebra g = new GreenZebra();
         ripen(g); // OOPS!
         slice(g); // OOPS!
         g.evaluate();
      }
   } ///:~
```

This seems a bit strange at first. Sure, fruit has qualities, but why not just put data members representing those qualities directly into the **Fruit** class? There are two potential reasons. The first is that you might want to easily insert or change the qualities. Note that **Fruit** has a **protected addQualities( )** method to allow derived classes to do this. (You might think the logical thing to do is to have a **protected** constructor in **Fruit** that takes a **FruitQualities** argument, but constructors don't inherit so it wouldn't be available in second or greater level classes.) By making the fruit qualities into a separate class, you have greater flexibility, including the ability to change the qualities midway through the lifetime of a particular **Fruit** object.

The second reason for making **FruitQualities** a separate object is in case you want to add new qualities or to change the behavior via inheritance and polymorphism. Note that for **GreenZebra** (which really is a type of tomato – I've grown them and they're fabulous), the constructor calls **addQualities( )** and passes it a **ZebraQualities** object, which is derived from **FruitQualities** so it can be attached to the **FruitQualities** handle in the base class. Of course, when **GreenZebra** uses the **FruitQualities** it must downcast it to the correct type (as seen in **evaluate( )**), but it always knows that type is **ZebraQualities**.

You'll also see that there's a **Seed** class, and that **Fruit** (which by definition carries its own seeds) contains an array of **Seed**s.

Finally, notice that each class has a copy constructor, and that each copy constructor must take care to call the copy constructors for the base class and member objects to produce a deep copy. The copy constructor is tested inside the class **CopyConstructor**. The method **ripen( )** takes a **Tomato** argument and performs copy-construction on it in order to duplicate the object:

```
t = new Tomato(t);
```

while **slice( )** takes a more generic **Fruit** object and also duplicates it:

```
f = new Fruit(f);
```

These are tested with different kinds of **Fruit** in **main( )**. Here's the output:

```
In ripen, t is a Tomato
In slice, f is a Fruit
In ripen, t is a Tomato
In slice, f is a Fruit
```

This is where the problem shows up. After the copy-construction that happens to the **Tomato** inside **slice( )**, the result is no longer a **Tomato** object, but just a **Fruit**. It has lost all of its tomato-ness. Further, when you take a **GreenZebra**, both **ripen( )** and **slice( )** turn it into a **Tomato** and a **Fruit**, respectively. Thus, unfortunately, the copy constructor scheme is no good to us in Java when attempting to make a local copy of an object.

Why does it work in C++ and not Java?

The copy constructor is a fundamental part of C++, since it automatically makes a local copy of an object. Yet the example above proves that it does not work for Java. Why? In Java everything that we manipulate is a handle, while in C++ you can have handle-like entities and you can *also* pass around the objects directly. That's what the C++ copy constructor is for: when you want to take an object and pass it in by value, thus duplicating the object. So it works fine in C++, but you should keep in mind that this scheme fails in Java, so don't use it.

Read-only classes

While the local copy produced by **clone( )** gives the desired results in the appropriate cases, it is an example of forcing the programmer (the author of the method) to be responsible for preventing the ill effects of aliasing. What if you're making a library that's so general purpose and commonly used that you cannot make the assumption that it will always be cloned in the proper places? Or more likely, what if you *want* to allow aliasing for efficiency – to prevent the needless duplication of objects – but you don't want the negative side effects of aliasing?

One solution is to create *immutable objects* which belong to read-only classes. You can define a class such that no methods in the class cause changes to the internal state of the object. In such a class, aliasing has no impact since you can read only the internal state, so if many pieces of code are reading the same object there's no problem.

As a simple example of immutable objects, Java's standard library contains "wrapper" classes for all the primitive types. You might have already discovered that, if you want to store an **int** inside a collection such as a **Vector** (which takes only **Object** handles), you can wrap your **int** inside the standard library **Integer** class:

```
//: ImmutableInteger.java
// The Integer class cannot be changed
import java.util.*;

public class ImmutableInteger {
  public static void main(String[] args) {
    Vector v = new Vector();
    for(int i = 0; i < 10; i++)
      v.addElement(new Integer(i));
    // But how do you change the int
    // inside the Integer?
  }
} ///:~
```

The **Integer** class (as well as all the primitive "wrapper" classes) implements immutability in a simple fashion: they have no methods that allow you to change the object.

If you do need an object that holds a primitive type that can be modified, you must create it yourself. Fortunately, this is trivial:

```
//: MutableInteger.java
// A changeable wrapper class
import java.util.*;

class IntValue {
  int n;
  IntValue(int x) { n = x; }
  public String toString() {
    return Integer.toString(n);
  }
```

```
    }

public class MutableInteger {
  public static void main(String[] args) {
    Vector v = new Vector();
    for(int i = 0; i < 10; i++)
      v.addElement(new IntValue(i));
    System.out.println(v);
    for(int i = 0; i < v.size(); i++)
      ((IntValue)v.elementAt(i)).n++;
    System.out.println(v);
  }
} ///:~
```

Note that **n** is friendly to simplify coding.

IntValue can be even simpler if the default initialization to zero is adequate (then you don't need the constructor) and you don't care about printing it out (then you don't need the **toString( )**):

```
class IntValue { int n; }
```

Fetching the element out and casting it is a bit awkward, but that's a feature of **Vector**, not of **IntValue**.

Creating read-only classes

It's possible to create your own read-only class. Here's an example:

```
//: Immutable1.java
// Objects that cannot be modified
// are immune to aliasing.

public class Immutable1 {
  private int data;
  public Immutable1(int initVal) {
    data = initVal;
  }
  public int read() { return data; }
  public boolean nonzero() { return data != 0; }
  public Immutable1 quadruple() {
    return new Immutable1(data * 4);
  }
  static void f(Immutable1 i1) {
    Immutable1 quad = i1.quadruple();
```

```
      System.out.println("i1 = " + i1.read());
      System.out.println("quad = " + quad.read());
   }
   public static void main(String[] args) {
      Immutable1 x = new Immutable1(47);
      System.out.println("x = " + x.read());
      f(x);
      System.out.println("x = " + x.read());
   }
} ///:~
```

All data is **private**, and you'll see that none of the **public** methods modify that data. Indeed, the method that does appear to modify an object is **quadruple( )**, but this creates a new **Immutable1** object and leaves the original one untouched.

The method **f( )** takes an **Immutable1** object and performs various operations on it, and the output of **main( )** demonstrates that there is no change to **x**. Thus, **x**'s object could be aliased many times without harm because the **Immutable1** class is designed to guarantee that objects cannot be changed.

The drawback to immutability

Creating an immutable class seems at first to provide an elegant solution. However, whenever you do need a modified object of that new type you must suffer the overhead of a new object creation, as well as potentially causing more frequent garbage collections. For some classes this is not a problem, but for others (such as the **String** class) it is prohibitively expensive.

The solution is to create a companion class that *can* be modified. Then when you're doing a lot of modifications, you can switch to using the modifiable companion class and switch back to the immutable class when you're done.

The example above can be modified to show this:

```
//: Immutable2.java
// A companion class for making changes
// to immutable objects.

class Mutable {
   private int data;
   public Mutable(int initVal) {
```

```
      data = initVal;
    }
    public Mutable add(int x) {
      data += x;
      return this;
    }
    public Mutable multiply(int x) {
      data *= x;
      return this;
    }
    public Immutable2 makeImmutable2() {
      return new Immutable2(data);
    }
}

public class Immutable2 {
    private int data;
    public Immutable2(int initVal) {
      data = initVal;
    }
    public int read() { return data; }
    public boolean nonzero() { return data != 0; }
    public Immutable2 add(int x) {
      return new Immutable2(data + x);
    }
    public Immutable2 multiply(int x) {
      return new Immutable2(data * x);
    }
    public Mutable makeMutable() {
      return new Mutable(data);
    }
    public static Immutable2 modify1(Immutable2 y){
      Immutable2 val = y.add(12);
      val = val.multiply(3);
      val = val.add(11);
      val = val.multiply(2);
      return val;
    }
    // This produces the same result:
    public static Immutable2 modify2(Immutable2 y){
      Mutable m = y.makeMutable();
      m.add(12).multiply(3).add(11).multiply(2);
      return m.makeImmutable2();
    }
```

```
    public static void main(String[] args) {
        Immutable2 i2 = new Immutable2(47);
        Immutable2 r1 = modify1(i2);
        Immutable2 r2 = modify2(i2);
        System.out.println("i2 = " + i2.read());
        System.out.println("r1 = " + r1.read());
        System.out.println("r2 = " + r2.read());
    }
} ///:~
```

Immutable2 contains methods that, as before, preserve the immutability of the objects by producing new objects whenever a modification is desired. These are the **add( )** and **multiply( )** methods. The companion class is called **Mutable**, and it also has **add( )** and **multiply( )** methods, but these modify the **Mutable** object rather than making a new one. In addition, **Mutable** has a method to use its data to produce an **Immutable2** object and vice versa.

The two static methods **modify1( )** and **modify2( )** show two different approaches to producing the same result. In **modify1( )**, everything is done within the **Immutable2** class and you can see that four new **Immutable2** objects are created in the process. (And each time **val** is reassigned, the previous object becomes garbage.)

In the method **modify2( )**, you can see that the first action is to take the **Immutable2 y** and produce a **Mutable** from it. (This is just like calling **clone( )** as you saw earlier, but this time a different type of object is created.) Then the **Mutable** object is used to perform a lot of change operations *without* requiring the creation of many new objects. Finally, it's turned back into an **Immutable2**. Here, two new objects are created (the **Mutable** and the result **Immutable2**) instead of four.

This approach makes sense, then, when:

1. You need immutable objects and

2. You often need to make a lot of modifications or

3. It's expensive to create new immutable objects

Immutable Strings

Consider the following code:

```
//: Stringer.java
```

```
public class Stringer {
  static String upcase(String s) {
    return s.toUpperCase();
  }
  public static void main(String[] args) {
    String q = new String("howdy");
    System.out.println(q); // howdy
    String qq = upcase(q);
    System.out.println(qq); // HOWDY
    System.out.println(q); // howdy
  }
} ///:~
```

When **q** is passed in to **upcase( )** it's actually a copy of the handle to **q**. The object this handle is connected to stays put in a single physical location. The handles are copied as they are passed around.

Looking at the definition for **upcase( )**, you can see that the handle that's passed in has the name **s**, and it exists for only as long as the body of **upcase( )** is being executed. When **upcase( )** completes, the local handle **s** vanishes. **upcase( )** returns the result, which is the original string with all the characters set to uppercase. Of course, it actually returns a handle to the result. But it turns out that the handle that it returns is for a new object, and the original **q** is left alone. How does this happen?

Implicit constants

If you say:

```
String s = "asdf";
String x = Stringer.upcase(s);
```

do you really want the **upcase( )** method to *change* the argument? In general, you don't, because an argument usually looks to the reader of the code as a piece of information provided to the method, not something to be modified. This is an important guarantee, since it makes code easier to write and understand.

In C++, the availability of this guarantee was important enough to put in a special keyword, **const**, to allow the programmer to ensure that a handle (pointer or reference in C++) could not be used to modify the original object. But then the C++ programmer was required to be diligent and remember to use **const** everywhere. It can be confusing and easy to forget.

Overloading '+' and the StringBuffer

Objects of the **String** class are designed to be immutable, using the technique shown previously. If you examine the online documentation for the **String** class (which is summarized a little later in this chapter), you'll see that every method in the class that appears to modify a **String** really creates and returns a brand new **String** object containing the modification. The original **String** is left untouched. Thus, there's no feature in Java like C++'s **const** to make the compiler support the immutability of your objects. If you want it, you have to wire it in yourself, like **String** does.

Since **String** objects are immutable, you can alias to a particular **String** as many times as you want. Because it's read-only there's no possibility that one handle will change something that will affect the other handles. So a read-only object solves the aliasing problem nicely.

It also seems possible to handle all the cases in which you need a modified object by creating a brand new version of the object with the modifications, as **String** does. However, for some operations this isn't efficient. A case in point is the operator '+' that has been overloaded for **String** objects. Overloading means that it has been given an extra meaning when used with a particular class. (The '+' and '+=' for **String** are the only operators that are overloaded in Java and Java does not allow the programmer to overload any others[4]).

When used with **String** objects, the '+' allows you to concatenate **String**s together:

```
String s = "abc" + foo + "def" +
Integer.toString(47);
```

You could imagine how this *might* work: the **String** "abc" could have a method **append( )** that creates a new **String** object containing "abc" concatenated with the contents of **foo**. The new **String** object would then create another new **String** that added "def" and so on.

---

[4] C++ allows the programmer to overload operators at will. Because this can often be a complicated process (see Chapter 10 of *Thinking in C++* Prentice-Hall, 1995), the Java designers deemed it a "bad" feature that shouldn't be included in Java. It wasn't so bad that they didn't end up doing it themselves, and ironically enough, operator overloading would be much easier to use in Java than in C++.

This would certainly work, but it requires the creation of a lot of **String** objects just to put together this new **String**, and then you have a bunch of the intermediate **String** objects that need to be garbage-collected. I suspect that the Java designers tried this approach first (which is a lesson in software design – you don't really know anything about a system until you try it out in code and get something working). I also suspect they discovered that it delivered unacceptable performance.

The solution is a mutable companion class similar to the one shown previously. For **String**, this companion class is called **StringBuffer**, and the compiler automatically creates a **StringBuffer** to evaluate certain expressions, in particular when the overloaded operators **+** and **+=** are used with **String** objects. This example shows what happens:

```
//: ImmutableStrings.java
// Demonstrating StringBuffer

public class ImmutableStrings {
  public static void main(String[] args) {
    String foo = "foo";
    String s = "abc" + foo +
      "def" + Integer.toString(47);
    System.out.println(s);
    // The "equivalent" using StringBuffer:
    StringBuffer sb =
      new StringBuffer("abc"); // Creates String!
    sb.append(foo);
    sb.append("def"); // Creates String!
    sb.append(Integer.toString(47));
    System.out.println(sb);
  }
} ///:~
```

In the creation of **String s**, the compiler is doing the rough equivalent of the subsequent code that uses **sb**: a **StringBuffer** is created and **append( )** is used to add new characters directly into the **StringBuffer** object (rather than making new copies each time). While this is more efficient, it's worth noting that each time you create a quoted character string such as **"abc"** and **"def"**, the compiler turns those into **String** objects. So there can be more objects created than you expect, despite the efficiency afforded through **StringBuffer**.

The **String** and **StringBuffer** classes

Here is an overview of the methods available for both **String** and **StringBuffer** so you can get a feel for the way they interact. These tables don't contain every single method, but rather the ones that are important to this discussion. Methods that are overloaded are summarized in a single row.

First, the **String** class:

Method	Arguments, Overloading	Use
Constructor	Overloaded: Default, **String**, **StringBuffer**, **char** arrays, **byte** arrays.	Creating **String** objects.
length( )		Number of characters in **String**.
charAt()	**int Index**	The **char** at a location in the **String**.
getChars( ), **getBytes( )**	The beginning and end from which to copy, the array to copy into, an index into the destination array.	Copy **char**s or **byte**s into an external array.
toCharArray( )		Produces a **char[]** containing the characters in the **String**.
equals( ), **equals-IgnoreCase( )**	A **String** to compare with.	An equality check on the contents of the two **String**s.
compareTo( )	A **String** to compare with.	Result is negative, zero, or positive depending on the lexicographical ordering of the **String** and the argument. Uppercase and lowercase are not equal!
regionMatches( )	Offset into this **String**, the other **String** and its offset and length to compare. Overload adds "ignore case."	Boolean result indicates whether the region matches.

Method	Arguments, Overloading	Use
startsWith( )	**String** that it might start with. Overload adds offset into argument.	Boolean result indicates whether the **String** starts with the argument.
endsWith( )	**String** that might be a suffix of this **String**.	Boolean result indicates whether the argument is a suffix.
indexOf( ), **lastIndexOf( )**	Overloaded: **char**, **char** and starting index, **String**, **String**, and starting index	Returns –1 if the argument is not found within this **String**, otherwise returns the index where the argument starts. **lastIndexOf( )** searches backward from end.
substring( )	Overloaded: Starting index, starting index, and ending index.	Returns a new **String** object containing the specified character set.
concat( )	The **String** to concatenate	Returns a new **String** object containing the original **String**'s characters followed by the characters in the argument.
replace( )	The old character to search for, the new character to replace it with.	Returns a new **String** object with the replacements made. Uses the old **String** if no match is found.
toLowerCase( ) **toUpperCase( )**		Returns a new **String** object with the case of all letters changed. Uses the old **String** if no changes need to be made.
trim( )		Returns a new **String** object with the white space removed from each end. Uses the old **String** if no changes need to be made.
valueOf( )	Overloaded: **Object**, **char[]**, **char[]** and offset and count, **boolean**, **char**,	Returns a **String** containing a character representation of the argument.

Method	Arguments, Overloading	Use
	int, long, float, double.	
intern( )		Produces one and only one **String** handle for each unique character sequence.

You can see that every **String** method carefully returns a new **String** object when it's necessary to change the contents. Also notice that if the contents don't need changing the method will just return a handle to the original **String**. This saves storage and overhead.

Here's the **StringBuffer** class:

Method	Arguments, overloading	Use
Constructor	Overloaded: default, length of buffer to create, **String** to create from.	Create a new **StringBuffer** object.
toString( )		Creates a **String** from this **StringBuffer**.
length( )		Number of characters in the **StringBuffer**.
capacity( )		Returns current number of spaces allocated.
ensure-Capacity( )	Integer indicating desired capacity.	Makes the **StringBuffer** hold at least the desired number of spaces.
setLength( )	Integer indicating new length of character string in buffer.	Truncates or expands the previous character string. If expanding, pads with nulls.
charAt( )	Integer indicating the location of the desired element.	Returns the **char** at that location in the buffer.
setCharAt( )	Integer indicating the location of the desired element and the new **char** value for the element.	Modifies the value at that location.
getChars( )	The beginning and end from which to copy, the array to copy into, an index into the	Copy **chars** into an external array. There's no **getBytes( )** as in

Method	Arguments, overloading	Use
	destination array.	**String**.
append( )	Overloaded: **Object**, **String**, **char[]**, **char[]** with offset and length, **boolean**, **char**, **int**, **long**, **float**, **double**.	The argument is converted to a string and appended to the end of the current buffer, increasing the buffer if necessary.
insert( )	Overloaded, each with a first argument of the offset at which to start inserting: **Object**, **String**, **char[]**, **boolean**, **char**, **int**, **long**, **float**, **double**.	The second argument is converted to a string and inserted into the current buffer beginning at the offset. The buffer is increased if necessary.
reverse( )		The order of the characters in the buffer is reversed.

The most commonly-used method is **append( )**, which is used by the compiler when evaluating **String** expressions that contain the '+' and '+=' operators. The **insert( )** method has a similar form, and both methods perform significant manipulations to the buffer instead of creating new objects.

Strings are special

By now you've seen that the **String** class is not just another class in Java. There are a lot of special cases in **String**, not the least of which is that it's a built-in class and fundamental to Java. Then there's the fact that a quoted character string is converted to a **String** by the compiler and the special overloaded operators + and +=. In this chapter you've seen the remaining special case: the carefully-built immutability using the companion **StringBuffer** and some extra magic in the compiler.

Summary

Because everything is a handle in Java, and because every object is created on the heap and garbage collected only when it is no longer used, the flavor of object manipulation changes, especially when passing and returning objects. For example, in C or C++, if you wanted to initialize some piece of storage in a method, you'd probably request that the user pass the address of that piece of storage into the method. Otherwise you'd have to worry about who was responsible for destroying that storage. Thus, the interface and understanding of such methods is more complicated. But in Java, you never have to worry about responsibility or whether an object will still exist when it is needed, since that is always taken care of for you. Your programs can create an object at the point that it is needed, and no sooner, and never worry about the mechanics of passing around responsibility for that object: you simply pass the handle. Sometimes the simplification that this provides is unnoticed, other times it is staggering.

The downside to all this underlying magic is twofold:

1. You always take the efficiency hit for the extra memory management (although this can be quite small), and there's always a slight amount of uncertainty about the time something can take to run (since the garbage collector can be forced into action whenever you get low on memory). For most applications, the benefits outweigh the drawbacks, and particularly time-critical sections can be written using **native** methods (see Appendix A).

2. Aliasing: sometimes you can accidentally end up with two handles to the same object, which is a problem only if both handles are assumed to point to a *distinct* object. This is where you need to pay a little closer attention and, when necessary, **clone( )** an object to prevent the other handle from being surprised by an unexpected change. Alternatively, you can support aliasing for efficiency by creating immutable objects whose operations can return a new object of the same type or some different type, but never change the original object so that anyone aliased to that object sees no change.

Some people say that cloning in Java is a botched design, and to heck with it, so they implement their own version of cloning[5] and never call the **Object.clone( )** method, thus eliminating the need to implement **Cloneable** and catch the **CloneNotSupportedException**. This is certainly a reasonable approach and since **clone( )** is supported so rarely within the standard Java library, it is apparently a safe one as well. But as long as you don't call **Object.clone( )** you don't need to implement **Cloneable** or catch the exception, so that would seem acceptable as well.

---

[5] Doug Lea, who was helpful in resolving this issue, suggested this to me, saying that he simply creates a function called **duplicate( )** for each class.

It's interesting to notice that one of the "reserved but not implemented" keywords in Java is **byvalue**. After seeing the issues of aliasing and cloning, you can imagine that **byvalue** might someday be used to implement an automatic local copy in Java. This could eliminate the more complex issues of cloning and make coding in these situations simpler and more robust.

Exercises

1. Create a class **myString** containing a **String** object that you initialize in the constructor using the constructor's argument. Add a **toString( )** method and a method **concatenate( )** that appends a **String** object to your internal string. Implement **clone( )** in **myString**. Create two **static** methods that each take a **myString x** handle as an argument and call **x.concatenate("test")**, but in the second method call **clone( )** first. Test the two methods and show the different effects.

2. Create a class called **Battery** containing an **int** that is a battery number (as a unique identifier). Make it cloneable and give it a **toString( )** method. Now create a class called **Toy** that contains an array of **Battery** and a **toString( )** that prints out all the batteries. Write a **clone( )** for **Toy** that automatically clones all of its **Battery** objects. Test this by cloning **Toy** and printing the result.

3. Change **CheckCloneable.java** so that all of the **clone( )** methods catch the **CloneNotSupportedException** rather than passing it to the caller.

4. Modify **Compete.java** to add more member objects to classes **Thing2** and **Thing4** and see if you can determine how the timings vary with complexity – whether it's a simple linear relationship or if it seems more complicated.

5. Starting with **Snake.java**, create a deep-copy version of the snake.

13: Creating windows and applets

The original design goal of the graphical user interface (GUI) library in Java 1.0 was to allow the programmer to build a GUI that looks good on all platforms.

That goal was not achieved. Instead, the Java 1.0 *Abstract Window Toolkit* (AWT) produces a GUI that looks equally mediocre on all systems. In addition it's restrictive: you can use only four fonts and you cannot access any of the more sophisticated GUI elements that exist in your operating system (OS). The Java 1.0 AWT programming model is also awkward and non–object-oriented.

Much of this situation has been improved with the Java 1.1 AWT event model, which takes a much clearer, object–oriented approach, along with the introduction of Java Beans, a component programming model that is particularly oriented toward the easy creation of visual programming environments. Java 1.2 finishes the transformation away from the old Java 1.0 AWT by adding the *Java Foundation Classes* (JFC), the GUI portion of which is called "Swing." These are a rich set of easy-to-use, easy-to-understand Java Beans that can be dragged and dropped (as well as hand programmed) to create a GUI that you can (finally) be satisfied with. The "revision 3" rule of the software industry (a product isn't good until revision 3) seems to hold true with programming languages as well.

One of Java's primary design goals is to create *applets*, which are little programs that run inside a Web browser. Because they must be safe, applets are limited in what they can accomplish. However, they are a powerful tool in supporting client-side programming, a major issue for the Web.

Programming within an applet is so restrictive that it's often referred to as being "inside the sandbox," since you always have someone – the Java run-time security system – watching over you. Java 1.1 offers digital signing for applets so you can choose to allow trusted applets to have access to your machine. However, you can also step outside the sandbox and write regular applications, in which case you can access the other features of your OS. We've been writing regular applications all along in this book, but they've been *console applications* without any graphical components. The AWT can also be used to build GUI interfaces for regular applications.

In this chapter you'll first learn the use of the original "old" AWT, which is still supported and used by many of the code examples that you will come across. Although it's a bit painful to learn the old AWT, it's necessary because you must read and maintain legacy code that uses the old AWT. Sometimes you'll even need to write old AWT code to support environments that haven't upgraded past Java 1.0. In the second part of the chapter you'll learn about the structure of the "new" AWT in Java 1.1 and see how much better the event model is. (If you can, you should use the newest tools when you're creating new programs.) Finally, you'll learn about the new JFC/Swing components, which can be added to Java 1.1 as a library – this means you can use the library without requiring a full upgrade to Java 1.2.

Most of the examples will show the creation of applets, not only because it's easier but also because that's where the AWT's primary usefulness might reside. In addition you'll see how things are different when you want to create a regular application using the AWT, and how to create programs that are both applets and applications so they can be run either inside a browser or from the command line.

Please be aware that this is not a comprehensive glossary of all the methods for the described classes. This chapter will just get you started with the essentials. When you're looking for more sophistication, make sure you go to your information browser to look for the classes and methods that will solve your problem. (If you're using a development environment your information browser might be built in; if you're using the Sun JDK then you use your Web browser and start in the java root directory.) Appendix F lists other resources for learning library details.

Why use the AWT?

One of the problems with the "old" AWT that you'll learn about in this chapter is that it is a poor example of both object-oriented design and GUI development kit design. It throws us back into the dark ages of programming (some suggest that the 'A' in AWT stands for "awkward," "awful," "abominable," etc.). You must write lines of code to do *everything*, including tasks that are accomplished much more easily using *resources* in other environments.

Many of these problems are reduced or eliminated in Java 1.1 because:

1. The new AWT in Java 1.1 is a much better programming model and a significant step towards a better library. Java Beans is the framework for that library.

2. "GUI builders" (visual programming environments) will become *de rigeur* for all development systems. Java Beans and the new AWT allow the GUI builder to write code for you as you place components onto forms using graphical tools. Other component technologies such as ActiveX will be supported in the same fashion.

So why learn to use the old AWT? "Because it's there." In this case, "there" has a much more ominous meaning and points to a tenet of object-oriented library design: *Once you publicize a component in your library, you can never take it out*. If you do, you'll wreck somebody's existing code. In addition, there are many existing code examples out there that you'll read as you learn about Java and they all use the old AWT.

The AWT must reach into the GUI components of the native OS, which means that it performs a task that an applet cannot otherwise accomplish. An untrusted applet cannot make any direct calls into an OS because otherwise it could do bad things to the user's machine. The only way an untrusted applet can access important functionality such as "draw a window on the screen" is through calls in the standard Java library that's been specially ported and safety checked for that machine. The original model that Sun created is that this "trusted library" will be provided only by the trusted vendor of the Java system in your Web browser, and the vendor will control what goes into that library.

But what if you want to extend the system by adding a new component that accesses functionality in the OS? Waiting for Sun to decide that your extension should be incorporated into the standard Java library isn't going to solve your problem. The new model in Java 1.1 is "trusted code" or "signed code" whereby a special server verifies that a piece of code that you download is in fact "signed" by the stated author using a public-key encryption system. This way, you'll know for sure where the code comes from, that it's Bob's code and not just someone pretending to be Bob. This doesn't prevent Bob from making mistakes or doing something malicious, but it does prevent Bob from shirking responsibility – anonymity is what makes computer viruses possible. A digitally signed applet – a "trusted applet" – in Java 1.1 *can* reach into your machine and manipulate it directly, just like any other application you get from a "trusted" vendor and install onto your computer.

But the point of all this is that the old AWT is *there*. There will always be old AWT code floating around and new Java programmers learning from old books will encounter that code. Also, the old AWT is worth studying as an example of poor library design. The coverage of the old AWT given here will be relatively painless since it won't go into depth and enumerate every single method and class, but instead give you an overview of the old AWT design.

The basic applet

Libraries are often grouped according to their functionality. Some libraries, for example, are used as is, off the shelf. The standard Java library **String** and **Vector** classes are examples of these. Other libraries are designed specifically as building blocks to build other classes. A certain class of library is the *application framework*, whose goal is to help you build applications by providing a class or set of classes that produces the basic behavior that you need in every application of a particular type.

Then, to customize the behavior to your own needs you inherit from the application class and override the methods of interest. The application framework's default control mechanism will call your overridden methods at the appropriate time. An application framework is a good example of "separating the things that change from the things that stay the same," since it attempts to localize all the unique parts of a program in the overridden methods.

Applets are built using an application framework. You inherit from class **Applet** and override the appropriate methods. Most of the time you'll be concerned with only a few important methods that have to do with how the applet is built and used on a Web page. These methods are:

Method	Operation
init( )	Called when the applet is first created to perform first-time initialization of the applet
start( )	Called every time the applet moves into sight on the Web browser to allow the applet to start up its normal operations (especially those that are shut off by **stop( )**). Also called after **init( )**.
paint( )	Part of the base class **Component** (three levels of inheritance up). Called as part of an **update( )** to perform special painting on the canvas of an applet.
stop( )	Called every time the applet moves out of sight on the Web browser to allow the applet to shut off expensive operations. Also called right before **destroy( )**.
destroy( )	Called when the applet is being unloaded from the page to perform final release of resources when the applet is no longer used

Consider the **paint( )** method. This method is called automatically when the **Component** (in this case, the applet) decides that it needs to update itself – perhaps because it's being moved back onto the screen or placed on the screen for the first time, or perhaps some other window had been temporarily placed over your Web browser. The applet calls its **update( )** method (defined in the base class **Component**), which goes about restoring everything, and as a part of that restoration calls **paint( )**. You don't have to override **paint( )**, but it turns out to be an easy way to make a simple applet, so we'll start out with **paint( )**.

When **update( )** calls **paint( )** it hands it a handle to a **Graphics** object that represents the surface on which you can paint. This is important because you're limited to the surface of that particular component and thus cannot paint outside that area, which is a good thing or else you'd be painting outside the lines. In the case of an applet, the surface is the area inside the applet.

The **Graphics** object also has a set of operations you can perform on it. These operations revolve around painting on the canvas, so most of them have to do with drawing images, shapes, arcs, etc. (Note that you can look all this up in your online Java documentation if you're curious.) There are some methods that allow you to draw characters, however, and the most commonly used one is **drawString( )**. For this, you must specify the **String** you want to draw and its starting location on the applet's drawing surface. This location is given in pixels, so it will look different on different machines, but at least it's portable.

With this information you can create a simple applet:

```
//: Applet1.java
// Very simple applet
package c13;
import java.awt.*;
import java.applet.*;

public class Applet1 extends Applet {
  public void paint(Graphics g) {
    g.drawString("First applet", 10, 10);
  }
} ///:~
```

Note that applets are not required to have a **main( )**. That's all wired in to the application framework; you put any startup code in **init( )**.

To run this program you must place it inside a Web page and view that page inside your Java-enabled Web browser. To place an applet inside a Web page you put a special tag inside the HTML source for that Web page[1] to tell the page how to load and run the applet. This is the **applet** tag, and it looks like this for Applet1:

```
<applet
code=Applet1
width=200
height=200>
</applet>
```

---

[1] It is assumed that the reader is familiar with the basics of HTML. It's not too hard to figure out, and there are lots of books and resources.

The **code** value gives the name of the **.class** file where the applet resides. The **width** and **height** specify the initial size of the applet (in pixels, as before). There are other items you can place within the applet tag: a place to find other **.class** files on the Internet (**codebase**), alignment information (**align**), a special identifier that makes it possible for applets to communicate with each other (**name**), and applet parameters to provide information that the applet can retrieve. Parameters are in the form

```
<param name=identifier value = "information">
```

and there can be as many as you want.

For simple applets all you need to do is place an applet tag in the above form inside your Web page and that will load and run the applet.

Testing applets

You can perform a simple test without any network connection by starting up your Web browser and opening the HTML file containing the applet tag. (Sun's JDK also contains a tool called the *appletviewer* that picks the <APPLET> tags out of the HTML file and runs the applets without displaying the surrounding HTML text.[2]) As the HTML file is loaded, the browser will discover the applet tag and go hunt for the **.class** file specified by the **code** value. Of course, it looks at the CLASSPATH to find out where to hunt, and if your **.class** file isn't in the CLASSPATH then it will give an error message on the status line of the browser to the effect that it couldn't find that **.class** file.

When you want to try this out on your Web site things are a little more complicated. First of all, you must *have* a Web site, which for most people means a third-party Internet Service Provider (ISP) at a remote location. Then you must have a way to move the HTML files and the **.class** files from your site to the correct directory (your WWW directory) on the ISP machine. This is typically done with a File Transfer Protocol (FTP) program, of which there are many different types freely available. So it would seem that all you need to do is move the files to the ISP machine

---

[2] Because the appletviewer ignores everything but APPLET tags, you can put those tags in the Java source file as comments:
```
// <applet code=MyApplet.class width=200 height=100></applet>
```
This way, you can run "**appletviewer MyApplet.java**" and you don't need to create tiny HTML files to run tests.

with FTP, then connect to the site and HTML file using your browser; if the applet comes up and works, then everything checks out, right?

Here's where you can get fooled. If the browser cannot locate the **.class** file on the server, it will hunt through the CLASSPATH on your *local* machine. Thus, the applet might not be loading properly from the server, but to you it looks fine because the browser finds it on your machine. When someone else logs in, however, his or her browser can't find it. So when you're testing, make sure you erase the relevant **.class** files on your machine to be safe.

One of the most insidious places where this happened to me is when I innocently placed an applet inside a **package**. After uploading the HTML file and applet, it turned out that the server path to the applet was confused because of the package name. However, my browser found it in the local CLASSPATH. So I was the only one who could properly load the applet. It took some time to discover that the **package** statement was the culprit. In general, you'll want to leave the **package** statement out of an applet.

A more graphical example

The example above isn't too thrilling, so let's try adding a slightly more interesting graphic component:

```
//: Applet2.java
// Easy graphics
import java.awt.*;
import java.applet.*;

public class Applet2 extends Applet {
  public void paint(Graphics g) {
    g.drawString("Second applet", 10, 15);
    g.draw3DRect(0, 0, 100, 20, true);
  }
} ///:~
```

This puts a box around the string. Of course, all the numbers are hard-coded and are based on pixels, so on some machines the box will fit nicely around the string and on others it will probably be off, because fonts will be different on different machines.

There are other interesting things you can find in the documentation for the **Graphic** class. Any sort of graphics activity is usually entertaining, so further experiments of this sort are left to the reader.

Demonstrating the framework methods

It's interesting to see some of the framework methods in action. (This example will look only at **init( )**, **start( )**, and **stop( )** because **paint( )** and **destroy( )** are self-evident and not so easily traceable.) The following applet keeps track of the number of times these methods are called and displays them using **paint( )**:

```
//: Applet3.java
// Shows init(), start() and stop() activities
import java.awt.*;
import java.applet.*;

public class Applet3 extends Applet {
  String s;
  int inits = 0;
  int starts = 0;
  int stops = 0;
  public void init() { inits++; }
  public void start() { starts++; }
  public void stop() { stops++; }
  public void paint(Graphics g) {
    s = "inits: " + inits +
      ", starts: " + starts +
      ", stops: " + stops;
    g.drawString(s, 10, 10);
  }
} ///:~
```

Normally when you override a method you'll want to look to see whether you need to call the base-class version of that method, in case it does something important. For example, with **init( )** you might need to call **super.init( )**. However, the **Applet** documentation specifically states that the **init( )**, **start( )**, and **stop( )** methods in **Applet** do nothing, so it's not necessary to call them here.

When you experiment with this applet you'll discover that if you minimize the Web browser or cover it up with another window you might not get calls to **stop( )** and **start( )**. (This behavior seems to vary among implementations; you might wish to contrast the behavior of Web browsers with that of applet viewers.) The only time the calls will occur is when you move to a different Web page and then come back to the one containing the applet.

Making a button

Making a button is quite simple: you just call the **Button** constructor with the label you want on the button. (You can also use the default constructor if you want a button with no label, but this is not very useful.) Usually you'll want to create a handle for the button so you can refer to it later.

The **Button** is a component, like its own little window, that will automatically get repainted as part of an update. This means that you don't explicitly paint a button or any other kind of control; you simply place them on the form and let them automatically take care of painting themselves. So to place a button on a form you override **init( )** instead of overriding **paint( )**:

```
//: Button1.java
// Putting buttons on an applet
import java.awt.*;
import java.applet.*;

public class Button1 extends Applet {
  Button
    b1 = new Button("Button 1"),
    b2 = new Button("Button 2");
  public void init() {
    add(b1);
    add(b2);
  }
} ///:~
```

It's not enough to create the **Button** (or any other control). You must also call the **Applet add( )** method to cause the button to be placed on the applet's form. This seems a lot simpler than it is, because the call to **add( )** actually decides, implicitly, where to place the control on the form. Controlling the layout of a form is examined shortly.

Capturing an event

You'll notice that if you compile and run the applet above, nothing happens when you press the buttons. This is where you must step in and write some code to determine what will happen. The basis of event–driven programming, which comprises a lot of what a GUI is about, is tying events to code that responds to those events.

After working your way this far through the book and grasping some of the fundamentals of object-oriented programming, you might think that of course there will be some sort of object-oriented approach to handling events. For example, you might have to inherit each button and override some "button pressed" method (this, it turns out, is too tedious and restrictive). You might also think there's some master "event" class that contains a method for each event you want to respond to.

Before objects, the typical approach to handling events was the "giant switch statement." Each event would have a unique integer value and inside the master event handling method you'd write a **switch** on that value.

The AWT in Java 1.0 doesn't use any object-oriented approach. Neither does it use a giant **switch** statement that relies on the assignment of numbers to events. Instead, you must create a cascaded set of **if** statements. What you're trying to do with the **if** statements is detect the object that was the *target* of the event. That is, if you click on a button, then that particular button is the target. Normally, that's all you care about – if a button is the target of an event, then it was most certainly a mouse click and you can continue based on that assumption. However, events can contain other information as well. For example, if you want to find out the pixel location where a mouse click occurred so you can draw a line to that location, the **Event** object will contain the location. (You should also be aware that Java 1.0 components can be limited in the kinds of events they generate, while Java 1.1 and Swing/JFC components produce a full set of events.)

The Java 1.0 AWT method where your cascaded **if** statement resides is called **action( )**. Although the whole Java 1.0 Event model has been deprecated in Java 1.1, it is still widely used for simple applets and in systems that do not yet support Java 1.1, so I recommend you become comfortable with it, including the use of the following **action()** method approach.

action( ) has two arguments: the first is of type **Event** and contains all the information about the event that triggered this call to **action( )**. For example, it could be a mouse click, a normal keyboard press or release, a special key press or release, the fact that the component got or lost the focus, mouse movements, or drags, etc. The second argument is usually the target of the event, which you'll often ignore. The second argument is also encapsulated in the **Event** object so it is redundant as an argument.

The situations in which **action( )** gets called are extremely limited: When you place controls on a form, some types of controls (buttons, check boxes, drop-down lists, menus) have a "standard action" that occurs, which causes the call to **action( )** with the appropriate **Event** object. For example, with a button the **action( )** method is called when the button is pressed and at no other time. Usually this is just fine, since that's what you ordinarily look for with a button. However, it's possible to deal with many other types of events via the **handleEvent( )** method as we will see later in this chapter.

The previous example can be extended to handle button clicks as follows:

```
//: Button2.java
// Capturing button presses
import java.awt.*;
import java.applet.*;

public class Button2 extends Applet {
  Button
    b1 = new Button("Button 1"),
    b2 = new Button("Button 2");
  public void init() {
    add(b1);
    add(b2);
  }
  public boolean action(Event evt, Object arg) {
    if(evt.target.equals(b1))
      getAppletContext().showStatus("Button 1");
    else if(evt.target.equals(b2))
      getAppletContext().showStatus("Button 2");
    // Let the base class handle it:
    else
      return super.action(evt, arg);
    return true; // We've handled it here
  }
} ///:~
```

To see what the target is, ask the **Event** object what its **target** member is and then use the **equals( )** method to see if it matches the target object handle you're interested in. When you've written handlers for all the objects you're interested in you must call **super.action(evt, arg)** in the **else** statement at the end, as shown above. Remember from Chapter 7 (polymorphism) that your overridden method is called instead of the base class version. However, the base-class version contains code to handle all of the cases that you're not interested in, and it won't get called unless you call it explicitly. The return value indicates whether you've handled it or not, so if you do match an event you should return **true**, otherwise return whatever the base-class **event( )** returns.

For this example, the simplest action is to print what button is pressed. Some systems allow you to pop up a little window with a message in it, but applets discourage this. However, you can put a message at the bottom of the Web browser window on its *status line* by calling the **Applet** method **getAppletContext( )** to get access to the browser and then **showStatus( )** to put a string on the status line.[3] You can print out a complete description of an event the same way, with **getAppletContext().showStatus(evt + "")**. (The empty **String** forces the compiler to convert **evt** to a **String**.) Both of these reports are really useful only for testing and debugging since the browser might overwrite your message.

Strange as it might seem, you can also match an event to the *text* that's on a button through the second argument in **event( )**. Using this technique, the example above becomes:

```
//: Button3.java
// Matching events on button text
import java.awt.*;
import java.applet.*;

public class Button3 extends Applet {
  Button
    b1 = new Button("Button 1"),
    b2 = new Button("Button 2");
  public void init() {
    add(b1);
    add(b2);
  }
  public boolean action (Event evt, Object arg) {
    if(arg.equals("Button 1"))
      getAppletContext().showStatus("Button 1");
    else if(arg.equals("Button 2"))
      getAppletContext().showStatus("Button 2");
    // Let the base class handle it:
    else
      return super.action(evt, arg);
    return true; // We've handled it here
  }
} ///:~
```

---

[3] **ShowStatus( )** is also a method of Applet, so you can call it directly, without calling **getAppletContext( )**.

It's difficult to know exactly what the **equals( )** method is doing here. The biggest problem with this approach is that most new Java programmers who start with this technique spend at least one frustrating session discovering that they've gotten the capitalization or spelling wrong when comparing to the text on a button. (I had this experience.) Also, if you change the text of the button, the code will no longer work (but you won't get any compile-time or run-time error messages). You should avoid this approach if possible.

Text fields

A **TextField** is a one line area that allows the user to enter and edit text. **TextField** is inherited from **TextComponent**, which lets you select text, get the selected text as a **String**, get or set the text, and set whether the **TextField** is editable, along with other associated methods that you can find in your online reference. The following example demonstrates some of the functionality of a **TextField**; you can see that the method names are fairly obvious:

```
//: TextField1.java
// Using the text field control
import java.awt.*;
import java.applet.*;

public class TextField1 extends Applet {
  Button
    b1 = new Button("Get Text"),
    b2 = new Button("Set Text");
  TextField
    t = new TextField("Starting text", 30);
  String s = new String();
  public void init() {
    add(b1);
    add(b2);
    add(t);
  }
  public boolean action (Event evt, Object arg) {
    if(evt.target.equals(b1)) {
      getAppletContext().showStatus(t.getText());
      s = t.getSelectedText();
      if(s.length() == 0) s = t.getText();
      t.setEditable(true);
    }
```

```
    else if(evt.target.equals(b2)) {
      t.setText("Inserted by Button 2: " + s);
      t.setEditable(false);
    }
    // Let the base class handle it:
    else
      return super.action(evt, arg);
    return true; // We've handled it here
  }
} ///:~
```

There are several ways to construct a **TextField**; the one shown here provides an initial string and sets the size of the field in characters.

Pressing button 1 either gets the text you've selected with the mouse or it gets all the text in the field and places the result in **String s**. It also allows the field to be edited. Pressing button 2 puts a message and **s** into the text field and prevents the field from being edited (although you can still select the text). The editability of the text is controlled by passing **setEditable( )** a **true** or **false**.

Text areas

A **TextArea** is like a **TextField** except that it can have multiple lines and has significantly more functionality. In addition to what you can do with a **TextField**, you can append text and insert or replace text at a given location. It seems like this functionality could be useful for **TextField** as well, so it's a little confusing to try to detect how the distinction is made. You might think that if you want **TextArea** functionality everywhere you can simply use a one line **TextArea** in places where you would otherwise use a **TextField**. In Java 1.0, you also got scroll bars with a **TextArea** even when they weren't appropriate; that is, you got both vertical and horizontal scroll bars for a one line **TextArea**. In Java 1.1 this was remedied with an extra constructor that allows you to select which scroll bars (if any) are present. The following example shows only the Java 1.0 behavior, in which the scrollbars are always on. Later in the chapter you'll see an example that demonstrates Java 1.1 **TextArea**s.

```
//: TextArea1.java
// Using the text area control
import java.awt.*;
import java.applet.*;

public class TextArea1 extends Applet {
```

```java
Button b1 = new Button("Text Area 1");
Button b2 = new Button("Text Area 2");
Button b3 = new Button("Replace Text");
Button b4 = new Button("Insert Text");
TextArea t1 = new TextArea("t1", 1, 30);
TextArea t2 = new TextArea("t2", 4, 30);
public void init() {
  add(b1);
  add(t1);
  add(b2);
  add(t2);
  add(b3);
  add(b4);
}
public boolean action (Event evt, Object arg) {
  if(evt.target.equals(b1))
    getAppletContext().showStatus(t1.getText());
  else if(evt.target.equals(b2)) {
    t2.setText("Inserted by Button 2");
    t2.appendText(": " + t1.getText());
    getAppletContext().showStatus(t2.getText());
  }
  else if(evt.target.equals(b3)) {
    String s = " Replacement ";
    t2.replaceText(s, 3, 3 + s.length());
  }
  else if(evt.target.equals(b4))
    t2.insertText(" Inserted ", 10);
  // Let the base class handle it:
  else
    return super.action(evt, arg);
  return true; // We've handled it here
}
} ///:~
```

There are several different **TextArea** constructors, but the one shown here gives a starting string and the number of rows and columns. The different buttons show getting, appending, replacing, and inserting text.

Labels

A **Label** does exactly what it sounds like it should: places a label on the form. This is particularly important for text fields and text areas that don't have labels of their own, and can also be useful if you simply want to place textual information on a form. You can, as shown in the first example in this chapter, use **drawString( )** inside **paint( )** to place text in an exact location. When you use a **Label** it allows you to (approximately) associate the text with some other component via the layout manager (which will be discussed later in this chapter).

With the constructor you can create a blank label, a label with initial text in it (which is what you'll typically do), and a label with an alignment of **CENTER**, **LEFT**, or **RIGHT** (**static final int**s defined in class **Label**). You can also change the label and its alignment with **setText( )** and **setAlignment( )**, and if you've forgotten what you've set these to you can read the values with **getText( )** and **getAlignment( )**. This example shows what you can do with labels:

```
//: Label1.java
// Using labels
import java.awt.*;
import java.applet.*;

public class Label1 extends Applet {
  TextField t1 = new TextField("t1", 10);
  Label lab1 = new Label("TextField t1");
  Label lab2 = new Label("                    ");
  Label lab3 = new Label("                    ",
    Label.RIGHT);
  Button b1 = new Button("Test 1");
  Button b2 = new Button("Test 2");
  public void init() {
    add(lab1); add(t1);
    add(b1); add(lab2);
    add(b2); add(lab3);
  }
  public boolean action (Event evt, Object arg) {
    if(evt.target.equals(b1))
      lab2.setText("Text set into Label");
    else if(evt.target.equals(b2)) {
      if(lab3.getText().trim().length() == 0)
        lab3.setText("lab3");
      if(lab3.getAlignment() == Label.LEFT)
        lab3.setAlignment(Label.CENTER);
      else if(lab3.getAlignment()==Label.CENTER)
        lab3.setAlignment(Label.RIGHT);
      else if(lab3.getAlignment() == Label.RIGHT)
        lab3.setAlignment(Label.LEFT);
```

```
      }
      else
        return super.action(evt, arg);
      return true;
    }
  } ///:~
```

The first use of the label is the most typical: labeling a **TextField** or **TextArea**. In the second part of the example, a bunch of empty spaces are reserved and when you press the "Test 1" button **setText( )** is used to insert text into the field. Because a number of blank spaces do not equal the same number of characters (in a proportionally–spaced font) you'll see that the text gets truncated when inserted into the label.

The third part of the example reserves empty space, then the first time you press the "Test 2" button it sees that there are no characters in the label (since **trim( )** removes all of the blank spaces at each end of a **String**) and inserts a short label, which is initially left-aligned. The rest of the times you press the button it changes the alignment so you can see the effect.

You might think that you could create an empty label and then later put text in it with **setText( )**. However, you cannot put text into an empty label – presumably because it has zero width – so creating a label with no text seems to be a useless thing to do. In the example above, the "blank" label is filled with empty spaces so it has enough width to hold text that's placed inside later.

Similarly, **setAlignment( )** has no effect on a label that you'd typically create with text in the constructor. The label width is the width of the text, so changing the alignment doesn't do anything. However, if you start with a long label and then change it to a shorter one you can see the effect of the alignment.

These behaviors occur because of the default *layout manager* that's used for applets, which causes things to be squished together to their smallest size. Layout managers will be covered later in this chapter, when you'll see that other layouts don't have the same effect.

Check boxes

A check box provides a way to make a single on–off choice; it consists of a tiny box and a label. The box typically holds a little 'x' (or some other indication that it is set) or is empty depending on whether that item was selected.

You'll normally create a **Checkbox** using a constructor that takes the label as an argument. You can get and set the state, and also get and set the label if you want to read or change it after the **Checkbox** has been created. Note that the capitalization of **Checkbox** is inconsistent with the other controls, which could catch you by surprise since you might expect it to be "CheckBox."

Whenever a **Checkbox** is set or cleared an event occurs, which you can capture the same way you do a button. The following example uses a **TextArea** to enumerate all the check boxes that have been checked:

```
//: CheckBox1.java
// Using check boxes
import java.awt.*;
import java.applet.*;

public class CheckBox1 extends Applet {
  TextArea t = new TextArea(6, 20);
  Checkbox cb1 = new Checkbox("Check Box 1");
  Checkbox cb2 = new Checkbox("Check Box 2");
  Checkbox cb3 = new Checkbox("Check Box 3");
  public void init() {
    add(t); add(cb1); add(cb2); add(cb3);
  }
  public boolean action (Event evt, Object arg) {
    if(evt.target.equals(cb1))
      trace("1", cb1.getState());
    else if(evt.target.equals(cb2))
      trace("2", cb2.getState());
    else if(evt.target.equals(cb3))
      trace("3", cb3.getState());
    else
      return super.action(evt, arg);
    return true;
  }
  void trace(String b, boolean state) {
    if(state)
      t.appendText("Box " + b + " Set\n");
    else
      t.appendText("Box " + b + " Cleared\n");
  }
} ///:~
```

The **trace( )** method sends the name of the selected **Checkbox** and its current state to the **TextArea** using **appendText( )** so you'll see a cumulative list of the checkboxes that were selected and what their state is.

Radio buttons

The concept of a radio button in GUI programming comes from pre-electronic car radios with mechanical buttons: when you push one in, any other button that was pressed pops out. Thus it allows you to force a single choice among many.

The AWT does not have a separate class to represent the radio button; instead it reuses the **Checkbox**. However, to put the **Checkbox** in a radio button group (and to change its shape so it's visually different from an ordinary **Checkbox**) you must use a special constructor that takes a **CheckboxGroup** object as an argument. (You can also call **setCheckboxGroup( )** after the **Checkbox** has been created.)

A **CheckboxGroup** has no constructor argument; its sole reason for existence is to collect some **Checkbox**es into a group of radio buttons. One of the **Checkbox** objects must have its state set to **true** before you try to display the group of radio buttons; otherwise you'll get an exception at run time. If you try to set more than one radio button to **true** then only the final one set will be **true**.

Here's a simple example of the use of radio buttons. Note that you capture radio button events like all others:

```
//: RadioButton1.java
// Using radio buttons
import java.awt.*;
import java.applet.*;

public class RadioButton1 extends Applet {
  TextField t =
    new TextField("Radio button 2", 30);
  CheckboxGroup g = new CheckboxGroup();
  Checkbox
    cb1 = new Checkbox("one", g, false),
    cb2 = new Checkbox("two", g, true),
    cb3 = new Checkbox("three", g, false);
  public void init() {
```

```
        t.setEditable(false);
        add(t);
        add(cb1); add(cb2); add(cb3);
    }
    public boolean action (Event evt, Object arg) {
        if(evt.target.equals(cb1))
            t.setText("Radio button 1");
        else if(evt.target.equals(cb2))
            t.setText("Radio button 2");
        else if(evt.target.equals(cb3))
            t.setText("Radio button 3");
        else
            return super.action(evt, arg);
        return true;
    }
} ///:~
```

To display the state, an text field is used. This field is set to non-editable because it's used only to display data, not to collect it. This is shown as an alternative to using a **Label**. Notice the text in the field is initialized to "Radio button 2" since that's the initial selected radio button.

You can have any number of **CheckboxGroup**s on a form.

Drop-down lists

Like a group of radio buttons, a drop-down list is a way to force the user to select only one element from a group of possibilities. However, it's a much more compact way to accomplish this, and it's easier to change the elements of the list without surprising the user. (You can change radio buttons dynamically, but that tends to be visibly jarring).

Java's **Choice** box is not like the combo box in Windows, which lets you select from a list *or* type in your own selection. With a **Choice** box you choose one and only one element from the list. In the following example, the **Choice** box starts with a certain number of entries and then new entries are added to the box when a button is pressed. This allows you to see some interesting behaviors in **Choice** boxes:

```
//: Choice1.java
// Using drop-down lists
import java.awt.*;
import java.applet.*;
```

```java
public class Choice1 extends Applet {
  String[] description = { "Ebullient", "Obtuse",
    "Recalcitrant", "Brilliant", "Somnescent",
    "Timorous", "Florid", "Putrescent" };
  TextField t = new TextField(30);
  Choice c = new Choice();
  Button b = new Button("Add items");
  int count = 0;
  public void init() {
    t.setEditable(false);
    for(int i = 0; i < 4; i++)
      c.addItem(description[count++]);
    add(t);
    add(c);
    add(b);
  }
  public boolean action (Event evt, Object arg) {
    if(evt.target.equals(c))
      t.setText("index: " +  c.getSelectedIndex()
        + "    " + (String)arg);
    else if(evt.target.equals(b)) {
      if(count < description.length)
        c.addItem(description[count++]);
    }
    else
      return super.action(evt, arg);
    return true;
  }
} ///:~
```

The **TextField** displays the "selected index," which is the sequence number of the currently selected element, as well as the **String** representation of the second argument of **action( )**, which is in this case the string that was selected.

When you run this applet, pay attention to the determination of the size of the **Choice** box: in Windows, the size is fixed from the first time you drop down the list. This means that if you drop down the list, then add more elements to the list, the elements will be there but the drop–down list won't get any longer[4] (you can scroll through the elements). However, if you add all the elements before the first time the list is

---

[4] This behavior is apparently a bug and will be fixed in a later version of Java.

dropped down, then it will be sized correctly. Of course, the user will expect to see the whole list when it's dropped down, so this behavior puts some significant limitations on adding elements to **Choice** boxes.

List boxes

List boxes are significantly different from **Choice** boxes, and not just in appearance. While a **Choice** box drops down when you activate it, a **List** occupies some fixed number of lines on a screen all the time and doesn't change. In addition, a **List** allows multiple selection: if you click on more than one item the original item stays highlighted and you can select as many as you want. If you want to see the items in a list, you simply call **getSelectedItems( )**, which produces an array of **String** of the items that have been selected. To remove an item from a group you have to click it again.

A problem with a **List** is that the default action is double clicking, not single clicking. A single click adds or removes elements from the selected group and a double click calls **action( )**. One way around this is to re-educate your user, which is the assumption made in the following program:

```
//: List1.java
// Using lists with action()
import java.awt.*;
import java.applet.*;

public class List1 extends Applet {
  String[] flavors = { "Chocolate", "Strawberry",
    "Vanilla Fudge Swirl", "Mint Chip",
    "Mocha Almond Fudge", "Rum Raisin",
    "Praline Cream", "Mud Pie" };
  // Show 6 items, allow multiple selection:
  List lst = new List(6, true);
  TextArea t = new TextArea(flavors.length, 30);
  Button b = new Button("test");
  int count = 0;
  public void init() {
    t.setEditable(false);
    for(int i = 0; i < 4; i++)
      lst.addItem(flavors[count++]);
    add(t);
    add(lst);
```

```
      add(b);
    }
    public boolean action (Event evt, Object arg) {
      if(evt.target.equals(lst)) {
        t.setText("");
        String[] items = lst.getSelectedItems();
        for(int i = 0; i < items.length; i++)
          t.appendText(items[i] + "\n");
      }
      else if(evt.target.equals(b)) {
        if(count < flavors.length)
          lst.addItem(flavors[count++], 0);
      }
      else
        return super.action(evt, arg);
      return true;
    }
} ///:~
```

When you press the button it adds items to the *top* of the list (because of the second argument 0 to **addItem( )**). Adding elements to a **List** is more reasonable than the **Choice** box because users expect to scroll a list box (for one thing, it has a built-in scroll bar) but they don't expect to have to figure out how to get a drop-down list to scroll, as in the previous example.

However, the only way for **action( )** to be called is through a double-click. If you need to monitor other activities that the user is doing on your **List** (in particular, single clicks) you must take an alternative approach.

handleEvent( )

So far we've been using **action( )**, but there's another method that gets first crack at everything: **handleEvent( )**. Any time an event happens, it happens "over" or "to" a particular object. The **handleEvent( )** method for that object is automatically called and an **Event** object is created and passed to **handleEvent( )**. The default **handleEvent( )** (which is defined in **Component**, the base class for virtually all the "controls" in the AWT) will call either **action( )**, as we've been using, or other similar methods to indicate mouse activity, keyboard activity, or to indicate that the focus has moved. We'll look at those later in this chapter.

What if these other methods – **action( )** in particular – don't satisfy your needs? In the case of **List**, for example, what if you want to catch single mouse clicks but **action( )** responds to only double clicks? The solution is to override **handleEvent( )** for your applet, which after all is derived from **Applet** and can therefore override any non-**final** methods. When you override **handleEvent( )** for the applet you're getting all the applet events before they are routed, so you cannot just assume "This has to do with my button so I can assume it's been pressed," since that's true only for **action( )**. Inside **handleEvent( )** it's possible that the button has the focus and someone is typing to it. Whether it makes sense or not, those are events that you can detect and act upon in **handleEvent( )**.

To modify the **List** example so that it will react to single mouse clicks, the button detection will be left in **action( )** but the code to handle the **List** will be moved into **handleEvent( )** as follows:

```
//: List2.java
// Using lists with handleEvent()
import java.awt.*;
import java.applet.*;

public class List2 extends Applet {
  String[] flavors = { "Chocolate", "Strawberry",
    "Vanilla Fudge Swirl", "Mint Chip",
    "Mocha Almond Fudge", "Rum Raisin",
    "Praline Cream", "Mud Pie" };
  // Show 6 items, allow multiple selection:
  List lst = new List(6, true);
  TextArea t = new TextArea(flavors.length, 30);
  Button b = new Button("test");
  int count = 0;
  public void init() {
    t.setEditable(false);
    for(int i = 0; i < 4; i++)
      lst.addItem(flavors[count++]);
    add(t);
    add(lst);
    add(b);
  }
  public boolean handleEvent(Event evt) {
    if(evt.id == Event.LIST_SELECT ||
       evt.id == Event.LIST_DESELECT) {
      if(evt.target.equals(lst)) {
        t.setText("");
        String[] items = lst.getSelectedItems();
        for(int i = 0; i < items.length; i++)
          t.appendText(items[i] + "\n");
```

```
        }
      else
         return super.handleEvent(evt);
    }
    else
       return super.handleEvent(evt);
    return true;
  }
  public boolean action(Event evt, Object arg) {
    if(evt.target.equals(b)) {
      if(count < flavors.length)
         lst.addItem(flavors[count++], 0);
    }
    else
       return super.action(evt, arg);
    return true;
  }
} ///:~
```

The example is the same as before except for the addition of
handleEvent( ). Inside, a check is made to see whether a list selection or
deselection has occurred. Now remember, **handleEvent( )** is being
overridden for the applet, so this occurrence could be anywhere on the
form and it could be happening to another list. Thus, you must also
check to see what the target is. (Although in this case there's only one list
on the applet so we could have made the assumption that all list events
must be about that list. This is bad practice since it's going to be a
problem as soon as another list is added.) If the list matches the one we're
interested in, the same code as before will do the trick.

Note that the form for **handleEvent( )** is similar to **action( )**: if you deal
with a particular event you **return true**, but if you're not interested in
any of the other events via **handleEvent( )** you must **return
super.handleEvent(evt)**. This is vital because if you don't do this, none
of the other event-handling code will get called. For example, try
commenting out the **return super.handleEvent(evt)** in the code above.
You'll discover that **action( )** never gets called, certainly not what you
want. For both **action( )** and **handleEvent( )** it's important to follow the
format above and always return the base-class version of the method
when you do not handle the event yourself (in which case you should
return **true**). (Fortunately, these kinds of bug-prone details are relegated
to Java 1.0. The new design in Java 1.1 that you will see later in the
chapter eliminates these kinds of issues.)

In Windows, a list box automatically allows multiple selections if you hold down the shift key. This is nice because it allows the user to choose a single or multiple selection rather than fixing it during programming. You might think you'll be clever and implement this yourself by checking to see if the shift key is held down when a mouse click was made by testing for **evt.shiftDown( )**. Alas, the design of the AWT stymies you – you'd have to be able to know which item was clicked on if the shift key *wasn't* pressed so you could deselect all the rest and select only that one. However, you cannot figure that out in Java 1.0. (Java 1.1 sends all mouse, keyboard, and focus events to a **List**, so you'll be able to accomplish this.)

Controlling layout

The way that you place components on a form in Java is probably different from any other GUI system you've used. First, it's all code; there are no "resources" that control placement of components. Second, the way components are placed on a form is controlled by a "layout manager" that decides how the components lie based on the order that you **add( )** them. The size, shape, and placement of components will be remarkably different from one layout manager to another. In addition, the layout managers adapt to the dimensions of your applet or application window, so if that window dimension is changed (for example, in the HTML page's applet specification) the size, shape, and placement of the components could change.

Both the **Applet** and **Frame** classes are derived from **Container**, whose job it is to contain and display **Component**s. (The **Container** is a **Component** so it can also react to events.) In **Container,** there's a method called **setLayout( )** that allows you to choose a different layout manager.

In this section we'll explore the various layout managers by placing buttons in them (since that's the simplest thing to do). There won't be any capturing of button events since this is just intended to show how the buttons are laid out.

FlowLayout

So far, all the applets that have been created seem to have laid out their components using some mysterious internal logic. That's because the applet uses a default layout scheme: the **FlowLayout**. This simply "flows" the components onto the form, from left to right until the top

space is full, then moves down a row and continues flowing the
components.

Here's an example that explicitly (redundantly) sets the layout manager
in an applet to **FlowLayout** and then places buttons on the form. You'll
notice that with **FlowLayout** the components take on their "natural"
size. A **Button**, for example, will be the size of its string.

```
//: FlowLayout1.java
// Demonstrating the FlowLayout
import java.awt.*;
import java.applet.*;

public class FlowLayout1 extends Applet {
  public void init() {
    setLayout(new FlowLayout());
    for(int i = 0; i < 20; i++)
      add(new Button("Button " + i));
  }
} ///:~
```

All components will be compacted to their smallest size in a **FlowLayout**,
so you might get a little bit of surprising behavior. For example, a label
will be the size of its string, so right-justifying it yields an unchanged
display.

BorderLayout

This layout manager has the concept of four border regions and a center
area. When you add something to a panel that's using a **BorderLayout**
you must use an **add( )** method that takes a **String** object as its first
argument, and that string must specify (with proper capitalization)
"North" (top), "South" (bottom), "East" (right), "West" (left), or "Center."
If you misspell or mis-capitalize, you won't get a compile-time error, but
the applet simply won't do what you expect. Fortunately, as you will see
shortly, there's a much-improved approach in Java 1.1.

Here's a simple example:

```
//: BorderLayout1.java
// Demonstrating the BorderLayout
import java.awt.*;
import java.applet.*;

public class BorderLayout1 extends Applet {
```

```
   public void init() {
      int i = 0;
      setLayout(new BorderLayout());
      add("North", new Button("Button " + i++));
      add("South", new Button("Button " + i++));
      add("East", new Button("Button " + i++));
      add("West", new Button("Button " + i++));
      add("Center", new Button("Button " + i++));
   }
} ///:~
```

For every placement but "Center," the element that you add is compressed to fit in the smallest amount of space along one dimension while it is stretched to the maximum along the other dimension. "Center," however, spreads out along both dimensions to occupy the middle.

The **BorderLayout** is the default layout manager for applications and dialogs.

GridLayout

A **GridLayout** allows you to build a table of components, and as you add them they are placed left-to-right and top-to-bottom in the grid. In the constructor you specify the number of rows and columns that you need and these are laid out in equal proportions.

```
//: GridLayout1.java
// Demonstrating the FlowLayout
import java.awt.*;
import java.applet.*;

public class GridLayout1 extends Applet {
   public void init() {
      setLayout(new GridLayout(7,3));
      for(int i = 0; i < 20; i++)
         add(new Button("Button " + i));
   }
} ///:~
```

In this case there are 21 slots but only 20 buttons. The last slot is left empty; no "balancing" goes on with a **GridLayout**.

CardLayout

The **CardLayout** allows you to create the rough equivalent of a "tabbed dialog," which in more sophisticated environments has actual file-folder tabs running across one edge, and all you have to do is press a tab to bring forward a different dialog. Not so in the AWT: The **CardLayout** is simply a blank space and you're responsible for bringing forward new cards. (The JFC/Swing library contains tabbed panes that look much better and take care of all the details for you.)

Combining layouts

This example will combine more than one layout type, which seems rather difficult at first since only one layout manager can be operating for an applet or application. This is true, but if you create more **Panel** objects, each one of those **Panels** can have its own layout manager and then be integrated into the applet or application as simply another component, using the applet or application's layout manager. This gives you much greater flexibility as seen in the following example:

```
//: CardLayout1.java
// Demonstrating the CardLayout
import java.awt.*;
import java.applet.Applet;

class ButtonPanel extends Panel {
  ButtonPanel(String id) {
    setLayout(new BorderLayout());
    add("Center", new Button(id));
  }
}

public class CardLayout1 extends Applet {
  Button
    first = new Button("First"),
    second = new Button("Second"),
    third = new Button("Third");
  Panel cards = new Panel();
  CardLayout cl = new CardLayout();
  public void init() {
    setLayout(new BorderLayout());
    Panel p = new Panel();
    p.setLayout(new FlowLayout());
    p.add(first);
```

```
      p.add(second);
      p.add(third);
      add("North", p);
      cards.setLayout(cl);
      cards.add("First card",
        new ButtonPanel("The first one"));
      cards.add("Second card",
        new ButtonPanel("The second one"));
      cards.add("Third card",
        new ButtonPanel("The third one"));
      add("Center", cards);
   }
   public boolean action(Event evt, Object arg) {
      if (evt.target.equals(first)) {
        cl.first(cards);
      }
      else if (evt.target.equals(second)) {
        cl.first(cards);
        cl.next(cards);
      }
      else if (evt.target.equals(third)) {
        cl.last(cards);
      }
      else
        return super.action(evt, arg);
      return true;
   }
} ///:~
```

This example begins by creating a new kind of **Panel**: a **ButtonPanel**.
This contains a single button, placed at the center of a **BorderLayout**,
which means that it will expand to fill the entire panel. The label on the
button will let you know which panel you're on in the **CardLayout**.

In the applet, both the **Panel cards** where the cards will live and the
layout manager **cl** for the **CardLayout** must be members of the class
because you need to have access to those handles when you want to
manipulate the cards.

The applet is changed to use a **BorderLayout** instead of its default
FlowLayout, a **Panel** is created to hold three buttons (using a
FlowLayout), and this panel is placed at the "North" end of the applet.
The **cards** panel is added to the "Center" of the applet, effectively
occupying the rest of the real estate.

When you add the **ButtonPanel**s (or whatever other components you want) to the panel of cards, the **add( )** method's first argument is not "North," "South," etc. Instead, it's a string that describes the card. Although this string doesn't show up anywhere on the card, you can use it if you want to flip that card using the string. This approach is not used in **action( )**; instead the **first( )**, **next( )**, and **last( )** methods are used. Check your documentation for the other approach.

In Java, the use of some sort of "tabbed panel" mechanism is quite important because (as you'll see later) in applet programming the use of pop-up dialogs is heavily discouraged. For Java 1.0 applets, the **CardLayout** is the only viable way for the applet to have a number of different forms that "pop up" on command.

GridBagLayout

Some time ago, it was believed that all the stars, planets, the sun, and the moon revolved around the earth. It seemed intuitive from observation. But then astronomers became more sophisticated and started tracking the motion of individual objects, some of which seemed at times to go backward in their paths. Since it was known that everything revolved around the earth, those astronomers spent large amounts of time coming up with equations and theories to explain the motion of the stellar objects.

When trying to work with **GridBagLayout**, you can consider yourself the analog of one of those early astronomers. The basic precept (decreed, interestingly enough, by the designers at "Sun") is that everything should be done in code. The Copernican revolution (again dripping with irony, the discovery that the planets in the solar system revolve around the sun) is the use of *resources* to determine the layout and make the programmer's job easy. Until these are added to Java, you're stuck (to continue the metaphor) in the Spanish Inquisition of **GridBagLayout** and **GridBagConstraints**.

My recommendation is to avoid **GridBagLayout**. Instead, use the other layout managers and especially the technique of combining several panels using different layout managers within a single program. Your applets won't look *that* different; at least not enough to justify the trouble that **GridBagLayout** entails. For my part, it's just too painful to come up with an example for this (and I wouldn't want to encourage this kind of library design). Instead, I'll refer you to *Core Java* by Cornell & Horstmann (2nd ed., Prentice-Hall, 1997) to get started.

There's another light on the horizon: in the JFC/Swing library there is a new layout manager that uses Smalltalk's popular "Springs and Struts," and this could significantly reduce the need for **GridBagLayout**.

Alternatives to **action**

As noted previously, **action( )** isn't the only method that's automatically called by **handleEvent( )** once it sorts everything out for you. There are three other sets of methods that are called, and if you want to capture certain types of events (keyboard, mouse, and focus events) all you have to do is override the provided method. These methods are defined in the base class **Component**, so they're available in virtually all the controls that you might place on a form. However, you should be aware that this approach is deprecated in Java 1.1, so although you might see legacy code using this technique you should use the Java 1.1 approaches (described later in this chapter) instead.

Component method	When it's called
action (Event evt, Object what)	When the "typical" event occurs for this component (for example, when a button is pushed or a drop-down list item is selected)
keyDown (Event evt, int key)	A key is pressed when this component has the focus. The second argument is the key that was pressed and is redundantly copied from **evt.key**.
keyUp(Event evt, int key)	A key is released when this component has the focus.
lostFocus(Event evt, Object what)	The focus has moved away from the target. Normally, **what** is redundantly copied from **evt.arg**.
gotFocus(Event evt, Object what)	The focus has moved into the target.
mouseDown(Event evt, int x, int y)	A mouse down has occurred over the component, at the coordinates **x**, **y**.
mouseUp(Event evt, int x, int y)	A mouse up has occurred over the component.

Component method	When it's called
mouseMove(Event evt, int x, int y)	The mouse has moved while it's over the component.
mouseDrag(Event evt, int x, int y)	The mouse is being dragged after a **mouseDown** occurred over the component. All drag events are reported to the component in which the **mouseDown** occurred until there is a **mouseUp**.
mouseEnter(Event evt, int x, int y)	The mouse wasn't over the component before, but now it is.
mouseExit(Event evt, int x, int y)	The mouse used to be over the component, but now it isn't.

You can see that each method receives an **Event** object along with some information that you'll typically need when you're handling that particular situation – with a mouse event, for example, it's likely that you'll want to know the coordinates where the mouse event occurred. It's interesting to note that when **Component**'s **handleEvent( )** calls any of these methods (the typical case), the extra arguments are always redundant as they are contained within the **Event** object. In fact, if you look at the source code for **Component.handleEvent( )** you can see that it explicitly plucks the additional arguments out of the **Event** object. (This might be considered inefficient coding in some languages, but remember that Java's focus is on safety, not necessarily speed.)

To prove to yourself that these events are in fact being called and as an interesting experiment, it's worth creating an applet that overrides each of the methods above (except for **action( )**, which is overridden in many other places in this chapter) and displays data about each of the events as they happen.

This example also shows you how to make your own button object because that's what is used as the target of all the events of interest. You might first (naturally) assume that to make a new button, you'd inherit from **Button**. But this doesn't work. Instead, you inherit from **Canvas** (a much more generic component) and paint your button on that canvas by overriding the **paint( )** method. As you'll see, it's really too bad that overriding **Button** doesn't work, since there's a bit of code involved to paint the button. (If you don't believe me, try exchanging **Button** for **Canvas** in this example, and remember to call the base-class constructor **super(label)**. You'll see that the button doesn't get painted and the events don't get handled.)

The **myButton** class is specific: it works only with an **AutoEvent** "parent window" (not a base class, but the window in which this button is created and lives). With this knowledge, **myButton** can reach into the parent window and manipulate its text fields, which is what's necessary to be able to write the status information into the fields of the parent. Of course this is a much more limited solution, since **myButton** can be used only in conjunction with **AutoEvent**. This kind of code is sometimes called "highly coupled." However, to make **myButton** more generic requires a lot more effort that isn't warranted for this example (and possibly for many of the applets that you will write). Again, keep in mind that the following code uses APIs that are deprecated in Java 1.1.

```
//: AutoEvent.java
// Alternatives to action()
import java.awt.*;
import java.applet.*;
import java.util.*;

class MyButton extends Canvas {
  AutoEvent parent;
  Color color;
  String label;
  MyButton(AutoEvent parent,
           Color color, String label) {
    this.label = label;
    this.parent = parent;
    this.color = color;
  }
  public void paint(Graphics  g) {
    g.setColor(color);
    int rnd = 30;
    g.fillRoundRect(0, 0, size().width,
                    size().height, rnd, rnd);
    g.setColor(Color.black);
    g.drawRoundRect(0, 0, size().width,
                    size().height, rnd, rnd);
    FontMetrics fm = g.getFontMetrics();
    int width = fm.stringWidth(label);
    int height = fm.getHeight();
    int ascent = fm.getAscent();
    int leading = fm.getLeading();
    int horizMargin = (size().width - width)/2;
    int verMargin = (size().height - height)/2;
    g.setColor(Color.white);
    g.drawString(label, horizMargin,
```

```
                    verMargin + ascent + leading);
    }
    public boolean keyDown(Event evt, int key) {
      TextField t =
        (TextField)parent.h.get("keyDown");
      t.setText(evt.toString());
      return true;
    }
    public boolean keyUp(Event evt, int key) {
      TextField t =
        (TextField)parent.h.get("keyUp");
      t.setText(evt.toString());
      return true;
    }
    public boolean lostFocus(Event evt, Object w) {
      TextField t =
        (TextField)parent.h.get("lostFocus");
      t.setText(evt.toString());
      return true;
    }
    public boolean gotFocus(Event evt, Object w) {
      TextField t =
        (TextField)parent.h.get("gotFocus");
      t.setText(evt.toString());
      return true;
    }
    public boolean
    mouseDown(Event evt,int x,int y) {
      TextField t =
        (TextField)parent.h.get("mouseDown");
      t.setText(evt.toString());
      return true;
    }
    public boolean
    mouseDrag(Event evt,int x,int y) {
      TextField t =
        (TextField)parent.h.get("mouseDrag");
      t.setText(evt.toString());
      return true;
    }
    public boolean
    mouseEnter(Event evt,int x,int y) {
      TextField t =
        (TextField)parent.h.get("mouseEnter");
```

```
          t.setText(evt.toString());
          return true;
        }
        public boolean
        mouseExit(Event evt,int x,int y) {
          TextField t =
            (TextField)parent.h.get("mouseExit");
          t.setText(evt.toString());
          return true;
        }
        public boolean
        mouseMove(Event evt,int x,int y) {
          TextField t =
            (TextField)parent.h.get("mouseMove");
          t.setText(evt.toString());
          return true;
        }
        public boolean mouseUp(Event evt,int x,int y) {
          TextField t =
            (TextField)parent.h.get("mouseUp");
          t.setText(evt.toString());
          return true;
        }
      }

    public class AutoEvent extends Applet {
      Hashtable h = new Hashtable();
      String[] event = {
        "keyDown", "keyUp", "lostFocus",
        "gotFocus", "mouseDown", "mouseUp",
        "mouseMove", "mouseDrag", "mouseEnter",
        "mouseExit"
      };
      MyButton
        b1 = new MyButton(this, Color.blue, "test1"),
        b2 = new MyButton(this, Color.red, "test2");
      public void init() {
        setLayout(new GridLayout(event.length+1,2));
        for(int i = 0; i < event.length; i++) {
          TextField t = new TextField();
          t.setEditable(false);
          add(new Label(event[i], Label.CENTER));
          add(t);
          h.put(event[i], t);
```

```
        }
        add(b1);
        add(b2);
    }
} ///:~
```

You can see the constructor uses the technique of using the same name for the argument as what it's assigned to, and differentiating between the two using **this**:

```
    this.label = label;
```

The **paint( )** method starts out simple: it fills a "round rectangle" with the button's color, and then draws a black line around it. Notice the use of **size( )** to determine the width and height of the component (in pixels, of course). After this, **paint( )** seems quite complicated because there's a lot of calculation going on to figure out how to center the button's label inside the button using the "font metrics." You can get a pretty good idea of what's going on by looking at the method call, and it turns out that this is pretty stock code, so you can just cut and paste it when you want to center a label inside any component.

You can't understand exactly how the **keyDown( )**, **keyUp( )**, etc. methods work until you look down at the **AutoEvent** class. This contains a **Hashtable** to hold the strings representing the type of event and the **TextField** where information about that event is held. Of course, these could have been created statically rather than putting them in a **Hashtable**, but I think you'll agree that it's a lot easier to use and change. In particular, if you need to add or remove a new type of event in **AutoEvent**, you simply add or remove a string in the **event** array – everything else happens automatically.

The place where you look up the strings is in the **keyDown( )**, **keyUp( )**, etc. methods back in **MyButton**. Each of these methods uses the **parent** handle to reach back to the parent window. Since that parent is an **AutoEvent** it contains the **Hashtable h**, and the **get( )** method, when provided with the appropriate **String**, will produce a handle to an **Object** that we happen to know is a **TextField** – so it is cast to that. Then the **Event** object is converted to its **String** representation, which is displayed in the **TextField**.

It turns out this example is rather fun to play with since you can really see what's going on with the events in your program.

Applet restrictions

For safety's sake, applets are quite restricted and there are many things you can't do. You can generally answer the question of what an applet is able to do by looking at what it is *supposed* to do: extend the functionality of a Web page in a browser. Since, as a net surfer, you never really know if a Web page is from a friendly place or not, you want any code that it runs to be safe. So the biggest restrictions you'll notice are probably:

1) *An applet can't touch the local disk*. This means writing *or* reading, since you wouldn't want an applet to read and transmit important information about you across the Web. Writing is prevented, of course, since that would be an open invitation to a virus. These restrictions can be relaxed when digital signing is fully implemented.

2) *An applet can't have menus.* (Note: this is fixed in Swing) This is probably less oriented toward safety and more toward reducing confusion. You might have noticed that an applet looks like it blends right in as part of a Web page; you often don't see the boundaries of the applet. There's no frame or title bar to hang the menu from, other than the one belonging to the Web browser. Perhaps the design could be changed to allow you to merge your applet menu with the browser menu – that would be complicated and would also get a bit too close to the edge of safety by allowing the applet to affect its environment.

3) *Dialog boxes are "untrusted."* In Java, dialog boxes present a bit of a quandary. First of all, they're not exactly disallowed in applets but they're heavily discouraged. If you pop up a dialog box from within an applet you'll get an "untrusted applet" message attached to that dialog. This is because, in theory, it would be possible to fool the user into thinking that they're dealing with a regular native application and to get them to type in their credit card number, which then goes across the Web. After seeing the kinds of GUIs that the AWT produces you might have a hard time believing *anybody* could be fooled that way. But an applet is always attached to a Web page and visible within your Web browser, while a dialog box is detached so in theory it could be possible. As a result it will be rare to see an applet that uses a dialog box.

Many applet restrictions are relaxed for trusted applets (those signed by a trusted source) in newer browsers.

There are other issues when thinking about applet development:

♦ Applets take longer to download since you must download the whole thing every time, including a separate server hit for each different class. Your browser can cache the applet, but there are no guarantees. One improvement in Java 1.1 is the JAR (Java ARchive) file that allows packaging of all the applet components (including other **.class** files as well as images and sounds) together into a single compressed file that can be downloaded in a single server transaction. "Digital signing" (the ability to verify the creator of a class) is available for each individual entry in the JAR file.

♦ Because of security issues you must work harder to do certain things such as accessing databases and sending email. In addition, the security restrictions make accessing multiple hosts difficult, since everything has to be routed through the Web server, which then becomes a performance bottleneck and a single failure point that can stop the entire process.

♦ An applet within the browser doesn't have the same kind of control that a native application does. For example, you can't have a modal dialog box within an applet, since the user can always switch the page. When the user *does* change from a Web page or even exit the browser, the results can be catastrophic for your applet – there's no way to save the state so if you're in the middle of a transaction or other operation the information can be lost. In addition, different browsers do different things to your applet when you leave a Web page so the results are essentially undefined.

Applet advantages

If you can live within the restrictions, applets have definite advantages, especially when building client/server or other networked applications:

♦ There is no installation issue. An applet has true platform independence (including the ability to easily play audio files, etc.) so you don't need to make any changes in your code for different platforms nor does anyone have to perform any "tweaking" upon installation. In fact, installation is automatic every time the user loads the Web page along with the applets, so updates happen silently and automatically. In traditional client/server systems, building and installing a new version of the client software is often a nightmare.

♦ Because of the security built into the core Java language and the applet structure, you don't have to worry about bad code causing damage to someone's system. This, along with the previous point, makes Java (as well as alternative client-side Web programming tools like JavaScript and VBScript) popular for so-called *Intranet* client/server applications that live only within the company and don't move out onto the Internet.

♦ Because applets are automatically integrated with HTML, you have a built-in platform-independent documentation system to support the applet. It's an interesting twist, since we're used to having the documentation part of the program rather than vice versa.

Windowed applications

It's possible to see that for safety's sake you can have only limited behavior within an applet. In a real sense, the applet is a temporary extension to the Web browser so its functionality must be limited along with its knowledge and control. There are times, however, when you'd like to make a windowed program do something else than sit on a Web page, and perhaps you'd like it to do some of the things a "regular" application can do and yet have the vaunted instant portability provided by Java. In previous chapters in this book we've made command-line applications, but in some operating environments (the Macintosh, for example) there isn't a command line. So for any number of reasons you'd like to build a windowed, non-applet program using Java. This is certainly a reasonable desire.

A Java windowed application can have menus and dialog boxes (impossible or difficult with an applet), and yet if you're using an older version of Java you sacrifice the native operating environment's look and feel. The JFC/Swing library allows you to make an application that preserves the look and feel of the underlying operating environment. If you want to build windowed applications, it makes sense to do so only if you can use the latest version of Java and associated tools so you can deliver applications that won't confound your users. If for some reason you're forced to use an older version of Java, think hard before committing to building a significant windowed application.

Menus

It's impossible to put a menu directly on an applet (in Java 1.0 and Java 1.1; the Swing library *does* allow it), so they're for applications. Go ahead, try it if you don't believe me and you're sure that it would make sense to have menus on applets. There's no **setMenuBar( )** method in **Applet** and that's the way a menu is attached. (You'll see later that it's possible to spawn a **Frame** from within an **Applet**, and the **Frame** can contain menus.)

There are four different types of **MenuComponent**, all derived from that abstract class: **MenuBar** (you can have one **MenuBar** only on a particular **Frame**), **Menu** to hold one individual drop-down menu or submenu, **MenuItem** to represent one single element on a menu, and **CheckboxMenuItem**, which is derived from **MenuItem** and produces a checkmark to indicate whether that menu item is selected.

Unlike a system that uses resources, with Java and the AWT you must hand assemble all the menus in source code. Here are the ice cream flavors again, used to create menus:

```java
//: Menu1.java
// Menus work only with Frames.
// Shows submenus, checkbox menu items
// and swapping menus.
import java.awt.*;

public class Menu1 extends Frame {
  String[] flavors = { "Chocolate", "Strawberry",
    "Vanilla Fudge Swirl", "Mint Chip",
    "Mocha Almond Fudge", "Rum Raisin",
    "Praline Cream", "Mud Pie" };
  TextField t = new TextField("No flavor", 30);
  MenuBar mb1 = new MenuBar();
  Menu f = new Menu("File");
  Menu m = new Menu("Flavors");
  Menu s = new Menu("Safety");
  // Alternative approach:
  CheckboxMenuItem[] safety = {
    new CheckboxMenuItem("Guard"),
    new CheckboxMenuItem("Hide")
  };
  MenuItem[] file = {
    new MenuItem("Open"),
    new MenuItem("Exit")
  };
  // A second menu bar to swap to:
  MenuBar mb2 = new MenuBar();
  Menu fooBar = new Menu("fooBar");
  MenuItem[] other = {
    new MenuItem("Foo"),
    new MenuItem("Bar"),
```

```
      new MenuItem("Baz"),
  };
  Button b = new Button("Swap Menus");
  public Menu1() {
    for(int i = 0; i < flavors.length; i++) {
      m.add(new MenuItem(flavors[i]));
      // Add separators at intervals:
      if((i+1) % 3 == 0)
        m.addSeparator();
    }
    for(int i = 0; i < safety.length; i++)
      s.add(safety[i]);
    f.add(s);
    for(int i = 0; i < file.length; i++)
      f.add(file[i]);
    mb1.add(f);
    mb1.add(m);
    setMenuBar(mb1);
    t.setEditable(false);
    add("Center", t);
    // Set up the system for swapping menus:
    add("North", b);
    for(int i = 0; i < other.length; i++)
      fooBar.add(other[i]);
    mb2.add(fooBar);
  }
  public boolean handleEvent(Event evt) {
    if(evt.id == Event.WINDOW_DESTROY)
      System.exit(0);
    else
      return super.handleEvent(evt);
    return true;
  }
  public boolean action(Event evt, Object arg) {
    if(evt.target.equals(b)) {
      MenuBar m = getMenuBar();
      if(m == mb1) setMenuBar(mb2);
      else if (m == mb2) setMenuBar(mb1);
    }
    else if(evt.target instanceof MenuItem) {
      if(arg.equals("Open")) {
        String s = t.getText();
        boolean chosen = false;
        for(int i = 0; i < flavors.length; i++)
```

```
                    if(s.equals(flavors[i])) chosen = true;
                  if(!chosen)
                    t.setText("Choose a flavor first!");
                  else
                    t.setText("Opening "+ s +". Mmm, mm!");
                }
                else if(evt.target.equals(file[1]))
                  System.exit(0);
                // CheckboxMenuItems cannot use String
                // matching; you must match the target:
                else if(evt.target.equals(safety[0]))
                  t.setText("Guard the Ice Cream! " +
                      "Guarding is " + safety[0].getState());
                else if(evt.target.equals(safety[1]))
                  t.setText("Hide the Ice Cream! " +
                      "Is it cold? " + safety[1].getState());
                else
                  t.setText(arg.toString());
              }
              else
                return super.action(evt, arg);
              return true;
            }
            public static void main(String[] args) {
              Menu1 f = new Menu1();
              f.resize(300,200);
              f.show();
            }
          } ///:~
```

In this program I avoided the typical long lists of **add( )** calls for each menu because that seemed like a lot of unnecessary typing. Instead, I placed the menu items into arrays and then simply stepped through each array calling **add( )** in a **for** loop. This makes adding or subtracting a menu item less tedious.

As an alternative approach (which I find less desirable since it requires more typing), the **CheckboxMenuItem**s are created in an array of handles called **safety**; this is true for the arrays **file** and **other** as well.

This program creates not one but two **MenuBar**s to demonstrate that menu bars can be actively swapped while the program is running. You can see how a **MenuBar** is made up of **Menu**s, and each **Menu** is made up of **MenuItem**s, **CheckboxMenuItem**s, or even other **Menu**s (which produce submenus). When a **MenuBar** is assembled it can be installed into the current program with the **setMenuBar( )** method. Note that when the button is pressed, it checks to see which menu is currently installed using **getMenuBar( )**, then puts the other menu bar in its place.

When testing for "Open," notice that spelling and capitalization are critical, but Java signals no error if there is no match with "Open." This kind of string comparison is a clear source of programming errors.

The checking and un-checking of the menu items is taken care of automatically, but dealing with CheckboxMenuItems can be a bit surprising since for some reason they don't allow string matching. (Although string matching isn't a good approach, this seems inconsistent.) So you can match only the target object and not its label. As shown, the **getState( )** method can be used to reveal the state. You can also change the state of a **CheckboxMenuItem** with **setState( )**.

You might think that one menu could reasonably reside on more than one menu bar. This does seem to make sense because all you're passing to the **MenuBar add( )** method is a handle. However, if you try this, the behavior will be strange and not what you expect. (It's difficult to know if this is a bug or if they intended it to work this way.)

This example also shows what you need to do to create an application instead of an applet. (Again, because an application can support menus and an applet cannot directly have a menu.) Instead of inheriting from **Applet**, you inherit from **Frame**. Instead of **init( )** to set things up, you make a constructor for your class. Finally, you create a **main( )** and in that you build an object of your new type, resize it, and then call **show( )**. It's different from an applet in only a few small places, but it's now a standalone windowed application and you've got menus.

Dialog boxes

A dialog box is a window that pops up out of another window. Its purpose is to deal with some specific issue without cluttering the original window with those details. Dialog boxes are heavily used in windowed programming environments, but as mentioned previously, rarely used in applets.

To create a dialog box, you inherit from **Dialog**, which is just another kind of **Window**, like a **Frame**. Unlike a **Frame**, a **Dialog** cannot have a menu bar or change the cursor, but other than that they're quite similar. A dialog has a layout manager (which defaults to **BorderLayout**) and you override **action( )** etc., or **handleEvent( )** to deal with events. One significant difference you'll want to note in **handleEvent( )**: when the

WINDOW_DESTROY event occurs, you don't want to shut down the application! Instead, you release the resources used by the dialog's window by calling **dispose( )**.

In the following example, the dialog box is made up of a grid (using **GridLayout**) of a special kind of button that is defined here as class **ToeButton**. This button draws a frame around itself and, depending on its state, a blank, an "x," or an "o" in the middle. It starts out blank, and then depending on whose turn it is, changes to an "x" or an "o." However, it will also flip back and forth between "x" and "o" when you click on the button. (This makes the tic-tac-toe concept only slightly more annoying than it already is.) In addition, the dialog box can be set up for any number of rows and columns by changing numbers in the main application window.

```java
//: ToeTest.java
// Demonstration of dialog boxes
// and creating your own components
import java.awt.*;

class ToeButton extends Canvas {
  int state = ToeDialog.BLANK;
  ToeDialog parent;
  ToeButton(ToeDialog parent) {
    this.parent = parent;
  }
  public void paint(Graphics  g) {
    int x1 = 0;
    int y1 = 0;
    int x2 = size().width - 1;
    int y2 = size().height - 1;
    g.drawRect(x1, y1, x2, y2);
    x1 = x2/4;
    y1 = y2/4;
    int wide = x2/2;
    int high = y2/2;
    if(state == ToeDialog.XX) {
      g.drawLine(x1, y1, x1 + wide, y1 + high);
      g.drawLine(x1, y1 + high, x1 + wide, y1);
    }
    if(state == ToeDialog.OO) {
      g.drawOval(x1, y1, x1+wide/2, y1+high/2);
    }
  }
  public boolean
```

```
    mouseDown(Event evt, int x, int y) {
      if(state == ToeDialog.BLANK) {
        state = parent.turn;
        parent.turn= (parent.turn == ToeDialog.XX ?
          ToeDialog.OO : ToeDialog.XX);
      }
      else
        state = (state == ToeDialog.XX ?
          ToeDialog.OO : ToeDialog.XX);
      repaint();
      return true;
    }
}

class ToeDialog extends Dialog {
  // w = number of cells wide
  // h = number of cells high
  static final int BLANK = 0;
  static final int XX = 1;
  static final int OO = 2;
  int turn = XX; // Start with x's turn
  public ToeDialog(Frame parent, int w, int h) {
    super(parent, "The game itself", false);
    setLayout(new GridLayout(w, h));
    for(int i = 0; i < w * h; i++)
      add(new ToeButton(this));
    resize(w * 50, h * 50);
  }
  public boolean handleEvent(Event evt) {
    if(evt.id == Event.WINDOW_DESTROY)
      dispose();
    else
      return super.handleEvent(evt);
    return true;
  }
}

public class ToeTest extends Frame {
  TextField rows = new TextField("3");
  TextField cols = new TextField("3");
  public ToeTest() {
    setTitle("Toe Test");
    Panel p = new Panel();
    p.setLayout(new GridLayout(2,2));
```

```
      p.add(new Label("Rows", Label.CENTER));
      p.add(rows);
      p.add(new Label("Columns", Label.CENTER));
      p.add(cols);
      add("North", p);
      add("South", new Button("go"));
    }
    public boolean handleEvent(Event evt) {
      if(evt.id == Event.WINDOW_DESTROY)
        System.exit(0);
      else
        return super.handleEvent(evt);
      return true;
    }
    public boolean action(Event evt, Object arg) {
      if(arg.equals("go")) {
        Dialog d = new ToeDialog(
          this,
          Integer.parseInt(rows.getText()),
          Integer.parseInt(cols.getText()));
        d.show();
      }
      else
        return super.action(evt, arg);
      return true;
    }
    public static void main(String[] args) {
      Frame f = new ToeTest();
      f.resize(200,100);
      f.show();
    }
  } ///:~
```

The **ToeButton** class keeps a handle to its parent, which must be of type
ToeDialog. As before, this introduces high coupling because a **ToeButton**
can be used only with a **ToeDialog**, but it solves a number of problems,
and in truth it doesn't seem like such a bad solution because there's no
other kind of dialog that's keeping track of whose turn it is. Of course,
you can take another approach, which is to make **ToeDialog.turn** a
static member of **ToeButton**. This eliminates the coupling, but prevents
you from having more than one **ToeDialog** at a time. (More than one
that works properly, anyway.)

The **paint( )** method is concerned with the graphics: drawing the square around the button and drawing the "x" or the "o." This is full of tedious calculations, but it's straightforward.

A mouse click is captured by the overridden **mouseDown( )** method, which first checks to see if the button has anything written on it. If not, the parent window is queried to find out whose turn it is and that is used to establish the state of the button. Note that the button then reaches back into the parent and changes the turn. If the button is already displaying an "x" or an "o" then that is flopped. You can see in these calculations the convenient use of the ternary if-else described in Chapter 3. After a button state change, the button is repainted.

The constructor for **ToeDialog** is quite simple: it adds into a **GridLayout** as many buttons as you request, then resizes it for 50 pixels on a side for each button. (If you don't resize a **Window**, it won't show up!) Note that **handleEvent( )** just calls **dispose( )** for a **WINDOW_DESTROY** so the whole application doesn't go away.

ToeTest sets up the whole application by creating the **TextField**s (for inputting the rows and columns of the button grid) and the "go" button. You'll see in **action( )** that this program uses the less-desirable "string match" technique for detecting the button press (make sure you get spelling and capitalization right!). When the button is pressed, the data in the **TextField**s must be fetched, and, since they are in **String** form, turned into **int**s using the **static Integer.parseInt( )** method. Once the **Dialog** is created, the **show( )** method must be called to display and activate it.

You'll notice that the **ToeDialog** object is assigned to a **Dialog** handle **d**. This is an example of upcasting, although it really doesn't make much difference here since all that's happening is the **show( )** method is called. However, if you wanted to call some method that existed only in **ToeDialog** you would want to assign to a **ToeDialog** handle and not lose the information in an upcast.

File dialogs

Some operating systems have a number of special built-in dialog boxes to handle the selection of things such as fonts, colors, printers, and the like. Virtually all graphical operating systems support the opening and saving of files, however, and so Java's **FileDialog** encapsulates these for easy use. This, of course, makes no sense at all to use from an applet since an applet can neither read nor write files on the local disk. (This will change for trusted applets in newer browsers.)

The following application exercises the two forms of file dialogs, one for opening and one for saving. Most of the code should by now be familiar, and all the interesting activities happen in **action( )** for the two different button clicks:

```
//: FileDialogTest.java
// Demonstration of File dialog boxes
import java.awt.*;

public class FileDialogTest extends Frame {
  TextField filename = new TextField();
  TextField directory = new TextField();
  Button open = new Button("Open");
  Button save = new Button("Save");
  public FileDialogTest() {
    setTitle("File Dialog Test");
    Panel p = new Panel();
    p.setLayout(new FlowLayout());
    p.add(open);
    p.add(save);
    add("South", p);
    directory.setEditable(false);
    filename.setEditable(false);
    p = new Panel();
    p.setLayout(new GridLayout(2,1));
    p.add(filename);
    p.add(directory);
    add("North", p);
  }
  public boolean handleEvent(Event evt) {
    if(evt.id == Event.WINDOW_DESTROY)
      System.exit(0);
    else
      return super.handleEvent(evt);
    return true;
  }
  public boolean action(Event evt, Object arg) {
    if(evt.target.equals(open)) {
      // Two arguments, defaults to open file:
      FileDialog d = new FileDialog(this,
        "What file do you want to open?");
      d.setFile("*.java"); // Filename filter
      d.setDirectory("."); // Current directory
      d.show();
      String openFile;
```

```
          if((openFile = d.getFile()) != null) {
            filename.setText(openFile);
            directory.setText(d.getDirectory());
          } else {
            filename.setText("You pressed cancel");
            directory.setText("");
          }
        }
        else if(evt.target.equals(save)) {
          FileDialog d = new FileDialog(this,
            "What file do you want to save?",
            FileDialog.SAVE);
          d.setFile("*.java");
          d.setDirectory(".");
          d.show();
          String saveFile;
          if((saveFile = d.getFile()) != null) {
            filename.setText(saveFile);
            directory.setText(d.getDirectory());
          } else {
            filename.setText("You pressed cancel");
            directory.setText("");
          }
        }
        else
          return super.action(evt, arg);
        return true;
      }
      public static void main(String[] args) {
        Frame f = new FileDialogTest();
        f.resize(250,110);
        f.show();
      }
    } ///:~
```

For an "open file" dialog, you use the constructor that takes two
arguments; the first is the parent window handle and the second is the
title for the title bar of the **FileDialog**. The method **setFile( )** provides an
initial file name – presumably the native OS supports wildcards, so in this
example all the **.java** files will initially be displayed. The **setDirectory( )**
method chooses the directory where the file selection will begin. (In
general, the OS allows the user to change directories.)

The **show( )** command doesn't return until the dialog is closed. The
FileDialog object still exists, so you can read data from it. If you call

---

getFile( ) and it returns **null** it means the user canceled out of the dialog. Both the file name and the results of **getDirectory( )** are displayed in the **TextField**s.

The button for saving works the same way, except that it uses a different constructor for the **FileDialog**. This constructor takes three arguments and the third argument must be either **FileDialog.SAVE** or **FileDialog.OPEN**.

The new AWT

In Java 1.1 a dramatic change has been accomplished in the creation of the new AWT. Most of this change revolves around the new event model used in Java 1.1: as bad, awkward, and non-object-oriented as the old event model was, the new event model is possibly the most elegant I have seen. It's difficult to understand how such a bad design (the old AWT) and such a good one (the new event model) could come out of the same group. This new way of thinking about events seems to drop so easily into your mind that the issue no longer becomes an impediment; instead, it's a tool that helps you design the system. It's also essential for Java Beans, described later in the chapter.

Instead of the non-object-oriented cascaded **if** statements in the old AWT, the new approach designates objects as "sources" and "listeners" of events. As you will see, the use of inner classes is integral to the object-oriented nature of the new event model. In addition, events are now represented in a class hierarchy instead of a single class, and you can create your own event types.

You'll also find, if you've programmed with the old AWT, that Java 1.1 has made a number of what might seem like gratuitous name changes. For example, **setSize( )** replaces **resize( )**. This will make sense when you learn about Java Beans, because Beans use a particular naming convention. The names had to be modified to make the standard AWT components into Beans.

Java 1.1 continues to support the old AWT to ensure backward compatibility with existing programs. Without fully admitting disaster, the online documents for Java 1.1 list all the problems involved with programming the old AWT and describe how those problems are addressed in the new AWT.

Clipboard operations are supported in 1.1, although drag-and-drop "will be supported in a future release." You can access the desktop color scheme so your Java program can fit in with the rest of the desktop. Pop-up menus are available, and there are some improvements for graphics and images. Mouseless operation is supported. There is a simple API for printing and simplified support for scrolling.

The new event model

In the new event model a component can initiate ("fire") an event. Each type of event is represented by a distinct class. When an event is fired, it is received by one or more "listeners," which act on that event. Thus, the source of an event and the place where the event is handled can be separate.

Each event listener is an object of a class that implements a particular type of listener **interface**. So as a programmer, all you do is create a listener object and register it with the component that's firing the event. This registration is performed by calling a **addXXXListener( )** method in the event-firing component, in which **XXX** represents the type of event listened for. You can easily know what types of events can be handled by noticing the names of the addListener methods, and if you try to listen for the wrong events you'll find out your mistake at compile time. Java Beans also uses the names of the addListener methods to determine what a Bean can do.

All of your event logic, then, will go inside a listener class. When you create a listener class, the sole restriction is that it must implement the appropriate interface. You can create a global listener class, but this is a situation in which inner classes tend to be quite useful, not only because they provide a logical grouping of your listener classes inside the UI or business logic classes they are serving, but because (as you shall see later) the fact that an inner class object keeps a handle to its parent object provides a nice way to call across class and subsystem boundaries.

A simple example will make this clear. Consider the **Button2.java** example from earlier in this chapter.

```
//: Button2New.java
// Capturing button presses
import java.awt.*;
import java.awt.event.*; // Must add this
import java.applet.*;

public class Button2New extends Applet {
  Button
    b1 = new Button("Button 1"),
```

```
      b2 = new Button("Button 2");
   public void init() {
      b1.addActionListener(new B1());
      b2.addActionListener(new B2());
      add(b1);
      add(b2);
   }
   class B1 implements ActionListener {
      public void actionPerformed(ActionEvent e) {
         getAppletContext().showStatus("Button 1");
      }
   }
   class B2 implements ActionListener {
      public void actionPerformed(ActionEvent e) {
         getAppletContext().showStatus("Button 2");
      }
   }
   /* The old way:
   public boolean action(Event evt, Object arg) {
      if(evt.target.equals(b1))
         getAppletContext().showStatus("Button 1");
      else if(evt.target.equals(b2))
         getAppletContext().showStatus("Button 2");
      // Let the base class handle it:
      else
         return super.action(evt, arg);
      return true; // We've handled it here
   }
   */
} ///:~
```

So you can compare the two approaches, the old code is left in as a
comment. In **init( )**, the only change is the addition of the two lines:

```
b1.addActionListener(new B1());
b2.addActionListener(new B2());
```

addActionListener( ) tells a button which object to activate when the
button is pressed. The classes **B1** and **B2** are inner classes that implement
the **interface ActionListener**. This interface contains a single method
actionPerformed( ) (meaning "This is the action that will be performed
when the event is fired"). Note that **actionPerformed( )** does not take a
generic event, but rather a specific type of event, **ActionEvent**. So you
don't need to bother testing and downcasting the argument if you want
to extract specific **ActionEvent** information.

One of the nicest things about **actionPerformed( )** is how simple it is. It's just a method that gets called. Compare it to the old **action( )** method, in which you must figure out what happened and act appropriately, and also worry about calling the base class version of **action( )** and return a value to indicate whether it's been handled. With the new event model you know that all the event-detection logic is taken care of so you don't have to figure that out; you just say what happens and you're done. If you're don't already prefer this approach over the old one, you will soon.

Event and listener types

All the AWT components have been changed to include **addXXXListener( )** and **removeXXXListener( )** methods so that the appropriate types of listeners can be added and removed from each component. You'll notice that the "**XXX**" in each case also represents the argument for the method, for example, **addFooListener(FooListener fl)**. The following table includes the associated events, listeners, methods, and the components that support those particular events by providing the **addXXXListener( )** and **removeXXXListener( )** methods.

Event, listener interface and add- and remove-methods	Components supporting this event
ActionEvent **ActionListener** **addActionListener( )** **removeActionListener( )**	**Button, List, TextField, MenuItem,** and its derivatives including **CheckboxMenuItem, Menu,** and **PopupMenu**
AdjustmentEvent **AdjustmentListener** **addAdjustmentListener( )** **removeAdjustmentListener( )**	**Scrollbar** Anything you create that implements the **Adjustable** interface
ComponentEvent **ComponentListener** **addComponentListener( )** **removeComponentListener( )**	**Component** and its derivatives, including **Button, Canvas, Checkbox, Choice, Container, Panel, Applet, ScrollPane, Window, Dialog, FileDialog, Frame, Label, List, Scrollbar, TextArea,** and **TextField**
ContainerEvent **ContainerListener** **addContainerListener( )** **removeContainerListener( )**	**Container** and its derivatives, including **Panel, Applet, ScrollPane, Window, Dialog, FileDialog,** and **Frame**
FocusEvent **FocusListener**	**Component** and its derivatives, including **Button, Canvas,**

Event, listener interface and add- and remove-methods	Components supporting this event
addFocusListener( ) removeFocusListener( )	**Checkbox, Choice, Container, Panel, Applet, ScrollPane, Window, Dialog, FileDialog, Frame Label, List, Scrollbar, TextArea**, and **TextField**
KeyEvent KeyListener addKeyListener( ) removeKeyListener( )	**Component** and its derivatives, including **Button, Canvas, Checkbox, Choice, Container, Panel, Applet, ScrollPane, Window, Dialog, FileDialog, Frame, Label, List, Scrollbar, TextArea**, and **TextField**
MouseEvent (for both clicks and motion) **MouseListener** addMouseListener( ) removeMouseListener( )	**Component** and its derivatives, including **Button, Canvas, Checkbox, Choice, Container, Panel, Applet, ScrollPane, Window, Dialog, FileDialog, Frame, Label, List, Scrollbar, TextArea**, and **TextField**
MouseEvent[5] (for both clicks and motion) **MouseMotionListener** addMouseMotionListener( ) removeMouseMotionListener( )	**Component** and its derivatives, including **Button, Canvas, Checkbox, Choice, Container, Panel, Applet, ScrollPane, Window, Dialog, FileDialog, Frame, Label, List, Scrollbar, TextArea**, and **TextField**
WindowEvent WindowListener addWindowListener( ) removeWindowListener( )	**Window** and its derivatives, including **Dialog, FileDialog**, and **Frame**
ItemEvent ItemListener addItemListener( ) removeItemListener( )	**Checkbox, CheckboxMenuItem, Choice, List**, and anything that implements the **ItemSelectable** interface
TextEvent TextListener	Anything derived from **TextComponent**, including

---

[5] There is no **MouseMotionEvent** even though it seems like there ought to be. Clicking and motion is combined into **MouseEvent**, so this second appearance of **MouseEvent** in the table is not an error.

Event, listener interface and add- and remove-methods	Components supporting this event
addTextListener( ) **removeTextListener( )**	**TextArea** and **TextField**

You can see that each type of component supports only certain types of events. It's helpful to see the events supported by each component, as shown in the following table:

Component type	Events supported by this component
Adjustable	**AdjustmentEvent**
Applet	**ContainerEvent, FocusEvent, KeyEvent, MouseEvent, ComponentEvent**
Button	**ActionEvent, FocusEvent, KeyEvent, MouseEvent, ComponentEvent**
Canvas	**FocusEvent, KeyEvent, MouseEvent, ComponentEvent**
Checkbox	**ItemEvent, FocusEvent, KeyEvent, MouseEvent, ComponentEvent**
CheckboxMenuItem	**ActionEvent, ItemEvent**
Choice	**ItemEvent, FocusEvent, KeyEvent, MouseEvent, ComponentEvent**
Component	**FocusEvent, KeyEvent, MouseEvent, ComponentEvent**
Container	**ContainerEvent, FocusEvent, KeyEvent, MouseEvent, ComponentEvent**
Dialog	**ContainerEvent, WindowEvent, FocusEvent, KeyEvent, MouseEvent, ComponentEvent**
FileDialog	**ContainerEvent, WindowEvent, FocusEvent, KeyEvent, MouseEvent, ComponentEvent**
Frame	**ContainerEvent, WindowEvent, FocusEvent, KeyEvent, MouseEvent, ComponentEvent**
Label	**FocusEvent, KeyEvent, MouseEvent, ComponentEvent**
List	**ActionEvent, FocusEvent, KeyEvent, MouseEvent, ItemEvent, ComponentEvent**
Menu	**ActionEvent**

Component type	Events supported by this component
MenuItem	**ActionEvent**
Panel	**ContainerEvent, FocusEvent, KeyEvent, MouseEvent, ComponentEvent**
PopupMenu	**ActionEvent**
Scrollbar	**AdjustmentEvent, FocusEvent, KeyEvent, MouseEvent, ComponentEvent**
ScrollPane	**ContainerEvent, FocusEvent, KeyEvent, MouseEvent, ComponentEvent**
TextArea	**TextEvent, FocusEvent, KeyEvent, MouseEvent, ComponentEvent**
TextComponent	**TextEvent, FocusEvent, KeyEvent, MouseEvent, ComponentEvent**
TextField	**ActionEvent, TextEvent, FocusEvent, KeyEvent, MouseEvent, ComponentEvent**
Window	**ContainerEvent, WindowEvent, FocusEvent, KeyEvent, MouseEvent, ComponentEvent**

Once you know which events a particular component supports, you don't need to look anything up to react to that event. You simply:

1. Take the name of the event class and remove the word "**Event**." Add the word "**Listener**" to what remains. This is the listener interface you need to implement in your inner class.

2. Implement the interface above and write out the methods for the events you want to capture. For example, you might be looking for mouse movements, so you write code for the **mouseMoved( )** method of the **MouseMotionListener** interface. (You must implement the other methods, of course, but there's a shortcut for that which you'll see soon.)

3. Create an object of the listener class in step 2. Register it with your component with the method produced by prefixing "**add**" to your listener name. For example, **addMouseMotionListener( )**.

To finish what you need to know, here are the listener interfaces:

Listener interface w/ adapter	Methods in interface

Listener interface w/ adapter	Methods in interface
ActionListener	actionPerformed(ActionEvent)
AdjustmentListener	adjustmentValueChanged(AdjustmentEvent)
ComponentListener ComponentAdapter	componentHidden(ComponentEvent) componentShown(ComponentEvent) componentMoved(ComponentEvent) componentResized(ComponentEvent)
ContainerListener ContainerAdapter	componentAdded(ContainerEvent) componentRemoved(ContainerEvent)
FocusListener FocusAdapter	focusGained(FocusEvent) focusLost(FocusEvent)
KeyListener KeyAdapter	keyPressed(KeyEvent) keyReleased(KeyEvent) keyTyped(KeyEvent)
MouseListener MouseAdapter	mouseClicked(MouseEvent) mouseEntered(MouseEvent) mouseExited(MouseEvent) mousePressed(MouseEvent) mouseReleased(MouseEvent)
MouseMotionListener MouseMotionAdapter	mouseDragged(MouseEvent) mouseMoved(MouseEvent)
WindowListener WindowAdapter	windowOpened(WindowEvent) windowClosing(WindowEvent) windowClosed(WindowEvent) windowActivated(WindowEvent) windowDeactivated(WindowEvent) windowIconified(WindowEvent) windowDeiconified(WindowEvent)
ItemListener	itemStateChanged(ItemEvent)
TextListener	textValueChanged(TextEvent)

Using listener adapters for simplicity

In the table above, you can see that some listener interfaces have only one method. These are trivial to implement since you'll implement them only when you want to write that particular method. However, the listener interfaces that have multiple methods could be less pleasant to use. For example, something you must always do when creating an application is provide a **WindowListener** to the **Frame** so that when you get the **windowClosing( )** event you can call **System.exit(0)** to exit the application. But since **WindowListener** is an **interface**, you must implement all of the other methods even if they don't do anything. This can be annoying.

To solve the problem, each of the listener interfaces that have more than one method are provided with *adapters*, the names of which you can see in the table above. Each adapter provides default methods for each of the interface methods. (Alas, **WindowAdapter** does *not* have a default **windowClosing( )** that calls **System.exit(0)**.) Then all you need to do is inherit from the adapter and override only the methods you need to change. For example, the typical **WindowListener** you'll use looks like this:

```
class MyWindowListener extends WindowAdapter {
  public void windowClosing(WindowEvent e) {
    System.exit(0);
  }
}
```

The whole point of the adapters is to make the creation of listener classes easy.

There is a downside to adapters, however, in the form of a pitfall. Suppose you write a **WindowAdapter** like the one above:

```
class MyWindowListener extends WindowAdapter {
  public void WindowClosing(WindowEvent e) {
    System.exit(0);
  }
}
```

This doesn't work, but it will drive you crazy trying to figure out why, since everything will compile and run fine – except that closing the window won't exit the program. Can you see the problem? It's in the name of the method: **WindowClosing( )** instead of **windowClosing( )**. A simple slip in capitalization results in the addition of a completely new method. However, this is not the method that's called when the window is closing, so you don't get the desired results.

Making windows and applets with the Java 1.1 AWT

Often you'll want to be able to create a class that can be invoked as either a window or an applet. To accomplish this, you simply add a **main( )** to your applet that builds an instance of the applet inside a **Frame**. As a simple example, let's look at **Button2New.java** modified to work as both an application and an applet:

```
//: Button2NewB.java
// An application and an applet
import java.awt.*;
import java.awt.event.*; // Must add this
import java.applet.*;

public class Button2NewB extends Applet {
  Button
    b1 = new Button("Button 1"),
    b2 = new Button("Button 2");
  TextField t = new TextField(20);
  public void init() {
    b1.addActionListener(new B1());
    b2.addActionListener(new B2());
    add(b1);
    add(b2);
    add(t);
  }
  class B1 implements ActionListener {
    public void actionPerformed(ActionEvent e) {
      t.setText("Button 1");
    }
  }
  class B2 implements ActionListener {
    public void actionPerformed(ActionEvent e) {
      t.setText("Button 2");
    }
  }
  // To close the application:
  static class WL extends WindowAdapter {
    public void windowClosing(WindowEvent e) {
      System.exit(0);
    }
  }
  // A main() for the application:
  public static void main(String[] args) {
    Button2NewB applet = new Button2NewB();
    Frame aFrame = new Frame("Button2NewB");
    aFrame.addWindowListener(new WL());
    aFrame.add(applet, BorderLayout.CENTER);
    aFrame.setSize(300,200);
    applet.init();
```

```
        applet.start();
        aFrame.setVisible(true);
    }
} ///:~
```

The inner class **WL** and the **main( )** are the only two elements added to
the applet, and the rest of the applet is untouched. In fact, you can
usually copy and paste the **WL** class and **main( )** into your own applets
with little modification. The **WL** class is **static** so it can be easily created
in **main( )**. (Remember that an inner class normally needs an outer class
handle when it's created. Making it **static** eliminates this need.) You can
see that in **main( )**, the applet is explicitly initialized and started since in
this case the browser isn't available to do it for you. Of course, this
doesn't provide the full behavior of the browser, which also calls **stop( )**
and **destroy( )**, but for most situations it's acceptable. If it's a problem,
you can:

1. Make the handle **applet** a **static** member of the class (instead of a
    local variable of **main( )**), and then:

2. Call **applet.stop( )** and **applet.destroy( )** inside
    WindowAdapter.windowClosing( ) before you call **System.exit( )**.

Notice the last line:

```
    aFrame.setVisible(true);
```

This is one of the changes in the Java 1.1 AWT. The **show( )** method is
deprecated and **setVisible(true)** replaces it. These sorts of seemingly
capricious changes will make more sense when you learn about Java
Beans later in the chapter.

This example is also modified to use a **TextField** rather than printing to
the console or to the browser status line. One restriction in making a
program that's both an applet and an application is that you must
choose input and output forms that work for both situations.

There's another small new feature of the Java 1.1 AWT shown here. You
no longer need to use the error-prone approach of specifying
BorderLayout positions using a **String**. When adding an element to a
BorderLayout in Java 1.1, you can say:

```
    aFrame.add(applet, BorderLayout.CENTER);
```

You name the location with one of the **BorderLayout** constants, which
can then be checked at compile-time (rather than just quietly doing the

wrong thing, as with the old form). This is a definite improvement, and will be used throughout the rest of the book.

Making the window listener
an anonymous class

Any of the listener classes could be implemented as anonymous classes, but there's always a chance that you might want to use their functionality elsewhere. However, the window listener is used here only to close the application's window so you can safely make it an anonymous class. Then, in **main( )**, the line:

```
aFrame.addWindowListener(new WL());
```

will become:

```
aFrame.addWindowListener(
    new WindowAdapter() {
        public void windowClosing(WindowEvent e) {
            System.exit(0);
        }
    });
```

This has the advantage that it doesn't require yet another class name. You must decide for yourself whether it makes the code easier to understand or more difficult. However, for the remainder of the book an anonymous inner class will usually be used for the window listener.

Packaging the applet into a JAR file

An important JAR use is to optimize applet loading. In Java 1.0, people tended to try to cram all their code into a single **Applet** class so the client would need only a single server hit to download the applet code. Not only did this result in messy, hard to read (and maintain) programs, but the **.class** file was still uncompressed so downloading wasn't as fast as it could have been.

JAR files change all of that by compressing all of your **.class** files into a single file that is downloaded by the browser. Now you don't need to create an ugly design to minimize the number of classes you create, and the user will get a much faster download time.

Consider the example above. It looks like **Button2NewB** is a single class, but in fact it contains three inner classes, so that's four in all. Once you've compiled the program, you package it into a JAR file with the line:

```
jar cf Button2NewB.jar *.class
```

This assumes that the only **.class** files in the current directory are the ones from **Button2NewB.java** (otherwise you'll get extra baggage).

Now you can create an HTML page with the new **archive** tag to indicate the name of the JAR file, like this:

```
<head><title>Button2NewB Example Applet
</title></head>
<body>
<applet code="Button2NewB.class"
        archive="Button2NewB.jar"
        width=200 height=150>
</applet>
</body>
```

Everything else about applet tags in HTML files remains the same.

Revisiting the earlier examples

To see a number of examples using the new event model and to study the way a program can be converted from the old to the new event model, the following examples revisit many of the issues demonstrated in the first part of this chapter using the old event model. In addition, each program is now both an applet and an application so you can run it with or without a browser.

Text fields

This is similar to **TextField1.java**, but it adds significant extra behavior:

```
//: TextNew.java
// Text fields with Java 1.1 events
import java.awt.*;
import java.awt.event.*;
import java.applet.*;

public class TextNew extends Applet {
  Button
    b1 = new Button("Get Text"),
    b2 = new Button("Set Text");
```

```
TextField
  t1 = new TextField(30),
  t2 = new TextField(30),
  t3 = new TextField(30);
String s = new String();
public void init() {
  b1.addActionListener(new B1());
  b2.addActionListener(new B2());
  t1.addTextListener(new T1());
  t1.addActionListener(new T1A());
  t1.addKeyListener(new T1K());
  add(b1);
  add(b2);
  add(t1);
  add(t2);
  add(t3);
}
class T1 implements TextListener {
  public void textValueChanged(TextEvent e) {
    t2.setText(t1.getText());
  }
}
class T1A implements ActionListener {
  private int count = 0;
  public void actionPerformed(ActionEvent e) {
    t3.setText("t1 Action Event " + count++);
  }
}
class T1K extends KeyAdapter {
  public void keyTyped(KeyEvent e) {
    String ts = t1.getText();
    if(e.getKeyChar() ==
        KeyEvent.VK_BACK_SPACE) {
      // Ensure it's not empty:
      if( ts.length() > 0) {
        ts = ts.substring(0, ts.length() - 1);
        t1.setText(ts);
      }
    }
    else
      t1.setText(
        t1.getText() +
          Character.toUpperCase(
            e.getKeyChar())));
```

```
        t1.setCaretPosition(
          t1.getText().length());
        // Stop regular character from appearing:
        e.consume();
      }
    }
    class B1 implements ActionListener {
      public void actionPerformed(ActionEvent e) {
        s = t1.getSelectedText();
        if(s.length() == 0) s = t1.getText();
        t1.setEditable(true);
      }
    }
    class B2 implements ActionListener {
      public void actionPerformed(ActionEvent e) {
        t1.setText("Inserted by Button 2: " + s);
        t1.setEditable(false);
      }
    }
    public static void main(String[] args) {
      TextNew applet = new TextNew();
      Frame aFrame = new Frame("TextNew");
      aFrame.addWindowListener(
        new WindowAdapter() {
          public void windowClosing(WindowEvent e) {
            System.exit(0);
          }
        });
      aFrame.add(applet, BorderLayout.CENTER);
      aFrame.setSize(300,200);
      applet.init();
      applet.start();
      aFrame.setVisible(true);
    }
} ///:~
```

The **TextField t3** is included as a place to report when the action listener
for the **TextField t1** is fired. You'll see that the action listener for a
TextField is fired only when you press the "enter" key.

The **TextField t1** has several listeners attached to it. The **T1** listener
copies all text from **t1** into **t2** and the **T1K** listener forces all characters to
upper case. You'll notice that the two work together, and if you add the
T1K listener *after* you add the **T1** listener, it doesn't matter: all characters
will still be forced to upper case in both text fields. It would seem that

keyboard events are always fired before **TextComponent** events, and if you want the characters in **t2** to retain the original case that was typed in, you must do some extra work.

T1K has some other activities of interest. You must detect a backspace (since you're controlling everything now) and perform the deletion. The caret must be explicitly set to the end of the field; otherwise it won't behave as you expect. Finally, to prevent the original character from being handled by the default mechanism, the event must be "consumed" using the **consume( )** method that exists for event objects. This tells the system to stop firing the rest of the event handlers for this particular event.

This example also quietly demonstrates one of the benefits of the design of inner classes. Note that in the inner class:

```
class T1 implements TextListener {
  public void textValueChanged(TextEvent e) {
    t2.setText(t1.getText());
  }
}
```

t1 and **t2** are *not* members of **T1**, and yet they're accessible without any special qualification. This is because an object of an inner class automatically captures a handle to the outer object that created it, so you can treat members and methods of the enclosing class object as if they're yours. As you can see, this is quite convenient.[6]

Text areas

The most significant change to text areas in Java 1.1 concerns scroll bars. With the **TextArea** constructor, you can now control whether a **TextArea** will have scroll bars: vertical, horizontal, both, or neither. This example modifies the earlier Java 1.0 **TextArea1.java** to show the Java 1.1 scrollbar constructors:

```
//: TextAreaNew.java
// Controlling scrollbars with the TextArea
// component in Java 1.1
import java.awt.*;
import java.awt.event.*;
```

---

[6] It also solves the problem of "callbacks" without adding any awkward "method pointer" feature to Java.

```java
import java.applet.*;

public class TextAreaNew extends Applet {
  Button b1 = new Button("Text Area 1");
  Button b2 = new Button("Text Area 2");
  Button b3 = new Button("Replace Text");
  Button b4 = new Button("Insert Text");
  TextArea t1 = new TextArea("t1", 1, 30);
  TextArea t2 = new TextArea("t2", 4, 30);
  TextArea t3 = new TextArea("t3", 1, 30,
    TextArea.SCROLLBARS_NONE);
  TextArea t4 = new TextArea("t4", 10, 10,
    TextArea.SCROLLBARS_VERTICAL_ONLY);
  TextArea t5 = new TextArea("t5", 4, 30,
    TextArea.SCROLLBARS_HORIZONTAL_ONLY);
  TextArea t6 = new TextArea("t6", 10, 10,
    TextArea.SCROLLBARS_BOTH);
  public void init() {
    b1.addActionListener(new B1L());
    add(b1);
    add(t1);
    b2.addActionListener(new B2L());
    add(b2);
    add(t2);
    b3.addActionListener(new B3L());
    add(b3);
    b4.addActionListener(new B4L());
    add(b4);
    add(t3); add(t4); add(t5); add(t6);
  }
  class B1L implements ActionListener {
    public void actionPerformed(ActionEvent e) {
      t5.append(t1.getText() + "\n");
    }
  }
  class B2L implements ActionListener {
    public void actionPerformed(ActionEvent e) {
      t2.setText("Inserted by Button 2");
      t2.append(": " + t1.getText());
      t5.append(t2.getText() + "\n");
    }
  }
  class B3L implements ActionListener {
    public void actionPerformed(ActionEvent e) {
```

```
      String s = " Replacement ";
      t2.replaceRange(s, 3, 3 + s.length());
    }
  }
  class B4L implements ActionListener {
    public void actionPerformed(ActionEvent e) {
      t2.insert(" Inserted ", 10);
    }
  }
  public static void main(String[] args) {
    TextAreaNew applet = new TextAreaNew();
    Frame aFrame = new Frame("TextAreaNew");
    aFrame.addWindowListener(
      new WindowAdapter() {
        public void windowClosing(WindowEvent e) {
          System.exit(0);
        }
      });
    aFrame.add(applet, BorderLayout.CENTER);
    aFrame.setSize(300,725);
    applet.init();
    applet.start();
    aFrame.setVisible(true);
  }
} ///:~
```

You'll notice that you can control the scrollbars only at the time of
construction of the **TextArea**. Also, even if a **TextArea** doesn't have a
scrollbar, you can move the cursor such that scrolling will be forced. (You
can see this behavior by playing with the example.)

Check boxes and radio buttons

As noted previously, check boxes and radio buttons are both created with
the same class, **Checkbox**, but radio buttons are **Checkbox**es placed into
a **CheckboxGroup**. In either case, the interesting event is **ItemEvent**, for
which you create an **ItemListener**.

When dealing with a group of check boxes or radio buttons, you have a
choice. You can either create a new inner class to handle the event for
each different **Checkbox** or you can create one inner class that
determines which **Checkbox** was clicked and register a single object of
that inner class with each **Checkbox** object. The following example shows
both approaches:

```
//: RadioCheckNew.java
// Radio buttons and Check Boxes in Java 1.1
import java.awt.*;
import java.awt.event.*;
import java.applet.*;

public class RadioCheckNew extends Applet {
  TextField t = new TextField(30);
  Checkbox[] cb = {
    new Checkbox("Check Box 1"),
    new Checkbox("Check Box 2"),
    new Checkbox("Check Box 3") };
  CheckboxGroup g = new CheckboxGroup();
  Checkbox
    cb4 = new Checkbox("four", g, false),
    cb5 = new Checkbox("five", g, true),
    cb6 = new Checkbox("six", g, false);
  public void init() {
    t.setEditable(false);
    add(t);
    ILCheck il = new ILCheck();
    for(int i = 0; i < cb.length; i++) {
      cb[i].addItemListener(il);
      add(cb[i]);
    }
    cb4.addItemListener(new IL4());
    cb5.addItemListener(new IL5());
    cb6.addItemListener(new IL6());
    add(cb4); add(cb5); add(cb6);
  }
  // Checking the source:
  class ILCheck implements ItemListener {
    public void itemStateChanged(ItemEvent e) {
      for(int i = 0; i < cb.length; i++) {
        if(e.getSource().equals(cb[i])) {
          t.setText("Check box " + (i + 1));
          return;
        }
      }
    }
  }
  // vs. an individual class for each item:
  class IL4 implements ItemListener {
    public void itemStateChanged(ItemEvent e) {
```

```
          t.setText("Radio button four");
        }
      }
      class IL5 implements ItemListener {
        public void itemStateChanged(ItemEvent e) {
          t.setText("Radio button five");
        }
      }
      class IL6 implements ItemListener {
        public void itemStateChanged(ItemEvent e) {
          t.setText("Radio button six");
        }
      }
      public static void main(String[] args) {
        RadioCheckNew applet = new RadioCheckNew();
        Frame aFrame = new Frame("RadioCheckNew");
        aFrame.addWindowListener(
          new WindowAdapter() {
            public void windowClosing(WindowEvent e) {
              System.exit(0);
            }
          });
        aFrame.add(applet, BorderLayout.CENTER);
        aFrame.setSize(300,200);
        applet.init();
        applet.start();
        aFrame.setVisible(true);
      }
    } ///:~
```

ILCheck has the advantage that it automatically adapts when you add or subtract **Checkbox**es. Of course, you can use this with radio buttons as well. It should be used, however, only when your logic is general enough to support this approach. Otherwise you'll end up with a cascaded **if** statement, a sure sign that you should revert to using independent listener classes.

Drop-down lists

Drop-down lists (**Choice**) in Java 1.1 also use **ItemListeners** to notify you when a choice has changed:

```
//: ChoiceNew.java
// Drop-down lists with Java 1.1
import java.awt.*;
```

```
import java.awt.event.*;
import java.applet.*;

public class ChoiceNew extends Applet {
  String[] description = { "Ebullient", "Obtuse",
    "Recalcitrant", "Brilliant", "Somnescent",
    "Timorous", "Florid", "Putrescent" };
  TextField t = new TextField(100);
  Choice c = new Choice();
  Button b = new Button("Add items");
  int count = 0;
  public void init() {
    t.setEditable(false);
    for(int i = 0; i < 4; i++)
      c.addItem(description[count++]);
    add(t);
    add(c);
    add(b);
    c.addItemListener(new CL());
    b.addActionListener(new BL());
  }
  class CL implements ItemListener {
    public void itemStateChanged(ItemEvent e) {
      t.setText("index: " +  c.getSelectedIndex()
        + "    " + e.toString());
    }
  }
  class BL implements ActionListener {
    public void actionPerformed(ActionEvent e) {
      if(count < description.length)
        c.addItem(description[count++]);
    }
  }
  public static void main(String[] args) {
    ChoiceNew applet = new ChoiceNew();
    Frame aFrame = new Frame("ChoiceNew");
    aFrame.addWindowListener(
      new WindowAdapter() {
        public void windowClosing(WindowEvent e) {
          System.exit(0);
        }
      });
    aFrame.add(applet, BorderLayout.CENTER);
    aFrame.setSize(750,100);
```

```
        applet.init();
        applet.start();
        aFrame.setVisible(true);
    }
} ///:~
```

Nothing else here is particularly new (except that Java 1.1 has
significantly fewer bugs in the UI classes).

Lists

You'll recall that one of the problems with the Java 1.0 **List** design is that
it took extra work to make it do what you'd expect: react to a single click
on one of the list elements. Java 1.1 has solved this problem:

```
//: ListNew.java
// Java 1.1 Lists are easier to use
import java.awt.*;
import java.awt.event.*;
import java.applet.*;

public class ListNew extends Applet {
  String[] flavors = { "Chocolate", "Strawberry",
    "Vanilla Fudge Swirl", "Mint Chip",
    "Mocha Almond Fudge", "Rum Raisin",
    "Praline Cream", "Mud Pie" };
  // Show 6 items, allow multiple selection:
  List lst = new List(6, true);
  TextArea t = new TextArea(flavors.length, 30);
  Button b = new Button("test");
  int count = 0;
  public void init() {
    t.setEditable(false);
    for(int i = 0; i < 4; i++)
      lst.addItem(flavors[count++]);
    add(t);
    add(lst);
    add(b);
    lst.addItemListener(new LL());
    b.addActionListener(new BL());
  }
  class LL implements ItemListener {
    public void itemStateChanged(ItemEvent e) {
      t.setText("");
      String[] items = lst.getSelectedItems();
```

```
        for(int i = 0; i < items.length; i++)
          t.append(items[i] + "\n");
      }
    }
    class BL implements ActionListener {
      public void actionPerformed(ActionEvent e) {
        if(count < flavors.length)
          lst.addItem(flavors[count++], 0);
      }
    }
    public static void main(String[] args) {
      ListNew applet = new ListNew();
      Frame aFrame = new Frame("ListNew");
      aFrame.addWindowListener(
        new WindowAdapter() {
          public void windowClosing(WindowEvent e) {
            System.exit(0);
          }
        });
      aFrame.add(applet, BorderLayout.CENTER);
      aFrame.setSize(300,200);
      applet.init();
      applet.start();
      aFrame.setVisible(true);
    }
} ///:~
```

You can see that no extra logic is required to support a single click on a
list item. You just attach a listener like you do everywhere else.

Menus

The event handling for menus does seem to benefit from the Java 1.1
event model, but Java's approach to menus is still messy and requires a
lot of hand coding. The right medium for a menu seems to be a resource
rather than a lot of code. Keep in mind that program-building tools will
generally handle the creation of menus for you, so that will reduce the
pain somewhat (as long as they will also handle the maintenance!).

In addition, you'll find the events for menus are inconsistent and can lead
to confusion: **MenuItem**s use **ActionListener**s, but
CheckboxMenuItems use **ItemListener**s. The **Menu** objects can also
support **ActionListener**s, but that's not usually helpful. In general,
you'll attach listeners to each **MenuItem** or **CheckboxMenuItem**, but
the following example (revised from the earlier version) also shows ways

to combine the capture of multiple menu components into a single listener class. As you'll see, it's probably not worth the hassle to do this.

```
//: MenuNew.java
// Menus in Java 1.1
import java.awt.*;
import java.awt.event.*;

public class MenuNew extends Frame {
  String[] flavors = { "Chocolate", "Strawberry",
    "Vanilla Fudge Swirl", "Mint Chip",
    "Mocha Almond Fudge", "Rum Raisin",
    "Praline Cream", "Mud Pie" };
  TextField t = new TextField("No flavor", 30);
  MenuBar mb1 = new MenuBar();
  Menu f = new Menu("File");
  Menu m = new Menu("Flavors");
  Menu s = new Menu("Safety");
  // Alternative approach:
  CheckboxMenuItem[] safety = {
    new CheckboxMenuItem("Guard"),
    new CheckboxMenuItem("Hide")
  };
  MenuItem[] file = {
    // No menu shortcut:
    new MenuItem("Open"),
    // Adding a menu shortcut is very simple:
    new MenuItem("Exit",
      new MenuShortcut(KeyEvent.VK_E))
  };
  // A second menu bar to swap to:
  MenuBar mb2 = new MenuBar();
  Menu fooBar = new Menu("fooBar");
  MenuItem[] other = {
    new MenuItem("Foo"),
    new MenuItem("Bar"),
    new MenuItem("Baz"),
  };
  // Initialization code:
  {
    ML ml = new ML();
    CMIL cmil = new CMIL();
    safety[0].setActionCommand("Guard");
    safety[0].addItemListener(cmil);
    safety[1].setActionCommand("Hide");
```

```
      safety[1].addItemListener(cmil);
      file[0].setActionCommand("Open");
      file[0].addActionListener(ml);
      file[1].setActionCommand("Exit");
      file[1].addActionListener(ml);
      other[0].addActionListener(new FooL());
      other[1].addActionListener(new BarL());
      other[2].addActionListener(new BazL());
    }
  Button b = new Button("Swap Menus");
  public MenuNew() {
    FL fl = new FL();
    for(int i = 0; i < flavors.length; i++) {
      MenuItem mi = new MenuItem(flavors[i]);
      mi.addActionListener(fl);
      m.add(mi);
      // Add separators at intervals:
      if((i+1) % 3 == 0)
        m.addSeparator();
    }
    for(int i = 0; i < safety.length; i++)
      s.add(safety[i]);
    f.add(s);
    for(int i = 0; i < file.length; i++)
      f.add(file[i]);
    mb1.add(f);
    mb1.add(m);
    setMenuBar(mb1);
    t.setEditable(false);
    add(t, BorderLayout.CENTER);
    // Set up the system for swapping menus:
    b.addActionListener(new BL());
    add(b, BorderLayout.NORTH);
    for(int i = 0; i < other.length; i++)
      fooBar.add(other[i]);
    mb2.add(fooBar);
  }
  class BL implements ActionListener {
    public void actionPerformed(ActionEvent e) {
      MenuBar m = getMenuBar();
      if(m == mb1) setMenuBar(mb2);
      else if (m == mb2) setMenuBar(mb1);
    }
  }
```

```
class ML implements ActionListener {
  public void actionPerformed(ActionEvent e) {
    MenuItem target = (MenuItem)e.getSource();
    String actionCommand =
      target.getActionCommand();
    if(actionCommand.equals("Open")) {
      String s = t.getText();
      boolean chosen = false;
      for(int i = 0; i < flavors.length; i++)
        if(s.equals(flavors[i])) chosen = true;
      if(!chosen)
        t.setText("Choose a flavor first!");
      else
        t.setText("Opening "+ s +". Mmm, mm!");
    } else if(actionCommand.equals("Exit")) {
      dispatchEvent(
        new WindowEvent(MenuNew.this,
          WindowEvent.WINDOW_CLOSING));
    }
  }
}
class FL implements ActionListener {
  public void actionPerformed(ActionEvent e) {
    MenuItem target = (MenuItem)e.getSource();
    t.setText(target.getLabel());
  }
}
// Alternatively, you can create a different
// class for each different MenuItem. Then you
// Don't have to figure out which one it is:
class FooL implements ActionListener {
  public void actionPerformed(ActionEvent e) {
    t.setText("Foo selected");
  }
}
class BarL implements ActionListener {
  public void actionPerformed(ActionEvent e) {
    t.setText("Bar selected");
  }
}
class BazL implements ActionListener {
  public void actionPerformed(ActionEvent e) {
    t.setText("Baz selected");
  }
```

```
  }
class CMIL implements ItemListener {
  public void itemStateChanged(ItemEvent e) {
    CheckboxMenuItem target =
      (CheckboxMenuItem)e.getSource();
    String actionCommand =
      target.getActionCommand();
    if(actionCommand.equals("Guard"))
      t.setText("Guard the Ice Cream! " +
        "Guarding is " + target.getState());
    else if(actionCommand.equals("Hide"))
      t.setText("Hide the Ice Cream! " +
        "Is it cold? " + target.getState());
  }
}
public static void main(String[] args) {
  MenuNew f = new MenuNew();
  f.addWindowListener(
    new WindowAdapter() {
      public void windowClosing(WindowEvent e) {
        System.exit(0);
      }
    });
  f.setSize(300,200);
  f.setVisible(true);
}
} ///:~
```

This code is similar to the previous (Java 1.0) version, until you get to the initialization section (marked by the opening brace right after the comment "Initialization code:"). Here you can see the **ItemListener**s and **ActionListener**s attached to the various menu components.

Java 1.1 supports "menu shortcuts," so you can select a menu item using the keyboard instead of the mouse. These are quite simple; you just use the overloaded **MenuItem** constructor that takes as a second argument a **MenuShortcut** object. The constructor for **MenuShortcut** takes the key of interest, which magically appears on the menu item when it drops down. The example above adds Control-E to the "Exit" menu item.

You can also see the use of **setActionCommand( )**. This seems a bit strange because in each case the "action command" is exactly the same as the label on the menu component. Why not just use the label instead of this alternative string? The problem is internationalization. If you retarget this program to another language, you want to change only the label in the menu, and not go through the code changing all the logic that will no doubt introduce new errors. So to make this easy for code that checks the text string associated with a menu component, the "action command" can be immutable while the menu label can change. All the code works with the "action command," so it's unaffected by changes to the menu labels. Note that in this program, not all the menu components are examined for their action commands, so those that aren't don't have their action command set.

Much of the constructor is the same as before, with the exception of a couple of calls to add listeners. The bulk of the work happens in the listeners. In **BL**, the **MenuBar** swapping happens as in the previous example. In **ML**, the "figure out who rang" approach is taken by getting the source of the **ActionEvent** and casting it to a **MenuItem**, then getting the action command string to pass it through a cascaded **if** statement. Much of this is the same as before, but notice that if "Exit" is chosen, a new **WindowEvent** is created, passing in the handle of the enclosing class object (**MenuNew.this**) and creating a **WINDOW_CLOSING** event. This is handed to the **dispatchEvent( )** method of the enclosing class object, which then ends up calling **windowClosing( )** inside the window listener for the **Frame** (this listener is created as an anonymous inner class, inside **main( )**), just as if the message had been generated the "normal" way. Through this mechanism, you can dispatch any message you want in any circumstances, so it's quite powerful.

The **FL** listener is simple even though it's handling all the different flavors in the flavor menu. This approach is useful if you have enough simplicity in your logic, but in general, you'll want to take the approach used with **FooL**, **BarL**, and **BazL**, in which they are each attached to only a single menu component so no extra detection logic is necessary and you know exactly who called the listener. Even with the profusion of classes generated this way, the code inside tends to be smaller and the process is more foolproof.

Dialog boxes

This is a direct rewrite of the earlier **ToeTest.java.** In this version, however, everything is placed inside an inner class. Although this completely eliminates the need to keep track of the object that spawned any class, as was the case in **ToeTest.java**, it could be taking the concept of inner classes a bit too far. At one point, the inner classes are nested four deep! This is the kind of design in which you need to decide whether the benefit of inner classes is worth the increased complexity. In addition, when you create a non-**static** inner class you're tying that class to its surrounding class. Sometimes a standalone class can more easily be reused.

```java
//: ToeTestNew.java
// Demonstration of dialog boxes
// and creating your own components
import java.awt.*;
import java.awt.event.*;

public class ToeTestNew extends Frame {
  TextField rows = new TextField("3");
  TextField cols = new TextField("3");
  public ToeTestNew() {
    setTitle("Toe Test");
    Panel p = new Panel();
    p.setLayout(new GridLayout(2,2));
    p.add(new Label("Rows", Label.CENTER));
    p.add(rows);
    p.add(new Label("Columns", Label.CENTER));
    p.add(cols);
    add(p, BorderLayout.NORTH);
    Button b = new Button("go");
    b.addActionListener(new BL());
    add(b, BorderLayout.SOUTH);
  }
  static final int BLANK = 0;
  static final int XX = 1;
  static final int OO = 2;
  class ToeDialog extends Dialog {
    // w = number of cells wide
    // h = number of cells high
    int turn = XX; // Start with x's turn
    public ToeDialog(int w, int h) {
      super(ToeTestNew.this,
        "The game itself", false);
      setLayout(new GridLayout(w, h));
      for(int i = 0; i < w * h; i++)
        add(new ToeButton());
      setSize(w * 50, h * 50);
      addWindowListener(new WindowAdapter() {
        public void windowClosing(WindowEvent e){
          dispose();
        }
      });
    }
```

```
class ToeButton extends Canvas {
  int state = BLANK;
  ToeButton() {
    addMouseListener(new ML());
  }
  public void paint(Graphics  g) {
    int x1 = 0;
    int y1 = 0;
    int x2 = getSize().width - 1;
    int y2 = getSize().height - 1;
    g.drawRect(x1, y1, x2, y2);
    x1 = x2/4;
    y1 = y2/4;
    int wide = x2/2;
    int high = y2/2;
    if(state == XX) {
      g.drawLine(x1, y1,
        x1 + wide, y1 + high);
      g.drawLine(x1, y1 + high,
        x1 + wide, y1);
    }
    if(state == OO) {
      g.drawOval(x1, y1,
        x1 + wide/2, y1 + high/2);
    }
  }
  class ML extends MouseAdapter {
    public void mousePressed(MouseEvent e) {
      if(state == BLANK) {
        state = turn;
        turn = (turn == XX ? OO : XX);
      }
      else
        state = (state == XX ? OO : XX);
      repaint();
    }
  }
}
}
class BL implements ActionListener {
  public void actionPerformed(ActionEvent e) {
    Dialog d = new ToeDialog(
      Integer.parseInt(rows.getText()),
      Integer.parseInt(cols.getText()));
```

```
        d.show();
      }
    }
    public static void main(String[] args) {
      Frame f = new ToeTestNew();
      f.addWindowListener(
        new WindowAdapter() {
          public void windowClosing(WindowEvent e) {
            System.exit(0);
          }
        });
      f.setSize(200,100);
      f.setVisible(true);
    }
} ///:~
```

Because **statics** can be at only the outer level of the class, inner classes cannot have **static** data or **static** inner classes.

File dialogs

Converting from **FileDialogTest.java** to the new event model is straightforward:

```
//: FileDialogNew.java
// Demonstration of File dialog boxes
import java.awt.*;
import java.awt.event.*;

public class FileDialogNew extends Frame {
  TextField filename = new TextField();
  TextField directory = new TextField();
  Button open = new Button("Open");
  Button save = new Button("Save");
  public FileDialogNew() {
    setTitle("File Dialog Test");
    Panel p = new Panel();
    p.setLayout(new FlowLayout());
    open.addActionListener(new OpenL());
    p.add(open);
    save.addActionListener(new SaveL());
    p.add(save);
    add(p, BorderLayout.SOUTH);
    directory.setEditable(false);
    filename.setEditable(false);
```

```
    p = new Panel();
    p.setLayout(new GridLayout(2,1));
    p.add(filename);
    p.add(directory);
    add(p, BorderLayout.NORTH);
  }
  class OpenL implements ActionListener {
    public void actionPerformed(ActionEvent e) {
      // Two arguments, defaults to open file:
      FileDialog d = new FileDialog(
        FileDialogNew.this,
        "What file do you want to open?");
      d.setFile("*.java");
      d.setDirectory("."); // Current directory
      d.show();
      String yourFile = "*.*";
      if((yourFile = d.getFile()) != null) {
        filename.setText(yourFile);
        directory.setText(d.getDirectory());
      } else {
        filename.setText("You pressed cancel");
        directory.setText("");
      }
    }
  }
  class SaveL implements ActionListener {
    public void actionPerformed(ActionEvent e) {
      FileDialog d = new FileDialog(
        FileDialogNew.this,
        "What file do you want to save?",
        FileDialog.SAVE);
      d.setFile("*.java");
      d.setDirectory(".");
      d.show();
      String saveFile;
      if((saveFile = d.getFile()) != null) {
        filename.setText(saveFile);
        directory.setText(d.getDirectory());
      } else {
        filename.setText("You pressed cancel");
        directory.setText("");
      }
    }
  }
}
```

```
      public static void main(String[] args) {
        Frame f = new FileDialogNew();
        f.addWindowListener(
          new WindowAdapter() {
            public void windowClosing(WindowEvent e) {
              System.exit(0);
            }
          });
        f.setSize(250,110);
        f.setVisible(true);
      }
    } ///:~
```

It would be nice if all the conversions were this easy, but they're usually easy enough, and your code benefits from the improved readability.

Binding events dynamically

One of the benefits of the new AWT event model is flexibility. In the old model you were forced to hard code the behavior of your program, but with the new model you can add and remove event behavior with single method calls. The following example demonstrates this:

```
//: DynamicEvents.java
// The new Java 1.1 event model allows you to
// change event behavior dynamically. Also
// demonstrates multiple actions for an event.
import java.awt.*;
import java.awt.event.*;
import java.util.*;

public class DynamicEvents extends Frame {
  Vector v = new Vector();
  int i = 0;
  Button
    b1 = new Button("Button 1"),
    b2 = new Button("Button 2");
  public DynamicEvents() {
    setLayout(new FlowLayout());
    b1.addActionListener(new B());
    b1.addActionListener(new B1());
    b2.addActionListener(new B());
    b2.addActionListener(new B2());
    add(b1);
```

```
    add(b2);
  }
  class B implements ActionListener {
    public void actionPerformed(ActionEvent e) {
      System.out.println("A button was pressed");
    }
  }
  class CountListener implements ActionListener {
    int index;
    public CountListener(int i) { index = i; }
    public void actionPerformed(ActionEvent e) {
      System.out.println(
        "Counted Listener " + index);
    }
  }
  class B1 implements ActionListener {
    public void actionPerformed(ActionEvent e) {
      System.out.println("Button 1 pressed");
      ActionListener a = new CountListener(i++);
      v.addElement(a);
      b2.addActionListener(a);
    }
  }
  class B2 implements ActionListener {
    public void actionPerformed(ActionEvent e) {
      System.out.println("Button 2 pressed");
      int end = v.size() -1;
      if(end >= 0) {
        b2.removeActionListener(
          (ActionListener)v.elementAt(end));
        v.removeElementAt(end);
      }
    }
  }
  public static void main(String[] args) {
    Frame f = new DynamicEvents();
    f.addWindowListener(
      new WindowAdapter() {
        public void windowClosing(WindowEvent e){
          System.exit(0);
        }
      });
    f.setSize(300,200);
    f.show();
```

```
        }
} ///:~
```

The new twists in this example are:

1. There is more than one listener attached to each **Button**. Usually, components handle events as *multicast*, meaning that you can register many listeners for a single event. In the special components in which an event is handled as *unicast*, you'll get a **TooManyListenersException**.

2. During the execution of the program, listeners are dynamically added and removed from the **Button b2**. Adding is accomplished in the way you've seen before, but each component also has a **removeXXXListener( )** method to remove each type of listener.

This kind of flexibility provides much greater power in your programming.

You should notice that event listeners are not guaranteed to be called in the order they are added (although most implementations do in fact work that way).

Separating business logic from UI logic

In general you'll want to design your classes so that each one does "only one thing." This is particularly important when user-interface code is concerned, since it's easy to wrap up "what you're doing" with "how you're displaying it." This kind of coupling prevents code reuse. It's much more desirable to separate your "business logic" from the GUI. This way, you can not only reuse the business logic more easily, it's also easier to reuse the GUI.

Another issue is *multi-tiered* systems, where the "business objects" reside on a completely separate machine. This central location of the business rules allows changes to be instantly effective for all new transactions, and is thus a compelling way to set up a system. However, these business objects can be used in many different applications and so should not be tied to any particular mode of display. They should just perform the business operations and nothing more.

The following example shows how easy it is to separate the business logic from the GUI code:

```
//: Separation.java
// Separating GUI logic and business objects
import java.awt.*;
import java.awt.event.*;
import java.applet.*;

class BusinessLogic {
  private int modifier;
  BusinessLogic(int mod) {
    modifier = mod;
  }
  public void setModifier(int mod) {
    modifier = mod;
  }
  public int getModifier() {
    return modifier;
  }
  // Some business operations:
  public int calculation1(int arg) {
    return arg * modifier;
  }
  public int calculation2(int arg) {
    return arg + modifier;
  }
}

public class Separation extends Applet {
  TextField
    t = new TextField(20),
    mod = new TextField(20);
  BusinessLogic bl = new BusinessLogic(2);
  Button
    calc1 = new Button("Calculation 1"),
    calc2 = new Button("Calculation 2");
  public void init() {
    add(t);
    calc1.addActionListener(new Calc1L());
    calc2.addActionListener(new Calc2L());
    add(calc1); add(calc2);
    mod.addTextListener(new ModL());
    add(new Label("Modifier:"));
    add(mod);
  }
  static int getValue(TextField tf) {
```

```
        try {
          return Integer.parseInt(tf.getText());
        } catch(NumberFormatException e) {
          return 0;
        }
      }
    }
    class Calc1L implements ActionListener {
      public void actionPerformed(ActionEvent e) {
        t.setText(Integer.toString(
          bl.calculation1(getValue(t))));
      }
    }
    class Calc2L implements ActionListener {
      public void actionPerformed(ActionEvent e) {
        t.setText(Integer.toString(
          bl.calculation2(getValue(t))));
      }
    }
    class ModL implements TextListener {
      public void textValueChanged(TextEvent e) {
        bl.setModifier(getValue(mod));
      }
    }
    public static void main(String[] args) {
      Separation applet = new Separation();
      Frame aFrame = new Frame("Separation");
      aFrame.addWindowListener(
        new WindowAdapter() {
          public void windowClosing(WindowEvent e) {
            System.exit(0);
          }
        });
      aFrame.add(applet, BorderLayout.CENTER);
      aFrame.setSize(200,200);
      applet.init();
      applet.start();
      aFrame.setVisible(true);
    }
  } ///:~
```

You can see that **BusinessLogic** is a straightforward class that performs its operations without even a hint that it might be used in a GUI environment. It just does its job.

Separation keeps track of all the UI details, and it talks to **BusinessLogic** only through its **public** interface. All the operations are centered around getting information back and forth through the UI and the **BusinessLogic** object. So **Separation**, in turn, just does its job. Since **Separation** knows only that it's talking to a **BusinessLogic** object (that is, it isn't highly coupled), it could be massaged into talking to other types of objects without much trouble.

Thinking in terms of separating UI from business logic also makes life easier when you're adapting legacy code to work with Java.

Recommended coding approaches

Inner classes, the new event model, and the fact that the old event model is still supported along with new library features that rely on old-style programming has added a new element of confusion. Now there are even more different ways for people to write unpleasant code. Unfortunately, this kind of code is showing up in books and article examples, and even in documentation and examples distributed from Sun! In this section we'll look at some misunderstandings about what you should and shouldn't do with the new AWT, and end by showing that except in extenuating circumstances you can always use listener classes (written as inner classes) to solve your event-handling needs. Since this is also the simplest and clearest approach, it should be a relief for you to learn this.

Before looking at anything else, you should know that although Java 1.1 is backward-compatible with Java 1.0 (that is, you can compile and run 1.0 programs with 1.1), you cannot mix the event models within the same program. That is, you cannot use the old-style **action( )** method in the same program in which you employ listeners. This can be a problem in a larger program when you're trying to integrate old code with a new program, since you must decide whether to use the old, hard-to-maintain approach with the new program or to update the old code. This shouldn't be too much of a battle since the new approach is so superior to the old.

Baseline: the good way to do it

To give you something to compare with, here's an example showing the recommended approach. By now it should be reasonably familiar and comfortable:

```
//: GoodIdea.java
// The best way to design classes using the new
// Java 1.1 event model: use an inner class for
```

```
// each different event. This maximizes
// flexibility and modularity.
import java.awt.*;
import java.awt.event.*;
import java.util.*;

public class GoodIdea extends Frame {
  Button
    b1 = new Button("Button 1"),
    b2 = new Button("Button 2");
  public GoodIdea() {
    setLayout(new FlowLayout());
    b1.addActionListener(new B1L());
    b2.addActionListener(new B2L());
    add(b1);
    add(b2);
  }
  public class B1L implements ActionListener {
    public void actionPerformed(ActionEvent e) {
      System.out.println("Button 1 pressed");
    }
  }
  public class B2L implements ActionListener {
    public void actionPerformed(ActionEvent e) {
      System.out.println("Button 2 pressed");
    }
  }
  public static void main(String[] args) {
    Frame f = new GoodIdea();
    f.addWindowListener(
      new WindowAdapter() {
        public void windowClosing(WindowEvent e){
          System.out.println("Window Closing");
          System.exit(0);
        }
      });
    f.setSize(300,200);
    f.setVisible(true);
  }
} ///:~
```

This is fairly trivial: each button has its own listener that prints
something out to the console. But notice that there isn't an **if** statement
in the entire program, or any statement that says, "I wonder what
caused this event." Each piece of code is concerned with *doing*, not type-

checking. This is the best way to write your code; not only is it easier to conceptualize, but much easier to read and maintain. Cutting and pasting to create new programs is also much easier.

Implementing the main class as a listener

The first bad idea is a common and recommended approach. This makes the main class (typically **Applet** or **Frame**, but it could be any class) implement the various listeners. Here's an example:

```
//: BadIdea1.java
// Some literature recommends this approach,
// but it's missing the point of the new event
// model in Java 1.1
import java.awt.*;
import java.awt.event.*;
import java.util.*;

public class BadIdea1 extends Frame
    implements ActionListener, WindowListener {
  Button
    b1 = new Button("Button 1"),
    b2 = new Button("Button 2");
  public BadIdea1() {
    setLayout(new FlowLayout());
    addWindowListener(this);
    b1.addActionListener(this);
    b2.addActionListener(this);
    add(b1);
    add(b2);
  }
  public void actionPerformed(ActionEvent e) {
    Object source = e.getSource();
    if(source == b1)
      System.out.println("Button 1 pressed");
    else if(source == b2)
      System.out.println("Button 2 pressed");
    else
      System.out.println("Something else");
  }
  public void windowClosing(WindowEvent e) {
    System.out.println("Window Closing");
    System.exit(0);
  }
  public void windowClosed(WindowEvent e) {}
```

```
      public void windowDeiconified(WindowEvent e) {}
      public void windowIconified(WindowEvent e) {}
      public void windowActivated(WindowEvent e) {}
      public void windowDeactivated(WindowEvent e) {}
      public void windowOpened(WindowEvent e) {}

      public static void main(String[] args) {
        Frame f = new BadIdea1();
        f.setSize(300,200);
        f.setVisible(true);
      }
    } ///:~
```

The use of this shows up in the three lines:

```
      addWindowListener(this);
      b1.addActionListener(this);
      b2.addActionListener(this);
```

Since **BadIdea1** implements **ActionListener** and **WindowListener**, these lines are certainly acceptable, and if you're still stuck in the mode of trying to make fewer classes to reduce server hits during applet loading, it seems to be a good idea. However:

1. Java 1.1 supports JAR files so all your files can be placed in a single compressed JAR archive that requires only one server hit. You no longer need to reduce class count for Internet efficiency.

2. The code above is much less modular so it's harder to grab and paste. Note that you must not only implement the various interfaces for your main class, but in **actionPerformed( )** you've got to detect which action was performed using a cascaded **if** statement. Not only is this going backwards, *away* from the listener model, but you can't easily reuse the **actionPerformed( )** method since it's specific to this particular application. Contrast this with **GoodIdea.java**, in which you can just grab one listener class and paste it in anywhere else with minimal fuss. Plus you can register multiple listener classes with a single event, allowing even more modularity in what each listener class does.

Mixing the approaches

The second bad idea is to mix the two approaches: use inner listener classes, but also implement one or more listener interfaces as part of the main class. This approach has appeared without explanation in books and documentation, and I can only assume that the authors thought they must use the different approaches for different purposes. But you don't – in your programming you can probably use inner listener classes exclusively.

```
//: BadIdea2.java
// An improvement over BadIdea1.java, since it
// uses the WindowAdapter as an inner class
// instead of implementing all the methods of
// WindowListener, but still misses the
// valuable modularity of inner classes
import java.awt.*;
import java.awt.event.*;
import java.util.*;

public class BadIdea2 extends Frame
    implements ActionListener {
  Button
    b1 = new Button("Button 1"),
    b2 = new Button("Button 2");
  public BadIdea2() {
    setLayout(new FlowLayout());
    addWindowListener(new WL());
    b1.addActionListener(this);
    b2.addActionListener(this);
    add(b1);
    add(b2);
  }
  public void actionPerformed(ActionEvent e) {
    Object source = e.getSource();
    if(source == b1)
      System.out.println("Button 1 pressed");
    else if(source == b2)
      System.out.println("Button 2 pressed");
    else
      System.out.println("Something else");
  }
  class WL extends WindowAdapter {
    public void windowClosing(WindowEvent e) {
      System.out.println("Window Closing");
      System.exit(0);
    }
  }
  public static void main(String[] args) {
    Frame f = new BadIdea2();
    f.setSize(300,200);
```

```
        f.setVisible(true);
      }
    } ///:~
```

Since **actionPerformed( )** is still tightly coupled to the main class, it's hard to reuse that code. It's also messier and less pleasant to read than the inner class approach.

There's no reason that you have to use any of the old thinking for events in Java 1.1 – so why do it?

Inheriting a component

Another place where you'll often see variations on the old way of doing things is when creating a new type of component. Here's an example showing that here, too, the new way works:

```
//: GoodTechnique.java
// Your first choice when overriding components
// should be to install listeners. The code is
// much safer, more modular and maintainable.
import java.awt.*;
import java.awt.event.*;

class Display {
  public static final int
      EVENT = 0, COMPONENT = 1,
      MOUSE = 2, MOUSE_MOVE = 3,
      FOCUS = 4, KEY = 5, ACTION = 6,
      LAST = 7;
  public String[] evnt;
  Display() {
    evnt = new String[LAST];
    for(int i = 0; i < LAST; i++)
      evnt[i] = new String();
  }
  public void show(Graphics g) {
    for(int i = 0; i < LAST; i++)
      g.drawString(evnt[i], 0, 10 * i + 10);
  }
}

class EnabledPanel extends Panel {
  Color c;
  int id;
```

```
    Display display = new Display();
    public EnabledPanel(int i, Color mc) {
      id = i;
      c = mc;
      setLayout(new BorderLayout());
      add(new MyButton(), BorderLayout.SOUTH);
      addComponentListener(new CL());
      addFocusListener(new FL());
      addKeyListener(new KL());
      addMouseListener(new ML());
      addMouseMotionListener(new MML());
    }
    // To eliminate flicker:
    public void update(Graphics g) {
      paint(g);
    }
    public void paint(Graphics  g) {
      g.setColor(c);
      Dimension s = getSize();
      g.fillRect(0, 0, s.width, s.height);
      g.setColor(Color.black);
      display.show(g);
    }
    // Don't need to enable anything for this:
    public void processEvent(AWTEvent e) {
      display.evnt[Display.EVENT]= e.toString();
      repaint();
      super.processEvent(e);
    }
    class CL implements ComponentListener {
      public void componentMoved(ComponentEvent e){
        display.evnt[Display.COMPONENT] =
          "Component moved";
        repaint();
      }
      public void
      componentResized(ComponentEvent e) {
        display.evnt[Display.COMPONENT] =
          "Component resized";
        repaint();
      }
      public void
      componentHidden(ComponentEvent e) {
        display.evnt[Display.COMPONENT] =
```

```
          "Component hidden";
        repaint();
      }
      public void componentShown(ComponentEvent e){
        display.evnt[Display.COMPONENT] =
          "Component shown";
        repaint();
      }
    }
    class FL implements FocusListener {
      public void focusGained(FocusEvent e) {
        display.evnt[Display.FOCUS] =
          "FOCUS gained";
        repaint();
      }
      public void focusLost(FocusEvent e) {
        display.evnt[Display.FOCUS] =
          "FOCUS lost";
        repaint();
      }
    }
    class KL implements KeyListener {
      public void keyPressed(KeyEvent e) {
        display.evnt[Display.KEY] =
          "KEY pressed: ";
        showCode(e);
      }
      public void keyReleased(KeyEvent e) {
        display.evnt[Display.KEY] =
          "KEY released: ";
        showCode(e);
      }
      public void keyTyped(KeyEvent e) {
        display.evnt[Display.KEY] =
          "KEY typed: ";
        showCode(e);
      }
      void showCode(KeyEvent e) {
        int code = e.getKeyCode();
        display.evnt[Display.KEY] +=
          KeyEvent.getKeyText(code);
        repaint();
      }
    }
```

```
class ML implements MouseListener {
  public void mouseClicked(MouseEvent e) {
    requestFocus(); // Get FOCUS on click
    display.evnt[Display.MOUSE] =
      "MOUSE clicked";
    showMouse(e);
  }
  public void mousePressed(MouseEvent e) {
    display.evnt[Display.MOUSE] =
      "MOUSE pressed";
    showMouse(e);
  }
  public void mouseReleased(MouseEvent e) {
    display.evnt[Display.MOUSE] =
      "MOUSE released";
    showMouse(e);
  }
  public void mouseEntered(MouseEvent e) {
    display.evnt[Display.MOUSE] =
      "MOUSE entered";
    showMouse(e);
  }
  public void mouseExited(MouseEvent e) {
    display.evnt[Display.MOUSE] =
      "MOUSE exited";
    showMouse(e);
  }
  void showMouse(MouseEvent e) {
    display.evnt[Display.MOUSE] +=
      ", x = " + e.getX() +
      ", y = " + e.getY();
    repaint();
  }
}
class MML implements MouseMotionListener {
  public void mouseDragged(MouseEvent e) {
    display.evnt[Display.MOUSE_MOVE] =
      "MOUSE dragged";
    showMouse(e);
  }
  public void mouseMoved(MouseEvent e) {
    display.evnt[Display.MOUSE_MOVE] =
      "MOUSE moved";
    showMouse(e);
```

```
      }
    void showMouse(MouseEvent e) {
      display.evnt[Display.MOUSE_MOVE] +=
        ", x = " + e.getX() +
        ", y = " + e.getY();
      repaint();
    }
  }
}

class MyButton extends Button {
  int clickCounter;
  String label = "";
  public MyButton() {
    addActionListener(new AL());
  }
  public void paint(Graphics g) {
    g.setColor(Color.green);
    Dimension s = getSize();
    g.fillRect(0, 0, s.width, s.height);
    g.setColor(Color.black);
    g.drawRect(0, 0, s.width - 1, s.height - 1);
    drawLabel(g);
  }
  private void drawLabel(Graphics g) {
    FontMetrics fm = g.getFontMetrics();
    int width = fm.stringWidth(label);
    int height = fm.getHeight();
    int ascent = fm.getAscent();
    int leading = fm.getLeading();
    int horizMargin =
      (getSize().width - width)/2;
    int verMargin =
      (getSize().height - height)/2;
    g.setColor(Color.red);
    g.drawString(label, horizMargin,
      verMargin + ascent + leading);
  }
  class AL implements ActionListener {
    public void actionPerformed(ActionEvent e) {
      clickCounter++;
      label = "click #" + clickCounter +
        " " + e.toString();
      repaint();
```

```
            }
         }
      }

      public class GoodTechnique extends Frame {
         GoodTechnique() {
            setLayout(new GridLayout(2,2));
            add(new EnabledPanel(1, Color.cyan));
            add(new EnabledPanel(2, Color.lightGray));
            add(new EnabledPanel(3, Color.yellow));
         }
         public static void main(String[] args) {
            Frame f = new GoodTechnique();
            f.setTitle("Good Technique");
            f.addWindowListener(
               new WindowAdapter() {
                  public void windowClosing(WindowEvent e){
                     System.out.println(e);
                     System.out.println("Window Closing");
                     System.exit(0);
                  }
               });
            f.setSize(700,700);
            f.setVisible(true);
         }
      } ///:~
```

This example also demonstrates the various events that occur and displays the information about them. The class **Display** is a way to centralize that information display. There's an array of **String**s to hold information about each type of event, and the method **show( )** takes a handle to whatever **Graphic**s object you have and writes directly on that surface. The scheme is intended to be somewhat reusable.

EnabledPanel represents the new type of component. It's a colored panel with a button at the bottom, and it captures all the events that happen over it by using inner listener classes for every single event *except* those in which **EnabledPanel** overrides **processEvent( )** in the old style (notice it must also call **super.processEvent( )**). The only reason for using this method is that it captures every event that happens, so you can view everything that goes on. **processEvent( )** does nothing more than show the string representation of each event, otherwise it would have to use a cascade of **if** statements to figure out what event it was. On the other hand, the inner listener classes already know precisely what event occurred. (Assuming you register them to components in which you don't need any control logic, which should be your goal.) Thus, they don't have to check anything out; they just do their stuff.

Each listener modifies the **Display** string associated with its particular event and calls **repaint( )** so the strings get displayed. You can also see a trick that will usually eliminate flicker:

```
public void update(Graphics g) {
  paint(g);
}
```

You don't always need to override **update( )**, but if you write something that flickers, try it. The default version of update clears the background and then calls **paint( )** to redraw any graphics. This clearing is usually what causes flicker but is not necessary since **paint( )** redraws the entire surface.

You can see that there are a lot of listeners – however, type checking occurs for the listeners, and you can't listen for something that the component doesn't support (unlike **BadTechnique.java**, which you will see momentarily).

Experimenting with this program is quite educational since you learn a lot about the way that events occur in Java. For one thing, it shows a flaw in the design of most windowing systems: it's pretty hard to click and release the mouse without moving it, and the windowing system will often think you're dragging when you're actually just trying to click on something. A solution to this is to use **mousePressed( )** and **mouseReleased( )** instead of **mouseClicked( )**, and then determine whether to call your own "mouseReallyClicked( )" method based on time and about 4 pixels of mouse hysteresis.

Ugly component inheritance

The alternative, which you will see put forward in many published works, is to call **enableEvents( )** and pass it the masks corresponding to the events you want to handle. This causes those events to be sent to the old-style methods (although they're new to Java 1.1) with names like **processFocusEvent( )**. You must also remember to call the base-class version. Here's what it looks like:

```
//: BadTechnique.java
// It's possible to override components this way,
// but the listener approach is much better, so
// why would you?
import java.awt.*;
```

```
import java.awt.event.*;

class Display {
  public static final int
    EVENT = 0, COMPONENT = 1,
    MOUSE = 2, MOUSE_MOVE = 3,
    FOCUS = 4, KEY = 5, ACTION = 6,
    LAST = 7;
  public String[] evnt;
  Display() {
    evnt = new String[LAST];
    for(int i = 0; i < LAST; i++)
      evnt[i] = new String();
  }
  public void show(Graphics g) {
    for(int i = 0; i < LAST; i++)
      g.drawString(evnt[i], 0, 10 * i + 10);
  }
}

class EnabledPanel extends Panel {
  Color c;
  int id;
  Display display = new Display();
  public EnabledPanel(int i, Color mc) {
    id = i;
    c = mc;
    setLayout(new BorderLayout());
    add(new MyButton(), BorderLayout.SOUTH);
    // Type checking is lost. You can enable and
    // process events that the component doesn't
    // capture:
    enableEvents(
      // Panel doesn't handle these:
      AWTEvent.ACTION_EVENT_MASK |
      AWTEvent.ADJUSTMENT_EVENT_MASK |
      AWTEvent.ITEM_EVENT_MASK |
      AWTEvent.TEXT_EVENT_MASK |
      AWTEvent.WINDOW_EVENT_MASK |
      // Panel can handle these:
      AWTEvent.COMPONENT_EVENT_MASK |
      AWTEvent.FOCUS_EVENT_MASK |
      AWTEvent.KEY_EVENT_MASK |
      AWTEvent.MOUSE_EVENT_MASK |
```

```
      AWTEvent.MOUSE_MOTION_EVENT_MASK |
      AWTEvent.CONTAINER_EVENT_MASK);
      // You can enable an event without
      // overriding its process method.
  }
  // To eliminate flicker:
  public void update(Graphics g) {
    paint(g);
  }
  public void paint(Graphics  g) {
    g.setColor(c);
    Dimension s = getSize();
    g.fillRect(0, 0, s.width, s.height);
    g.setColor(Color.black);
    display.show(g);
  }
  public void processEvent(AWTEvent e) {
    display.evnt[Display.EVENT]= e.toString();
    repaint();
    super.processEvent(e);
  }
  public void
  processComponentEvent(ComponentEvent e) {
    switch(e.getID()) {
      case ComponentEvent.COMPONENT_MOVED:
        display.evnt[Display.COMPONENT] =
          "Component moved";
        break;
      case ComponentEvent.COMPONENT_RESIZED:
        display.evnt[Display.COMPONENT] =
          "Component resized";
        break;
      case ComponentEvent.COMPONENT_HIDDEN:
        display.evnt[Display.COMPONENT] =
          "Component hidden";
        break;
      case ComponentEvent.COMPONENT_SHOWN:
        display.evnt[Display.COMPONENT] =
          "Component shown";
        break;
      default:
    }
    repaint();
    // Must always remember to call the "super"
```

```java
      // version of whatever you override:
      super.processComponentEvent(e);
  }
  public void processFocusEvent(FocusEvent e) {
    switch(e.getID()) {
      case FocusEvent.FOCUS_GAINED:
        display.evnt[Display.FOCUS] =
          "FOCUS gained";
        break;
      case FocusEvent.FOCUS_LOST:
        display.evnt[Display.FOCUS] =
          "FOCUS lost";
        break;
      default:
    }
    repaint();
    super.processFocusEvent(e);
  }
  public void processKeyEvent(KeyEvent e) {
    switch(e.getID()) {
      case KeyEvent.KEY_PRESSED:
        display.evnt[Display.KEY] =
          "KEY pressed: ";
        break;
      case KeyEvent.KEY_RELEASED:
        display.evnt[Display.KEY] =
          "KEY released: ";
        break;
      case KeyEvent.KEY_TYPED:
        display.evnt[Display.KEY] =
          "KEY typed: ";
        break;
      default:
    }
    int code = e.getKeyCode();
    display.evnt[Display.KEY] +=
      KeyEvent.getKeyText(code);
    repaint();
    super.processKeyEvent(e);
  }
  public void processMouseEvent(MouseEvent e) {
    switch(e.getID()) {
      case MouseEvent.MOUSE_CLICKED:
        requestFocus(); // Get FOCUS on click
```

```
            display.evnt[Display.MOUSE] =
              "MOUSE clicked";
            break;
          case MouseEvent.MOUSE_PRESSED:
            display.evnt[Display.MOUSE] =
              "MOUSE pressed";
            break;
          case MouseEvent.MOUSE_RELEASED:
            display.evnt[Display.MOUSE] =
              "MOUSE released";
            break;
          case MouseEvent.MOUSE_ENTERED:
            display.evnt[Display.MOUSE] =
              "MOUSE entered";
            break;
          case MouseEvent.MOUSE_EXITED:
            display.evnt[Display.MOUSE] =
              "MOUSE exited";
            break;
          default:
      }
      display.evnt[Display.MOUSE] +=
        ", x = " + e.getX() +
        ", y = " + e.getY();
      repaint();
      super.processMouseEvent(e);
    }
    public void
    processMouseMotionEvent(MouseEvent e) {
      switch(e.getID()) {
        case MouseEvent.MOUSE_DRAGGED:
          display.evnt[Display.MOUSE_MOVE] =
            "MOUSE dragged";
          break;
        case MouseEvent.MOUSE_MOVED:
          display.evnt[Display.MOUSE_MOVE] =
            "MOUSE moved";
          break;
        default:
      }
      display.evnt[Display.MOUSE_MOVE] +=
        ", x = " + e.getX() +
        ", y = " + e.getY();
      repaint();
```

```
        super.processMouseMotionEvent(e);
      }
    }

    class MyButton extends Button {
      int clickCounter;
      String label = "";
      public MyButton() {
        enableEvents(AWTEvent.ACTION_EVENT_MASK);
      }
      public void paint(Graphics g) {
        g.setColor(Color.green);
        Dimension s = getSize();
        g.fillRect(0, 0, s.width, s.height);
        g.setColor(Color.black);
        g.drawRect(0, 0, s.width - 1, s.height - 1);
        drawLabel(g);
      }
      private void drawLabel(Graphics g) {
        FontMetrics fm = g.getFontMetrics();
        int width = fm.stringWidth(label);
        int height = fm.getHeight();
        int ascent = fm.getAscent();
        int leading = fm.getLeading();
        int horizMargin =
          (getSize().width - width)/2;
        int verMargin =
          (getSize().height - height)/2;
        g.setColor(Color.red);
        g.drawString(label, horizMargin,
                     verMargin + ascent + leading);
      }
      public void processActionEvent(ActionEvent e) {
        clickCounter++;
        label = "click #" + clickCounter +
          " " + e.toString();
        repaint();
        super.processActionEvent(e);
      }
    }

    public class BadTechnique extends Frame {
      BadTechnique() {
        setLayout(new GridLayout(2,2));
```

```
      add(new EnabledPanel(1, Color.cyan));
      add(new EnabledPanel(2, Color.lightGray));
      add(new EnabledPanel(3, Color.yellow));
      // You can also do it for Windows:
      enableEvents(AWTEvent.WINDOW_EVENT_MASK);
   }
   public void processWindowEvent(WindowEvent e) {
      System.out.println(e);
      if(e.getID() == WindowEvent.WINDOW_CLOSING) {
         System.out.println("Window Closing");
         System.exit(0);
      }
   }
   public static void main(String[] args) {
      Frame f = new BadTechnique();
      f.setTitle("Bad Technique");
      f.setSize(700,700);
      f.setVisible(true);
   }
} ///:~
```

Sure, it works. But it's ugly and hard to write, read, debug, maintain, and reuse. So why bother when you can use inner listener classes?

Java 1.1 UI APIs

Java 1.1 has also added some important new functionality, including focus traversal, desktop color access, printing "inside the sandbox," and the beginnings of clipboard support.

Focus traversal is quite easy, since it's transparently present in the AWT library components and you don't have to do anything to make it work. If you make your own components and want them to handle focus traversal, you override **isFocusTraversable( )** to return **true**. If you want to capture the keyboard focus on a mouse click, you catch the mouse down event and call **requestFocus( )**.

Desktop colors

The desktop colors provide a way for you to know what the various color choices are on the current user's desktop. This way, you can use those colors in your program if you desire. The colors are automatically initialized and placed in **static** members of class **SystemColor**, so all you need to do is read the member you're interested in. The names are intentionally self-explanatory: **desktop**, **activeCaption**, **activeCaptionText**, **activeCaptionBorder**, **inactiveCaption**, **inactiveCaptionText**, **inactiveCaptionBorder**, **window**, **windowBorder**, **windowText**, **menu**, **menuText**, **text**, **textText**, **textHighlight**, **textHighlightText**, **textInactiveText**, **control**, **controlText**, **controlHighlight**, **controlLtHighlight**, **controlShadow**, **controlDkShadow**, **scrollbar**, **info** (for help), and **infoText** (for help text).

Printing

Unfortunately, there isn't much that's automatic with printing. Instead you must go through a number of mechanical, non-OO steps in order to print. Printing a component graphically can be slightly more automatic: by default, the **print( )** method calls **paint( )** to do its work. There are times when this is satisfactory, but if you want to do anything more specialized you must know that you're printing so you can in particular find out the page dimensions.

The following example demonstrates the printing of both text and graphics, and the different approaches you can use for printing graphics. In addition, it tests the printing support:

```
//: PrintDemo.java
// Printing with Java 1.1
import java.awt.*;
import java.awt.event.*;

public class PrintDemo extends Frame {
  Button
    printText = new Button("Print Text"),
    printGraphics = new Button("Print Graphics");
  TextField ringNum = new TextField(3);
  Choice faces = new Choice();
  Graphics g = null;
  Plot plot = new Plot3(); // Try different plots
  Toolkit tk = Toolkit.getDefaultToolkit();
  public PrintDemo() {
    ringNum.setText("3");
    ringNum.addTextListener(new RingL());
    Panel p = new Panel();
    p.setLayout(new FlowLayout());
    printText.addActionListener(new TBL());
```

```
      p.add(printText);
      p.add(new Label("Font:"));
      p.add(faces);
      printGraphics.addActionListener(new GBL());
      p.add(printGraphics);
      p.add(new Label("Rings:"));
      p.add(ringNum);
      setLayout(new BorderLayout());
      add(p, BorderLayout.NORTH);
      add(plot, BorderLayout.CENTER);
      String[] fontList = tk.getFontList();
      for(int i = 0; i < fontList.length; i++)
        faces.add(fontList[i]);
      faces.select("Serif");
    }
  class PrintData {
    public PrintJob pj;
    public int pageWidth, pageHeight;
    PrintData(String jobName) {
      pj = getToolkit().getPrintJob(
        PrintDemo.this, jobName, null);
      if(pj != null) {
        pageWidth = pj.getPageDimension().width;
        pageHeight= pj.getPageDimension().height;
        g = pj.getGraphics();
      }
    }
    void end() { pj.end(); }
  }
  class ChangeFont {
    private int stringHeight;
    ChangeFont(String face, int style,int point){
      if(g != null) {
        g.setFont(new Font(face, style, point));
        stringHeight =
          g.getFontMetrics().getHeight();
      }
    }
    int stringWidth(String s) {
      return g.getFontMetrics().stringWidth(s);
    }
    int stringHeight() { return stringHeight; }
  }
  class TBL implements ActionListener {
```

```java
    public void actionPerformed(ActionEvent e) {
      PrintData pd =
        new PrintData("Print Text Test");
      // Null means print job canceled:
      if(pd == null) return;
      String s = "PrintDemo";
      ChangeFont cf = new ChangeFont(
        faces.getSelectedItem(), Font.ITALIC,72);
      g.drawString(s,
        (pd.pageWidth - cf.stringWidth(s)) / 2,
        (pd.pageHeight - cf.stringHeight()) / 3);

      s = "A smaller point size";
      cf = new ChangeFont(
        faces.getSelectedItem(), Font.BOLD, 48);
      g.drawString(s,
        (pd.pageWidth - cf.stringWidth(s)) / 2,
        (int)((pd.pageHeight -
            cf.stringHeight())/1.5));
      g.dispose();
      pd.end();
    }
  }
  class GBL implements ActionListener {
    public void actionPerformed(ActionEvent e) {
      PrintData pd =
        new PrintData("Print Graphics Test");
      if(pd == null) return;
      plot.print(g);
      g.dispose();
      pd.end();
    }
  }
  class RingL implements TextListener {
    public void textValueChanged(TextEvent e) {
      int i = 1;
      try {
        i = Integer.parseInt(ringNum.getText());
      } catch(NumberFormatException ex) {
        i = 1;
      }
      plot.rings = i;
      plot.repaint();
    }
```

```
    }
  public static void main(String[] args) {
    Frame pdemo = new PrintDemo();
    pdemo.setTitle("Print Demo");
    pdemo.addWindowListener(
      new WindowAdapter() {
        public void windowClosing(WindowEvent e) {
          System.exit(0);
        }
      });
    pdemo.setSize(500, 500);
    pdemo.setVisible(true);
  }
}

class Plot extends Canvas {
  public int rings = 3;
}

class Plot1 extends Plot {
  // Default print() calls paint():
  public void paint(Graphics g) {
    int w = getSize().width;
    int h = getSize().height;
    int xc = w / 2;
    int yc = w / 2;
    int x = 0, y = 0;
    for(int i = 0; i < rings; i++) {
      if(x < xc && y < yc) {
        g.drawOval(x, y, w, h);
        x += 10; y += 10;
        w -= 20; h -= 20;
      }
    }
  }
}

class Plot2 extends Plot {
  // To fit the picture to the page, you must
  // know whether you're printing or painting:
  public void paint(Graphics g) {
    int w, h;
    if(g instanceof PrintGraphics) {
      PrintJob pj =
```

```
          ((PrintGraphics)g).getPrintJob();
      w = pj.getPageDimension().width;
      h = pj.getPageDimension().height;
    }
    else {
      w = getSize().width;
      h = getSize().height;
    }
    int xc = w / 2;
    int yc = w / 2;
    int x = 0, y = 0;
    for(int i = 0; i < rings; i++) {
      if(x < xc && y < yc) {
        g.drawOval(x, y, w, h);
        x += 10; y += 10;
        w -= 20; h -= 20;
      }
    }
  }
}

class Plot3 extends Plot {
  // Somewhat better. Separate
  // printing from painting:
  public void print(Graphics g) {
    // Assume it's a PrintGraphics object:
    PrintJob pj =
      ((PrintGraphics)g).getPrintJob();
    int w = pj.getPageDimension().width;
    int h = pj.getPageDimension().height;
    doGraphics(g, w, h);
  }
  public void paint(Graphics g) {
    int w = getSize().width;
    int h = getSize().height;
    doGraphics(g, w, h);
  }
  private void doGraphics(
      Graphics g, int w, int h) {
    int xc = w / 2;
    int yc = w / 2;
    int x = 0, y = 0;
    for(int i = 0; i < rings; i++) {
      if(x < xc && y < yc) {
```

```
            g.drawOval(x, y, w, h);
            x += 10; y += 10;
            w -= 20; h -= 20;
          }
        }
      }
    } ///:~
```

The program allows you to select fonts from a **Choice** list (and you'll see that the number of fonts available in Java 1.1 is still extremely limited, and has nothing to do with any extra fonts you install on your machine). It uses these to print out text in bold, italic, and in different sizes. In addition, a new type of component called a **Plot** is created to demonstrate graphics. A **Plot** has rings that it will display on the screen and print onto paper, and the three derived classes **Plot1**, **Plot2**, and **Plot3** perform these tasks in different ways so that you can see your alternatives when printing graphics. Also, you can change the number of rings in a plot – this is interesting because it shows the printing fragility in Java 1.1. On my system, the printer gave error messages and didn't print correctly when the ring count got "too high" (whatever that means), but worked fine when the count was "low enough." You will notice, too, that the page dimensions produced when printing do not seem to correspond to the actual dimensions of the page. This might be fixed in a future release of Java, and you can use this program to test it.

This program encapsulates functionality inside inner classes whenever possible, to facilitate reuse. For example, whenever you want to begin a print job (whether for graphics or text), you must create a **PrintJob** object, which has its own **Graphics** object along with the width and height of the page. The creation of a **PrintJob** and extraction of page dimensions is encapsulated in the **PrintData** class.

Printing text

Conceptually, printing text is straightforward: you choose a typeface and size, decide where the string should go on the page, and draw it with **Graphics.drawString( )**. This means, however, that you must perform the calculations of exactly where each line will go on the page to make sure it doesn't run off the end of the page or collide with other lines. If you want to make a word processor, your work is cut out for you.

ChangeFont encapsulates a little of the process of changing from one font to another by automatically creating a new **Font** object with your desired typeface, style (**Font.BOLD** or **Font.ITALIC** – there's no support for underline, strikethrough, etc.), and point size. It also simplifies the calculation of the width and height of a string.

When you press the "Print text" button, the **TBL** listener is activated. You can see that it goes through two iterations of creating a **ChangeFont** object and calling **drawString( )** to print out the string in a calculated position, centered, one-third, and two-thirds down the page, respectively. Notice whether these calculations produce the expected results. (They didn't with the version I used.)

Printing graphics

When you press the "Print graphics" button the **GBL** listener is activated. The creation of a **PrintData** object initializes **g**, and then you simply call **print( )** for the component you want to print. To force printing you must call **dispose( )** for the **Graphics** object and **end( )** for the **PrintData** object (which turns around and calls **end( )** for the **PrintJob**).

The work is going on inside the **Plot** object. You can see that the base-class **Plot** is simple – it extends **Canvas** and contains an **int** called **rings** to indicate how many concentric rings to draw on this particular **Canvas**. The three derived classes show different approaches to accomplishing the same goal: drawing on both the screen and on the printed page.

Plot1 takes the simplest approach to coding: ignore the fact that there are differences in painting and printing, and just override **paint( )**. The reason this works is that the default **print( )** method simply turns around and calls **paint( )**. However, you'll notice that the size of the output depends on the size of the on-screen canvas, which makes sense since the **width** and **height** are determined by calling **Canvas.getSize( )**. The other situation in which this is acceptable is if your image is always a fixed size.

When the size of the drawing surface is important, then you must discover the dimensions. Unfortunately, this turns out to be awkward, as you can see in **Plot2**. For some possibly good reason that I don't know, you cannot simply ask the **Graphics** object the dimensions of its drawing surface. This would have made the whole process quite elegant. Instead, to see if you're printing rather than painting, you must detect the **PrintGraphics** using the RTTI **instanceof** keyword (described in Chapter 11), then downcast and call the sole **PrintGraphics** method: **getPrintJob( )**. Now you have a handle to the **PrintJob** and you can find out the width and height of the paper. This is a hacky approach, but perhaps there is some rational reason for it. (On the other hand, you've seen some of the other library designs by now so you might get the impression that the designers were, in fact, just hacking around…)

You can see that **paint( )** in **Plot2** goes through both possibilities of printing or painting. But since the **print( )** method should be called when printing, why not use that? This approach is used in **Plot3**, and it eliminates the need to use **instanceof** since inside **print( )** you can assume that you can cast to a **PrintGraphics** object. This is a little better. The situation is improved by placing the common drawing code (once the dimensions have been detected) inside a separate method **doGraphics( )**.

Running Frames within applets

What if you'd like to print from within an applet? Well, to print anything you must get a **PrintJob** object through a **Toolkit** object's **getPrintJob( )** method, which takes only a **Frame** object and not an **Applet**. Thus it would seem that it's possible to print from within an application, but not an applet. However, it turns out that you can create a **Frame** from within an applet (which is the reverse of what I've been doing for the applet/application examples so far, which has been making an applet and putting inside a **Frame**). This is a useful technique since it allows you to use many applications within applets (as long as they don't violate applet security). When the application window comes up within an applet, however, you'll notice that the Web browser sticks a little caveat on it, something to the effect of "Warning: Applet Window."

You can see that it's quite straightforward to put a **Frame** inside an applet. The only thing that you must add is code to **dispose( )** of the **Frame** when the user closes it (instead of calling **System.exit( )**):

```
//: PrintDemoApplet.java
// Creating a Frame from within an Applet
import java.applet.*;
import java.awt.*;
import java.awt.event.*;

public class PrintDemoApplet extends Applet {
  public void init() {
    Button b = new Button("Run PrintDemo");
    b.addActionListener(new PDL());
    add(b);
  }
  class PDL implements ActionListener {
    public void actionPerformed(ActionEvent e) {
      final PrintDemo pd = new PrintDemo();
```

```
        pd.addWindowListener(new WindowAdapter() {
          public void windowClosing(WindowEvent e){
            pd.dispose();
          }
        });
        pd.setSize(500, 500);
        pd.show();
      }
    }
  } ///:~
```

There's some confusion involved with Java 1.1 printing support. Some of the publicity seemed to claim that you'd be able to print from within an applet. However, the Java security system contains a feature that could lock out an applet from initiating its own print job, requiring that the initiation be done via a Web browser or applet viewer. At the time of this writing, this seemed to remain an unresolved issue. When I ran this program from within a Web browser, the **PrintDemo** window came up just fine, but it wouldn't print from the browser.

The clipboard

Java 1.1 supports limited operations with the system clipboard (in the **java.awt.datatransfer** package). You can copy **String** objects to the clipboard as text, and you can paste text from the clipboard into **String** objects. Of course, the clipboard is designed to hold any type of data, but how this data is represented on the clipboard is up to the program doing the cutting and pasting. Although it currently supports only string data, the Java clipboard API provides for extensibility through the concept of a "flavor." When data comes off the clipboard, it has an associated set of flavors that it can be converted to (for example, a graph might be represented as a string of numbers or as an image) and you can see if that particular clipboard data supports the flavor you're interested in.

The following program is a simple demonstration of cut, copy, and paste with **String** data in a **TextArea**. One thing you'll notice is that the keyboard sequences you normally use for cutting, copying, and pasting also work. But if you look at any **TextField** or **TextArea** in any other program you'll find that they also automatically support the clipboard key sequences. This example simply adds programmatic control of the clipboard, and you could use these techniques if you want to capture clipboard text into some non-**TextComponent**.

```
//: CutAndPaste.java
// Using the clipboard from Java 1.1
```

```java
import java.awt.*;
import java.awt.event.*;
import java.awt.datatransfer.*;

public class CutAndPaste extends Frame {
  MenuBar mb = new MenuBar();
  Menu edit = new Menu("Edit");
  MenuItem
    cut = new MenuItem("Cut"),
    copy = new MenuItem("Copy"),
    paste = new MenuItem("Paste");
  TextArea text = new TextArea(20,20);
  Clipboard clipbd =
    getToolkit().getSystemClipboard();
  public CutAndPaste() {
    cut.addActionListener(new CutL());
    copy.addActionListener(new CopyL());
    paste.addActionListener(new PasteL());
    edit.add(cut);
    edit.add(copy);
    edit.add(paste);
    mb.add(edit);
    setMenuBar(mb);
    add(text, BorderLayout.CENTER);
  }
  class CopyL implements ActionListener {
    public void actionPerformed(ActionEvent e) {
      String selection = text.getSelectedText();
      StringSelection clipString =
        new StringSelection(selection);
      clipbd.setContents(clipString, clipString);
    }
  }
  class CutL implements ActionListener {
    public void actionPerformed(ActionEvent e) {
      String selection = text.getSelectedText();
      StringSelection clipString =
        new StringSelection(selection);
      clipbd.setContents(clipString, clipString);
      text.replaceRange("",
        text.getSelectionStart(),
        text.getSelectionEnd());
    }
  }
```

```
class PasteL implements ActionListener {
  public void actionPerformed(ActionEvent e) {
    Transferable clipData =
      clipbd.getContents(CutAndPaste.this);
    try {
      String clipString =
        (String)clipData.
          getTransferData(
            DataFlavor.stringFlavor);
      text.replaceRange(clipString,
        text.getSelectionStart(),
        text.getSelectionEnd());
    } catch(Exception ex) {
      System.out.println("not String flavor");
    }
  }
}
public static void main(String[] args) {
  CutAndPaste cp = new CutAndPaste();
  cp.addWindowListener(
    new WindowAdapter() {
      public void windowClosing(WindowEvent e) {
        System.exit(0);
      }
    });
  cp.setSize(300,200);
  cp.setVisible(true);
}
} ///:~
```

The creation and addition of the menu and **TextArea** should by now seem
a pedestrian activity. What's different is the creation of the **Clipboard**
field **clipbd**, which is done through the **Toolkit**.

All the action takes place in the listeners. The **CopyL** and **CutL** listeners
are the same except for the last line of **CutL**, which erases the line that's
been copied. The special two lines are the creation of a **StringSelection**
object from the **String** and the call to **setContents( )** with this
StringSelection. That's all there is to putting a **String** on the clipboard.

In **PasteL**, data is pulled off the clipboard using **getContents( )**. What
comes back is a fairly anonymous **Transferable** object, and you don't
really know what it contains. One way to find out is to call
getTransferDataFlavors( ), which returns an array of **DataFlavor**
objects indicating which flavors are supported by this particular object.

You can also ask it directly with **isDataFlavorSupported( )**, passing in the flavor you're interested in. Here, however, the bold approach is taken: **getTransferData( )** is called assuming that the contents supports the **String** flavor, and if it doesn't the problem is sorted out in the exception handler.

In the future you can expect more data flavors to be supported.

Visual programming and Beans

So far in this book you've seen how valuable Java is for creating reusable pieces of code. The "most reusable" unit of code has been the class, since it comprises a cohesive unit of characteristics (fields) and behaviors (methods) that can be reused either directly via composition or through inheritance.

Inheritance and polymorphism are essential parts of object-oriented programming, but in the majority of cases when you're putting together an application, what you really want is components that do exactly what you need. You'd like to drop these parts into your design like the electronic engineer puts together chips on a circuit board (or even, in the case of Java, onto a Web page). It seems, too, that there should be some way to accelerate this "modular assembly" style of programming.

"Visual programming" first became successful – *very* successful – with Microsoft's Visual Basic (VB), followed by a second-generation design in Borland's Delphi (the primary inspiration for the Java Beans design). With these programming tools the components are represented visually, which makes sense since they usually display some kind of visual component such as a button or a text field. The visual representation, in fact, is often exactly the way the component will look in the running program. So part of the process of visual programming involves dragging a component from a pallet and dropping it onto your form. The application builder tool writes code as you do this, and that code will cause the component to be created in the running program.

Simply dropping the component onto a form is usually not enough to complete the program. Often, you must change the characteristics of a component, such as what color it is, what text is on it, what database it's connected to, etc. Characteristics that can be modified at design time are referred to as *properties*. You can manipulate the properties of your component inside the application builder tool, and when you create the program this configuration data is saved so that it can be rejuvenated when the program is started.

By now you're probably used to the idea that an object is more than characteristics; it's also a set of behaviors. At design-time, the behaviors of a visual component are partially represented by *events*, meaning "Here's something that can happen to the component." Ordinarily, you decide what you want to happen when an event occurs by tying code to that event.

Here's the critical part: the application builder tool is able to dynamically interrogate (using reflection) the component to find out which properties and events the component supports. Once it knows what they are, it can display the properties and allow you to change those (saving the state when you build the program), and also display the events. In general, you do something like double clicking on an event and the application builder tool creates a code body and ties it to that particular event. All you have to do at that point is write the code that executes when the event occurs.

All this adds up to a lot of work that's done for you by the application builder tool. As a result you can focus on what the program looks like and what it is supposed to do, and rely on the application builder tool to manage the connection details for you. The reason that visual programming tools have been so successful is that they dramatically speed up the process of building an application – certainly the user interface, but often other portions of the application as well.

What is a Bean?

After the dust settles, then, a component is really just a block of code, typically embodied in a class. The key issue is the ability for the application builder tool to discover the properties and events for that component. To create a VB component, the programmer had to write a fairly complicated piece of code following certain conventions to expose the properties and events. Delphi was a second-generation visual programming tool and the language was actively designed around visual programming so it is much easier to create a visual component. However, Java has brought the creation of visual components to its most advanced state with Java Beans, because a Bean is just a class. You don't have to write any extra code or use special language extensions in order to make something a Bean. The only thing you need to do, in fact, is slightly modify the way that you name your methods. It is the method name that tells the application builder tool whether this is a property, an event, or just an ordinary method.

In the Java documentation, this naming convention is mistakenly termed a "design pattern." This is unfortunate since design patterns (see Chapter 16) are challenging enough without this sort of confusion. It's not a design pattern, it's just a naming convention and it's fairly simple:

1. For a property named **xxx**, you typically create two methods: **getXxx( )** and **setXxx( )**. Note that the first letter after get or set is automatically lowercased to produce the property name. The type produced by the "get" method is the same as the type of the argument to the "set" method. The name of the property and the type for the "get" and "set" are not related.

2. For a boolean property, you can use the "get" and "set" approach above, but you can also use "is" instead of "get."

3. Ordinary methods of the Bean don't conform to the above naming convention, but they're **public**.

4. For events, you use the "listener" approach. It's exactly the same as you've been seeing: **addFooBarListener(FooBarListener)** and **removeFooBarListener(FooBarListener)** to handle a **FooBarEvent**. Most of the time the built-in events and listeners will satisfy your needs, but you can also create your own events and listener interfaces.

Point 1 above answers a question about something you might have noticed in the change from Java 1.0 to Java 1.1: a number of method names have had small, apparently meaningless name changes. Now you can see that most of those changes had to do with adapting to the "get" and "set" naming conventions in order to make that particular component into a Bean.

We can use these guidelines to create a simple Bean:

```
//: Frog.java
// A trivial Java Bean
package frogbean;
import java.awt.*;
import java.awt.event.*;

class Spots {}

public class Frog {
```

```
      private int jumps;
      private Color color;
      private Spots spots;
      private boolean jmpr;
      public int getJumps() { return jumps; }
      public void setJumps(int newJumps) {
         jumps = newJumps;
      }
      public Color getColor() { return color; }
      public void setColor(Color newColor) {
         color = newColor;
      }
      public Spots getSpots() { return spots; }
      public void setSpots(Spots newSpots) {
         spots = newSpots;
      }
      public boolean isJumper() { return jmpr; }
      public void setJumper(boolean j) { jmpr = j; }
      public void addActionListener(
          ActionListener l) {
         //...
      }
      public void removeActionListener(
          ActionListener l) {
         // ...
      }
      public void addKeyListener(KeyListener l) {
         // ...
      }
      public void removeKeyListener(KeyListener l) {
         // ...
      }
      // An "ordinary" public method:
      public void croak() {
         System.out.println("Ribbet!");
      }
    } ///:~
```

First, you can see that it's just a class. Usually, all your fields will be
private, and accessible only through methods. Following the naming
convention, the properties are **jumps**, **color**, **spots**, and **jumper** (notice
the change in case of the first letter in the property name). Although the
name of the internal identifier is the same as the name of the property in
the first three cases, in **jumper** you can see that the property name does

not force you to use any particular name for internal variables (or, indeed, to even *have* any internal variable for that property).

The events this Bean handles are **ActionEvent** and **KeyEvent**, based on the naming of the "add" and "remove" methods for the associated listener. Finally, you can see that the ordinary method **croak( )** is still part of the Bean simply because it's a **public** method, not because it conforms to any naming scheme.

Extracting **BeanInfo** with the **Introspector**

One of the most critical parts of the Bean scheme occurs when you drag a Bean off a palette and plop it down on a form. The application builder tool must be able to create the Bean (which it can do if there's a default constructor) and then, without access to the Bean's source code, extract all the necessary information to create the property sheet and event handlers.

Part of the solution is already evident from the end of Chapter 11: Java 1.1 *reflection* allows all the methods of an anonymous class to be discovered. This is perfect for solving the Bean problem without requiring you to use any extra language keywords like those required in other visual programming languages. In fact, one of the prime reasons that reflection was added to Java 1.1 was to support Beans (although reflection also supports object serialization and remote method invocation). So you might expect that the creator of the application builder tool would have to reflect each Bean and hunt through its methods to find the properties and events for that Bean.

This is certainly possible, but the Java designers wanted to provide a standard interface for everyone to use, not only to make Beans simpler to use but also to provide a standard gateway to the creation of more complex Beans. This interface is the **Introspector** class, and the most important method in this class is the **static getBeanInfo( )**. You pass a **Class** handle to this method and it fully interrogates that class and returns a **BeanInfo** object that you can then dissect to find properties, methods, and events.

Usually you won't care about any of this – you'll probably get most of your Beans off the shelf from vendors, and you don't need to know all the magic that's going on underneath. You'll simply drag your Beans onto your form, then configure their properties and write handlers for the events you're interested in. However, it's an interesting and educational exercise to use the **Introspector** to display information about a Bean, so here's a tool that does it (you'll find it in the **frogbean** subdirectory):

```
//: BeanDumper.java
// A method to introspect a Bean
import java.beans.*;
import java.lang.reflect.*;

public class BeanDumper {
  public static void dump(Class bean){
    BeanInfo bi = null;
    try {
      bi = Introspector.getBeanInfo(
        bean, java.lang.Object.class);
    } catch(IntrospectionException ex) {
      System.out.println("Couldn't introspect " +
        bean.getName());
      System.exit(1);
    }
    PropertyDescriptor[] properties =
      bi.getPropertyDescriptors();
    for(int i = 0; i < properties.length; i++) {
      Class p = properties[i].getPropertyType();
      System.out.println(
        "Property type:\n  " + p.getName());
      System.out.println(
        "Property name:\n  " +
        properties[i].getName());
      Method readMethod =
        properties[i].getReadMethod();
      if(readMethod != null)
        System.out.println(
          "Read method:\n  " +
          readMethod.toString());
      Method writeMethod =
        properties[i].getWriteMethod();
      if(writeMethod != null)
        System.out.println(
          "Write method:\n  " +
          writeMethod.toString());
      System.out.println("====================");
    }
    System.out.println("Public methods:");
    MethodDescriptor[] methods =
```

```
      bi.getMethodDescriptors();
    for(int i = 0; i < methods.length; i++)
      System.out.println(
        methods[i].getMethod().toString());
    System.out.println("======================");
    System.out.println("Event support:");
    EventSetDescriptor[] events =
      bi.getEventSetDescriptors();
    for(int i = 0; i < events.length; i++) {
      System.out.println("Listener type:\n   " +
        events[i].getListenerType().getName());
      Method[] lm =
        events[i].getListenerMethods();
      for(int j = 0; j < lm.length; j++)
        System.out.println(
          "Listener method:\n   " +
          lm[j].getName());
      MethodDescriptor[] lmd =
        events[i].getListenerMethodDescriptors();
      for(int j = 0; j < lmd.length; j++)
        System.out.println(
          "Method descriptor:\n   " +
          lmd[j].getMethod().toString());
      Method addListener =
        events[i].getAddListenerMethod();
      System.out.println(
          "Add Listener Method:\n   " +
        addListener.toString());
      Method removeListener =
        events[i].getRemoveListenerMethod();
      System.out.println(
        "Remove Listener Method:\n   " +
        removeListener.toString());
      System.out.println("====================");
    }
  }
  // Dump the class of your choice:
  public static void main(String[] args) {
    if(args.length < 1) {
      System.err.println("usage: \n" +
        "BeanDumper fully.qualified.class");
      System.exit(0);
    }
    Class c = null;
```

```
        try {
          c = Class.forName(args[0]);
        } catch(ClassNotFoundException ex) {
          System.err.println(
            "Couldn't find " + args[0]);
          System.exit(0);
        }
        dump(c);
      }
    } ///:~
```

BeanDumper.dump( ) is the method that does all the work. First it tries to create a **BeanInfo** object, and if successful calls the methods of **BeanInfo** that produce information about properties, methods, and events. In **Introspector.getBeanInfo( )**, you'll see there is a second argument. This tells the **Introspector** where to stop in the inheritance hierarchy. Here, it stops before it parses all the methods from **Object**, since we're not interested in seeing those.

For properties, **getPropertyDescriptors( )** returns an array of **PropertyDescriptor**s. For each **PropertyDescriptor** you can call **getPropertyType( )** to find the class of object that is passed in and out via the property methods. Then, for each property you can get its pseudonym (extracted from the method names) with **getName( )**, the method for reading with **getReadMethod( )**, and the method for writing with **getWriteMethod( )**. These last two methods return a **Method** object that can actually be used to invoke the corresponding method on the object (this is part of reflection).

For the public methods (including the property methods), **getMethodDescriptors( )** returns an array of **MethodDescriptor**s. For each one you can get the associated **Method** object and print out its name.

For the events, **getEventSetDescriptors( )** returns an array of (what else?) **EventSetDescriptor**s. Each of these can be queried to find out the class of the listener, the methods of that listener class, and the add- and remove-listener methods. The **BeanDumper** program prints out all of this information.

If you invoke **BeanDumper** on the **Frog** class like this:

```
java BeanDumper frogbean.Frog
```

the output, after removing extra details that are unnecessary here, is:

```
class name: Frog
Property type:
  Color
Property name:
  color
Read method:
  public Color getColor()
Write method:
  public void setColor(Color)
====================
Property type:
  Spots
Property name:
  spots
Read method:
  public Spots getSpots()
Write method:
  public void setSpots(Spots)
====================
Property type:
  boolean
Property name:
  jumper
Read method:
  public boolean isJumper()
Write method:
  public void setJumper(boolean)
====================
Property type:
  int
Property name:
  jumps
Read method:
  public int getJumps()
Write method:
  public void setJumps(int)
====================
Public methods:
public void setJumps(int)
public void croak()
public void removeActionListener(ActionListener)
public void addActionListener(ActionListener)
public int getJumps()
public void setColor(Color)
```

```
public void setSpots(Spots)
public void setJumper(boolean)
public boolean isJumper()
public void addKeyListener(KeyListener)
public Color getColor()
public void removeKeyListener(KeyListener)
public Spots getSpots()
======================
Event support:
Listener type:
  KeyListener
Listener method:
  keyTyped
Listener method:
  keyPressed
Listener method:
  keyReleased
Method descriptor:
  public void keyTyped(KeyEvent)
Method descriptor:
  public void keyPressed(KeyEvent)
Method descriptor:
  public void keyReleased(KeyEvent)
Add Listener Method:
  public void addKeyListener(KeyListener)
Remove Listener Method:
  public void removeKeyListener(KeyListener)
====================
Listener type:
  ActionListener
Listener method:
  actionPerformed
Method descriptor:
  public void actionPerformed(ActionEvent)
Add Listener Method:
  public void addActionListener(ActionListener)
Remove Listener Method:
  public void removeActionListener(ActionListener)
====================
```

This reveals most of what the **Introspector** sees as it produces a **BeanInfo** object from your Bean. You can see that the type of the property and its name are independent. Notice the lowercasing of the property name. (The only time this doesn't occur is when the property name begins with more than one capital letter in a row.) And remember that the method names you're seeing here (such as the read and write methods) are actually produced from a **Method** object that can be used to invoke the associated method on the object.

The public method list includes the methods that are not associated with a property or event, such as **croak( )**, as well as those that are. These are all the methods that you can call programmatically for a Bean, and the application builder tool can choose to list all of these while you're making method calls, to ease your task.

Finally, you can see that the events are fully parsed out into the listener, its methods, and the add- and remove-listener methods. Basically, once you have the **BeanInfo**, you can find out everything of importance for the Bean. You can also call the methods for that Bean, even though you don't have any other information except the object (again, a feature of reflection).

A more sophisticated Bean

This next example is slightly more sophisticated, albeit frivolous. It's a canvas that draws a little circle around the mouse whenever the mouse is moved. When you press the mouse, the word "Bang!" appears in the middle of the screen, and an action listener is fired.

The properties you can change are the size of the circle as well as the color, size, and text of the word that is displayed when you press the mouse. A **BangBean** also has its own **addActionListener( )** and **removeActionListener( )** so you can attach your own listener that will be fired when the user clicks on the **BangBean**. You should be able to recognize the property and event support:

```
//: BangBean.java
// A graphical Bean
package bangbean;
import java.awt.*;
import java.awt.event.*;
import java.io.*;
import java.util.*;

public class BangBean extends Canvas
        implements Serializable {
  protected int xm, ym;
  protected int cSize = 20; // Circle size
  protected String text = "Bang!";
  protected int fontSize = 48;
```

```
  protected Color tColor = Color.red;
  protected ActionListener actionListener;
  public BangBean() {
    addMouseListener(new ML());
    addMouseMotionListener(new MML());
  }
  public int getCircleSize() { return cSize; }
  public void setCircleSize(int newSize) {
    cSize = newSize;
  }
  public String getBangText() { return text; }
  public void setBangText(String newText) {
    text = newText;
  }
  public int getFontSize() { return fontSize; }
  public void setFontSize(int newSize) {
    fontSize = newSize;
  }
  public Color getTextColor() { return tColor; }
  public void setTextColor(Color newColor) {
    tColor = newColor;
  }
  public void paint(Graphics g) {
    g.setColor(Color.black);
    g.drawOval(xm - cSize/2, ym - cSize/2,
      cSize, cSize);
  }
  // This is a unicast listener, which is
  // the simplest form of listener management:
  public void addActionListener (
      ActionListener l)
        throws TooManyListenersException {
    if(actionListener != null)
      throw new TooManyListenersException();
    actionListener = l;
  }
  public void removeActionListener(
      ActionListener l) {
    actionListener = null;
  }
  class ML extends MouseAdapter {
    public void mousePressed(MouseEvent e) {
      Graphics g = getGraphics();
      g.setColor(tColor);
```

```
        g.setFont(
          new Font(
            "TimesRoman", Font.BOLD, fontSize));
        int width =
          g.getFontMetrics().stringWidth(text);
        g.drawString(text,
          (getSize().width - width) /2,
          getSize().height/2);
        g.dispose();
        // Call the listener's method:
        if(actionListener != null)
          actionListener.actionPerformed(
            new ActionEvent(BangBean.this,
              ActionEvent.ACTION_PERFORMED, null));
      }
    }
    class MML extends MouseMotionAdapter {
      public void mouseMoved(MouseEvent e) {
        xm = e.getX();
        ym = e.getY();
        repaint();
      }
    }
    public Dimension getPreferredSize() {
      return new Dimension(200, 200);
    }
    // Testing the BangBean:
    public static void main(String[] args) {
      BangBean bb = new BangBean();
      try {
        bb.addActionListener(new BBL());
      } catch(TooManyListenersException e) {}
      Frame aFrame = new Frame("BangBean Test");
      aFrame.addWindowListener(
        new WindowAdapter() {
          public void windowClosing(WindowEvent e) {
            System.exit(0);
          }
        });
      aFrame.add(bb, BorderLayout.CENTER);
      aFrame.setSize(300,300);
      aFrame.setVisible(true);
    }
    // During testing, send action information
```

```
      // to the console:
      static class BBL implements ActionListener {
        public void actionPerformed(ActionEvent e) {
          System.out.println("BangBean action");
        }
      }
    } ///:~
```

The first thing you'll notice is that **BangBean** implements the
Serializable interface. This means that the application builder tool can
"pickle" all the information for the **BangBean** using serialization after
the program designer has adjusted the values of the properties. When the
Bean is created as part of the running application, these "pickled"
properties are restored so that you get exactly what you designed.

You can see that all the fields are **private**, which is what you'll usually
do with a Bean – allow access only through methods, usually using the
"property" scheme.

When you look at the signature for **addActionListener( )**, you'll see that
it can throw a **TooManyListenersException**. This indicates that it is
unicast, which means it notifies only one listener when the event occurs.
Ordinarily, you'll use *multicast* events so that many listeners can be
notified of an event. However, that runs into issues that you won't be
ready for until the next chapter, so it will be revisited there (under the
heading "Java Beans revisited"). A unicast event sidesteps the problem.

When you press the mouse, the text is put in the middle of the
BangBean, and if the **actionListener** field is not **null**, its
actionPerformed( ) is called, creating a new **ActionEvent** object in the
process. Whenever the mouse is moved, its new coordinates are captured
and the canvas is repainted (erasing any text that's on the canvas, as
you'll see).

The **main( )** is added to allow you to test the program from the
command line. When a Bean is in a development environment, **main( )**
will not be used, but it's helpful to have a **main( )** in each of your Beans
because it provides for rapid testing. **main( )** creates a **Frame** and places
a **BangBean** within it, attaching a simple **ActionListener** to the
BangBean to print to the console whenever an **ActionEvent** occurs.
Usually, of course, the application builder tool would create most of the
code that uses the Bean.

When you run the **BangBean** through **BeanDumper** or put the
BangBean inside a Bean-enabled development environment, you'll notice
that there are many more properties and actions than are evident from

the above code. That's because **BangBean** is inherited from **Canvas**, and **Canvas** is a Bean, so you're seeing its properties and events as well.

Packaging a Bean

Before you can bring a Bean into a Bean-enabled visual builder tool, it must be put into the standard Bean container, which is a JAR (Java ARchive) file that includes all the Bean classes as well as a "manifest" file that says "This is a Bean." A manifest file is simply a text file that follows a particular form. For the **BangBean**, the manifest file looks like this:

```
Manifest-Version: 1.0

Name: bangbean/BangBean.class
Java-Bean: True
```

The first line indicates the version of the manifest scheme, which until further notice from Sun is 1.0. The second line (empty lines are ignored) names the **BangBean.class** file, and the third says, "It's a Bean." Without the third line, the program builder tool will not recognize the class as a Bean.

The only tricky part is that you must make sure that you get the proper path in the "Name:" field. If you look back at **BangBean.java**, you'll see it's in **package bangbean** (and thus in a subdirectory called "bangbean" that's off of the classpath), and the name in the manifest file must include this package information. In addition, you must place the manifest file in the directory *above* the root of your package path, which in this case means placing the file in the directory above the "bangbean" subdirectory. Then you must invoke **jar** from the same directory as the manifest file, as follows:

```
jar cfm BangBean.jar BangBean.mf bangbean
```

This assumes that you want the resulting JAR file to be named **BangBean.jar** and that you've put the manifest in a file called **BangBean.mf**.

You might wonder "What about all the other classes that were generated when I compiled **BangBean.java**?" Well, they all ended up inside the **bangbean** subdirectory, and you'll see that the last argument for the above **jar** command line is the **bangbean** subdirectory. When you give **jar** the name of a subdirectory, it packages that entire subdirectory into the jar file (including, in this case, the original **BangBean.java** source-code file – you might not choose to include the source with your own

Beans). In addition, if you turn around and unpack the JAR file you've just created, you'll discover that your manifest file isn't inside, but that **jar** has created its own manifest file (based partly on yours) called **MANIFEST.MF** and placed it inside the subdirectory **META-INF** (for "meta-information"). If you open this manifest file you'll also notice that digital signature information has been added by **jar** for each file, of the form:

```
Digest-Algorithms: SHA MD5
SHA-Digest: pDpEAG9NaeCx8aFtqPI4udSX/OO=
MD5-Digest: O4NcS1hE3Smnzlp2hj6qeg==
```

In general, you don't need to worry about any of this, and if you make changes you can just modify your original manifest file and re-invoke **jar** to create a new JAR file for your Bean. You can also add other Beans to the JAR file simply by adding their information to your manifest.

One thing to notice is that you'll probably want to put each Bean in its own subdirectory, since when you create a JAR file you hand the **jar** utility the name of a subdirectory and it puts everything in that subdirectory into the JAR file. You can see that both **Frog** and **BangBean** are in their own subdirectories.

Once you have your Bean properly inside a JAR file you can bring it into a Beans-enabled program-builder environment. The way you do this varies from one tool to the next, but Sun provides a freely-available test bed for Java Beans in their "Beans Development Kit" (BDK) called the "beanbox." (Download the BDK from *www.javasoft.com.*) To place your Bean in the beanbox, copy the JAR file into the BDK's "jars" subdirectory before you start up the beanbox.

More complex Bean support

You can see how remarkably simple it is to make a Bean. But you aren't limited to what you've seen here. The Java Bean design provides a simple point of entry but can also scale to more complex situations. These situations are beyond the scope of this book but they will be briefly introduced here. You can find more details at *http://java.sun.com/beans*.

One place where you can add sophistication is with properties. The examples above have shown only single properties, but it's also possible to represent multiple properties in an array. This is called an *indexed property*. You simply provide the appropriate methods (again following a naming convention for the method names) and the **Introspector**

---

recognizes an indexed property so your application builder tool can respond appropriately.

Properties can be *bound*, which means that they will notify other objects via a **PropertyChangeEvent**. The other objects can then choose to change themselves based on the change to the Bean.

Properties can be *constrained*, which means that other objects can veto a change to that property if it is unacceptable. The other objects are notified using a **PropertyChangeEvent**, and they can throw a **ProptertyVetoException** to prevent the change from happening and to restore the old values.

You can also change the way your Bean is represented at design time:

1. You can provide a custom property sheet for your particular Bean. The ordinary property sheet will be used for all other Beans, but yours is automatically invoked when your Bean is selected.

2. You can create a custom editor for a particular property, so the ordinary property sheet is used, but when your special property is being edited, your editor will automatically be invoked.

3. You can provide a custom **BeanInfo** class for your Bean that produces information that's different from the default created by the **Introspector**.

4. It's also possible to turn "expert" mode on and off in all **FeatureDescriptor**s to distinguish between basic features and more complicated ones.

More to Beans

There's another issue that couldn't be addressed here. Whenever you create a Bean, you should expect that it will be run in a multithreaded environment. This means that you must understand the issues of threading, which will be introduced in the next chapter. You'll find a section there called "Java Beans revisited" that will look at the problem and its solution.

Introduction to Swing[7]

After working your way through this chapter and seeing the huge changes that have occurred within the AWT (although, if you can remember back that far, Sun claimed Java was a "stable" language when it first appeared), you might still have the feeling that it's not quite done. Sure, there's now a good event model, and JavaBeans is an excellent component-reuse design. But the GUI components still seem rather minimal, primitive, and awkward.

That's where Swing comes in. The Swing library appeared after Java 1.1 so you might naturally assume that it's part of Java 1.2. However, it is designed to work with Java 1.1 as an add-on. This way, you don't have to wait for your platform to support Java 1.2 in order to enjoy a good UI component library. Your users might actually need to download the Swing library if it isn't part of their Java 1.1 support, and this could cause a few snags. But it works.

Swing contains all the components that you've been missing throughout the rest of this chapter: those you expect to see in a modern UI, everything from buttons that contain pictures to trees and grids. It's a big library, but it's designed to have appropriate complexity for the task at hand – if something is simple, you don't have to write much code but as you try to do more your code becomes increasingly complex. This means an easy entry point, but you've got the power if you need it.

Swing has great depth. This section does not attempt to be comprehensive, but instead introduces the power and simplicity of Swing to get you started using the library. Please be aware that what you see here is intended to be simple. If you need to do more, then Swing can probably give you what you want if you're willing to do the research by hunting through the online documentation from Sun.

---

[7] At the time this section was written, the Swing library had been pronounced "frozen" by Sun, so this code should compile and run without problems as long as you've downloaded and installed the Swing library. (You should be able to compile one of Sun's included demonstration programs to test your installation.) If you do encounter difficulties, check *www.BruceEckel.com* for updated code.

Benefits of Swing

When you begin to use the Swing library, you'll see that it's a huge step forward. Swing components are Beans (and thus use the Java 1.1 event model), so they can be used in any development environment that supports Beans. Swing provides a full set of UI components. For speed, all the components are lightweight (no "peer" components are used), and Swing is written entirely in Java for portability.

Much of what you'll like about Swing could be called "orthogonality of use;" that is, once you pick up the general ideas about the library you can apply them everywhere. Primarily because of the Beans naming conventions, much of the time I was writing these examples I could guess at the method names and get it right the first time, without looking anything up. This is certainly the hallmark of a good library design. In addition, you can generally plug components into other components and things will work correctly.

Keyboard navigation is automatic – you can use a Swing application without the mouse, but you don't have to do any extra programming (the old AWT required some ugly code to achieve keyboard navigation). Scrolling support is effortless – you simply wrap your component in a **JScrollPane** as you add it to your form. Other features such as tool tips typically require a single line of code to implement.

Swing also supports something called "pluggable look and feel," which means that the appearance of the UI can be dynamically changed to suit the expectations of users working under different platforms and operating systems. It's even possible to invent your own look and feel.

Easy conversion

If you've struggled long and hard to build your UI using Java 1.1, you don't want to throw it away to convert to Swing. Fortunately, the library is designed to allow easy conversion – in many cases you can simply put a 'J' in front of the class names of each of your old AWT components. Here's an example that should have a familiar flavor to it:

```
//: JButtonDemo.java
// Looks like Java 1.1 but with J's added
package c13.swing;
import java.awt.*;
import java.awt.event.*;
import java.applet.*;
import com.sun.java.swing.*;
```

```
public class JButtonDemo extends Applet {
  JButton
    b1 = new JButton("JButton 1"),
    b2 = new JButton("JButton 2");
  JTextField t = new JTextField(20);
  public void init() {
    ActionListener al = new ActionListener() {
      public void actionPerformed(ActionEvent e){
        String name =
          ((JButton)e.getSource()).getText();
        t.setText(name + " Pressed");
      }
    };
    b1.addActionListener(al);
    add(b1);
    b2.addActionListener(al);
    add(b2);
    add(t);
  }
  public static void main(String args[]) {
    JButtonDemo applet = new JButtonDemo();
    JFrame frame = new JFrame("TextAreaNew");
    frame.addWindowListener(new WindowAdapter() {
      public void windowClosing(WindowEvent e){
        System.exit(0);
      }
    });
    frame.getContentPane().add(
      applet, BorderLayout.CENTER);
    frame.setSize(300,100);
    applet.init();
    applet.start();
    frame.setVisible(true);
  }
} ///:~
```

There's a new **import** statement, but everything else looks like the Java 1.1 AWT with the addition of some J's. Also, you don't just **add( )** something to a Swing **JFrame**, but you must get the "content pane" first, as seen above. But you can easily get many of the benefits of Swing with a simple conversion.

Because of the **package** statement, you'll have to invoke this program by saying:

```
java c13.swing.JbuttonDemo
```

All of the programs in this section will require a similar form to run
them.

A display framework

Although the programs that are both applets and applications can be
valuable, if used everywhere they become distracting and waste paper.
Instead, a display framework will be used for the Swing examples in the
rest of this section:

```
//: Show.java
// Tool for displaying Swing demos
package c13.swing;
import java.awt.*;
import java.awt.event.*;
import com.sun.java.swing.*;

public class Show {
  public static void
  inFrame(JPanel jp, int width, int height) {
    String title = jp.getClass().toString();
    // Remove the word "class":
    if(title.indexOf("class") != -1)
      title = title.substring(6);
    JFrame frame = new JFrame(title);
    frame.addWindowListener(new WindowAdapter() {
      public void windowClosing(WindowEvent e){
        System.exit(0);
      }
    });
    frame.getContentPane().add(
      jp, BorderLayout.CENTER);
    frame.setSize(width, height);
    frame.setVisible(true);
  }
} ///:~
```

Classes that want to display themselves should inherit from **JPanel** and
then add any visual components to themselves. Finally, they create a
main( ) containing the line:

```
Show.inFrame(new MyClass(), 500, 300);
```

in which the last two arguments are the display width and height.

Note that the title for the **JFrame** is produced using RTTI.

Tool tips

Almost all of the classes that you'll be using to create your user interfaces are derived from **JComponent**, which contains a method called **setToolTipText(String)** So, for virtually anything you place on your form, all you need to do is say (for an object **jc** of any **JComponent**-derived class):

```
jc.setToolTipText("My tip");
```

and when the mouse stays over that **JComponent** for a predetermined period of time, a tiny box containing your text will pop up next to the mouse.

Borders

JComponent also contains a method called **setBorder( )**, which allows you to place various interesting borders on any visible component. The following example demonstrates a number of the different borders that are available, using a method called **showBorder( )** that creates a **JPanel** and puts on the border in each case. Also, it uses RTTI to find the name of the border that you're using (stripping off all the path information), then puts that name in a **JLabel** in the middle of the panel:

```
//: Borders.java
// Different Swing borders
package c13.swing;
import java.awt.*;
import java.awt.event.*;
import com.sun.java.swing.*;
import com.sun.java.swing.border.*;

public class Borders extends JPanel {
  static JPanel showBorder(Border b) {
    JPanel jp = new JPanel();
    jp.setLayout(new BorderLayout());
    String nm = b.getClass().toString();
    nm = nm.substring(nm.lastIndexOf('.') + 1);
    jp.add(new JLabel(nm, JLabel.CENTER),
      BorderLayout.CENTER);
```

```
      jp.setBorder(b);
      return jp;
    }
    public Borders() {
      setLayout(new GridLayout(2,4));
      add(showBorder(new TitledBorder("Title")));
      add(showBorder(new EtchedBorder()));
      add(showBorder(new LineBorder(Color.blue)));
      add(showBorder(
        new MatteBorder(5,5,30,30,Color.green)));
      add(showBorder(
        new BevelBorder(BevelBorder.RAISED)));
      add(showBorder(
        new SoftBevelBorder(BevelBorder.LOWERED)));
      add(showBorder(new CompoundBorder(
        new EtchedBorder(),
        new LineBorder(Color.red))));
    }
    public static void main(String args[]) {
      Show.inFrame(new Borders(), 500, 300);
    }
} ///:~
```

Most of the examples in this section use **TitledBorder**, but you can see that the rest of the borders are as easy to use. You can also create your own borders and put them inside buttons, labels, etc. – anything derived from **JComponent**.

Buttons

Swing adds a number of different types of buttons, and it also changes the organization of the selection components: all buttons, checkboxes, radio buttons, and even menu items are inherited from **AbstractButton** (which, since menu items are included, would probably have been better named "AbstractChooser" or something equally general). You'll see the use of menu items shortly, but the following example shows the various types of buttons available:

```
//: Buttons.java
// Various Swing buttons
package c13.swing;
import java.awt.*;
import java.awt.event.*;
import com.sun.java.swing.*;
```

```java
import com.sun.java.swing.basic.*;
import com.sun.java.swing.border.*;

public class Buttons extends JPanel {
  JButton jb = new JButton("JButton");
  BasicArrowButton
    up = new BasicArrowButton(
      BasicArrowButton.NORTH),
    down = new BasicArrowButton(
      BasicArrowButton.SOUTH),
    right = new BasicArrowButton(
      BasicArrowButton.EAST),
    left = new BasicArrowButton(
      BasicArrowButton.WEST);
  Spinner spin = new Spinner(47, "");
  StringSpinner stringSpin =
    new StringSpinner(3, "",
      new String[] {
        "red", "green", "blue", "yellow" });
  public Buttons() {
    add(jb);
    add(new JToggleButton("JToggleButton"));
    add(new JCheckBox("JCheckBox"));
    add(new JRadioButton("JRadioButton"));
    up.addActionListener(new ActionListener() {
      public void actionPerformed(ActionEvent e){
        spin.setValue(spin.getValue() + 1);
      }
    });
    down.addActionListener(new ActionListener() {
      public void actionPerformed(ActionEvent e){
        spin.setValue(spin.getValue() - 1);
      }
    });
    JPanel jp = new JPanel();
    jp.add(spin);
    jp.add(up);
    jp.add(down);
    jp.setBorder(new TitledBorder("Spinner"));
    add(jp);
    left.addActionListener(new ActionListener() {
      public void actionPerformed(ActionEvent e){
        stringSpin.setValue(
          stringSpin.getValue() + 1);
```

```
      }
    });
    right.addActionListener(new ActionListener(){
      public void actionPerformed(ActionEvent e){
        stringSpin.setValue(
          stringSpin.getValue() - 1);
      }
    });
    jp = new JPanel();
    jp.add(stringSpin);
    jp.add(left);
    jp.add(right);
    jp.setBorder(
      new TitledBorder("StringSpinner"));
    add(jp);
  }
  public static void main(String args[]) {
    Show.inFrame(new Buttons(), 300, 200);
  }
} ///:~
```

The **JButton** looks like the AWT button, but there's more you can do to it (like add images, as you'll see later). In **com.sun.java.swing.basic**, there is a **BasicArrowButton** that is convenient, but what to test it on? There are two types of "spinners" that just beg to be used with arrow buttons: **Spinner**, which changes an **int** value, and **StringSpinner**, which moves through an array of **String** (even automatically wrapping when it reaches the end of the array). The **ActionListeners** attached to the arrow buttons shows how relatively obvious it is to use these spinners: you just get and set values, using method names you would expect since they're Beans.

When you run the example, you'll see that the toggle button holds its last position, in or out. But the check boxes and radio buttons behave identically to each other, just clicking on or off (they are inherited from **JToggleButton**).

Button groups

If you want radio buttons to behave in an "exclusive or" fashion, you must add them to a button group, in a similar but less awkward way as the old AWT. But as the example below demonstrates, any **AbstractButton** can be added to a **ButtonGroup**.

To avoid repeating a lot of code, this example uses reflection to generate the groups of different types of buttons. This is seen in **makeBPanel**, which creates a button group and a **JPanel**, and for each **String** in the array that's the second argument to **makeBPanel( )**, it adds an object of the class represented by the first argument:

```
//: ButtonGroups.java
// Uses reflection to create groups of different
// types of AbstractButton.
package c13.swing;
import java.awt.*;
import java.awt.event.*;
import com.sun.java.swing.*;
import com.sun.java.swing.border.*;
import java.lang.reflect.*;

public class ButtonGroups extends JPanel {
  static String[] ids = {
    "June", "Ward", "Beaver",
    "Wally", "Eddie", "Lumpy",
  };
  static JPanel
  makeBPanel(Class bClass, String[] ids) {
    ButtonGroup bg = new ButtonGroup();
    JPanel jp = new JPanel();
    String title = bClass.getName();
    title = title.substring(
      title.lastIndexOf('.') + 1);
    jp.setBorder(new TitledBorder(title));
    for(int i = 0; i < ids.length; i++) {
      AbstractButton ab = new JButton("failed");
      try {
        // Get the dynamic constructor method
        // that takes a String argument:
        Constructor ctor = bClass.getConstructor(
          new Class[] { String.class });
        // Create a new object:
        ab = (AbstractButton)ctor.newInstance(
          new Object[]{ids[i]});
      } catch(Exception ex) {
        System.out.println("can't create " +
          bClass);
      }
      bg.add(ab);
      jp.add(ab);
```

```
      }
      return jp;
    }
    public ButtonGroups() {
      add(makeBPanel(JButton.class, ids));
      add(makeBPanel(JToggleButton.class, ids));
      add(makeBPanel(JCheckBox.class, ids));
      add(makeBPanel(JRadioButton.class, ids));
    }
    public static void main(String args[]) {
      Show.inFrame(new ButtonGroups(), 500, 300);
    }
} ///:~
```

The title for the border is taken from the name of the class, stripping off all the path information. The **AbstractButton** is initialized to a **JButton** that has the label "Failed" so if you ignore the exception message, you'll still see the problem on screen. The **getConstructor( )** method produces a **Constructor** object that takes the array of arguments of the types in the **Class** array passed to **getConstructor( )**. Then all you do is call **newInstance( )**, passing it an array of **Object** containing your actual arguments – in this case, just the **String** from the **ids** array.

This adds a little complexity to what is a simple process. To get "exclusive or" behavior with buttons, you create a button group and add each button for which you want that behavior to the group. When you run the program, you'll see that all the buttons except **JButton** exhibit this "exclusive or" behavior.

Icons

You can use an **Icon** inside a **JLabel** or anything that inherits from **AbstractButton** (including **JButton**, **JCheckbox**, **JradioButton**, and the different kinds of **JMenuItem**). Using **Icon**s with **JLabel**s is quite straightforward (you'll see an example later). The following example explores all the additional ways you can use **Icon**s with buttons and their descendants.

You can use any **gif** files you want, but the ones used in this example are part of the book's code distribution, available at *www.BruceEckel.com*. To open a file and bring in the image, simply create an **ImageIcon** and hand it the file name. From then on, you can use the resulting **Icon** in your program.

```
//: Faces.java
```

```
// Icon behavior in JButtons
package c13.swing;
import java.awt.*;
import java.awt.event.*;
import com.sun.java.swing.*;

public class Faces extends JPanel {
  static Icon[] faces = {
    new ImageIcon("face0.gif"),
    new ImageIcon("face1.gif"),
    new ImageIcon("face2.gif"),
    new ImageIcon("face3.gif"),
    new ImageIcon("face4.gif"),
  };
  JButton
    jb = new JButton("JButton", faces[3]),
    jb2 = new JButton("Disable");
  boolean mad = false;
  public Faces() {
    jb.addActionListener(new ActionListener() {
      public void actionPerformed(ActionEvent e){
        if(mad) {
          jb.setIcon(faces[3]);
          mad = false;
        } else {
          jb.setIcon(faces[0]);
          mad = true;
        }
        jb.setVerticalAlignment(JButton.TOP);
        jb.setHorizontalAlignment(JButton.LEFT);
      }
    });
    jb.setRolloverEnabled(true);
    jb.setRolloverIcon(faces[1]);
    jb.setPressedIcon(faces[2]);
    jb.setDisabledIcon(faces[4]);
    jb.setToolTipText("Yow!");
    add(jb);
    jb2.addActionListener(new ActionListener() {
      public void actionPerformed(ActionEvent e){
        if(jb.isEnabled()) {
          jb.setEnabled(false);
          jb2.setText("Enable");
        } else {
```

```
            jb.setEnabled(true);
            jb2.setText("Disable");
          }
        }
      });
      add(jb2);
    }
    public static void main(String args[]) {
      Show.inFrame(new Faces(), 300, 200);
    }
  } ///:~
```

An **Icon** can be used in many constructors, but you can also use
setIcon( ) to add or change an **Icon**. This example also shows how a
JButton (or any **AbstractButton**) can set the various different sorts of
icons that appear when things happen to that button: when it's pressed,
disabled, or "rolled over" (the mouse moves over it without clicking).
You'll see that this gives the button a rather animated feel.

Note that a tool tip is also added to the button.

Menus

Menus are much improved and more flexible in Swing – for example, you
can use them just about anywhere, including panels and applets. The
syntax for using them is much the same as it was in the old AWT, and
this preserves the same problem present in the old AWT: you must hard-
code your menus and there isn't any support for menus as resources
(which, among other things, would make them easier to change for other
languages). In addition, menu code gets long-winded and sometimes
messy. The following approach takes a step in the direction of solving
this problem by putting all the information about each menu into a two-
dimensional array of **Object** (that way you can put anything you want
into the array). This array is organized so that the first row represents
the menu name, and the remaining rows represent the menu items and
their characteristics. You'll notice the rows of the array do not have to be
uniform from one to the next – as long as your code knows where
everything should be, each row can be completely different.

```
//: Menus.java
// A menu-building system; also demonstrates
// icons in labels and menu items.
package c13.swing;
import java.awt.*;
import java.awt.event.*;
```

```
import com.sun.java.swing.*;

public class Menus extends JPanel {
  static final Boolean
    bT = new Boolean(true),
    bF = new Boolean(false);
  // Dummy class to create type identifiers:
  static class MType { MType(int i) {} };
  static final MType
    mi = new MType(1), // Normal menu item
    cb = new MType(2), // Checkbox menu item
    rb = new MType(3); // Radio button menu item
  JTextField t = new JTextField(10);
  JLabel l = new JLabel("Icon Selected",
    Faces.faces[0], JLabel.CENTER);
  ActionListener a1 = new ActionListener() {
    public void actionPerformed(ActionEvent e) {
      t.setText(
        ((JMenuItem)e.getSource()).getText());
    }
  };
  ActionListener a2 = new ActionListener() {
    public void actionPerformed(ActionEvent e) {
      JMenuItem mi = (JMenuItem)e.getSource();
      l.setText(mi.getText());
      l.setIcon(mi.getIcon());
    }
  };
  // Store menu data as "resources":
  public Object[][] fileMenu = {
    // Menu name and accelerator:
    { "File", new Character('F') },
    // Name type accel listener enabled
    { "New", mi, new Character('N'), a1, bT },
    { "Open", mi, new Character('O'), a1, bT },
    { "Save", mi, new Character('S'), a1, bF },
    { "Save As", mi, new Character('A'), a1, bF},
    { null }, // Separator
    { "Exit", mi, new Character('x'), a1, bT },
  };
  public Object[][] editMenu = {
    // Menu name:
    { "Edit", new Character('E') },
    // Name type accel listener enabled
```

```
          { "Cut", mi, new Character('t'), a1, bT },
          { "Copy", mi, new Character('C'), a1, bT },
          { "Paste", mi, new Character('P'), a1, bT },
          { null }, // Separator
          { "Select All", mi,new Character('l'),a1,bT},
        };
        public Object[][] helpMenu = {
          // Menu name:
          { "Help", new Character('H') },
          // Name type accel listener enabled
          { "Index", mi, new Character('I'), a1, bT },
          { "Using help", mi,new Character('U'),a1,bT},
          { null }, // Separator
          { "About", mi, new Character('t'), a1, bT },
        };
        public Object[][] optionMenu = {
          // Menu name:
          { "Options", new Character('O') },
          // Name type accel listener enabled
          { "Option 1", cb, new Character('1'), a1,bT},
          { "Option 2", cb, new Character('2'), a1,bT},
        };
        public Object[][] faceMenu = {
          // Menu name:
          { "Faces", new Character('a') },
          // Optinal last element is icon
          { "Face 0", rb, new Character('0'), a2, bT,
            Faces.faces[0] },
          { "Face 1", rb, new Character('1'), a2, bT,
            Faces.faces[1] },
          { "Face 2", rb, new Character('2'), a2, bT,
            Faces.faces[2] },
          { "Face 3", rb, new Character('3'), a2, bT,
            Faces.faces[3] },
          { "Face 4", rb, new Character('4'), a2, bT,
            Faces.faces[4] },
        };
        public Object[] menuBar = {
          fileMenu, editMenu, faceMenu,
          optionMenu, helpMenu,
        };
        static public JMenuBar
        createMenuBar(Object[] menuBarData) {
          JMenuBar menuBar = new JMenuBar();
```

```
      for(int i = 0; i < menuBarData.length; i++)
        menuBar.add(
          createMenu((Object[][])menuBarData[i]));
      return menuBar;
    }
    static ButtonGroup bgroup;
    static public JMenu
    createMenu(Object[][] menuData) {
      JMenu menu = new JMenu();
      menu.setText((String)menuData[0][0]);
      menu.setKeyAccelerator(
        ((Character)menuData[0][1]).charValue());
      // Create redundantly, in case there are
      // any radio buttons:
      bgroup = new ButtonGroup();
      for(int i = 1; i < menuData.length; i++) {
        if(menuData[i][0] == null)
          menu.add(new JSeparator());
        else
          menu.add(createMenuItem(menuData[i]));
      }
      return menu;
    }
    static public JMenuItem
    createMenuItem(Object[] data) {
      JMenuItem m = null;
      MType type = (MType)data[1];
      if(type == mi)
        m = new JMenuItem();
      else if(type == cb)
        m = new JCheckBoxMenuItem();
      else if(type == rb) {
        m = new JRadioButtonMenuItem();
        bgroup.add(m);
      }
      m.setText((String)data[0]);
      m.setKeyAccelerator(
        ((Character)data[2]).charValue());
      m.addActionListener(
        (ActionListener)data[3]);
      m.setEnabled(
        ((Boolean)data[4]).booleanValue());
      if(data.length == 6)
        m.setIcon((Icon)data[5]);
```

```
      return m;
    }
  Menus() {
    setLayout(new BorderLayout());
    add(createMenuBar(menuBar),
      BorderLayout.NORTH);
    JPanel p = new JPanel();
    p.setLayout(new BorderLayout());
    p.add(t, BorderLayout.NORTH);
    p.add(l, BorderLayout.CENTER);
    add(p, BorderLayout.CENTER);
  }
  public static void main(String args[]) {
    Show.inFrame(new Menus(), 300, 200);
  }
} ///:~
```

The goal is to allow the programmer to simply create tables to represent each menu, rather than typing lines of code to build the menus. Each table produces one menu, and the first row in the table contains the menu name and its keyboard accelerator. The remaining rows contain the data for each menu item: the string to be placed on the menu item, what type of menu item it is, its keyboard accelerator, the actionlistener that is fired when this menu item is selected, and whether this menu item is enabled. If a row starts with **null** it is treated as a separator.

To prevent wasteful and tedious multiple creations of **Boolean** objects and type flags, these are created as **static final** values at the beginning of the class: **bT** and **bF** to represent **Boolean**s and different objects of the dummy class **MType** to describe normal menu items (**mi**), checkbox menu items (**cb**), and radio button menu items (**rb**). Remember that an array of **Object** may hold only **Object** handles and not primitive values.

This example also shows how **JLabel**s and **JMenuItem**s (and their descendants) may hold **Icon**s. An **Icon** is placed into the **JLabel** via its constructor and changed when the corresponding menu item is selected.

The **menuBar** array contains the handles to all the file menus in the order that you want them to appear on the menu bar. You pass this array to **createMenuBar( )**, which breaks it up into individual arrays of menu data, passing each to **createMenu( )**. This method, in turn, takes the first line of the menu data and creates a **JMenu** from it, then calls **createMenuItem( )** for each of the remaining lines of menu data. Finally, **createMenuItem( )** parses each line of menu data and determines the type of menu and its attributes, and creates that menu item

---

Thinking in Java   *www.BruceEckel.com*

appropriately. In the end, as you can see in the **Menus( )** constructor, to create a menu from these tables say **createMenuBar(menuBar)** and everything is handled recursively.

This example does not take care of building cascading menus, but you should have enough of the concept that you can add that capability if you need it.

Popup menus

The implementation of **JPopupMenu** seems a bit strange: you must call **enableEvents( )** and select for mouse events instead of using an event listener. That is, it's possible to add a mouse listener but the **MouseEvent** that comes through doesn't return **true** from **isPopupTrigger( )** – it doesn't know that it should trigger a popup menu.[8] In addition, when I tried the listener approach it behaved strangely, possibly from recursive click handling. In any event, the following example produces the desired popup behavior:

```
//: Popup.java
// Creating popup menus with Swing
package c13.swing;
import java.awt.*;
import java.awt.event.*;
import com.sun.java.swing.*;

public class Popup extends JPanel {
  JPopupMenu popup = new JPopupMenu();
  JTextField t = new JTextField(10);
  public Popup() {
    add(t);
    ActionListener al = new ActionListener() {
      public void actionPerformed(ActionEvent e){
        t.setText(
          ((JMenuItem)e.getSource()).getText());
      }
    };
    JMenuItem m = new JMenuItem("Hither");
    m.addActionListener(al);
    popup.add(m);
    m = new JMenuItem("Yon");
```

---

[8] This may also be a result of using pre-beta software.

```
      m.addActionListener(al);
      popup.add(m);
      m = new JMenuItem("Afar");
      m.addActionListener(al);
      popup.add(m);
      popup.addSeparator();
      m = new JMenuItem("Stay Here");
      m.addActionListener(al);
      popup.add(m);
      enableEvents(AWTEvent.MOUSE_EVENT_MASK);
    }
    protected void processMouseEvent(MouseEvent e){
      if (e.isPopupTrigger())
        popup.show(
          e.getComponent(), e.getX(), e.getY());
      super.processMouseEvent(e);
    }
    public static void main(String args[]) {
      Show.inFrame(new Popup(),200,150);
    }
} ///:~
```

The same **ActionListener** is added to each **JMenuItem**, so that it fetches the text from the menu label and inserts it into the **JTextField**.

List boxes and combo boxes

List boxes and combo boxes in Swing work much as they do in the old AWT, but they also have increased functionality if you need it. In addition, some conveniences have been added. For example, the **JList** has a constructor that takes an array of **Strings** to display (oddly enough this same feature is not available in **JComboBox**). Here's a simple example that shows the basic use of each:

```
//: ListCombo.java
// List boxes & Combo boxes
package c13.swing;
import java.awt.*;
import java.awt.event.*;
import com.sun.java.swing.*;

public class ListCombo extends JPanel {
  public ListCombo() {
    setLayout(new GridLayout(2,1));
```

```
      JList list = new JList(ButtonGroups.ids);
      add(new JScrollPane(list));
      JComboBox combo = new JComboBox();
      for(int i = 0; i < 100; i++)
        combo.addItem(Integer.toString(i));
      add(combo);
    }
  public static void main(String args[]) {
      Show.inFrame(new ListCombo(),200,200);
    }
} ///:~
```

Something else that seems a bit odd at first is that **JList**s do not
automatically provide scrolling, even though that's something you
always expect. Adding support for scrolling turns out to be quite easy, as
shown above – you simply wrap the **JList** in a **JScrollPane** and all the
details are automatically managed for you.

Sliders and progress bars

A slider allows the user to input data by moving a point back and forth,
which is intuitive in some situations (volume controls, for example). A
progress bar displays data in a relative fashion from "full" to "empty" so
the user gets a perspective. My favorite example for these is to simply
hook the slider to the progress bar so when you move the slider the
progress bar changes accordingly:

```
//: Progress.java
// Using progress bars and sliders
package c13.swing;
import java.awt.*;
import java.awt.event.*;
import com.sun.java.swing.*;
import com.sun.java.swing.event.*;
import com.sun.java.swing.border.*;

public class Progress extends JPanel {
  JProgressBar pb = new JProgressBar();
  JSlider sb =
    new JSlider(JSlider.HORIZONTAL, 0, 100, 60);
  public Progress() {
    setLayout(new GridLayout(2,1));
    add(pb);
    sb.setValue(0);
```

```
        sb.setPaintTicks(true);
        sb.setMajorTickSpacing(20);
        sb.setMinorTickSpacing(5);
        sb.setBorder(new TitledBorder("Slide Me"));
        sb.addChangeListener(new ChangeListener() {
          public void stateChanged(ChangeEvent e) {
            pb.setValue(sb.getValue());
          }
        });
        add(sb);
      }
      public static void main(String args[]) {
        Show.inFrame(new Progress(),200,150);
      }
    } ///:~
```

The **JProgressBar** is fairly straightforward, but the **JSlider** has a lot of options, such as the orientation and major and minor tick marks. Notice how straightforward it is to add a titled border.

Trees

Using a **JTree** can be as simple as saying:

```
add(new JTree(
  new Object[] {"this", "that", "other"}));
```

This displays a primitive tree. The API for trees is vast, however – certainly one of the largest in Swing. It appears that you can do just about anything with trees, but more sophisticated tasks might require quite a bit of research and experimentation.

Fortunately, there is a middle ground provided in the library: the "default" tree components, which generally do what you need. So most of the time you can use these components, and only in special cases will you need to delve in and understand trees more deeply.

The following example uses the "default" tree components to display a tree in an applet. When you press the button, a new subtree is added under the currently-selected node (if no node is selected, the root node is used):

```
//: Trees.java
// Simple Swing tree example. Trees can be made
// vastly more complex than this.
```

```java
package c13.swing;
import java.awt.*;
import java.awt.event.*;
import com.sun.java.swing.*;
import com.sun.java.swing.tree.*;

// Takes an array of Strings and makes the first
// element a node and the rest leaves:
class Branch {
  DefaultMutableTreeNode r;
  public Branch(String[] data) {
    r = new DefaultMutableTreeNode(data[0]);
    for(int i = 1; i < data.length; i++)
      r.add(new DefaultMutableTreeNode(data[i]));
  }
  public DefaultMutableTreeNode node() {
    return r;
  }
}

public class Trees extends JPanel {
  String[][] data = {
    { "Colors", "Red", "Blue", "Green" },
    { "Flavors", "Tart", "Sweet", "Bland" },
    { "Length", "Short", "Medium", "Long" },
    { "Volume", "High", "Medium", "Low" },
    { "Temperature", "High", "Medium", "Low" },
    { "Intensity", "High", "Medium", "Low" },
  };
  static int i = 0;
  DefaultMutableTreeNode root, child, chosen;
  JTree tree;
  DefaultTreeModel model;
  public Trees() {
    setLayout(new BorderLayout());
    root = new DefaultMutableTreeNode("root");
    tree = new JTree(root);
    // Add it and make it take care of scrolling:
    add(new JScrollPane(tree),
      BorderLayout.CENTER);
    // Capture the tree's model:
    model =(DefaultTreeModel)tree.getModel();
    JButton test = new JButton("Press me");
    test.addActionListener(new ActionListener() {
```

```
        public void actionPerformed(ActionEvent e){
          if(i < data.length) {
            child = new Branch(data[i++]).node();
            // What's the last one you clicked?
            chosen = (DefaultMutableTreeNode)
              tree.getLastSelectedPathComponent();
            if(chosen == null) chosen = root;
            // The model will create the
            // appropriate event. In response, the
            // tree will update itself:
            model.insertNodeInto(child, chosen, 0);
            // This puts the new node on the
            // currently chosen node.
          }
        }
      });
      // Change the button's colors:
      test.setBackground(Color.blue);
      test.setForeground(Color.white);
      JPanel p = new JPanel();
      p.add(test);
      add(p, BorderLayout.SOUTH);
    }
    public static void main(String args[]) {
      Show.inFrame(new Trees(),200,500);
    }
  } ///:~
```

The first class, **Branch**, is a tool to take an array of **String** and build a **DefaultMutableTreeNode** with the first **String** as the root and the rest of the **String**s in the array as leaves. Then **node( )** can be called to produce the root of this "branch."

The **Trees** class contains a two-dimensional array of **Strings** from which **Branch**es can be made and a **static int i** to count through this array. The **DefaultMutableTreeNode** objects hold the nodes, but the physical representation on screen is controlled by the **JTree** and its associated model, the **DefaultTreeModel**. Note that when the **JTree** is added to the applet, it is wrapped in a **JScrollPane** – this is all it takes to provide automatic scrolling.

The **JTree** is controlled through its *model*. When you make a change to the model, the model generates an event that causes the **JTree** to perform any necessary updates to the visible representation of the tree. In **init( )**, the model is captured by calling **getModel( )**. When the button is pressed, a new "branch" is created. Then the currently selected component is found (or the root if nothing is selected) and the model's **insertNodeInto( )** method does all the work of changing the tree and causing it to be updated.

Most of the time an example like the one above will give you what you need in a tree. However, trees have the power to do just about anything you can imagine – everywhere you see the word "default" in the example above, you can substitute your own class to get different behavior. But beware: almost all of these classes have a large interface, so you could spend a lot of time struggling to understand the intricacies of trees.

Tables

Like trees, tables in Swing are vast and powerful. They are primarily intended to be the popular "grid" interface to databases via Java Database Connectivity (JDBC, discussed in Chapter 15) and thus they have a tremendous amount of flexibility, which you pay for in complexity. There's easily enough here to be the basis of a full-blown spreadsheet and could probably justify an entire book. However, it is also possible to create a relatively simple **JTable** if you understand the basics.

The **JTable** controls how the data is displayed, but the **TableModel** controls the data itself. So to create a **JTable** you'll typically create a **TableModel** first. You can fully implement the **TableModel** interface, but it's usually simpler to inherit from the helper class **AbstractTableModel**:

```
//: Table.java
// Simple demonstration of JTable
package c13.swing;
import java.awt.*;
import java.awt.event.*;
import com.sun.java.swing.*;
import com.sun.java.swing.table.*;
import com.sun.java.swing.event.*;

// The TableModel controls all the data:
class DataModel extends AbstractTableModel {
  Object[][] data = {
    {"one", "two", "three", "four"},
    {"five", "six", "seven", "eight"},
    {"nine", "ten", "eleven", "twelve"},
  };
  // Prints data when table changes:
  class TML implements TableModelListener {
```

```java
    public void tableChanged(TableModelEvent e) {
      for(int i = 0; i < data.length; i++) {
        for(int j = 0; j < data[0].length; j++)
          System.out.print(data[i][j] + " ");
        System.out.println();
      }
    }
  }
  DataModel() {
    addTableModelListener(new TML());
  }
  public int getColumnCount() {
    return data[0].length;
  }
  public int getRowCount() {
    return data.length;
  }
  public Object getValueAt(int row, int col) {
    return data[row][col];
  }
  public void
  setValueAt(Object val, int row, int col) {
    data[row][col] = val;
    // Indicate the change has happened:
    fireTableDataChanged();
  }
  public boolean
  isCellEditable(int row, int col) {
    return true;
  }
};

public class Table extends JPanel {
  public Table() {
    setLayout(new BorderLayout());
    JTable table = new JTable(new DataModel());
    JScrollPane scrollpane =
      JTable.createScrollPaneForTable(table);
    add(scrollpane, BorderLayout.CENTER);
  }
  public static void main(String args[]) {
    Show.inFrame(new Table(),200,200);
  }
} ///:~
```

DataModel contains an array of data, but you could also get the data from some other source such as a database. The constructor adds a **TableModelListener** which prints the array every time the table is changed. The rest of the methods follow the Beans naming convention, and are used by **JTable** when it wants to present the information in **DataModel**. **AbstractTableModel** provides default methods for **setValueAt( )** and **isCellEditable( )** that prevent changes to the data, so if you want to be able to edit the data, you must override these methods.

Once you have a **TableModel**, you only need to hand it to the **JTable** constructor. All the details of displaying, editing and updating will be taken care of for you. Notice that this example also puts the **JTable** in a **JScrollPane**, which requires a special **JTable** method.

Tabbed Panes

Earlier in this chapter you were introduced to the positively medieval **CardLayout**, and saw how you had to manage all the switching of the ugly cards yourself. Someone actually thought this was a good design. Fortunately, Swing remedies this by providing **JTabbedPane**, which handles all the tabs, the switching, and everything. The contrast between **CardLayout** and **JTabbedPane** is breathtaking.

The following example is quite fun because it takes advantage of the design of the previous examples. They are all built as descendants of **JPanel**, so this example will place each one of the previous examples in its own pane on a **JTabbedPane**. You'll notice that the use of RTTI makes the example quite small and elegant:

```
//: Tabbed.java
// Using tabbed panes
package c13.swing;
import java.awt.*;
import com.sun.java.swing.*;
import com.sun.java.swing.border.*;

public class Tabbed extends JPanel {
  static Object[][] q = {
    { "Felix", Borders.class },
    { "The Professor", Buttons.class },
    { "Rock Bottom", ButtonGroups.class },
    { "Theodore", Faces.class },
    { "Simon", Menus.class },
    { "Alvin", Popup.class },
    { "Tom", ListCombo.class },
```

```
      { "Jerry", Progress.class },
      { "Bugs", Trees.class },
      { "Daffy", Table.class },
  };
  static JPanel makePanel(Class c) {
    String title = c.getName();
    title = title.substring(
      title.lastIndexOf('.') + 1);
    JPanel sp = null;
    try {
      sp = (JPanel)c.newInstance();
    } catch(Exception e) {
      System.out.println(e);
    }
    sp.setBorder(new TitledBorder(title));
    return sp;
  }
  public Tabbed() {
    setLayout(new BorderLayout());
    JTabbedPane tabbed = new JTabbedPane();
    for(int i = 0; i < q.length; i++)
      tabbed.addTab((String)q[i][0],
        makePanel((Class)q[i][1]));
    add(tabbed, BorderLayout.CENTER);
    tabbed.setSelectedIndex(q.length/2);
  }
  public static void main(String args[]) {
    Show.inFrame(new Tabbed(),460,350);
  }
} ///:~
```

Again, you can see the theme of an array used for configuration: the first element is the **String** to be placed on the tab and the second is the **JPanel** class that will be displayed inside of the corresponding pane. In the **Tabbed( )** constructor, you can see the two important **JTabbedPane** methods that are used: **addTab( )** to put a new pane in, and **setSelectedIndex( )** to choose the pane to start with. (One in the middle is chosen just to show that you don't have to start with the first pane.)

When you call **addTab( )** you supply it with the **String** for the tab and any **Component** (that is, an AWT **Component**, not just a **JComponent**, which is derived from the AWT **Component**). The **Component** will be displayed in the pane. Once you do this, no further management is necessary – the **JTabbedPane** takes care of everything else for you (as it should).

The **makePanel( )** method takes the **Class** object of the class you want to create and uses **newInstance( )** to create one, casting it to a **JPanel** (of course, this assumes that any class you want to add must inherit from **JPanel**, but that's been the structure used for the examples in this section). It adds a **TitledBorder** that contains the name of the class and returns the result as a **JPanel** to be used in **addTab( )**.

When you run the program you'll see that the **JTabbedPane** automatically stacks the tabs if there are too many of them to fit on one row.

The Swing message box

Windowing environments commonly contain a standard set of message boxes that allow you to quickly post information to the user or to capture information from the user. In Swing, these message boxes are contained in **JOptionPane**. You have many different possibilities (some quite sophisticated), but the ones you'll most commonly use are probably the message dialog and confirmation dialog, invoked using the **static JOptionPane.showMessageDialog( )** and **JOptionPane. showConfirmDialog( )**.

More to Swing

This section was meant only to give you an introduction to the power of Swing and to get you started so you could see how relatively simple it is to feel your way through the libraries. What you've seen so far will probably suffice for a good portion of your UI design needs. However, there's a lot more to Swing – it's intended to be a fully-powered UI design tool kit. If you don't see what you need here, delve into the online documentation from Sun and search the Web. There's probably a way to accomplish just about everything you can imagine.

Some of the topics that were not covered in this section include:

◆ More specific components such as **JColorChooser**, **JFileChooser**, **JPasswordField**, **JHTMLPane** (which performs simple HTML formatting and display), and **JTextPane** (a text editor that supports formatting, word wrap, and images). These are fairly straightforward to use.

◆ The new event types for Swing. In many ways, these are like exceptions: the type is what's important, and the name can be used to infer just about everything else about them.

- New layout managers: Springs & Struts (a la Smalltalk) and **BoxLayout**.

- Splitter control: a divider style splitter bar that allows you to dynamically manipulate the position of other components.

- **JLayeredPane** and **JInternalFrame**, used together to create child frame windows inside parent frame windows, to produce *multiple-document interface* (MDI) applications.

- Pluggable look and feel, so you can write a single program that can dynamically adapt to behave as expected under different platforms and operating systems.

- Custom cursors.

- Dockable floating toolbars with the **JToolbar** API.

- Double-buffering and Automatic repaint batching for smoother screen redraws.

- Built-in "undo" support.

- Drag and drop support.

Summary

Of all the libraries in Java, the AWT has seen the most dramatic changes from Java 1.0 to Java 1.2. The Java 1.0 AWT was roundly criticized as being one of the worst designs seen, and while it would allow you to create portable programs, the resulting GUI was "equally mediocre on all platforms." It was also limiting, awkward, and unpleasant to use compared with native application development tools on a particular platform.

When Java 1.1 introduced the new event model and Java Beans, the stage was set – now it was possible to create GUI components that could be easily dragged and dropped inside visual application builder tools. In addition, the design of the event model and Beans clearly shows strong consideration for ease of programming and maintainable code (something that was not evident in the 1.0 AWT). But it wasn't until the GUI components – the JFC/Swing classes – appeared that the job was finished. With the Swing components, cross-platform GUI programming can be a civilized experience.

Actually, the only thing that's missing is the application builder tool, and this is where the real revolution lies. Microsoft's Visual Basic and Visual C++ require their application builder tools, as does Borland's Delphi and C++ Builder. If you want the application builder tool to get better, you have to cross your fingers and hope the vendor will give you what you want. But Java is an open environment, and so not only does it allow for competing application builder environments, it encourages them. And for these tools to be taken seriously, they must support Java Beans. This means a leveled playing field: if a better application builder tool comes along, you're not tied to the one you've been using – you can pick up and move to the new one and increase your productivity. This kind of competitive environment for GUI application builder tools has not been seen before, and the resulting competition can generate only positive results for the productivity of the programmer.

Exercises

1. Create an applet with a text field and three buttons. When you press each button, make some different text appear in the text field.

2. Add a check box to the applet created in Exercise 1, capture the event, and insert different text into the text field.

3. Create an applet and add all the components that cause **action( )** to be called, then capture their events and display an appropriate message for each inside a text field.

4. Add to Exercise 3 the components that can be used only with events detected by **handleEvent( )**. Override **handleEvent( )** and display appropriate messages for each inside a text field.

5. Create an applet with a **Button** and a **TextField**. Write a **handleEvent( )** so that if the button has the focus, characters typed into it will appear in the **TextField**.

6. Create an application and add to the main frame all the components described in this chapter, including menus and a dialog box.

7. Modify **TextNew.java** so that the characters in **t2** retain the original case that they were typed in, instead of automatically being forced to upper case.

8. Modify **CardLayout1.java** so that it uses the Java 1.1 event model.

9. Add **Frog.class** to the manifest file shown in this chapter and run **jar** to create a JAR file containing both **Frog** and **BangBean**. Now either download and install the BDK from Sun or use your own Beans-enabled program builder tool and add the JAR file to your environment so you can test the two Beans.

10. Create your own Java Bean called **Valve** that contains two properties: a Boolean called "on" and an integer called "level." Create a manifest file, use **jar** to package your Bean, then load it into the beanbox or into your own Beans-enabled program builder tool so that you can test it.

11. (Somewhat challenging) Change **Menus.java** so that it handles cascading menus.

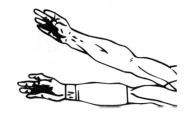

14: Multiple threads

Objects provide a way to divide a program up into independent sections. Often, you also need to turn a program into separate, independently-running subtasks.

Each of these independent subtasks is called a *thread*, and you program as if each thread runs by itself and has the CPU to itself. Some underlying mechanism is actually dividing up the CPU time for you, but in general, you don't have to think about it, which makes programming with multiple threads a much easier task.

Some definitions are useful at this point. A *process* is a self-contained running program with its own address space. A *multitasking* operating system is capable of running more than one process (program) at a time, while making it look like each one is chugging along by periodically providing CPU cycles to each process. A thread is a single sequential flow of control within a process. A single process can thus have multiple concurrently executing threads.

There are many possible uses for multithreading, but in general, you'll have some part of your program tied to a particular event or resource, and you don't want to hang up the rest of your program because of that. So you create a thread associated with that event or resource and let it run independently of the main program. A good example is a "quit" button – you don't want to be forced to poll the quit button in every piece of code you write in your program and yet you want the quit button to be responsive, as if you *were* checking it regularly. In fact, one of the most immediately compelling reasons for multithreading is to produce a responsive user interface.

Responsive user interfaces

As a starting point, consider a program that performs some CPU-intensive operation and thus ends up ignoring user input and being unresponsive. This one, a combined applet/application, will simply display the result of a running counter:

```java
//: Counter1.java
// A non-responsive user interface
package c14;
import java.awt.*;
import java.awt.event.*;
import java.applet.*;

public class Counter1 extends Applet {
  private int count = 0;
  private Button
    onOff = new Button("Toggle"),
    start = new Button("Start");
  private TextField t = new TextField(10);
  private boolean runFlag = true;
  public void init() {
    add(t);
    start.addActionListener(new StartL());
    add(start);
    onOff.addActionListener(new OnOffL());
    add(onOff);
  }
  public void go() {
```

```
        while (true) {
          try {
            Thread.currentThread().sleep(100);
          } catch (InterruptedException e){}
          if(runFlag)
            t.setText(Integer.toString(count++));
        }
      }
      class StartL implements ActionListener {
        public void actionPerformed(ActionEvent e) {
          go();
        }
      }
      class OnOffL implements ActionListener {
        public void actionPerformed(ActionEvent e) {
          runFlag = !runFlag;
        }
      }
      public static void main(String[] args) {
        Counter1 applet = new Counter1();
        Frame aFrame = new Frame("Counter1");
        aFrame.addWindowListener(
          new WindowAdapter() {
            public void windowClosing(WindowEvent e) {
              System.exit(0);
            }
          });
        aFrame.add(applet, BorderLayout.CENTER);
        aFrame.setSize(300,200);
        applet.init();
        applet.start();
        aFrame.setVisible(true);
      }
    } ///:~
```

At this point, the AWT and applet code should be reasonably familiar
from Chapter 13. The **go( )** method is where the program stays busy: it
puts the current value of **count** into the **TextField t**, then increments
count.

Part of the infinite loop inside **go( )** is to call **sleep( )**. **sleep( )** must be
associated with a **Thread** object, and it turns out that every application
has *some* thread associated with it. (Indeed, Java is based on threads and
there are always some running along with your application.) So
regardless of whether you're explicitly using threads, you can produce

the current thread used by your program with **Thread. currentThread()** (a static method of the **Thread** class) and then call **sleep( )** for that thread.

Note that **sleep( )** can throw **InterruptedException**, although throwing such an exception is considered a hostile way to break from a thread and should be discouraged. (Once again, exceptions are for exceptional conditions, not normal flow of control.) Interrupting a sleeping thread is included to support a future language feature.

When the **start** button is pressed, **go( )** is invoked. And upon examining **go( )**, you might naively think (as I did) that it should allow multithreading because it goes to sleep. That is, while the method is asleep, it seems like the CPU could be busy monitoring other button presses. But it turns out that the real problem is that **go( )** never returns, since it's in an infinite loop, and this means that **actionPerformed( )** never returns. Since you're stuck inside **actionPerformed( )** for the first keypress, the program can't handle any other events. (To get out, you must somehow kill the process; the easiest way to do this is to press Control-C in the console window.)

The basic problem here is that **go( )** needs to continue performing its operations, and at the same time it needs to return so **actionPerformed( )** can complete and the user interface can continue responding to the user. But in a conventional method like **go( )** it cannot continue *and* at the same time return control to the rest of the program. This sounds like an impossible thing to accomplish, as if the CPU must be in two places at once, but this is precisely the illusion that threading provides. The thread model (and programming support in Java) is a programming convenience to simplify juggling several operations at the same time within a single program. With threads, the CPU will pop around and give each thread some of its time. Each thread has the consciousness of constantly having the CPU to itself, but the CPU's time is actually sliced between all the threads.

Threading reduces computing efficiency somewhat, but the net improvement in program design, resource balancing, and user convenience is often quite valuable. Of course, if you have more than one CPU, then the operating system can dedicate each CPU to a set of threads or even a single thread and the whole program can run much faster. Multitasking and multithreading tend to be the most reasonable ways to utilize multiprocessor systems.

Inheriting from **Thread**

The simplest way to create a thread is to inherit from class **Thread**, which has all the wiring necessary to create and run threads. The most important method for **Thread** is **run( )**, which you must override to make the thread do your bidding. Thus, **run( )** is the code that will be executed "simultaneously" with the other threads in a program.

The following example creates any number of threads that it keeps track of by assigning each thread a unique number, generated with a **static** variable. The **Thread**'s **run( )** method is overridden to count down each time it passes through its loop and to finish when the count is zero (at the point when **run( )** returns, the thread is terminated).

```java
//: SimpleThread.java
// Very simple Threading example

public class SimpleThread extends Thread {
  private int countDown = 5;
  private int threadNumber;
  private static int threadCount = 0;
  public SimpleThread() {
    threadNumber = ++threadCount;
    System.out.println("Making " + threadNumber);
  }
  public void run() {
    while(true) {
      System.out.println("Thread " +
        threadNumber + "(" + countDown + ")");
      if(--countDown == 0) return;
    }
  }
  public static void main(String[] args) {
    for(int i = 0; i < 5; i++)
      new SimpleThread().start();
    System.out.println("All Threads Started");
  }
} ///:~
```

A **run( )** method virtually always has some kind of loop that continues until the thread is no longer necessary, so you must establish the condition on which to break out of this loop (or, in the case above, simply **return** from **run( )**). Often, **run( )** is cast in the form of an infinite loop, which means that, barring some external call to **stop( )** or **destroy( )** for that thread, it will run forever (until the program completes).

In **main( )** you can see a number of threads being created and run. The special method that comes with the **Thread** class is **start( )**, which performs special initialization for the thread and then calls **run( )**. So the steps are: the constructor is called to build the object, then **start( )** configures the thread and calls **run( )**. If you don't call **start( )** (which you can do in the constructor, if that's appropriate) the thread will never be started.

The output for one run of this program (it will be different every time) is:

```
Making 1
Making 2
Making 3
Making 4
Making 5
Thread 1(5)
Thread 1(4)
Thread 1(3)
Thread 1(2)
Thread 2(5)
Thread 2(4)
Thread 2(3)
Thread 2(2)
Thread 2(1)
Thread 1(1)
All Threads Started
Thread 3(5)
Thread 4(5)
Thread 4(4)
Thread 4(3)
Thread 4(2)
Thread 4(1)
Thread 5(5)
Thread 5(4)
Thread 5(3)
Thread 5(2)
Thread 5(1)
Thread 3(4)
Thread 3(3)
Thread 3(2)
Thread 3(1)
```

You'll notice that nowhere in this example is **sleep( )** called, and yet the output indicates that each thread gets a portion of the CPU's time in which to execute. This shows that **sleep( )**, while it relies on the existence of a thread in order to execute, is not involved with either enabling or disabling threading. It's simply another method.

You can also see that the threads are not run in the order that they're created. In fact, the order that the CPU attends to an existing set of threads is indeterminate, unless you go in and adjust the priorities using **Thread**'s **setPriority( )** method.

When **main( )** creates the **Thread** objects it isn't capturing the handles for any of them. An ordinary object would be fair game for garbage collection, but not a **Thread**. Each **Thread** "registers" itself so there is actually a reference to it someplace and the garbage collector can't clean it up.

Threading for a responsive interface

Now it's possible to solve the problem in **Counter1.java** with a thread. The trick is to place the subtask – that is, the loop that's inside **go( )** – inside the **run( )** method of a thread. When the user presses the **start** button, the thread is started, but then the *creation* of the thread completes, so even though the thread is running, the main job of the program (watching for and responding to user-interface events) can continue. Here's the solution:

```
//: Counter2.java
// A responsive user interface with threads
import java.awt.*;
import java.awt.event.*;
import java.applet.*;

class SeparateSubTask extends Thread {
  private int count = 0;
  private Counter2 c2;
  private boolean runFlag = true;
  public SeparateSubTask(Counter2 c2) {
    this.c2 = c2;
    start();
  }
  public void invertFlag() { runFlag = !runFlag; }
  public void run() {
    while (true) {
      try {
        sleep(100);
      } catch (InterruptedException e){}
      if(runFlag)
```

```
                  c2.t.setText(Integer.toString(count++));
          }
      }
  }

  public class Counter2 extends Applet {
    TextField t = new TextField(10);
    private SeparateSubTask sp = null;
    private Button
      onOff = new Button("Toggle"),
      start = new Button("Start");
    public void init() {
      add(t);
      start.addActionListener(new StartL());
      add(start);
      onOff.addActionListener(new OnOffL());
      add(onOff);
    }
    class StartL implements ActionListener {
      public void actionPerformed(ActionEvent e) {
        if(sp == null)
          sp = new SeparateSubTask(Counter2.this);
      }
    }
    class OnOffL implements ActionListener {
      public void actionPerformed(ActionEvent e) {
        if(sp != null)
          sp.invertFlag();
      }
    }
    public static void main(String[] args) {
      Counter2 applet = new Counter2();
      Frame aFrame = new Frame("Counter2");
      aFrame.addWindowListener(
        new WindowAdapter() {
          public void windowClosing(WindowEvent e) {
            System.exit(0);
          }
        });
      aFrame.add(applet, BorderLayout.CENTER);
      aFrame.setSize(300,200);
      applet.init();
      applet.start();
      aFrame.setVisible(true);
```

```
      }
    } ///:~
```

Counter2 is now a straightforward program, whose job is only to set up
and maintain the user interface. But now, when the user presses the **start**
button, a method is not called. Instead a thread of class
SeparateSubTask is created (the constructor starts it, in this case), and
then the **Counter2** event loop continues. Note that the handle to the
SeparateSubTask is stored so that when you press the **onOff** button it
can toggle the **runFlag** inside the **SeparateSubTask** object. That thread
(when it looks at the flag) can then start and stop itself. (This could also
have been accomplished by making **SeparateSubTask** an inner class.)

The class **SeparateSubTask** is a simple extension of **Thread** with a
constructor (that stores the **Counter2** handle and then runs the thread
by calling **start( )**) and a **run( )** that essentially contains the code from
inside **go( )** in **Counter1.java**. Because **SeparateSubTask** knows that it
holds a handle to a **Counter2**, it can reach in and access **Counter2**'s
TextField when it needs to.

When you press the **onOff** button, you'll see a virtually instant response.
Of course, the response isn't really instant, not like that of a system
that's driven by interrupts. The counter stops only when the thread has
the CPU and notices that the flag has changed.

Improving the code with an inner class

As an aside, look at the coupling that occurs between the
SeparateSubTask and **Counter2** classes. The **SeparateSubTask** is
intimately tied to **Counter2** – it must keep a handle to its "parent"
Counter2 object so it can call back and manipulate it. And yet the two
classes shouldn't really merge together into a single class (although in the
next section you'll see that Java provides a way to combine them)
because they're doing separate things and are created at different times.
They are tightly connected (what I call a "couplet") and this makes the
coding awkward. This is a situation in which an inner class can improve
the code significantly:

```
//: Counter2i.java
// Counter2 using an inner class for the thread
import java.awt.*;
import java.awt.event.*;
import java.applet.*;

public class Counter2i extends Applet {
```

```java
private class SeparateSubTask extends Thread {
  int count = 0;
  boolean runFlag = true;
  SeparateSubTask() { start(); }
  public void run() {
    while (true) {
      try {
        sleep(100);
      } catch (InterruptedException e) {}
      if(runFlag)
        t.setText(Integer.toString(count++));
    }
  }
}
private SeparateSubTask sp = null;
private TextField t = new TextField(10);
private Button
  onOff = new Button("Toggle"),
  start = new Button("Start");
public void init() {
  add(t);
  start.addActionListener(new StartL());
  add(start);
  onOff.addActionListener(new OnOffL());
  add(onOff);
}
class StartL implements ActionListener {
  public void actionPerformed(ActionEvent e) {
    if(sp == null)
      sp = new SeparateSubTask();
  }
}
class OnOffL implements ActionListener {
  public void actionPerformed(ActionEvent e) {
    if(sp != null)
      sp.runFlag = !sp.runFlag; // invertFlag();
  }
}
public static void main(String[] args) {
  Counter2i applet = new Counter2i();
  Frame aFrame = new Frame("Counter2i");
  aFrame.addWindowListener(
    new WindowAdapter() {
      public void windowClosing(WindowEvent e) {
```

```
                    System.exit(0);
            }
        });
        aFrame.add(applet, BorderLayout.CENTER);
        aFrame.setSize(300,200);
        applet.init();
        applet.start();
        aFrame.setVisible(true);
    }
} ///:~
```

This **SeparateSubTask** name will not collide with the **SeparateSubTask** in the previous example even though they're in the same directory, since it's hidden as an inner class. You can also see that the inner class is **private**, which means that its fields and methods can be given default access (except for **run( )**, which must be **public** since it is **public** in the base class). The **private** inner class is not accessible to anyone but **Counter2i**, and since the two classes are tightly coupled it's convenient to loosen the access restrictions between them. In **SeparateSubTask** you can see that the **invertFlag( )** method has been removed since **Counter2i** can now directly access **runFlag**.

Also, notice that **SeparateSubTask**'s constructor has been simplified – now it only starts the thread. The handle to the **Counter2i** object is still being captured as in the previous version, but instead of doing it by hand and referencing the outer object by hand, the inner class mechanism takes care of it automatically. In **run( )**, you can see that **t** is simply accessed, as if it were a field of **SeparateSubTask**. The **t** field in the parent class can now be made **private** since **SeparateSubTask** can access it without getting any special permission – and it's always good to make fields "as private as possible" so they cannot be accidentally changed by forces outside your class.

Anytime you notice classes that appear to have high coupling with each other, consider the coding and maintenance improvements you might get by using inner classes.

Combining the thread with the main class

In the example above you can see that the thread class is separate from the program's main class. This makes a lot of sense and is relatively easy to understand. There is, however, an alternate form that you will often see used that is not so clear but is usually more concise (which probably

accounts for its popularity). This form combines the main program class
with the thread class by making the main program class a thread. Since
for a GUI program the main program class must be inherited from either
Frame or **Applet**, an interface must be used to paste on the additional
functionality. This interface is called **Runnable**, and it contains the same
basic method that **Thread** does. In fact, **Thread** also implements
Runnable, which specifies only that there be a **run( )** method.

The use of the combined program/thread is not quite so obvious. When
you start the program, you create an object that's **Runnable**, but you
don't start the thread. This must be done explicitly. You can see this in the
following program, which reproduces the functionality of **Counter2**:

```
//: Counter3.java
// Using the Runnable interface to turn the
// main class into a thread.
import java.awt.*;
import java.awt.event.*;
import java.applet.*;

public class Counter3
    extends Applet implements Runnable {
  private int count = 0;
  private boolean runFlag = true;
  private Thread selfThread = null;
  private Button
    onOff = new Button("Toggle"),
    start = new Button("Start");
  private TextField t = new TextField(10);
  public void init() {
    add(t);
    start.addActionListener(new StartL());
    add(start);
    onOff.addActionListener(new OnOffL());
    add(onOff);
  }
  public void run() {
    while (true) {
      try {
        selfThread.sleep(100);
      } catch (InterruptedException e){}
      if(runFlag)
        t.setText(Integer.toString(count++));
    }
  }
```

```
class StartL implements ActionListener {
  public void actionPerformed(ActionEvent e) {
    if(selfThread == null) {
      selfThread = new Thread(Counter3.this);
      selfThread.start();
    }
  }
}
class OnOffL implements ActionListener {
  public void actionPerformed(ActionEvent e) {
    runFlag = !runFlag;
  }
}
public static void main(String[] args) {
  Counter3 applet = new Counter3();
  Frame aFrame = new Frame("Counter3");
  aFrame.addWindowListener(
    new WindowAdapter() {
      public void windowClosing(WindowEvent e) {
        System.exit(0);
      }
    });
  aFrame.add(applet, BorderLayout.CENTER);
  aFrame.setSize(300,200);
  applet.init();
  applet.start();
  aFrame.setVisible(true);
}
} ///:~
```

Now the **run( )** is inside the class, but it's still dormant after **init( )** completes. When you press the **start** button, the thread is created (if it doesn't already exist) in the somewhat obscure expression:

```
new Thread(Counter3.this);
```

When something has a **Runnable** interface, it simply means that it has a **run( )** method, but there's nothing special about that – it doesn't produce any innate threading abilities, like those of a class inherited from **Thread**. So to produce a thread from a **Runnable** object, you must create a thread separately and hand it the **Runnable** object; there's a special constructor for this that takes a **Runnable** as its argument. You can then call **start( )** for that thread:

```
selfThread.start();
```

This performs the usual initialization and then calls **run( )**.

The convenient aspect about the **Runnable interface** is that everything belongs to the same class. If you need to access something, you simply do it without going through a separate object. The penalty for this convenience is strict, though – you can have only a single thread running for that particular object (although you can create more objects of that type, or create other threads in different classes).

Note that the **Runnable** interface is not what imposes this restriction. It's the combination of **Runnable** and your main class that does it, since you can have only one object of your main class per application.

Making many threads

Consider the creation of many different threads. You can't do this with the previous example, so you must go back to having separate classes inherited from **Thread** to encapsulate the **run( )**. But this is a more general solution and easier to understand, so while the previous example shows a coding style you'll often see, I can't recommend it for most cases because it's just a little bit more confusing and less flexible.

The following example repeats the form of the examples above with counters and toggle buttons. But now all the information for a particular counter, including the button and text field, is inside its own object that is inherited from **Thread**. All the fields in **Ticker** are **private**, which means that the **Ticker** implementation can be changed at will, including the quantity and type of data components to acquire and display information. When a **Ticker** object is created, the constructor requires a handle to an AWT **Container**, which **Ticker** fills with its visual components. This way, if you change the visual components, the code that uses **Ticker** doesn't need to be modified.

```
//: Counter4.java
// If you separate your thread from the main
// class, you can have as many threads as you
// want.
import java.awt.*;
import java.awt.event.*;
import java.applet.*;

class Ticker extends Thread {
  private Button b = new Button("Toggle");
  private TextField t = new TextField(10);
  private int count = 0;
```

```
    private boolean runFlag = true;
    public Ticker(Container c) {
      b.addActionListener(new ToggleL());
      Panel p = new Panel();
      p.add(t);
      p.add(b);
      c.add(p);
    }
    class ToggleL implements ActionListener {
      public void actionPerformed(ActionEvent e) {
        runFlag = !runFlag;
      }
    }
    public void run() {
      while (true) {
        if(runFlag)
          t.setText(Integer.toString(count++));
         try {
          sleep(100);
        } catch (InterruptedException e){}
      }
    }
  }

public class Counter4 extends Applet {
  private Button start = new Button("Start");
  private boolean started = false;
  private Ticker[] s;
  private boolean isApplet = true;
  private int size;
  public void init() {
    // Get parameter "size" from Web page:
    if(isApplet)
      size =
        Integer.parseInt(getParameter("size"));
    s = new Ticker[size];
    for(int i = 0; i < s.length; i++)
      s[i] = new Ticker(this);
    start.addActionListener(new StartL());
    add(start);
  }
  class StartL implements ActionListener {
    public void actionPerformed(ActionEvent e) {
      if(!started) {
```

```
            started = true;
            for(int i = 0; i < s.length; i++)
               s[i].start();
         }
      }
   }
   public static void main(String[] args) {
      Counter4 applet = new Counter4();
      // This isn't an applet, so set the flag and
      // produce the parameter values from args:
      applet.isApplet = false;
      applet.size =
         (args.length == 0 ? 5 :
            Integer.parseInt(args[0]));
      Frame aFrame = new Frame("Counter4");
      aFrame.addWindowListener(
         new WindowAdapter() {
            public void windowClosing(WindowEvent e) {
               System.exit(0);
            }
         });
      aFrame.add(applet, BorderLayout.CENTER);
      aFrame.setSize(200, applet.size * 50);
      applet.init();
      applet.start();
      aFrame.setVisible(true);
   }
} ///:~
```

Ticker contains not only its threading equipment but also the way to control and display the thread. You can create as many threads as you want without explicitly creating the windowing components.

In **Counter4** there's an array of **Ticker** objects called **s**. For maximum flexibility, the size of this array is initialized by reaching out into the Web page using applet parameters. Here's what the size parameter looks like on the page, embedded inside the applet description:

```
<applet code=Counter4 width=600 height=600>
<param name=size value="20">
</applet>
```

The **param**, **name**, and **value** are all Web-page keywords. **name** is what you'll be referring to in your program, and **value** can be any string, not just something that resolves to a number.

You'll notice that the determination of the size of the array **s** is done inside **init( )**, and not as part of an inline definition of **s**. That is, you *cannot* say as part of the class definition (outside of any methods):

```
int size = Integer.parseInt(getParameter("size"));
Ticker[] s = new Ticker[size];
```

You can compile this, but you'll get a strange null-pointer exception at run time. It works fine if you move the **getParameter( )** initialization inside of **init( )**. The applet framework performs the necessary startup to grab the parameters before entering **init( )**.

In addition, this code is set up to be either an applet or an application. When it's an application the **size** argument is extracted from the command line (or a default value is provided).

Once the size of the array is established, new **Ticker** objects are created; as part of the **Ticker** constructor the button and text field for each **Ticker** is added to the applet.

Pressing the **start** button means looping through the entire array of **Ticker**s and calling **start( )** for each one. Remember, **start( )** performs necessary thread initialization and then calls **run( )** for that thread.

The **ToggleL** listener simply inverts the flag in **Ticker** and when the associated thread next takes note it can react accordingly.

One value of this example is that it allows you to easily create large sets of independent subtasks and to monitor their behavior. In this case, you'll see that as the number of subtasks gets larger, your machine will probably show more divergence in the displayed numbers because of the way that the threads are served.

You can also experiment to discover how important the **sleep(100)** is inside **Ticker.run( )**. If you remove the **sleep( )**, things will work fine until you press a toggle button. Then that particular thread has a false **runFlag** and the **run( )** is just tied up in a tight infinite loop, which appears difficult to break during multithreading, so the responsiveness and speed of the program really bogs down.

Daemon threads

A "daemon" thread is one that is supposed to provide a general service in the background as long as the program is running, but is not part of the essence of the program. Thus, when all of the non-daemon threads complete the program is terminated. Conversely, if there are any non-daemon threads still running the program doesn't terminate. (There is, for instance, a thread that runs **main( )**.)

You can find out if a thread is a daemon by calling **isDaemon( )**, and you can turn the daemonhood of a thread on and off with **setDaemon( )**. If a thread is a daemon, then any threads it creates will automatically be daemons.

The following example demonstrates daemon threads:

```java
//: Daemons.java
// Daemonic behavior
import java.io.*;

class Daemon extends Thread {
  private static final int SIZE = 10;
  private Thread[] t = new Thread[SIZE];
  public Daemon() {
    setDaemon(true);
    start();
  }
  public void run() {
    for(int i = 0; i < SIZE; i++)
      t[i] = new DaemonSpawn(i);
    for(int i = 0; i < SIZE; i++)
      System.out.println(
        "t[" + i + "].isDaemon() = "
        + t[i].isDaemon());
    while(true)
      yield();
  }
}

class DaemonSpawn extends Thread {
  public DaemonSpawn(int i) {
    System.out.println(
      "DaemonSpawn " + i + " started");
    start();
  }
  public void run() {
    while(true)
      yield();
  }
}
```

Thinking in Java   *www.BruceEckel.com*

```
public class Daemons {
  public static void main(String[] args) {
    Thread d = new Daemon();
    System.out.println(
      "d.isDaemon() = " + d.isDaemon());
    // Allow the daemon threads to finish
    // their startup processes:
    BufferedReader stdin =
      new BufferedReader(
        new InputStreamReader(System.in));
    System.out.println("Waiting for CR");
    try {
      stdin.readLine();
    } catch(IOException e) {}
  }
} ///:~
```

The **Daemon** thread sets its daemon flag to "true" and then spawns a bunch of other threads to show that they are also daemons. Then it goes into an infinite loop that calls **yield( )** to give up control to the other processes. In an earlier version of this program, the infinite loops would increment **int** counters, but this seemed to bring the whole program to a stop. Using **yield( )** makes the program quite peppy.

There's nothing to keep the program from terminating once **main( )** finishes its job since there are nothing but daemon threads running. So that you can see the results of starting all the daemon threads, **System.in** is set up to read so the program waits for a carriage return before terminating. Without this you see only some of the results from the creation of the daemon threads. (Try replacing the **readLine( )** code with **sleep( )** calls of various lengths to see this behavior.)

Sharing limited resources

You can think of a single-threaded program as one lonely entity moving around through your problem space and doing one thing at a time. Because there's only one entity, you never have to think about the problem of two entities trying to use the same resource at the same time, like two people trying to park in the same space, walk through a door at the same time, or even talk at the same time.

With multithreading, things aren't lonely anymore, but you now have the possibility of two or more threads trying to use the same limited resource at once. Colliding over a resource must be prevented or else

---

you'll have two threads trying to access the same bank account at the same time, print to the same printer, or adjust the same valve, etc.

Improperly accessing resources

Consider a variation on the counters that have been used so far in this chapter. In the following example, each thread contains two counters that are incremented and displayed inside **run( )**. In addition, there's another thread of class **Watcher** that is watching the counters to see if they're always equivalent. This seems like a needless activity, since looking at the code it appears obvious that the counters will always be the same. But that's where the surprise comes in. Here's the first version of the program:

```
//: Sharing1.java
// Problems with resource sharing while threading
import java.awt.*;
import java.awt.event.*;
import java.applet.*;

class TwoCounter extends Thread {
  private boolean started = false;
  private TextField
    t1 = new TextField(5),
    t2 = new TextField(5);
  private Label l =
    new Label("count1 == count2");
  private int count1 = 0, count2 = 0;
  // Add the display components as a panel
  // to the given container:
  public TwoCounter(Container c) {
    Panel p = new Panel();
    p.add(t1);
    p.add(t2);
    p.add(l);
    c.add(p);
  }
  public void start() {
    if(!started) {
      started = true;
      super.start();
    }
  }
  public void run() {
```

```
      while (true) {
        t1.setText(Integer.toString(count1++));
        t2.setText(Integer.toString(count2++));
        try {
          sleep(500);
        } catch (InterruptedException e){}
      }
    }
  }
  public void synchTest() {
    Sharing1.incrementAccess();
    if(count1 != count2)
      l.setText("Unsynched");
  }
}

class Watcher extends Thread {
  private Sharing1 p;
  public Watcher(Sharing1 p) {
    this.p = p;
    start();
  }
  public void run() {
    while(true) {
      for(int i = 0; i < p.s.length; i++)
        p.s[i].synchTest();
      try {
        sleep(500);
      } catch (InterruptedException e){}
    }
  }
}

public class Sharing1 extends Applet {
  TwoCounter[] s;
  private static int accessCount = 0;
  private static TextField aCount =
    new TextField("0", 10);
  public static void incrementAccess() {
    accessCount++;
    aCount.setText(Integer.toString(accessCount));
  }
  private Button
    start = new Button("Start"),
    observer = new Button("Observe");
```

```java
  private boolean isApplet = true;
  private int numCounters = 0;
  private int numObservers = 0;
  public void init() {
    if(isApplet) {
      numCounters =
        Integer.parseInt(getParameter("size"));
      numObservers =
        Integer.parseInt(
          getParameter("observers"));
    }
    s = new TwoCounter[numCounters];
    for(int i = 0; i < s.length; i++)
      s[i] = new TwoCounter(this);
    Panel p = new Panel();
    start.addActionListener(new StartL());
    p.add(start);
    observer.addActionListener(new ObserverL());
    p.add(observer);
    p.add(new Label("Access Count"));
    p.add(aCount);
    add(p);
  }
  class StartL implements ActionListener {
    public void actionPerformed(ActionEvent e) {
      for(int i = 0; i < s.length; i++)
        s[i].start();
    }
  }
  class ObserverL implements ActionListener {
    public void actionPerformed(ActionEvent e) {
      for(int i = 0; i < numObservers; i++)
        new Watcher(Sharing1.this);
    }
  }
  public static void main(String[] args) {
    Sharing1 applet = new Sharing1();
    // This isn't an applet, so set the flag and
    // produce the parameter values from args:
    applet.isApplet = false;
    applet.numCounters =
      (args.length == 0 ? 5 :
        Integer.parseInt(args[0]));
    applet.numObservers =
```

```
        (args.length < 2 ? 5 :
          Integer.parseInt(args[1]));
      Frame aFrame = new Frame("Sharing1");
      aFrame.addWindowListener(
        new WindowAdapter() {
          public void windowClosing(WindowEvent e){
            System.exit(0);
          }
        });
      aFrame.add(applet, BorderLayout.CENTER);
      aFrame.setSize(350, applet.numCounters *100);
      applet.init();
      applet.start();
      aFrame.setVisible(true);
    }
  } ///:~
```

As before, each counter contains its own display components: two text fields and a label that initially indicates that the counts are equivalent. These components are added to the **Container** in the **TwoCounter** constructor. Because this thread is started via a button press by the user, it's possible that **start( )** could be called more than once. It's illegal for **Thread.start( )** to be called more than once for a thread (an exception is thrown). You can see that the machinery to prevent this in the **started** flag and the overridden **start( )** method.

In **run( )**, **count1** and **count2** are incremented and displayed in a manner that would seem to keep them identical. Then **sleep( )** is called; without this call the program balks because it becomes hard for the CPU to swap tasks.

The **synchTest( )** method performs the apparently useless activity of checking to see if **count1** is equivalent to **count2**; if they are not equivalent it sets the label to "Unsynched" to indicate this. But first, it calls a static member of the class **Sharing1** that increments and displays an access counter to show how many times this check has occurred successfully. (The reason for this will become apparent in future variations of this example.)

The **Watcher** class is a thread whose job is to call **synchTest( )** for all of the **TwoCounter** objects that are active. It does this by stepping through the array that's kept in the **Sharing1** object. You can think of the **Watcher** as constantly peeking over the shoulders of the **TwoCounter** objects.

Sharing1 contains an array of **TwoCounter** objects that it initializes in **init( )** and starts as threads when you press the "start" button. Later, when you press the "Observe" button, one or more observers are created and freed upon the unsuspecting **TwoCounter** threads.

Note that to run this as an applet in a browser, your Web page will need to contain the lines:

```
<applet code=Sharing1 width=650 height=500>
<param name=size value="20">
<param name=observers value="1">
</applet>
```

You can change the width, height, and parameters to suit your experimental tastes. By changing the **size** and **observers** you'll change the behavior of the program. You can also see that this program is set up to run as a stand-alone application by pulling the arguments from the command line (or providing defaults).

Here's the surprising part. In **TwoCounter.run( )**, the infinite loop is just repeatedly passing over the adjacent lines:

```
t1.setText(Integer.toString(count1++));
t2.setText(Integer.toString(count2++));
```

(as well as sleeping, but that's not important here). When you run the program, however, you'll discover that **count1** and **count2** will be observed (by the **Watcher**) to be unequal at times! This is because of the nature of threads – they can be suspended at any time. So at times, the suspension occurs *between* the execution of the above two lines, and the **Watcher** thread happens to come along and perform the comparison at just this moment, thus finding the two counters to be different.

This example shows a fundamental problem with using threads. You never know when a thread might be run. Imagine sitting at a table with a fork, about to spear the last piece of food on your plate and as your fork reaches for it, the food suddenly vanishes (because your thread was suspended and another thread came in and stole the food). That's the problem that you're dealing with.

Sometimes you don't care if a resource is being accessed at the same time you're trying to use it (the food is on some other plate). But for multithreading to work, you need some way to prevent two threads from accessing the same resource, at least during critical periods.

Preventing this kind of collision is simply a matter of putting a lock on a resource when one thread is using it. The first thread that accesses a resource locks it, and then the other threads cannot access that resource until it is unlocked, at which time another thread locks and uses it, etc. If the front seat of the car is the limited resource, the child who shouts "Dibs!" asserts the lock.

How Java shares resources

Java has built-in support to prevent collisions over one kind of resource: the memory in an object. Since you typically make the data elements of a class **private** and access that memory only through methods, you can prevent collisions by making a particular method **synchronized**. Only one thread at a time can call a **synchronized** method for a particular object (although that thread can call more than one of the object's synchronized methods). Here are simple **synchronized** methods:

```
synchronized void f() { /* ... */ }
synchronized void g(){ /* ... */ }
```

Each object contains a single lock (also called a *monitor*) that is automatically part of the object (you don't have to write any special code). When you call any **synchronized** method, that object is locked and no other **synchronized** method of that object can be called until the first one finishes and releases the lock. In the example above, if **f( )** is called for an object, **g( )** cannot be called for the same object until **f( )** is completed and releases the lock. Thus, there's a single lock that's shared by all the **synchronized** methods of a particular object, and this lock prevents common memory from being written by more than one method at a time (i.e. more than one thread at a time).

There's also a single lock per class (as part of the **Class** object for the class), so that **synchronized static** methods can lock each other out from **static** data on a class-wide basis.

Note that if you want to guard some other resource from simultaneous access by multiple threads, you can do so by forcing access to that resource through **synchronized** methods.

Synchronizing the counters

Armed with this new keyword it appears that the solution is at hand: we'll simply use the **synchronized** keyword for the methods in **TwoCounter**. The following example is the same as the previous one, with the addition of the new keyword:

```
//: Sharing2.java
```

```
// Using the synchronized keyword to prevent
// multiple access to a particular resource.
import java.awt.*;
import java.awt.event.*;
import java.applet.*;

class TwoCounter2 extends Thread {
  private boolean started = false;
  private TextField
    t1 = new TextField(5),
    t2 = new TextField(5);
  private Label l =
    new Label("count1 == count2");
  private int count1 = 0, count2 = 0;
  public TwoCounter2(Container c) {
    Panel p = new Panel();
    p.add(t1);
    p.add(t2);
    p.add(l);
    c.add(p);
  }
  public void start() {
    if(!started) {
      started = true;
      super.start();
    }
  }
  public synchronized void run() {
    while (true) {
      t1.setText(Integer.toString(count1++));
      t2.setText(Integer.toString(count2++));
      try {
        sleep(500);
      } catch (InterruptedException e){}
    }
  }
  public synchronized void synchTest() {
    Sharing2.incrementAccess();
    if(count1 != count2)
      l.setText("Unsynched");
  }
}

class Watcher2 extends Thread {
```

```
    private Sharing2 p;
    public Watcher2(Sharing2 p) {
      this.p = p;
      start();
    }
    public void run() {
      while(true) {
        for(int i = 0; i < p.s.length; i++)
          p.s[i].synchTest();
        try {
          sleep(500);
        } catch (InterruptedException e){}
      }
    }
  }

public class Sharing2 extends Applet {
  TwoCounter2[] s;
  private static int accessCount = 0;
  private static TextField aCount =
    new TextField("0", 10);
  public static void incrementAccess() {
    accessCount++;
    aCount.setText(Integer.toString(accessCount));
  }
  private Button
    start = new Button("Start"),
    observer = new Button("Observe");
  private boolean isApplet = true;
  private int numCounters = 0;
  private int numObservers = 0;
  public void init() {
    if(isApplet) {
      numCounters =
        Integer.parseInt(getParameter("size"));
      numObservers =
        Integer.parseInt(
          getParameter("observers"));
    }
    s = new TwoCounter2[numCounters];
    for(int i = 0; i < s.length; i++)
      s[i] = new TwoCounter2(this);
    Panel p = new Panel();
    start.addActionListener(new StartL());
```

```
          p.add(start);
          observer.addActionListener(new ObserverL());
          p.add(observer);
          p.add(new Label("Access Count"));
          p.add(aCount);
          add(p);
      }
      class StartL implements ActionListener {
        public void actionPerformed(ActionEvent e) {
          for(int i = 0; i < s.length; i++)
            s[i].start();
        }
      }
      class ObserverL implements ActionListener {
        public void actionPerformed(ActionEvent e) {
          for(int i = 0; i < numObservers; i++)
            new Watcher2(Sharing2.this);
        }
      }
      public static void main(String[] args) {
        Sharing2 applet = new Sharing2();
        // This isn't an applet, so set the flag and
        // produce the parameter values from args:
        applet.isApplet = false;
        applet.numCounters =
          (args.length == 0 ? 5 :
            Integer.parseInt(args[0]));
        applet.numObservers =
          (args.length < 2 ? 5 :
            Integer.parseInt(args[1]));
        Frame aFrame = new Frame("Sharing2");
        aFrame.addWindowListener(
          new WindowAdapter() {
            public void windowClosing(WindowEvent e){
              System.exit(0);
            }
          });
        aFrame.add(applet, BorderLayout.CENTER);
        aFrame.setSize(350, applet.numCounters *100);
        applet.init();
        applet.start();
        aFrame.setVisible(true);
      }
    } ///:~
```

You'll notice that *both* **run( )** and **synchTest( )** are **synchronized**. If you synchronize only one of the methods, then the other is free to ignore the object lock and can be called with impunity. This is an important point: Every method that accesses a critical shared resource must be **synchronized** or it won't work right.

Now a new issue arises. The **Watcher2** can never get a peek at what's going on because the entire **run( )** method has been **synchronized**, and since **run( )** is always running for each object the lock is always tied up and **synch Test( )** can never be called. You can see this because the **accessCount** never changes.

What we'd like for this example is a way to isolate only *part* of the code inside **run( )**. The section of code you want to isolate this way is called a *critical section* and you use the **synchronized** keyword in a different way to set up a critical section. Java supports critical sections with the *synchronized block*; this time **synchronized** is used to specify the object whose lock is being used to synchronize the enclosed code:

```
synchronized(syncObject) {
    // This code can be accessed by only
    // one thread at a time, assuming all
    // threads respect syncObject's lock
}
```

Before the synchronized block can be entered, the lock must be acquired on **syncObject**. If some other thread already has this lock, then the block cannot be entered until the lock is given up.

The **Sharing2** example can be modified by removing the **synchronized** keyword from the entire **run( )** method and instead putting a **synchronized** block around the two critical lines. But what object should be used as the lock? The one that is already respected by **synchTest( )**, which is the current object (**this**)! So the modified **run( )** looks like this:

```
public void run() {
    while (true) {
        synchronized(this) {
            t1.setText(Integer.toString(count1++));
            t2.setText(Integer.toString(count2++));
        }
        try {
            sleep(500);
        } catch (InterruptedException e){}
    }
}
```

This is the only change that must be made to **Sharing2.java**, and you'll see that while the two counters are never out of synch (according to when the **Watcher** is allowed to look at them), there is still adequate access provided to the **Watcher** during the execution of **run( )**.

Of course, all synchronization depends on programmer diligence: every piece of code that can access a shared resource must be wrapped in an appropriate synchronized block.

Synchronized efficiency

Since having two methods write to the same piece of data *never* sounds like a particularly good idea, it might seem to make sense for all methods to be automatically **synchronized** and eliminate the **synchronized** keyword altogether. (Of course, the example with a **synchronized run( )** shows that this wouldn't work either.) But it turns out that acquiring a lock is not a cheap operation – it multiplies the cost of a method call (that is, entering and exiting from the method, not executing the body of the method) by a minimum of four times, and could be more depending on your implementation. So if you know that a particular method will not cause contention problems it is expedient to leave off the **synchronized** keyword.

Java Beans revisited

Now that you understand synchronization you can take another look at Java Beans. Whenever you create a Bean, you must assume that it will run in a multithreaded environment. This means that:

1. Whenever possible, all the public methods of a Bean should be **synchronized**. Of course, this incurs the **synchronized** runtime overhead. If that's a problem, methods that will not cause problems in critical sections can be left un-**synchronized**, but keep in mind that this is not always obvious. Methods that qualify tend to be small (such as **getCircleSize( )** in the following example) and/or "atomic," that is, the method call executes in such a short amount of code that the object cannot be changed during execution. Making such methods un-**synchronized** might not have a significant effect on the execution speed of your program. You might as well make all **public** methods of a Bean **synchronized** and remove the **synchronized** keyword only when you know for sure that it's necessary and that it makes a difference.

2. When firing a multicast event to a bunch of listeners interested in that event, you must assume that listeners might be added or removed while moving through the list.

The first point is fairly easy to deal with, but the second point requires a little more thought. Consider the **BangBean.java** example presented in the last chapter. That ducked out of the multithreading question by ignoring the **synchronized** keyword (which hadn't been introduced yet) and making the event unicast. Here's that example modified to work in a multithreaded environment and to use multicasting for events:

```
//: BangBean2.java
// You should write your Beans this way so they
// can run in a multithreaded environment.
import java.awt.*;
import java.awt.event.*;
import java.util.*;
import java.io.*;

public class BangBean2 extends Canvas
    implements Serializable {
  private int xm, ym;
  private int cSize = 20; // Circle size
  private String text = "Bang!";
  private int fontSize = 48;
  private Color tColor = Color.red;
  private Vector actionListeners = new Vector();
  public BangBean2() {
    addMouseListener(new ML());
    addMouseMotionListener(new MM());
  }
  public synchronized int getCircleSize() {
    return cSize;
  }
  public synchronized void
  setCircleSize(int newSize) {
    cSize = newSize;
  }
  public synchronized String getBangText() {
    return text;
  }
  public synchronized void
  setBangText(String newText) {
    text = newText;
  }
```

```
public synchronized int getFontSize() {
  return fontSize;
}
public synchronized void
setFontSize(int newSize) {
  fontSize = newSize;
}
public synchronized Color getTextColor() {
  return tColor;
}
public synchronized void
setTextColor(Color newColor) {
  tColor = newColor;
}
public void paint(Graphics g) {
  g.setColor(Color.black);
  g.drawOval(xm - cSize/2, ym - cSize/2,
    cSize, cSize);
}
// This is a multicast listener, which is
// more typically used than the unicast
// approach taken in BangBean.java:
public synchronized void addActionListener (
    ActionListener l) {
  actionListeners.addElement(l);
}
public synchronized void removeActionListener(
    ActionListener l) {
  actionListeners.removeElement(l);
}
// Notice this isn't synchronized:
public void notifyListeners() {
  ActionEvent a =
    new ActionEvent(BangBean2.this,
      ActionEvent.ACTION_PERFORMED, null);
  Vector lv = null;
  // Make a copy of the vector in case someone
  // adds a listener while we're
  // calling listeners:
  synchronized(this) {
    lv = (Vector)actionListeners.clone();
  }
  // Call all the listener methods:
  for(int i = 0; i < lv.size(); i++) {
```

```
        ActionListener al =
            (ActionListener)lv.elementAt(i);
        al.actionPerformed(a);
      }
    }
    class ML extends MouseAdapter {
      public void mousePressed(MouseEvent e) {
        Graphics g = getGraphics();
        g.setColor(tColor);
        g.setFont(
          new Font(
            "TimesRoman", Font.BOLD, fontSize));
        int width =
          g.getFontMetrics().stringWidth(text);
        g.drawString(text,
          (getSize().width - width) /2,
          getSize().height/2);
        g.dispose();
        notifyListeners();
      }
    }
    class MM extends MouseMotionAdapter {
      public void mouseMoved(MouseEvent e) {
        xm = e.getX();
        ym = e.getY();
        repaint();
      }
    }
    // Testing the BangBean2:
    public static void main(String[] args) {
      BangBean2 bb = new BangBean2();
      bb.addActionListener(new ActionListener() {
        public void actionPerformed(ActionEvent e){
          System.out.println("ActionEvent" + e);
        }
      });
      bb.addActionListener(new ActionListener() {
        public void actionPerformed(ActionEvent e){
          System.out.println("BangBean2 action");
        }
      });
      bb.addActionListener(new ActionListener() {
        public void actionPerformed(ActionEvent e){
          System.out.println("More action");
```

```
      }
    });
    Frame aFrame = new Frame("BangBean2 Test");
    aFrame.addWindowListener(new WindowAdapter(){
      public void windowClosing(WindowEvent e) {
        System.exit(0);
      }
    });
    aFrame.add(bb, BorderLayout.CENTER);
    aFrame.setSize(300,300);
    aFrame.setVisible(true);
  }
} ///:~
```

Adding **synchronized** to the methods is an easy change. However, notice in **addActionListener( )** and **removeActionListener( )** that the **ActionListeners** are now added to and removed from a **Vector**, so you can have as many as you want.

You can see that the method **notifyListeners( )** is *not* **synchronized**. It can be called from more than one thread at a time. It's also possible for **addActionListener( )** or **removeActionListener( )** to be called in the middle of a call to **notifyListeners( )**, which is a problem since it traverses the **Vector actionListeners**. To alleviate the problem, the **Vector** is cloned inside a **synchronized** clause and the clone is traversed. This way the original **Vector** can be manipulated without impact on **notifyListeners( )**.

The **paint( )** method is also not **synchronized**. Deciding whether to synchronize overridden methods is not as clear as when you're just adding your own methods. In this example it turns out that **paint( )** seems to work OK whether it's **synchronized** or not. But the issues you must consider are:

1. Does the method modify the state of "critical" variables within the object? To discover whether the variables are "critical" you must determine whether they will be read or set by other threads in the program. (In this case, the reading or setting is virtually always accomplished via **synchronized** methods, so you can just examine those.) In the case of **paint( )**, no modification takes place.

2. Does the method depend on the state of these "critical" variables? If a **synchronized** method modifies a variable that your method uses, then you might very well want to make your method **synchronized** as well. Based on this, you might observe that **cSize** is changed by **synchronized** methods and therefore **paint( )** should be

synchronized. Here, however, you can ask "What's the worst thing that will happen if **cSize** is changed during a **paint( )**?" When you see that it's nothing too bad, and a transient effect at that, it's best to leave **paint( )** un-**synchronized** to prevent the extra overhead from the **synchronized** method call.

3. A third clue is to notice whether the base-class version of **paint( )** is **synchronized**, which it isn't. This isn't an airtight argument, just a clue. In this case, for example, a field that *is* changed via **synchronized** methods (that is **cSize**) has been mixed into the **paint( )** formula and might have changed the situation. Notice, however, that **synchronized** doesn't inherit – that is, if a method is **synchronized** in the base class then it *is not* automatically **synchronized** in the derived class overridden version.

The test code in **TestBangBean2** has been modified from that in the previous chapter to demonstrate the multicast ability of **BangBean2** by adding extra listeners.

Blocking

A thread can be in any one of four states:

1. *New*: the thread object has been created but it hasn't been started yet so it cannot run.

2. *Runnable*: This means that a thread *can* be run when the time-slicing mechanism has CPU cycles available for the thread. Thus, the thread might or might not be running, but there's nothing to prevent it from being run if the scheduler can arrange it; it's not dead or blocked.

3. *Dead*: the normal way for a thread to die is by returning from its **run( )** method. You can also call **stop( )**, but this throws an exception that's a subclass of **Error** (which means you usually don't catch it). Remember that throwing an exception should be a special event and not part of normal program execution; thus the use of **stop( )** is discouraged (and it's deprecated in Java 1.2). There's also a **destroy( )** method (which has never been implemented) that you should never call if you can avoid it since it's drastic and doesn't release object locks.

4. *Blocked*: the thread could be run but there's something that prevents it. While a thread is in the blocked state the scheduler will simply skip

over it and not give it any CPU time. Until a thread re-enters the runnable state it won't perform any operations.

Becoming blocked

The blocked state is the most interesting and is worth further examination. A thread can become blocked for five reasons:

1. You've put the thread to sleep by calling **sleep(milliseconds)**, in which case it will not be run for the specified time.

2. You've suspended the execution of the thread with **suspend( )**. It will not become runnable again until the thread gets the **resume( )** message.

3. You've suspended the execution of the thread with **wait( )**. It will not become runnable again until the thread gets the **notify( )** or **notifyAll( )** message. (Yes, this looks just like number 2, but there's a distinct difference that will be revealed.)

4. The thread is waiting for some IO to complete.

5. The thread is trying to call a **synchronized** method on another object and that object's lock is not available.

You can also call **yield( )** (a method of the **Thread** class) to voluntarily give up the CPU so that other threads can run. However, the same thing happens if the scheduler decides that your thread has had enough time and jumps to another thread. That is, nothing prevents the scheduler from re-starting your thread. When a thread is blocked, there's some reason that it cannot continue running.

The following example shows all five ways of becoming blocked. It all exists in a single file called **Blocking.java,** but it will be examined here in discrete pieces. (You'll notice the "Continued" and "Continuing" tags that allow the tool shown in Chapter 17 to piece everything together.) First, the basic framework:

```
//: Blocking.java
// Demonstrates the various ways a thread
// can be blocked.
import java.awt.*;
import java.awt.event.*;
import java.applet.*;
import java.io.*;
```

```
//////////// The basic framework ///////////
class Blockable extends Thread {
  private Peeker peeker;
  protected TextField state = new TextField(40);
  protected int i;
  public Blockable(Container c) {
    c.add(state);
    peeker = new Peeker(this, c);
  }
  public synchronized int read() { return i; }
  protected synchronized void update() {
    state.setText(getClass().getName()
      + " state: i = " + i);
  }
  public void stopPeeker() {
    // peeker.stop(); Deprecated in Java 1.2
    peeker.terminate(); // The preferred approach
  }
}

class Peeker extends Thread {
  private Blockable b;
  private int session;
  private TextField status = new TextField(40);
  private boolean stop = false;
  public Peeker(Blockable b, Container c) {
    c.add(status);
    this.b = b;
    start();
  }
  public void terminate() { stop = true; }
  public void run() {
    while (!stop) {
      status.setText(b.getClass().getName()
        + " Peeker " + (++session)
        + "; value = " + b.read());
      try {
        sleep(100);
      } catch (InterruptedException e){}
    }
  }
} ///:Continued
```

The **Blockable** class is meant to be a base class for all the classes in this example that demonstrate blocking. A **Blockable** object contains a

TextField called **state** that is used to display information about the object. The method that displays this information is **update( )**. You can see it uses **getClass( ).getName( )** to produce the name of the class instead of just printing it out; this is because **update( )** cannot know the exact name of the class it is called for, since it will be a class derived from **Blockable**.

The indicator of change in **Blockable** is an **int i**, which will be incremented by the **run( )** method of the derived class.

There's a thread of class **Peeker** that is started for each **Blockable** object, and the **Peeker**'s job is to watch its associated **Blockable** object to see changes in **i** by calling **read( )** and reporting them in its **status TextField**. This is important: Note that **read( )** and **update( )** are both **synchronized**, which means they require that the object lock be free.

Sleeping

The first test in this program is with **sleep( )**:

```
///:Continuing
///////////// Blocking via sleep() //////////
class Sleeper1 extends Blockable {
  public Sleeper1(Container c) { super(c); }
  public synchronized void run() {
    while(true) {
      i++;
      update();
       try {
        sleep(1000);
      } catch (InterruptedException e){}
    }
  }
}

class Sleeper2 extends Blockable {
  public Sleeper2(Container c) { super(c); }
  public void run() {
    while(true) {
      change();
       try {
        sleep(1000);
      } catch (InterruptedException e){}
    }
  }
}
```

```
    public synchronized void change() {
        i++;
        update();
    }
} ///:Continued
```

In **Sleeper1** the entire **run( )** method is **synchronized**. You'll see that the **Peeker** associated with this object will run along merrily *until* you start the thread, and then the **Peeker** stops cold. This is one form of blocking: since **Sleeper1.run( )** is **synchronized**, and once the thread starts it's always inside **run( )**, the method never gives up the object lock and the **Peeker** is blocked.

Sleeper2 provides a solution by making run un-**synchronized**. Only the **change( )** method is **synchronized**, which means that while **run( )** is in **sleep( )**, the **Peeker** can access the **synchronized** method it needs, namely **read( )**. Here you'll see that the **Peeker** continues running when you start the **Sleeper2** thread.

Suspending and resuming

The next part of the example introduces the concept of suspension. The **Thread** class has a method **suspend( )** to temporarily halt the thread and **resume( )** that re-starts it at the point it was halted. Presumably, **resume( )** is called by some thread outside the suspended one, and in this case there's a separate class called **Resumer** that does just that. Each of the classes demonstrating suspend/resume has an associated resumer:

```
///:Continuing
////////// Blocking via suspend() //////////
class SuspendResume extends Blockable {
  public SuspendResume(Container c) {
    super(c);
    new Resumer(this);
  }
}

class SuspendResume1 extends SuspendResume {
  public SuspendResume1(Container c) { super(c); }
  public synchronized void run() {
    while(true) {
      i++;
      update();
      suspend(); // Deprecated in Java 1.2
    }
```

```
      }
  }

  class SuspendResume2 extends SuspendResume {
    public SuspendResume2(Container c) { super(c);}
    public void run() {
      while(true) {
        change();
        suspend(); // Deprecated in Java 1.2
      }
    }
    public synchronized void change() {
        i++;
        update();
    }
  }

  class Resumer extends Thread {
    private SuspendResume sr;
    public Resumer(SuspendResume sr) {
      this.sr = sr;
      start();
    }
    public void run() {
      while(true) {
          try {
            sleep(1000);
          } catch (InterruptedException e){}
          sr.resume(); // Deprecated in Java 1.2
      }
    }
  } ///:Continued
```

SuspendResume1 also has a **synchronized run( )** method. Again, when you start this thread you'll see that its associated **Peeker** gets blocked waiting for the lock to become available, which never happens. This is fixed as before in **SuspendResume2**, which does not **synchronize** the entire **run( )** method but instead uses a separate **synchronized change( )** method.

You should be aware that Java 1.2 deprecates the use of **suspend( )** and **resume( )**, because **suspend( )** holds the object's lock and is thus deadlock-prone. That is, you can easily get a number of locked objects waiting on each other, and this will cause your program to freeze. Although you might see them used in older programs you should not use

suspend( ) and **resume( )**. The proper solution is described later in this chapter.

Wait and notify

The point with the first two examples is that both **sleep( )** and **suspend( )** *do not* release the lock as they are called. You must be aware of this when working with locks. On the other hand, the method **wait( )** *does* release the lock when it is called, which means that other **synchronized** methods in the thread object could be called during a **wait( )**. In the following two classes, you'll see that the **run( )** method is fully **synchronized** in both cases, however, the **Peeker** still has full access to the **synchronized** methods during a **wait( )**. This is because **wait( )** releases the lock on the object as it suspends the method it's called within.

You'll also see that there are two forms of **wait( )**. The first takes an argument in milliseconds that has the same meaning as in **sleep( )**: pause for this period of time. The difference is that in **wait( )**, the object lock is released *and* you can come out of the **wait( )** because of a **notify( )** as well as having the clock run out.

The second form takes no arguments, and means that the **wait( )** will continue until a **notify( )** comes along and will not automatically terminate after a time.

One fairly unique aspect of **wait( )** and **notify( )** is that both methods are part of the base class **Object** and not part of **Thread** as are **sleep( )**, **suspend( )**, and **resume( )**. Although this seems a bit strange at first – to have something that's exclusively for threading as part of the universal base class – it's essential because they manipulate the lock that's also part of every object. As a result, you can put a **wait( )** inside any **synchronized** method, regardless of whether there's any threading going on inside that particular class. In fact, the *only* place you can call **wait( )** is within a **synchronized** method or block. If you call **wait( )** or **notify( )** within a method that's not **synchronized**, the program will compile, but when you run it you'll get an **IllegalMonitorStateException** with the somewhat non-intuitive message "current thread not owner." Note that **sleep( )**, **suspend( )**, and **resume( )** can all be called within non-**synchronized** methods since they don't manipulate the lock.

You can call **wait( )** or **notify( )** only for your own lock. Again, you can compile code that tries to use the wrong lock, but it will produce the same **IllegalMonitorStateException** message as before. You can't fool with someone else's lock, but you can ask another object to perform an operation that manipulates its own lock. So one approach is to create a

synchronized method that calls **notify( )** for its own object. However, in **Notifier** you'll see the **notify( )** call inside a **synchronized** block:

```
synchronized(wn2) {
  wn2.notify();
}
```

where **wn2** is the object of type **WaitNotify2**. This method, which is not part of **WaitNotify2**, acquires the lock on the **wn2** object, at which point it's legal for it to call **notify( )** for **wn2** and you won't get the **IllegalMonitorStateException**.

```
///:Continuing
////////// Blocking via wait() //////////
class WaitNotify1 extends Blockable {
  public WaitNotify1(Container c) { super(c); }
  public synchronized void run() {
    while(true) {
      i++;
      update();
       try {
        wait(1000);
      } catch (InterruptedException e){}
    }
  }
}

class WaitNotify2 extends Blockable {
  public WaitNotify2(Container c) {
    super(c);
    new Notifier(this);
  }
  public synchronized void run() {
    while(true) {
      i++;
      update();
       try {
        wait();
      } catch (InterruptedException e){}
    }
  }
}

class Notifier extends Thread {
  private WaitNotify2 wn2;
```

```
      public Notifier(WaitNotify2 wn2) {
        this.wn2 = wn2;
        start();
      }
      public void run() {
        while(true) {
          try {
            sleep(2000);
          } catch (InterruptedException e){}
          synchronized(wn2) {
            wn2.notify();
          }
        }
      }
    } ///:Continued
```

wait( ) is typically used when you've gotten to the point where you're
waiting for some other condition, under the control of forces outside
your thread, to change and you don't want to idly wait by inside the
thread. So **wait( )** allows you to put the thread to sleep while waiting for
the world to change, and only when a **notify( )** or **notifyAll( )** occurs
does the thread wake up and check for changes. Thus, it provides a way
to synchronize between threads.

Blocking on IO

If a stream is waiting for some IO activity, it will automatically block. In
the following portion of the example, the two classes work with generic
Reader and **Writer** objects (using the Java 1.1 Streams), but in the test
framework a piped stream will be set up to allow the two threads to
safely pass data to each other (which is the purpose of piped streams).

The **Sender** puts data into the **Writer** and sleeps for a random amount of
time. However, **Receiver** has no **sleep( )**, **suspend( )**, or **wait( )**. But
when it does a **read( )** it automatically blocks when there is no more
data.

```
    ///:Continuing
    class Sender extends Blockable { // send
      private Writer out;
      public Sender(Container c, Writer out) {
        super(c);
        this.out = out;
      }
      public void run() {
```

```
        while(true) {
          for(char c = 'A'; c <= 'z'; c++) {
            try {
              i++;
              out.write(c);
              state.setText("Sender sent: "
                + (char)c);
              sleep((int)(3000 * Math.random()));
            } catch (InterruptedException e){}
            catch (IOException e) {}
          }
        }
      }
    }

    class Receiver extends Blockable {
      private Reader in;
      public Receiver(Container c, Reader in) {
        super(c);
        this.in = in;
      }
      public void run() {
        try {
          while(true) {
            i++; // Show peeker it's alive
            // Blocks until characters are there:
            state.setText("Receiver read: "
              + (char)in.read());
          }
        } catch(IOException e) { e.printStackTrace();}
      }
    } ///:Continued
```

Both classes also put information into their **state** fields and change **i** so the **Peeker** can see that the thread is running.

Testing

The main applet class is surprisingly simple because most of the work has been put into the **Blockable** framework. Basically, an array of **Blockable** objects is created, and since each one is a thread, they perform their own activities when you press the "start" button. There's also a button and **actionPerformed( )** clause to stop all of the **Peeker** objects, which provides a demonstration of the alternative to the deprecated (in Java 1.2) **stop( )** method of **Thread**.

To set up a connection between the **Sender** and **Receiver** objects, a **PipedWriter** and **PipedReader** are created. Note that the **PipedReader in** must be connected to the **PipedWriter out** via a constructor argument. After that, anything that's placed in **out** can later be extracted from **in**, as if it passed through a pipe (hence the name). The **in** and **out** objects are then passed to the **Receiver** and **Sender** constructors, respectively, which treat them as **Reader** and **Writer** objects of any type (that is, they are upcast).

The array of **Blockable** handles **b** is not initialized at its point of definition because the piped streams cannot be set up before that definition takes place (the need for the **try** block prevents this).

```
///:Continuing
////////// Testing Everything //////////
public class Blocking extends Applet {
  private Button
    start = new Button("Start"),
    stopPeekers = new Button("Stop Peekers");
  private boolean started = false;
  private Blockable[] b;
  private PipedWriter out;
  private PipedReader in;
  public void init() {
    out = new PipedWriter();
    try {
      in = new PipedReader(out);
    } catch(IOException e) {}
    b = new Blockable[] {
      new Sleeper1(this),
      new Sleeper2(this),
      new SuspendResume1(this),
      new SuspendResume2(this),
      new WaitNotify1(this),
      new WaitNotify2(this),
      new Sender(this, out),
      new Receiver(this, in)
    };
    start.addActionListener(new StartL());
    add(start);
    stopPeekers.addActionListener(
      new StopPeekersL());
    add(stopPeekers);
  }
  class StartL implements ActionListener {
```

```
      public void actionPerformed(ActionEvent e) {
        if(!started) {
          started = true;
          for(int i = 0; i < b.length; i++)
            b[i].start();
        }
      }
    }
    class StopPeekersL implements ActionListener {
      public void actionPerformed(ActionEvent e) {
        // Demonstration of the preferred
        // alternative to Thread.stop():
        for(int i = 0; i < b.length; i++)
          b[i].stopPeeker();
      }
    }
    public static void main(String[] args) {
      Blocking applet = new Blocking();
      Frame aFrame = new Frame("Blocking");
      aFrame.addWindowListener(
        new WindowAdapter() {
          public void windowClosing(WindowEvent e) {
            System.exit(0);
          }
        });
      aFrame.add(applet, BorderLayout.CENTER);
      aFrame.setSize(350,550);
      applet.init();
      applet.start();
      aFrame.setVisible(true);
    }
} ///:~
```

In **init( )**, notice the loop that moves through the entire array and adds the **state** and **peeker.status** text fields to the page.

When the **Blockable** threads are initially created, each one automatically creates and starts its own **Peeker**. So you'll see the **Peeker**s running before the **Blockable** threads are started. This is essential, as some of the **Peeker**s will get blocked and stop when the **Blockable** threads start, and it's essential to see this to understand that particular aspect of blocking.

Deadlock

Because threads can become blocked *and* because objects can have
synchronized methods that prevent threads from accessing that object
until the synchronization lock is released, it's possible for one thread to
get stuck waiting for another thread, which in turn waits for another
thread, etc., until the chain leads back to a thread waiting on the first
one. Thus, there's a continuous loop of threads waiting on each other
and no one can move. This is called *deadlock*. The claim is that it doesn't
happen that often, but when it happens to you it's frustrating to debug.

There is no language support to help prevent deadlock; it's up to you to
avoid it by careful design. These are not comforting words to the person
who's trying to debug a deadlocking program.

The deprecation of stop( ), suspend( ), resume( ), and destroy( ) in Java 1.2

One change that has been made in Java 1.2 to reduce the possibility of
deadlock is the deprecation of **Thread**'s **stop( )**, **suspend( )**, **resume( )**,
and **destroy( )** methods.

The reason that the **stop( )** method is deprecated is because it is unsafe. It
releases all the locks that the thread had acquired, and if the objects are in
an inconsistent state ("damaged") other threads can view and modify
them in that state. The resulting problems can be subtle and difficult to
detect. Instead of using **stop( )**, you should follow the example in
Blocking.java and use a flag to tell the thread when to terminate itself
by exiting its **run( )** method.

There are times when a thread blocks, such as when it is waiting for
input, and it cannot poll a flag as it does in **Blocking.java**. In these cases,
you still shouldn't use **stop( )**, but instead you can use the **interrupt( )**
method in **Thread** to break out of the blocked code:

```
//: Interrupt.java
// The alternative approach to using stop()
// when a thread is blocked
import java.awt.*;
import java.awt.event.*;
import java.applet.*;

class Blocked extends Thread {
  public synchronized void run() {
    try {
```

```
      wait(); // Blocks
    } catch(InterruptedException e) {
      System.out.println("InterruptedException");
    }
    System.out.println("Exiting run()");
  }
}

public class Interrupt extends Applet {
  private Button
    interrupt = new Button("Interrupt");
  private Blocked blocked = new Blocked();
  public void init() {
    add(interrupt);
    interrupt.addActionListener(
      new ActionListener() {
        public
        void actionPerformed(ActionEvent e) {
          System.out.println("Button pressed");
          if(blocked == null) return;
          Thread remove = blocked;
          blocked = null; // to release it
          remove.interrupt();
        }
      });
    blocked.start();
  }
  public static void main(String[] args) {
    Interrupt applet = new Interrupt();
    Frame aFrame = new Frame("Interrupt");
    aFrame.addWindowListener(
      new WindowAdapter() {
        public void windowClosing(WindowEvent e) {
          System.exit(0);
        }
      });
    aFrame.add(applet, BorderLayout.CENTER);
    aFrame.setSize(200,100);
    applet.init();
    applet.start();
    aFrame.setVisible(true);
  }
} ///:~
```

The **wait( )** inside **Blocked.run( )** produces the blocked thread. When you press the button, the **blocked** handle is set to **null** so the garbage collector will clean it up, and then the object's **interrupt( )** method is called. The first time you press the button you'll see that the thread quits, but after that there's no thread to kill so you just see that the button has been pressed.

The **suspend( )** and **resume( )** methods turn out to be inherently deadlock-prone. When you call **suspend( )**, the target thread stops but it still holds any locks that it has acquired up to that point. So no other thread can access the locked resources until the thread is resumed. Any thread that wants to resume the target thread and also tries to use any of the locked resources produces deadlock. You should not use **suspend( )** and **resume( )**, but instead put a flag in your **Thread** class to indicate whether the thread should be active or suspended. If the flag indicates that the thread is suspended, the thread goes into a wait using **wait( )**. When the flag indicates that the thread should be resumed the thread is restarted with **notify( )**. An example can be produced by modifying **Counter2.java**. Although the effect is similar, you'll notice that the code organization is quite different – anonymous inner classes are used for all of the listeners and the **Thread** is an inner class, which makes programming slightly more convenient since it eliminates some of the extra bookkeeping necessary in **Counter2.java**:

```
//: Suspend.java
// The alternative approach to using suspend()
// and resume(), which have been deprecated
// in Java 1.2.
import java.awt.*;
import java.awt.event.*;
import java.applet.*;

public class Suspend extends Applet {
  private TextField t = new TextField(10);
  private Button
    suspend = new Button("Suspend"),
    resume = new Button("Resume");
  class Suspendable extends Thread {
    private int count = 0;
    private boolean suspended = false;
    public Suspendable() { start(); }
    public void fauxSuspend() {
      suspended = true;
    }
    public synchronized void fauxResume() {
```

```
          suspended = false;
          notify();
        }
      public void run() {
        while (true) {
          try {
            sleep(100);
            synchronized(this) {
              while(suspended)
                wait();
            }
          } catch (InterruptedException e){}
          t.setText(Integer.toString(count++));
        }
      }
    }
    private Suspendable ss = new Suspendable();
    public void init() {
      add(t);
      suspend.addActionListener(
        new ActionListener() {
          public
          void actionPerformed(ActionEvent e) {
            ss.fauxSuspend();
          }
        });
      add(suspend);
      resume.addActionListener(
        new ActionListener() {
          public
          void actionPerformed(ActionEvent e) {
            ss.fauxResume();
          }
        });
      add(resume);
    }
    public static void main(String[] args) {
      Suspend applet = new Suspend();
      Frame aFrame = new Frame("Suspend");
      aFrame.addWindowListener(
        new WindowAdapter() {
          public void windowClosing(WindowEvent e){
            System.exit(0);
          }
```

```
        });
        aFrame.add(applet, BorderLayout.CENTER);
        aFrame.setSize(300,100);
        applet.init();
        applet.start();
        aFrame.setVisible(true);
    }
} ///:~
```

The flag **suspended** inside **Suspendable** is used to turn suspension on and off. To suspend, the flag is set to **true** by calling **fauxSuspend( )** and this is detected inside **run( )**. The **wait( )**, as described earlier in this chapter, must be **synchronized** so that it has the object lock. In **fauxResume( )**, the **suspended** flag is set to **false** and **notify( )** is called – since this wakes up **wait( )** inside a **synchronized** clause the **fauxResume( )** method must also be **synchronized** so that it acquires the lock before calling **notify( )** (thus the lock is available for the **wait( )** to wake up with). If you follow the style shown in this program you can avoid using **wait( )** and **notify( )**.

The **destroy( )** method of **Thread** has never been implemented; it's like a **suspend( )** that cannot resume, so it has the same deadlock issues as **suspend( )**. However, this is not a deprecated method and it might be implemented in a future version of Java (after 1.2) for special situations in which the risk of a deadlock is acceptable.

You might wonder why these methods, now deprecated, were included in Java in the first place. It seems a clear admission of a rather significant mistake to simply remove them outright (and pokes yet another hole in the arguments for Java's exceptional design and infallibility touted by Sun marketing people). The heartening part about the change is that it clearly indicates that the technical people and not the marketing people are running the show – they discovered a problem and they are fixing it. I find this much more promising and hopeful than leaving the problem in because fixing it would admit an error. It means that Java will continue to improve, even if it means a little discomfort on the part of Java programmers. I'd rather deal with the discomfort than watch the language stagnate.

Priorities

The *priority* of a thread tells the scheduler how important this thread is. If there are a number of threads blocked and waiting to be run, the scheduler will run the one with the highest priority first. However, this doesn't mean that threads with lower priority don't get run (that is, you can't get deadlocked because of priorities). Lower priority threads just tend to run less often.

You can read the priority of a thread with **getPriority( )** and change it with **setPriority( )**. The form of the prior "counter" examples can be used to show the effect of changing the priorities. In this applet you'll see that the counters slow down as the associated threads have their priorities lowered:

```java
//: Counter5.java
// Adjusting the priorities of threads
import java.awt.*;
import java.awt.event.*;
import java.applet.*;

class Ticker2 extends Thread {
  private Button
    b = new Button("Toggle"),
    incPriority = new Button("up"),
    decPriority = new Button("down");
  private TextField
    t = new TextField(10),
    pr = new TextField(3); // Display priority
  private int count = 0;
  private boolean runFlag = true;
  public Ticker2(Container c) {
    b.addActionListener(new ToggleL());
    incPriority.addActionListener(new UpL());
    decPriority.addActionListener(new DownL());
    Panel p = new Panel();
    p.add(t);
    p.add(pr);
    p.add(b);
    p.add(incPriority);
    p.add(decPriority);
    c.add(p);
  }
  class ToggleL implements ActionListener {
    public void actionPerformed(ActionEvent e) {
      runFlag = !runFlag;
    }
  }
  class UpL implements ActionListener {
    public void actionPerformed(ActionEvent e) {
```

```
         int newPriority = getPriority() + 1;
         if(newPriority > Thread.MAX_PRIORITY)
           newPriority = Thread.MAX_PRIORITY;
         setPriority(newPriority);
       }
     }
     class DownL implements ActionListener {
       public void actionPerformed(ActionEvent e) {
         int newPriority = getPriority() - 1;
         if(newPriority < Thread.MIN_PRIORITY)
           newPriority = Thread.MIN_PRIORITY;
         setPriority(newPriority);
       }
     }
     public void run() {
       while (true) {
         if(runFlag) {
           t.setText(Integer.toString(count++));
           pr.setText(
             Integer.toString(getPriority()));
         }
         yield();
       }
     }
   }

   public class Counter5 extends Applet {
     private Button
       start = new Button("Start"),
       upMax = new Button("Inc Max Priority"),
       downMax = new Button("Dec Max Priority");
     private boolean started = false;
     private static final int SIZE = 10;
     private Ticker2[] s = new Ticker2[SIZE];
     private TextField mp = new TextField(3);
     public void init() {
       for(int i = 0; i < s.length; i++)
         s[i] = new Ticker2(this);
       add(new Label("MAX_PRIORITY = "
         + Thread.MAX_PRIORITY));
       add(new Label("MIN_PRIORITY = "
         + Thread.MIN_PRIORITY));
       add(new Label("Group Max Priority = "));
       add(mp);
```

```
      add(start);
      add(upMax); add(downMax);
      start.addActionListener(new StartL());
      upMax.addActionListener(new UpMaxL());
      downMax.addActionListener(new DownMaxL());
      showMaxPriority();
      // Recursively display parent thread groups:
      ThreadGroup parent =
        s[0].getThreadGroup().getParent();
      while(parent != null) {
        add(new Label(
          "Parent threadgroup max priority = "
          + parent.getMaxPriority()));
        parent = parent.getParent();
      }
    }
    public void showMaxPriority() {
      mp.setText(Integer.toString(
        s[0].getThreadGroup().getMaxPriority()));
    }
    class StartL implements ActionListener {
      public void actionPerformed(ActionEvent e) {
        if(!started) {
          started = true;
          for(int i = 0; i < s.length; i++)
            s[i].start();
        }
      }
    }
    class UpMaxL implements ActionListener {
      public void actionPerformed(ActionEvent e) {
        int maxp =
          s[0].getThreadGroup().getMaxPriority();
        if(++maxp > Thread.MAX_PRIORITY)
          maxp = Thread.MAX_PRIORITY;
        s[0].getThreadGroup().setMaxPriority(maxp);
        showMaxPriority();
      }
    }
    class DownMaxL implements ActionListener {
      public void actionPerformed(ActionEvent e) {
        int maxp =
          s[0].getThreadGroup().getMaxPriority();
        if(--maxp < Thread.MIN_PRIORITY)
```

```
       maxp = Thread.MIN_PRIORITY;
       s[0].getThreadGroup().setMaxPriority(maxp);
       showMaxPriority();
     }
   }
 public static void main(String[] args) {
   Counter5 applet = new Counter5();
   Frame aFrame = new Frame("Counter5");
   aFrame.addWindowListener(
     new WindowAdapter() {
       public void windowClosing(WindowEvent e) {
         System.exit(0);
       }
     });
   aFrame.add(applet, BorderLayout.CENTER);
   aFrame.setSize(300, 600);
   applet.init();
   applet.start();
   aFrame.setVisible(true);
 }
} ///:~
```

Ticker2 follows the form established earlier in this chapter, but there's an extra **TextField** for displaying the priority of the thread and two more buttons for incrementing and decrementing the priority.

Also notice the use of **yield( )**, which voluntarily hands control back to the scheduler. Without this the multithreading mechanism still works, but you'll notice it runs slowly (try removing the call to **yield( )**!). You could also call **sleep( )**, but then the rate of counting would be controlled by the **sleep( )** duration instead of the priority.

The **init( )** in **Counter5** creates an array of 10 **Ticker2**s; their buttons and fields are placed on the form by the **Ticker2** constructor. **Counter5** adds buttons to start everything up as well as increment and decrement the maximum priority of the threadgroup. In addition, there are labels that display the maximum and minimum priorities possible for a thread and a **TextField** to show the thread group's maximum priority. (The next section will fully describe thread groups.) Finally, the priorities of the parent thread groups are also displayed as labels.

When you press an "up" or "down" button, that **Ticker2**'s priority is fetched and incremented or decremented accordingly.

When you run this program, you'll notice several things. First of all, the thread group's default priority is 5. Even if you decrement the maximum

---

priority below 5 before starting the threads (or before creating the threads, which requires a code change), each thread will have a default priority of 5.

The simple test is to take one counter and decrement its priority to one, and observe that it counts much slower. But now try to increment it again. You can get it back up to the thread group's priority, but no higher. Now decrement the thread group's priority a couple of times. The thread priorities are unchanged, but if you try to modify them either up or down you'll see that they'll automatically pop to the priority of the thread group. Also, new threads will still be given a default priority, even if that's higher than the group priority. (Thus the group priority is not a way to prevent new threads from having higher priorities than existing ones.)

Finally, try to increment the group maximum priority. It can't be done. You can only reduce thread group maximum priorities, not increase them.

Thread groups

All threads belong to a thread group. This can be either the default thread group or a group you explicitly specify when you create the thread. At creation, the thread is bound to a group and cannot change to a different group. Each application has at least one thread that belongs to the system thread group. If you create more threads without specifying a group, they will also belong to the system thread group.

Thread groups must also belong to other thread groups. The thread group that a new one belongs to must be specified in the constructor. If you create a thread group without specifying a thread group for it to belong to, it will be placed under the system thread group. Thus, all thread groups in your application will ultimately have the system thread group as the parent.

The reason for the existence of thread groups is hard to determine from the literature, which tends to be confusing on this subject. It's often cited as "security reasons." According to Arnold & Gosling,[1] "Threads within a thread group can modify the other threads in the group, including any farther down the hierarchy. A thread cannot modify threads outside of its

---

[1] *The Java Programming Language*, by Ken Arnold and James Gosling, Addison-Wesley 1996 pp 179.

own group or contained groups." It's hard to know what "modify" is supposed to mean here. The following example shows a thread in a "leaf" subgroup modifying the priorities of all the threads in its tree of thread groups as well as calling a method for all the threads in its tree.

```java
//: TestAccess.java
// How threads can access other threads
// in a parent thread group

public class TestAccess {
  public static void main(String[] args) {
    ThreadGroup
      x = new ThreadGroup("x"),
      y = new ThreadGroup(x, "y"),
      z = new ThreadGroup(y, "z");
    Thread
      one = new TestThread1(x, "one"),
      two = new TestThread2(z, "two");
  }
}

class TestThread1 extends Thread {
  private int i;
  TestThread1(ThreadGroup g, String name) {
    super(g, name);
  }
  void f() {
    i++; // modify this thread
    System.out.println(getName() + " f()");
  }
}

class TestThread2 extends TestThread1 {
  TestThread2(ThreadGroup g, String name) {
    super(g, name);
    start();
  }
  public void run() {
    ThreadGroup g =
      getThreadGroup().getParent().getParent();
    g.list();
    Thread[] gAll = new Thread[g.activeCount()];
    g.enumerate(gAll);
    for(int i = 0; i < gAll.length; i++) {
      gAll[i].setPriority(Thread.MIN_PRIORITY);
```

```
        ((TestThread1)gAll[i]).f();
      }
      g.list();
    }
  } ///:~
```

In **main( )**, several **ThreadGroup**s are created, leafing off from each other: **x** has no argument but its name (a **String**), so it is automatically placed in the "system" thread group, while **y** is under **x** and **z** is under **y**. Note that initialization happens in textual order so this code is legal.

Two threads are created and placed in different thread groups. **TestThread1** doesn't have a **run( )** method but it does have an **f( )** that modifies the thread and prints something so you can see it was called. **TestThread2** is a subclass of **TestThread1** and its **run( )** is fairly elaborate. It first gets the thread group of the current thread, then moves up the heritage tree by two levels using **getParent( )**. (This is contrived since I purposely place the **TestThread2** object two levels down in the hierarchy.) At this point, an array of handles to **Thread**s is created using the method **activeCount( )** to ask how many threads are in this thread group and all the child thread groups. The **enumerate( )** method places handles to all of these threads in the array **gAll**, then I simply move through the entire array calling the **f( )** method for each thread, as well as modifying the priority. Thus, a thread in a "leaf" thread group modifies threads in parent thread groups.

The debugging method **list( )** prints all the information about a thread group to standard output and is helpful when investigating thread group behavior. Here's the output of the program:

```
java.lang.ThreadGroup[name=x,maxpri=10]
    Thread[one,5,x]
    java.lang.ThreadGroup[name=y,maxpri=10]
        java.lang.ThreadGroup[name=z,maxpri=10]
            Thread[two,5,z]
one f()
two f()
java.lang.ThreadGroup[name=x,maxpri=10]
    Thread[one,1,x]
    java.lang.ThreadGroup[name=y,maxpri=10]
        java.lang.ThreadGroup[name=z,maxpri=10]
            Thread[two,1,z]
```

Not only does **list( )** print the class name of **ThreadGroup** or **Thread**, but it also prints the thread group name and its maximum priority. For threads, the thread name is printed, followed by the thread priority and the group that it belongs to. Note that **list( )** indents the threads and thread groups to indicate that they are children of the un-indented thread group.

You can see that **f( )** is called by the **TestThread2 run( )** method, so it's obvious that all threads in a group are vulnerable. However, you can access only the threads that branch off from your own **system** thread group tree, and perhaps this is what is meant by "safety." You cannot access anyone else's system thread group tree.

Controlling thread groups

Putting aside the safety issue, one thing thread groups do seem to be useful for is control: you can perform certain operations on an entire thread group with a single command. The following example demonstrates this and the restrictions on priorities within thread groups. The commented numbers in parentheses provide a reference to compare to the output.

```
//: ThreadGroup1.java
// How thread groups control priorities
// of the threads inside them.

public class ThreadGroup1 {
  public static void main(String[] args) {
    // Get the system thread & print its Info:
    ThreadGroup sys =
      Thread.currentThread().getThreadGroup();
    sys.list(); // (1)
    // Reduce the system thread group priority:
    sys.setMaxPriority(Thread.MAX_PRIORITY - 1);
    // Increase the main thread priority:
    Thread curr = Thread.currentThread();
    curr.setPriority(curr.getPriority() + 1);
    sys.list(); // (2)
    // Attempt to set a new group to the max:
    ThreadGroup g1 = new ThreadGroup("g1");
    g1.setMaxPriority(Thread.MAX_PRIORITY);
    // Attempt to set a new thread to the max:
    Thread t = new Thread(g1, "A");
    t.setPriority(Thread.MAX_PRIORITY);
    g1.list(); // (3)
    // Reduce g1's max priority, then attempt
    // to increase it:
    g1.setMaxPriority(Thread.MAX_PRIORITY - 2);
```

```
      g1.setMaxPriority(Thread.MAX_PRIORITY);
      g1.list(); // (4)
      // Attempt to set a new thread to the max:
      t = new Thread(g1, "B");
      t.setPriority(Thread.MAX_PRIORITY);
      g1.list(); // (5)
      // Lower the max priority below the default
      // thread priority:
      g1.setMaxPriority(Thread.MIN_PRIORITY + 2);
      // Look at a new thread's priority before
      // and after changing it:
      t = new Thread(g1, "C");
      g1.list(); // (6)
      t.setPriority(t.getPriority() -1);
      g1.list(); // (7)
      // Make g2 a child Threadgroup of g1 and
      // try to increase its priority:
      ThreadGroup g2 = new ThreadGroup(g1, "g2");
      g2.list(); // (8)
      g2.setMaxPriority(Thread.MAX_PRIORITY);
      g2.list(); // (9)
      // Add a bunch of new threads to g2:
      for (int i = 0; i < 5; i++)
        new Thread(g2, Integer.toString(i));
      // Show information about all threadgroups
      // and threads:
      sys.list(); // (10)
      System.out.println("Starting all threads:");
      Thread[] all = new Thread[sys.activeCount()];
      sys.enumerate(all);
      for(int i = 0; i < all.length; i++)
        if(!all[i].isAlive())
          all[i].start();
      // Suspends & Stops all threads in
      // this group and its subgroups:
      System.out.println("All threads started");
      sys.suspend(); // Deprecated in Java 1.2
      // Never gets here...
      System.out.println("All threads suspended");
      sys.stop(); // Deprecated in Java 1.2
      System.out.println("All threads stopped");
  }
} ///:~
```

The output that follows has been edited to allow it to fit on the page (the **java.lang.** has been removed) and to add numbers to correspond to the commented numbers in the listing above.

```
(1)  ThreadGroup[name=system,maxpri=10]
        Thread[main,5,system]
(2)  ThreadGroup[name=system,maxpri=9]
        Thread[main,6,system]
(3)  ThreadGroup[name=g1,maxpri=9]
        Thread[A,9,g1]
(4)  ThreadGroup[name=g1,maxpri=8]
        Thread[A,9,g1]
(5)  ThreadGroup[name=g1,maxpri=8]
        Thread[A,9,g1]
        Thread[B,8,g1]
(6)  ThreadGroup[name=g1,maxpri=3]
        Thread[A,9,g1]
        Thread[B,8,g1]
        Thread[C,6,g1]
(7)  ThreadGroup[name=g1,maxpri=3]
        Thread[A,9,g1]
        Thread[B,8,g1]
        Thread[C,3,g1]
(8)  ThreadGroup[name=g2,maxpri=3]
(9)  ThreadGroup[name=g2,maxpri=3]
(10) ThreadGroup[name=system,maxpri=9]
        Thread[main,6,system]
        ThreadGroup[name=g1,maxpri=3]
           Thread[A,9,g1]
           Thread[B,8,g1]
           Thread[C,3,g1]
           ThreadGroup[name=g2,maxpri=3]
              Thread[0,6,g2]
              Thread[1,6,g2]
              Thread[2,6,g2]
              Thread[3,6,g2]
              Thread[4,6,g2]
Starting all threads:
All threads started
```

All programs have at least one thread running, and the first action in **main( )** is to call the **static** method of **Thread** called **currentThread( )**. From this thread, the thread group is produced and **list( )** is called for the result. The output is:

```
(1)  ThreadGroup[name=system,maxpri=10]
       Thread[main,5,system]
```

You can see that the name of the main thread group is **system**, and the name of the main thread is **main**, and it belongs to the **system** thread group.

The second exercise shows that the **system** group's maximum priority can be reduced and the **main** thread can have its priority increased:

```
(2)  ThreadGroup[name=system,maxpri=9]
       Thread[main,6,system]
```

The third exercise creates a new thread group, **g1**, which automatically belongs to the **system** thread group since it isn't otherwise specified. A new thread **A** is placed in **g1**. After attempting to set this group's maximum priority to the highest level and **A**'s priority to the highest level, the result is:

```
(3)  ThreadGroup[name=g1,maxpri=9]
       Thread[A,9,g1]
```

Thus, it's not possible to change the thread group's maximum priority to be higher than its parent thread group.

The fourth exercise reduces **g1**'s maximum priority by two and then tries to increase it up to **Thread.MAX_PRIORITY**. The result is:

```
(4)  ThreadGroup[name=g1,maxpri=8]
       Thread[A,9,g1]
```

You can see that the increase in maximum priority didn't work. You can only decrease a thread group's maximum priority, not increase it. Also, notice that thread **A**'s priority didn't change, and now it is higher than the thread group's maximum priority. Changing a thread group's maximum priority doesn't affect existing threads.

The fifth exercise attempts to set a new thread to maximum priority:

```
(5)  ThreadGroup[name=g1,maxpri=8]
       Thread[A,9,g1]
       Thread[B,8,g1]
```

The new thread cannot be changed to anything higher than the maximum thread group priority.

The default thread priority for this program is 6; that's the priority a new thread will be created at and where it will stay if you don't manipulate the priority. Exercise six lowers the maximum thread group priority below the default thread priority to see what happens when you create a new thread under this condition:

```
(6)  ThreadGroup[name=g1,maxpri=3]
        Thread[A,9,g1]
        Thread[B,8,g1]
        Thread[C,6,g1]
```

Even though the maximum priority of the thread group is 3, the new thread is still created using the default priority of 6. Thus, maximum thread group priority does not affect default priority. (In fact, there appears to be no way to set the default priority for new threads.)

After changing the priority, attempting to decrement it by one, the result is:

```
(7)  ThreadGroup[name=g1,maxpri=3]
        Thread[A,9,g1]
        Thread[B,8,g1]
        Thread[C,3,g1]
```

Only when you attempt to change the priority is the thread group's maximum priority enforced.

A similar experiment is performed in (8) and (9), in which a new thread group **g2** is created as a child of **g1** and its maximum priority is changed. You can see that it's impossible for **g2**'s maximum to go higher than **g1**'s:

```
(8)  ThreadGroup[name=g2,maxpri=3]
(9)  ThreadGroup[name=g2,maxpri=3]
```

Also notice that **g2** is automatically set to the thread group maximum priority of **g1** as **g2** is created.

After all of these experiments, the entire system of thread groups and threads is printed out:

```
(10) ThreadGroup[name=system,maxpri=9]
        Thread[main,6,system]
        ThreadGroup[name=g1,maxpri=3]
          Thread[A,9,g1]
          Thread[B,8,g1]
          Thread[C,3,g1]
          ThreadGroup[name=g2,maxpri=3]
            Thread[0,6,g2]
```

```
Thread[1,6,g2]
Thread[2,6,g2]
Thread[3,6,g2]
Thread[4,6,g2]
```

So because of the rules of thread groups, a child group must always have a maximum priority that's less than or equal to its parent's maximum priority.

The last part of this program demonstrates methods for an entire group of threads. First the program moves through the entire tree of threads and starts each one that hasn't been started. For drama, the **system** group is then suspended and finally stopped. (Although it's interesting to see that **suspend( )** and **stop( )** work on entire thread groups, you should keep in mind that these methods are deprecated in Java 1.2.) But when you suspend the **system** group you also suspend the **main** thread and the whole program shuts down, so it never gets to the point where the threads are stopped. Actually, if you do stop the **main** thread it throws a **ThreadDeath** exception, so this is not a typical thing to do. Since **ThreadGroup** is inherited from **Object**, which contains the **wait( )** method, you can also choose to suspend the program for any number of seconds by calling **wait(seconds * 1000)**. This must acquire the lock inside a synchronized block, of course.

The **ThreadGroup** class also has **suspend( )** and **resume( )** methods so you can stop and start an entire thread group and all of its threads and subgroups with a single command. (Again, **suspend( )** and **resume( )** are deprecated in Java 1.2.)

Thread groups can seem a bit mysterious at first, but keep in mind that you probably won't be using them directly very often.

Runnable revisited

Earlier in this chapter, I suggested that you think carefully before making an applet or main **Frame** as an implementation of **Runnable**. If you take that approach, you can make only one of those threads in your program. This limits your flexibility if you decide that you want to have more than one thread of that type.

Of course, if you must inherit from a class *and* you want to add threading behavior to the class, **Runnable** is the correct solution. The final example in this chapter exploits this by making a **Runnable Canvas** class that paints different colors on itself. This application is set up to take values from the command line to determine how big the grid of colors is and how long to **sleep( )** between color changes. By playing with these values you'll discover some interesting and possibly inexplicable features of threads:

```
//: ColorBoxes.java
// Using the Runnable interface
import java.awt.*;
import java.awt.event.*;

class CBox extends Canvas implements Runnable {
  private Thread t;
  private int pause;
  private static final Color[] colors = {
    Color.black, Color.blue, Color.cyan,
    Color.darkGray, Color.gray, Color.green,
    Color.lightGray, Color.magenta,
    Color.orange, Color.pink, Color.red,
    Color.white, Color.yellow
  };
  private Color cColor = newColor();
  private static final Color newColor() {
    return colors[
      (int)(Math.random() * colors.length)
    ];
  }
  public void paint(Graphics  g) {
    g.setColor(cColor);
    Dimension s = getSize();
    g.fillRect(0, 0, s.width, s.height);
  }
  public CBox(int pause) {
    this.pause = pause;
    t = new Thread(this);
    t.start();
  }
  public void run() {
    while(true) {
      cColor = newColor();
      repaint();
      try {
        t.sleep(pause);
      } catch(InterruptedException e) {}
    }
  }
}
```

```
    }

  public class ColorBoxes extends Frame {
    public ColorBoxes(int pause, int grid) {
      setTitle("ColorBoxes");
      setLayout(new GridLayout(grid, grid));
      for (int i = 0; i < grid * grid; i++)
        add(new CBox(pause));
      addWindowListener(new WindowAdapter() {
        public void windowClosing(WindowEvent e) {
          System.exit(0);
        }
      });
    }
    public static void main(String[] args) {
      int pause = 50;
      int grid = 8;
      if(args.length > 0)
        pause = Integer.parseInt(args[0]);
      if(args.length > 1)
        grid = Integer.parseInt(args[1]);
      Frame f = new ColorBoxes(pause, grid);
      f.setSize(500, 400);
      f.setVisible(true);
    }
  } ///:~
```

ColorBoxes is a typical application with a constructor that sets up the
GUI. This constructor takes an argument of **int grid** to set up the
GridLayout so that it has **grid** cells in each dimension. Then it adds the
appropriate number of **CBox** objects to fill the grid, passing the **pause**
value to each one. In **main( )** you can see how **pause** and **grid** have
default values that can be changed if you pass in command-line
arguments.

CBox is where all the work takes place. This is inherited from **Canvas**
and it implements the **Runnable** interface so each **Canvas** can also be a
Thread. Remember that when you implement **Runnable**, you don't
make a **Thread** object, just a class that has a **run( )** method. Thus, you
must explicitly create a **Thread** object and hand the **Runnable** object to
the constructor, then call **start( )** (this happens in the constructor). In
CBox this thread is called **t**.

Notice the array **colors**, which is an enumeration of all the colors in class **Color**. This is used in **newColor( )** to produce a randomly-selected color. The current cell color is **cColor**.

paint( ) is quite simple – it just sets the color to **cColor** and fills the entire canvas with that color.

In **run( )**, you see the infinite loop that sets the **cColor** to a new random color and then calls **repaint( )** to show it. Then the thread goes to **sleep( )** for the amount of time specified on the command line.

Precisely because this design is flexible and threading is tied to each **Canvas** element, you can experiment by making as many threads as you want. (In reality, there is a restriction imposed by the number of threads your JVM can comfortably handle.)

This program also makes an interesting benchmark, since it can show dramatic speed differences between one JVM implementation and another.

Too many threads

At some point, you'll find that **ColorBoxes** bogs down. On my machine, this occurred somewhere after a 10 x 10 grid. Why does this happen? You're naturally suspicious that the AWT might have something to do with it, so here's an example that tests that premise by making fewer threads. The code is reorganized so that a **Vector implements Runnable** and that **Vector** holds a number of color blocks and randomly chooses ones to update. Then a number of these **Vector** objects are created, depending roughly on the grid dimension you choose. As a result, you have far fewer threads than color blocks, so if there's a speedup we'll know it was because there were too many threads in the previous example:

```
//: ColorBoxes2.java
// Balancing thread use
import java.awt.*;
import java.awt.event.*;
import java.util.*;

class CBox2 extends Canvas {
  private static final Color[] colors = {
    Color.black, Color.blue, Color.cyan,
    Color.darkGray, Color.gray, Color.green,
    Color.lightGray, Color.magenta,
```

```
          Color.orange, Color.pink, Color.red,
          Color.white, Color.yellow
      };
      private Color cColor = newColor();
      private static final Color newColor() {
        return colors[
          (int)(Math.random() * colors.length)
        ];
      }
      void nextColor() {
        cColor = newColor();
        repaint();
      }
      public void paint(Graphics  g) {
        g.setColor(cColor);
        Dimension s = getSize();
        g.fillRect(0, 0, s.width, s.height);
      }
    }

    class CBoxVector
      extends Vector implements Runnable {
      private Thread t;
      private int pause;
      public CBoxVector(int pause) {
        this.pause = pause;
        t = new Thread(this);
      }
      public void go() { t.start(); }
      public void run() {
        while(true) {
          int i = (int)(Math.random() * size());
          ((CBox2)elementAt(i)).nextColor();
          try {
            t.sleep(pause);
          } catch(InterruptedException e) {}
        }
      }
    }

    public class ColorBoxes2 extends Frame {
      private CBoxVector[] v;
      public ColorBoxes2(int pause, int grid) {
        setTitle("ColorBoxes2");
```

```
      setLayout(new GridLayout(grid, grid));
      v = new CBoxVector[grid];
      for(int i = 0; i < grid; i++)
        v[i] = new CBoxVector(pause);
      for (int i = 0; i < grid * grid; i++) {
        v[i % grid].addElement(new CBox2());
        add((CBox2)v[i % grid].lastElement());
      }
      for(int i = 0; i < grid; i++)
        v[i].go();
      addWindowListener(new WindowAdapter() {
        public void windowClosing(WindowEvent e) {
          System.exit(0);
        }
      });
    }
    public static void main(String[] args) {
      // Shorter default pause than ColorBoxes:
      int pause = 5;
      int grid = 8;
      if(args.length > 0)
        pause = Integer.parseInt(args[0]);
      if(args.length > 1)
        grid = Integer.parseInt(args[1]);
      Frame f = new ColorBoxes2(pause, grid);
      f.setSize(500, 400);
      f.setVisible(true);
    }
} ///:~
```

In **ColorBoxes2** an array of **CBoxVector** is created and initialized to hold **grid CBoxVector**s, each of which knows how long to sleep. An equal number of **Cbox2** objects is then added to each **CBoxVector**, and each vector is told to **go( )**, which starts its thread.

CBox2 is similar to **CBox**: it paints itself with a randomly-chosen color. But that's *all* a **CBox2** does. All of the threading has been moved into **CBoxVector**.

The **CBoxVector** could also have inherited **Thread** and had a member object of type **Vector**. That design has the advantage that the **addElement( )** and **elementAt( )** methods could then be given specific argument and return value types instead of generic **Objects**. (Their names could also be changed to something shorter.) However, the design used here seemed at first glance to require less code. In addition, it

---

automatically retains all the other behaviors of a **Vector**. With all the casting and parentheses necessary for **elementAt( )**, this might not be the case as your body of code grows.

As before, when you implement **Runnable** you don't get all of the equipment that comes with **Thread**, so you have to create a new **Thread** and hand yourself to its constructor in order to have something to **start( )**, as you can see in the **CBoxVector** constructor and in **go( )**. The **run( )** method simply chooses a random element number within the vector and calls **nextColor( )** for that element to cause it to choose a new randomly-selected color.

Upon running this program, you see that it does indeed run faster and respond more quickly (for instance, when you interrupt it, it stops more quickly), and it doesn't seem to bog down as much at higher grid sizes. Thus, a new factor is added into the threading equation: you must watch to see that you don't have "too many threads" (whatever that turns out to mean for your particular program and platform). If you do, you must try to use techniques like the one above to "balance" the number of threads in your program. If you see performance problems in a multithreaded program you now have a number of issues to examine:

1. Do you have enough calls to **sleep( )**, **yield( )**, and/or **wait( )**?

2. Are calls to **sleep( )** long enough?

3. Are you running too many threads?

4. Have you tried different platforms and JVMs?

Issues like this are one reason that multithreaded programming is often considered an art.

Summary

It is vital to learn when to use multithreading and when to avoid it. The main reason to use it is to manage a number of tasks whose intermingling will make more efficient use of the computer or be more convenient for the user. The classic example of resource balancing is using the CPU during I/O waits. The classic example of user convenience is monitoring a "stop" button during long downloads.

The main drawbacks to multithreading are:

1. Slowdown while waiting for shared resources

---

2. Additional CPU overhead required to manage threads

3. Unrewarded complexity, such as the silly idea of having a separate thread to update each element of an array

4. Pathologies including starving, racing, and deadlock

An additional advantage to threads is that they substitute "light" execution context switches (of the order of 100 instructions) for "heavy" process context switches (of the order of 1000s of instructions). Since all threads in a given process share the same memory space, a light context switch changes only program execution and local variables. On the other hand, a process change, the heavy context switch, must exchange the full memory space.

Threading is like stepping into an entirely new world and learning a whole new programming language, or at least a new set of language concepts. With the appearance of thread support in most microcomputer operating systems, extensions for threads have also been appearing in programming languages or libraries. In all cases, thread programming (1) seems mysterious and requires a shift in the way you think about programming and (2) looks similar to thread support in other languages, so when you understand threads, you understand a common tongue. And although support for threads can make Java seem like a more complicated language, don't blame Java. Threads are tricky.

One of the biggest difficulties with threads occurs because more than one thread might be sharing a resource, such as the memory in an object, and you must make sure that multiple threads don't try to read and change that resource at the same time. This requires judicious use of the **synchronized** keyword, which is a helpful tool but must be understood thoroughly because it can quietly introduce deadlock situations.

In addition, there's a certain art to the application of threads. Java is designed to allow you to create as many objects as you need to solve your problem – at least in theory. (Creating millions of objects for an engineering finite-element analysis, for example, might not be practical in Java.) However, it seems that there is an upper bound to the number of threads you'll want to create because at some point a large number of threads seems to become unwieldy. This critical point is not in the many thousands as it might be with objects, but rather in the neighborhood of less than 100. As you often create only a handful of threads to solve a problem, this is typically not much of a limit, yet in a more general design it becomes a constraint.

A significant non-intuitive issue in threading is that, because of thread scheduling, you can typically make your applications run *faster* by inserting calls to **sleep( )** inside **run( )**'s main loop. This definitely makes it feel like an art, in particular when the longer delays seem to speed up performance. Of course, the reason this happens is that shorter delays can cause the end-of-**sleep( )** scheduler interrupt to happen before the running thread is ready to go to sleep, forcing the scheduler to stop it and restart it later so it can finish what it was doing and then go to sleep. It takes extra thought to realize how messy things can get.

One thing you might notice missing in this chapter is an animation example, which is one of the most popular things to do with applets. However, a complete solution (with sound) to this problem comes with the Java JDK (available at *java.sun.com*) in the demo section. In addition, we can expect better animation support to become part of future versions of Java, while completely different non–Java, non–programming solutions to animation for the Web are appearing that will probably be superior to traditional approaches. For explanations about how Java animation works, see *Core Java* by Cornell & Horstmann, Prentice-Hall 1997. For more advanced discussions of threading, see *Concurrent Programming in Java* by Doug Lea, Addison-Wesley 1997, or *Java Threads* by Oaks & Wong, O'Reilly 1997.

Exercises

1. Inherit a class from **Thread** and override the **run( )** method. Inside **run( )**, print a message, then call **sleep( )**. Repeat this three times, then return from **run( )**. Put a start-up message in the constructor and override **finalize( )** to print a shut-down message. Make a separate thread class that calls **System.gc( )** and **System.runFinalization( )** inside **run( )**, printing a message as it does so. Make several thread objects of both types and run them to see what happens.

2. Modify **Counter2.java** so that the thread is an inner class and doesn't need to explicitly store a handle to a **Counter2**.

3. Modify **Sharing2.java** to add a **synchronized** block inside the **run( )** method of **TwoCounter** instead of synchronizing the entire **run( )** method.

4. Create two **Thread** subclasses, one with a **run( )** that starts up, captures the handle of the second **Thread** object and then calls **wait( )**.

The other class' **run( )** should call **notifyAll( )** for the first thread after some number of seconds have passed, so the first thread can print out a message.

5. In **Counter5.java** inside **Ticker2**, remove the **yield( )** and explain the results. Replace the **yield( )** with a **sleep( )** and explain the results.

6. In **ThreadGroup1.java**, replace the call to **sys.suspend( )** with a call to **wait( )** for the thread group, causing it to wait for two seconds. For this to work correctly you must acquire the lock for **sys** inside a **synchronized** block.

7. Change **Daemons.java** so that **main( )** has a **sleep( )** instead of a **readLine( )**. Experiment with different sleep times to see what happens.

8. (Intermediate) In Chapter 7, locate the **GreenhouseControls.java** example, which consists of three files. In **Event.java**, the class **Event** is based on watching the time. Change **Event** so that it is a **Thread**, and change the rest of the design so that it works with this new **Thread**-based **Event**.

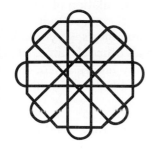

15: Network
programming

Historically, network programming has been error-prone, difficult, and complex.

The programmer had to know many details about the network and sometimes even the hardware. You usually needed to understand the various "layers" of the networking protocol, and there were a lot of different functions in each different networking library concerned with connecting, packing, and unpacking blocks of information; shipping those blocks back and forth; and handshaking. It was a daunting task.

However, the concept of networking is not so difficult. You want to get some information from that machine over there and move it to this machine here, or vice versa. It's quite similar to reading and writing files, except that the file exists on a remote machine and the remote machine can decide exactly what it wants to do about the information you're requesting or sending.

One of Java's great strengths is painless networking. As much as possible, the underlying details of networking have been abstracted away and taken care of within the JVM and local machine installation of Java. The programming model you use is that of a file; in fact, you actually wrap the network connection (a "socket") with stream objects, so you end up using the same method calls as you do with all other streams. In addition, Java's built-in multithreading is exceptionally handy when dealing with another networking issue: handling multiple connections at once.

This chapter introduces Java's networking support using easy-to-understand examples.

Identifying a machine

Of course, in order to tell one machine from another and to make sure that you are connected with the machine you want, there must be some way of uniquely identifying machines on a network. Early networks were satisfied to provide unique names for machines within the local network. However, Java works within the Internet, which requires a way to uniquely identify a machine from all the others *in the world*. This is accomplished with the IP (Internet Protocol) address that can exist in two forms:

1. The familiar DNS (Domain Name Service) form. My domain name is **bruceeckel.com**, so suppose I have a computer called **Opus** in my domain. Its domain name would be **Opus.bruceeckel.com**. This is exactly the kind of name that you use when you send email to people, and is often incorporated into a World-Wide-Web address.

2. Alternatively, you can use the "dotted quad" form, which is four numbers separated by dots, such as **123.255.28.120**.

In both cases, the IP address is represented internally as a 32-bit number[1] (so each of the quad numbers cannot exceed 255), and you can get a special Java object to represent this number from either of the forms above by using the **static InetAddress.getByName( )** method that's in

---

[1] This means a maximum of just over four billion numbers, which is rapidly running out. The new standard for IP addresses will use a 128-bit number, which should produce enough unique IP addresses for the foreseeable future.

java.net. The result is an object of type **InetAddress** that you can use to build a "socket" as you will see later.

As a simple example of using **InetAddress.getByName( )**, consider what happens if you have a dial-up Internet service provider (ISP). Each time you dial up, you are assigned a temporary IP address. But while you're connected, your IP address has the same validity as any other IP address on the Internet. If someone connects to your machine using your IP address then they can connect to a Web server or FTP server that you have running on your machine. Of course, they need to know your IP address, and since it's assigned each time you dial up, how can you find out what it is?

The following program uses **InetAddress.getByName( )** to produce your IP address. To use it, you must know the name of your computer. It has been tested only on Windows 95, but there you can go to "Settings," "Control Panel," "Network," and then select the "Identification" tab. "Computer name" is the name to put on the command line.

```
//: WhoAmI.java
// Finds out your network address when you're
// connected to the Internet.
package c15;
import java.net.*;

public class WhoAmI {
  public static void main(String[] args)
      throws Exception {
    if(args.length != 1) {
      System.err.println(
        "Usage: WhoAmI MachineName");
      System.exit(1);
    }
    InetAddress a =
      InetAddress.getByName(args[0]);
    System.out.println(a);
  }
} ///:~
```

In my case, the machine is called "Colossus" (from the movie of the same name, because I keep putting bigger disks on it). So, once I've connected to my ISP I run the program:

```
java WhoAmI Colossus
```

I get back a message like this (of course, the address is different each time):

```
Colossus/199.190.87.75
```

If I tell my friend this address, he can log onto my personal Web server by going to the URL *http://199.190.87.75* (only as long as I continue to stay connected during that session). This can sometimes be a handy way to distribute information to someone else or to test out a Web site configuration before posting it to a "real" server.

Servers and clients

The whole point of a network is to allow two machines to connect and talk to each other. Once the two machines have found each other they can have a nice, two-way conversation. But how do they find each other? It's like getting lost in an amusement park: one machine has to stay in one place and listen while the other machine says, "Hey, where are you?"

The machine that "stays in one place" is called the *server*, and the one that seeks is called the *client*. This distinction is important only while the client is trying to connect to the server. Once they've connected, it becomes a two-way communication process and it doesn't matter anymore that one happened to take the role of server and the other happened to take the role of the client.

So the job of the server is to listen for a connection, and that's performed by the special server object that you create. The job of the client is to try to make a connection to a server, and this is performed by the special client object you create. Once the connection is made, you'll see that at both server and client ends, the connection is just magically turned into an IO stream object, and from then on you can treat the connection as if you were reading from and writing to a file. Thus, after the connection is made you will just use the familiar IO commands from Chapter 10. This is one of the nice features of Java networking.

Testing programs without a network

For many reasons, you might not have a client machine, a server machine, and a network available to test your programs. You might be performing exercises in a classroom situation, or you could be writing programs that aren't yet stable enough to put onto the network. The creators of the Internet Protocol were aware of this issue, and they created a special address called **localhost** to be the "local loopback" IP address for testing without a network. The generic way to produce this address in Java is:

```
InetAddress addr = InetAddress.getByName(null);
```

If you hand **getByName( )** a **null**, it defaults to using the **localhost**. The **InetAddress** is what you use to refer to the particular machine, and you must produce this before you can go any further. You can't manipulate the contents of an **InetAddress** (but you can print them out, as you'll see in the next example). The only way you can create an **InetAddress** is through one of that class's **static** member methods **getByName( )** (which is what you'll usually use), **getAllByName( )**, or **getLocalHost( )**.

You can also produce the local loopback address by handing it the string **localhost**:

```
InetAddress.getByName("localhost");
```

or by using its dotted quad form to name the reserved IP number for the loopback:

```
InetAddress.getByName("127.0.0.1");
```

All three forms produce the same result.

Port: a unique place within the machine

An IP address isn't enough to identify a unique server, since many servers can exist on one machine. Each IP machine also contains *ports*, and when you're setting up a client or a server you must choose a port where both client and server agree to connect; if you're meeting someone, the IP address is the neighborhood and the port is the bar.

The port is not a physical location in a machine, but a software abstraction (mainly for bookkeeping purposes). The client program knows how to connect to the machine via its IP address, but how does it connect to a desired service (potentially one of many on that machine)? That's where the port numbers come in as second level of addressing. The idea is that if you ask for a particular port, you're requesting the service that's associated with the port number. The time of day is a simple example of a service. Typically, each service is associated with a unique port number on a given server machine. It's up to the client to know ahead of time which port number the desired service is running on.

The system services reserve the use of ports 1 through 1024, so you shouldn't use those or any other port that you know to be in use. The first choice for examples in this book will be port 8080 (in memory of the venerable old 8-bit Intel 8080 chip in my first computer, a CP/M machine).

Sockets

The *socket* is the software abstraction used to represent the "terminals" of a connection between two machines. For a given connection, there's a socket on each machine, and you can imagine a hypothetical "cable" running between the two machines with each end of the "cable" plugged into a socket. Of course, the physical hardware and cabling between machines is completely unknown. The whole point of the abstraction is that we don't have to know more than is necessary.

In Java, you create a socket to make the connection to the other machine, then you get an **InputStream** and **OutputStream** (or, with the appropriate converters, **Reader** and **Writer**) from the socket in order to be able to treat the connection as an IO stream object. There are two stream-based socket classes: a **ServerSocket** that a server uses to "listen" for incoming connections and a **Socket** that a client uses in order to initiate a connection. Once a client makes a socket connection, the **ServerSocket** returns (via the **accept( )** method) a corresponding server side **Socket** through which direct communications will take place. From then on, you have a true **Socket** to **Socket** connection and you treat both ends the same way because they *are* the same. At this point, you use the methods **getInputStream( )** and **getOutputStream( )** to produce the corresponding **InputStream** and **OutputStream** objects from each **Socket**. These must be wrapped inside buffers and formatting classes just like any other stream object described in Chapter 10.

The use of the term **ServerSocket** would seem to be another example of a confusing name scheme in the Java libraries. You might think **ServerSocket** would be better named "ServerConnector" or something without the word "Socket" in it. You might also think that **ServerSocket** and **Socket** should both be inherited from some common base class. Indeed, the two classes do have several methods in common but not enough to give them a common base class. Instead, **ServerSocket**'s job is to wait until some other machine connects to it, then to return an actual **Socket**. This is why **ServerSocket** seems to be a bit misnamed, since its job isn't really to be a socket but instead to make a **Socket** object when someone else connects to it.

However, the **ServerSocket** does create a physical "server" or listening socket on the host machine. This socket listens for incoming connections and then returns an "established" socket (with the local and remote endpoints defined) via the **accept( )** method. The confusing part is that both of these sockets (listening and established) are associated with the same server socket. The listening socket can accept only new connection requests and not data packets. So while **ServerSocket** doesn't make much sense programmatically, it does "physically."

When you create a **ServerSocket**, you give it only a port number. You don't have to give it an IP address because it's already on the machine it represents. When you create a **Socket**, however, you must give both the IP address and the port number where you're trying to connect. (On the other hand, the **Socket** that comes back from **ServerSocket.accept( )** already contains all this information.)

A simple server and client

This example makes the simplest use of servers and clients using sockets. All the server does is wait for a connection, then uses the **Socket** produced by that connection to create an **InputStream** and **OutputStream**. After that, everything it reads from the **InputStream** it echoes to the **OutputStream** until it receives the line END, at which time it closes the connection.

The client makes the connection to the server, then creates an **OutputStream**. Lines of text are sent through the **OutputStream**. The client also creates an **InputStream** to hear what the server is saying (which, in this case, is just the words echoed back).

Both the server and client use the same port number and the client uses the local loopback address to connect to the server on the same machine so you don't have to test it over a network. (For some configurations, you might need to be *connected* to a network for the programs to work, even if you aren't communicating over that network.)

Here is the server:

```
//: JabberServer.java
// Very simple server that just
// echoes whatever the client sends.
import java.io.*;
import java.net.*;

public class JabberServer {
```

```java
    // Choose a port outside of the range 1-1024:
    public static final int PORT = 8080;
    public static void main(String[] args)
        throws IOException {
      ServerSocket s = new ServerSocket(PORT);
      System.out.println("Started: " + s);
      try {
        // Blocks until a connection occurs:
        Socket socket = s.accept();
        try {
          System.out.println(
            "Connection accepted: "+ socket);
          BufferedReader in =
            new BufferedReader(
              new InputStreamReader(
                socket.getInputStream()));
          // Output is automatically flushed
          // by PrintWriter:
          PrintWriter out =
            new PrintWriter(
              new BufferedWriter(
                new OutputStreamWriter(
                  socket.getOutputStream())),true);
          while (true) {
            String str = in.readLine();
            if (str.equals("END")) break;
            System.out.println("Echoing: " + str);
            out.println(str);
          }
        // Always close the two sockets...
        } finally {
          System.out.println("closing...");
          socket.close();
        }
      } finally {
        s.close();
      }
    }
} ///:~
```

You can see that the **ServerSocket** just needs a port number, not an IP address (since it's running on *this* machine!). When you call **accept( )**, the method *blocks* until some client tries to connect to it. That is, it's there waiting for a connection but other processes can run (see Chapter

14). When a connection is made, **accept( )** returns with a **Socket** object representing that connection.

The responsibility for cleaning up the sockets is crafted carefully here. If the **ServerSocket** constructor fails, the program just quits (notice we must assume that the constructor for **ServerSocket** doesn't leave any open network sockets lying around if it fails). For this case, **main( ) throws IOException** so a **try** block is not necessary. If the **ServerSocket** constructor is successful then all other method calls must be guarded in a **try-finally** block to ensure that, no matter how the block is left, the **ServerSocket** is properly closed.

The same logic is used for the **Socket** returned by **accept( )**. If **accept( )** fails, then we must assume that the **Socket** doesn't exist or hold any resources, so it doesn't need to be cleaned up. If it's successful, however, the following statements must be in a **try-finally** block so that if they fail the **Socket** will still be cleaned up. Care is required here because sockets use important non-memory resources, so you must be diligent in order to clean them up (since there is no destructor in Java to do it for you).

Both the **ServerSocket** and the **Socket** produced by **accept( )** are printed to **System.out**. This means that their **toString( )** methods are automatically called. These produce:

```
ServerSocket[addr=0.0.0.0,PORT=0,localport=8080]
Socket[addr=127.0.0.1,PORT=1077,localport=8080]
```

Shortly, you'll see how these fit together with what the client is doing.

The next part of the program looks just like opening files for reading and writing except that the **InputStream** and **OutputStream** are created from the **Socket** object. Both the **InputStream** and **OutputStream** objects are converted to Java 1.1 **Reader** and **Writer** objects using the "converter" classes **InputStreamReader** and **OutputStreamWriter**, respectively. You could also have used the Java 1.0 **InputStream** and **OutputStream** classes directly, but with output there's a distinct advantage to using the **Writer** approach. This appears with **PrintWriter**, which has an overloaded constructor that takes a second argument, a **boolean** flag that indicates whether to automatically flush the output at the end of each **println( )** (but *not* **print( )**) statement. Every time you write to **out**, its buffer must be flushed so the information goes out over the network. Flushing is important for this particular example because the client and server each wait for a line from the other party before proceeding. If flushing doesn't occur, the information will not be put onto the network until the buffer is full, which causes lots of problems in this example.

When writing network programs you need to be careful about using automatic flushing. Every time you flush the buffer a packet must be created and sent. In this case, that's exactly what we want, since if the packet containing the line isn't sent then the handshaking back and forth between server and client will stop. Put another way, the end of a line is the end of a message. But in many cases messages aren't delimited by lines so it's much more efficient to not use auto flushing and instead let the built-in buffering decide when to build and send a packet. This way, larger packets can be sent and the process will be faster.

Note that, like virtually all streams you open, these are buffered. There's an exercise at the end of the chapter to show you what happens if you don't buffer the streams (things get slow).

The infinite **while** loop reads lines from the **BufferedReader in** and writes information to **System.out** and to the **PrintWriter out**. Note that these could be any streams, they just happen to be connected to the network.

When the client sends the line consisting of "END" the program breaks out of the loop and closes the **Socket**.

Here's the client:

```
//: JabberClient.java
// Very simple client that just sends
// lines to the server and reads lines
// that the server sends.
import java.net.*;
import java.io.*;

public class JabberClient {
  public static void main(String[] args)
      throws IOException {
    // Passing null to getByName() produces the
    // special "Local Loopback" IP address, for
    // testing on one machine w/o a network:
    InetAddress addr =
      InetAddress.getByName(null);
    // Alternatively, you can use
    // the address or name:
    // InetAddress addr =
    //    InetAddress.getByName("127.0.0.1");
```

```
    // InetAddress addr =
    //    InetAddress.getByName("localhost");
    System.out.println("addr = " + addr);
    Socket socket =
      new Socket(addr, JabberServer.PORT);
    // Guard everything in a try-finally to make
    // sure that the socket is closed:
    try {
      System.out.println("socket = " + socket);
      BufferedReader in =
        new BufferedReader(
          new InputStreamReader(
            socket.getInputStream()));
      // Output is automatically flushed
      // by PrintWriter:
      PrintWriter out =
        new PrintWriter(
          new BufferedWriter(
            new OutputStreamWriter(
              socket.getOutputStream())),true);
      for(int i = 0; i < 10; i ++) {
        out.println("howdy " + i);
        String str = in.readLine();
        System.out.println(str);
      }
      out.println("END");
    } finally {
      System.out.println("closing...");
      socket.close();
    }
  }
} ///:~
```

In **main( )** you can see all three ways to produce the **InetAddress** of the
local loopback IP address: using **null**, **localhost**, or the explicit reserved
address **127.0.0.1**. Of course, if you want to connect to a machine across
a network you substitute that machine's IP address. When the
InetAddress addr is printed (via the automatic call to its **toString( )**
method) the result is:

```
localhost/127.0.0.1
```

By handing **getByName( )** a **null**, it defaulted to finding the **localhost**,
and that produced the special address **127.0.0.1**.

Note that the **Socket** called **socket** is created with both the **InetAddress** and the port number. To understand what it means when you print out one of these **Socket** objects, remember that an Internet connection is determined uniquely by these four pieces of data: **clientHost**, **clientPortNumber**, **serverHost**, and **serverPortNumber**. When the server comes up, it takes up its assigned port (8080) on the localhost (127.0.0.1). When the client comes up, it is allocated to the next available port on its machine, 1077 in this case, which also happens to be on the same machine (127.0.0.1) as the server. Now, in order for data to move between the client and server, each side has to know where to send it. Therefore, during the process of connecting to the "known" server, the client sends a "return address" so the server knows where to send its data. This is what you see in the example output for the server side:

```
Socket[addr=127.0.0.1,port=1077,localport=8080]
```

This means that the server just accepted a connection from 127.0.0.1 on port 1077 while listening on its local port (8080). On the client side:

```
Socket[addr=localhost/127.0.0.1,PORT=8080,localpor
t=1077]
```

which means that the client made a connection to 127.0.0.1 on port 8080 using the local port 1077.

You'll notice that every time you start up the client anew, the local port number is incremented. It starts at 1025 (one past the reserved block of ports) and keeps going up until you reboot the machine, at which point it starts at 1025 again. (On UNIX machines, once the upper limit of the socket range is reached, the numbers will wrap around to the lowest available number again.)

Once the **Socket** object has been created, the process of turning it into a **BufferedReader** and **PrintWriter** is the same as in the server (again, in both cases you start with a **Socket**). Here, the client initiates the conversation by sending the string "howdy" followed by a number. Note that the buffer must again be flushed (which happens automatically via the second argument to the **PrintWriter** constructor). If the buffer isn't flushed, the whole conversation will hang because the initial "howdy" will never get sent (the buffer isn't full enough to cause the send to happen automatically). Each line that is sent back from the server is written to **System.out** to verify that everything is working correctly. To terminate the conversation, the agreed-upon "END" is sent. If the client simply hangs up, then the server throws an exception.

You can see that the same care is taken here to ensure that the network resources represented by the **Socket** are properly cleaned up, using a **try-finally** block.

Sockets produce a "dedicated" connection that persists until it is explicitly disconnected. (The dedicated connection can still be disconnected un-explicitly if one side, or an intermediary link, of the connection crashes.) This means the two parties are locked in communication and the connection is constantly open. This seems like a logical approach to networking, but it puts an extra load on the network. Later in the chapter you'll see a different approach to networking, in which the connections are only temporary.

Serving multiple clients

The **JabberServer** works, but it can handle only one client at a time. In a typical server, you'll want to be able to deal with many clients at once. The answer is multithreading, and in languages that don't directly support multithreading this means all sorts of complications. In Chapter 14 you saw that multithreading in Java is about as simple as possible, considering that multithreading is a rather complex topic. Because threading in Java is reasonably straightforward, making a server that handles multiple clients is relatively easy.

The basic scheme is to make a single **ServerSocket** in the server and call **accept( )** to wait for a new connection. When **accept( )** returns, you take the resulting **Socket** and use it to create a new thread whose job is to serve that particular client. Then you call **accept( )** again to wait for a new client.

In the following server code, you can see that it looks similar to the **JabberServer.java** example except that all of the operations to serve a particular client have been moved inside a separate thread class:

```
//: MultiJabberServer.java
// A server that uses multithreading to handle
// any number of clients.
import java.io.*;
import java.net.*;

class ServeOneJabber extends Thread {
  private Socket socket;
  private BufferedReader in;
  private PrintWriter out;
```

```java
  public ServeOneJabber(Socket s)
      throws IOException {
    socket = s;
    in =
      new BufferedReader(
        new InputStreamReader(
          socket.getInputStream()));
    // Enable auto-flush:
    out =
      new PrintWriter(
        new BufferedWriter(
          new OutputStreamWriter(
            socket.getOutputStream())), true);
    // If any of the above calls throw an
    // exception, the caller is responsible for
    // closing the socket. Otherwise the thread
    // will close it.
    start(); // Calls run()
  }
  public void run() {
    try {
      while (true) {
        String str = in.readLine();
        if (str.equals("END")) break;
        System.out.println("Echoing: " + str);
        out.println(str);
      }
      System.out.println("closing...");
    } catch (IOException e) {
    } finally {
      try {
        socket.close();
      } catch(IOException e) {}
    }
  }
}

public class MultiJabberServer {
  static final int PORT = 8080;
  public static void main(String[] args)
      throws IOException {
    ServerSocket s = new ServerSocket(PORT);
    System.out.println("Server Started");
    try {
```

```
        while(true) {
          // Blocks until a connection occurs:
          Socket socket = s.accept();
          try {
            new ServeOneJabber(socket);
          } catch(IOException e) {
            // If it fails, close the socket,
            // otherwise the thread will close it:
            socket.close();
          }
        }
      } finally {
        s.close();
      }
    }
  } ///:~
```

The **ServeOneJabber** thread takes the **Socket** object that's produced by
accept( ) in **main( )** every time a new client makes a connection. Then,
as before, it creates a **BufferedReader** and auto-flushed **PrintWriter**
object using the **Socket**. Finally, it calls the special **Thread** method
start( ), which performs thread initialization and then calls **run( )**. This
performs the same kind of action as in the previous example: reading
something from the socket and then echoing it back until it reads the
special "END" signal.

The responsibility for cleaning up the socket must again be carefully
designed. In this case, the socket is created outside of the
ServeOneJabber so the responsibility can be shared. If the
ServeOneJabber constructor fails, it will just throw the exception to the
caller, who will then clean up the thread. But if the constructor succeeds,
then the **ServeOneJabber** object takes over responsibility for cleaning up
the thread, in its **run( )**.

Notice the simplicity of the **MultiJabberServer**. As before, a
ServerSocket is created and **accept( )** is called to allow a new connection.
But this time, the return value of **accept( )** (a **Socket**) is passed to the
constructor for **ServeOneJabber,** which creates a new thread to handle
that connection. When the connection is terminated, the thread simply
goes away.

If the creation of the **ServerSocket** fails, the exception is again thrown
through **main( )**. But if it succeeds, the outer **try-finally** guarantees its
cleanup. The inner **try-catch** guards only against the failure of the

---

ServeOneJabber constructor; if the constructor succeeds, then the
ServeOneJabber thread will close the associated socket.

To test that the server really does handle multiple clients, the following
program creates many clients (using threads) that connect to the same
server. Each thread has a limited lifetime, and when it goes away, that
leaves space for the creation of a new thread. The maximum number of
threads allowed is determined by the **final int maxthreads**. You'll notice
that this value is rather critical, since if you make it too high the threads
seem to run out of resources and the program mysteriously fails.

```java
//: MultiJabberClient.java
// Client that tests the MultiJabberServer
// by starting up multiple clients.
import java.net.*;
import java.io.*;

class JabberClientThread extends Thread {
  private Socket socket;
  private BufferedReader in;
  private PrintWriter out;
  private static int counter = 0;
  private int id = counter++;
  private static int threadcount = 0;
  public static int threadCount() {
    return threadcount;
  }
  public JabberClientThread(InetAddress addr) {
    System.out.println("Making client " + id);
    threadcount++;
    try {
      socket =
        new Socket(addr, MultiJabberServer.PORT);
    } catch(IOException e) {
      // If the creation of the socket fails,
      // nothing needs to be cleaned up.
    }
    try {
      in =
        new BufferedReader(
          new InputStreamReader(
            socket.getInputStream()));
      // Enable auto-flush:
      out =
        new PrintWriter(
```

```
            new BufferedWriter(
              new OutputStreamWriter(
                socket.getOutputStream()))), true);
          start();
        } catch(IOException e) {
          // The socket should be closed on any
          // failures other than the socket
          // constructor:
          try {
            socket.close();
          } catch(IOException e2) {}
        }
        // Otherwise the socket will be closed by
        // the run() method of the thread.
      }
      public void run() {
        try {
          for(int i = 0; i < 25; i++) {
            out.println("Client " + id + ": " + i);
            String str = in.readLine();
            System.out.println(str);
          }
          out.println("END");
        } catch(IOException e) {
        } finally {
          // Always close it:
          try {
            socket.close();
          } catch(IOException e) {}
          threadcount--; // Ending this thread
        }
      }
    }

    public class MultiJabberClient {
      static final int MAX_THREADS = 40;
      public static void main(String[] args)
          throws IOException, InterruptedException {
        InetAddress addr =
          InetAddress.getByName(null);
        while(true) {
          if(JabberClientThread.threadCount()
             < MAX_THREADS)
            new JabberClientThread(addr);
```

```
                  Thread.currentThread().sleep(100);
            }
        }
    } ///:~
```

The **JabberClientThread** constructor takes an **InetAddress** and uses it to open a **Socket**. You're probably starting to see the pattern: the **Socket** is always used to create some kind of **Reader** and/or **Writer** (or **InputStream** and/or **OutputStream**) object, which is the only way that the **Socket** can be used. (You can, of course, write a class or two to automate this process instead of doing all the typing if it becomes painful.) Again, **start( )** performs thread initialization and calls **run( )**. Here, messages are sent to the server and information from the server is echoed to the screen. However, the thread has a limited lifetime and eventually completes. Note that the socket is cleaned up if the constructor fails after the socket is created but before the constructor completes. Otherwise the responsibility for calling **close( )** for the socket is relegated to the **run( )** method.

The **threadcount** keeps track of how many **JabberClientThread** objects currently exist. It is incremented as part of the constructor and decremented as **run( )** exits (which means the thread is terminating). In **MultiJabberClient.main( )**, you can see that the number of threads is tested, and if there are too many, no more are created. Then the method sleeps. This way, some threads will eventually terminate and more can be created. You can experiment with **MAX_THREADS** to see where your particular system begins to have trouble with too many connections.

Datagrams

The examples you've seen so far use the *Transmission Control Protocol* (TCP, also known as *stream-based sockets*), which is designed for ultimate reliability and guarantees that the data will get there. It allows retransmission of lost data, it provides multiple paths through different routers in case one goes down, and bytes are delivered in the order they are sent. All this control and reliability comes at a cost: TCP has a high overhead.

There's a second protocol, called *User Datagram Protocol* (UDP), which doesn't guarantee that the packets will be delivered and doesn't guarantee that they will arrive in the order they were sent. It's called an "unreliable protocol" (TCP is a "reliable protocol"), which sounds bad, but because it's much faster it can be useful. There are some applications, such as an audio signal, in which it isn't so critical if a few packets are dropped here or there but speed is vital. Or consider a time-of-day server, where it really doesn't matter if one of the messages is lost. Also, some applications might be able to fire off a UDP message to a server and can then assume, if there is no response in a reasonable period of time, that the message was lost.

The support for datagrams in Java has the same feel as its support for TCP sockets, but there are significant differences. With datagrams, you put a **DatagramSocket** on both the client and server, but there is no analogy to the **ServerSocket** that waits around for a connection. That's because there is no "connection," but instead a datagram just shows up. Another fundamental difference is that with TCP sockets, once you've made the connection you don't need to worry about who's talking to whom anymore; you just send the data back and forth through conventional streams. However, with datagrams, the datagram packet must know where it came from and where it's supposed to go. That means you must know these things for each datagram packet that you load up and ship off.

A **DatagramSocket** sends and receives the packets, and the **DatagramPacket** contains the information. When you're receiving a datagram, you need only provide a buffer in which the data will be placed; the information about the Internet address and port number where the information came from will be automatically initialized when the packet arrives through the **DatagramSocket**. So the constructor for a **DatagramPacket** to receive datagrams is:

```
DatagramPacket(buf, buf.length)
```

in which **buf** is an array of **byte**. Since **buf** is an array, you might wonder why the constructor couldn't figure out the length of the array on its own. I wondered this, and can only guess that it's a throwback to C-style programming, in which of course arrays can't tell you how big they are.

You can reuse a receiving datagram; you don't have to make a new one each time. Every time you reuse it, the data in the buffer is overwritten.

The maximum size of the buffer is restricted only by the allowable datagram packet size, which limits it to slightly less than 64Kbytes. However, in many applications you'll want it to be much smaller, certainly when you're sending data. Your chosen packet size depends on what you need for your particular application.

When you send a datagram, the **DatagramPacket** must contain not only the data, but also the Internet address and port where it will be sent. So the constructor for an outgoing **DatagramPacket** is:

```
DatagramPacket(buf, length, inetAddress, port)
```

This time, **buf** (which is a **byte** array) already contains the data that you want to send out. The **length** might be the length of **buf**, but it can also be shorter, indicating that you want to send only that many bytes. The other two arguments are the Internet address where the packet is going and the destination port within that machine.[2]

You might think that the two constructors create two different objects: one for receiving datagrams and one for sending them. Good OO design would suggest that these should be two different classes, rather than one class with different behavior depending on how you construct the object. This is probably true, but fortunately the use of **DatagramPacket**s is simple enough that you're not tripped up by the problem, as you can see in the following example. This example is similar to the **MultiJabberServer** and **MultiJabberClient** example for TCP sockets. Multiple clients will send datagrams to a server, which will echo them back to the same client that sent the message.

To simplify the creation of a **DatagramPacket** from a **String** and vice-versa, the example begins with a utility class, **Dgram**, to do the work for you:

```
//: Dgram.java
// A utility class to convert back and forth
// Between Strings and DataGramPackets.
import java.net.*;

public class Dgram {
  public static DatagramPacket toDatagram(
      String s, InetAddress destIA, int destPort) {
      // Deprecated in Java 1.1, but it works:
      byte[] buf = new byte[s.length() + 1];
      s.getBytes(0, s.length(), buf, 0);
      // The correct Java 1.1 approach, but it's
      // Broken (it truncates the String):
      // byte[] buf = s.getBytes();
```

---

[2] TCP and UDP ports are considered unique. That is, you can simultaneously run a TCP and UDP server on port 8080 without interference.

```
      return new DatagramPacket(buf, buf.length,
        destIA, destPort);
  }
  public static String toString(DatagramPacket p){
    // The Java 1.0 approach:
    // return new String(p.getData(),
    //   0, 0, p.getLength());
    // The Java 1.1 approach:
    return
      new String(p.getData(), 0, p.getLength());
  }
} ///:~
```

The first method of **Dgram** takes a **String**, an **InetAddress**, and a port number and builds a **DatagramPacket** by copying the contents of the **String** into a **byte** buffer and passing the buffer into the **DatagramPacket** constructor. Notice the "+1" in the buffer allocation – this was necessary to prevent truncation. The **getBytes( )** method of **String** is a special operation that copies the **chars** of a **String** into a **byte** buffer. This method is now deprecated; Java 1.1 has a "better" way to do this but it's commented out here because it truncates the **String**. So you'll get a deprecation message when you compile it under Java 1.1, but the behavior will be correct. (This bug might be fixed by the time you read this.)

The **Dgram.toString( )** method shows both the Java 1.0 approach and the Java 1.1 approach (which is different because there's a new kind of **String** constructor).

Here is the server for the datagram demonstration:

```
//: ChatterServer.java
// A server that echoes datagrams
import java.net.*;
import java.io.*;
import java.util.*;

public class ChatterServer {
  static final int INPORT = 1711;
  private byte[] buf = new byte[1000];
  private DatagramPacket dp =
    new DatagramPacket(buf, buf.length);
  // Can listen & send on the same socket:
  private DatagramSocket socket;
```

```
    public ChatterServer() {
      try {
        socket = new DatagramSocket(INPORT);
        System.out.println("Server started");
        while(true) {
          // Block until a datagram appears:
          socket.receive(dp);
          String rcvd = Dgram.toString(dp) +
            ", from address: " + dp.getAddress() +
            ", port: " + dp.getPort();
          System.out.println(rcvd);
          String echoString =
            "Echoed: " + rcvd;
          // Extract the address and port from the
          // received datagram to find out where to
          // send it back:
          DatagramPacket echo =
            Dgram.toDatagram(echoString,
              dp.getAddress(), dp.getPort());
          socket.send(echo);
        }
      } catch(SocketException e) {
        System.err.println("Can't open socket");
        System.exit(1);
      } catch(IOException e) {
        System.err.println("Communication error");
        e.printStackTrace();
      }
    }
    public static void main(String[] args) {
      new ChatterServer();
    }
  } ///:~
```

The **ChatterServer** contains a single **DatagramSocket** for receiving
messages, instead of creating one each time you're ready to receive a new
message. The single **DatagramSocket** can be used repeatedly. This
DatagramSocket has a port number because this is the server and the
client must have an exact address where it wants to send the datagram. It
is given a port number but not an Internet address because it resides on
"this" machine so it knows what its Internet address is (in this case, the
default **localhost**). In the infinite **while** loop, the **socket** is told to
receive( ), whereupon it blocks until a datagram shows up, and then
sticks it into our designated receiver, the **DatagramPacket dp**. The
packet is converted to a **String** along with information about the Internet

address and socket where the packet came from. This information is displayed, and then an extra string is added to indicate that it is being echoed back from the server.

Now there's a bit of a quandary. As you will see, there are potentially many different Internet addresses and port numbers that the messages might come from – that is, the clients can reside on any machine. (In this demonstration they all reside on the **localhost**, but the port number for each client is different.) To send a message back to the client that originated it, you need to know that client's Internet address and port number. Fortunately, this information is conveniently packaged inside the **DatagramPacket** that sent the message, so all you have to do is pull it out using **getAddress( )** and **getPort( )**, which are used to build the **DatagramPacket echo** that is sent back through the same socket that's doing the receiving. In addition, when the socket sends the datagram, it automatically adds the Internet address and port information of *this* machine, so that when the client receives the message, it can use **getAddress( )** and **getPort( )** to find out where the datagram came from. In fact, the only time that **getAddress( )** and **getPort( )** don't tell you where the datagram came from is if you create a datagram to send and you call **getAddress( )** and **getPort( )** *before* you send the datagram (in which case it tells the address and port of this machine, the one the datagram is being sent from). This is an essential part of datagrams: you don't need to keep track of where a message came from because it's always stored inside the datagram. In fact, the most reliable way to program is if you don't try to keep track, but instead always extract the address and port from the datagram in question (as is done here).

To test this server, here's a program that makes a number of clients, all of which fire datagram packets to the server and wait for the server to echo them back.

```
//: ChatterClient.java
// Tests the ChatterServer by starting multiple
// clients, each of which sends datagrams.
import java.lang.Thread;
import java.net.*;
import java.io.*;

public class ChatterClient extends Thread {
    // Can listen & send on the same socket:
    private DatagramSocket s;
    private InetAddress hostAddress;
    private byte[] buf = new byte[1000];
    private DatagramPacket dp =
```

```
      new DatagramPacket(buf, buf.length);
  private int id;

  public ChatterClient(int identifier) {
    id = identifier;
    try {
      // Auto-assign port number:
      s = new DatagramSocket();
      hostAddress =
        InetAddress.getByName("localhost");
    } catch(UnknownHostException e) {
      System.err.println("Cannot find host");
      System.exit(1);
    } catch(SocketException e) {
      System.err.println("Can't open socket");
      e.printStackTrace();
      System.exit(1);
    }
    System.out.println("ChatterClient starting");
  }
  public void run() {
    try {
      for(int i = 0; i < 25; i++) {
        String outMessage = "Client #" +
          id + ", message #" + i;
        // Make and send a datagram:
        s.send(Dgram.toDatagram(outMessage,
          hostAddress,
          ChatterServer.INPORT));
        // Block until it echoes back:
        s.receive(dp);
        // Print out the echoed contents:
        String rcvd = "Client #" + id +
          ", rcvd from " +
          dp.getAddress() + ", " +
          dp.getPort() + ": " +
          Dgram.toString(dp);
        System.out.println(rcvd);
      }
    } catch(IOException e) {
      e.printStackTrace();
      System.exit(1);
    }
  }
}
```

```
public static void main(String[] args) {
    for(int i = 0; i < 10; i++)
        new ChatterClient(i).start();
}
} ///:~
```

ChatterClient is created as a **Thread** so that multiple clients can be made to bother the server. Here you can see that the receiving **DatagramPacket** looks just like the one used for **ChatterServer**. In the constructor, the **DatagramSocket** is created with no arguments since it doesn't need to advertise itself as being at a particular port number. The Internet address used for this socket will be "this machine" (for the example, **localhost**) and the port number will be automatically assigned, as you will see from the output. This **DatagramSocket**, like the one for the server, will be used both for sending and receiving.

The **hostAddress** is the Internet address of the host machine you want to talk to. The one part of the program in which you must know an exact Internet address and port number is the part in which you make the outgoing **DatagramPacket**. As is always the case, the host must be at a known address and port number so that clients can originate conversations with the host.

Each thread is given a unique identification number (although the port number automatically assigned to the thread would also provide a unique identifier). In **run( )**, a message **String** is created that contains the thread's identification number and the message number this thread is currently sending. This **String** is used to create a datagram that is sent to the host at its address; the port number is taken directly from a constant in **ChatterServer**. Once the message is sent, **receive( )** blocks until the server replies with an echoing message. All of the information that's shipped around with the message allows you to see that what comes back to this particular thread is derived from the message that originated from it. In this example, even though UDP is an "unreliable" protocol, you'll see that all of the datagrams get where they're supposed to. (This will be true for localhost and LAN situations, but you might begin to see some failures for non-local connections.)

When you run this program, you'll see that each of the threads finishes, which means that each of the datagram packets sent to the server is turned around and echoed to the correct recipient; otherwise one or more threads would hang, blocking until their input shows up.

You might think that the only right way to, for example, transfer a file from one machine to another is through TCP sockets, since they're "reliable." However, because of the speed of datagrams they can actually be a better solution. You simply break the file up into packets and number each packet. The receiving machine takes the packets and reassembles them; a "header packet" tells the machine how many to expect and any other important information. If a packet is lost, the receiving machine sends a datagram back telling the sender to retransmit.

A Web application

Now let's consider creating an application to run on the Web, which will show Java in all its glory. Part of this application will be a Java program running on the Web server, and the other part will be an applet that's downloaded to the browser. The applet collects information from the user and sends it back to the application running on the Web server. The task of the program will be simple: the applet will ask for the email address of the user, and after verifying that this address is reasonably legitimate (it doesn't contain spaces, and it does contain an '@' symbol) the applet will send the email address to the Web server. The application running on the server will capture the data and check a data file in which all of the email addresses are kept. If that address is already in the file, it will send back a message to that effect, which is displayed by the applet. If the address isn't in the file, it is placed in the list and the applet is informed that the address was added successfully.

Traditionally, the way to handle such a problem is to create an HTML page with a text field and a "submit" button. The user can type whatever he or she wants into the text field, and it will be submitted to the server without question. As it submits the data, the Web page also tells the server what to do with the data by mentioning the Common Gateway Interface (CGI) program that the server should run after receiving this data. This CGI program is typically written in either Perl or C (and sometimes C++, if the server supports it), and it must handle everything. First it looks at the data and decides whether it's in the correct format. If not, the CGI program must create an HTML page to describe the problem; this page is handed to the server, which sends it back to the user. The user must then back up a page and try again. If the data is correct, the CGI program opens the data file and either adds the email address to the file or discovers that the address is already in the file. In both cases it must format an appropriate HTML page for the server to return to the user.

As Java programmers, this seems like an awkward way for us to solve the problem, and naturally, we'd like to do the whole thing in Java. First, we'll use a Java applet to take care of data validation at the client site, without all that tedious Web traffic and page formatting. Then let's skip the Perl CGI script in favor of a Java application running on the server. In fact, let's skip the Web server altogether and simply make our own network connection from the applet to the Java application on the server!

As you'll see, there are a number of issues that make this a more complicated problem than it seems. It would be ideal to write the applet using Java 1.1 but that's hardly practical. At this writing, the number of users running Java 1.1-enabled browsers is small, and although such browsers are now commonly available, you'll probably need to take into account that a significant number of users will be slow to upgrade. So to be on the safe side, the applet will be programmed using only Java 1.0 code. With this in mind, there will be no JAR files to combine **.class** files in the applet, so the applet should be designed to create as few **.class** files as possible to minimize download time.

Well, it turns out the Web server (the one available to me when I wrote the example) *does* have Java in it, but only Java 1.0! So the server application must also be written using Java 1.0.

The server application

Now consider the server application, which will be called **NameCollector**. What happens if more than one user at a time tries to submit their email addresses? If **NameCollector** uses TCP/IP sockets, then it must use the multithreading approach shown earlier to handle more than one client at a time. But all of these threads will try to write to a single file where all the email addresses will be kept. This would require a locking mechanism to make sure that more than one thread doesn't access the file at once. A semaphore will do the trick, but perhaps there's a simpler way.

If we use datagrams instead, multithreading is unnecessary. A single datagram socket will listen for incoming datagrams, and when one appears the program will process the message and send the reply as a datagram back to whomever sent the request. If the datagram gets lost, then the user will notice that no reply comes and can then re-submit the request.

When the server application receives a datagram and unpacks it, it must extract the email address and check the file to see if that address is there already (and if it isn't, add it). And now we run into another problem. It turns out that Java 1.0 doesn't quite have the horsepower to easily manipulate the file containing the email addresses (Java 1.1 does). However, the problem can be solved in C quite readily, and this will provide an excuse to show you the easiest way to connect a non–Java program to a Java program. A **Runtime** object for a program has a method called **exec( )** that will start up a separate program on the machine and return a **Process** object. You can get an **OutputStream** that connects to standard input for this separate program and an **InputStream** that connects to standard output. All you need to do is write a program using any language that takes its input from standard input and writes the output to standard output. This is a convenient trick when you run into a problem that can't be solved easily or quickly enough in Java (or when you have legacy code you don't want to rewrite). You can also use Java's *native methods* (see Appendix A) but those are much more involved.

The C program

The job of this non–Java application (written in C because Java wasn't appropriate for CGI programming; if nothing else, the startup time is prohibitive) is to manage the list of email addresses. Standard input will accept an email address and the program will look up the name in the list to see if it's already there. If not, it will add it and report success, but if the name is already there then it will report that. Don't worry if you don't completely understand what the following code means; it's just one example of how you can write a program in another language and use it from Java. The particular programming language doesn't really matter as long as it can read from standard input and write to standard output.

```c
//: Listmgr.c
// Used by NameCollector.java to manage
// the email list file on the server
#include <stdio.h>
#include <stdlib.h>
#include <string.h>
#define BSIZE 250

int alreadyInList(FILE* list, char* name) {
  char lbuf[BSIZE];
  // Go to the beginning of the list:
  fseek(list, 0, SEEK_SET);
  // Read each line in the list:
  while(fgets(lbuf, BSIZE, list)) {
    // Strip off the newline:
    char * newline = strchr(lbuf, '\n');
    if(newline != 0)
      *newline = '\0';
    if(strcmp(lbuf, name) == 0)
      return 1;
```

```
        }
        return 0;
    }

    int main() {
        char buf[BSIZE];
        FILE* list = fopen("emlist.txt", "a+t");
        if(list == 0) {
            perror("could not open emlist.txt");
            exit(1);
        }
        while(1) {
            gets(buf); /* From stdin */
            if(alreadyInList(list, buf)) {
                printf("Already in list: %s", buf);
                fflush(stdout);
            }
            else {
                fseek(list, 0, SEEK_END);
                fprintf(list, "%s\n", buf);
                fflush(list);
                printf("%s added to list", buf);
                fflush(stdout);
            }
        }
    } ///:~
```

This assumes that the C compiler accepts '//' style comments. (Many do, and you can also compile this program with a C++ compiler.) If yours doesn't, simply delete those comments.

The first function in the file checks to see whether the name you hand it as a second argument (a pointer to a **char**) is in the file. Here, the file is passed as a **FILE** pointer to an already-opened file (the file is opened inside **main( )**). The function **fseek( )** moves around in the file; here it is used to move to the top of the file. **fgets( )** reads a line from the file **list** into the buffer **lbuf**, not exceeding the buffer size **BSIZE**. This is inside a **while** loop so that each line in the file is read. Next, **strchr( )** is used to locate the newline character so that it can be stripped off. Finally, **strcmp( )** is used to compare the name you've passed into the function to the current line int the file. **strcmp( )** returns zero if it finds a match. In this case the function exits and a one is returned to indicate that yes, the name was already in the list. (Note that the function returns as soon as it discovers the match, so it doesn't waste time looking at the rest of the list.) If you get all the way through the list without a match, the function returns zero.

In **main( )**, the file is opened using **fopen( )**. The first argument is the file name and the second is the way to open the file; **a+** means "Append, and open (or create if the file does not exist) for update at the end of the file." The **fopen( )** function returns a **FILE** pointer which, if it's zero, means that the open was unsuccessful. This is dealt with by printing an error message with **perror( )** and terminating the program with **exit( )**.

Assuming that the file was opened successfully, the program enters an infinite loop. The function call **gets(buf)** gets a line from standard input (which will be connected to the Java program, remember) and places it in the buffer **buf**. This is simply passed to the **alreadyInList( )** function, and if it's already in the list, **printf( )** sends that message to standard output (where the Java program is listening). **fflush( )** is a way to flush the output buffer.

If the name is not already in the list, **fseek( )** is used to move to the end of the list and **fprintf( )** "prints" the name to the end of the list. Then **printf( )** is used to indicate that the name was added to the list (again flushing standard output) and the infinite loop goes back to waiting for a new name.

Remember that you usually cannot compile this program on your computer and load it onto the Web server machine, since that machine might use a different processor and operating system. For example, my Web server runs on an Intel processor but it uses Linux, so I must download the source code and compile using remote commands (via telnet) with the C compiler that comes with the Linux distribution.

The Java program

This program will first start the C program above and make the necessary connections to talk to it. Then it will create a datagram socket that will be used to listen for datagram packets from the applet.

```
//: NameCollector.java
// Extracts email names from datagrams and stores
// them inside a file, using Java 1.02.
import java.net.*;
import java.io.*;
import java.util.*;

public class NameCollector {
  final static int COLLECTOR_PORT = 8080;
```

```
final static int BUFFER_SIZE = 1000;
byte[] buf = new byte[BUFFER_SIZE];
DatagramPacket dp =
  new DatagramPacket(buf, buf.length);
// Can listen & send on the same socket:
DatagramSocket socket;
Process listmgr;
PrintStream nameList;
DataInputStream addResult;
public NameCollector() {
  try {
    listmgr =
      Runtime.getRuntime().exec("listmgr.exe");
    nameList = new PrintStream(
      new BufferedOutputStream(
        listmgr.getOutputStream()));
    addResult = new DataInputStream(
      new BufferedInputStream(
        listmgr.getInputStream()));

  } catch(IOException e) {
    System.err.println(
      "Cannot start listmgr.exe");
    System.exit(1);
  }
  try {
    socket =
      new DatagramSocket(COLLECTOR_PORT);
    System.out.println(
      "NameCollector Server started");
    while(true) {
      // Block until a datagram appears:
      socket.receive(dp);
      String rcvd = new String(dp.getData(),
          0, 0, dp.getLength());
      // Send to listmgr.exe standard input:
      nameList.println(rcvd.trim());
      nameList.flush();
      byte[] resultBuf = new byte[BUFFER_SIZE];
      int byteCount =
        addResult.read(resultBuf);
      if(byteCount != -1) {
        String result =
          new String(resultBuf, 0).trim();
```

```
                // Extract the address and port from
                // the received datagram to find out
                // where to send the reply:
                InetAddress senderAddress =
                  dp.getAddress();
                int senderPort = dp.getPort();
                byte[] echoBuf = new byte[BUFFER_SIZE];
                result.getBytes(
                  0, byteCount, echoBuf, 0);
                DatagramPacket echo =
                  new DatagramPacket(
                    echoBuf, echoBuf.length,
                    senderAddress, senderPort);
                socket.send(echo);
              }
              else
                System.out.println(
                  "Unexpected lack of result from " +
                  "listmgr.exe");
            }
        } catch(SocketException e) {
          System.err.println("Can't open socket");
          System.exit(1);
        } catch(IOException e) {
          System.err.println("Communication error");
          e.printStackTrace();
        }
      }
      public static void main(String[] args) {
        new NameCollector();
      }
    } ///:~
```

The first definitions in **NameCollector** should look familiar: the port is chosen, a datagram packet is created, and there's a handle to a **DatagramSocket**. The next three definitions concern the connection to the C program: a **Process** object is what comes back when the C program is fired up by the Java program, and that **Process** object produces the **InputStream** and **OutputStream** objects representing, respectively, the standard output and standard input of the C program. These must of course be "wrapped" as is usual with Java IO, so we end up with a **PrintStream** and **DataInputStream**.

All the work for this program happens inside the constructor. To start up the C program, the current **Runtime** object is procured. This is used to call **exec( )**, which returns the **Process** object. You can see that there are simple calls to produce the streams from the **Process** object: **getOutputStream( )** and **getInputStream( )**. From this point on, all you need to consider is sending data to the stream **nameList** and getting the results from **addResult**.

As before, a **DatagramSocket** is connected to a port. Inside the infinite **while** loop, the program calls **receive( )**, which blocks until a datagram shows up. When the datagram appears, its contents are extracted into the **String rcvd**. This is trimmed to remove white space at each end and sent to the C program in the line:

```
nameList.println(rcvd.trim());
```

This is only possible because Java's **exec( )** provides access to any executable that reads from standard input and writes to standard output. There are other ways to talk to non-Java code, which are discussed in Appendix A.

Capturing the result from the C program is slightly more complicated. You must call **read( )** and provide a buffer where the results will be placed. The return value for **read( )** is the number of bytes that came from the C program, and if this value is -1 it means that something is wrong. Otherwise, the **resultBuf** is turned into a **String** and the spaces are trimmed off. This string is then placed into a **DatagramPacket** as before and shipped back to the same address that sent the request in the first place. Note that the sender's address is part of the **DatagramPacket** we received.

Remember that although the C program must be compiled on the Web server, the Java program can be compiled anywhere since the resulting byte codes will be the same regardless of the platform on which the program will be running.

The *NameSender* applet

As mentioned earlier, the applet must be written with Java 1.0 so that it will run on the largest number of browsers, so it's best if the number of classes produced is minimized. Thus, instead of using the **Dgram** class developed earlier, all of the datagram manipulations will be placed in line. In addition, the applet needs a thread to listen for the reply from the server, and instead of making this a separate thread it's integrated into the applet by implementing the **Runnable** interface. This isn't as easy to read, but it produces a one-class (and one-server-hit) applet:

```
//: NameSender.java
// An applet that sends an email address
// as a datagram, using Java 1.02.
import java.awt.*;
import java.applet.*;
import java.net.*;
import java.io.*;

public class NameSender extends Applet
    implements Runnable {
  private Thread pl = null;
  private Button send = new Button(
    "Add email address to mailing list");
  private TextField t = new TextField(
    "type your email address here", 40);
  private String str = new String();
  private Label
    l = new Label(), l2 = new Label();
  private DatagramSocket s;
  private InetAddress hostAddress;
  private byte[] buf =
    new byte[NameCollector.BUFFER_SIZE];
  private DatagramPacket dp =
    new DatagramPacket(buf, buf.length);
  private int vcount = 0;
  public void init() {
    setLayout(new BorderLayout());
    Panel p = new Panel();
    p.setLayout(new GridLayout(2, 1));
    p.add(t);
    p.add(send);
    add("North", p);
    Panel labels = new Panel();
    labels.setLayout(new GridLayout(2, 1));
    labels.add(l);
    labels.add(l2);
    add("Center", labels);
    try {
      // Auto-assign port number:
      s = new DatagramSocket();
      hostAddress = InetAddress.getByName(
        getCodeBase().getHost());
    } catch(UnknownHostException e) {
      l.setText("Cannot find host");
```

```java
      } catch(SocketException e) {
        l.setText("Can't open socket");
      }
      l.setText("Ready to send your email address");
    }
    public boolean action (Event evt, Object arg) {
      if(evt.target.equals(send)) {
        if(pl != null) {
          // pl.stop(); Deprecated in Java 1.2
          Thread remove = pl;
          pl = null;
          remove.interrupt();
        }
        l2.setText("");
        // Check for errors in email name:
        str = t.getText().toLowerCase().trim();
        if(str.indexOf(' ') != -1) {
          l.setText("Spaces not allowed in name");
          return true;
        }
        if(str.indexOf(',') != -1) {
          l.setText("Commas not allowed in name");
          return true;
        }
        if(str.indexOf('@') == -1) {
          l.setText("Name must include '@'");
          l2.setText("");
          return true;
        }
        if(str.indexOf('@') == 0) {
          l.setText("Name must preceed '@'");
          l2.setText("");
          return true;
        }
        String end =
          str.substring(str.indexOf('@'));
        if(end.indexOf('.') == -1) {
          l.setText("Portion after '@' must " +
            "have an extension, such as '.com'");
          l2.setText("");
          return true;
        }
        // Everything's OK, so send the name. Get a
        // fresh buffer, so it's zeroed. For some
```

```
            // reason you must use a fixed size rather
            // than calculating the size dynamically:
            byte[] sbuf =
               new byte[NameCollector.BUFFER_SIZE];
            str.getBytes(0, str.length(), sbuf, 0);
            DatagramPacket toSend =
               new DatagramPacket(
                  sbuf, 100, hostAddress,
                  NameCollector.COLLECTOR_PORT);
            try {
               s.send(toSend);
            } catch(Exception e) {
               l.setText("Couldn't send datagram");
               return true;
            }
            l.setText("Sent: " + str);
            send.setLabel("Re-send");
            pl = new Thread(this);
            pl.start();
            l2.setText(
               "Waiting for verification " + ++vcount);
         }
      else return super.action(evt, arg);
      return true;
   }
   // The thread portion of the applet watches for
   // the reply to come back from the server:
   public void run() {
      try {
         s.receive(dp);
      } catch(Exception e) {
         l2.setText("Couldn't receive datagram");
         return;
      }
      l2.setText(new String(dp.getData(),
         0, 0, dp.getLength()));
   }
} ///:~
```

The UI for the applet is quite simple. There's a **TextField** in which you type your email address, and a **Button** to send the email address to the server. Two **Labels** are used to report status back to the user.

By now you can recognize the **DatagramSocket**, **InetAddress**, buffer, and **DatagramPacket** as trappings of the network connection. Lastly, you can see the **run( )** method that implements the thread portion so the applet can listen for the reply sent back by the server.

The **init( )** method sets up the GUI with the familiar layout tools, then creates the **DatagramSocket** that will be used both for sending and receiving datagrams.

The **action( )** method (remember, we're confined to Java 1.0 now, so we can't use any slick inner listener classes) watches only to see if you press the "send" button. When the button is pressed, the first action is to check the **Thread pl** to see if it's **null**. If it's not **null**, there's a live thread running. The first time the message is sent a thread is started up to watch for the reply. Thus, if a thread is running, it means this is not the first time the user has tried to send the message. The **pl** handle is set to **null** and the old listener is interrupted. (This is the preferred approach, since **stop( )** is deprecated in Java 1.2 as explained in the previous chapter.)

Regardless of whether this is the first time the button was pressed, the text in **l2** is erased.

The next group of statements checks the email name for errors. The **String.indexOf( )** method is used to search for illegal characters, and if one is found it is reported to the user. Note that all of this happens without any network activity, so it's fast and it doesn't bog down the Internet.

Once the name is verified, it is packaged into a datagram and sent to the host address and port number in the same way that was described in the earlier datagram example. The first label is changed to show you that the send has occurred, and the button text is changed so that it reads "re-send." At this point, the thread is started up and the second label informs you that the applet is waiting for a reply from the server.

The **run( )** method for the thread uses the **DatagramSocket** that lives in **NameSender** to **receive( )**, which blocks until the datagram packet comes from the server. The resulting packet is placed into **NameSender**'s **DatagramPacket dp**. The data is retrieved from the packet and placed into the second label in **NameSender**. At this point, the thread terminates and becomes dead. If the reply doesn't come back from the server in a reasonable amount of time, the user might become impatient and press the button again, thus terminating the current thread (and, after re-sending the data, starting a new one). Because a thread is used to listen for the reply, the user still has full use of the UI.

The Web page

Of course, the applet must go inside a Web page. Here is the complete Web page; you can see that it's intended to be used to automatically collect names for my mailing list:

```
<HTML>
<HEAD>
<META CONTENT="text/html">
<TITLE>
Add Yourself to Bruce Eckel's Java Mailing List
</TITLE>
</HEAD>
<BODY LINK="#0000ff" VLINK="#800080" BGCOLOR="#ffffff">
<FONT SIZE=6><P>
Add Yourself to Bruce Eckel's Java Mailing List
</P></FONT>
The applet on this page will automatically add your
email address to the mailing list, so you will receive
update information about changes to the online version
of "Thinking in Java," notification when the book is in
print, information about upcoming Java seminars, and
notification about the "Hands-on Java Seminar"
Multimedia CD. Type in your email address and press the
button to automatically add yourself to this mailing
list. <HR>
<applet code=NameSender width=400 height=100>
</applet>
<HR>
If after several tries, you do not get verification it
means that the Java application on the server is having
problems. In this case, you can add yourself to the list
by sending email to
<A HREF="mailto:Bruce@EckelObjects.com">
Bruce@EckelObjects.com</A>
</BODY>
</HTML>
```

The applet tag is quite trivial, no different from the first one presented in Chapter 13.

Problems with this approach

This certainly seems like an elegant approach. There's no CGI programming and so there are no delays while the server starts up a CGI program. The datagram approach seems to produce a nice quick response. In addition, when Java 1.1 is available everywhere, the server portion can be written entirely in Java. (Although it's quite interesting to see how easy it is to connect to a non-Java program using standard input and output.)

There are problems, however. One problem is rather subtle: since the Java application is running constantly on the server and it spends most of its time blocked in the **Datagram.receive( )** method, there *might* be some CPU hogging going on. At least, that's the way it appeared on the server where I was experimenting. On the other hand, there wasn't much else happening on that server, and starting the program using "nice" (a Unix program to prevent a process from hogging the CPU) or its equivalent could solve the problem if you have a more heavily-loaded server. In any event, it's worth keeping your eye on an application like this – a blocked **receive( )** could hog the CPU.

The second problem is a show stopper. It concerns firewalls. A firewall is a machine that sits between your network and the Internet. It monitors all traffic coming in from the Internet and going out to the Internet, and makes sure that traffic conforms to what it expects.

Firewalls are conservative little beasts. They demand strict conformance to all the rules, and if you're not conforming they assume that you're doing something sinful and shut you out (not quite so bad as the Spanish Inquisition, but close). For example, if you are on a network behind a firewall and you start connecting to the Internet using a Web browser, the firewall expects that all your transactions will connect to the server using the accepted http port, which is 80. Now along comes this Java applet **NameSender**, which is trying to send a datagram to port 8080, which is way outside the range of the "protected" ports 0-1024. The firewall naturally assumes the worst – that someone has a virus – and it doesn't allow the transaction to happen.

As long as your customers have raw connections to the Internet (for example, using a typical Internet service provider) there's no problem, but you might have some important customers dwelling behind firewalls, and they won't be able to use your program.

This is rather disheartening after learning so much Java, because it would seem that you must give up Java on the server and learn how to write CGI scripts in C or Perl. But as it turns out, despair is not in order.

One scenario is part of Sun's grand scheme. If everything goes as planned, Web servers will be equipped with *servlet servers*. These will take a request from the client (going through the firewall-accepted port 80) and instead of starting up a CGI program they will start up a Java program called a *servlet*. This is a little application that's designed to run only on the server. A servlet server will automatically start up the servlet to handle the client request, which means you can write all your programs in Java (further enabling the "100 percent pure Java initiative"). It is admittedly an appealing idea: once you're comfortable with Java, you don't have to switch to a more primitive language to handle requests on the server.

Since it's only for handling requests on the server, the servlet API has no GUI abilities. This fits quite well with **NameCollector.java**, which doesn't have a GUI anyway.

At this writing, a low-cost servlet server was available from *java.sun.com*. In addition, Sun is encouraging other Web server manufacturers to add servlet capabilities to their servers.

Connecting Java to CGI

A Java program can send a CGI request to a server just like an HTML page can. As with HTML pages, this request can be either a GET or a POST. In addition, the Java program can intercept the output of the CGI program, so you don't have to rely on the program to format a new page and force the user to back up from one page to another if something goes wrong. In fact, the appearance of the program can be the same as the previous version.

It also turns out that the code is simpler, and that CGI isn't difficult to write after all. (An innocent statement that's true of many things – *after* you understand them.) So in this section you'll get a crash course in CGI programming. To solve the general problem, some CGI tools will be created in C++ that will allow you to easily write a CGI program to solve any problem. The benefit to this approach is portability – the example you are about to see will work on any system that supports CGI, and there's no problem with firewalls.

This example also works out the basics of creating any connection with applets and CGI programs, so you can easily adapt it to your own projects.

Encoding data for CGI

In this version, the name *and* the email address will be collected and stored in the file in the form:

```
First Last <email@domain.com>;
```

This is a convenient form for many mailers. Since two fields are being collected, there are no shortcuts because CGI has a particular format for encoding the data in fields. You can see this for yourself if you make an ordinary HTML page and add the lines:

```
<Form method="GET" ACTION="/cgi-bin/Listmgr2.exe">
<P>Name: <INPUT TYPE = "text" NAME = "name"
VALUE = "" size = "40"></p>
<P>Email Address: <INPUT TYPE = "text"
NAME = "email" VALUE = "" size = "40"></p>
<p><input type = "submit" name = "submit" > </p>
</Form>
```

This creates two data entry fields called **name** and **email**, along with a **submit** button that collects the data and sends it to a CGI program. **Listmgr2.exe** is the name of the executable program that resides in the directory that's typically called "cgi-bin" on your Web server.[3] (If the named program is not in the cgi-bin directory, you won't see any results.) If you fill out this form and press the "submit" button, you will see in the URL address window of the browser something like:

```
http://www.myhome.com/cgi-bin/Listmgr2.exe?
name=First+Last&email=email@domain.com&submit=Subm
it
```

(Without the line break, of course). Here you see a little bit of the way that data is encoded to send to CGI. For one thing, spaces are not allowed

---

[3] You can test this under Windows32 using the Microsoft Personal Web Server that comes with Microsoft Office 97 and some of their other products. This is a nice way to experiment since you can perform local tests (and it's also fast). If you're on a different platform or if you don't have Office 97, you might be able to find a freeware Web server for testing by searching the Internet.

(since spaces typically separate command-line arguments). Spaces are replaced by '+' signs. In addition, each field contains the field name (which is determined by the HTML page) followed by an '=' and the field data, and terminated by a '&'.

At this point, you might wonder about the '+', '=,' and '&'. What if those are used in the field, as in "John & Marsha Smith"? This is encoded to:

```
John+%26+Marsha+Smith
```

That is, the special character is turned into a '%' followed by its ASCII value in hex.

Fortunately, Java has a tool to perform this encoding for you. It's a static method of the class **URLEncoder** called **encode( )**. You can experiment with this method using the following program:

```
//: EncodeDemo.java
// Demonstration of URLEncoder.encode()
import java.net.*;

public class EncodeDemo {
  public static void main(String[] args) {
    String s = "";
    for(int i = 0; i < args.length; i++)
      s += args[i] + " ";
    s = URLEncoder.encode(s.trim());
    System.out.println(s);
  }
} ///:~
```

This takes the command-line arguments and combines them into a string of words separated by spaces (the final space is removed using **String.trim( )**). These are then encoded and printed.

To invoke a CGI program, all the applet needs to do is collect the data from its fields (or wherever it needs to collect the data from), URL-encode each piece of data, and then assemble it into a single string, placing the name of each field followed by an '=', followed by the data, followed by an '&'. To form the entire CGI command, this string is placed after the URL of the CGI program and a '?'. That's all it takes to invoke any CGI program, and as you'll see you can easily do it within an applet.

The applet

The applet is actually considerably simpler than **NameSender.java**, partly because it's so easy to send a GET request and also because no thread is required to wait for the reply. There are now two fields instead of one, but you'll notice that much of the applet looks familiar, from **NameSender.java**.

```
//: NameSender2.java
// An applet that sends an email address
// via a CGI GET, using Java 1.02.
import java.awt.*;
import java.applet.*;
import java.net.*;
import java.io.*;

public class NameSender2 extends Applet {
  final String CGIProgram = "Listmgr2.exe";
  Button send = new Button(
    "Add email address to mailing list");
  TextField name = new TextField(
    "type your name here", 40),
    email = new TextField(
    "type your email address here", 40);
  String str = new String();
  Label l = new Label(), l2 = new Label();
  int vcount = 0;
  public void init() {
    setLayout(new BorderLayout());
    Panel p = new Panel();
    p.setLayout(new GridLayout(3, 1));
    p.add(name);
    p.add(email);
    p.add(send);
    add("North", p);
    Panel labels = new Panel();
    labels.setLayout(new GridLayout(2, 1));
    labels.add(l);
    labels.add(l2);
    add("Center", labels);
    l.setText("Ready to send email address");
  }
  public boolean action (Event evt, Object arg) {
    if(evt.target.equals(send)) {
```

```java
        l2.setText("");
        // Check for errors in data:
        if(name.getText().trim()
            .indexOf(' ') == -1) {
          l.setText(
            "Please give first and last name");
          l2.setText("");
          return true;
        }
        str = email.getText().trim();
        if(str.indexOf(' ') != -1) {
          l.setText(
            "Spaces not allowed in email name");
          l2.setText("");
          return true;
        }
        if(str.indexOf(',') != -1) {
          l.setText(
            "Commas not allowed in email name");
          return true;
        }
        if(str.indexOf('@') == -1) {
          l.setText("Email name must include '@'");
          l2.setText("");
          return true;
        }
        if(str.indexOf('@') == 0) {
          l.setText(
            "Name must preceed '@' in email name");
          l2.setText("");
          return true;
        }
        String end =
          str.substring(str.indexOf('@'));
        if(end.indexOf('.') == -1) {
          l.setText("Portion after '@' must " +
            "have an extension, such as '.com'");
          l2.setText("");
          return true;
        }
        // Build and encode the email data:
        String emailData =
          "name=" + URLEncoder.encode(
            name.getText().trim()) +
```

```
          "&email=" + URLEncoder.encode(
            email.getText().trim().toLowerCase()) +
          "&submit=Submit";
        // Send the name using CGI's GET process:
        try {
          l.setText("Sending...");
          URL u = new URL(
            getDocumentBase(), "cgi-bin/" +
            CGIProgram + "?" + emailData);
          l.setText("Sent: " + email.getText());
          send.setLabel("Re-send");
          l2.setText(
            "Waiting for reply " + ++vcount);
          DataInputStream server =
            new DataInputStream(u.openStream());
          String line;
          while((line = server.readLine()) != null)
            l2.setText(line);
        } catch(MalformedURLException e) {
          l.setText("Bad URl");
        } catch(IOException e) {
          l.setText("IO Exception");
        }
      }
      else return super.action(evt, arg);
      return true;
    }
  } ///:~
```

The name of the CGI program (which you'll see later) is **Listmgr2.exe**. Many Web servers are Unix machines (mine runs Linux) that don't traditionally use the **.exe** extension for their executable programs, but you can call the program anything you want under Unix. By using the **.exe** extension the program can be tested without change under both Unix and Win32.

As before, the applet sets up its user interface (with two fields this time instead of one). The only significant difference occurs inside the **action( )** method, which handles the button press. After the name has been checked, you see the lines:

```
        String emailData =
          "name=" + URLEncoder.encode(
            name.getText().trim()) +
          "&email=" + URLEncoder.encode(
```

```
      email.getText().trim().toLowerCase()) +
   "&submit=Submit";
// Send the name using CGI's GET process:
try {
   l.setText("Sending...");
   URL u = new URL(
      getDocumentBase(), "cgi-bin/" +
      CGIProgram + "?" + emailData);
   l.setText("Sent: " + email.getText());
   send.setLabel("Re-send");
   l2.setText(
      "Waiting for reply " + ++vcount);
   DataInputStream server =
      new DataInputStream(u.openStream());
   String line;
   while((line = server.readLine()) != null)
      l2.setText(line);
   // ...
```

The **name** and **email** data are extracted from their respective text boxes, and the spaces are trimmed off both ends using **trim( )**. The **email** name is forced to lower case so all email addresses in the list can be accurately compared (to prevent accidental duplicates based on capitalization). The data from each field is URL-encoded, and then the GET string is assembled in the same way that an HTML page would do it. (This way you can use a Java applet in concert with any existing CGI program designed to work with regular HTML GET requests.)

At this point, some Java magic happens: if you want to connect to any URL, just create a **URL** object and hand the address to the constructor. The constructor makes the connection with the server (and, with Web servers, all the action happens in making the connection, via the string used as the URL). In this case, the URL points to the cgi–bin directory of the current Web site (the base address of the current Web site is produced with **getDocumentBase( )**). When the Web server sees "cgi-bin" in a URL, it expects that to be followed by the name of the program inside the cgi-bin directory that you want it to run. Following the program name is a question mark and the argument string that the CGI program will look for in the QUERY_STRING environment variable, as you'll see.

Usually when you make any sort of request, you get back (you're forced to accept in return) an HTML page. With Java **URL** objects, however, you can intercept anything that comes back from the CGI program by getting an **InputStream** from the **URL** object. This is performed with the **URL openStream( )** method, which is in turn wrapped in a

DataInputStream. Then you can read lines, and when **readLine( )** returns **null** the CGI program has finished its output.

The CGI program you're about to see returns only one line, a string indicating success or failure (and the details of the failure). This line is captured and placed into the second **Label** field so the user can see the results.

Displaying a Web page from within an applet

It's also possible for the applet to display the result of the CGI program as a Web page, just as if it were running in normal HTML mode. You can do this with the following line:

```
getAppletContext().showDocument(u);
```

in which **u** is the **URL** object. Here's a simple example that redirects you to another Web page. The page happens to be the output of a CGI program, but you can as easily go to an ordinary HTML page, so you could build on this applet to produce a password-protected gateway to a particular portion of your Web site:

```
//: ShowHTML.java
import java.awt.*;
import java.applet.*;
import java.net.*;
import java.io.*;

public class ShowHTML extends Applet {
  static final String CGIProgram = "MyCGIProgram";
  Button send = new Button("Go");
  Label l = new Label();
  public void init() {
    add(send);
    add(l);
  }
  public boolean action (Event evt, Object arg) {
    if(evt.target.equals(send)) {
      try {
        // This could be an HTML page instead of
        // a CGI program. Notice that this CGI
        // program doesn't use arguments, but
        // you can add them in the usual way.
        URL u = new URL(
          getDocumentBase(),
```

```
        "cgi-bin/" + CGIProgram);
      // Display the output of the URL using
      // the Web browser, as an ordinary page:
      getAppletContext().showDocument(u);
    } catch(Exception e) {
      l.setText(e.toString());
    }
  }
  else return super.action(evt, arg);
  return true;
}
} ///:~
```

The beauty of the **URL** class is how much it shields you from. You can connect to Web servers without knowing much at all about what's going on under the covers.

The CGI program in C++

At this point you could follow the previous example and write the CGI program for the server using ANSI C. One argument for doing this is that ANSI C can be found virtually everywhere. However, C++ has become quite ubiquitous, especially in the form of the GNU C++ Compiler[4] (**g++**) that can be downloaded free from the Internet for virtually any platform (and often comes pre-installed with operating systems such as Linux). As you will see, this means that you can get the benefit of object-oriented programming in a CGI program.

To avoid throwing too many new concepts at you all at once, this program will not be a "pure" C++ program; some code will be written in plain C even though C++ alternatives exist. This isn't a significant issue because the biggest benefit in using C++ for this program is the ability to create classes. Since what we're concerned with when parsing the CGI information is the field name-value pairs, one class (**Pair**) will be used to represent a single name-value pair and a second class (**CGI_vector**) will automatically parse the CGI string into **Pair** objects that it will hold (as a **vector**) so you can fetch each **Pair** out at your leisure.

---

[4] GNU stands for "Gnu's Not Unix." The project, created by the Free Software Foundation, was originally intended to replace the Unix operating system with a free version of that OS. Linux appears to have replaced this initiative, but the GNU tools have played an integral part in the development of Linux, which comes packaged with many GNU components.

This program is also interesting because it demonstrates some of the pluses and minuses of C++ in contrast with Java. You'll see some similarities; for example the **class** keyword. Access control has identical keywords **public** and **private**, but they're used differently: they control a block instead of a single method or field (that is, if you say **private:** each following definition is **private** until you say **public:**). Also, when you create a class, all the definitions automatically default to **private**.

One of the reasons for using C++ here is the convenience of the C++ *Standard Template Library*. Among other things, the STL contains a **vector** class. This is a C++ **template**, which means that it will be configured at compile time so it will hold objects of only a particular type (in this case, **Pair** objects). Unlike the Java **Vector**, which will accept anything, the C++ **vector** template will cause a compile-time error message if you try to put anything but a **Pair** object into the **vector**, and when you get something out of the **vector** it will automatically be a **Pair** object, without casting. Thus, the checking happens at compile time and produces a more robust program. In addition, the program can run faster since you don't have to perform run-time casts. The **vector** also overloads the **operator[]** so you have a convenient syntax for extracting **Pair** objects. The **vector** template will be used in the creation of **CGI_vector**, which you'll see is a fairly short definition considering how powerful it is.

On the down side, look at the complexity of the definition of **Pair** in the following code. **Pair** has more method definitions than you're used to seeing in Java code, because the C++ programmer must know how to control copying with the copy-constructor and assignment with the overloaded **operator=**. As described in Chapter 12, occasionally you need to concern yourself with similar things in Java, but in C++ you must be aware of them almost constantly.

The project will start with a reusable portion, which consists of **Pair** and **CGI_vector** in a C++ header file. Technically, you shouldn't cram this much into a header file, but for these examples it doesn't hurt anything and it will also look more Java-like, so it will be easier for you to read:

```
//: CGITools.h
// Automatically extracts and decodes data
// from CGI GETs and POSTs. Tested with GNU C++
// (available for most server machines).
#include <string.h>
#include <vector> // STL vector
using namespace std;
```

```
// A class to hold a single name-value pair from
// a CGI query. CGI_vector holds Pair objects and
// returns them from its operator[].
class Pair {
  char* nm;
  char* val;
public:
  Pair() { nm = val = 0; }
  Pair(char* name, char* value) {
    // Creates new memory:
    nm = decodeURLString(name);
    val = decodeURLString(value);
  }
  const char* name() const { return nm; }
  const char* value() const { return val; }
  // Test for "emptiness"
  bool empty() const {
    return (nm == 0) || (val == 0);
  }
  // Automatic type conversion for boolean test:
  operator bool() const {
    return (nm != 0) && (val != 0);
  }
  // The following constructors & destructor are
  // necessary for bookkeeping in C++.
  // Copy-constructor:
  Pair(const Pair& p) {
    if(p.nm == 0 || p.val == 0) {
      nm = val = 0;
    } else {
      // Create storage & copy rhs values:
      nm = new char[strlen(p.nm) + 1];
      strcpy(nm, p.nm);
      val = new char[strlen(p.val) + 1];
      strcpy(val, p.val);
    }
  }
  // Assignment operator:
  Pair& operator=(const Pair& p) {
    // Clean up old lvalues:
    delete nm;
    delete val;
    if(p.nm == 0 || p.val == 0) {
      nm = val = 0;
```

```
    } else {
      // Create storage & copy rhs values:
      nm = new char[strlen(p.nm) + 1];
      strcpy(nm, p.nm);
      val = new char[strlen(p.val) + 1];
      strcpy(val, p.val);
    }
    return *this;
  }
  ~Pair() { // Destructor
    delete nm; // 0 value OK
    delete val;
  }
  // If you use this method outide this class,
  // you're responsible for calling 'delete' on
  // the pointer that's returned:
  static char*
  decodeURLString(const char* URLstr) {
    int len = strlen(URLstr);
    char* result = new char[len + 1];
    memset(result, len + 1, 0);
    for(int i = 0, j = 0; i <= len; i++, j++) {
      if(URLstr[i] == '+')
        result[j] = ' ';
      else if(URLstr[i] == '%') {
        result[j] =
          translateHex(URLstr[i + 1]) * 16 +
          translateHex(URLstr[i + 2]);
        i += 2; // Move past hex code
      } else // An ordinary character
        result[j] = URLstr[i];
    }
    return result;
  }
  // Translate a single hex character; used by
  // decodeURLString():
  static char translateHex(char hex) {
    if(hex >= 'A')
      return (hex & 0xdf) - 'A' + 10;
    else
      return hex - '0';
  }
};
```

```
// Parses any CGI query and turns it
// into an STL vector of Pair objects:
class CGI_vector : public vector<Pair> {
  char* qry;
  const char* start; // Save starting position
  // Prevent assignment and copy-construction:
  void operator=(CGI_vector&);
  CGI_vector(CGI_vector&);
public:
  // const fields must be initialized in the C++
  // "Constructor initializer list":
  CGI_vector(char* query) :
      start(new char[strlen(query) + 1]) {
    qry = (char*)start; // Cast to non-const
    strcpy(qry, query);
    Pair p;
    while((p = nextPair()) != 0)
      push_back(p);
  }
  // Destructor:
  ~CGI_vector() { delete start; }
private:
  // Produces name-value pairs from the query
  // string. Returns an empty Pair when there's
  // no more query string left:
  Pair nextPair() {
    char* name = qry;
    if(name == 0 || *name == '\0')
      return Pair(); // End, return null Pair
    char* value = strchr(name, '=');
    if(value == 0)
      return Pair(); // Error, return null Pair
    // Null-terminate name, move value to start
    // of its set of characters:
    *value = '\0';
    value++;
    // Look for end of value, marked by '&':
    qry = strchr(value, '&');
    if(qry == 0) qry = ""; // Last pair found
    else {
      *qry = '\0'; // Terminate value string
      qry++; // Move to next pair
    }
    return Pair(name, value);
```

```
        }
};  ///:~
```

After the **#include** statements, you see a line that says:

```
using namespace std;
```

Namespaces in C++ solve one of the problems taken care of by the **package** scheme in Java: hiding library names. The **std** namespace refers to the Standard C++ library, and **vector** is in this library so the line is required.

The **Pair** class starts out looking pretty simple: it just holds two (**private**) character pointers, one for the name and one for the value. The default constructor simply sets these pointers to zero, since in C++ an object's memory isn't automatically zeroed. The second constructor calls the method **decodeURLString( )** that produces a decoded string in newly-allocated heap memory. This memory must be managed and destroyed by the object, as you will see in the destructor. The **name( )** and **value( )** methods produce read-only pointers to the respective fields. The **empty( )** method is a way for you to ask the **Pair** object whether either of its fields are empty; it returns a **bool,** which is C++'s built-in primitive Boolean data type. The **operator bool( )** uses a special case of C++ *operator overloading*, which allows you to control automatic type conversion. If you have a **Pair** object called **p** and you use it in an expression in which a Boolean result is expected, such as **if(p) {** //..., then the compiler will recognize that it has a **Pair** and it needs a Boolean, so it will automatically call **operator bool( )** to perform the necessary conversion.

The next three methods are part of the bookkeeping that's necessary when you create a class in C++. In the so-called "canonical form" for a C++ class, you must define the necessary "ordinary" constructors as well as a copy-constructor and the assignment operator, **operator=** (and the destructor, to clean up the memory). You must define these because they can be quietly called by the compiler when you pass objects in and out of a function (this calls the copy-constructor) or when you assign objects (the assignment operator). Once you've gone through the trouble to understand how the copy-constructor and assignment operator work you can write robust classes in C++, but it is a bit of a learning experience.[5]

---

[5] My book *Thinking in C++* (Prentice-Hall, 1995) devotes an entire chapter to this subject. Refer to this if you need further information on the subject.

The copy-constructor **Pair(const Pair&)** is automatically called whenever you pass an object into or out of a function *by value*. That is, you aren't passing the address of the object you're making a copy of the whole object inside the function frame. This isn't an option in Java since you pass only handles, thus there's no copy-constructor in Java. (If you want to make a local duplicate, you **clone( )** the object – see Chapter 12.) Likewise, if you assign a handle in Java, it's simply copied. But assignment in C++ means that the entire object is copied. In the copy-constructor, you create new storage and copy the source data, but with the assignment operator you must release the old storage before allocating new storage. What you're seeing is probably the worst-case complexity scenario for a C++ class, but it's one of the reasons Java proponents can argue that Java is a lot simpler than C++. In Java you pass handles and there's a garbage collector, so you don't have to do this kind of thing.

This isn't quite the whole story. The **Pair** class is using **char*** for **nm** and **val**, and the worst-case complexity occurs primarily around pointers. If you use the more modern Standard C++ **string** class instead of **char***, things get much simpler (however, not all compilers have caught up enough to come with **string**). Then, the first part of **Pair** looks like this:

```
class Pair {
    string nm;
    string val;
public:
    Pair() { }
    Pair(char* name, char* value) {
        // Creates new memory:
        nm = decodeURLString(name);
        val = decodeURLString(value);
    }
    const char* name() const { return nm.c_str(); }
    const char* value() const { return val.c_str();
}
    // Test for "emptiness"
    bool empty() const {
        return (nm.length() == 0) || (val.length() ==
0);
    }
    // Automatic type conversion for boolean test:
    operator bool() const {
        return (nm.length() != 0) && (val.length() !=
0);
    }
```

(Also, for this case **decodeURLString( )** returns a **string** instead of a **char***.) You don't need to define a copy-constructor, **operator=**, or destructor because the compiler does that for you, and does it correctly. But even if it sometimes works automatically, C++ programmers must still know the details of copy-construction and assignment.

The remainder of the **Pair** class consists of the two methods **decodeURLString( )** and a helper method **translateHex( )**, which is used by **decodeURLString( )**. (Note that **translateHex( )** does not guard against bad user input such as "%1H.") After allocating adequate storage (which must be released by the destructor), **decodeURLString( )** moves through and replaces each '+' with a space and each hex code (beginning with a '%') with the appropriate character.

CGI_vector parses and holds an entire CGI GET command. It is inherited from the STL **vector,** which is instantiated to hold **Pair**s. Inheritance in C++ is denoted by using a colon at the point you'd say **extends** in Java. In addition, inheritance defaults to **private** so you'll almost always need to use the **public** keyword as was done here. You can also see that **CGI_vector** has a copy-constructor and an **operator=**, but they're both declared as **private**. This is to prevent the compiler from synthesizing the two functions (which it will do if you don't declare them yourself), but it also prevents the client programmer from passing a **CGI_vector** by value or from using assignment.

CGI_vector's job is to take the QUERY_STRING and parse it into name-value pairs, which it will do with the aid of **Pair**. First it copies the string into locally-allocated memory and keeps track of the starting address with the constant pointer **start.** (This is later used in the destructor to release the memory.) Then it uses its method **nextPair( )** to parse the string into raw name-value pairs, delimited by '=' and '&' signs. These are handed by **nextPair( )** to the **Pair** constructor so **nextPair( )** can return the **Pair** object, which is then added to the **vector** with **push_back( )**. When **nextPair( )** runs out of QUERY_STRING, it returns zero.

Now that the basic tools are defined, they can easily be used in a CGI program, like this:

```
//: Listmgr2.cpp
// CGI version of Listmgr.c in C++, which
// extracts its input via the GET submission
// from the associated applet. Also works as
// an ordinary CGI program with HTML forms.
#include <stdio.h>
```

```cpp
#include "CGITools.h"
const char* dataFile = "list2.txt";
const char* notify = "Bruce@EckelObjects.com";
#undef DEBUG

// Similar code as before, except that it looks
// for the email name inside of '<>':
int inList(FILE* list, const char* emailName) {
  const int BSIZE = 255;
  char lbuf[BSIZE];
  char emname[BSIZE];
  // Put the email name in '<>' so there's no
  // possibility of a match within another name:
  sprintf(emname, "<%s>", emailName);
  // Go to the beginning of the list:
  fseek(list, 0, SEEK_SET);
  // Read each line in the list:
  while(fgets(lbuf, BSIZE, list)) {
    // Strip off the newline:
    char * newline = strchr(lbuf, '\n');
    if(newline != 0)
      *newline = '\0';
    if(strstr(lbuf, emname) != 0)
      return 1;
  }
  return 0;
}

void main() {
  // You MUST print this out, otherwise the
  // server will not send the response:
  printf("Content-type: text/plain\n\n");
  FILE* list = fopen(dataFile, "a+t");
  if(list == 0) {
    printf("error: could not open database. ");
    printf("Notify %s", notify);
    return;
  }
  // For a CGI "GET," the server puts the data
  // in the environment variable QUERY_STRING:
  CGI_vector query(getenv("QUERY_STRING"));
  #if defined(DEBUG)
  // Test: dump all names and values
  for(int i = 0; i < query.size(); i++) {
```

```
    printf("query[%d].name() = [%s], ",
       i, query[i].name());
    printf("query[%d].value() = [%s]\n",
       i, query[i].value());
  }
#endif(DEBUG)
  Pair name = query[0];
  Pair email = query[1];
  if(name.empty() || email.empty()) {
    printf("error: null name or email");
    return;
  }
  if(inList(list, email.value())) {
    printf("Already in list: %s", email.value());
    return;
  }
  // It's not in the list, add it:
  fseek(list, 0, SEEK_END);
  fprintf(list, "%s <%s>;\n",
    name.value(), email.value());
  fflush(list);
  fclose(list);
  printf("%s <%s> added to list\n",
    name.value(), email.value());
} ///:~
```

The **alreadyInList( )** function is almost identical to the previous version, except that it assumes all email names are inside '**<>**'.

When you use the GET approach (which is normally done in the HTML METHOD tag of the FORM directive, but which is controlled here by the way the data is sent), the Web server grabs everything after the '?' and puts in into the environment variable QUERY_STRING. So to read that information you have to get the value of QUERY_STRING, which you do using the standard C library function **getenv( )**. In **main( )**, notice how simple the act of parsing the QUERY_STRING is: you just hand it to the constructor for the **CGI_vector** object called **query** and all the work is done for you. From then on you can pull out the names and values from **query** as if it were an array. (This is because the **operator[]** is overloaded in **vector**.) You can see how this works in the debug code, which is surrounded by the preprocessor directives **#if defined(DEBUG)** and **#endif(DEBUG)**.

Now it's important to understand something about CGI. A CGI program is handed its input in one of two ways: through QUERY_STRING during a

GET (as in this case) or through standard input during a POST. But a CGI program sends its output through standard output, typically using **printf( )** in a C program. Where does this output go? Back to the Web server, which decides what to do with it. The server makes this decision based on the **content-type** header, which means that if the **content-type** header isn't the first thing it sees, it won't know what to do with the data. Thus, it's essential that you start the output of all CGI programs with the **content-type** header.

In this case, we want the server to feed all the information directly back to the client program (which is our applet, waiting for its reply). The information should be unchanged, so the **content-type** is **text/plain**. Once the server sees this, it will echo all strings right back to the client. So each of the strings you see, three for error conditions and one for a successful add, will end up back at the applet.

Adding the email name uses the same code. In the case of the CGI script, however, there isn't an infinite loop – the program just responds and then terminates. Each time a CGI request comes in, the program is started in response to that request, and then it shuts down. Thus there is no possibility of CPU hogging, and the only performance issue concerns starting the program up and opening the file, which are dwarfed by the overhead of the Web server as it handles the CGI request.

One of the advantages of this design is that, now that **Pair** and **CGI_vector** are defined, most of the work is done for you so you can easily create your own CGI program simply by modifying **main( )**. Eventually, servlet servers will probably be ubiquitous, but in the meantime C++ is still handy for creating fast CGI programs.

What about POST?

Using a GET is fine for many applications. However, GET passes its data to the CGI program through an environment variable, and some Web servers can run out of environment space with long GET strings (you should start worrying at about 200 characters). CGI provides a solution for this: POST. With POST, the data is encoded and concatenated the same way as a GET, but POST uses standard input to pass the encoded query string to the CGI program. All you have to do is determine the length of the query string, and this length is stored in the environment variable CONTENT_LENGTH. Once you know the length, you can allocate storage and read the precise number of bytes from standard input.

The **Pair** and **CGI_vector** from **CGITools.h** can be used as is for a CGI program that handles POSTs. The following listing shows how simple it is to write such a CGI program. In this example, "pure" C++ will be used so the **stdio.h** library will be dropped in favor of **iostream**s. With **iostream**s, two predefined objects are available: **cin**, which connects to standard input, and **cout**, which connects to standard output. There are several ways to read from **cin** and write to **cout**, but the following program take the common approach of using '**<<**' to send information to **cout**, and the use of a member function (in this case, **read( )**) to read from **cin**.

```cpp
//: POSTtest.cpp
// CGI_vector works as easily with POST as it
// does with GET. Written in "pure" C++.
#include <iostream.h>
#include "CGITools.h"

void main() {
  cout << "Content-type: text/plain\n" << endl;
  // For a CGI "POST," the server puts the length
  // of the content string in the environment
  // variable CONTENT_LENGTH:
  char* clen = getenv("CONTENT_LENGTH");
  if(clen == 0) {
    cout << "Zero CONTENT_LENGTH" << endl;
    return;
  }
  int len = atoi(clen);
  char* query_str = new char[len + 1];
  cin.read(query_str, len);
  query_str[len] = '\0';
  CGI_vector query(query_str);
  // Test: dump all names and values
  for(int i = 0; i < query.size(); i++)
    cout << "query[" << i << "].name() = [" <<
      query[i].name() << "], " <<
      "query[" << i << "].value() = [" <<
      query[i].value() << "]" << endl;
  delete query_str; // Release storage
} ///:~
```

The **getenv( )** function returns a pointer to a character string representing the content length. If this pointer is zero, the CONTENT_LENGTH environment variable has not been set, so something is wrong. Otherwise, the character string must be converted to an integer using the ANSI C library function **atoi( )**. The length is used with **new** to allocate enough storage to hold the query string (plus its null terminator), and then **read( )** is called for **cin**. The **read( )** function takes a pointer to the destination buffer and the number of bytes to read. The **query_str** is then null-terminated to indicate the end of the character string.

At this point, the query string is no different from a GET query string, so it is handed to the constructor for **CGI_vector**. The different fields in the vector are then available just as in the previous example.

To test this program, you must compile it in the cgi-bin directory of your host Web server. Then you can perform a simple test by writing an HTML page like this:

```
<HTML>
<HEAD>
<META CONTENT="text/html">
<TITLE>A test of standard HTML POST</TITLE>
</HEAD>
Test, uses standard html POST
<Form method="POST" ACTION="/cgi-bin/POSTtest">
<P>Field1: <INPUT TYPE = "text" NAME = "Field1"
VALUE = "" size = "40"></p>
<P>Field2: <INPUT TYPE = "text" NAME = "Field2"
VALUE = "" size = "40"></p>
<P>Field3: <INPUT TYPE = "text" NAME = "Field3"
VALUE = "" size = "40"></p>
<P>Field4: <INPUT TYPE = "text" NAME = "Field4"
VALUE = "" size = "40"></p>
<P>Field5: <INPUT TYPE = "text" NAME = "Field5"
VALUE = "" size = "40"></p>
<P>Field6: <INPUT TYPE = "text" NAME = "Field6"
VALUE = "" size = "40"></p>
<p><input type = "submit" name = "submit" > </p>
</Form>
</HTML>
```

When you fill this out and submit it, you'll get back a simple text page containing the parsed results, so you can see that the CGI program works correctly.

Of course, it's a little more interesting to submit the data using an applet. Submitting POST data is a different process, however. After you invoke the CGI program in the usual way, you must make a direct connection to the server so you can feed it the query string. The server then turns around and feeds the query string to the CGI program via standard input.

Thinking in Java *www.BruceEckel.com*

To make a direct connection to the server, you must take the URL you've created and call **openConnection( )** to produce a **URLConnection**. Then, because a **URLConnection** doesn't usually allow you to send data to it, you must call the magic function **setDoOutput(true)** along with **setDoInput(true)** and **setAllowUserInteraction(false)**.[6] Finally, you can call **getOutputStream( )** to produce an **OutputStream**, which you wrap inside a **DataOutputStream** so you can talk to it conveniently. Here's an applet that does just that, after collecting data from its various fields:

```
//: POSTtest.java
// An applet that sends its data via a CGI POST
import java.awt.*;
import java.applet.*;
import java.net.*;
import java.io.*;

public class POSTtest extends Applet {
   final static int SIZE = 10;
   Button submit = new Button("Submit");
   TextField[] t = new TextField[SIZE];
   String query = "";
   Label l = new Label();
   TextArea ta = new TextArea(15, 60);
   public void init() {
      Panel p = new Panel();
      p.setLayout(new GridLayout(t.length + 2, 2));
      for(int i = 0; i < t.length; i++) {
         p.add(new Label(
            "Field " + i + "   ", Label.RIGHT));
         p.add(t[i] = new TextField(30));
      }
      p.add(l);
      p.add(submit);
      add("North", p);
      add("South", ta);
   }
```

[6] I can't say I really understand what's going on here, but I managed to get it working by studying *Java Network Programming* by Elliotte Rusty Harold (O'Reilly 1997). He alludes to a number of confusing bugs in the Java networking libraries, so this is an area in which you can't just write code and have it work right away. Be warned.

```java
public boolean action (Event evt, Object arg) {
  if(evt.target.equals(submit)) {
    query = "";
    ta.setText("");
    // Encode the query from the field data:
    for(int i = 0; i < t.length; i++)
      query += "Field" + i + "=" +
        URLEncoder.encode(
          t[i].getText().trim()) +
        "&";
    query += "submit=Submit";
    // Send the name using CGI's POST process:
    try {
      URL u = new URL(
        getDocumentBase(), "cgi-bin/POSTtest");
      URLConnection urlc = u.openConnection();
      urlc.setDoOutput(true);
      urlc.setDoInput(true);
      urlc.setAllowUserInteraction(false);
      DataOutputStream server =
        new DataOutputStream(
          urlc.getOutputStream());
      // Send the data
      server.writeBytes(query);
      server.close();
      // Read and display the response. You
      // cannot use
      // getAppletContext().showDocument(u);
      // to display the results as a Web page!
      DataInputStream in =
        new DataInputStream(
          urlc.getInputStream());
      String s;
      while((s = in.readLine()) != null) {
        ta.appendText(s + "\n");
      }
      in.close();
    }
    catch (Exception e) {
      l.setText(e.toString());
    }
  }
  else return super.action(evt, arg);
  return true;
```

```
      }
    } ///:~
```

Once the information is sent to the server, you can call
getInputStream( ) and wrap the return value in a **DataInputStream** so
that you can read the results. One thing you'll notice is that the results
are displayed as lines of text in a **TextArea**. Why not simply use
getAppletContext().showDocument(u)? Well, this is one of those
mysteries. The code above works fine, but if you try to use
showDocument( ) instead, everything stops working – almost. That is,
showDocument( ) *does* work, but what you get back from **POSTtest** is
"Zero CONTENT_LENGTH." So somehow, **showDocument( )** prevents the
POST query from being passed on to the CGI program. It's difficult to
know whether this is a bug that will be fixed, or some lack of
understanding on my part (the books I looked at were equally abstruse).
In any event, if you can stand to limit yourself to looking at the text that
comes back from the CGI program, the above applet works fine.

Connecting to databases with JDBC

It has been estimated that half of all software development involves
client/server operations. A great promise of Java has been the ability to
build platform-independent client/server database applications. In Java
1.1 this has come to fruition with Java DataBase Connectivity (JDBC).

One of the major problems with databases has been the feature wars
between the database companies. There is a "standard" database
language, Structured Query Language (SQL-92), but usually you must
know which database vendor you're working with despite the standard.
JDBC is designed to be platform-independent, so you don't need to worry
about the database you're using while you're programming. However,
it's still possible to make vendor-specific calls from JDBC so you aren't
restricted from doing what you must.

JDBC, like many of the APIs in Java, is designed for simplicity. The
method calls you make correspond to the logical operations you'd think
of doing when gathering data from a database: connect to the database,
create a statement and execute the query, and look at the result set.

To allow this platform independence, JDBC provides a *driver manager* that
dynamically maintains all the driver objects that your database queries

---

will need. So if you have three different kinds of vendor databases to connect to, you'll need three different driver objects. The driver objects register themselves with the driver manager at the time of loading, and you can force the loading using **Class.forName( )**.

To open a database, you must create a "database URL" that specifies:

1. That you're using JDBC with "jdbc"

2. The "subprotocol": the name of the driver or the name of a database connectivity mechanism. Since the design of JDBC was inspired by ODBC, the first subprotocol available is the "jdbc-odbc bridge," specified by "odbc"

3. The database identifier. This varies with the database driver used, but it generally provides a logical name that is mapped by the database administration software to a physical directory where the database tables are located. For your database identifier to have any meaning, you must register the name using your database administration software. (The process of registration varies from platform to platform.)

All this information is combined into one string, the "database URL." For example, to connect through the ODBC subprotocol to a database identified as "people," the database URL could be:

```
String dbUrl = "jdbc:odbc:people";
```

If you're connecting across a network, the database URL will also contain the information identifying the remote machine.

When you're ready to connect to the database, you call the **static** method **DriverManager.getConnection( )**, passing it the database URL, the user name, and a password to get into the database. You get back a **Connection** object that you can then use to query and manipulate the database.

The following example opens a database of contact information and looks for a person's last name as given on the command line. It selects only the names of people that have email addresses, then prints out all the ones that match the given last name:

```
//: Lookup.java
// Looks up email addresses in a
// local database using JDBC
import java.sql.*;
```

```
public class Lookup {
  public static void main(String[] args) {
    String dbUrl = "jdbc:odbc:people";
    String user = "";
    String password = "";
    try {
      // Load the driver (registers itself)
      Class.forName(
        "sun.jdbc.odbc.JdbcOdbcDriver");
      Connection c = DriverManager.getConnection(
        dbUrl, user, password);
      Statement s = c.createStatement();
      // SQL code:
      ResultSet r =
        s.executeQuery(
          "SELECT FIRST, LAST, EMAIL " +
          "FROM people.csv people " +
          "WHERE " +
          "(LAST='" + args[0] + "') " +
          " AND (EMAIL Is Not Null) " +
          "ORDER BY FIRST");
      while(r.next()) {
        // Capitalization doesn't matter:
        System.out.println(
          r.getString("Last") + ", "
          + r.getString("fIRST")
          + ": " + r.getString("EMAIL") );
      }
      s.close(); // Also closes ResultSet
    } catch(Exception e) {
      e.printStackTrace();
    }
  }
} ///:~
```

You can see the creation of the database URL as previously described. In this example, there is no password protection on the database so the user name and password are empty strings.

Once the connection is made with **DriverManager.getConnection( )**, you can use the resulting **Connection** object to create a **Statement** object using the **createStatement( )** method. With the resulting **Statement**, you can call **executeQuery( )**, passing in a string containing an SQL-92 standard SQL statement. (You'll see shortly how you can generate this statement automatically, so you don't have to know much about SQL.)

The **executeQuery( )** method returns a **ResultSet** object, which is quite a bit like an iterator: the **next( )** method moves the iterator to the next record in the statement, or returns **null** if the end of the result set has been reached. You'll always get a **ResultSet** object back from **executeQuery( )** even if a query results in an empty set (that is, an exception is not thrown). Note that you must call **next( )** once before trying to read any record data. If the result set is empty, this first call to **next( )** will return **false**. For each record in the result set, you can select the fields using (among other approaches) the field name as a string. Also note that the capitalization of the field name is ignored – it doesn't matter with an SQL database. You determine the type you'll get back by calling **getInt( )**, **getString( )**, **getFloat( )**, etc. At this point, you've got your database data in Java native format and can do whatever you want with it using ordinary Java code.

Getting the example to work

With JDBC, understanding the code is relatively simple. The confusing part is making it work on your particular system. The reason this is confusing is that it requires you to figure out how to get your JDBC driver to load properly, and how to set up a database using your database administration software.

Of course, this process can vary radically from machine to machine, but the process I used to make it work under 32-bit Windows might give you clues to help you attack your own situation.

Step 1: Find the JDBC Driver

The program above contains the statement:

```
Class.forName("sun.jdbc.odbc.JdbcOdbcDriver");
```

This implies a directory structure, which is deceiving. With this particular installation of JDK 1.1, there was no file called **JdbcOdbcDriver.class**, so if you looked at this example and went searching for it you'd be frustrated. Other published examples use a pseudo name, such as "myDriver.ClassName," which is less than helpful. In fact, the load statement above for the jdbc-odbc driver (the only one that actually comes with JDK 1.1) appears in only a few places in the online documentation (in particular, a page labeled "JDBC-ODBC Bridge Driver"). If the load statement above doesn't work, then the name might have been changed as part of a Java version change, so you should hunt through the documentation again.

If the load statement is wrong, you'll get an exception at this point. To test whether your driver load statement is working correctly, comment out the code after the statement and up to the **catch** clause; if the program throws no exceptions it means that the driver is loading properly.

Step 2: Configure the database

Again, this is specific to 32-bit Windows; you might need to do some research to figure it out for your own platform.

First, open the control panel. You might find two icons that say "ODBC." You must use the one that says "32bit ODBC," since the other one is for backwards compatibility with 16-bit ODBC software and will produce no results for JDBC. When you open the "32bit ODBC" icon, you'll see a tabbed dialog with a number of tabs, including "User DSN," "System DSN," "File DSN," etc., in which "DSN" means "Data Source Name." It turns out that for the JDBC-ODBC bridge, the only place where it's important to set up your database is "System DSN," but you'll also want to test your configuration and create queries, and for that you'll also need to set up your database in "File DSN." This will allow the Microsoft Query tool (that comes with Microsoft Office) to find the database. Note that other query tools are also available from other vendors.

The most interesting database is one that you're already using. Standard ODBC supports a number of different file formats including such venerable workhorses as DBase. However, it also includes the simple "comma-separated ASCII" format, which virtually every data tool has the ability to write. In my case, I just took my "people" database that I've been maintaining for years using various contact-management tools and exported it as a comma-separated ASCII file (these typically have an extension of **.csv**). In the "File DSN" section I chose "Add," chose the text driver to handle my comma-separated ASCII file, and then un-checked "use current directory" to allow me to specify the directory where I exported the data file.

You'll notice when you do this that you don't actually specify a file, only a directory. That's because a database is typically represented as a collection of files under a single directory (although it could be represented in other forms as well). Each file usually contains a single table, and the SQL statements can produce results that are culled from multiple tables in the database (this is called a *join*). A database that contains only a single table (like this one) is usually called a *flat-file database*. Most problems that go beyond the simple storage and retrieval

---

of data generally require multiple tables that must be related by joins to produce the desired results, and these are called *relational* databases.

Step 3: Test the configuration

To test the configuration you'll need a way to discover whether the database is visible from a program that queries it. Of course, you can simply run the JDBC program example above up to and including the statement:

```
Connection c = DriverManager.getConnection(
    dbUrl, user, password);
```

If an exception is thrown, your configuration was incorrect.

However, it's useful to get a query-generation tool involved at this point. I used Microsoft Query that came with Microsoft Office, but you might prefer something else. The query tool must know where the database is, and Microsoft Query required that I go to the ODBC Administrator's "File DSN" tab and add a new entry there, again specifying the text driver and the directory where my database lives. You can name the entry anything you want, but it's helpful to use the same name you used in "System DSN."

Once you've done this, you will see that your database is available when you create a new query using your query tool.

Step 4: Generate your SQL query

The query that I created using Microsoft Query not only showed me that my database was there and in good order, but it also automatically created the SQL code that I needed to insert into my Java program. I wanted a query that would search for records that had the last name that was typed on the command line when starting the Java program. So as a starting point, I searched for a specific last name, 'Eckel'. I also wanted to display only those names that had email addresses associated with them. The steps I took to create this query were:

1. Start a new query and use the Query Wizard. Select the "people" database. (This is the equivalent of opening the database connection using the appropriate database URL.)

2. Select the "people" table within the database. From within the table, choose the columns FIRST, LAST, and EMAIL.

---

3. Under "Filter Data," choose LAST and select "equals" with an argument of Eckel. Click the "And" radio button.

4. Choose EMAIL and select "Is not Null."

5. Under "Sort By," choose FIRST.

The result of this query will show you whether you're getting what you want.

Now you can press the SQL button and without any research on your part, up will pop the correct SQL code, ready for you to cut and paste. For this query, it looked like this:

```
SELECT people.FIRST, people.LAST, people.EMAIL
FROM people.csv people
WHERE (people.LAST='Eckel') AND
(people.EMAIL Is Not Null)
ORDER BY people.FIRST
```

With more complicated queries it's easy to get things wrong, but with a query tool you can interactively test your queries and automatically generate the correct code. It's hard to argue the case for doing this by hand.

Step 5: Modify and paste in your query

You'll notice that the code above looks different from what's used in the program. That's because the query tool uses full qualification for all of the names, even when there's only one table involved. (When more than one table is involved, the qualification prevents collisions between columns from different tables that have the same names.) Since this query involves only one table, you can optionally remove the "people" qualifier from most of the names, like this:

```
SELECT FIRST, LAST, EMAIL
FROM people.csv people
WHERE (LAST='Eckel') AND
(EMAIL Is Not Null)
ORDER BY FIRST
```

In addition, you don't want this program to be hard coded to look for only one name. Instead, it should hunt for the name given as the command-line argument. Making these changes and turning the SQL statement into a dynamically-created **String** produces:

```
"SELECT FIRST, LAST, EMAIL " +
```

```
"FROM people.csv people " +
"WHERE " +
"(LAST='" + args[0] + "') " +
" AND (EMAIL Is Not Null) " +
"ORDER BY FIRST");
```

SQL has another way to insert names into a query called *stored
procedures*, which is used for speed. But for much of your database
experimentation and for your first cut, building your own query strings
in Java is fine.

You can see from this example that by using the tools currently available
– in particular the query-building tool – database programming with SQL
and JDBC can be quite straightforward.

A GUI version of the lookup program

It's more useful to leave the lookup program running all the time and
simply switch to it and type in a name whenever you want to look
someone up. The following program creates the lookup program as an
application/applet, and it also adds name completion so the data will
show up without forcing you to type the entire last name:

```
//: VLookup.java
// GUI version of Lookup.java
import java.awt.*;
import java.awt.event.*;
import java.applet.*;
import java.sql.*;

public class VLookup extends Applet {
  String dbUrl = "jdbc:odbc:people";
  String user = "";
  String password = "";
  Statement s;
  TextField searchFor = new TextField(20);
  Label completion =
    new Label("                              ");
  TextArea results = new TextArea(40, 20);
  public void init() {
    searchFor.addTextListener(new SearchForL());
    Panel p = new Panel();
    p.add(new Label("Last name to search for:"));
    p.add(searchFor);
    p.add(completion);
```

```
      setLayout(new BorderLayout());
      add(p, BorderLayout.NORTH);
      add(results, BorderLayout.CENTER);
      try {
        // Load the driver (registers itself)
        Class.forName(
          "sun.jdbc.odbc.JdbcOdbcDriver");
        Connection c = DriverManager.getConnection(
          dbUrl, user, password);
        s = c.createStatement();
      } catch(Exception e) {
        results.setText(e.getMessage());
      }
    }
    class SearchForL implements TextListener {
      public void textValueChanged(TextEvent te) {
        ResultSet r;
        if(searchFor.getText().length() == 0) {
          completion.setText("");
          results.setText("");
          return;
        }
        try {
          // Name completion:
          r = s.executeQuery(
            "SELECT LAST FROM people.csv people " +
            "WHERE (LAST Like '" +
            searchFor.getText()   +
            "%') ORDER BY LAST");
          if(r.next())
            completion.setText(
              r.getString("last"));
          r = s.executeQuery(
            "SELECT FIRST, LAST, EMAIL " +
            "FROM people.csv people " +
            "WHERE (LAST='" +
            completion.getText() +
            "') AND (EMAIL Is Not Null) " +
            "ORDER BY FIRST");
        } catch(Exception e) {
          results.setText(
            searchFor.getText() + "\n");
          results.append(e.getMessage());
          return;
```

```
        }
        results.setText("");
        try {
          while(r.next()) {
            results.append(
              r.getString("Last") + ", "
              + r.getString("fIRST") +
              ": " + r.getString("EMAIL") + "\n");
          }
        } catch(Exception e) {
          results.setText(e.getMessage());
        }
      }
    }
  public static void main(String[] args) {
    VLookup applet = new VLookup();
    Frame aFrame = new Frame("Email lookup");
    aFrame.addWindowListener(
      new WindowAdapter() {
        public void windowClosing(WindowEvent e) {
          System.exit(0);
        }
      });
    aFrame.add(applet, BorderLayout.CENTER);
    aFrame.setSize(500,200);
    applet.init();
    applet.start();
    aFrame.setVisible(true);
  }
} ///:~
```

Much of the database logic is the same, but you can see that a **TextListener** is added to listen to the **TextField**, so that whenever you type a new character it first tries to do a name completion by looking up the last name in the database and using the first one that shows up. (It places it in the **completion Label**, and uses that as the lookup text.) This way, as soon as you've typed enough characters for the program to uniquely find the name you're looking for, you can stop.

Why the JDBC API
seems so complex

When you browse the online documentation for JDBC it can seem daunting. In particular, in the **DatabaseMetaData** interface – which is just huge, contrary to most of the interfaces you see in Java – there are methods such as **dataDefinitionCausesTransactionCommit( )**, **getMaxColumnNameLength( )**, **getMaxStatementLength( )**, **storesMixedCaseQuotedIdentifiers( )**, **supportsANSI92IntermediateSQL( )**, **supportsLimitedOuterJoins( )**, and so on. What's this all about?

As mentioned earlier, databases have seemed from their inception to be in a constant state of turmoil, primarily because the demand for database applications, and thus database tools, is so great. Only recently has there been any convergence on the common language of SQL (and there are plenty of other database languages in common use). But even with an SQL "standard" there are so many variations on that theme that JDBC must provide the large **DatabaseMetaData** interface so that your code can discover the capabilities of the particular "standard" SQL database that it's currently connected to. In short, you can write simple, transportable SQL, but if you want to optimize speed your coding will multiply tremendously as you investigate the capabilities of a particular vendor's database.

This, of course, is not Java's fault. The discrepancies between database products are just something that JDBC tries to help compensate for. But bear in mind that your life will be easier if you can either write generic queries and not worry too much about performance, or, if you must tune for performance, know the platform you're writing for so you don't need to write all that investigation code.

There is more JDBC information available in the electronic documents that come as part of the Java 1.1 distribution from Sun. In addition, you can find more in the book *JDBC Database Access with Java* (Hamilton, Cattel, and Fisher, Addison-Wesley 1997). Other JDBC books are appearing regularly.

Remote methods

Traditional approaches to executing code on other machines across a network have been confusing as well as tedious and error-prone to

---

implement. The nicest way to think about this problem is that some object happens to live on another machine, and you can send a message to that object and get a result as if the object lived on your local machine. This simplification is exactly what Java 1.1 *Remote Method Invocation* (RMI) allows you to do. This section walks you through the steps necessary to create your own RMI objects.

Remote interfaces

RMI makes heavy use of interfaces. When you want to create a remote object, you mask the underlying implementation by passing around an interface. Thus, when the client gets a handle to a remote object, what they really get is an interface handle, which *happens* to connect to some local stub code that talks across the network. But you don't think about this, you just send messages via your interface handle.

When you create a remote interface, you must follow these guidelines:

1. The remote interface must be **public** (it cannot have "package access," that is, it cannot be "friendly"). Otherwise, a client will get an error when attempting to load a remote object that implements the remote interface.

2. The remote interface must extend the interface **java.rmi.Remote**.

3. Each method in the remote interface must declare **java.rmi.RemoteException** in its **throws** clause in addition to any application-specific exceptions.

4. A remote object passed as an argument or return value (either directly or embedded within a local object) must be declared as the remote interface, not the implementation class.

Here's a simple remote interface that represents an accurate time service:

```
//: PerfectTimeI.java
// The PerfectTime remote interface
package c15.ptime;
import java.rmi.*;

interface PerfectTimeI extends Remote {
  long getPerfectTime() throws RemoteException;
} ///:~
```

It looks like any other interface except that it extends **Remote** and all of its methods throw **RemoteException**. Remember that an **interface** and all of its methods are automatically **public**.

Implementing the remote interface

The server must contain a class that extends **UnicastRemoteObject** and implements the remote interface. This class can also have additional methods, but only the methods in the remote interface will be available to the client, of course, since the client will get only a handle to the interface, not the class that implements it.

You must explicitly define the constructor for the remote object even if you're only defining a default constructor that calls the base-class constructor. You must write it out since it must throw **RemoteException**.

Here's the implementation of the remote interface **PerfectTimeI**:

```
//: PerfectTime.java
// The implementation of the PerfectTime
// remote object
package c15.ptime;
import java.rmi.*;
import java.rmi.server.*;
import java.rmi.registry.*;
import java.net.*;

public class PerfectTime
    extends UnicastRemoteObject
    implements PerfectTimeI {
  // Implementation of the interface:
  public long getPerfectTime()
      throws RemoteException {
    return System.currentTimeMillis();
  }
  // Must implement constructor to throw
  // RemoteException:
  public PerfectTime() throws RemoteException {
    // super(); // Called automatically
  }
  // Registration for RMI serving:
  public static void main(String[] args) {
    System.setSecurityManager(
      new RMISecurityManager());
```

```
    try {
      PerfectTime pt = new PerfectTime();
      Naming.bind(
        "//colossus:2005/PerfectTime", pt);
      System.out.println("Ready to do time");
    } catch(Exception e) {
      e.printStackTrace();
    }
  }
} ///:~
```

Here, **main( )** handles all the details of setting up the server. When you're serving RMI objects, at some point in your program you must:

1. Create and install a security manager that supports RMI. The only one available for RMI as part of the Java distribution is **RMISecurityManager**.

2. Create one or more instances of a remote object. Here, you can see the creation of the **PerfectTime** object.

3. Register at least one of the remote objects with the RMI remote object registry for bootstrapping purposes. One remote object can have methods that produce handles to other remote objects. This allows you to set it up so the client must go to the registry only once, to get the first remote object.

Setting up the registry

Here, you see a call to the **static** method **Naming.bind( )**. However, this call requires that the registry be running as a separate process on the computer. The name of the registry server is **rmiregistry**, and under 32-bit Windows you say:

```
start rmiregistry
```

to start it in the background. On Unix, it is:

```
rmiregistry &
```

Like many network programs, the **rmiregistry** is located at the IP address of whatever machine started it up, but it must also be listening at a port. If you invoke the **rmiregistry** as above, with no argument, the registry's port will default to 1099. If you want it to be at some other port, you add an argument on the command line to specify the port. For this example, the port will be located at 2005, so the **rmiregistry** should be started like this under 32-bit Windows:

```
start rmiregistry 2005
```

or for Unix:

```
rmiregistry 2005 &
```

The information about the port must also be given to the **bind( )** command, as well as the IP address of the machine where the registry is located. But this brings up what can be a frustrating problem if you're expecting to test RMI programs locally the way the network programs have been tested so far in this chapter. In the JDK 1.1.1 release, there are a couple of problems:[7]

1. **localhost** does not work with RMI. Thus, to experiment with RMI on a single machine, you must provide the name of the machine. To find out the name of your machine under 32-bit Windows, go to the control panel and select "Network." Select the "Identification" tab, and you'll see your computer name. In my case, I called my computer "Colossus" (for all the hard disks I've had to put on to hold all the different development systems). It appears that capitalization is ignored.

2. RMI will not work unless your computer has an active TCP/IP connection, even if all your components are just talking to each other on the local machine. This means that you must connect to your Internet service provider before trying to run the program or you'll get some obscure exception messages.

Will all this in mind, the **bind( )** command becomes:

```
Naming.bind("//colossus:2005/PerfectTime", pt);
```

If you are using the default port 1099, you don't need to specify a port, so you could say:

```
Naming.bind("//colossus/PerfectTime", pt);
```

In a future release of the JDK (after 1.1) when the **localhost** bug is fixed, you will be able to perform local testing by leaving off the IP address and using only the identifier:

---

[7] Many brain cells died in agony to discover this information.

```
Naming.bind("PerfectTime", pt);
```

The name for the service is arbitrary; it happens to be PerfectTime here, just like the name of the class, but you could call it anything you want. The important thing is that it's a unique name in the registry that the client knows to look for to procure the remote object. If the name is already in the registry, you'll get an **AlreadyBoundException**. To prevent this, you can always use **rebind( )** instead of **bind( )**, since **rebind( )** either adds a new entry or replaces the one that's already there.

Even though **main( )** exits, your object has been created and registered so it's kept alive by the registry, waiting for a client to come along and request it. As long as the **rmiregistry** is running and you don't call **Naming.unbind( )** on your name, the object will be there. For this reason, when you're developing your code you need to shut down the **rmiregistry** and restart it when you compile a new version of your remote object.

You aren't forced to start up **rmiregistry** as an external process. If you know that your application is the only one that's going to use the registry, you can start it up inside your program with the line:

```
LocateRegistry.createRegistry(2005);
```

Like before, 2005 is the port number we happen to be using in this example. This is the equivalent of running **rmiregistry 2005** from a command line, but it can often be more convenient when you're developing RMI code since it eliminates the extra steps of starting and stopping the registry. Once you've executed this code, you can **bind( )** using **Naming** as before.

Creating stubs and skeletons

If you compile and run **PerfectTime.java**, it won't work even if you have the **rmiregistry** running correctly. That's because the framework for RMI isn't all there yet. You must first create the stubs and skeletons that provide the network connection operations and allow you to pretend that the remote object is just another local object on your machine.

What's going on behind the scenes is complex. Any objects that you pass into or return from a remote object must **implement Serializable** (if you want to pass remote references instead of the entire objects, the object arguments can **implement Remote**), so you can imagine that the stubs and skeletons are automatically performing serialization and deserialization as they "marshal" all of the arguments across the network and return the result. Fortunately, you don't have to know any of this, but you *do* have to create the stubs and skeletons. This is a simple process: you invoke the **rmic** tool on your compiled code, and it creates the necessary files. So the only requirement is that another step be added to your compilation process.

The **rmic** tool is particular about packages and classpaths, however. **PerfectTime.java** is in the package **c15.Ptime**, and even if you invoke **rmic** in the same directory in which **PerfectTime.class** is located, **rmic** won't find the file, since it searches the classpath. So you must specify the location off the class path, like so:

```
rmic c15.PTime.PerfectTime
```

You don't have to be in the directory containing **PerfectTime.class** when you execute this command, but the results will be placed in the current directory.

When **rmic** runs successfully, you'll have two new classes in the directory:

```
PerfectTime_Stub.class
PerfectTime_Skel.class
```

corresponding to the stub and skeleton. Now you're ready to get the server and client to talk to each other.

Using the remote object

The whole point of RMI is to make the use of remote objects simple. The only extra thing that you must do in your client program is to look up and fetch the remote interface from the server. From then on, it's just regular Java programming: sending messages to objects. Here's the program that uses **PerfectTime**:

```java
//: DisplayPerfectTime.java
// Uses remote object PerfectTime
package c15.ptime;
import java.rmi.*;
import java.rmi.registry.*;

public class DisplayPerfectTime {
  public static void main(String[] args) {
    System.setSecurityManager(
      new RMISecurityManager());
    try {
```

```
         PerfectTimeI t =
           (PerfectTimeI)Naming.lookup(
             "//colossus:2005/PerfectTime");
         for(int i = 0; i < 10; i++)
           System.out.println("Perfect time = " +
             t.getPerfectTime());
       } catch(Exception e) {
         e.printStackTrace();
       }
     }
   } ///:~
```

The ID string is the same as the one used to register the object with
Naming, and the first part represents the URL and port number. Since
you're using a URL, you can also specify a machine on the Internet.

What comes back from **Naming.lookup( )** must be cast to the remote
interface, *not* to the class. If you use the class instead, you'll get an
exception.

You can see in the method call

```
    t.getPerfectTime( )
```

that once you have a handle to the remote object, programming with it is
indistinguishable from programming with a local object (with one
difference: remote methods throw **RemoteException**).

Alternatives to RMI

RMI is just one way to create objects that can be distributed across a
network. It has the advantage of being a "pure Java" solution, but if you
have a lot of code written in some other language, it might not meet
your needs. The two most compelling alternatives are Microsoft's DCOM
(which, according to Microsoft's plan, will eventually be hosted on
platforms other than Windows) and CORBA, which is supported in Java
1.1 and was designed from the start to be cross-platform. You can get an
introduction to distributed objects in Java (albeit with a clear bias
towards CORBA) in *Client/Server Programming with Java and CORBA* by
Orfali & Harkey (John Wiley & Sons, 1997). A more serious treatment of
CORBA is given by *Java Programming with CORBA* by Andreas Vogel
and Keith Duddy (John Wiley & Sons, 1997).

Summary

There's actually a lot more to networking than can be covered in this introductory treatment. Java networking also provides fairly extensive support for URLs, including protocol handlers for different types of content that can be discovered at an Internet site.

In addition, an up-and-coming technology is the *Servlet Server*, which is an Internet server that uses Java to handle requests instead of the slow and rather awkward CGI (Common Gateway Interface) protocol. This means that to provide services on the server side you'll be able to write in Java instead of using some other language that you might not know as well. You'll also get the portability benefits of Java so you won't have to worry about the particular platform the server is hosted on.

These and other features are fully and carefully described in *Java Network Programming* by Elliotte Rusty Harold (O'Reilly, 1997).

Exercises

1. Compile and run the **JabberServer** and **JabberClient** programs in this chapter. Now edit the files to remove all of the buffering for the input and output, then compile and run them again to observe the results.

2. Create a server that asks for a password, then opens a file and sends the file over the network connection. Create a client that connects to this server, gives the appropriate password, then captures and saves the file. Test the pair of programs on your machine using the **localhost** (the local loopback IP address **127.0.0.1** produced by calling **InetAddress.getByName(null)**).

3. Modify the server in Exercise 2 so that it uses multithreading to handle multiple clients.

4. Modify **JabberClient** so that output flushing doesn't occur and observe the effect.

5. Build on **ShowHTML.java** to produce an applet that is a password-protected gateway to a particular portion of your Web site.

---

6.   (More challenging) Create a client/server pair of programs that use datagrams to transmit a file from one machine to the other. (See the description at the end of the datagram section of this chapter.)

7.   (More challenging) Take the **VLookup.java** program and modify it so that when you click on the resulting name it automatically takes that name and copies it to the clipboard (so you can simply paste it into your email). You'll need to look back at the IO stream chapter to remember how to use the Java 1.1 clipboard.

16: Design patterns

This chapter introduces the important and yet non-traditional "patterns" approach to program design.

Probably the most important step forward in object-oriented design is the "design patterns" movement, chronicled in *Design Patterns*, by Gamma, Helm, Johnson & Vlissides (Addison-Wesley 1995).[1] That book shows 23 different solutions to particular classes of problems. In this chapter, the basic concepts of design patterns will be introduced along with several examples. This should whet your appetite to read *Design Patterns* (a source of what has now become an essential, almost mandatory, vocabulary for OOP programmers).

---

[1] But be warned: the examples are in C++.

The latter part of this chapter contains an example of the design evolution process, starting with an initial solution and moving through the logic and process of evolving the solution to more appropriate designs. The program shown (a trash sorting simulation) has evolved over time, and you can look at that evolution as a prototype for the way your own design can start as an adequate solution to a particular problem and evolve into a flexible approach to a class of problems.

The pattern concept

Initially, you can think of a pattern as an especially clever and insightful way of solving a particular class of problems. That is, it looks like a lot of people have worked out all the angles of a problem and have come up with the most general, flexible solution for it. The problem could be one you have seen and solved before, but your solution probably didn't have the kind of completeness you'll see embodied in a pattern.

Although they're called "design patterns," they really aren't tied to the realm of design. A pattern seems to stand apart from the traditional way of thinking about analysis, design, and implementation. Instead, a pattern embodies a complete idea within a program, and thus it can sometimes appear at the analysis phase or high-level design phase. This is interesting because a pattern has a direct implementation in code and so you might not expect it to show up before low-level design or implementation (and in fact you might not realize that you need a particular pattern until you get to those phases).

The basic concept of a pattern can also be seen as the basic concept of program design: adding a layer of abstraction. Whenever you abstract something you're isolating particular details, and one of the most compelling motivations behind this is to *separate things that change from things that stay the same*. Another way to put this is that once you find some part of your program that's likely to change for one reason or another, you'll want to keep those changes from propagating other changes throughout your code. Not only does this make the code much cheaper to maintain, but it also turns out that it is usually simpler to understand (which results in lowered costs).

Often, the most difficult part of developing an elegant and cheap-to-maintain design is in discovering what I call "the vector of change." (Here, "vector" refers to the maximum gradient and not a collection class.) This means finding the most important thing that changes in your system, or put another way, discovering where your greatest cost is.

Once you discover the vector of change, you have the focal point around which to structure your design.

So the goal of design patterns is to isolate changes in your code. If you look at it this way, you've been seeing some design patterns already in this book. For example, inheritance can be thought of as a design pattern (albeit one implemented by the compiler). It allows you to express differences in behavior (that's the thing that changes) in objects that all have the same interface (that's what stays the same). Composition can also be considered a pattern, since it allows you to change – dynamically or statically – the objects that implement your class, and thus the way that class works.

You've also already seen another pattern that appears in *Design Patterns*: the *iterator* (Java 1.0 and 1.1 capriciously calls it the **Enumeration**; Java 1.2 collections use "iterator"). This hides the particular implementation of the collection as you're stepping through and selecting the elements one by one. The iterator allows you to write generic code that performs an operation on all of the elements in a sequence without regard to the way that sequence is built. Thus your generic code can be used with any collection that can produce an iterator.

The singleton

Possibly the simplest design pattern is the *singleton*, which is a way to provide one and only one instance of an object. This is used in the Java libraries, but here's a more direct example:

```
//: SingletonPattern.java
// The Singleton design pattern: you can
// never instantiate more than one.
package c16;

// Since this isn't inherited from a Cloneable
// base class and cloneability isn't added,
// making it final prevents cloneability from
// being added in any derived classes:
final class Singleton {
  private static Singleton s = new Singleton(47);
  private int i;
  private Singleton(int x) { i = x; }
  public static Singleton getHandle() {
    return s;
  }
  public int getValue() { return i; }
```

```
      public void setValue(int x) { i = x; }
}

public class SingletonPattern {
  public static void main(String[] args) {
    Singleton s = Singleton.getHandle();
    System.out.println(s.getValue());
    Singleton s2 = Singleton.getHandle();
    s2.setValue(9);
    System.out.println(s.getValue());
    try {
      // Can't do this: compile-time error.
      // Singleton s3 = (Singleton)s2.clone();
    } catch(Exception e) {}
  }
} ///:~
```

The key to creating a singleton is to prevent the client programmer from having any way to create an object except the ways you provide. You must make all constructors **private**, and you must create at least one constructor to prevent the compiler from synthesizing a default constructor for you (which it will create as "friendly").

At this point, you decide how you're going to create your object. Here, it's created statically, but you can also wait until the client programmer asks for one and create it on demand. In any case, the object should be stored privately. You provide access through public methods. Here, **getHandle( )** produces the handle to the **Singleton** object. The rest of the interface (**getValue( )** and **setValue( )**) is the regular class interface.

Java also allows the creation of objects through cloning. In this example, making the class **final** prevents cloning. Since **Singleton** is inherited directly from **Object**, the **clone( )** method remains **protected** so it cannot be used (doing so produces a compile-time error). However, if you're inheriting from a class hierarchy that has already overridden **clone( )** as **public** and implemented **Cloneable**, the way to prevent cloning is to override **clone( )** and throw a **CloneNotSupportedException** as described in Chapter 12. (You could also override **clone( )** and simply return **this**, but that would be deceiving since the client programmer would think they were cloning the object, but would instead still be dealing with the original.)

Note that you aren't restricted to creating only one object. This is also a technique to create a limited pool of objects. In that situation, however, you can be confronted with the problem of sharing objects in the pool. If this is an issue, you can create a solution involving a check-out and check-in of the shared objects.

Classifying patterns

The *Design Patterns* book discusses 23 different patterns, classified under three purposes (all of which revolve around the particular aspect that can vary). The three purposes are:

1. **Creational**: how an object can be created. This often involves isolating the details of object creation so your code isn't dependent on what types of objects there are and thus doesn't have to be changed when you add a new type of object. The aforementioned *Singleton* is classified as a creational pattern, and later in this chapter you'll see examples of *Factory Method* and *Prototype*.

2. **Structural**: designing objects to satisfy particular project constraints. These work with the way objects are connected with other objects to ensure that changes in the system don't require changes to those connections.

3. **Behavioral**: objects that handle particular types of actions within a program. These encapsulate processes that you want to perform, such as interpreting a language, fulfilling a request, moving through a sequence (as in an iterator), or implementing an algorithm. This chapter contains examples of the *Observer* and the *Visitor* patterns.

The *Design Patterns* book has a section on each of its 23 patterns along with one or more examples for each, typically in C++ but sometimes in Smalltalk. (You'll find that this doesn't matter too much since you can easily translate the concepts from either language into Java.) This book will not repeat all the patterns shown in *Design Patterns* since that book stands on its own and should be studied separately. Instead, this chapter will give some examples that should provide you with a decent feel for what patterns are about and why they are so important.

The observer pattern

The observer pattern solves a fairly common problem: What if a group of objects needs to update themselves when some object changes state? This can be seen in the "model-view" aspect of Smalltalk's MVC (model-view-controller), or the almost-equivalent "Document-View Architecture." Suppose that you have some data (the "document") and more than one

---

view, say a plot and a textual view. When you change the data, the two views must know to update themselves, and that's what the observer facilitates. It's a common enough problem that its solution has been made a part of the standard **java.util** library.

There are two types of objects used to implement the observer pattern in Java. The **Observable** class keeps track of everybody who wants to be informed when a change happens, whether the "state" has changed or not. When someone says "OK, everybody should check and potentially update themselves," the **Observable** class performs this task by calling the **notifyObservers( )** method for each one on the list. The **notifyObservers( )** method is part of the base class **Observable**.

There are actually two "things that change" in the observer pattern: the quantity of observing objects and the way an update occurs. That is, the observer pattern allows you to modify both of these without affecting the surrounding code.

The following example is similar to the **ColorBoxes** example from Chapter 14. Boxes are placed in a grid on the screen and each one is initialized to a random color. In addition, each box **implements** the **Observer** interface and is registered with an **Observable** object. When you click on a box, all of the other boxes are notified that a change has been made because the **Observable** object automatically calls each **Observer** object's **update( )** method. Inside this method, the box checks to see if it's adjacent to the one that was clicked, and if so it changes its color to match the clicked box.

```
//: BoxObserver.java
// Demonstration of Observer pattern using
// Java's built-in observer classes.
import java.awt.*;
import java.awt.event.*;
import java.util.*;

// You must inherit a new type of Observable:
class BoxObservable extends Observable {
  public void notifyObservers(Object b) {
    // Otherwise it won't propagate changes:
    setChanged();
    super.notifyObservers(b);
  }
}

public class BoxObserver extends Frame {
```

```
    Observable notifier = new BoxObservable();
    public BoxObserver(int grid) {
      setTitle("Demonstrates Observer pattern");
      setLayout(new GridLayout(grid, grid));
      for(int x = 0; x < grid; x++)
        for(int y = 0; y < grid; y++)
          add(new OCBox(x, y, notifier));
    }
    public static void main(String[] args) {
      int grid = 8;
      if(args.length > 0)
        grid = Integer.parseInt(args[0]);
      Frame f = new BoxObserver(grid);
      f.setSize(500, 400);
      f.setVisible(true);
      f.addWindowListener(
        new WindowAdapter() {
          public void windowClosing(WindowEvent e) {
            System.exit(0);
          }
        });
    }
}

class OCBox extends Canvas implements Observer {
  Observable notifier;
  int x, y; // Locations in grid
  Color cColor = newColor();
  static final Color[] colors = {
    Color.black, Color.blue, Color.cyan,
    Color.darkGray, Color.gray, Color.green,
    Color.lightGray, Color.magenta,
    Color.orange, Color.pink, Color.red,
    Color.white, Color.yellow
  };
  static final Color newColor() {
    return colors[
      (int)(Math.random() * colors.length)
    ];
  }
  OCBox(int x, int y, Observable notifier) {
    this.x = x;
    this.y = y;
    notifier.addObserver(this);
```

```
      this.notifier = notifier;
      addMouseListener(new ML());
    }
    public void paint(Graphics  g) {
      g.setColor(cColor);
      Dimension s = getSize();
      g.fillRect(0, 0, s.width, s.height);
    }
    class ML extends MouseAdapter {
      public void mousePressed(MouseEvent e) {
        notifier.notifyObservers(OCBox.this);
      }
    }
    public void update(Observable o, Object arg) {
      OCBox clicked = (OCBox)arg;
      if(nextTo(clicked)) {
        cColor = clicked.cColor;
        repaint();
      }
    }
    private final boolean nextTo(OCBox b) {
      return Math.abs(x - b.x) <= 1 &&
             Math.abs(y - b.y) <= 1;
    }
} ///:~
```

When you first look at the online documentation for **Observable**, it's a bit confusing because it appears that you can use an ordinary **Observable** object to manage the updates. But this doesn't work; try it – inside **BoxObserver**, create an **Observable** object instead of a **BoxObservable** object and see what happens: nothing. To get an effect, you *must* inherit from **Observable** and somewhere in your derived-class code call **setChanged( )**. This is the method that sets the "changed" flag, which means that when you call **notifyObservers( )** all of the observers will, in fact, get notified. In the example above **setChanged( )** is simply called within **notifyObservers( )**, but you could use any criterion you want to decide when to call **setChanged( )**.

BoxObserver contains a single **Observable** object called **notifier**, and every time an **OCBox** object is created, it is tied to **notifier**. In **OCBox**, whenever you click the mouse the **notifyObservers( )** method is called, passing the clicked object in as an argument so that all the boxes receiving the message (in their **update( )** method) know who was clicked and can decide whether to change themselves or not. Using a combination of code in **notifyObservers( )** and **update( )** you can work out some fairly complex schemes.

It might appear that the way the observers are notified must be frozen at compile time in the **notifyObservers( )** method. However, if you look more closely at the code above you'll see that the only place in **BoxObserver** or **OCBox** where you're aware that you're working with a **BoxObservable** is at the point of creation of the **Observable** object – from then on everything uses the basic **Observable** interface. This means that you could inherit other **Observable** classes and swap them at run-time if you want to change notification behavior then.

Simulating the trash recycler

The nature of this problem is that the trash is thrown unclassified into a single bin, so the specific type information is lost. But later, the specific type information must be recovered to properly sort the trash. In the initial solution, RTTI (described in Chapter 11) is used.

This is not a trivial design because it has an added constraint. That's what makes it interesting – it's more like the messy problems you're likely to encounter in your work. The extra constraint is that the trash arrives at the trash recycling plant all mixed together. The program must model the sorting of that trash. This is where RTTI comes in: you have a bunch of anonymous pieces of trash, and the program figures out exactly what type they are.

```
//: RecycleA.java
// Recycling with RTTI
package c16.recyclea;
import java.util.*;
import java.io.*;

abstract class Trash {
  private double weight;
  Trash(double wt) { weight = wt; }
  abstract double value();
  double weight() { return weight; }
  // Sums the value of Trash in a bin:
  static void sumValue(Vector bin) {
    Enumeration e = bin.elements();
    double val = 0.0f;
    while(e.hasMoreElements()) {
      // One kind of RTTI:
```

```
      // A dynamically-checked cast
      Trash t = (Trash)e.nextElement();
      // Polymorphism in action:
      val += t.weight() * t.value();
      System.out.println(
        "weight of " +
        // Using RTTI to get type
        // information about the class:
        t.getClass().getName() +
        " = " + t.weight());
    }
    System.out.println("Total value = " + val);
  }
}

class Aluminum extends Trash {
  static double val  = 1.67f;
  Aluminum(double wt) { super(wt); }
  double value() { return val; }
  static void value(double newval) {
    val = newval;
  }
}

class Paper extends Trash {
  static double val = 0.10f;
  Paper(double wt) { super(wt); }
  double value() { return val; }
  static void value(double newval) {
    val = newval;
  }
}

class Glass extends Trash {
  static double val = 0.23f;
  Glass(double wt) { super(wt); }
  double value() { return val; }
  static void value(double newval) {
    val = newval;
  }
}

public class RecycleA {
  public static void main(String[] args) {
```

```
    Vector bin = new Vector();
    // Fill up the Trash bin:
    for(int i = 0; i < 30; i++)
      switch((int)(Math.random() * 3)) {
        case 0 :
          bin.addElement(new
            Aluminum(Math.random() * 100));
          break;
        case 1 :
          bin.addElement(new
            Paper(Math.random() * 100));
          break;
        case 2 :
          bin.addElement(new
            Glass(Math.random() * 100));
      }
    Vector
      glassBin = new Vector(),
      paperBin = new Vector(),
      alBin = new Vector();
    Enumeration sorter = bin.elements();
    // Sort the Trash:
    while(sorter.hasMoreElements()) {
      Object t = sorter.nextElement();
      // RTTI to show class membership:
      if(t instanceof Aluminum)
        alBin.addElement(t);
      if(t instanceof Paper)
        paperBin.addElement(t);
      if(t instanceof Glass)
        glassBin.addElement(t);
    }
    Trash.sumValue(alBin);
    Trash.sumValue(paperBin);
    Trash.sumValue(glassBin);
    Trash.sumValue(bin);
  }
} ///:~
```

The first thing you'll notice is the **package** statement:

```
package c16.recyclea;
```

This means that in the source code listings available for the book, this file will be placed in the subdirectory **recyclea** that branches off from the subdirectory **c16** (for Chapter 16). The unpacking tool in Chapter 17 takes care of placing it into the correct subdirectory. The reason for doing this is that this chapter rewrites this particular example a number of times and by putting each version in its own **package** the class names will not clash.

Several **Vector** objects are created to hold **Trash** handles. Of course, **Vector**s actually hold **Object**s so they'll hold anything at all. The reason they hold **Trash** (or something derived from **Trash**) is only because you've been careful to not put in anything except **Trash**. If you do put something "wrong" into the **Vector**, you won't get any compile-time warnings or errors – you'll find out only via an exception at run-time.

When the **Trash** handles are added, they lose their specific identities and become simply **Object** handles (they are *upcast*). However, because of polymorphism the proper behavior still occurs when the dynamically-bound methods are called through the **Enumeration sorter**, once the resulting **Object** has been cast back to **Trash**. **sumValue( )** also uses an **Enumeration** to perform operations on every object in the **Vector**.

It looks silly to upcast the types of **Trash** into a collection holding base type handles, and then turn around and downcast. Why not just put the trash into the appropriate receptacle in the first place? (Indeed, this is the whole enigma of recycling). In this program it would be easy to repair, but sometimes a system's structure and flexibility can benefit greatly from downcasting.

The program satisfies the design requirements: it works. This might be fine as long as it's a one-shot solution. However, a useful program tends to evolve over time, so you must ask, "What if the situation changes?" For example, cardboard is now a valuable recyclable commodity, so how will that be integrated into the system (especially if the program is large and complicated). Since the above type-check coding in the **switch** statement could be scattered throughout the program, you must go find all that code every time a new type is added, and if you miss one the compiler won't give you any help by pointing out an error.

The key to the misuse of RTTI here is that *every type is tested*. If you're looking for only a subset of types because that subset needs special treatment, that's probably fine. But if you're hunting for every type inside a switch statement, then you're probably missing an important point, and definitely making your code less maintainable. In the next section we'll look at how this program evolved over several stages to become much more flexible. This should prove a valuable example in program design.

Improving the design

The solutions in *Design Patterns* are organized around the question "What will change as this program evolves?" This is usually the most important question that you can ask about any design. If you can build your system around the answer, the results will be two-pronged: not only will your system allow easy (and inexpensive) maintenance, but you might also produce components that are reusable, so that other systems can be built more cheaply. This is the promise of object-oriented programming, but it doesn't happen automatically; it requires thought and insight on your part. In this section we'll see how this process can happen during the refinement of a system.

The answer to the question "What will change?" for the recycling system is a common one: more types will be added to the system. The goal of the design, then, is to make this addition of types as painless as possible. In the recycling program, we'd like to encapsulate all places where specific type information is mentioned, so (if for no other reason) any changes can be localized to those encapsulations. It turns out that this process also cleans up the rest of the code considerably.

"Make more objects"

This brings up a general object-oriented design principle that I first heard spoken by Grady Booch: "If the design is too complicated, make more objects." This is simultaneously counterintuitive and ludicrously simple, and yet it's the most useful guideline I've found. (You might observe that "making more objects" is often equivalent to "add another level of indirection.") In general, if you find a place with messy code, consider what sort of class would clean that up. Often the side effect of cleaning up the code will be a system that has better structure and is more flexible.

Consider first the place where **Trash** objects are created, which is a **switch** statement inside **main( )**:

```
for(int i = 0; i < 30; i++)
  switch((int)(Math.random() * 3)) {
    case 0 :
      bin.addElement(new
        Aluminum(Math.random() * 100));
      break;
    case 1 :
```

```
           bin.addElement(new
              Paper(Math.random() * 100));
           break;
        case 2 :
           bin.addElement(new
              Glass(Math.random() * 100));
      }
```

This is definitely messy, and also a place where you must change code whenever a new type is added. If new types are commonly added, a better solution is a single method that takes all of the necessary information and produces a handle to an object of the correct type, already upcast to a trash object. In *Design Patterns* this is broadly referred to as a *creational pattern* (of which there are several). The specific pattern that will be applied here is a variant of the *Factory Method*. Here, the factory method is a **static** member of **Trash**, but more commonly it is a method that is overridden in the derived class.

The idea of the factory method is that you pass it the essential information it needs to know to create your object, then stand back and wait for the handle (already upcast to the base type) to pop out as the return value. From then on, you treat the object polymorphically. Thus, you never even need to know the exact type of object that's created. In fact, the factory method hides it from you to prevent accidental misuse. If you want to use the object without polymorphism, you must explicitly use RTTI and casting.

But there's a little problem, especially when you use the more complicated approach (not shown here) of making the factory method in the base class and overriding it in the derived classes. What if the information required in the derived class requires more or different arguments? "Creating more objects" solves this problem. To implement the factory method, the **Trash** class gets a new method called **factory**. To hide the creational data, there's a new class called **Info** that contains all of the necessary information for the **factory** method to create the appropriate **Trash** object. Here's a simple implementation of **Info**:

```
class Info {
   int type;
   // Must change this to add another type:
   static final int MAX_NUM = 4;
   double data;
   Info(int typeNum, double dat) {
      type = typeNum % MAX_NUM;
      data = dat;
```

```
      }
   }
```

An **Info** object's only job is to hold information for the **factory( )**
method. Now, if there's a situation in which **factory( )** needs more or
different information to create a new type of **Trash** object, the **factory( )**
interface doesn't need to be changed. The **Info** class can be changed by
adding new data and new constructors, or in the more typical object-
oriented fashion of subclassing.

The **factory( )** method for this simple example looks like this:

```
static Trash factory(Info i) {
   switch(i.type) {
      default: // To quiet the compiler
      case 0:
         return new Aluminum(i.data);
      case 1:
         return new Paper(i.data);
      case 2:
         return new Glass(i.data);
      // Two lines here:
      case 3:
         return new Cardboard(i.data);
   }
}
```

Here, the determination of the exact type of object is simple, but you can
imagine a more complicated system in which **factory( )** uses an elaborate
algorithm. The point is that it's now hidden away in one place, and you
know to come to this place when you add new types.

The creation of new objects is now much simpler in **main( )**:

```
for(int i = 0; i < 30; i++)
   bin.addElement(
      Trash.factory(
         new Info(
            (int)(Math.random() * Info.MAX_NUM),
            Math.random() * 100)));
```

An **Info** object is created to pass the data into **factory( )**, which in turn
produces some kind of **Trash** object on the heap and returns the handle
that's added to the **Vector bin**. Of course, if you change the quantity and
type of argument, this statement will still need to be modified, but that
can be eliminated if the creation of the **Info** object is automated. For

example, a **Vector** of arguments can be passed into the constructor of an **Info** object (or directly into a **factory( )** call, for that matter). This requires that the arguments be parsed and checked at runtime, but it does provide the greatest flexibility.

You can see from this code what "vector of change" problem the factory is responsible for solving: if you add new types to the system (the change), the only code that must be modified is within the factory, so the factory isolates the effect of that change.

A pattern for prototyping creation

A problem with the design above is that it still requires a central location where all the types of the objects must be known: inside the **factory( )** method. If new types are regularly being added to the system, the **factory( )** method must be changed for each new type. When you discover something like this, it is useful to try to go one step further and move *all* of the information about the type – including its creation – into the class representing that type. This way, the only thing you need to do to add a new type to the system is to inherit a single class.

To move the information concerning type creation into each specific type of **Trash**, the "prototype" pattern (from the *Design Patterns* book) will be used. The general idea is that you have a master sequence of objects, one of each type you're interested in making. The objects in this sequence are used *only* for making new objects, using an operation that's not unlike the **clone( )** scheme built into Java's root class **Object**. In this case, we'll name the cloning method **tClone( )**. When you're ready to make a new object, presumably you have some sort of information that establishes the type of object you want to create, then you move through the master sequence comparing your information with whatever appropriate information is in the prototype objects in the master sequence. When you find one that matches your needs, you clone it.

In this scheme there is no hard-coded information for creation. Each object knows how to expose appropriate information and how to clone itself. Thus, the **factory( )** method doesn't need to be changed when a new type is added to the system.

One approach to the problem of prototyping is to add a number of methods to support the creation of new objects. However, in Java 1.1 there's already support for creating new objects if you have a handle to the **Class** object. With Java 1.1 *reflection* (introduced in Chapter 11) you can call a constructor even if you have only a handle to the **Class** object. This is the perfect solution for the prototyping problem.

The list of prototypes will be represented indirectly by a list of handles to all the **Class** objects you want to create. In addition, if the prototyping fails, the **factory( )** method will assume that it's because a particular **Class** object wasn't in the list, and it will attempt to load it. By loading the prototypes dynamically like this, the **Trash** class doesn't need to know what types it is working with, so it doesn't need any modifications when you add new types. This allows it to be easily reused throughout the rest of the chapter.

```
//: Trash.java
// Base class for Trash recycling examples
package c16.trash;
import java.util.*;
import java.lang.reflect.*;

public abstract class Trash {
  private double weight;
  Trash(double wt) { weight = wt; }
  Trash() {}
  public abstract double value();
  public double weight() { return weight; }
  // Sums the value of Trash in a bin:
  public static void sumValue(Vector bin) {
    Enumeration e = bin.elements();
    double val = 0.0f;
    while(e.hasMoreElements()) {
      // One kind of RTTI:
      // A dynamically-checked cast
      Trash t = (Trash)e.nextElement();
      val += t.weight() * t.value();
      System.out.println(
        "weight of " +
        // Using RTTI to get type
        // information about the class:
        t.getClass().getName() +
        " = " + t.weight());
    }
    System.out.println("Total value = " + val);
  }
  // Remainder of class provides support for
  // prototyping:
  public static class PrototypeNotFoundException
      extends Exception {}
  public static class CannotCreateTrashException
      extends Exception {}
```

```
private static Vector trashTypes =
  new Vector();
public static Trash factory(Info info)
    throws PrototypeNotFoundException,
    CannotCreateTrashException {
  for(int i = 0; i < trashTypes.size(); i++) {
    // Somehow determine the new type
    // to create, and create one:
    Class tc =
      (Class)trashTypes.elementAt(i);
    if (tc.getName().indexOf(info.id) != -1) {
      try {
        // Get the dynamic constructor method
        // that takes a double argument:
        Constructor ctor =
          tc.getConstructor(
            new Class[] {double.class});
        // Call the constructor to create a
        // new object:
        return (Trash)ctor.newInstance(
          new Object[]{new Double(info.data)});
      } catch(Exception ex) {
        ex.printStackTrace();
        throw new CannotCreateTrashException();
      }
    }
  }
  // Class was not in the list. Try to load it,
  // but it must be in your class path!
  try {
    System.out.println("Loading " + info.id);
    trashTypes.addElement(
      Class.forName(info.id));
  } catch(Exception e) {
    e.printStackTrace();
    throw new PrototypeNotFoundException();
  }
  // Loaded successfully. Recursive call
  // should work this time:
  return factory(info);
}
public static class Info {
  public String id;
  public double data;
```

```
        public Info(String name, double data) {
          id = name;
          this.data = data;
        }
      }
    } ///:~
```

The basic **Trash** class and **sumValue( )** remain as before. The rest of the class supports the prototyping pattern. You first see two inner classes (which are made **static**, so they are inner classes only for code organization purposes) describing exceptions that can occur. This is followed by a **Vector trashTypes**, which is used to hold the **Class** handles.

In **Trash.factory( )**, the **String** inside the **Info** object **id** (a different version of the **Info** class than that of the prior discussion) contains the type name of the **Trash** to be created; this **String** is compared to the **Class** names in the list. If there's a match, then that's the object to create. Of course, there are many ways to determine what object you want to make. This one is used so that information read in from a file can be turned into objects.

Once you've discovered which kind of **Trash** to create, then the reflection methods come into play. The **getConstructor( )** method takes an argument that's an array of **Class** handles. This array represents the arguments, in their proper order, for the constructor that you're looking for. Here, the array is dynamically created using the Java 1.1 array-creation syntax:

```
new Class[] {double.class}
```

This code assumes that every **Trash** type has a constructor that takes a **double** (and notice that **double.class** is distinct from **Double.class**). It's also possible, for a more flexible solution, to call **getConstructors( )**, which returns an array of the possible constructors.

What comes back from **getConstructor( )** is a handle to a **Constructor** object (part of **java.lang.reflect**). You call the constructor dynamically with the method **newInstance( )**, which takes an array of **Object** containing the actual arguments. This array is again created using the Java 1.1 syntax:

```
new Object[]{new Double(info.data)}
```

In this case, however, the **double** must be placed inside a wrapper class so that it can be part of this array of objects. The process of calling

newInstance( ) extracts the **double**, but you can see it is a bit confusing – an argument might be a **double** or a **Double**, but when you make the call you must always pass in a **Double**. Fortunately, this issue exists only for the primitive types.

Once you understand how to do it, the process of creating a new object given only a **Class** handle is remarkably simple. Reflection also allows you to call methods in this same dynamic fashion.

Of course, the appropriate **Class** handle might not be in the **trashTypes** list. In this case, the **return** in the inner loop is never executed and you'll drop out at the end. Here, the program tries to rectify the situation by loading the **Class** object dynamically and adding it to the **trashTypes** list. If it still can't be found something is really wrong, but if the load is successful then the **factory** method is called recursively to try again.

As you'll see, the beauty of this design is that this code doesn't need to be changed, regardless of the different situations it will be used in (assuming that all **Trash** subclasses contain a constructor that takes a single **double** argument).

Trash subclasses

To fit into the prototyping scheme, the only thing that's required of each new subclass of **Trash** is that it contain a constructor that takes a **double** argument. Java 1.1 reflection handles everything else.

Here are the different types of **Trash**, each in their own file but part of the **Trash** package (again, to facilitate reuse within the chapter):

```
//: Aluminum.java
// The Aluminum class with prototyping
package c16.trash;

public class Aluminum extends Trash {
   private static double val = 1.67f;
   public Aluminum(double wt) { super(wt); }
   public double value() { return val; }
   public static void value(double newVal) {
      val = newVal;
   }
} ///:~

//: Paper.java
// The Paper class with prototyping
package c16.trash;
```

```
public class Paper extends Trash {
  private static double val = 0.10f;
  public Paper(double wt) { super(wt); }
  public double value() { return val; }
  public static void value(double newVal) {
    val = newVal;
  }
} ///:~
```

```
//: Glass.java
// The Glass class with prototyping
package c16.trash;

public class Glass extends Trash {
  private static double val = 0.23f;
  public Glass(double wt) { super(wt); }
  public double value() { return val; }
  public static void value(double newVal) {
    val = newVal;
  }
} ///:~
```

And here's a new type of **Trash**:

```
//: Cardboard.java
// The Cardboard class with prototyping
package c16.trash;

public class Cardboard extends Trash {
  private static double val = 0.23f;
  public Cardboard(double wt) { super(wt); }
  public double value() { return val; }
  public static void value(double newVal) {
    val = newVal;
  }
} ///:~
```

You can see that, other than the constructor, there's nothing special about any of these classes.

Parsing **Trash** from an external file

The information about **Trash** objects will be read from an outside file. The file has all of the necessary information about each piece of trash on a single line in the form **Trash:weight**, such as:

```
c16.Trash.Glass:54
c16.Trash.Paper:22
c16.Trash.Paper:11
c16.Trash.Glass:17
c16.Trash.Aluminum:89
c16.Trash.Paper:88
c16.Trash.Aluminum:76
c16.Trash.Cardboard:96
c16.Trash.Aluminum:25
c16.Trash.Aluminum:34
c16.Trash.Glass:11
c16.Trash.Glass:68
c16.Trash.Glass:43
c16.Trash.Aluminum:27
c16.Trash.Cardboard:44
c16.Trash.Aluminum:18
c16.Trash.Paper:91
c16.Trash.Glass:63
c16.Trash.Glass:50
c16.Trash.Glass:80
c16.Trash.Aluminum:81
c16.Trash.Cardboard:12
c16.Trash.Glass:12
c16.Trash.Glass:54
c16.Trash.Aluminum:36
c16.Trash.Aluminum:93
c16.Trash.Glass:93
c16.Trash.Paper:80
c16.Trash.Glass:36
c16.Trash.Glass:12
c16.Trash.Glass:60
c16.Trash.Paper:66
c16.Trash.Aluminum:36
c16.Trash.Cardboard:22
```

Note that the class path must be included when giving the class names, otherwise the class will not be found.

To parse this, the line is read and the **String** method **indexOf( )** produces the index of the ':'. This is first used with the **String** method **substring( )** to extract the name of the trash type, and next to get the weight that is turned into a **double** with the **static Double.valueOf( )** method. The **trim( )** method removes white space at both ends of a string.

The **Trash** parser is placed in a separate file since it will be reused throughout this chapter:

```
//: ParseTrash.java
// Open a file and parse its contents into
// Trash objects, placing each into a Vector
package c16.trash;
import java.util.*;
import java.io.*;

public class ParseTrash {
  public static void
  fillBin(String filename, Fillable bin) {
    try {
      BufferedReader data =
        new BufferedReader(
          new FileReader(filename));
      String buf;
      while((buf = data.readLine()) != null) {
        String type = buf.substring(0,
          buf.indexOf(':')).trim();
        double weight = Double.valueOf(
          buf.substring(buf.indexOf(':') + 1)
          .trim()).doubleValue();
        bin.addTrash(
          Trash.factory(
            new Trash.Info(type, weight)));
      }
      data.close();
    } catch(IOException e) {
      e.printStackTrace();
    } catch(Exception e) {
      e.printStackTrace();
    }
  }
  // Special case to handle Vector:
  public static void
  fillBin(String filename, Vector bin) {
    fillBin(filename, new FillableVector(bin));
```

```
    }
} ///:~
```

In **RecycleA.java**, a **Vector** was used to hold the **Trash** objects. However, other types of collections can be used as well. To allow for this, the first version of **fillBin( )** takes a handle to a **Fillable**, which is simply an **interface** that supports a method called **addTrash( )**:

```
//: Fillable.java
// Any object that can be filled with Trash
package c16.trash;

public interface Fillable {
   void addTrash(Trash t);
} ///:~
```

Anything that supports this interface can be used with **fillBin**. Of course, **Vector** doesn't implement **Fillable**, so it won't work. Since **Vector** is used in most of the examples, it makes sense to add a second overloaded **fillBin( )** method that takes a **Vector**. The **Vector** can be used as a **Fillable** object using an adapter class:

```
//: FillableVector.java
// Adapter that makes a Vector Fillable
package c16.trash;
import java.util.*;

public class FillableVector implements Fillable {
   private Vector v;
   public FillableVector(Vector vv) { v = vv; }
   public void addTrash(Trash t) {
      v.addElement(t);
   }
} ///:~
```

You can see that the only job of this class is to connect **Fillable**'s **addTrash( )** method to **Vector**'s **addElement( )**. With this class in hand, the overloaded **fillBin( )** method can be used with a **Vector** in **ParseTrash.java**:

```
public static void
fillBin(String filename, Vector bin) {
   fillBin(filename, new FillableVector(bin));
}
```

This approach works for any collection class that's used frequently. Alternatively, the collection class can provide its own adapter that implements **Fillable**. (You'll see this later, in **DynaTrash.java**.)

Recycling with prototyping

Now you can see the revised version of **RecycleA.java** using the prototyping technique:

```
//: RecycleAP.java
// Recycling with RTTI and Prototypes
package c16.recycleap;
import c16.trash.*;
import java.util.*;

public class RecycleAP {
  public static void main(String[] args) {
    Vector bin = new Vector();
    // Fill up the Trash bin:
    ParseTrash.fillBin("Trash.dat", bin);
    Vector
      glassBin = new Vector(),
      paperBin = new Vector(),
      alBin = new Vector();
    Enumeration sorter = bin.elements();
    // Sort the Trash:
    while(sorter.hasMoreElements()) {
      Object t = sorter.nextElement();
      // RTTI to show class membership:
      if(t instanceof Aluminum)
        alBin.addElement(t);
      if(t instanceof Paper)
        paperBin.addElement(t);
      if(t instanceof Glass)
        glassBin.addElement(t);
    }
    Trash.sumValue(alBin);
    Trash.sumValue(paperBin);
    Trash.sumValue(glassBin);
    Trash.sumValue(bin);
  }
} ///:~
```

All of the **Trash** objects, as well as the **ParseTrash** and support classes, are now part of the package **c16.trash** so they are simply imported.

The process of opening the data file containing **Trash** descriptions and the parsing of that file have been wrapped into the **static** method **ParseTrash.fillBin( )**, so now it's no longer a part of our design focus. You will see that throughout the rest of the chapter, no matter what new classes are added, **ParseTrash.fillBin( )** will continue to work without change, which indicates a good design.

In terms of object creation, this design does indeed severely localize the changes you need to make to add a new type to the system. However, there's a significant problem in the use of RTTI that shows up clearly here. The program seems to run fine, and yet it never detects any cardboard, even though there is cardboard in the list! This happens *because* of the use of RTTI, which looks for only the types that you tell it to look for. The clue that RTTI is being misused is that *every type in the system* is being tested, rather than a single type or subset of types. As you will see later, there are ways to use polymorphism instead when you're testing for every type. But if you use RTTI a lot in this fashion, and you add a new type to your system, you can easily forget to make the necessary changes in your program and produce a difficult-to-find bug. So it's worth trying to eliminate RTTI in this case, not just for aesthetic reasons – it produces more maintainable code.

Abstracting usage

With creation out of the way, it's time to tackle the remainder of the design: where the classes are used. Since it's the act of sorting into bins that's particularly ugly and exposed, why not take that process and hide it inside a class? This is the principle of "If you must do something ugly, at least localize the ugliness inside a class." It looks like this:

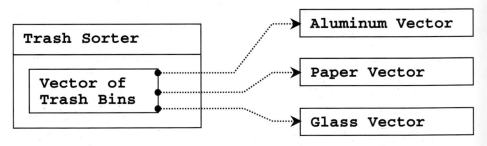

The **TrashSorter** object initialization must now be changed whenever a new type of **Trash** is added to the model. You could imagine that the **TrashSorter** class might look something like this:

```
class TrashSorter extends Vector {
   void sort(Trash t) { /* ... */ }
}
```

That is, **TrashSorter** is a **Vector** of handles to **Vectors** of **Trash** handles, and with **addElement( )** you can install another one, like so:

```
TrashSorter ts = new TrashSorter();
ts.addElement(new Vector());
```

Now, however, **sort( )** becomes a problem. How does the statically-coded method deal with the fact that a new type has been added? To solve this, the type information must be removed from **sort( )** so that all it needs to do is call a generic method that takes care of the details of type. This, of course, is another way to describe a dynamically-bound method. So **sort( )** will simply move through the sequence and call a dynamically-bound method for each **Vector**. Since the job of this method is to grab the pieces of trash it is interested in, it's called **grab(Trash)**. The structure now looks like:

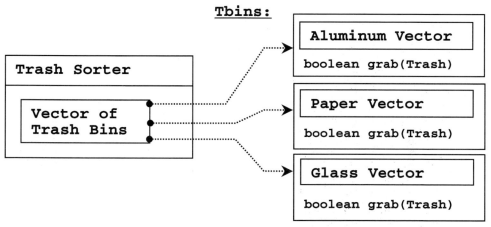

TrashSorter needs to call each **grab( )** method and get a different result depending on what type of **Trash** the current **Vector** is holding. That is, each **Vector** must be aware of the type it holds. The classic approach to this problem is to create a base "Trash bin" class and inherit a new derived class for each different type you want to hold. If Java had a parameterized type mechanism that would probably be the most straightforward approach. But rather than hand-coding all the classes that such a mechanism should be building for us, further observation can produce a better approach.

A basic OOP design principle is "Use data members for variation in state, use polymorphism for variation in behavior." Your first thought might be that the **grab( )** method certainly behaves differently for a **Vector** that holds **Paper** than for one that holds **Glass**. But what it does is strictly dependent on the type, and nothing else. This could be interpreted as a different state, and since Java has a class to represent type (**Class**) this can be used to determine the type of **Trash** a particular **Tbin** will hold.

The constructor for this **Tbin** requires that you hand it the **Class** of your choice. This tells the **Vector** what type it is supposed to hold. Then the **grab( )** method uses **Class BinType** and RTTI to see if the **Trash** object you've handed it matches the type it's supposed to grab.

Here is the whole program. The commented numbers (e.g. (*1*)) mark sections that will be described following the code.

```java
//: RecycleB.java
// Adding more objects to the recycling problem
package c16.recycleb;
import c16.trash.*;
import java.util.*;

// A vector that admits only the right type:
class Tbin extends Vector {
  Class binType;
  Tbin(Class binType) {
    this.binType = binType;
  }
  boolean grab(Trash t) {
    // Comparing class types:
    if(t.getClass().equals(binType)) {
      addElement(t);
      return true; // Object grabbed
    }
    return false; // Object not grabbed
  }
}

class TbinList extends Vector { //(*1*)
  boolean sort(Trash t) {
    Enumeration e = elements();
    while(e.hasMoreElements()) {
      Tbin bin = (Tbin)e.nextElement();
      if(bin.grab(t)) return true;
    }
```

```
          return false; // bin not found for t
        }
      void sortBin(Tbin bin) { // (*2*)
        Enumeration e = bin.elements();
        while(e.hasMoreElements())
          if(!sort((Trash)e.nextElement()))
            System.out.println("Bin not found");
      }
    }

    public class RecycleB {
      static Tbin bin = new Tbin(Trash.class);
      public static void main(String[] args) {
        // Fill up the Trash bin:
        ParseTrash.fillBin("Trash.dat", bin);

        TbinList trashBins = new TbinList();
        trashBins.addElement(
          new Tbin(Aluminum.class));
        trashBins.addElement(
          new Tbin(Paper.class));
        trashBins.addElement(
          new Tbin(Glass.class));
        // add one line here: (*3*)
        trashBins.addElement(
          new Tbin(Cardboard.class));

        trashBins.sortBin(bin); // (*4*)

        Enumeration e = trashBins.elements();
        while(e.hasMoreElements()) {
          Tbin b = (Tbin)e.nextElement();
          Trash.sumValue(b);
        }
        Trash.sumValue(bin);
      }
    } ///:~
```

1. **TbinList** holds a set of **Tbin** handles, so that **sort( )** can iterate
   through the **Tbin**s when it's looking for a match for the **Trash** object
   you've handed it.

2. **sortBin( )** allows you to pass an entire **Tbin** in, and it moves through
   the **Tbin**, picks out each piece of **Trash**, and sorts it into the
   appropriate specific **Tbin**. Notice the genericity of this code: it doesn't

---

change at all if new types are added. If the bulk of your code doesn't need changing when a new type is added (or some other change occurs) then you have an easily-extensible system.

3. Now you can see how easy it is to add a new type. Few lines must be changed to support the addition. If it's really important, you can squeeze out even more by further manipulating the design.

4. One method call causes the contents of **bin** to be sorted into the respective specifically-typed bins.

Multiple dispatching

The above design is certainly satisfactory. Adding new types to the system consists of adding or modifying distinct classes without causing code changes to be propagated throughout the system. In addition, RTTI is not "misused" as it was in **RecycleA.java**. However, it's possible to go one step further and take a purist viewpoint about RTTI and say that it should be eliminated altogether from the operation of sorting the trash into bins.

To accomplish this, you must first take the perspective that all type-dependent activities – such as detecting the type of a piece of trash and putting it into the appropriate bin – should be controlled through polymorphism and dynamic binding.

The previous examples first sorted by type, then acted on sequences of elements that were all of a particular type. But whenever you find yourself picking out particular types, stop and think. The whole idea of polymorphism (dynamically-bound method calls) is to handle type-specific information for you. So why are you hunting for types?

The answer is something you probably don't think about: Java performs only single dispatching. That is, if you are performing an operation on more than one object whose type is unknown, Java will invoke the dynamic binding mechanism on only one of those types. This doesn't solve the problem, so you end up detecting some types manually and effectively producing your own dynamic binding behavior.

The solution is called *multiple dispatching*, which means setting up a configuration such that a single method call produces more than one dynamic method call and thus determines more than one type in the process. To get this effect, you need to work with more than one type hierarchy: you'll need a type hierarchy for each dispatch. The following example works with two hierarchies: the existing **Trash** family and a hierarchy of the types of trash bins that the trash will be placed into. This second hierarchy isn't always obvious and in this case it needed to be created in order to produce multiple dispatching (in this case there will be only two dispatches, which is referred to as *double dispatching*).

Implementing the double dispatch

Remember that polymorphism can occur only via method calls, so if you want double dispatching to occur, there must be two method calls: one used to determine the type within each hierarchy. In the **Trash** hierarchy there will be a new method called **addToBin( )**, which takes an argument of an array of **TypedBin**. It uses this array to step through and try to add itself to the appropriate bin, and this is where you'll see the double dispatch.

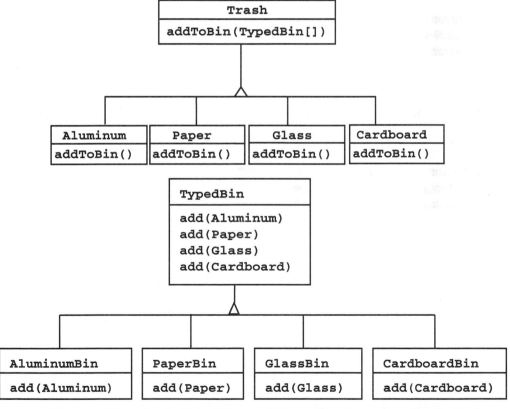

The new hierarchy is **TypedBin**, and it contains its own method called **add( )** that is also used polymorphically. But here's an additional twist: **add( )** is *overloaded* to take arguments of the different types of trash. So

---

an essential part of the double dispatching scheme also involves overloading.

Redesigning the program produces a dilemma: it's now necessary for the base class **Trash** to contain an **addToBin( )** method. One approach is to copy all of the code and change the base class. Another approach, which you can take when you don't have control of the source code, is to put the **addToBin( )** method into an **interface**, leave **Trash** alone, and inherit new specific types of **Aluminum**, **Paper**, **Glass**, and **Cardboard**. This is the approach that will be taken here.

Most of the classes in this design must be **public**, so they are placed in their own files. Here's the interface:

```
//: TypedBinMember.java
// An interface for adding the double dispatching
// method to the trash hierarchy without
// modifying the original hierarchy.
package c16.doubledispatch;

interface TypedBinMember {
  // The new method:
  boolean addToBin(TypedBin[] tb);
} ///:~
```

In each particular subtype of **Aluminum**, **Paper**, **Glass**, and **Cardboard**, the **addToBin( )** method in the **interface TypedBinMember** is implemented,, but it *looks* like the code is exactly the same in each case:

```
//: DDAluminum.java
// Aluminum for double dispatching
package c16.doubledispatch;
import c16.trash.*;

public class DDAluminum extends Aluminum
    implements TypedBinMember {
  public DDAluminum(double wt) { super(wt); }
  public boolean addToBin(TypedBin[] tb) {
    for(int i = 0; i < tb.length; i++)
      if(tb[i].add(this))
        return true;
    return false;
  }
} ///:~

//: DDPaper.java
```

```
    // Paper for double dispatching
    package c16.doubledispatch;
    import c16.trash.*;

    public class DDPaper extends Paper
        implements TypedBinMember {
      public DDPaper(double wt) { super(wt); }
      public boolean addToBin(TypedBin[] tb) {
        for(int i = 0; i < tb.length; i++)
          if(tb[i].add(this))
            return true;
        return false;
      }
    } ///:~

    //: DDGlass.java
    // Glass for double dispatching
    package c16.doubledispatch;
    import c16.trash.*;

    public class DDGlass extends Glass
        implements TypedBinMember {
      public DDGlass(double wt) { super(wt); }
      public boolean addToBin(TypedBin[] tb) {
        for(int i = 0; i < tb.length; i++)
          if(tb[i].add(this))
            return true;
        return false;
      }
    } ///:~

    //: DDCardboard.java
    // Cardboard for double dispatching
    package c16.doubledispatch;
    import c16.trash.*;

    public class DDCardboard extends Cardboard
        implements TypedBinMember {
      public DDCardboard(double wt) { super(wt); }
      public boolean addToBin(TypedBin[] tb) {
        for(int i = 0; i < tb.length; i++)
          if(tb[i].add(this))
            return true;
        return false;
      }
    }
```

```
} ///:~
```

The code in each **addToBin( )** calls **add( )** for each **TypedBin** object in the array. But notice the argument: **this**. The type of **this** is different for each subclass of **Trash**, so the code is different. (Although this code will benefit if a parameterized type mechanism is ever added to Java.) So this is the first part of the double dispatch, because once you're inside this method you know you're **Aluminum**, or **Paper**, etc. During the call to **add( )**, this information is passed via the type of **this**. The compiler resolves the call to the proper overloaded version of **add( )**. But since **tb[i]** produces a handle to the base type **TypedBin**, this call will end up calling a different method depending on the type of **TypedBin** that's currently selected. That is the second dispatch.

Here's the base class for **TypedBin**:

```
//: TypedBin.java
// Vector that knows how to grab the right type
package c16.doubledispatch;
import c16.trash.*;
import java.util.*;

public abstract class TypedBin {
  Vector v = new Vector();
  protected boolean addIt(Trash t) {
    v.addElement(t);
    return true;
  }
  public Enumeration elements() {
    return v.elements();
  }
  public boolean add(DDAluminum a) {
    return false;
  }
  public boolean add(DDPaper a) {
    return false;
  }
  public boolean add(DDGlass a) {
    return false;
  }
  public boolean add(DDCardboard a) {
    return false;
  }
} ///:~
```

You can see that the overloaded **add( )** methods all return **false**. If the method is not overloaded in a derived class, it will continue to return **false**, and the caller (**addToBin( )**, in this case) will assume that the current **Trash** object has not been added successfully to a collection, and continue searching for the right collection.

In each of the subclasses of **TypedBin**, only one overloaded method is overridden, according to the type of bin that's being created. For example, **CardboardBin** overrides **add(DDCardboard)**. The overridden method adds the trash object to its collection and returns **true**, while all the rest of the **add( )** methods in **CardboardBin** continue to return **false**, since they haven't been overridden. This is another case in which a parameterized type mechanism in Java would allow automatic generation of code. (With C++ **templates**, you wouldn't have to explicitly write the subclasses or place the **addToBin( )** method in **Trash**.)

Since for this example the trash types have been customized and placed in a different directory, you'll need a different trash data file to make it work. Here's a possible **DDTrash.dat**:

```
c16.DoubleDispatch.DDGlass:54
c16.DoubleDispatch.DDPaper:22
c16.DoubleDispatch.DDPaper:11
c16.DoubleDispatch.DDGlass:17
c16.DoubleDispatch.DDAluminum:89
c16.DoubleDispatch.DDPaper:88
c16.DoubleDispatch.DDAluminum:76
c16.DoubleDispatch.DDCardboard:96
c16.DoubleDispatch.DDAluminum:25
c16.DoubleDispatch.DDAluminum:34
c16.DoubleDispatch.DDGlass:11
c16.DoubleDispatch.DDGlass:68
c16.DoubleDispatch.DDGlass:43
c16.DoubleDispatch.DDAluminum:27
c16.DoubleDispatch.DDCardboard:44
c16.DoubleDispatch.DDAluminum:18
c16.DoubleDispatch.DDPaper:91
c16.DoubleDispatch.DDGlass:63
c16.DoubleDispatch.DDGlass:50
c16.DoubleDispatch.DDGlass:80
c16.DoubleDispatch.DDAluminum:81
c16.DoubleDispatch.DDCardboard:12
c16.DoubleDispatch.DDGlass:12
c16.DoubleDispatch.DDGlass:54
c16.DoubleDispatch.DDAluminum:36
```

```
c16.DoubleDispatch.DDAluminum:93
c16.DoubleDispatch.DDGlass:93
c16.DoubleDispatch.DDPaper:80
c16.DoubleDispatch.DDGlass:36
c16.DoubleDispatch.DDGlass:12
c16.DoubleDispatch.DDGlass:60
c16.DoubleDispatch.DDPaper:66
c16.DoubleDispatch.DDAluminum:36
c16.DoubleDispatch.DDCardboard:22
```

Here's the rest of the program:

```
//: DoubleDispatch.java
// Using multiple dispatching to handle more
// than one unknown type during a method call.
package c16.doubledispatch;
import c16.trash.*;
import java.util.*;

class AluminumBin extends TypedBin {
  public boolean add(DDAluminum a) {
    return addIt(a);
  }
}

class PaperBin extends TypedBin {
  public boolean add(DDPaper a) {
    return addIt(a);
  }
}

class GlassBin extends TypedBin {
  public boolean add(DDGlass a) {
    return addIt(a);
  }
}

class CardboardBin extends TypedBin {
  public boolean add(DDCardboard a) {
    return addIt(a);
  }
}

class TrashBinSet {
  private TypedBin[] binSet = {
```

```
          new AluminumBin(),
          new PaperBin(),
          new GlassBin(),
          new CardboardBin()
      };
    public void sortIntoBins(Vector bin) {
      Enumeration e = bin.elements();
      while(e.hasMoreElements()) {
        TypedBinMember t =
          (TypedBinMember)e.nextElement();
        if(!t.addToBin(binSet))
          System.err.println("Couldn't add " + t);
      }
    }
    public TypedBin[] binSet() { return binSet; }
}

public class DoubleDispatch {
    public static void main(String[] args) {
      Vector bin = new Vector();
      TrashBinSet bins = new TrashBinSet();
      // ParseTrash still works, without changes:
      ParseTrash.fillBin("DDTrash.dat", bin);
      // Sort from the master bin into the
      // individually-typed bins:
      bins.sortIntoBins(bin);
      TypedBin[] tb = bins.binSet();
      // Perform sumValue for each bin...
      for(int i = 0; i < tb.length; i++)
        Trash.sumValue(tb[i].v);
      // ... and for the master bin
      Trash.sumValue(bin);
    }
} ///:~
```

TrashBinSet encapsulates all of the different types of **TypedBins**, along with the **sortIntoBins( )** method, which is where all the double dispatching takes place. You can see that once the structure is set up, sorting into the various **TypedBins** is remarkably easy. In addition, the efficiency of two dynamic method calls is probably better than any other way you could sort.

Notice the ease of use of this system in **main( )**, as well as the complete independence of any specific type information within **main( )**. All other methods that talk only to the **Trash** base-class interface will be equally invulnerable to changes in **Trash** types.

The changes necessary to add a new type are relatively isolated: you inherit the new type of **Trash** with its **addToBin( )** method, then you inherit a new **TypedBin** (this is really just a copy and simple edit), and finally you add a new type into the aggregate initialization for **TrashBinSet**.

The "visitor" pattern

Now consider applying a design pattern with an entirely different goal to the trash-sorting problem.

For this pattern, we are no longer concerned with optimizing the addition of new types of **Trash** to the system. Indeed, this pattern makes adding a new type of **Trash** *more* complicated. The assumption is that you have a primary class hierarchy that is fixed; perhaps it's from another vendor and you can't make changes to that hierarchy. However, you'd like to add new polymorphic methods to that hierarchy, which means that normally you'd have to add something to the base class interface. So the dilemma is that you need to add methods to the base class, but you can't touch the base class. How do you get around this?

The design pattern that solves this kind of problem is called a "visitor" (the final one in the *Design Patterns* book), and it builds on the double dispatching scheme shown in the last section.

The visitor pattern allows you to extend the interface of the primary type by creating a separate class hierarchy of type **Visitor** to virtualize the operations performed upon the primary type. The objects of the primary type simply "accept" the visitor, then call the visitor's dynamically-bound method. It looks like this:

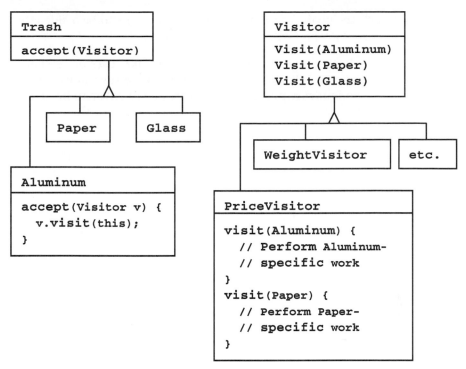

Now, if **v** is a **Visitable** handle to an **Aluminum** object, the code:

```
PriceVisitor pv = new PriceVisitor();
v.accept(pv);
```

causes two polymorphic method calls: the first one to select **Aluminum**'s version of **accept( )**, and the second one within **accept( )** when the specific version of **visit( )** is called dynamically using the base-class **Visitor** handle **v**.

This configuration means that new functionality can be added to the system in the form of new subclasses of **Visitor**. The **Trash** hierarchy doesn't need to be touched. This is the prime benefit of the visitor pattern: you can add new polymorphic functionality to a class hierarchy without touching that hierarchy (once the **accept( )** methods have been installed). Note that the benefit is helpful here but not exactly what we started out to accomplish, so at first blush you might decide that this isn't the desired solution.

But look at one thing that's been accomplished: the visitor solution avoids sorting from the master **Trash** sequence into individual typed sequences. Thus, you can leave everything in the single master sequence and simply pass through that sequence using the appropriate visitor to accomplish the goal. Although this behavior seems to be a side effect of visitor, it does give us what we want (avoiding RTTI).

The double dispatching in the visitor pattern takes care of determining both the type of **Trash** and the type of **Visitor**. In the following example, there are two implementations of **Visitor**: **PriceVisitor** to both determine and sum the price, and **WeightVisitor** to keep track of the weights.

You can see all of this implemented in the new, improved version of the recycling program. As with **DoubleDispatch.java**, the **Trash** class is left alone and a new interface is created to add the **accept( )** method:

```
//: Visitable.java
// An interface to add visitor functionality to
// the Trash hierarchy without modifying the
// base class.
package c16.trashvisitor;
import c16.trash.*;

interface Visitable {
  // The new method:
  void accept(Visitor v);
} ///:~
```

The subtypes of **Aluminum**, **Paper**, **Glass**, and **Cardboard** implement the **accept( )** method:

```
//: VAluminum.java
// Aluminum for the visitor pattern
package c16.trashvisitor;
import c16.trash.*;

public class VAluminum extends Aluminum
    implements Visitable {
  public VAluminum(double wt) { super(wt); }
  public void accept(Visitor v) {
    v.visit(this);
  }
} ///:~

//: VPaper.java
// Paper for the visitor pattern
package c16.trashvisitor;
import c16.trash.*;

public class VPaper extends Paper
```

```
        implements Visitable {
    public VPaper(double wt) { super(wt); }
    public void accept(Visitor v) {
      v.visit(this);
    }
} ///:~

//: VGlass.java
// Glass for the visitor pattern
package c16.trashvisitor;
import c16.trash.*;

public class VGlass extends Glass
        implements Visitable {
    public VGlass(double wt) { super(wt); }
    public void accept(Visitor v) {
      v.visit(this);
    }
} ///:~

//: VCardboard.java
// Cardboard for the visitor pattern
package c16.trashvisitor;
import c16.trash.*;

public class VCardboard extends Cardboard
        implements Visitable {
    public VCardboard(double wt) { super(wt); }
    public void accept(Visitor v) {
      v.visit(this);
    }
} ///:~
```

Since there's nothing concrete in the **Visitor** base class, it can be created as an **interface**:

```
//: Visitor.java
// The base interface for visitors
package c16.trashvisitor;
import c16.trash.*;

interface Visitor {
    void visit(VAluminum a);
    void visit(VPaper p);
    void visit(VGlass g);
```

```
    void visit(VCardboard c);
} ///:~
```

Once again custom **Trash** types have been created in a different
subdirectory. The new **Trash** data file is **VTrash.dat** and looks like this:

```
c16.TrashVisitor.VGlass:54
c16.TrashVisitor.VPaper:22
c16.TrashVisitor.VPaper:11
c16.TrashVisitor.VGlass:17
c16.TrashVisitor.VAluminum:89
c16.TrashVisitor.VPaper:88
c16.TrashVisitor.VAluminum:76
c16.TrashVisitor.VCardboard:96
c16.TrashVisitor.VAluminum:25
c16.TrashVisitor.VAluminum:34
c16.TrashVisitor.VGlass:11
c16.TrashVisitor.VGlass:68
c16.TrashVisitor.VGlass:43
c16.TrashVisitor.VAluminum:27
c16.TrashVisitor.VCardboard:44
c16.TrashVisitor.VAluminum:18
c16.TrashVisitor.VPaper:91
c16.TrashVisitor.VGlass:63
c16.TrashVisitor.VGlass:50
c16.TrashVisitor.VGlass:80
c16.TrashVisitor.VAluminum:81
c16.TrashVisitor.VCardboard:12
c16.TrashVisitor.VGlass:12
c16.TrashVisitor.VGlass:54
c16.TrashVisitor.VAluminum:36
c16.TrashVisitor.VAluminum:93
c16.TrashVisitor.VGlass:93
c16.TrashVisitor.VPaper:80
c16.TrashVisitor.VGlass:36
c16.TrashVisitor.VGlass:12
c16.TrashVisitor.VGlass:60
c16.TrashVisitor.VPaper:66
c16.TrashVisitor.VAluminum:36
c16.TrashVisitor.VCardboard:22
```

The rest of the program creates specific **Visitor** types and sends them
through a single list of **Trash** objects:

```
//: TrashVisitor.java
```

```
// The "visitor" pattern
package c16.trashvisitor;
import c16.trash.*;
import java.util.*;

// Specific group of algorithms packaged
// in each implementation of Visitor:
class PriceVisitor implements Visitor {
  private double alSum; // Aluminum
  private double pSum;  // Paper
  private double gSum;  // Glass
  private double cSum;  // Cardboard
  public void visit(VAluminum al) {
    double v = al.weight() * al.value();
    System.out.println(
      "value of Aluminum= " + v);
    alSum += v;
  }
  public void visit(VPaper p) {
    double v = p.weight() * p.value();
    System.out.println(
      "value of Paper= " + v);
    pSum += v;
  }
  public void visit(VGlass g) {
    double v = g.weight() * g.value();
    System.out.println(
      "value of Glass= " + v);
    gSum += v;
  }
  public void visit(VCardboard c) {
    double v = c.weight() * c.value();
    System.out.println(
      "value of Cardboard = " + v);
    cSum += v;
  }
  void total() {
    System.out.println(
      "Total Aluminum: $" + alSum + "\n" +
      "Total Paper: $" + pSum + "\n" +
      "Total Glass: $" + gSum + "\n" +
      "Total Cardboard: $" + cSum);
  }
}
```

```java
class WeightVisitor implements Visitor {
  private double alSum; // Aluminum
  private double pSum; // Paper
  private double gSum; // Glass
  private double cSum; // Cardboard
  public void visit(VAluminum al) {
    alSum += al.weight();
    System.out.println("weight of Aluminum = "
        + al.weight());
  }
  public void visit(VPaper p) {
    pSum += p.weight();
    System.out.println("weight of Paper = "
        + p.weight());
  }
  public void visit(VGlass g) {
    gSum += g.weight();
    System.out.println("weight of Glass = "
        + g.weight());
  }
  public void visit(VCardboard c) {
    cSum += c.weight();
    System.out.println("weight of Cardboard = "
        + c.weight());
  }
  void total() {
    System.out.println("Total weight Aluminum:"
        + alSum);
    System.out.println("Total weight Paper:"
        + pSum);
    System.out.println("Total weight Glass:"
        + gSum);
    System.out.println("Total weight Cardboard:"
        + cSum);
  }
}

public class TrashVisitor {
  public static void main(String[] args) {
    Vector bin = new Vector();
    // ParseTrash still works, without changes:
    ParseTrash.fillBin("VTrash.dat", bin);
    // You could even iterate through
```

```
      // a list of visitors!
      PriceVisitor pv = new PriceVisitor();
      WeightVisitor wv = new WeightVisitor();
      Enumeration it = bin.elements();
      while(it.hasMoreElements()) {
        Visitable v = (Visitable)it.nextElement();
        v.accept(pv);
        v.accept(wv);
      }
      pv.total();
      wv.total();
    }
} ///:~
```

Note that the shape of **main( )** has changed again. Now there's only a single **Trash** bin. The two **Visitor** objects are accepted into every element in the sequence, and they perform their operations. The visitors keep their own internal data to tally the total weights and prices.

Finally, there's no run-time type identification other than the inevitable cast to **Trash** when pulling things out of the sequence. This, too, could be eliminated with the implementation of parameterized types in Java.

One way you can distinguish this solution from the double dispatching solution described previously is to note that, in the double dispatching solution, only one of the overloaded methods, **add( )**, was overridden when each subclass was created, while here *each* one of the overloaded **visit( )** methods is overridden in every subclass of **Visitor**.

More coupling?

There's a lot more code here, and there's definite coupling between the **Trash** hierarchy and the **Visitor** hierarchy. However, there's also high cohesion within the respective sets of classes: they each do only one thing (**Trash** describes Trash, while **Visitor** describes actions performed on **Trash**), which is an indicator of a good design. Of course, in this case it works well only if you're adding new **Visitor**s, but it gets in the way when you add new types of **Trash**.

Low coupling between classes and high cohesion within a class is definitely an important design goal. Applied mindlessly, though, it can prevent you from achieving a more elegant design. It seems that some classes inevitably have a certain intimacy with each other. These often occur in pairs that could perhaps be called *couplets*, for example, collections and iterators (**Enumeration**s). The **Trash-Visitor** pair above appears to be another such couplet.

RTTI considered harmful?

Various designs in this chapter attempt to remove RTTI, which might give you the impression that it's "considered harmful" (the condemnation used for poor, ill-fated **goto**, which was thus never put into Java). This isn't true; it is the *misuse* of RTTI that is the problem. The reason our designs removed RTTI is because the misapplication of that feature prevented extensibility, while the stated goal was to be able to add a new type to the system with as little impact on surrounding code as possible. Since RTTI is often misused by having it look for every single type in your system, it causes code to be non-extensible: when you add a new type, you have to go hunting for all the code in which RTTI is used, and if you miss any you won't get help from the compiler.

However, RTTI doesn't automatically create non-extensible code. Let's revisit the trash recycler once more. This time, a new tool will be introduced, which I call a **TypeMap**. It contains a **Hashtable** that holds **Vector**s, but the interface is simple: you can **add( )** a new object, and you can **get( )** a **Vector** containing all the objects of a particular type. The keys for the contained **Hashtable** are the types in the associated **Vector**. The beauty of this design (suggested by Larry O'Brien) is that the **TypeMap** dynamically adds a new pair whenever it encounters a new type, so whenever you add a new type to the system (even if you add the new type at run-time), it adapts.

Our example will again build on the structure of the **Trash** types in **package c16.Trash** (and the **Trash.dat** file used there can be used here without change):

```
//: DynaTrash.java
// Using a Hashtable of Vectors and RTTI
// to automatically sort trash into
// vectors. This solution, despite the
// use of RTTI, is extensible.
package c16.dynatrash;
import c16.trash.*;
import java.util.*;

// Generic TypeMap works in any situation:
class TypeMap {
  private Hashtable t = new Hashtable();
```

```
    public void add(Object o) {
      Class type = o.getClass();
      if(t.containsKey(type))
        ((Vector)t.get(type)).addElement(o);
      else {
        Vector v = new Vector();
        v.addElement(o);
        t.put(type,v);
      }
    }
    public Vector get(Class type) {
      return (Vector)t.get(type);
    }
    public Enumeration keys() { return t.keys(); }
    // Returns handle to adapter class to allow
    // callbacks from ParseTrash.fillBin():
    public Fillable filler() {
      // Anonymous inner class:
      return new Fillable() {
        public void addTrash(Trash t) { add(t); }
      };
    }
  }

  public class DynaTrash {
    public static void main(String[] args) {
      TypeMap bin = new TypeMap();
      ParseTrash.fillBin("Trash.dat",bin.filler());
      Enumeration keys = bin.keys();
      while(keys.hasMoreElements())
        Trash.sumValue(
          bin.get((Class)keys.nextElement()));
    }
  } ///:~
```

Although powerful, the definition for **TypeMap** is simple. It contains a
Hashtable, and the **add( )** method does most of the work. When you
add( ) a new object, the handle for the **Class** object for that type is
extracted. This is used as a key to determine whether a **Vector** holding
objects of that type is already present in the **Hashtable**. If so, that **Vector**
is extracted and the object is added to the **Vector**. If not, the **Class** object
and a new **Vector** are added as a key-value pair.

You can get an **Enumeration** of all the **Class** objects from **keys( )**, and use each **Class** object to fetch the corresponding **Vector** with **get( )**. And that's all there is to it.

The **filler( )** method is interesting because it takes advantage of the design of **ParseTrash.fillBin( )**, which doesn't just try to fill a **Vector** but instead anything that implements the **Fillable** interface with its **addTrash( )** method. All **filler( )** needs to do is to return a handle to an **interface** that implements **Fillable**, and then this handle can be used as an argument to **fillBin( )** like this:

```
ParseTrash.fillBin("Trash.dat", bin.filler());
```

To produce this handle, an *anonymous inner class* (described in Chapter 7) is used. You never need a named class to implement **Fillable**, you just need a handle to an object of that class, thus this is an appropriate use of anonymous inner classes.

An interesting thing about this design is that even though it wasn't created to handle the sorting, **fillBin( )** is performing a sort every time it inserts a **Trash** object into **bin**.

Much of **class DynaTrash** should be familiar from the previous examples. This time, instead of placing the new **Trash** objects into a **bin** of type **Vector**, the **bin** is of type **TypeMap**, so when the trash is thrown into **bin** it's immediately sorted by **TypeMap**'s internal sorting mechanism. Stepping through the **TypeMap** and operating on each individual **Vector** becomes a simple matter:

```
Enumeration keys = bin.keys();
while(keys.hasMoreElements())
  Trash.sumValue(
     bin.get((Class)keys.nextElement()));
```

As you can see, adding a new type to the system won't affect this code at all, nor the code in **TypeMap**. This is certainly the smallest solution to the problem, and arguably the most elegant as well. It does rely heavily on RTTI, but notice that each key-value pair in the **Hashtable** is looking for only one type. In addition, there's no way you can "forget" to add the proper code to this system when you add a new type, since there isn't any code you need to add.

Summary

Coming up with a design such as **TrashVisitor.java** that contains a larger amount of code than the earlier designs can seem at first to be counterproductive. It pays to notice what you're trying to accomplish with various designs. Design patterns in general strive to *separate the things that change from the things that stay the same*. The "things that change" can refer to many different kinds of changes. Perhaps the change occurs because the program is placed into a new environment or because something in the current environment changes (this could be: "The user wants to add a new shape to the diagram currently on the screen"). Or, as in this case, the change could be the evolution of the code body. While previous versions of the trash-sorting example emphasized the addition of new *types* of **Trash** to the system, **TrashVisitor.java** allows you to easily add new *functionality* without disturbing the **Trash** hierarchy. There's more code in **TrashVisitor.java**, but adding new functionality to **Visitor** is cheap. If this is something that happens a lot, then it's worth the extra effort and code to make it happen more easily.

The discovery of the vector of change is no trivial matter; it's not something that an analyst can usually detect before the program sees its initial design. The necessary information will probably not appear until later phases in the project: sometimes only at the design or implementation phases do you discover a deeper or more subtle need in your system. In the case of adding new types (which was the focus of most of the "recycle" examples) you might realize that you need a particular inheritance hierarchy only when you are in the maintenance phase and you begin extending the system!

One of the most important things that you'll learn by studying design patterns seems to be an about-face from what has been promoted so far in this book. That is: "OOP is all about polymorphism." This statement can produce the "two-year-old with a hammer" syndrome (everything looks like a nail). Put another way, it's hard enough to "get" polymorphism, and once you do, you try to cast all your designs into that one particular mold.

What design patterns say is that OOP isn't just about polymorphism. It's about "separating the things that change from the things that stay the same." Polymorphism is an especially important way to do this, and it turns out to be helpful if the programming language directly supports polymorphism (so you don't have to wire it in yourself, which would tend to make it prohibitively expensive). But design patterns in general

---

show *other* ways to accomplish the basic goal, and once your eyes have been opened to this you will begin to search for more creative designs.

Since the *Design Patterns* book came out and made such an impact, people have been searching for other patterns. You can expect to see more of these appear as time goes on. Here are some sites recommended by Jim Coplien, of C++ fame (*http://www.bell-labs.com/~cope*), who is one of the main proponents of the patterns movement:

http://st-www.cs.uiuc.edu/users/patterns
http://c2.com/cgi/wiki
http://c2.com/ppr
http://www.bell-labs.com/people/cope/Patterns/Process/index.html
http://www.bell-labs.com/cgi-user/OrgPatterns/OrgPatterns
http://st-www.cs.uiuc.edu/cgi-bin/wikic/wikic
http://www.cs.wustl.edu/~schmidt/patterns.html
http://www.espinc.com/patterns/overview.html

Also note there has been a yearly conference on design patterns, called PLOP, that produces a published proceedings, the third of which came out in late 1997 (all published by Addison-Wesley).

Exercises

1. Using **SingletonPattern.java** as a starting point, create a class that manages a fixed number of its own objects.

2. Add a class Plastic to TrashVisitor.java.

3. Add a class Plastic to DynaTrash.java.

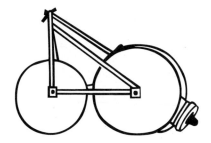

17: Projects

This chapter includes a set of projects that build on the material presented in this book or otherwise didn't fit in earlier chapters.

Most of these projects are significantly more complex than the examples in the rest of the book, and they often demonstrate new techniques and uses of class libraries.

Text processing

If you come from a C or C++ background, you might be skeptical at first of Java's power when it comes to handling text. Indeed, one drawback is that execution speed is slower and that could hinder some of your efforts. However, the tools (in particular the **String** class) are quite powerful, as the examples in this section show (and performance improvements have been promised for Java).

As you'll see, these examples were created to solve problems that arose in the creation of this book. However, they are not restricted to that and the solutions they offer can easily be adapted to other situations. In addition, they show the power of Java in an area that has not previously been emphasized in this book.

Extracting code listings

You've no doubt noticed that each complete code listing (not code fragment) in this book begins and ends with special comment tag marks '//:' and '///:~'. This meta-information is included so that the code can be automatically extracted from the book into compilable source-code files. In my previous book, I had a system that allowed me to automatically incorporate tested code files into the book. In this book, however, I discovered that it was often easier to paste the code into the book once it was initially tested and, since it's hard to get right the first time, to perform edits to the code within the book. But how to extract it and test the code? This program is the answer, and it could come in handy when you set out to solve a text processing problem. It also demonstrates many of the **String** class features.

I first save the entire book in ASCII text format into a separate file. The **CodePackager** program has two modes (which you can see described in **usageString**): if you use the **-p** flag, it expects to see an input file containing the ASCII text from the book. It will go through this file and use the comment tag marks to extract the code, and it uses the file name on the first line to determine the name of the file. In addition, it looks for the **package** statement in case it needs to put the file into a special directory (chosen via the path indicated by the **package** statement).

But that's not all. It also watches for the change in chapters by keeping track of the package names. Since all packages for each chapter begin with **c02**, **c03**, **c04**, etc. to indicate the chapter where they belong (except for those beginning with **com**, which are ignored for the purpose of keeping track of chapters), as long as the first listing in each chapter contains a **package** statement with the chapter number, the **CodePackager** program can keep track of when the chapter changed and put all the subsequent files in the new chapter subdirectory.

As each file is extracted, it is placed into a **SourceCodeFile** object that is then placed into a collection. (This process will be more thoroughly described later.) These **SourceCodeFile** objects could simply be stored in files, but that brings us to the second use for this project. If you invoke **CodePackager** *without* the **-p** flag it expects a "packed" file as input, which it will then extract into separate files. So the **-p** flag means that the extracted files will be found "packed" into this single file.

Why bother with the packed file? Because different computer platforms have different ways of storing text information in files. A big issue is the end-of-line character or characters, but other issues can also exist. However, Java has a special type of IO stream – the **DataOutputStream** – which promises that, regardless of what machine the data is coming from, the storage of that data will be in a form that can be correctly retrieved by any other machine by using a **DataInputStream**. That is, Java handles all of the platform-specific details, which is a large part of the promise of Java. So the **-p** flag stores everything into a single file in a universal format. You download this file and the Java program from the Web, and when you run **CodePackager** on this file *without* the -p flag the files will all be extracted to appropriate places on your system. (You can specify an alternate subdirectory; otherwise the subdirectories will just be created in the current directory.) To ensure that no system-specific formats remain, **File** objects are used everywhere a path or a file is described. In addition, there's a sanity check: an empty file is placed in each subdirectory; the name of that file indicates how many files you should find in that subdirectory.

Here is the code, which will be described in detail at the end of the listing:

```
//: CodePackager.java
// "Packs" and "unpacks" the code in "Thinking
// in Java" for cross-platform distribution.
/* Commented so CodePackager sees it and starts
    a new chapter directory, but so you don't
    have to worry about the directory where this
    program lives:
package c17;
*/
import java.util.*;
import java.io.*;

class Pr {
  static void error(String e) {
    System.err.println("ERROR: " + e);
    System.exit(1);
  }
}

class IO {
  static BufferedReader disOpen(File f) {
    BufferedReader in = null;
    try {
      in = new BufferedReader(
```

```java
          new FileReader(f));
    } catch(IOException e) {
      Pr.error("could not open " + f);
    }
    return in;
  }
  static BufferedReader disOpen(String fname) {
    return disOpen(new File(fname));
  }
  static DataOutputStream dosOpen(File f) {
    DataOutputStream in = null;
    try {
      in = new DataOutputStream(
        new BufferedOutputStream(
          new FileOutputStream(f)));
    } catch(IOException e) {
      Pr.error("could not open " + f);
    }
    return in;
  }
  static DataOutputStream dosOpen(String fname) {
    return dosOpen(new File(fname));
  }
  static PrintWriter psOpen(File f) {
    PrintWriter in = null;
    try {
      in = new PrintWriter(
        new BufferedWriter(
          new FileWriter(f)));
    } catch(IOException e) {
      Pr.error("could not open " + f);
    }
    return in;
  }
  static PrintWriter psOpen(String fname) {
    return psOpen(new File(fname));
  }
  static void close(Writer os) {
    try {
      os.close();
    } catch(IOException e) {
      Pr.error("closing " + os);
    }
  }
}
```

```
    static void close(DataOutputStream os) {
      try {
        os.close();
      } catch(IOException e) {
        Pr.error("closing " + os);
      }
    }
    static void close(Reader os) {
      try {
        os.close();
      } catch(IOException e) {
        Pr.error("closing " + os);
      }
    }
}

class SourceCodeFile {
  public static final String
    startMarker = "//:", // Start of source file
    endMarker = "} ///:~", // End of source
    endMarker2 = "}; ///:~", // C++ file end
    beginContinue = "} ///:Continued",
    endContinue = "///:Continuing",
    packMarker = "###", // Packed file header tag
    eol = // Line separator on current system
      System.getProperty("line.separator"),
    filesep = // System's file path separator
      System.getProperty("file.separator");
  public static String copyright = "";
  static {
    try {
      BufferedReader cr =
        new BufferedReader(
          new FileReader("Copyright.txt"));
      String crin;
      while((crin = cr.readLine()) != null)
        copyright += crin + "\n";
      cr.close();
    } catch(Exception e) {
      copyright = "";
    }
  }
  private String filename, dirname,
    contents = new String();
```

```java
private static String chapter = "c02";
// The file name separator from the old system:
public static String oldsep;
public String toString() {
  return dirname + filesep + filename;
}
// Constructor for parsing from document file:
public SourceCodeFile(String firstLine,
    BufferedReader in) {
  dirname = chapter;
  // Skip past marker:
  filename = firstLine.substring(
      startMarker.length()).trim();
  // Find space that terminates file name:
  if(filename.indexOf(' ') != -1)
    filename = filename.substring(
        0, filename.indexOf(' '));
  System.out.println("found: " + filename);
  contents = firstLine + eol;
  if(copyright.length() != 0)
    contents += copyright + eol;
  String s;
  boolean foundEndMarker = false;
  try {
    while((s = in.readLine()) != null) {
      if(s.startsWith(startMarker))
        Pr.error("No end of file marker for " +
          filename);
      // For this program, no spaces before
      // the "package" keyword are allowed
      // in the input source code:
      else if(s.startsWith("package")) {
        // Extract package name:
        String pdir = s.substring(
          s.indexOf(' ')).trim();
        pdir = pdir.substring(
          0, pdir.indexOf(';')).trim();
        // Capture the chapter from the package
        // ignoring the 'com' subdirectories:
        if(!pdir.startsWith("com")) {
          int firstDot = pdir.indexOf('.');
          if(firstDot != -1)
            chapter =
              pdir.substring(0,firstDot);
```

```
        else
          chapter = pdir;
      }
      // Convert package name to path name:
      pdir = pdir.replace(
        '.', filesep.charAt(0));
      System.out.println("package " + pdir);
      dirname = pdir;
    }
    contents += s + eol;
    // Move past continuations:
    if(s.startsWith(beginContinue))
      while((s = in.readLine()) != null)
        if(s.startsWith(endContinue)) {
          contents += s + eol;
          break;
        }
    // Watch for end of code listing:
    if(s.startsWith(endMarker) ||
       s.startsWith(endMarker2)) {
      foundEndMarker = true;
      break;
    }
  }
  if(!foundEndMarker)
    Pr.error(
      "End marker not found before EOF");
  System.out.println("Chapter: " + chapter);
} catch(IOException e) {
  Pr.error("Error reading line");
}
}
// For recovering from a packed file:
public SourceCodeFile(BufferedReader pFile) {
  try {
    String s = pFile.readLine();
    if(s == null) return;
    if(!s.startsWith(packMarker))
      Pr.error("Can't find " + packMarker
        + " in " + s);
    s = s.substring(
      packMarker.length()).trim();
    dirname = s.substring(0, s.indexOf('#'));
    filename = s.substring(s.indexOf('#') + 1);
```

```java
      dirname = dirname.replace(
        oldsep.charAt(0), filesep.charAt(0));
      filename = filename.replace(
        oldsep.charAt(0), filesep.charAt(0));
      System.out.println("listing: " + dirname
        + filesep + filename);
      while((s = pFile.readLine()) != null) {
        // Watch for end of code listing:
        if(s.startsWith(endMarker) ||
           s.startsWith(endMarker2)) {
          contents += s;
          break;
        }
        contents += s + eol;
      }
    } catch(IOException e) {
      System.err.println("Error reading line");
    }
  }
  public boolean hasFile() {
    return filename != null;
  }
  public String directory() { return dirname; }
  public String filename() { return filename; }
  public String contents() { return contents; }
  // To write to a packed file:
  public void writePacked(DataOutputStream out) {
    try {
      out.writeBytes(
        packMarker + dirname + "#"
        + filename + eol);
      out.writeBytes(contents);
    } catch(IOException e) {
      Pr.error("writing " + dirname +
        filesep + filename);
    }
  }
  // To generate the actual file:
  public void writeFile(String rootpath) {
    File path = new File(rootpath, dirname);
    path.mkdirs();
    PrintWriter p =
      IO.psOpen(new File(path, filename));
    p.print(contents);
```

```
        IO.close(p);
    }
}

class DirMap {
  private Hashtable t = new Hashtable();
  private String rootpath;
  DirMap() {
    rootpath = System.getProperty("user.dir");
  }
  DirMap(String alternateDir) {
    rootpath = alternateDir;
  }
  public void add(SourceCodeFile f){
    String path = f.directory();
    if(!t.containsKey(path))
      t.put(path, new Vector());
    ((Vector)t.get(path)).addElement(f);
  }
  public void writePackedFile(String fname) {
    DataOutputStream packed = IO.dosOpen(fname);
    try {
      packed.writeBytes("###Old Separator:" +
        SourceCodeFile.filesep + "###\n");
    } catch(IOException e) {
      Pr.error("Writing separator to " + fname);
    }
    Enumeration e = t.keys();
    while(e.hasMoreElements()) {
      String dir = (String)e.nextElement();
      System.out.println(
        "Writing directory " + dir);
      Vector v = (Vector)t.get(dir);
      for(int i = 0; i < v.size(); i++) {
        SourceCodeFile f =
          (SourceCodeFile)v.elementAt(i);
        f.writePacked(packed);
      }
    }
    IO.close(packed);
  }
  // Write all the files in their directories:
  public void write() {
    Enumeration e = t.keys();
```

```
      while(e.hasMoreElements()) {
        String dir = (String)e.nextElement();
        Vector v = (Vector)t.get(dir);
        for(int i = 0; i < v.size(); i++) {
          SourceCodeFile f =
            (SourceCodeFile)v.elementAt(i);
          f.writeFile(rootpath);
        }
        // Add file indicating file quantity
        // written to this directory as a check:
        IO.close(IO.dosOpen(
          new File(new File(rootpath, dir),
            Integer.toString(v.size())+".files")));
      }
    }
}

public class CodePackager {
  private static final String usageString =
  "usage: java CodePackager packedFileName" +
  "\nExtracts source code files from packed \n" +
  "version of Tjava.doc sources into " +
  "directories off current directory\n" +
  "java CodePackager packedFileName newDir\n" +
  "Extracts into directories off newDir\n" +
  "java CodePackager -p source.txt packedFile" +
  "\nCreates packed version of source files" +
  "\nfrom text version of Tjava.doc";
  private static void usage() {
    System.err.println(usageString);
    System.exit(1);
  }
  public static void main(String[] args) {
    if(args.length == 0) usage();
    if(args[0].equals("-p")) {
      if(args.length != 3)
        usage();
      createPackedFile(args);
    }
    else {
      if(args.length > 2)
        usage();
      extractPackedFile(args);
    }
```

```
      }
    private static String currentLine;
    private static BufferedReader in;
    private static DirMap dm;
    private static void
    createPackedFile(String[] args) {
      dm = new DirMap();
      in = IO.disOpen(args[1]);
      try {
        while((currentLine = in.readLine())
            != null) {
          if(currentLine.startsWith(
              SourceCodeFile.startMarker)) {
            dm.add(new SourceCodeFile(
                    currentLine, in));
          }
          else if(currentLine.startsWith(
              SourceCodeFile.endMarker))
            Pr.error("file has no start marker");
          // Else ignore the input line
        }
      } catch(IOException e) {
        Pr.error("Error reading " + args[1]);
      }
      IO.close(in);
      dm.writePackedFile(args[2]);
    }
    private static void
    extractPackedFile(String[] args) {
      if(args.length == 2) // Alternate directory
        dm = new DirMap(args[1]);
      else // Current directory
        dm = new DirMap();
      in = IO.disOpen(args[0]);
      String s = null;
      try {
         s = in.readLine();
      } catch(IOException e) {
        Pr.error("Cannot read from " + in);
      }
      // Capture the separator used in the system
      // that packed the file:
      if(s.indexOf("###Old Separator:") != -1 ) {
        String oldsep = s.substring(
```

```
        "###Old Separator:".length());
    oldsep = oldsep.substring(
      0, oldsep. indexOf('#'));
    SourceCodeFile.oldsep = oldsep;
  }
  SourceCodeFile sf = new SourceCodeFile(in);
  while(sf.hasFile()) {
    dm.add(sf);
    sf = new SourceCodeFile(in);
  }
  dm.write();
  }
} ///:~
```

You'll first notice the **package** statement that is commented out. Since this is the first program in the chapter, the **package** statement is necessary to tell **CodePackager** that the chapter has changed, but putting it in a package would be a problem. When you create a **package**, you tie the resulting program to a particular directory structure, which is fine for most of the examples in this book. Here, however, the **CodePackager** program must be compiled and run from an arbitrary directory, so the **package** statement is commented out. It will still *look* like an ordinary **package** statement to **CodePackager**, though, since the program isn't sophisticated enough to detect multi-line comments. (It has no need for such sophistication, a fact that comes in handy here.)

The first two classes are support/utility classes designed to make the rest of the program more consistent to write and easier to read. The first, **Pr**, is similar to the ANSI C library **perror**, since it prints an error message (but also exits the program). The second class encapsulates the creation of files, a process that was shown in Chapter 10 as one that rapidly becomes verbose and annoying. In Chapter 10, the proposed solution created new classes, but here **static** method calls are used. Within those methods the appropriate exceptions are caught and dealt with. These methods make the rest of the code much cleaner to read.

The first class that helps solve the problem is **SourceCodeFile**, which represents all the information (including the contents, file name, and directory) for one source code file in the book. It also contains a set of **String** constants representing the markers that start and end a file, a marker used inside the packed file, the current system's end-of-line separator and file path separator (notice the use of **System.getProperty( )** to get the local version), and a copyright notice, which is extracted from the following file **Copyright.txt**.

```
///////////////////////////////////////////////
// Copyright (c) Bruce Eckel, 1998
// Source code file from the book "Thinking in Java"
// All rights reserved EXCEPT as allowed by the
// following statements: You may freely use this file
// for your own work (personal or commercial),
// including modifications and distribution in
// executable form only. Permission is granted to use
// this file in classroom situations, including its
// use in presentation materials, as long as the book
// "Thinking in Java" is cited as the source.
// Except in classroom situations, you may not copy
// and distribute this code; instead, the sole
// distribution point is http://www.BruceEckel.com
// (and official mirror sites) where it is
// freely available. You may not remove this
// copyright and notice. You may not distribute
// modified versions of the source code in this
// package. You may not use this file in printed
// media without the express permission of the
// author. Bruce Eckel makes no representation about
// the suitability of this software for any purpose.
// It is provided "as is" without express or implied
// warranty of any kind, including any implied
// warranty of merchantability, fitness for a
// particular purpose or non-infringement. The entire
// risk as to the quality and performance of the
// software is with you. Bruce Eckel and the
// publisher shall not be liable for any damages
// suffered by you or any third party as a result of
// using or distributing software. In no event will
// Bruce Eckel or the publisher be liable for any
// lost revenue, profit, or data, or for direct,
// indirect, special, consequential, incidental, or
// punitive damages, however caused and regardless of
// the theory of liability, arising out of the use of
// or inability to use software, even if Bruce Eckel
// and the publisher have been advised of the
// possibility of such damages. Should the software
// prove defective, you assume the cost of all
// necessary servicing, repair, or correction. If you
// think you've found an error, please email all
// modified files with clearly commented changes to:
// Bruce@EckelObjects.com. (please use the same
```

```
// address for non-code errors found in the book).
/////////////////////////////////////////////////
```

When extracting files from a packed file, the file separator of the system that packed the file is also noted, so it can be replaced with the correct one for the local system.

The subdirectory name for the current chapter is kept in the field **chapter**, which is initialized to **c02**. (You'll notice that the listing in Chapter 2 doesn't contain a package statement.) The only time that the **chapter** field changes is when a **package** statement is discovered in the current file.

Building a packed file

The first constructor is used to extract a file from the ASCII text version of this book. The calling code (which appears further down in the listing) reads each line in until it finds one that matches the beginning of a listing. At that point, it creates a new **SourceCodeFile** object, passing it the first line (which has already been read by the calling code) and the **BufferedReader** object from which to extract the rest of the source code listing.

At this point, you begin to see heavy use of the **String** methods. To extract the file name, the overloaded version of **substring( )** is called that takes the starting offset and goes to the end of the **String**. This starting index is produced by finding the **length( )** of the **startMarker**. **trim( )** removes white space from both ends of the **String**. The first line can also have words after the name of the file; these are detected using **indexOf( )**, which returns –1 if it cannot find the character you're looking for and the value where the first instance of that character is found if it does. Notice there is also an overloaded version of **indexOf( )** that takes a **String** instead of a character.

Once the file name is parsed and stored, the first line is placed into the **contents String** (which is used to hold the entire text of the source code listing). At this point, the rest of the lines are read and concatenated into the **contents String**. It's not quite that simple, since certain situations require special handling. One case is error checking: if you run into a **startMarker**, it means that no end marker was placed at the end of the listing that's currently being collected. This is an error condition that aborts the program.

The second special case is the **package** keyword. Although Java is a free-form language, this program requires that the **package** keyword be at the beginning of the line. When the **package** keyword is seen, the package name is extracted by looking for the space at the beginning and the semicolon at the end. (Note that this could also have been performed in a single operation by using the overloaded **substring( )** that takes both the starting and ending indexes.) Then the dots in the package name are replaced by the file separator, although an assumption is made here that the file separator is only one character long. This is probably true on all systems, but it's a place to look if there are problems.

The default behavior is to concatenate each line to **contents**, along with the end-of-line string, until the **endMarker** is discovered, which indicates that the constructor should terminate. If the end of the file is encountered before the **endMarker** is seen, that's an error.

Extracting from a packed file

The second constructor is used to recover the source code files from a packed file. Here, the calling method doesn't have to worry about skipping over the intermediate text. The file contains all the source-code files, placed end-to-end. All you need to hand to this constructor is the **BufferedReader** where the information is coming from, and the constructor takes it from there. There is some meta-information, however, at the beginning of each listing, and this is denoted by the **packMarker**. If the **packMarker** isn't there, it means the caller is mistakenly trying to use this constructor where it isn't appropriate.

Once the **packMarker** is found, it is stripped off and the directory name (terminated by a '**#**') and the file name (which goes to the end of the line) are extracted. In both cases, the old separator character is replaced by the one that is current to this machine using the **String replace( )** method. The old separator is placed at the beginning of the packed file, and you'll see how that is extracted later in the listing.

The rest of the constructor is quite simple. It reads and concatenates each line to the **contents** until the **endMarker** is found.

Accessing and writing the listings

The next set of methods are simple accessors: **directory( )**, **filename( )** (notice the method can have the same spelling and capitalization as the field) and **contents( )**, and **hasFile( )** to indicate whether this object contains a file or not. (The need for this will be seen later.)

The final three methods are concerned with writing this code listing into a file, either a packed file via **writePacked( )** or a Java source file via **writeFile( )**. All **writePacked( )** needs is the **DataOutputStream**, which was opened elsewhere, and represents the file that's being written. It puts the header information on the first line and then calls **writeBytes( )** to write **contents** in a "universal" format.

When writing the Java source file, the file must be created. This is done via **IO.psOpen( )**, handing it a **File** object that contains not only the file name but also the path. But the question now is: does this path exist? The user has the option of placing all the source code directories into a completely different subdirectory, which might not even exist. So before each file is written, **File.mkdirs( )** is called with the path that you want to write the file into. This will make the entire path all at once.

Containing the entire collection of listings

It's convenient to organize the listings as subdirectories while the whole collection is being built in memory. One reason is another sanity check: as each subdirectory of listings is created, an additional file is added whose name contains the number of files in that directory.

The **DirMap** class produces this effect and demonstrates the concept of a "multimap." This is implemented using a **Hashtable** whose keys are the subdirectories being created and whose values are **Vector** objects containing the **SourceCodeFile** objects in that particular directory. Thus, instead of mapping a key to a single value, the "multimap" maps a key to a set of values via the associated **Vector**. Although this sounds complex, it's remarkably straightforward to implement. You'll see that most of the size of the **DirMap** class is due to the portions that write to files, not to the "multimap" implementation.

There are two ways you can make a **DirMap**: the default constructor assumes that you want the directories to branch off of the current one, and the second constructor lets you specify an alternate absolute path for the starting directory.

The **add( )** method is where quite a bit of dense action occurs. First, the **directory( )** is extracted from the **SourceCodeFile** you want to add, and then the **Hashtable** is examined to see if it contains that key already. If not, a new **Vector** is added to the **Hashtable** and associated with that key. At this point, the **Vector** is there, one way or another, and it is extracted so the **SourceCodeFile** can be added. Because **Vector**s can be easily combined with **Hashtable**s like this, the power of both is amplified.

Writing a packed file involves opening the file to write (as a **DataOutputStream** so the data is universally recoverable) and writing the header information about the old separator on the first line. Next, an **Enumeration** of the **Hashtable** keys is produced and stepped through to select each directory and to fetch the **Vector** associated with that directory so each **SourceCodeFile** in that **Vector** can be written to the packed file.

Writing the Java source files to their directories in **write( )** is almost identical to **writePackedFile( )** since both methods simply call the appropriate method in **SourceCodeFile**. Here, however, the root path is passed into **SourceCodeFile.writeFile( )** and when all the files have been written the additional file with the name containing the number of files is also written.

The main program

The previously described classes are used within **CodePackager**. First you see the usage string that gets printed whenever the end user invokes the program incorrectly, along with the **usage( )** method that calls it and exits the program. All **main( )** does is determine whether you want to create a packed file or extract from one, then it ensures the arguments are correct and calls the appropriate method.

When a packed file is created, it's assumed to be made in the current directory, so the **DirMap** is created using the default constructor. After the file is opened each line is read and examined for particular conditions:

1. If the line starts with the starting marker for a source code listing, a new **SourceCodeFile** object is created. The constructor reads in the rest of the source listing. The handle that results is directly added to the **DirMap**.

2. If the line starts with the end marker for a source code listing, something has gone wrong, since end markers should be found only by the **SourceCodeFile** constructor.

When extracting a packed file, the extraction can be into the current directory or into an alternate directory, so the **DirMap** object is created accordingly. The file is opened and the first line is read. The old file path separator information is extracted from this line. Then the input is used to create the first **SourceCodeFile** object, which is added to the **DirMap**. New **SourceCodeFile** objects are created and added as long as they contain a file. (The last one created will simply return when it runs out of input and then **hasFile( )** will return false.)

Checking capitalization style

Although the previous example can come in handy as a guide for some project of your own that involves text processing, this project will be directly useful because it performs a style check to make sure that your capitalization conforms to the de-facto Java style. It opens each **.java** file in the current directory and extracts all the class names and identifiers, then shows you if any of them don't meet the Java style.

For the program to operate correctly, you must first build a class name repository to hold all the class names in the standard Java library. You do this by moving into all the source code subdirectories for the standard Java library and running **ClassScanner** in each subdirectory. Provide as arguments the name of the repository file (using the same path and name each time) and the **-a** command-line option to indicate that the class names should be added to the repository.

To use the program to check your code, run it and hand it the path and name of the repository to use. It will check all the classes and identifiers in the current directory and tell you which ones don't follow the typical Java capitalization style.

You should be aware that the program isn't perfect; there a few times when it will point out what it thinks is a problem but on looking at the code you'll see that nothing needs to be changed. This is a little annoying, but it's still much easier than trying to find all these cases by staring at your code.

The explanation immediately follows the listing:

```
//: ClassScanner.java
// Scans all files in directory for classes
// and identifiers, to check capitalization.
// Assumes properly compiling code listings.
// Doesn't do everything right, but is a very
// useful aid.
import java.io.*;
import java.util.*;

class MultiStringMap extends Hashtable {
  public void add(String key, String value) {
    if(!containsKey(key))
      put(key, new Vector());
    ((Vector)get(key)).addElement(value);
  }
```

```java
    public Vector getVector(String key) {
      if(!containsKey(key)) {
        System.err.println(
          "ERROR: can't find key: " + key);
        System.exit(1);
      }
      return (Vector)get(key);
    }
    public void printValues(PrintStream p) {
      Enumeration k = keys();
      while(k.hasMoreElements()) {
        String oneKey = (String)k.nextElement();
        Vector val = getVector(oneKey);
        for(int i = 0; i < val.size(); i++)
          p.println((String)val.elementAt(i));
      }
    }
  }

public class ClassScanner {
  private File path;
  private String[] fileList;
  private Properties classes = new Properties();
  private MultiStringMap
    classMap = new MultiStringMap(),
    identMap = new MultiStringMap();
  private StreamTokenizer in;
  public ClassScanner() {
    path = new File(".");
    fileList = path.list(new JavaFilter());
    for(int i = 0; i < fileList.length; i++) {
      System.out.println(fileList[i]);
      scanListing(fileList[i]);
    }
  }
  void scanListing(String fname) {
    try {
      in = new StreamTokenizer(
          new BufferedReader(
            new FileReader(fname)));
      // Doesn't seem to work:
      // in.slashStarComments(true);
      // in.slashSlashComments(true);
      in.ordinaryChar('/');
```

```
        in.ordinaryChar('.');
        in.wordChars('_', '_');
        in.eolIsSignificant(true);
        while(in.nextToken() !=
              StreamTokenizer.TT_EOF) {
          if(in.ttype == '/')
            eatComments();
          else if(in.ttype ==
                  StreamTokenizer.TT_WORD) {
            if(in.sval.equals("class") ||
               in.sval.equals("interface")) {
              // Get class name:
                while(in.nextToken() !=
                      StreamTokenizer.TT_EOF
                      && in.ttype !=
                      StreamTokenizer.TT_WORD)
                  ;
                classes.put(in.sval, in.sval);
                classMap.add(fname, in.sval);
            }
            if(in.sval.equals("import") ||
               in.sval.equals("package"))
              discardLine();
            else // It's an identifier or keyword
              identMap.add(fname, in.sval);
          }
        }
      } catch(IOException e) {
        e.printStackTrace();
      }
    }
    void discardLine() {
      try {
        while(in.nextToken() !=
              StreamTokenizer.TT_EOF
              && in.ttype !=
              StreamTokenizer.TT_EOL)
          ; // Throw away tokens to end of line
      } catch(IOException e) {
        e.printStackTrace();
      }
    }
    // StreamTokenizer's comment removal seemed
    // to be broken. This extracts them:
```

```
void eatComments() {
  try {
    if(in.nextToken() !=
        StreamTokenizer.TT_EOF) {
      if(in.ttype == '/')
        discardLine();
      else if(in.ttype != '*')
        in.pushBack();
      else
        while(true) {
          if(in.nextToken() ==
              StreamTokenizer.TT_EOF)
            break;
          if(in.ttype == '*')
            if(in.nextToken() !=
                StreamTokenizer.TT_EOF
                && in.ttype == '/')
              break;
        }
    }
  } catch(IOException e) {
    e.printStackTrace();
  }
}
public String[] classNames() {
  String[] result = new String[classes.size()];
  Enumeration e = classes.keys();
  int i = 0;
  while(e.hasMoreElements())
    result[i++] = (String)e.nextElement();
  return result;
}
public void checkClassNames() {
  Enumeration files = classMap.keys();
  while(files.hasMoreElements()) {
    String file = (String)files.nextElement();
    Vector cls = classMap.getVector(file);
    for(int i = 0; i < cls.size(); i++) {
      String className =
        (String)cls.elementAt(i);
      if(Character.isLowerCase(
          className.charAt(0)))
        System.out.println(
          "class capitalization error, file: "
```

```
                + file + ", class: "
                + className);
        }
      }
    }
    public void checkIdentNames() {
      Enumeration files = identMap.keys();
      Vector reportSet = new Vector();
      while(files.hasMoreElements()) {
        String file = (String)files.nextElement();
        Vector ids = identMap.getVector(file);
        for(int i = 0; i < ids.size(); i++) {
          String id =
            (String)ids.elementAt(i);
          if(!classes.contains(id)) {
            // Ignore identifiers of length 3 or
            // longer that are all uppercase
            // (probably static final values):
            if(id.length() >= 3 &&
               id.equals(
                 id.toUpperCase()))
              continue;
            // Check to see if first char is upper:
            if(Character.isUpperCase(id.charAt(0))){
              if(reportSet.indexOf(file + id)
                 == -1){ // Not reported yet
                reportSet.addElement(file + id);
                System.out.println(
                  "Ident capitalization error in:"
                  + file + ", ident: " + id);
              }
            }
          }
        }
      }
    }
    static final String usage =
      "Usage: \n" +
      "ClassScanner classnames -a\n" +
      "\tAdds all the class names in this \n" +
      "\tdirectory to the repository file \n" +
      "\tcalled 'classnames'\n" +
      "ClassScanner classnames\n" +
      "\tChecks all the java files in this \n" +
```

```
          "\tdirectory for capitalization errors, \n" +
          "\tusing the repository file 'classnames'";
    private static void usage() {
      System.err.println(usage);
      System.exit(1);
    }
    public static void main(String[] args) {
      if(args.length < 1 || args.length > 2)
        usage();
      ClassScanner c = new ClassScanner();
      File old = new File(args[0]);
      if(old.exists()) {
        try {
          // Try to open an existing
          // properties file:
          InputStream oldlist =
            new BufferedInputStream(
              new FileInputStream(old));
          c.classes.load(oldlist);
          oldlist.close();
        } catch(IOException e) {
          System.err.println("Could not open "
            + old + " for reading");
          System.exit(1);
        }
      }
      if(args.length == 1) {
        c.checkClassNames();
        c.checkIdentNames();
      }
      // Write the class names to a repository:
      if(args.length == 2) {
        if(!args[1].equals("-a"))
          usage();
        try {
          BufferedOutputStream out =
            new BufferedOutputStream(
              new FileOutputStream(args[0]));
          c.classes.save(out,
            "Classes found by ClassScanner.java");
          out.close();
        } catch(IOException e) {
          System.err.println(
            "Could not write " + args[0]);
```

```
            System.exit(1);
        }
      }
    }
  }

  class JavaFilter implements FilenameFilter {
    public boolean accept(File dir, String name) {
      // Strip path information:
      String f = new File(name).getName();
      return f.trim().endsWith(".java");
    }
  } ///:~
```

The class **MultiStringMap** is a tool that allows you to map a group of strings onto each key entry. As in the previous example, it uses a **Hashtable** (this time with inheritance) with the key as the single string that's mapped onto the **Vector** value. The **add( )** method simply checks to see if there's a key already in the **Hashtable**, and if not it puts one there. The **getVector( )** method produces a **Vector** for a particular key, and **printValues( )**, which is primarily useful for debugging, prints out all the values **Vector** by **Vector**.

To keep life simple, the class names from the standard Java libraries are all put into a **Properties** object (from the standard Java library). Remember that a **Properties** object is a **Hashtable** that holds only **String** objects for both the key and value entries. However, it can be saved to disk and restored from disk in one method call, so it's ideal for the repository of names. Actually, we need only a list of names, and a **Hashtable** can't accept **null** for either its key or its value entry. So the same object will be used for both the key and the value.

For the classes and identifiers that are discovered for the files in a particular directory, two **MultiStringMaps** are used: **classMap** and **identMap**. Also, when the program starts up it loads the standard class name repository into the **Properties** object called **classes**, and when a new class name is found in the local directory that is also added to **classes** as well as to **classMap**. This way, **classMap** can be used to step through all the classes in the local directory, and **classes** can be used to see if the current token is a class name (which indicates a definition of an object or method is beginning, so grab the next tokens – until a semicolon – and put them into **identMap**).

The default constructor for **ClassScanner** creates a list of file names (using the **JavaFilter** implementation of **FilenameFilter**, as described in Chapter 10). Then it calls **scanListing( )** for each file name.

Inside **scanListing( )** the source code file is opened and turned into a **StreamTokenizer**. In the documentation, passing **true** to **slashStarComments( )** and **slashSlashComments( )** is supposed to strip those comments out, but this seems to be a bit flawed (it doesn't quite work in Java 1.0). Instead, those lines are commented out and the comments are extracted by another method. To do this, the '/' must be captured as an ordinary character rather than letting the **StreamTokenizer** absorb it as part of a comment, and the **ordinaryChar( )** method tells the **StreamTokenizer** to do this. This is also true for dots ('.'), since we want to have the method calls pulled apart into individual identifiers. However, the underscore, which is ordinarily treated by **StreamTokenizer** as an individual character, should be left as part of identifiers since it appears in such **static final** values as **TT_EOF** etc., used in this very program. The **wordChars( )** method takes a range of characters you want to add to those that are left inside a token that is being parsed as a word. Finally, when parsing for one-line comments or discarding a line we need to know when an end-of-line occurs, so by calling **eolIsSignificant(true)** the eol will show up rather than being absorbed by the **StreamTokenizer**.

The rest of **scanListing( )** reads and reacts to tokens until the end of the file, signified when **nextToken( )** returns the **final static** value **StreamTokenizer.TT_EOF**.

If the token is a '/' it is potentially a comment, so **eatComments( )** is called to deal with it. The only other situation we're interested in here is if it's a word, of which there are some special cases.

If the word is **class** or **interface** then the next token represents a class or interface name, and it is put into **classes** and **classMap**. If the word is **import** or **package**, then we don't want the rest of the line. Anything else must be an identifier (which we're interested in) or a keyword (which we're not, but they're all lowercase anyway so it won't spoil things to put those in). These are added to **identMap**.

The **discardLine( )** method is a simple tool that looks for the end of a line. Note that any time you get a new token, you must check for the end of the file.

The **eatComments( )** method is called whenever a forward slash is encountered in the main parsing loop. However, that doesn't necessarily mean a comment has been found, so the next token must be extracted to see if it's another forward slash (in which case the line is discarded) or an asterisk. But if it's neither of those, it means the token you've just pulled out is needed back in the main parsing loop! Fortunately, the **pushBack( )** method allows you to "push back" the current token onto the input stream so that when the main parsing loop calls **nextToken( )** it will get the one you just pushed back.

For convenience, the **classNames( )** method produces an array of all the names in the **classes** collection. This method is not used in the program but is helpful for debugging.

The next two methods are the ones in which the actual checking takes place. In **checkClassNames( )**, the class names are extracted from the **classMap** (which, remember, contains only the names in this directory, organized by file name so the file name can be printed along with the errant class name). This is accomplished by pulling each associated **Vector** and stepping through that, looking to see if the first character is lower case. If so, the appropriate error message is printed.

In **checkIdentNames( )**, a similar approach is taken: each identifier name is extracted from **identMap**. If the name is not in the **classes** list, it's assumed to be an identifier or keyword. A special case is checked: if the identifier length is 3 or more *and* all the characters are uppercase, this identifier is ignored because it's probably a **static final** value such as **TT_EOF**. Of course, this is not a perfect algorithm, but it assumes that you'll eventually notice any all-uppercase identifiers that are out of place.

Instead of reporting every identifier that starts with an uppercase character, this method keeps track of which ones have already been reported in a **Vector** called **reportSet( )**. This treats the **Vector** as a "set" that tells you whether an item is already in the set. The item is produced by concatenating the file name and identifier. If the element isn't in the set, it's added and then the report is made.

The rest of the listing is comprised of **main( )**, which busies itself by handling the command line arguments and figuring out whether you're building a repository of class names from the standard Java library or checking the validity of code you've written. In both cases it makes a **ClassScanner** object.

Whether you're building a repository or using one, you must try to open the existing repository. By making a **File** object and testing for existence, you can decide whether to open the file and **load( )** the **Properties** list **classes** inside **ClassScanner**. (The classes from the repository add to, rather than overwrite, the classes found by the **ClassScanner** constructor.) If you provide only one command-line argument it means that you want to perform a check of the class names and identifier names, but if you provide two arguments (the second being "**-a**") you're building a class name repository. In this case, an output file is opened and the method **Properties.save( )** is used to write the list into a file, along with a string that provides header file information.

A method lookup tool

Chapter 11 introduced the Java 1.1 concept of *reflection* and used that feature to look up methods for a particular class – either the entire list of methods or a subset of those whose names match a keyword you provide. The magic of this is that it can automatically show you *all* the methods for a class without forcing you to walk up the inheritance hierarchy examining the base classes at each level. Thus, it provides a valuable timesaving tool for programming: because the names of most Java method names are made nicely verbose and descriptive, you can search for the method names that contain a particular word of interest. When you find what you think you're looking for, check the online documentation.

However, by Chapter 11 you hadn't seen the AWT, so that tool was developed as a command-line application. Here is the more useful GUI version, which dynamically updates the output as you type and also allows you to cut and paste from the output:

```
//: DisplayMethods.java
// Display the methods of any class inside
// a window. Dynamically narrows your search.
import java.awt.*;
import java.awt.event.*;
import java.applet.*;
import java.lang.reflect.*;
import java.io.*;

public class DisplayMethods extends Applet {
  Class cl;
  Method[] m;
  Constructor[] ctor;
  String[] n = new String[0];
  TextField
    name = new TextField(40),
    searchFor = new TextField(30);
```

```
      Checkbox strip =
        new Checkbox("Strip Qualifiers");
      TextArea results = new TextArea(40, 65);
      public void init() {
        strip.setState(true);
        name.addTextListener(new NameL());
        searchFor.addTextListener(new SearchForL());
        strip.addItemListener(new StripL());
        Panel
          top = new Panel(),
          lower = new Panel(),
          p = new Panel();
        top.add(new Label("Qualified class name:"));
        top.add(name);
        lower.add(
          new Label("String to search for:"));
        lower.add(searchFor);
        lower.add(strip);
        p.setLayout(new BorderLayout());
        p.add(top, BorderLayout.NORTH);
        p.add(lower, BorderLayout.SOUTH);
        setLayout(new BorderLayout());
        add(p, BorderLayout.NORTH);
        add(results, BorderLayout.CENTER);
      }
      class NameL implements TextListener {
        public void textValueChanged(TextEvent e) {
          String nm = name.getText().trim();
          if(nm.length() == 0) {
            results.setText("No match");
            n = new String[0];
            return;
          }
          try {
            cl = Class.forName(nm);
          } catch (ClassNotFoundException ex) {
            results.setText("No match");
            return;
          }
          m = cl.getMethods();
          ctor = cl.getConstructors();
          // Convert to an array of Strings:
          n = new String[m.length + ctor.length];
          for(int i = 0; i < m.length; i++)
```

```
          n[i] = m[i].toString();
        for(int i = 0; i < ctor.length; i++)
          n[i + m.length] = ctor[i].toString();
        reDisplay();
      }
    }
    void reDisplay() {
      // Create the result set:
      String[] rs = new String[n.length];
      String find = searchFor.getText();
      int j = 0;
      // Select from the list if find exists:
      for (int i = 0; i < n.length; i++) {
        if(find == null)
          rs[j++] = n[i];
        else if(n[i].indexOf(find) != -1)
            rs[j++] = n[i];
      }
      results.setText("");
      if(strip.getState() == true)
        for (int i = 0; i < j; i++)
          results.append(
            StripQualifiers.strip(rs[i]) + "\n");
      else // Leave qualifiers on
        for (int i = 0; i < j; i++)
          results.append(rs[i] + "\n");
    }
    class StripL implements ItemListener {
      public void itemStateChanged(ItemEvent e) {
        reDisplay();
      }
    }
    class SearchForL implements TextListener {
      public void textValueChanged(TextEvent e) {
        reDisplay();
      }
    }
    public static void main(String[] args) {
      DisplayMethods applet = new DisplayMethods();
      Frame aFrame = new Frame("Display Methods");
      aFrame.addWindowListener(
        new WindowAdapter() {
          public void windowClosing(WindowEvent e) {
            System.exit(0);
```

```
            }
          });
       aFrame.add(applet, BorderLayout.CENTER);
       aFrame.setSize(500,750);
       applet.init();
       applet.start();
       aFrame.setVisible(true);
    }
}

class StripQualifiers {
  private StreamTokenizer st;
  public StripQualifiers(String qualified) {
      st = new StreamTokenizer(
        new StringReader(qualified));
      st.ordinaryChar(' ');
  }
  public String getNext() {
    String s = null;
    try {
      if(st.nextToken() !=
             StreamTokenizer.TT_EOF) {
        switch(st.ttype) {
          case StreamTokenizer.TT_EOL:
            s = null;
            break;
          case StreamTokenizer.TT_NUMBER:
            s = Double.toString(st.nval);
            break;
          case StreamTokenizer.TT_WORD:
            s = new String(st.sval);
            break;
          default: // single character in ttype
            s = String.valueOf((char)st.ttype);
        }
      }
    } catch(IOException e) {
      System.out.println(e);
    }
    return s;
  }
  public static String strip(String qualified) {
    StripQualifiers sq =
      new StripQualifiers(qualified);
```

```
    String s = "", si;
    while((si = sq.getNext()) != null) {
      int lastDot = si.lastIndexOf('.');
      if(lastDot != -1)
        si = si.substring(lastDot + 1);
      s += si;
    }
    return s;
  }
} ///:~
```

Some things you've seen before. As with many of the GUI programs in this book, this is created to perform both as an application and as an applet. Also, the **StripQualifiers** class is exactly the same as it was in Chapter 11.

The GUI contains a **TextField name** in which you can enter the fully-qualified class name you want to look up, and another one, **searchFor**, in which you can enter the optional text to search for within the list of methods. The **Checkbox** allows you to say whether you want to use the fully-qualified names in the output or if you want the qualification stripped off. Finally, the results are displayed in a **TextArea**.

You'll notice that there are no buttons or other components by which to indicate that you want the search to start. That's because both of the **TextField**s and the **Checkbox** are monitored by their listener objects. Whenever you make a change, the list is immediately updated. If you change the text within the **name** field, the new text is captured in **class NameL**. If the text isn't empty, it is used inside **Class.forName( )** to try to look up the class. As you're typing, of course, the name will be incomplete and **Class.forName( )** will fail, which means that it throws an exception. This is trapped and the **TextArea** is set to "No match". But as soon as you type in a correct name (capitalization counts), **Class.forName( )** is successful and **getMethods( )** and **getConstructors( )** will return arrays of **Method** and **Constructor** objects, respectively. Each of the objects in these arrays is turned into a **String** via **toString( )** (this produces the complete method or constructor signature) and both lists are combined into **n**, a single **String** array. The array **n** is a member of **class DisplayMethods** and is used in updating the display whenever **reDisplay( )** is called.

If you change the **Checkbox** or **searchFor** components, their listeners simply call **reDisplay( )**. **reDisplay( )** creates a temporary array of **String** called **rs** (for "result set"). The result set is either copied directly from **n** if there is no **find** word, or conditionally copied from the **String**s in **n** that contain the **find** word. Finally, the **strip Checkbox** is interrogated to see if the user wants the names to be stripped (the default is "yes"). If so, **StripQualifiers.strip( )** does the job; if not, the list is simply displayed.

In **init( )**, you might think that there's a lot of busy work involved in setting up the layout. In fact, it is possible to lay out the components with less work, but the advantage of using **BorderLayout**s this way is that it allows the user to resize the window and make – in particular – the **TextArea** larger, which means you can resize to allow you to see longer names without scrolling.

You might find that you'll keep this tool running while you're programming, since it provides one of the best "first lines of attack" when you're trying to figure out what method to call.

Complexity theory

This program was modified from code originally created by Larry O'Brien, and is based on the "Boids" program created by Craig Reynolds in 1986 to demonstrate an aspect of complexity theory called "emergence."

The goal here is to produce a reasonably lifelike reproduction of flocking or herding behavior in animals by establishing a small set of simple rules for each animal. Each animal can look at the entire scene and all the other animals in the scene, but it reacts only to a set of nearby "flockmates." The animal moves according to three simple steering behaviors:

1.   Separation: Avoid crowding local flockmates.

2.   Alignment: Follow the average heading of local flockmates.

3.   Cohesion: Move toward the center of the group of local flockmates.

More elaborate models can include obstacles and the ability for the animals to predict collisions and avoid them, so the animals can flow around fixed objects in the environment. In addition, the animals might also be given a goal, which can cause the herd to follow a desired path. For simplicity, obstacle avoidance and goal-seeking is not included in the model presented here.

Emergence means that, despite the limited nature of computers and the simplicity of the steering rules, the result seems realistic. That is, remarkably lifelike behavior "emerges" from this simple model.

The program is presented as a combined application/applet:

```java
//: FieldOBeasts.java
// Demonstration of complexity theory; simulates
// herding behavior in animals. Adapted from
// a program by Larry O'Brien lobrien@msn.com
import java.awt.*;
import java.awt.event.*;
import java.applet.*;
import java.util.*;

class Beast {
  int
    x, y,               // Screen position
    currentSpeed;       // Pixels per second
  float currentDirection;  // Radians
  Color color;          // Fill color
  FieldOBeasts field; // Where the Beast roams
  static final int GSIZE = 10; // Graphic size

  public Beast(FieldOBeasts f, int x, int y,
      float cD, int cS, Color c) {
    field = f;
    this.x = x;
    this.y = y;
    currentDirection = cD;
    currentSpeed = cS;
    color = c;
  }
  public void step() {
    // You move based on those within your sight:
    Vector seen = field.beastListInSector(this);
    // If you're not out in front
    if(seen.size() > 0) {
      // Gather data on those you see
      int totalSpeed = 0;
      float totalBearing = 0.0f;
      float distanceToNearest = 100000.0f;
      Beast nearestBeast =
        (Beast)seen.elementAt(0);
      Enumeration e = seen.elements();
```

```
    while(e.hasMoreElements()) {
      Beast aBeast = (Beast) e.nextElement();
      totalSpeed += aBeast.currentSpeed;
      float bearing =
        aBeast.bearingFromPointAlongAxis(
          x, y, currentDirection);
      totalBearing += bearing;
      float distanceToBeast =
        aBeast.distanceFromPoint(x, y);
      if(distanceToBeast < distanceToNearest) {
        nearestBeast = aBeast;
        distanceToNearest = distanceToBeast;
      }
    }
    // Rule 1: Match average speed of those
    // in the list:
    currentSpeed = totalSpeed / seen.size();
    // Rule 2: Move towards the perceived
    // center of gravity of the herd:
    currentDirection =
      totalBearing / seen.size();
    // Rule 3: Maintain a minimum distance
    // from those around you:
    if(distanceToNearest <=
       field.minimumDistance) {
      currentDirection =
        nearestBeast.currentDirection;
      currentSpeed = nearestBeast.currentSpeed;
      if(currentSpeed > field.maxSpeed) {
        currentSpeed = field.maxSpeed;
      }
    }
  }
  else {   // You are in front, so slow down
    currentSpeed =
      (int)(currentSpeed * field.decayRate);
  }
  // Make the beast move:
  x += (int)(Math.cos(currentDirection)
           * currentSpeed);
  y += (int)(Math.sin(currentDirection)
           * currentSpeed);
  x %= field.xExtent;
  y %= field.yExtent;
```

```
      if(x < 0)
        x += field.xExtent;
      if(y < 0)
        y += field.yExtent;
  }
  public float bearingFromPointAlongAxis (
      int originX, int originY, float axis) {
    // Returns bearing angle of the current Beast
    // in the world coordiante system
    try {
      double bearingInRadians =
        Math.atan(
          (this.y - originY) /
          (this.x - originX));
      // Inverse tan has two solutions, so you
      // have to correct for other quarters:
      if(x < originX) {
        if(y < originY) {
          bearingInRadians += - (float)Math.PI;
        }
        else {
          bearingInRadians =
            (float)Math.PI - bearingInRadians;
        }
      }
      // Just subtract the axis (in radians):
      return (float) (axis - bearingInRadians);
    } catch(ArithmeticException aE) {
      // Divide by 0 error possible on this
      if(x > originX) {
          return 0;
      }
      else
        return (float) Math.PI;
    }
  }
  public float distanceFromPoint(int x1, int y1){
    return (float) Math.sqrt(
      Math.pow(x1 - x, 2) +
      Math.pow(y1 - y, 2));
  }
  public Point position() {
    return new Point(x, y);
  }
```

```java
  // Beasts know how to draw themselves:
  public void draw(Graphics g) {
    g.setColor(color);
    int directionInDegrees = (int)(
      (currentDirection * 360) / (2 * Math.PI));
    int startAngle = directionInDegrees -
      FieldOBeasts.halfFieldOfView;
    int endAngle = 90;
    g.fillArc(x, y, GSIZE, GSIZE,
      startAngle, endAngle);
  }
}

public class FieldOBeasts extends Applet
    implements Runnable {
  private Vector beasts;
  static float
    fieldOfView =
      (float)(Math.PI / 4), // In radians
    // Deceleration % per second:
    decayRate = 1.0f,
    minimumDistance = 10f; // In pixels
  static int
    halfFieldOfView = (int)(
      (fieldOfView * 360) / (2 * Math.PI)),
    xExtent = 0,
    yExtent = 0,
    numBeasts = 50,
    maxSpeed = 20; // Pixels/second
  boolean uniqueColors = true;
  Thread thisThread;
  int delay = 25;
  public void init() {
    if (xExtent == 0 && yExtent == 0) {
      xExtent = Integer.parseInt(
        getParameter("xExtent"));
      yExtent = Integer.parseInt(
        getParameter("yExtent"));
    }
    beasts =
      makeBeastVector(numBeasts, uniqueColors);
    // Now start the beasts a-rovin':
    thisThread = new Thread(this);
    thisThread.start();
```

```
      }
      public void run() {
        while(true) {
          for(int i = 0; i < beasts.size(); i++){
            Beast b = (Beast) beasts.elementAt(i);
            b.step();
          }
          try {
            thisThread.sleep(delay);
          } catch(InterruptedException ex){}
          repaint(); // Otherwise it won't update
        }
      }
      Vector makeBeastVector(
          int quantity, boolean uniqueColors) {
        Vector newBeasts = new Vector();
        Random generator = new Random();
        // Used only if uniqueColors is on:
        double cubeRootOfBeastNumber =
          Math.pow((double)numBeasts, 1.0 / 3.0);
        float colorCubeStepSize =
          (float) (1.0 / cubeRootOfBeastNumber);
        float r = 0.0f;
        float g = 0.0f;
        float b = 0.0f;
        for(int i = 0; i < quantity; i++) {
          int x =
            (int) (generator.nextFloat() * xExtent);
          if(x > xExtent - Beast.GSIZE)
            x -= Beast.GSIZE;
          int y =
            (int) (generator.nextFloat() * yExtent);
          if(y > yExtent - Beast.GSIZE)
            y -= Beast.GSIZE;
          float direction = (float)(
            generator.nextFloat() * 2 * Math.PI);
          int speed = (int)(
            generator.nextFloat() * (float)maxSpeed);
          if(uniqueColors) {
            r += colorCubeStepSize;
            if(r > 1.0) {
              r -= 1.0f;
              g += colorCubeStepSize;
              if( g > 1.0) {
```

```
              g -= 1.0f;
              b += colorCubeStepSize;
              if(b > 1.0)
                 b -= 1.0f;
           }
         }
       }
       newBeasts.addElement(
          new Beast(this, x, y, direction, speed,
             new Color(r,g,b)));
     }
     return newBeasts;
  }
  public Vector beastListInSector(Beast viewer) {
     Vector output = new Vector();
     Enumeration e = beasts.elements();
     Beast aBeast = (Beast)beasts.elementAt(0);
     int counter = 0;
     while(e.hasMoreElements()) {
        aBeast = (Beast) e.nextElement();
        if(aBeast != viewer) {
           Point p = aBeast.position();
           Point v = viewer.position();
           float bearing =
              aBeast.bearingFromPointAlongAxis(
                 v.x, v.y, viewer.currentDirection);
           if(Math.abs(bearing) < fieldOfView / 2)
             output.addElement(aBeast);
        }
     }
     return output;
  }
  public void paint(Graphics g)   {
     Enumeration e = beasts.elements();
     while(e.hasMoreElements()) {
        ((Beast)e.nextElement()).draw(g);
     }
  }
  public static void main(String[] args)    {
     FieldOBeasts field = new FieldOBeasts();
     field.xExtent = 640;
     field.yExtent = 480;
     Frame frame = new Frame("Field 'O Beasts");
     // Optionally use a command-line argument
```

```
      // for the sleep time:
      if(args.length >= 1)
        field.delay = Integer.parseInt(args[0]);
      frame.addWindowListener(
        new WindowAdapter() {
          public void windowClosing(WindowEvent e) {
            System.exit(0);
          }
        });
      frame.add(field, BorderLayout.CENTER);
      frame.setSize(640,480);
      field.init();
      field.start();
      frame.setVisible(true);
    }
} ///:~
```

Although this isn't a perfect reproduction of the behavior in Craig
Reynold's "Boids" example, it exhibits its own fascinating characteristics,
which you can modify by adjusting the numbers. You can find out more
about the modeling of flocking behavior and see a spectacular 3-D
version of Boids at Craig Reynold's page
http://www.hmt.com/cwr/boids.html.

To run this program as an applet, put the following applet tag in an
HTML file:

```
<applet
code=FieldOBeasts
width=640
height=480>
<param name=xExtent value = "640">
<param name=yExtent value = "480">
</applet>
```

Summary

This chapter shows some of the more sophisticated things that you can
do with Java. It also makes the point that while Java must certainly have
its limits, those limits are primarily relegated to performance. (When the
text-processing programs were written, for example, C++ versions were
much faster – this might be due partly to an inefficient implementation
of the IO library, which should change in time.) The limits of Java *do not*
seem to be in the area of expressiveness. Not only does it seem possible to

express just about everything you can imagine, but Java seems oriented toward making that expression easy to write and read. Therefore you don't run into the wall of complexity that often occurs with languages that are more trivial to use than Java (at least they seem that way, at first). And with Java 1.2's JFC/Swing library, even the expressiveness and ease of use of the AWT is improving dramatically.

Exercises

1. (Challenging) Rewrite **FieldOBeasts.java** so that its state can be persistent. Implement buttons to allow you to save and recall different state files and continue running them where they left off. Use **CADState.java** from Chapter 10 as an example of how to do this.

2. (Term project) Taking **FieldOBeasts.java** as a starting point, build an automobile traffic simulation system.

3. (Term project) Using **ClassScanner.java** as a starting point, build a tool that points out methods and fields that are defined but never used.

4. (Term project) Using JDBC, build a contact management program using a flat-file database containing names, addresses, telephone numbers, email addresses, etc. You should be able to easily add new names to the database. When typing in the name to be looked up, use automatic name completion as shown in **VLookup.java** in Chapter 15.

A: Using non-Java code

This appendix was contributed by and used with the permission of Andrea Provaglio (*www.AndreaProvaglio.com*).

The Java language and its standard API are rich enough to write full-fledged applications. But in some cases you must call non-Java code; for example, if you want to access operating-system-specific features, interface with special hardware devices, reuse a pre-existing, non-Java code base, or implement time-critical sections of code. Interfacing with non–Java code requires dedicated support in the compiler and in the Virtual Machine, and additional tools to map the Java code to the non-Java code. (There's also a simple approach: in Chapter 15, the section titled "a Web application" contains an example of connecting to non–Java code using standard input and output.) Currently, different vendors offer different solutions: Java 1.1 has the Java Native Interface (JNI), Netscape has proposed its Java Runtime Interface, and Microsoft offers J/Direct, Raw Native Interface (RNI), and Java/COM integration.

This fragmentation among different vendors implies serious drawbacks for the programmer. If a Java application must call native methods, the programmer might need to implement different versions of the native methods depending on the platform the application will run on. The programmer might actually need different versions of the Java code as well as different Java virtual machines.

Another solution is CORBA (Common Object Request Broker Architecture), an integration technology developed by the OMG (Object Management Group, a non-profit consortium of companies). CORBA is not part of any language, but is a specification for implementing a common communication bus and services that allow interoperability among objects implemented in different languages. This communication bus, called an ORB (Object Request Broker), is a product implemented by third-party vendors, but it is not part of the Java language specification.

This appendix gives an overview of JNI, J/Direct, RNI, Java/COM integration, and CORBA. This is not an in-depth treatment, and in some cases you're assumed to have partial knowledge of the related concepts and techniques. But in the end, you should be able to compare the different approaches and choose the one that is most appropriate to the problem you want to solve.

The Java Native Interface

JNI is a fairly rich programming interface that allows you to call native methods from a Java application. It was added in Java 1.1, maintaining a certain degree of compatibility with its Java 1.0 equivalent, the native method interface (NMI). NMI has design characteristics that make it unsuitable for adoption in all virtual machines. For this reason, future versions of the language might no longer support NMI, and it will not be covered here.

Currently, JNI is designed to interface with native methods written only in C or C++. Using JNI, your native methods can:

♦ Create, inspect, and update Java objects (including arrays and **String**s)

♦ Call Java methods

- Catch and throw exceptions

- Load classes and obtain class information

- Perform runtime type checking

Thus, virtually everything you can do with classes and objects in ordinary Java you can also do in native methods.

Calling a native method

We'll start with a simple example: a Java program that calls a native method, which in turn calls the Win32 **MessageBox( )** API function to display a graphical text box. This example will also be used later with J/Direct. If your platform is not Win32, just replace the C header include:

```
#include <windows.h>
```

with

```
#include <stdio.h>
```

and replace the call to **MessageBox( )** with a call to **printf( )**.

The first step is to write the Java code declaring a native method and its arguments:

```
class ShowMsgBox {
  public static void main(String [] args) {
    ShowMsgBox app = new ShowMsgBox();
    app.ShowMessage("Generated with JNI");
  }
  private native void ShowMessage(String msg);
  static {
    System.loadLibrary("MsgImpl");
  }
}
```

The native method declaration is followed by a **static** block that calls **System.loadLibrary( )** (which you could call at any time, but this style is more appropriate). **System.loadLibrary( )** loads a DLL in memory and links to it. The DLL must be in your system path or in the directory containing the Java class file. The file name extension is automatically added by the JVM depending on the platform.

The C header file generator: javah

Now compile your Java source file and run **javah** on the resulting **.class** file. **Javah** was present in version 1.0, but since you are using Java 1.1 JNI you must specify the **–jni** switch:

```
javah -jni ShowMsgBox
```

Javah reads the Java class file and for each native method declaration it generates a function prototype in a C or C++ header file. Here's the output: the **ShowMsgBox.h** source file (edited slightly to fit into the book):

```
/* DO NOT EDIT THIS FILE
    - it is machine generated */
#include <jni.h>
/* Header for class ShowMsgBox */

#ifndef _Included_ShowMsgBox
#define _Included_ShowMsgBox
#ifdef __cplusplus
extern "C" {
#endif
/*
 * Class:      ShowMsgBox
 * Method:     ShowMessage
 * Signature: (Ljava/lang/String;)V
 */
JNIEXPORT void JNICALL
Java_ShowMsgBox_ShowMessage
    (JNIEnv *, jobject, jstring);

#ifdef __cplusplus
}
#endif
#endif
```

As you can see by the **#ifdef __cplusplus** preprocessor directive, this file can be compiled either by a C or a C++ compiler. The first **#include** directive includes **jni.h**, a header file that, among other things, defines the types that you can see used in the rest of the file. **JNIEXPORT** and **JNICALL** are macros that expand to match platform-specific directives; **JNIEnv**, **jobject** and **jstring** are JNI data type definitions.

Name mangling and function signatures

JNI imposes a naming convention (called *name mangling*) on native methods; this is important, since it's part of the mechanism by which the virtual machine links Java calls to native methods. Basically, all native methods start with the word "Java," followed by the name of the class in which the Java native declaration appears, followed by the name of the Java method; the underscore character is used as a separator. If the Java native method is overloaded, then the function signature is appended to the name as well; you can see the native signature in the comments preceding the prototype. For more information about name mangling and native method signatures, please refer to the JNI documentation.

Implementing your DLL

At this point, all you have to do is write a C or C++ source file that includes the javah-generated header file and implements the native method, then compile it and generate a dynamic link library. This part is platform-dependent, and I'll assume that you know how to create a DLL. The code below implements the native method by calling a Win32 API. It is then compiled and linked into a file called **MsgImpl.dll** (for "Message Implementation").

```
#include <windows.h>
#include "ShowMsgBox.h"

BOOL APIENTRY DllMain(HANDLE hModule,
   DWORD dwReason, void** lpReserved) {
   return TRUE;
}

JNIEXPORT void JNICALL
Java_ShowMsgBox_ShowMessage(JNIEnv * jEnv,
   jobject this, jstring jMsg) {
   const char * msg;
   msg = (*jEnv)->GetStringUTFChars(jEnv, jMsg,0);
   MessageBox(HWND_DESKTOP, msg,
      "Thinking in Java: JNI",
      MB_OK | MB_ICONEXCLAMATION);
   (*jEnv)->ReleaseStringUTFChars(jEnv, jMsg,msg);
}
```

If you have no interest in Win32, just skip the **MessageBox( )** call; the interesting part is the surrounding code. The arguments that are passed into the native method are the gateway back into Java. The first, of type

JNIEnv, contains all the hooks that allow you to call back into the JVM. (We'll look at this in the next section.) The second argument has a different meaning depending on the type of method. For non-**static** methods like the example above (also called *instance methods*), the second argument is the equivalent of the "this" pointer in C++ and similar to **this** in Java: it's a reference to the object that called the native method. For **static** methods, it's a reference to the **Class** object where the method is implemented.

The remaining arguments represent the Java objects passed into the native method call. Primitives are also passed in this way, but they come in by value.

In the following sections we'll explain this code by looking at how to access and control the JVM from inside a native method.

Accessing JNI functions: The **JNIEnv** argument

JNI functions are those that the programmer uses to interact with the JVM from inside a native method. As you can see in the example above, every JNI native method receives a special argument as its first parameter: the **JNIEnv** argument, which is a pointer to a special JNI data structure of type **JNIEnv_**. One element of the JNI data structure is a pointer to an array generated by the JVM; each element of this array is a pointer to a JNI function. The JNI functions can be called from the native method by dereferencing these pointers (it's simpler than it sounds). Every JVM provides its own implementation of the JNI functions, but their addresses will always be at predefined offsets.

Through the **JNIEnv** argument, the programmer has access to a large set of functions. These functions can be grouped into the following categories:

♦   Obtaining version information

♦   Performing class and object operations

♦   Handling global and local references to Java objects

♦   Accessing instance fields and static fields

♦   Calling instance methods and static methods

♦   Performing string and array operations

- Generating and handling Java exceptions

The number of JNI functions is quite large and won't be covered here. Instead, I'll show the rationale behind the use of these functions. For more detailed information, consult your compiler's JNI documentation.

If you take a look at the **jni.h** header file, you'll see that inside the **#ifdef __cplusplus** preprocessor conditional, the **JNIEnv_** structure is defined as a class when compiled by a C++ compiler. This class contains a number of inline functions that let you access the JNI functions with an easy and familiar syntax. For example, the line in the preceding example

```
(*jEnv)->ReleaseStringUTFChars(jEnv, jMsg,msg);
```

can be rewritten as follows in C++:

```
jEnv->ReleaseStringUTFChars(jMsg,msg);
```

You'll notice that you no longer need the double dereferencing of the **jEnv** pointer, and that the same pointer is no longer passed as the first parameter to the JNI function call. In the rest of these examples, I'll use the C++ style.

Accessing Java Strings

As an example of accessing a JNI function, consider the code shown above. Here, the **JNIEnv** argument **jEnv** is used to access a Java **String**. Java **String**s are in Unicode format, so if you receive one and want to pass it to a non-Unicode function (**printf( )**, for example), you must first convert it into ASCII characters with the JNI function **GetStringUTFChars( )**. This function takes a Java **String** and converts it to UTF-8 characters. (These are 8 bits wide to hold ASCII values or 16 bits wide to hold Unicode. If the content of the original string was composed only of ASCII, the resulting string will be ASCII as well.)

GetStringUTFChars is the name of one of the fields in the structure that **JNIEnv** is indirectly pointing to, and this field in turn is a pointer to a function. To access the JNI function, we use the traditional C syntax for calling a function though a pointer. You use the form above to access all of the JNI functions.

Passing and using Java objects

In the previous example we passed a **String** to the native method. You can also pass Java objects of your own creation to a native method.

Inside your native method, you can access the fields and methods of the object that was received.

To pass objects, use the ordinary Java syntax when declaring the native method. In the example below, **MyJavaClass** has one **public** field and one **public** method. The class **UseObjects** declares a native method that takes an object of class **MyJavaClass**. To see if the native method manipulates its argument, the **public** field of the argument is set, the native method is called, and then the value of the **public** field is printed.

```
class MyJavaClass {
  public void divByTwo() { aValue /= 2; }
  public int aValue;
}

public class UseObjects {
  public static void main(String [] args) {
    UseObjects app = new UseObjects();
    MyJavaClass anObj = new MyJavaClass();
    anObj.aValue = 2;
    app.changeObject(anObj);
    System.out.println("Java: " + anObj.aValue);
  }
  private native void
  changeObject(MyJavaClass obj);
  static {
    System.loadLibrary("UseObjImpl");
  }
}
```

After compiling the code and handing the **.class** file to **javah**, you can implement the native method. In the example below, once the field and method ID are obtained, they are accessed through JNI functions.

```
JNIEXPORT void JNICALL
Java_UseObjects_changeObject(
  JNIEnv * env, jobject jThis, jobject obj) {
  jclass cls;
  jfieldID fid;
  jmethodID mid;
  int value;
  cls = env->GetObjectClass(obj);
  fid = env->GetFieldID(cls,
        "aValue", "I");
  mid = env->GetMethodID(cls,
```

```
                "divByTwo", "()V");
        value = env->GetIntField(obj, fid);
        printf("Native: %d\n", value);
        env->SetIntField(obj, fid, 6);
        env->CallVoidMethod(obj, mid);
        value = env->GetIntField(obj, fid);
        printf("Native: %d\n", value);
    }
```

The first argument aside, the C++ function receives a **jobject**, which is the native side of the Java object reference we pass from the Java code. We simply read **aValue**, print it out, change the value, call the object's **divByTwo( )** method, and print the value out again.

To access a field or method, you must first obtain its identifier. Appropriate JNI functions take the class object, the element name, and the signature. These functions return an identifier that you use to access the element. This approach might seem convoluted, but your native method has no knowledge of the internal layout of the Java object. Instead, it must access fields and methods through indexes returned by the JVM. This allows different JVMs to implement different internal object layouts with no impact on your native methods.

If you run the Java program, you'll see that the object that's passed from the Java side is manipulated by your native method. But what exactly is passed? A pointer or a Java reference? And what is the garbage collector doing during native method calls?

The garbage collector continues to operate during native method execution, but it's guaranteed that your objects will not be garbage collected during a native method call. To ensure this, *local references* are created before, and destroyed right after, the native method call. Since their lifetime wraps the call, you know that the objects will be valid throughout the native method call.

Since these references are created and subsequently destroyed every time the function is called, you cannot make local copies in your native methods, in **static** variables. If you want a reference that lasts across function invocations, you need a global reference. Global references are not created by the JVM, but the programmer can make a global reference out of a local one by calling specific JNI functions. When you create a global reference, you become responsible for the lifetime of the referenced object. The global reference (and the object it refers to) will be in memory until the programmer explicitly frees the reference with the appropriate JNI function. It's similar to **malloc( )** and **free( )** in C.

JNI and Java exceptions

With JNI, Java exceptions can be thrown, caught, printed, and rethrown just as they are inside a Java program. But it's up to the programmer to call dedicated JNI functions to deal with exceptions. Here are the JNI functions for exception handling:

*   **Throw( )**
    Throws an existing exception object. Used in native methods to rethrow an exception.

*   **ThrowNew( )**
    Generates a new exception object and throws it.

*   **ExceptionOccurred( )**
    Determines if an exception was thrown and not yet cleared.

*   **ExceptionDescribe( )**
    Prints an exception and the stack trace.

*   **ExceptionClear( )**
    Clears a pending exception.

*   **FatalError( )**
    Raises a fatal error. Does not return.

Among these, you can't ignore **ExceptionOccurred( )** and **ExceptionClear( )**. Most JNI functions can generate exceptions, and there is no language feature that you can use in place of a Java try block, so you must call **ExceptionOccurred( )** after each JNI function call to see if an exception was thrown. If you detect an exception, you may choose to handle it (and possibly rethrow it). You must make certain, however, that the exception is eventually cleared. This can be done in your function using **ExceptionClear( )** or in some other function if the exception is rethrown, but it must be done.

You must ensure that the exception is cleared, because otherwise the results will be unpredictable if you call a JNI function while an exception is pending. There are few JNI functions that are safe to call during an exception; among these, of course, are all the exception handling functions.

JNI and threading

Since Java is a multithreaded language, several threads can call a native method concurrently. (The native method might be suspended in the middle of its operation when a second thread calls it.) It's entirely up to the programmer to guarantee that the native call is thread-safe, i.e. it does not modify shared data in an unmonitored way. Basically, you have two options: declare the native method as **synchronized** or implement some other strategy within the native method to ensure correct, concurrent data manipulation.

Also, you should never pass the **JNIEnv** pointer across threads, since the internal structure it points to is allocated on a per-thread basis and contains information that makes sense only in that particular thread.

Using a pre-existing code base

The easiest way to implement JNI native methods is to start writing native method prototypes in a Java class, compile that class, and run the **.class** file through **javah**. But what if you have a large, pre-existing code base that you want to call from Java? Renaming all the functions in your DLLs to match the JNI name mangling convention is not a viable solution. The best approach is to write a wrapper DLL "outside" your original code base. The Java code calls functions in this new DLL, which in turn calls your original DLL functions. This solution is not just a work-around; in most cases you must do this anyway because you must call JNI functions on the object references before you can use them.

The Microsoft way

At the time of this writing, Microsoft does not support JNI, but provides proprietary support to call non-Java code. This support is built into the compiler, the Microsoft JVM, and external tools. The features described in this section will work only if your program was compiled using the Microsoft Java compiler and run on the Microsoft Java Virtual Machine. If you plan to distribute your application on the Internet, or if your Intranet is built on different platforms, this can be a serious issue.

The Microsoft interface to Win32 code provides three ways to connect to Win32:

1. **J/Direct**: A way to easily call Win32 DLL functions, with some limitations.

---

2. **Raw Native Interface (RNI)**: You can call Win32 DLL functions, but you must then handle garbage collection.

3. **Java/COM integration**: You can expose or call COM services directly from Java.

I'll cover all three techniques in the following sections.

At the time of writing, these features were tested on the Microsoft SDK for Java 2.0 beta 2, which was downloaded (with a painful process they call "Active Setup") from the Microsoft Web site. The Java SDK is a set of command-line tools, but the compilation engine can be easily plugged into the Developer Studio environment, allowing you to use Visual J++ 1.1 to compile Java 1.1 code.

J/Direct

J/Direct is the simplest way to call functions in a Win32 DLL. It was designed primarily to interface with the Win32 API, but you can use it to call any other APIs. The ease of use of this feature is counterbalanced by some limitations and reduced performance (compared to RNI). But J/Direct has distinct advantages. First, there is no need to write additional non–Java code, except the code in the DLL you want to call. In other words, you do not need a wrapper or proxy/stub DLL. Second, function arguments are automatically converted to and from standard data types. (If you must pass user-defined data types, J/Direct might not be the way to go.) Third, it's simple and straightforward, as the example below shows. In just a few lines, this example calls the Win32 API function **MessageBox( )**, which pops up a little modal window with a title, a message, an optional icon, and a few buttons.

```
public class ShowMsgBox {
  public static void main(String args[])
  throws UnsatisfiedLinkError    {
    MessageBox(0,
      "Created by the MessageBox() Win32 func",
      "Thinking in Java", 0);
  }
  /** @dll.import("USER32") */
  private static native int
  MessageBox(int hwndOwner, String text,
    String title, int fuStyle);
}
```

Amazingly, this code is all you need to call a function in a Win32 DLL using J/Direct. The key is the @**dll.import** directive before the **MessageBox( )** declaration, at the bottom of the example code. It looks like a comment, but it's not: it tells the compiler that the function below the directive is implemented in the USER32 DLL, and should be called accordingly. All you must do is supply a prototype that matches the function implementation in the DLL and call the function. But instead of typing in the Java version of each Win32 API function that you need, a Microsoft Java package does this for you (I'll describe this shortly). For this example to work, the function must be exported *by name* by the DLL, but the @**dll.import** directive can be used to link *by ordinal* as well, i.e., you can specify the entry position of the function in the DLL. I'll cover the features of the @**dll.import** directive later.

An important issue in the process of linking with non-Java code is the automatic marshaling of the function parameters. As you can see, the Java declaration of **MessageBox( )** takes two String arguments, but the original C implementation takes two **char** pointers. The compiler automatically converts the standard data types for you, following the rules described in a later section.

Finally, you might have noticed the **UnsatisfiedLinkError** exception in the declaration of **main( )**. This exception occurs when the linker is unable to resolve the symbol for the non-Java function at run-time. This happens for a number of reasons: the **.dll** file was not found, it is not a valid DLL, or J/Direct is not supported by your virtual machine. For the DLL to be found, it must be in the Windows or Windows\System directory, in one of the directories listed in your PATH environment variable, or in the directory where the **.class** file is located. J/Direct is supported in the Microsoft Java compiler version 1.02.4213 or above, and in the Microsoft JVM version 4.79.2164 or above. To get the compiler version number, run JVC from the command line with no parameters. To get the JVM version number, locate the icon for **msjava.dll**, and using the context menu look at its properties.

The @**dll.import** directive

The @**dll.import** directive, your one and only way to J/Direct, is quite flexible. It has a number of modifiers that you can use to customize the way you link to the non-Java code. It can also be applied to some methods within a class or to a whole class, meaning that all of the methods you declare in that class are implemented in the same DLL. Let's look at these features.

Aliasing and linking by ordinal

For the **@dll.import** directive to work as shown above, the function in the DLL must be exported by name. However, you might want to use a different name than the original one in the DLL (aliasing), or the function might be exported by number (i.e. by ordinal) instead of by name. The example below declares **FinestraDiMessaggio( )** (the Italian equivalent of "MessageBox") as an alias to **MessageBox( )**. As you can see, the syntax is pretty simple.

```
public class Aliasing {
  public static void main(String args[])
  throws UnsatisfiedLinkError   {
    FinestraDiMessaggio(0,
      "Created by the MessageBox() Win32 func",
      "Thinking in Java", 0);
  }
  /** @dll.import("USER32",
  entrypoint="MessageBox") */
  private static native int
  FinestraDiMessaggio(int hwndOwner, String text,
    String title, int fuStyle);
}
```

The next example shows how to link to a function in a DLL that is not exported by name, but by its position inside of the DLL. The example assumes that there is a DLL named MYMATH somewhere along your path, and that this DLL contains at position 3 a function that takes two integers and gives you back the sum.

```
public class ByOrdinal {
  public static void main(String args[])
  throws UnsatisfiedLinkError {
    int j=3, k=9;
    System.out.println("Result of DLL function:"
      + Add(j,k));
  }
  /** @dll.import("MYMATH", entrypoint = "#3") */
  private static native int Add(int op1,int op2);
}
```

You can see the only difference is the form of the **entrypoint** argument.

Applying @dll.import to the entire class

The **@dll.import** directive can be applied to an entire class, meaning that all of the methods in that class are implemented in the same DLL and with the same linkage attributes. The directive is not inherited by subclasses; for this reason, and since functions in a DLL are by nature **static** functions, a better design approach is to encapsulate the API functions in a separate class, as shown here:

```
/** @dll.import("USER32") */
class MyUser32Access {
  public static native int
  MessageBox(int hwndOwner, String text,
    String title, int fuStyle);
  public native static boolean
  MessageBeep(int uType);
}

public class WholeClass {
  public static void main(String args[])
  throws UnsatisfiedLinkError {
    MyUser32Access.MessageBeep(4);
    MyUser32Access.MessageBox(0,
      "Created by the MessageBox() Win32 func",
      "Thinking in Java", 0);
  }
}
```

Since the **MessageBeep( )** and **MessageBox( )** functions are now declared as static in a different class, you must call them specifying their scope. You might think that you must use the approach above to map *all* of the Win32 API (functions, constants, and data types) to Java classes. Fortunately, you don't have to.

The com.ms.win32 package

The Win32 API is fairly big – on the order of a thousand functions, constants, and data types. Of course, you do not want to write the Java equivalent of every single Win32 API function. Microsoft took care of this, distributing a Java package that maps the Win32 API to Java classes using J/Direct. This package, named **com.ms.win32**, is installed in your classpath during the installation of the Java SDK 2.0 if you select it in the setup options. The package is made up of large number of Java classes that reproduce the constants, data structures, and functions of the Win32

API. The three richest classes are **User32.class**, **Kernel32.class**, and **Gdi32.class**. These contain the core of the Win32 API. To use them, just import them in your Java code. The **ShowMsgBox** example above can be rewritten using **com.ms.win32** as follows (I also took care of the **UnsatisfiedLinkError** in a more civilized way):

```
import com.ms.win32.*;

public class UseWin32Package {
  public static void main(String args[]) {
    try {
      User32.MessageBeep(
        winm.MB_ICONEXCLAMATION);
      User32.MessageBox(0,
        "Created by the MessageBox() Win32 func",
        "Thinking in Java",
        winm.MB_OKCANCEL |
        winm.MB_ICONEXCLAMATION);
    } catch(UnsatisfiedLinkError e) {
      System.out.println("Can't link Win32 API");
      System.out.println(e);
    }
  }
}
```

The package is imported in the first line. The **MessageBeep( )** and **MessageBox( )** functions can now be called with no other declarations. In **MessageBeep( )** you can see that importing the package has also declared the Win32 constants. These constants are defined in a number of Java interfaces, all named winx (x is the first letter of the constant you want to use).

At the time of this writing, the classes in the **com.ms.win32** package are still under development, but usable nonetheless.

Marshaling

Marshaling means converting a function argument from its native binary representation into some language-independent format, and then converting this generic representation into a binary format that is appropriate to the called function. In the example above, we called the **MessageBox( )** function and passed it a couple of **String**s. **MessageBox( )** is a C function, and the binary layout of Java **String**s is not the same as C strings, but the arguments are nonetheless correctly passed. That's because J/Direct takes care of converting a Java **String** into a C string before calling the C code. This happens with all standard Java types. Below is a table of the implicit conversions for simple data types:

Java	C
byte	BYTE or CHAR
short	SHORT or WORD
int	INT, UINT, LONG, ULONG, or DWORD
char	TCHAR
long	__int64
float	Float
double	Double
boolean	BOOL
String	LPCTSTR (Allowed as return value only in ole mode)
byte[]	BYTE *
short[]	WORD *
char[]	TCHAR *
int[]	DWORD *

The list continues, but this gives you the idea. In most cases, you do not need to worry about converting to and from simple data types, but things are different when you must pass arguments of user-defined data types. For example, you might need to pass the address of a structured, user-defined data type, or you might need to pass a pointer to a raw memory area. For these situations, there are special compiler directives to mark a Java class so that it can be passed as a pointer to a structure (the **@dll.struct** directive). For details on the use of these keywords, please refer to the product documentation.

Writing callback functions

Some Win32 API functions require a function pointer as one of the parameters. The Windows API function may then call the argument function, possibly at a later time when some event occurs. This technique is called a *callback function*. Examples include window procedures and the callbacks you set up during a print operation (you give the print spooler the address of your callback function so it can update the status and possibly interrupt printing).

Another example is the **EnumWindows( )** API function that enumerates all top-level windows currently present in the system. **EnumWindows( )** takes a function pointer, then traverses a list maintained internally by

---

Windows. For every window in the list, it calls the callback function, passing the window handle as an argument to the callback.

To do the same thing in Java, you must use the **Callback** class in the **com.ms.dll** package. You inherit from **Callback** and override **callback( )**. This method will accept only **int** parameters and will return **int** or **void**. The method signature and implementation depends on the Windows API function that's using this callback.

Now all we need to do is create an instance of this **Callback**-derived class and pass it as the function pointer argument to the API function. J/Direct will take care of the rest.

The example below calls the **EnumWindows( )** Win32 API; the **callback( )** method in the EnumWindowsProc class gets the window handle for each top-level window, obtains the caption text, and prints it to the console window.

```java
import com.ms.dll.*;
import com.ms.win32.*;

class EnumWindowsProc extends Callback {
  public boolean callback(int hwnd, int lparam) {
    StringBuffer text = new StringBuffer(50);
    User32.GetWindowText(
      hwnd, text, text.capacity()+1);
    if(text.length() != 0)
      System.out.println(text);
    return true;  // to continue enumeration.
  }
}

public class ShowCallback {
  public static void main(String args[])
  throws InterruptedException {
    boolean ok = User32.EnumWindows(
      new EnumWindowsProc(), 0);
    if(!ok)
      System.err.println("EnumWindows failed.");
    Thread.currentThread().sleep(3000);
  }
}
```

The call to **sleep( )** allows the windows procedure to complete before **main( )** exits.

Other J/Direct features

There are two more J/Direct features you can get using modifiers in the **@dll.import** directive. The first is simplified access to OLE functions, and the second is the selection of the ANSI versus Unicode version of API functions. Here is a short description of the two.

By convention, all OLE functions return a value of type HRESULT, which is a structured integer value defined by COM. If you program at the COM level and you want something different returned from an OLE function, you must pass it a pointer to a memory area that the function will fill with data. But in Java we don't have pointers; also, this style is not exactly elegant. With J/Direct, you can easily call OLE functions using the **ole** modifier in the **@dll.import** directive. A native method marked as an **ole** function is automatically translated from a Java-style method signature, which is where you decide the return type, into a COM-style function.

The second feature selects between ANSI and Unicode string handling. Most Win32 API functions that handle strings come in two versions. For example, if you look at the symbols exported by the USER32 DLL, you will not find a **MessageBox( )** function, but instead **MessageBoxA( )** and **MessageBoxW( )** functions, which are the ANSI and Unicode version, respectively. If you do not specify which version you want to call in the **@dll.import** directive, the JVM will try to figure it out. But this operation takes some time during program execution time that you can save with the **ansi**, **unicode**, or **auto** modifiers.

For a more detailed discussion of these features, consult the Microsoft documentation.

Raw Native Interface (RNI)

Compared to J/Direct, RNI is a fairly complex interface to non-Java code, but it's much more powerful. RNI is closer to the JVM than J/Direct, and this lets you write much more efficient code, manipulate Java objects in your native methods, and in general gives you a much higher degree of integration with the JVM internal operations.

RNI is conceptually similar to Sun's JNI. Because of this, and because the product is not yet completed, I'll just point out the major differences. For further information, please refer to Microsoft's documentation.

There are several notable differences between JNI and RNI. Below is the C header file generated by **msjavah**, the Microsoft equivalent of Sun's **javah**, applied to the **ShowMsgBox** Java class file used previously for the JNI example.

```
/*   DO NOT EDIT -
automatically generated by msjavah   */
#include <native.h>
#pragma warning(disable:4510)
#pragma warning(disable:4512)
#pragma warning(disable:4610)

struct Classjava_lang_String;
#define Hjava_lang_String Classjava_lang_String

/*   Header for class ShowMsgBox   */

#ifndef _Included_ShowMsgBox
#define _Included_ShowMsgBox

#define HShowMsgBox ClassShowMsgBox
typedef struct ClassShowMsgBox {
#include <pshpack4.h>
   long MSReserved;
#include <poppack.h>
} ClassShowMsgBox;

#ifdef __cplusplus
extern "C" {
#endif
__declspec(dllexport) void __cdecl
ShowMsgBox_ShowMessage (struct HShowMsgBox *,
   struct Hjava_lang_String *);
#ifdef __cplusplus
}
#endif

#endif   /* _Included_ShowMsgBox */

#pragma warning(default:4510)
#pragma warning(default:4512)
#pragma warning(default:4610)
```

Apart from being less readable, there are more technical issues disguised in the code, which we'll examine.

In RNI, the native method programmer knows the binary layout of the objects. This allows you to directly access the information you want; you don't need to get a field or method identifier as in JNI. But since not all virtual machines necessarily use the same binary layout for their objects, the native method above is guaranteed to run only under the Microsoft JVM.

In JNI, the **JNIEnv** argument gives access to a large number of functions to interact with the JVM. In RNI, the functions for controlling JVM operations are directly available. Some of them, like the one for handling exceptions, are similar to their JNI counterparts, but most of the RNI functions have different names and purposes from those in JNI.

One of the most remarkable differences between JNI and RNI is the garbage collection model. In JNI, the GC basically follows the same rules during native method execution that it follows for the Java code execution. In RNI, the programmer is responsible for starting and stopping the Garbage Collector during native method activity. By default, the GC is disabled upon entering the native method; doing so, the programmer can assume that the objects being used will not be garbage collected during that time. But if the native method, let's say, is going to take a long time, the programmer is free to enable the GC, calling the **GCEnable( )** RNI function.

There is also something similar to the global handles features – something the programmer can use to be sure that specific objects will not be garbage collected when the CG is enabled. The concept is similar but the name is different: in RNI these guys are called **GCFrame**s.

RNI Summary

The fact that RNI is tightly integrated with the Microsoft JVM is both its strength and its weakness. RNI is more complex than JNI, but it also gives you a high degree of control of the internal activities of the JVM, including garbage collection. Also, it is clearly designed for speed, adopting compromises and techniques that C programmers are familiar with. But it's not suitable for JVMs other than Microsoft's.

Java/COM integration

COM (formerly known as OLE) is the Microsoft Component Object Model, the foundation of all ActiveX technologies. These include ActiveX Controls, Automation, and ActiveX Documents. But COM is much more;

it's a specification (and a partial implementation) for developing component objects that can interoperate using dedicated features of the operating system. In practice, all of the new software developed for Win32 systems has some relationship with COM – the operating system exposes some of its features via COM objects. Third-party components can be COM, and you can create and register your own COM components. In one way or another, if you want to write Win32 code, you'll have to deal with COM. Here, I'll just recap the fundamentals of COM programming, and I'll assume that you are familiar with the concept of a COM server (any COM object that can expose services to COM clients) and a COM client (a COM object that uses the services provided by a COM server). This section kept things simple; the tools are actually much more powerful, and you can use them in a more sophisticated way. But this requires a deep knowledge of COM, which is beyond the scope of this appendix. If you're interested in this powerful but platform-dependent feature, you should investigate COM and the Microsoft documentation on Java/COM integration. For more information, Dale Rogerson's "Inside COM" (Microsoft Press, 1997) is an excellent book.

Since COM is the architectural heart of all the new Win32 applications, being able to use, or to expose, COM services from Java code can be important. The Java/COM integration is no doubt one of the most interesting features of the Microsoft Java compiler and virtual machine. Java and COM are so similar in their models that the integration is conceptually straightforward and technically seamless – there's almost no special code to write in order to access COM. Most the details are handled by the compiler and/or by the virtual machine. The effect is that the COM objects are seen as ordinary Java objects by the Java programmer, and COM clients can use COM servers implemented in Java just like any other COM server. Again, I use the generic term COM, but by extension this means that you can implement an ActiveX Automation server in Java, or you can use an ActiveX Control in your Java programs.

The most notable similarities between Java and COM revolve around the relationship between COM interfaces and the Java **interface** keyword. This is a near-perfect match because:

♦   A COM object exposes interfaces (and only interfaces).

♦   A COM interface has no implementation; the COM object exposing an interface is responsible for its implementation.

♦   A COM interface is a description of a group of functions semantically related; no data is exposed.

- A COM class groups together COM interfaces. A Java class can implement an arbitrary number of Java interfaces

- COM has a reference object model; the programmer never "has" an object, just references to one or more of its interfaces. Java has a reference object model as well – a reference to an object can be cast to a reference to one of its interfaces.

- The lifetime in memory of a COM object is determined by the number of clients using the object; when this count goes to zero, the object deletes itself from memory. In Java, the lifetime of an object is also determined by the number of clients. When there are no more references to that object, the object is a candidate to be released by the garbage collector.

This tight mapping between Java and COM not only allows the Java programmer to easily access COM features, but it also makes Java an interesting language for writing COM code. COM is language-independent, but the de facto languages for COM development are C++ and Visual Basic. Compared to Java, C++ is much more powerful for COM development and generates much more efficient code, but it's hard to use. Visual Basic is much easier than Java, but it's too far from the underlying operating system, and its object model does not map very well to COM. Java is an excellent compromise between the two.

Let's take a look at some of the keys points of COM development that you need to know to write Java/COM clients and servers.

COM Fundamentals

COM is a binary specification for implementing interoperable objects. For example, COM describes the binary layout an object should have to be able to call services in another COM object. Since it's a description of a binary layout, COM objects can be implemented in any language that's able to produce such a layout. Usually the programmer is freed from these low level details, since the compiler takes care of generating the correct layout. For example, if you program in C++, most compilers generate a virtual function table that is COM-compliant. With languages that do not produce executable code, such as VB and Java, the runtime takes care of hooking into COM.

The COM Library also supplies a few basic functions, such as the ones for creating an object or locating a COM class registered in your system.

The main goals of a component object model are:

- Let objects call services into other objects.

- Allow new types of objects, or upgrades to existing ones, to be seamlessly plugged into the environment.

The first point is exactly what object-oriented programming is about: you have a client object that makes requests to a server object. In this case, the terms "client" and "server" are used in a generic way, and not to refer to some particular hardware configuration. With any object-oriented language, the first goal is easy to achieve if your application is a monolithic piece of code that implements both the server object code and the client object code. If you make changes to the way client and the server objects interface with each other, you simply compile and link again. When you restart your application, it uses a new version of the components.

The situation is completely different when your application is made up of component objects that are not under your control – you don't control their source code and they can evolve separately from your application. This is exactly the case, for example, when you use a third-party ActiveX Control in your application. The control is installed in your system, and your application is able, at runtime, to locate the server code, activate the object, link to it, and use it. Later, you can install a newer version of the control, and your application should still be able to run; in the worst case, it should gracefully report an error condition, such as "Control not found," without hanging up.

In these scenarios, your components are implemented in separate executable code files: DLLs or EXEs. If the server object is implemented in a separate executable code file, you need a standard, operating system supplied method to activate these objects. Of course, in your code you do not want to use the physical name and location of the DLL or EXE, because these might change; you want some identifier maintained by the operating system. Also, your application needs a description of the services exposed by the server. This is exactly what I'll cover in the next two sections.

GUIDs and the Registry

COM uses structured integer numbers, 128 bits long, to unequivocally identify COM entities registered in the system. These numbers, called GUIDs (Globally Unique IDentifiers) can be generated by specific utilities, and are guaranteed to be unique "in space and in time," to quote Kraig Brockschmidt. In space, because the number is generator reads the id of your network card, and in time because the system date and time are used as well. A GUID can be used to identify a COM class (in which case it's called a CLSID) or a COM interface (IID). The names are different but the concept and the binary structure are the same. GUIDs are also used in other situations that I will not cover here.

GUIDs, along with their associated information, are stored in the Windows Registry, or Registration Database. It's a hierarchical database, built into the operating system, which holds a great amount of information about the hardware and software configuration of your system. For COM, the Registry keeps track of the components installed in your system, such as their CLSIDs, the name and location of the executable file that implement them, and a lot of other details. One of these details is the ProgID of the component; a ProgID is conceptually similar to a GUID in the sense that it identifies a COM component. The difference is that a GUID is a binary, algorithmically-generated value, whereas a ProgID is a programmer-defined string value. A ProgID is associated with a CLSID.

A COM component is said to be registered in the system when at least its CLSID and its executable file location are present in the Registry (the ProgID is usually present as well). Registering and using COM components is exactly what we'll do in the following examples.

One of the effects of the Registry is as a decoupling layer between the client and server objects. The client activates the server using some information that is stored in the Registry; one piece of information is the physical location of the server executables. If the location changes, the information in the Registry is updated accordingly, but this is transparent to the client, which just uses ProgIDs or CLSIDs. In other words, the Registry allows for location transparency of the server code. With the introduction of DCOM (Distributed COM), a server that was running on a local machine can even be moved to a remote machine on the network, without the client even noticing it (well, almost...).

Type Libraries

Because of COM's dynamic linking and the independent evolution of client and server code, the client always needs to dynamically detect the services that are exposed by the server. These services are described in a binary, language-independent way (as interfaces and method signatures) in the *type library*. This can be a separate file (usually with the .TLB extension), or a Win32 resource linked into the executable. At runtime, the client uses the information in the type library to call functions in the server.

You can generate a type library by writing a Microsoft Interface Definition Language (MIDL) source file and compiling it with the MIDL compiler to generate a .TLB file. MIDL is a language that describes COM classes, interfaces, and methods. It resembles the OMG/CORBA IDL in name, syntax, and purpose. The Java programmer has no need to use MIDL, though. A different Microsoft tool, described later, reads a Java class file and generates a type library.

Function return codes in COM: HRESULT

COM functions exposed by a server return a value of the predefined type HRESULT. An HRESULT is an integer containing three fields. This allows for multiple failure and success codes, along with additional information. Because a COM function returns an HRESULT, you cannot use the return value to hand back ordinary data from the function call. If you must return data, you pass a pointer to a memory area that the function will fill. This is known as an *out parameter*. You don't need to worry about this as a Java/COM programmer since the virtual machine takes care of it for you. This is described in the following sections.

MS Java/COM Integration

The Microsoft Java compiler, Virtual Machine, and tools make life a lot easier for the Java/COM programmer than it is for the C++/COM programmer. The compiler has special directives and packages for treating Java classes as COM classes, but in most cases, you'll just rely on the Microsoft JVM support for COM, and on a couple of external tools.

The Microsoft Java Virtual Machine acts as a bridge between COM and Java objects. If you create a Java object as a COM server, your object will still be running inside the JVM. The Microsoft JVM is implemented as a DLL, which exposes COM interfaces to the operating system. Internally, the JVM maps function calls to these COM interfaces to method calls in your Java objects. Of course, the JVM must know which Java class file corresponds to the server executable; it can discover this information because you previously registered the class file in the Windows Registry using **Javareg**, a utility in the Microsoft Java SDK. **Javareg** reads a Java class file, generates a corresponding type library and a GUID, and registers the class in the system. **Javareg** can be used to register remote servers as well, for example, servers that run on a different physical machine.

If you want to write a Java/COM client, you must go through a different process. A Java/COM client is Java code that wants to activate and use one of the COM servers registered on your system. Again, the virtual machine interfaces with the COM server and exposes its services as methods in a Java class. Another Microsoft tool, **jactivex**, reads a type library and generates Java source files that contain special compiler directives. The generated source files are part of a package named after the type library you specified. The next step is to import that package in your COM client Java source files.

Let's look at a couple of examples.

Developing COM servers in Java

This section shows the process you will apply to the development of ActiveX Controls, Automation Servers, or any other COM-compliant server. The following example implements a simple Automation server that adds integer numbers. You set the value of the **addend** with the **setAddend( )** method, and each time you call the **sum( )** method the **addend** is added to the current **result**. You retrieve the **result** with **getResult( )** and reset the values with **clear( )**. The Java class that implements this behavior is straightforward:

```
public class Adder {
   private int addend;
   private int result;
   public void setAddend(int a) { addend = a; }
   public int getAddend() { return addend; }
   public int getResult() { return result; }
   public void sum() { result += addend;   }
   public void clear() {
      result = 0;
      addend = 0;
   }
}
```

To use this Java class as a COM object, the **Javareg** tool is applied to the compiled **Adder.class** file. This tool has a number of options; in this case we specify the Java class file name ("Adder"), the ProgID we want to put in the Registry for this server ("JavaAdder.Adder.1"), and the name we want for the type library that will be generated ("JavaAdder.tlb"). Since no CLSID is given, **Javareg** will generate one; if we call **Javareg** again on the same server, the existing CLSID will be used.

```
javareg /register
   /class:Adder /progid:JavaAdder.Adder.1
/typelib:JavaAdder.tlb
```

Javareg also registers the new server in the Windows Registry. At this point, you must remember to copy your **Adder.class** file into the Windows\Java\trustlib directory. For security reasons, related mostly to the use of COM services by applets, your COM server will be activated only if it is installed in the trustlib directory.

You now have a new Automation server installed on your system. To test it, you need an Automation controller, and "the" Automation Controller is Visual Basic (VB). Below, you can see a few lines of VB code. On the VB form, I put a text box to input the value of the addend, a label to show the result, and two push buttons to invoke the **sum( )** and **clear( )** methods. At the beginning, an object variable named **Adder** is declared. In the **Form_Load** subroutine, executed when the form is first displayed, a new instance of the **Adder** automation server is instantiated and the text fields on the form are initialized. When the user presses the "Sum" or "Clear" buttons, appropriate methods in the server are invoked.

```
Dim Adder As Object

Private Sub Form_Load()
    Set Adder = CreateObject("JavaAdder.Adder.1")
    Addend.Text = Adder.getAddend
    Result.Caption = Adder.getResult
End Sub

Private Sub SumBtn_Click()
    Adder.setAddend (Addend.Text)
    Adder.Sum
    Result.Caption = Adder.getResult
End Sub

Private Sub ClearBtn_Click()
    Adder.Clear
    Addend.Text = Adder.getAddend
    Result.Caption = Adder.getResult
End Sub
```

Note that this code has no knowledge that the server was implemented in Java.

When you run this program and the **CreateObject( )** function is called, the Windows Registry is searched for the specified ProgID. Among the information related to the ProgID is the name of the Java class file, so in response the Java Virtual Machine is started, and the Java object instantiated inside the JVM. From then on, the JVM takes care of the interaction between the client and server code.

Developing COM clients in Java

Now let's jump to the other side and develop a COM client in Java. This program will call services in a COM server that's installed on your system. The example is a client for the server we implemented in the previous example. While the code will look familiar to a Java programmer, what happens behind the scenes is quite unusual. This example uses a server that happens to be written in Java but applies to any ActiveX Control, ActiveX Automation server, or ActiveX component installed in your system for which you have a type library.

First, the **Jactivex** tool is applied to the server's type library. **Jactivex** has a number of options and switches, but in its basic form it reads a type library and generates Java source files, which it stores in your **windows/Java/trustlib** directory. In the example line below, it is applied to the type library that was generated for out COM Automation server.

```
jactivex /javatlb JavaAdder.tlb
```

If, after **Jactivex** has finished, you take a look at your **windows/Java/trustlib** directory, you'll find a new subdirectory called **javaadder** that contains the source files for a new package. This is the Java equivalent of the type library. These files use compiler directives specific to the Microsoft compiler: the @**com** directives. The reason **jactivex** generated more than one file is that COM uses more than one entity to describe a COM server (and also because I did not fine-tune the use of MIDL files and the Java/COM tools).

The file named **Adder.java** is the equivalent of a **coclass** directive in a MIDL file: it's the declaration of a COM class. The other files are the Java equivalent of the COM interfaces exposed by the server. These interfaces, such as **Adder_DispatchDefault.java**, are dispatch interfaces, part of the mechanism of interaction between an Automation controller and an Automation server. The Java/COM integration feature also supports the implementation and use of dual interfaces. IDispatch and dual interfaces are beyond the scope of this appendix.

Below, you can see the client code. The first line just imports the package generated by **jactivex**. Then an instance of the COM Automation server is created and used, as if it was an ordinary Java class. Notice the typecast on the line where the COM object is instantiated. This is consistent with the COM object model. In COM, the programmer never has a reference to the whole object; instead, the programmer can only have references to one or more of the interfaces implemented in the class.

Instantiating a Java object of the Adder class tells COM to activate the server and to create an instance of this COM object. But then we must specify which interface we want to use, choosing among the ones implemented by the server. This is exactly what the typecast does. The interface used here is the *default dispatch interface*, the standard interface that an Automation controller uses to communicate with an Automation server (for details, see *Inside COM*, ibid.). Notice how simple it is to activate the server and select a COM interface:

```
import javaadder.*;

public class JavaClient {
    public static void main(String [] args) {
        Adder_DispatchDefault iAdder =
            (Adder_DispatchDefault) new Adder();
        iAdder.setAddend(3);
        iAdder.sum();
        iAdder.sum();
        iAdder.sum();
        System.out.println(iAdder.getResult());
    }
}
```

Now you can compile and run the code.

The com.ms.com package

The **com.ms.com** package defines a number of classes for COM development. It supports the use of GUIDs – the **Variant** and **SafeArray** Automation types – interfacing with ActiveX Controls at a deeper level and handling COM exceptions.

I cannot cover all of these topics here, but I want to point out something about COM exceptions. By convention, virtually all COM functions return an HRESULT value that tells you if the function invocation succeeded or not and why. But if you look at the Java method signature in our server and client code, there no HRESULT. Instead, we use the function return value to get data back from some functions. The virtual machine is translating Java-style function calls into COM-style function calls, even for the return parameter. But what happens inside the virtual machine if one of the functions you call in the server fails at the COM level? In this case, the JVM sees that the HRESULT value indicates a failure and generates a native Java exception of class **com.ms.com.ComFailException**. In this way, you can handle COM errors using Java exception handling instead of checking function return values.

To learn more about the classes in this package, please refer to the Microsoft documentation.

ActiveX/Beans integration

An interesting result of Java/COM integration is the ActiveX/Beans integration, by which a Java Bean can be hosted by an ActiveX container such as VB or any Microsoft Office product, and an ActiveX Control can be hosted by a Beans container such as Sun's BeanBox. The Microsoft JVM takes care of the details. An ActiveX Control is just a COM server exposing predefined, required interfaces. A Bean is just a Java class that is compliant with a specific programming style. At the time this was written, however, the integration was not perfect. For example, the virtual machine is not able to map the JavaBeans event model to the COM event model. If you want to handle events from a Bean inside an ActiveX container, the Bean must intercept system events such as mouse actions via low-level techniques, not the standard JavaBeans delegation event model.

Apart from this, the ActiveX/Beans integration is extremely interesting. The concept and tools are exactly the same as discussed above, so please consult Microsoft's documentation for more details.

A note about native methods and applets

Native methods face the security issue. When your Java code calls a native method, you pass control outside of the virtual machine "sandbox." The native method has complete access to the operating system. Of course, this is exactly what you want if you write native methods, but it is not acceptable for applets, at least not implicitly. You don't want an applet, downloaded from a remote Internet server, to be free to play with the file system and other critical areas of your machine unless you allow it to do so. To prevent this situation with J/Direct, RNI, and COM integration, only trusted Java code has permission to make native method calls. Different conditions must be met depending on the feature the applet is trying to use. For example, an applet that uses J/Direct must be digitally signed to indicate full trust. At the time of this writing, not all of these security mechanisms are implemented (in the Microsoft SDK for Java, beta 2), so keep an eye on the documentation as new versions become available.

CORBA

In large, distributed applications, your needs might not be satisfied by the preceding approaches. For example, you might want to interface with legacy datastores, or you might need services from a server object regardless of its physical location. These situations require some form of Remote Procedure Call (RPC), and possibly language independence. This is where CORBA can help.

CORBA is not a language feature; it's an integration technology. It's a specification that vendors can follow to implement CORBA-compliant integration products. CORBA is part of the OMG's effort to define a standard framework for distributed, language-independent object interoperability.

CORBA supplies the ability to make remote procedure calls into Java objects and non–Java objects, and to interface with legacy systems in a location-transparent way. Java adds networking support and a nice object-oriented language for building graphical and non-graphical applications. The Java and OMG object model map nicely to each other; for example, both Java and CORBA implement the interface concept and a reference object model.

CORBA Fundamentals

The object interoperability specification developed by the OMG is commonly referred to as the Object Management Architecture (OMA). The OMA defines two components: the Core Object Model and the OMA Reference Architecture. The Core Object Model states the basic concepts of object, interface, operation, and so on. (CORBA is a refinement of the Core Object Model.) The OMA Reference Architecture defines an underlying infrastructure of services and mechanisms that allow objects to interoperate. The OMA Reference Architecture includes the Object Request Broker (ORB), Object Services (also known as CORBAservices), and common facilities.

The ORB is the communication bus by which objects can request services from other objects, regardless of their physical location. This means that what looks like a method call in the client code is actually a complex

---

operation. First, a connection with the server object must exist, and to create a connection the ORB must know where the server implementation code resides. Once the connection is established, the method arguments must be marshaled, i.e. converted in a binary stream to be sent across a network. Other information that must be sent are the server machine name, the server process, and the identity of the server object inside that process. Finally, this information is sent through a low-level wire protocol, the information is decoded on the server side, and the call is executed. The ORB hides all of this complexity from the programmer and makes the operation almost as simple as calling a method on local object.

There is no specification for how an ORB Core should be implemented, but to provide a basic compatibility among different vendors' ORBs, the OMG defines a set of services that are accessible through standard interfaces.

CORBA Interface Definition Language (IDL)

CORBA is designed for language transparency: a client object can call methods on a server object of different class, regardless of the language they are implemented with. Of course, the client object must know the names and signatures of methods that the server object exposes. This is where IDL comes in. The CORBA IDL is a language-neutral way to specify data types, attributes, operations, interfaces, and more. The IDL syntax is similar to the C++ or Java syntax. The following table shows the correspondence between some of the concepts common to three languages that can be specified through CORBA IDL:

CORBA IDL	Java	C++
Module	Package	Namespace
Interface	Interface	Pure abstract class
Method	Method	Member function

The inheritance concept is supported as well, using the colon operator as in C++. The programmer writes an IDL description of the attributes, methods, and interfaces that will be implemented and used by the server and clients. The IDL is then compiled by a vendor-provided IDL/Java compiler, which reads the IDL source and generates Java code.

The IDL compiler is an extremely useful tool: it doesn't just generate a Java source equivalent of the IDL, it also generates the code that will be used to marshal method arguments and to make remote calls. This code, called the stub and skeleton code, is organized in multiple Java source files and is usually part of the same Java package.

The naming service

The naming service is one of the fundamental CORBA services. A CORBA object is accessed through a reference, a piece of information that's not meaningful for the human reader. But references can be assigned programmer-defined, string names. This operation is known as *stringifying the reference*, and one of the OMA components, the Naming Service, is devoted to performing string-to-object and object-to-string conversion and mapping. Since the Naming Service acts as a telephone directory that both servers and clients can consult and manipulate, it runs as a separate process. Creating an object-to-string mapping is called *binding an object*, and removing the mapping is called *unbinding*. Getting an object reference passing a string is called *resolving the name*.

For example, on startup, a server application could create a server object, bind the object into the name service, and then wait for clients to make requests. A client first obtains a server object reference, resolving the string name, and then can make calls into the server using the reference.

Again, the Naming Service specification is part of CORBA, but the application that implements it is provided by the ORB vendor. The way you get access to the Naming Service functionality can vary from vendor to vendor.

An example

The code shown here will not be elaborate because different ORBs have different ways to access CORBA services, so examples are vendor specific. (The example below uses JavaIDL, a free product from Sun that comes with a light-weight ORB, a naming service, and a IDL-to-Java compiler.) In addition, since Java is young and still evolving, not all CORBA features are present in the various Java/CORBA products.

We want to implement a server, running on some machine, that can be queried for the exact time. We also want to implement a client that asks for the exact time. In this case we'll be implementing both programs in Java, but we could also use two different languages (which often happens in real situations).

Writing the IDL source

The first step is to write an IDL description of the services provided. This is usually done by the server programmer, who is then free to implement the server in any language in which a CORBA IDL compiler exists. The

IDL file is distributed to the client side programmer and becomes the bridge between languages.

The example below shows the IDL description of our exact time server:

```
module RemoteTime {
    interface ExactTime {
        string getTime();
    };
};
```

This is a declaration of the **ExactTime** interface inside the **RemoteTime** namespace. The interface is made up of one single method the gives back the current time in **string** format.

Creating stubs and skeletons

The second step is to compile the IDL to create the Java stub and skeleton code that we'll use for implementing the client and the server. The tool that comes with the JavaIDL product is **idltojava**:

```
idltojava -fserver -fclient RemoteTime.idl
```

The two flags tell **idltojava** to generate code for both the stub and the skeleton. **Idltojava** generates a Java package named after the IDL module, **RemoteTime**, and the generated Java files are put in the **RemoteTime** subdirectory. **_ExactTimeImplBase.java** is the skeleton that we'll use to implement the server object, and **_ExactTimeStub.java** will be used for the client. There are Java representations of the IDL interface in **ExactTime.java** and a couple of other support files used, for example, to facilitate access to the naming service operations.

Implementing the server and the client

Below you can see the code for the server side. The server object implementation is in the **ExactTimeServer** class. The **RemoteTimeServer** is the application that creates a server object, registers it with the ORB, gives a name to the object reference, and then sits quietly waiting for client requests.

```
import RemoteTime.*;

import org.omg.CosNaming.*;
import org.omg.CosNaming.NamingContextPackage.*;
import org.omg.CORBA.*;
```

```java
import java.util.*;
import java.text.*;

// Server object implementation
class ExactTimeServer extends _ExactTimeImplBase{
  public String getTime(){
    return DateFormat.
        getTimeInstance(DateFormat.FULL).
          format(new Date(
              System.currentTimeMillis()));
  }
}

// Remote application implementation
public class RemoteTimeServer {
  public static void main(String args[])  {
    try {
      // ORB creation and initialization:
      ORB orb = ORB.init(args, null);
      // Create the server object and register it:
      ExactTimeServer timeServerObjRef =
        new ExactTimeServer();
      orb.connect(timeServerObjRef);
      // Get the root naming context:
      org.omg.CORBA.Object objRef =
        orb.resolve_initial_references(
          "NameService");
      NamingContext ncRef =
        NamingContextHelper.narrow(objRef);
      // Assign a string name to the
      // object reference (binding):
      NameComponent nc =
        new NameComponent("ExactTime", "");
      NameComponent path[] = {nc};
      ncRef.rebind(path, timeServerObjRef);
      // Wait for client requests:
      java.lang.Object sync =
        new java.lang.Object();
      synchronized(sync){
        sync.wait();
      }
    }
    catch (Exception e)  {
      System.out.println(
```

```
                    "Remote Time server error: " + e);
                e.printStackTrace(System.out);
            }
        }
    }
```

As you can see, implementing the server object is simple; it's a regular Java class that inherits from the skeleton code generated by the IDL compiler. Things get a bit more complicated when it comes to interacting with the ORB and other CORBA services.

Some CORBA services

This is a short description of what the JavaIDL-related code is doing (primarily ignoring the part of the CORBA code that is vendor dependent). The first line in **main( )** starts up the ORB, and of course, this is because our server object will need to interact with it. Right after the ORB initialization, a server object is created. Actually, the right term would be a *transient servant object*: an object that receives requests from clients, and whose lifetime is the same as the process that creates it. Once the transient servant object is created, it is registered with the ORB, which means that the ORB knows of its existence and can now forward requests to it.

Up to this point, all we have is **timeServerObjRef**, an object reference that is known only inside the current server process. The next step will be to assign a stringified name to this servant object; clients will use that name to locate the servant object. We accomplish this operation using the Naming Service. First, we need an object reference to the Naming Service; the call to **resolve_initial_references( )** takes the stringified object reference of the Naming Service that is "NameService," in JavaIDL, and returns an object reference. This is cast to a specific **NamingContext** reference using the **narrow( )** method. We can use now the naming services.

To bind the servant object with a stringified object reference, we first create a **NameComponent** object, initialized with "ExactTime," the name string we want to bind to the servant object. Then, using the **rebind( )** method, the stringified reference is bound to the object reference. We use **rebind( )** to assign a reference, even if it already exists, whereas **bind( )** raises an exception if the reference already exists. A name is made up in CORBA by a sequence of NameContexts – that's why we use an array to bind the name to the object reference.

The servant object is finally ready for use by clients. At this point, the server process enters a wait state. Again, this is because it is a transient servant, so its lifetime is confined to the server process. JavaIDL does not currently support persistent objects – objects that survive the execution of the process that creates them.

Now that we have an idea of what the server code is doing, let's look at the client code:

```
import RemoteTime.*;
import org.omg.CosNaming.*;
import org.omg.CORBA.*;

public class RemoteTimeClient {
  public static void main(String args[]) {
    try {
      // ORB creation and initialization:
      ORB orb = ORB.init(args, null);
      // Get the root naming context:
      org.omg.CORBA.Object objRef =
        orb.resolve_initial_references(
          "NameService");
      NamingContext ncRef =
        NamingContextHelper.narrow(objRef);
      // Get (resolve) the stringified object
      // reference for the time server:
      NameComponent nc =
        new NameComponent("ExactTime", "");
      NameComponent path[] = {nc};
      ExactTime timeObjRef =
        ExactTimeHelper.narrow(
          ncRef.resolve(path));
      // Make requests to the server object:
      String exactTime = timeObjRef.getTime();
      System.out.println(exactTime);
    } catch (Exception e) {
      System.out.println(
        "Remote Time server error: " + e);
      e.printStackTrace(System.out);
    }
  }
}
```

The first few lines do the same as they do in the server process: the ORB is initialized and a reference to the naming service server is resolved.

Next, we need an object reference for the servant object, so we pass the stringified object reference to the **resolve( )** method, and we cast the result into an **ExactTime** interface reference using the **narrow( )** method. Finally, we call **getTime( )**.

Activating the name service process

Finally we have a server and a client application ready to interoperate. You've seen that both need the naming service to bind and resolve stringified object references. You must start the naming service process before running either the server or the client. In JavaIDL, the naming service is a Java application that comes with the product package, but it can be different with other products. The JavaIDL naming service runs inside an instance of the JVM and listens by default to network port 900.

Activating the server and the client

Now you are ready to start your server and client application (in this order, since our server is transient). If everything is set up correctly, what you'll get is a single output line on the client console window, giving you the current time. Of course, this might be not very exciting by itself, but you should take one thing into account: even if they are on the same physical machine, the client and the server application are running inside different virtual machines and they can communicate via an underlying integration layer, the ORB and the Naming Service.

This is a simple example, designed to work without a network, but an ORB is usually configured for location transparency. When the server and the client are on different machines, the ORB can resolve remote stringified references using a component known as the *Implementation Repository*. Although the Implementation Repository is part of CORBA, there is almost no specification, so it differs from vendor to vendor.

As you can see, there is much more to CORBA than what has been covered here, but you should get the basic idea. If you want more information about CORBA, the place to start is the OMG Web site, at http://www.omg.org. There you'll find documentation, white papers, proceedings, and references to other CORBA sources and products.

Java Applets and CORBA

Java applets can act as CORBA clients. This way, an applet can access remote information and services exposed as CORBA objects. But an applet can connect only with the server from which it was downloaded, so all the CORBA objects the applet interacts with must be on that server. This is the opposite of what CORBA tries to do: give you complete location transparency.

This is an issue of network security. If you're on an Intranet, one solution is to loosen the security restrictions on the browser. Or, set up a firewall policy for connecting with external servers.

Some Java ORB products offer proprietary solutions to this problem. For example, some implement what is called HTTP Tunneling, while others have their special firewall features.

This is too complex a topic to be covered in an appendix, but it is definitely something you should be aware of.

CORBA vs. RMI

You saw that one of the main CORBA features is RPC support, which allows your local objects to call methods in remote objects. Of course, there already is a native Java feature that does exactly the same thing: RMI (see Chapter 15). While RMI makes RPC possible between Java objects, CORBA makes RPC possible between objects implemented in any language. It's a big difference.

However, RMI can be used to call services on remote, non-Java code. All you need is some kind of wrapper Java object around the non-Java code on the server side. The wrapper object connects externally to Java clients via RMI, and internally connects to the non-Java code using one of the techniques shown above, such as JNI or J/Direct.

This approach requires you to write a kind of integration layer, which is exactly what CORBA does for you, but then you don't need a third-party ORB.

Summary

What you've seen in this appendix are the most common techniques to call non-Java code from a Java application. Each technique has its pros and cons, but currently the major problem is that not all of these features are available on all JVMs, so a Java program that calls native methods on a specific platform might not work on a different platform with a different JVM.

Sun's JNI is flexible, reasonably simple (although it requires a lot of control over the JVM internals), powerful, and it's available on most

JVMs, but not all. Microsoft, at the time of this writing, does not support JNI, but offers J/Direct, a simple way to call Win32 DLL functions, and RNI, which is designed for high-performance code but requires a good understanding of the JVM internals. Microsoft also offers its proprietary Java/COM integration feature, which is powerful and makes Java an interesting language for writing COM servers and clients. J/Direct, RNI, and Java/COM integration are supported only by the Microsoft compiler and JVM.

Finally, we took a look at CORBA, which allows your Java objects to talk to other objects regardless of their physical location and implementation language. CORBA is different from the techniques above because it is not integrated with the Java language, but instead uses third-party integration technology and requires that you buy a third-party ORB. CORBA is an interesting and general solution, but it might not be the best approach if you just want to make calls into the operating system.

B: Comparing C++ and Java

As a C++ programmer, you already have the basic idea of object-oriented programming, and the syntax of Java no doubt looks familiar to you. This makes sense since Java was derived from C++.

However, there are a surprising number of differences between C++ and Java. These differences are intended to be significant improvements, and if you understand the differences you'll see why Java is such a beneficial programming language. This appendix takes you through the important features that distinguish Java from C++.

1. The biggest potential stumbling block is speed: interpreted Java runs in the range of 20 times slower than C. Nothing prevents the Java language from being compiled and there are just-in-time compilers appearing at this writing that offer significant speed-ups. It is not inconceivable that full native compilers will appear for the more

popular platforms, but without those there are classes of problems that will be insoluble with Java because of the speed issue.

2. Java has both kinds of comments like C++ does.

3. Everything must be in a class. There are no global functions or global data. If you want the equivalent of globals, make **static** methods and **static** data within a class. There are no structs or enumerations or unions, only classes.

4. All method definitions are defined in the body of the class. Thus, in C++ it would look like all the functions are inlined, but they're not (inlines are noted later).

5. Class definitions are roughly the same form in Java as in C++, but there's no closing semicolon. There are no class declarations of the form **class foo**, only class definitions.
```
class aType {
  void aMethod( ) { /* method body */ }
}
```

6. There's no scope resolution operator :: in Java. Java uses the dot for everything, but can get away with it since you can define elements only within a class. Even the method definitions must always occur within a class, so there is no need for scope resolution there either. One place where you'll notice the difference is in the calling of **static** methods: you say **ClassName.methodName( );**. In addition, **package** names are established using the dot, and to perform a kind of C++ **#include** you use the **import** keyword. For example: **import java.awt.*;**. (**#include** does not directly map to **import**, but it has a similar feel to it).

7. Java, like C++, has primitive types for efficient access. In Java, these are **boolean**, **char**, **byte**, **short**, **int**, **long**, **float**, and **double**. All the primitive types have specified sizes that are machine independent for portability. (This must have some impact on performance, varying with the machine.) Type-checking and type requirements are much tighter in Java. For example:
1. Conditional expressions can be only **boolean**, not integral.
2. The result of an expression like X + Y must be used; you can't just say "X + Y" for the side effect.

8. The **char** type uses the international 16-bit Unicode character set, so it can automatically represent most national characters.

9. Static quoted strings are automatically converted into **String** objects. There is no independent static character array string like there is in C and C++.

10. Java adds the triple right shift **>>>** to act as a "logical" right shift by inserting zeroes at the top end; the **>>** inserts the sign bit as it shifts (an "arithmetic" shift).

11. Although they look similar, arrays have a very different structure and behavior in Java than they do in C++. There's a read-only **length** member that tells you how big the array is, and run-time checking throws an exception if you go out of bounds. All arrays are created on the heap, and you can assign one array to another (the array handle is simply copied). The array identifier is a first-class object, with all of the methods commonly available to all other objects.

12. All objects of non-primitive types can be created only via **new**. There's no equivalent to creating non-primitive objects "on the stack" as in C++. All primitive types can be created only on the stack, without **new**. There are wrapper classes for all primitive classes so that you can create equivalent heap-based objects via **new**. (Arrays of primitives are a special case: they can be allocated via aggregate initialization as in C++, or by using **new**.)

13. No forward declarations are necessary in Java. If you want to use a class or a method before it is defined, you simply use it – the compiler ensures that the appropriate definition exists. Thus you don't have any of the forward referencing issues that you do in C++.

14. Java has no preprocessor. If you want to use classes in another library, you say **import** and the name of the library. There are no preprocessor-like macros.

15. Java uses packages in place of namespaces. The name issue is taken care of by putting everything into a class and by using a facility called "packages" that performs the equivalent namespace breakup for class names. Packages also collect library components under a single library name. You simply **import** a package and the compiler takes care of the rest.

16. Object handles defined as class members are automatically initialized to **null**. Initialization of primitive class data members is guaranteed in Java; if you don't explicitly initialize them they get a default value (a zero or equivalent). You can initialize them explicitly, either when you define them in the class or in the constructor. The syntax makes

more sense than that for C++, and is consistent for **static** and non-**static** members alike. You don't need to externally define storage for **static** members like you do in C++.

17. There are no Java pointers in the sense of C and C++. When you create an object with **new**, you get back a reference (which I've been calling a *handle* in this book). For example:

```
String s = new String("howdy");
```

However, unlike C++ references that must be initialized when created and cannot be rebound to a different location, Java references don't have to be bound at the point of creation. They can also be rebound at will, which eliminates part of the need for pointers. The other reason for pointers in C and C++ is to be able to point at any place in memory whatsoever (which makes them unsafe, which is why Java doesn't support them). Pointers are often seen as an efficient way to move through an array of primitive variables; Java arrays allow you to do that in a safer fashion. The ultimate solution for pointer problems is native methods (discussed in Appendix A). Passing pointers to methods isn't a problem since there are no global functions, only classes, and you can pass references to objects. The Java language promoters initially said "No pointers!", but when many programmers questioned how you can work without pointers, the promoters began saying "Restricted pointers." You can make up your mind whether it's "really" a pointer or not. In any event, there's no pointer *arithmetic*.

18. Java has constructors that are similar to constructors in C++. You get a default constructor if you don't define one, and if you define a non-default constructor, there's no automatic default constructor defined for you, just like in C++. There are no copy constructors, since all arguments are passed by reference.

19. There are no destructors in Java. There is no "scope" of a variable per se, to indicate when the object's lifetime is ended – the lifetime of an object is determined instead by the garbage collector. There is a **finalize( )** method that's a member of each class, something like a C++ destructor, but **finalize( )** is called by the garbage collector and is supposed to be responsible only for releasing "resources" (such as open files, sockets, ports, URLs, etc). If you need something done at a specific point, you must create a special method and call it, not rely upon **finalize( )**. Put another way, all objects in C++ will be (or rather, should be) destroyed, but not all objects in Java are garbage collected. Because Java doesn't support destructors, you must be careful to create a cleanup method if it's necessary and to explicitly

call all the cleanup methods for the base class and member objects in your class.

20. Java has method overloading that works virtually identically to C++ function overloading.

21. Java does not support default arguments.

22. There's no **goto** in Java. The one unconditional jump mechanism is the **break** *label* or **continue** *label*, which is used to jump out of the middle of multiply-nested loops.

23. Java uses a singly-rooted hierarchy, so all objects are ultimately inherited from the root class **Object**. In C++, you can start a new inheritance tree anywhere, so you end up with a forest of trees. In Java you get a single ultimate hierarchy. This can seem restrictive, but it gives a great deal of power since you know that every object is guaranteed to have at least the **Object** interface. C++ appears to be the only OO language that does not impose a singly rooted hierarchy.

24. Java has no templates or other implementation of parameterized types. There is a set of collections: **Vector**, **Stack**, and **Hashtable** that hold **Object** references, and through which you can satisfy your collection needs, but these collections are not designed for efficiency like the C++ Standard Template Library (STL). The new collections in Java 1.2 are more complete, but still don't have the same kind of efficiency as template implementations would allow.

25. Garbage collection means memory leaks are much harder to cause in Java, but not impossible. (If you make native method calls that allocate storage, these are typically not tracked by the garbage collector.) However, many memory leaks and resouce leaks can be tracked to a badly written **finalize( )** or to not releasing a resource at the end of the block where it is allocated (a place where a destructor would certainly come in handy). The garbage collector is a huge improvement over C++, and makes a lot of programming problems simply vanish. It might make Java unsuitable for solving a small subset of problems that cannot tolerate a garbage collector, but the advantage of a garbage collector seems to greatly outweigh this potential drawback.

26. Java has built-in multithreading support. There's a **Thread** class that you inherit to create a new thread (you override the **run( )** method). Mutual exclusion occurs at the level of objects using the **synchronized** keyword as a type qualifier for methods. Only one thread may use a **synchronized** method of a particular object at any

one time. Put another way, when a **synchronized** method is entered, it first "locks" the object against any other **synchronized** method using that object and "unlocks" the object only upon exiting the method. There are no explicit locks; they happen automatically. You're still responsible for implementing more sophisticated synchronization between threads by creating your own "monitor" class. Recursive **synchronized** methods work correctly. Time slicing is not guaranteed between equal priority threads.

27. Instead of controlling blocks of declarations like C++ does, the access specifiers (**public**, **private**, and **protected**) are placed on each definition for each member of a class. Without an explicit access specifier, an element defaults to "friendly," which means that it is accessible to other elements in the same package (equivalent to them all being C++ **friend**s) but inaccessible outside the package. The class, and each method within the class, has an access specifier to determine whether it's visible outside the file. Sometimes the **private** keyword is used less in Java because "friendly" access is often more useful than excluding access from other classes in the same package. (However, with multithreading the proper use of **private** is essential.) The Java **protected** keyword means "accessible to inheritors *and* to others in this package." There is no equivalent to the C++ **protected** keyword that means "accessible to inheritors *only*" (**private protected** used to do this, but the use of that keyword pair was removed).

28. Nested classes. In C++, nesting a class is an aid to name hiding and code organization (but C++ namespaces eliminate the need for name hiding). Java packaging provides the equivalence of namespaces, so that isn't an issue. Java 1.1 has *inner classes* that look just like nested classes. However, an object of an inner class secretly keeps a handle to the object of the outer class that was involved in the creation of the inner class object. This means that the inner class object may access members of the outer class object without qualification, as if those members belonged directly to the inner class object. This provides a much more elegant solution to the problem of callbacks, solved with pointers to members in C++.

29. Because of inner classes described in the previous point, there are no pointers to members in Java.

30. No **inline** methods. The Java compiler might decide on its own to inline a method, but you don't have much control over this. You can suggest inlining in Java by using the **final** keyword for a method.

However, **inline** functions are only suggestions to the C++ compiler as well.

31. Inheritance in Java has the same effect as in C++, but the syntax is different. Java uses the **extends** keyword to indicate inheritance from a base class and the **super** keyword to specify methods to be called in the base class that have the same name as the method you're in. (However, the **super** keyword in Java allows you to access methods only in the parent class, one level up in the hierarchy.) Base-class scoping in C++ allows you to access methods that are deeper in the hierarchy). The base-class constructor is also called using the **super** keyword. As mentioned before, all classes are ultimately automatically inherited from **Object**. There's no explicit constructor initializer list like in C++, but the compiler forces you to perform all base-class initialization at the beginning of the constructor body and it won't let you perform these later in the body. Member initialization is guaranteed through a combination of automatic initialization and exceptions for uninitialized object handles.

```
public class Foo extends Bar {
  public Foo(String msg) {
    super(msg); // Calls base constructor
  }
  public baz(int i) { // Override
    super.baz(i); // Calls base method
  }
}
```

32. Inheritance in Java doesn't change the protection level of the members in the base class. You cannot specify **public**, **private**, or **protected** inheritance in Java, as you can in C++. Also, overridden methods in a derived class cannot reduce the access of the method in the base class. For example, if a method is **public** in the base class and you override it, your overridden method must also be **public** (the compiler checks for this).

33. Java provides the **interface** keyword, which creates the equivalent of an abstract base class filled with abstract methods and with no data members. This makes a clear distinction between something designed to be just an interface and an extension of existing functionality via the **extends** keyword. It's worth noting that the **abstract** keyword produces a similar effect in that you can't create an object of that class. An **abstract** class *may* contain abstract methods (although it isn't required to contain any), but it is also able to contain implementations, so it is restricted to single inheritance. Together with interfaces, this scheme prevents the need for some mechanism

like virtual base classes in C++.

To create a version of the **interface** that can be instantiated, use the **implements** keyword, whose syntax looks like inheritance:

```
public interface Face {
  public void smile();
}
public class Baz extends Bar implements Face {
  public void smile( ) {
    System.out.println("a warm smile");
  }
}
```

34. There's no **virtual** keyword in Java because all non-**static** methods always use dynamic binding. In Java, the programmer doesn't have to decide whether to use dynamic binding. The reason **virtual** exists in C++ is so you can leave it off for a slight increase in efficiency when you're tuning for performance (or, put another way, "If you don't use it, you don't pay for it"), which often results in confusion and unpleasant surprises. The **final** keyword provides some latitude for efficiency tuning – it tells the compiler that this method cannot be overridden, and thus that it may be statically bound (and made inline, thus using the equivalent of a C++ non-**virtual** call). These optimizations are up to the compiler.

35. Java doesn't provide multiple inheritance (MI), at least not in the same sense that C++ does. Like **protected**, MI seems like a good idea but you know you need it only when you are face to face with a certain design problem. Since Java uses a singly-rooted hierarchy, you'll probably run into fewer situations in which MI is necessary. The **interface** keyword takes care of combining multiple interfaces.

36. Run-time type identification functionality is quite similar to that in C++. To get information about handle **X**, you can say, for example:
`X.getClass().getName();`
To perform a type-safe downcast you say:
`derived d = (derived)base;`
just like an old–style C cast. The compiler automatically invokes the dynamic casting mechanism without requiring extra syntax. Although this doesn't have the benefit of easy location of casts as in C++ "new casts," Java checks usage and throws exceptions so it won't allow bad casts like C++ does.

37. Exception handling in Java is different because there are no destructors. A **finally** clause can be added to force execution of statements that perform necessary cleanup. All exceptions in Java are

inherited from the base class **Throwable**, so you're guaranteed a common interface.

```
public void f(Obj b) throws IOException {
  myresource mr = b.createResource();
  try {
    mr.UseResource();
  } catch (MyException e) {
    // handle my exception
  } catch (Throwable e) {
    // handle all other exceptions
  } finally {
    mr.dispose(); // special cleanup
  }
}
```

38. Exception specifications in Java are vastly superior to those in C++. Instead of the C++ approach of calling a function at run-time when the wrong exception is thrown, Java exception specifications are checked and enforced at compile-time. In addition, overridden methods must conform to the exception specification of the base-class version of that method: they can throw the specified exceptions or exceptions derived from those. This provides much more robust exception-handling code.

39. Java has method overloading, but no operator overloading. The **String** class does use the **+** and **+=** operators to concatenate strings and **String** expressions use automatic type conversion, but that's a special built-in case.

40. The **const** issues in C++ are avoided in Java by convention. You pass only handles to objects and local copies are never made for you automatically. If you want the equivalent of C++'s pass-by-value, you call **clone( )** to produce a local copy of the argument (although the **clone( )** mechanism is somewhat poorly designed – see Chapter 12). There's no copy-constructor that's automatically called.
To create a compile-time constant value, you say, for example:
static final int SIZE = 255;
static final int BSIZE = 8 * SIZE;

41. Because of security issues, programming an "application" is quite different from programming an "applet." A significant issue is that an applet won't let you write to disk, because that would allow a program downloaded from an unknown machine to trash your disk. This changes somewhat with Java 1.1 digital signing, which allows you to unequivocally *know* everyone that wrote all the programs that

have special access to your system (one of which might have trashed your disk; you still have to figure out which one and what to do about it.). Java 1.2 also promises more power for applets

42. Since Java can be too restrictive in some cases, you could be prevented from doing important tasks such as directly accessing hardware. Java solves this with *native methods* that allow you to call a function written in another language (currently only C and C++ are supported). Thus, you can always solve a platform-specific problem (in a relatively non-portable fashion, but then that code is isolated). Applets cannot call native methods, only applications.

43. Java has built-in support for comment documentation, so the source code file can also contain its own documentation, which is stripped out and reformatted into HTML via a separate program. This is a boon for documentation maintenance and use.

44. Java contains standard libraries for solving specific tasks. C++ relies on non-standard third-party libraries. These tasks include (or will soon include):
    – Networking
    – Database Connection (via JDBC)
    – Multithreading
    – Distributed Objects (via RMI and CORBA)
    – Compression
    – Commerce
    The availability and standard nature of these libraries allow for more rapid application development.

45. Java 1.1 includes the Java Beans standard, which is a way to create components that can be used in visual programming environments. This promotes visual components that can be used under all vendor's development environments. Since you aren't tied to a particular vendor's design for visual components, this should result in greater selection and availability of components. In addition, the design for Java Beans is simpler for programmers to understand; vendor-specific component frameworks tend to involve a steeper learning curve.

46. If the access to a Java handle fails, an exception is thrown. This test doesn't have to occur right before the use of a handle; the Java specification just says that the exception must somehow be thrown. Many C++ runtime systems can also throw exceptions for bad pointers.

47. Generally, Java is more robust, via:
    – Object handles initialized to **null** (a keyword)
    – Handles are always checked and exceptions are thrown for failures
    – All array accesses are checked for bounds violations
    – Automatic garbage collection prevents memory leaks
    – Clean, relatively fool-proof exception handling
    – Simple language support for multithreading
    – Bytecode verification of network applets

C: Java programming guidelines

This appendix contains suggestions to help guide you while performing low-level program design, and also while writing code.

1. Capitalize the first letter of class names. The first letter of fields, methods, and objects (handles) should be lowercase. All identifiers should run their words together, and capitalize the first letter of all intermediate words. For example:
   ThisIsAClassName
   thisIsAMethodOrFieldName
   Capitalize *all* the letters of **static final** primitive identifiers that have

constant initializers in their definitions. This indicates they are compile-time constants.

Packages are a special case: they are all lowercase letters, even for intermediate words. The domain extension (com, org, net, edu, etc.) should also be lowercase. (This was a change between Java 1.1 and Java 1.2.)

2. When creating a class for general-purpose use, follow a "canonical form" and include definitions for **equals( )**, **hashCode( )**, **toString( )**, **clone( )** (implement **Cloneable**), and implement **Serializable**.

3. For each class you create, consider including a **main( )** that contains code to test that class. You don't need to remove the test code to use the class in a project, and if you make any changes you can easily re-run the tests. This code also provides examples of how to use your class.

4. Methods should be kept to brief, functional units that describe and implement a discrete part of a class interface. Ideally, methods should be concise; if they are long you might want to search for a way to break them up into several shorter methods. This will also foster reuse within your class. (Sometimes methods must be large, but they should still do just one thing.)

5. When you design a class, think about the client programmer's perspective (the class should be fairly obvious to use) and the perspective of the person maintaining the code (anticipate the kind of changes that will be made, to make them easy).

6. Try to keep classes small and focused. Clues to suggest redesign of a class are:
   1) A complicated switch statement: consider using polymorphism
   2) A large number of methods that cover broadly different types of operations: consider using several classes
   3) A large number of member variables that concern broadly different characteristics: consider using several classes

7. Keep things as "**private** as possible." Once you publicize an aspect of your library (a method, a class, a field), you can never take it out. If you do, you'll wreck somebody's existing code, forcing them to rewrite and redesign. If you publicize only what you must, you can change everything else with impunity, and since designs tend to evolve this is an important freedom. Privacy is especially important when dealing with multithreading – only **private** fields can be protected against un-**synchronized** use.

8. Watch out for "giant object syndrome." This is often an affliction of procedural programmers who are new to OOP and who end up writing a procedural program and sticking it inside one or two giant objects. With the exception of application frameworks, objects represent concepts in your application, not the application.

9. If you must do something ugly, at least localize the ugliness inside a class.

10. Anytime you notice classes that appear to have high coupling with each other, consider the coding and maintenance improvements you might get by using inner classes (see "Improving the code with an inner class" on page 759).

11. Use comments liberally, and use the **javadoc** comment-documentation syntax to produce your program documentation.

12. Avoid using "magic numbers," which are numbers hard-wired into code. These are a nightmare if you need to change them, since you never know if "100" means "the array size" or "something else entirely." Instead, create a constant with a descriptive name and use the constant identifier throughout your program. This makes the program easier to understand and much easier to maintain.

13. In terms of constructors and exceptions, you'll generally want to re-throw any exceptions that you catch while in a constructor if it causes failure of the creation of that object, so the caller doesn't continue blindly, thinking that the object was created correctly.

14. If your class requires any cleanup when the client programmer is finished with the object, place the cleanup code in a single, well-defined method with a name like **cleanup( )** that clearly suggests its purpose. In addition, place a **boolean** flag in the class to indicate whether the object has been cleaned up. In the **finalize( )** method for the class, check to make sure that the object has been cleaned up and throw a class derived from **RuntimeException** if it hasn't, to indicate a programming error. Before relying on such a scheme, ensure that **finalize( )** works on your system. (You might need to call **System.runFinalizersOnExit(true)** to ensure this behavior.)

15. If an object must be cleaned up (other than by garbage collection) within a particular scope, use the following approach: Initialize the object and, if successful, immediately enter a **try** block with a **finally** clause that performs the cleanup.

16. When overriding **finalize( )** during inheritance, remember to call **super.finalize( )** (this is not necessary if **Object** is your immediate superclass). You should call **super.finalize( )** as the *final* act of your overridden **finalize( )** rather than the first, to ensure that base-class components are still valid if you need them.

17. When you are creating a fixed-size collection of objects, transfer them to an array (especially if you're returning this collection from a method). This way you get the benefit of the array's compile-time type checking, and the recipient of the array might not need to cast the objects in the array in order to use them.

18. Choose **interfaces** over **abstract** classes. If you know something is going to be a base class, your first choice should be to make it an **interface**, and only if you're forced to have method definitions or member variables should you change it to an **abstract** class. An **interface** talks about what the client wants to do, while a class tends to focus on (or allow) implementation details.

19. Inside constructors, do only what is necessary to set the object into the proper state. Actively avoid calling other methods (except for **final** methods) since those methods can be overridden by someone else to produce unexpected results during construction. (See Chapter 7 for details.)

20. Objects should not simply hold some data; they should also have well-defined behaviors.

21. Choose composition first when creating new classes from existing classes. You should only used inheritance if it is required by your design. If you use inheritance where composition will work, your designs will become needlessly complicated.

22. Use inheritance and method overriding to express differences in behavior, and fields to express variations in state. An extreme example of what not to do is inheriting different classes to represent colors instead of using a "color" field.

23. To avoid a highly frustrating experience, make sure that there's only one class of each name anywhere in your classpath. Otherwise, the compiler can find the identically-named other class first, and report error messages that make no sense. If you suspect that you are having a classpath problem, try looking for **.class** files with the same names at each of the starting points in your classpath.

24. When using the event "adapters" in the Java 1.1 AWT, there's a particularly easy pitfall you can encounter. If you override one of the adapter methods and you don't quite get the spelling right, you'll end up adding a new method rather than overriding an existing method. However, this is perfectly legal, so you won't get any error message from the compiler or run-time system – your code simply won't work correctly.

25. Use design patterns to eliminate "naked functionality." That is, if only one object of your class should be created, don't bolt ahead to the application and write a comment "Make only one of these." Wrap it in a singleton. If you have a lot of messy code in your main program that creates your objects, look for a creational pattern like a factory method in which you can encapsulate that creation. Eliminating "naked functionality" will not only make your code much easier to understand and maintain, it will also make it more bulletproof against the well-intentioned maintainers that come after you.

26. Watch out for "analysis paralysis." Remember that you must usually move forward in a project before you know everything, and that often the best and fastest way to learn about some of your unknown factors is to go to the next step rather than trying to figure it out in your head.

27. Watch out for premature optimization. First make it work, then make it fast – but only if you must, and only if it's proven that there is a performance bottleneck in a particular section of your code. Unless you have used a profiler to discover a bottleneck, you will probably be wasting your time. The hidden cost of performance tweaks is that your code becomes less understandable and maintainable.

28. Remember that code is read much more than it is written. Clean designs make for easy-to-understand programs, but comments, detailed explanations, and examples are invaluable. They will help both you and everyone who comes after you. If nothing else, the frustration of trying to ferret out useful information from the online Java documentation should convince you.

29. When you think you've got a good analysis, design, or implementation, do a walkthrough. Bring someone in from outside your group – this doesn't have to be a consultant, but can be someone from another group within your company. Reviewing your work with a pair of fresh eyes can reveal problems at a stage where

it's much easier to fix them and more than pays for the time and money "lost" to the walkthrough process.

30. Elegance always pays off. In the short term it might seem like it takes much longer to come up with a truly graceful solution to a problem, but when it works the first time and easily adapts to new situations instead of requiring hours, days, or months of struggle, you'll see the rewards (even if no one can measure them). And there's nothing that matches the feeling that comes from knowing you've got an amazing design. Resist the urge to hurry; it will only slow you down.

31. You can find other programming guidelines on the Web. A good set of links can be found at
http://www.ulb.ac.be/esp/ip-Links/Java/joodcs/mm-WebBiblio.html

D: Performance

This appendix was contributed by and used with the permission of Joe Sharp, consultant (SharpJoe@aol.com).

The Java language emphasizes accurate, reliable behavior at the expense of performance. This is reflected in features such as automatic garbage collection, rigorous runtime checking, complete byte code checking, and conservative runtime synchronization. Availability on a wide choice of platforms leads, at present, to an interpreted virtual machine that further handicaps performance. About performance, Steve McConnell [16] quoted: "Complete it first, and then perfect it. The part that needs to be perfect is usually small." This appendix will aid you in locating and optimizing that "part that needs to be perfect."

Basic approach

You should address performance only after you have a correct and fully tested program:

1. Measure the program's performance under realistic conditions. If it meets your requirements, you are finished. If not, go to the next step.

2. Find the most critical performance bottleneck. This might require considerable ingenuity, but the effort will pay off. If you simply guess where the bottleneck is and try to optimize there, you'll waste your time.

3. Apply the speed improvement techniques discussed in this appendix, then return to Step 1.

Finding the critical bottleneck is the key to cost-effective effort – Donald Knuth [9] improved a program where 50 percent of the time was spent in less than 4 percent of the code. He changed a few lines in an hour of work and doubled the program speed. Working on the rest of the program would have dissipated his valuable time and effort. To quote Knuth, "Premature optimization is the root of all evil." It is wise to restrain your impulses to optimize early because you may forgo many useful programming techniques, resulting in code that's harder to understand, riskier, and requires more effort to maintain.

Locating the bottleneck

Three approaches to locating the performance-critical part of a program are:

1. Install your own instrumentation

"Profile" code by inserting explicit timing:

```
long start = System.currentTimeMillis();
    // Operation to be timed goes here
long time = System.currentTimeMillis() - start;
```

Have an infrequently-used method print cumulative times out to the console window with **System.out.println( )**. Since the compiler will ignore it when false, a **static final boolean** switch can turn the timing on and off so the code can efficiently be left in place in released code, ready for emergency use at any time. Even when more sophisticated profiling is available, this is a convenient way to time a specific task or operation.

System.currentTimeMillis( ) returns time in 1/1000ths of a second. However, some systems with time resolution less than a millisecond (such as a Windows PC) need to repeat an operation **n** times and divide the total time by **n** to get accurate estimates.

2. JDK profiling [2]

The JDK comes with a built-in profiler that keeps track of the time spent in each routine and writes the information to a file. Unfortunately, the JDK profilers have uneven performance. JDK 1.1.1 works, but subsequent releases have had various instabilities.

To run the profiler, use the **-prof** option when invoking the unoptimized versions of the Java interpreter, for example:

```
java_g -prof myClass
```

Or with an applet:

```
java_g -prof sun.applet.AppletViewer applet.html
```

The profiler output is not particularly easy to decipher. In fact, in JDK 1.0 it truncates the method names to 30 characters, so it might not be possible to distinguish between some methods. However, if your platform does support the **-prof** option, either Vladimir Bulatov's *HyperProf* [3] or Greg White's *ProfileViewer* [4] will help interpret the results.

3. Special tools

The best way to keep up with the exploding field of performance optimization tools is through a Web site such as Jonathan Hardwick's *Tools for Optimizing Java* [5] at *http://www.cs.cmu.edu/~jch/java/tools.html*.

Tips for measuring performance

♦ Since profiling uses clock time, make every effort to remove other processes during the measurement.

♦ Always time the code before and after making changes to verify that, at least on the test platform, your changes improved the program. (Jon Bentley mentioned that some of his most logical changes actually slowed the program down.)

♦ Try to make each timing test under identical conditions.

- If possible, contrive a test that doesn't rely on any user input to avoid variations in user response that can cause the results to fluctuate.

Speedup techniques

Now that the critical region has been isolated, you can apply two types of optimizations: generic techniques and those specific to Java.

Generic approaches

An effective generic speedup is to redefine the program in a more practical way. For example, in *Programming Pearls* [14], Bentley describes Doug McIlroy's representation of the English language with a novel data depiction that enabled him to produce a remarkably fast, compact spelling checker. In addition, choosing a better algorithm will probably give a bigger performance gain than any other approach, particularly as the size of the data set increases. For more of these generic approaches, see the general book listings [12–19] at the end of this appendix.

Language dependent approaches

To put things in perspective, it's useful to look at the time it takes to perform various operations. So that the results are relatively independent of the computer being used, they have been normalized by dividing by the time it takes to make a local assignment.

Operation	Example	Normalized time
Local assignment	i = n;	1.0
Instance assignment	this.i = n;	1.2
int increment	i++;	1.5
byte increment	b++;	2.0
short increment	s++;	2.0
float increment	f++;	2.0
double increment	d++;	2.0
Empty loop	while(true) n++;	2.0
Ternary expression	(x<0) ? -x : x	2.2
Math call	Math.abs(x);	2.5
Array assignment	a[0] = n;	2.7
long increment	l++;	3.5

Method call	funct( );	5.9
throw and **catch** exception	**try{ throw e; } catch(e){}**	320
synchronized method call	**synchMethod( );**	570
New Object	**new Object( );**	980
New array	**new int[10];**	3100

Using present systems (such as Pentium 200 pro, Netscape 3, and JDK 1.1.5), these relative times show the extraordinary cost of new objects and arrays, the heavy cost of synchronization, and the modest cost of an unsynchronized method call. References [5] and [6] give the Web address of measurement applets you can run on your own machine.

General modifications

Here are some modifications that you can make to speed up time-critical parts of your Java program. (Be sure to test the performance before and after you try them.)

Replace	With	Why
Interface	Abstract Class (when only one parent is needed)	Multiple inheritance of interfaces prevents some optimizations.
Non–local or array loop variable	Local loop variable	Time (above) shows an instance integer assignment is 1.2 local integer assignments, but an array assignment is 2.7 local integer assignments.
Linked list (fixed size)	Saving discarded link items or replacing the list with a circular array (in which approximate size is known)	Each new object takes 980 local assignments. See Reusing Objects (below), Van Wyk [12] p. 87 and Bentley[15] p. 81
x/2 (or any power of 2)	X >> 2 (or any power of 2)	Uses faster hardware instructions

Specific situations

The cost of Strings: The **String** concatenation operator + looks innocent but involves a lot of work. The compiler can efficiently concatenate constant strings, but a variable string requires considerable processing. For example, if **s** and **t** are **String** variables:

```
System.out.println("heading" + s + "trailer" + t);
```

this requires a new **StringBuffer**, appending arguments, and converting the result back to a **String** with **toString( )**. This costs both space and time. If you're appending more than one **String**, consider using a **StringBuffer** directly, especially if you can repeatedly reuse it in a loop. Preventing the creation of a new **StringBuffer** on each iteration saves the object creation time of 980 seen earlier. Using **substring( )** and the other **String** methods is usually an improvement. When feasible, character arrays are even faster. Also notice that **StringTokenizer** is costly because of synchronization.

Synchronization: In the JDK interpreter, calling a **synchronized** method is typically 10 times slower than calling an unsynchronized method. With JIT compilers, this performance gap has increased to 50 to 100 times (notice the timing above shows it to be 97 times slower). Avoid **synchronized** methods if you can – if you can't, synchronizing on methods rather than on code blocks is slightly faster.

Reusing objects: It takes a long time to create an object (the timing above shows 980 assignment times for a new **Object**, and 3100 assignment times for a small new array), so it's often worth saving and updating the fields of an old object instead of creating a new object. For example, rather than creating a new **Font** object in your **paint( )** method, you can declare it an instance object, initialize it once, and then just update it when necessary in **paint( )**. See also Bentley, *Programming Pearls* p. 81 [15].

Exceptions: You should only throw exceptions in abnormal situations, which are usually cases in which performance is not an issue since the program has run into a problem that it doesn't normally expect. When optimizing, combine small **try-catch** blocks, which thwart compiler optimization by breaking the code into small independent sections. On the other hand, be careful of sacrificing the robustness of your code by over-zealous removal of exception handling.

Hashing: The standard **Hashtable** class in Java 1.0 and 1.1 requires casting and costly synchronization (570 assignment times). Furthermore, the early JDK library doesn't deliberately choose prime number table sizes. Finally, a hashing function should be designed for the particular characteristics of the keys actually used. For all these reasons, the generic **Hashtable** can be improved by designing a hash class that fits a particular application. Note that the **HashMap** in the Java 1.2 collections library has much greater flexibility and isn't automatically **synchronized**.

Method inlining: Java compilers can inline a method only if it is **final**, **private**, or **static**, and in some cases it must have no local variables. If your code spends a lot of time calling a method that has none of these modifiers, consider writing a version that is **final**.

I/O: Use buffers wherever possible, otherwise you can end up doing I/O a single byte at a time. Note that the JDK 1.0 I/O classes use a lot of synchronization, so you might get better performance by using a single "bulk" call such as **readFully( )** and then interpreting the data yourself. Also notice that the Java 1.1 "reader" and "writer" classes were designed for improved performance.

Casts and instanceof: Casts take from 2 to 200 assignment times. The more costly ones require travel up the inheritance hierarchy. Other costly operations lose and restore capabilities of the lower level constructs.

Graphics: Use clipping to reduce the amount of work done in **repaint( )**, double buffering to improve perceived speed, and image strips or compression to speed downloading times. *Animation in Java Applets* from JavaWorld and *Performing Animation* from Sun are two good tutorials. Remember to use high-level primitives; it's much faster to call **drawPolygon( )** on a bunch of points than looping with **drawLine( )**. If you must draw a one-pixel-wide line, **drawLine(x,y,x,y)** is faster than **fillRect(x,y,1,1)**.

Using API classes: Use classes from the Java API when they offer native machine performance that you can't match using Java. For example, **arrayCopy( )** is much faster than using a loop to copy an array of any significant size.

Replacing API classes: Sometimes API classes do more than you need, with a corresponding increase in execution time. For these you can write specialized versions that do less but run faster. For example, one application that needed a container to store many arrays was speeded by replacing the original **Vector** with a faster dynamic array of objects.

Other suggestions

♦ Move repeated constant calculations out of a critical loop, for example, computing **buffer.length** for a constant-size **buffer**.

♦ **static final** constants can help the compiler optimize the program.

- Unroll fixed length loops.

- Use javac's optimization option, **-O**, which optimizes compiled code by inlining **static**, **final**, and **private** methods. Note that your classes may get larger in size (JDK 1.1 or later only – earlier versions might not perform byte verification). Newer just-in-time (JIT) compilers will dramatically speed the code.

- Count down to zero whenever possible – this uses a special JVM byte code.

References

Performance tools

[1] MicroBenchmark running on Pentium Pro (200Mh), Netscape 3.0, JDK 1.1.4 (see reference [5] below).

[2] Sun's Java document page on the JDK Java interpreter *http://java.sun.com/products/JDK/tools/win32/java.html*

[3] Vladimir Bulatov's *HyperProf* *http://www.physics.orst.edu/~bulatov/HyperProf*

[4] Greg White's *ProfileViewer* *http://www.inetmi.com/~gwhi/ProfileViewer/ProfileViewer.html*

Web sites

[5] The premiere online references for optimizing Java code are Jonathan Hardwick's Java Optimization site at *http://www.cs.cmu.edu/~jch/java/optimization.html*, "Tools for Optimizing Java" at *http://www.cs.cmu.edu/~jch/java/tools.html*, and "Java Microbenchmarks" (with a quick 45 second measurement benchmark) at *http://www.cs.cmu.edu/~jch/java/benchmarks.html*.

Articles

[6] *Make Java fast: Optimize! How to get the greatest performance out of your code through low-level optimizations in Java* by Doug Bell *http://www.javaworld.com/javaworld/jw-04-1997/jw-04-optimize.html*, complete with an extensive annotated measurement Benchmark applet.

[7] *Java Optimization Resources*
http://www.cs.cmu.edu/~jch/java/resources.html

[8] *Optimizing Java for Speed http://www.cs.cmu.edu/~jch/java/speed.html*

[9] *An Empirical Study of FORTRAN Programs* by Donald Knuth, 1971, Software – Practice and Experience, Volume 1 p. 105-33.

[10] *Building High-Performance Applications and Servers in Java: An Experiential Study*, by Jimmy Nguyen, Michael Fraenkel, Richard Redpath, Binh Q. Nguyen, and Sandeep K. Singhal; IBM Software Solutions, IBM T.J. Watson Research Center.
http://www.ibm.com/java/education/javahipr.html.

Java specific books

[11] *Advanced Java, Idioms, Pitfalls, Styles, and Programming Tips*, by Chris Laffra, Prentice Hall, 1997. (Java 1.0) Chapter Sections 11-20.

General books

[12] *Data Structures and C Programs* by Christopher J. Van Wyk, Addison-Wesley, 1988.

[13] *Writing Efficient Programs* by Jon Bentley, Prentice Hall, 1982, especially p. 110 and p. 145-151.

[14] *More Programming Pearls* by Jon Bentley. Association for Computing Machinery, February 1988.

[15] *Programming Pearls* by Jon Bentley, Addison-Wesley 1989. Part II addresses generic performance enhancements.

[16] *Code Complete: A Practical Handbook of Software Construction* by Steve McConnell, Microsoft Press 1993, Chapter 9.

[17] *Object-Oriented System Development* by Champeaux, Lea, and Faure, Chapter 25.

[18] *The Art of Programming* by Donald Knuth, Volume 1 *Fundamental Algorithms* 3rd Edition, 1997; Volume 2, *Seminumerical Algorithms* 3rd Edition; Volume 3 *Sorting and Searching* 2nd Edition, Addison-Wesley. The definitive encyclopedia of algorithms.

[19] *Algorithms in C: Fundamentals, Data Structures, Sorting, Searching* by Robert Sedgewick, 3rd Edition, Addison-Wesley 1997. The author is an

apprentice of Knuth's. This is one of seven editions devoted to several languages and contains timely, somewhat simpler treatments of algorithms.

E: A bit about garbage collection

It's hard to believe that Java could possibly be as fast or faster than C++.

This assertion has yet to be proven to my satisfaction. However, I've begun to see that many of my doubts about speed come from early implementations that were not particularly efficient so there was no model at which to point to explain how Java could be fast.

Part of the way I've thought about speed has come from being cloistered with the C++ model. C++ is very focused on everything happening statically, at compile time, so that the run-time image of the program is small and fast. C++ is also based directly on the C model, primarily for backwards compatibility, but sometimes simply because it worked a particular way in C so it was the easiest approach in C++. One of the most important cases is the way memory is managed in C and C++, and this has to do with one of my more fundamental assertions about why Java must be slow: in Java, all objects must be created on the heap.

In C++, creating objects on the stack is fast because when you enter a particular scope the stack pointer is moved down once to allocate storage for all the stack-based objects created in that scope, and when you leave the scope (after all the local destructors have been called) the stack pointer is moved up once. However, creating heap objects in C++ is typically much slower because it's based on the C concept of a heap as a big pool of memory that (and this is essential) must be recycled. When you call **delete** in C++ the released memory leaves a hole in the heap, so when you call **new**, the storage allocation mechanism must go seeking to try to fit the storage for your object into any existing holes in the heap or else you'll rapidly run out of heap storage. Searching for available pieces of memory is the reason that allocating heap storage has such a performance impact in C++, so it's far faster to create stack-based objects.

Again, because so much of C++ is based on doing everything at compile-time, this makes sense. But in Java there are certain places where things happen more dynamically and it changes the model. When it comes to creating objects, it turns out that the garbage collector can have a significant impact on increasing the speed of object creation. This might sound a bit odd at first – that storage release affects storage allocation – but it's the way some JVMs work and it means that allocating storage for heap objects in Java can be nearly as fast as creating storage on the stack in C++.

You can think of the C++ heap (and a slow implementation of a Java heap) as a yard where each object stakes out its own piece of turf. This real estate can become abandoned sometime later and must be reused. In some JVMs, the Java heap is quite different; it's more like a conveyor belt that moves forward every time you allocate a new object. This means that object storage allocation is remarkably rapid. The "heap pointer" is simply moved forward into virgin territory, so it's effectively the same as C++'s stack allocation. (Of course, there's a little extra overhead for bookkeeping but it's nothing like searching for storage.)

Now you might observe that the heap isn't in fact a conveyor belt, and if you treat it that way you'll eventually start paging memory a lot (which is a big performance hit) and later run out. The trick is that the garbage collector steps in and while it collects the garbage it compacts all the objects in the heap so that you've effectively moved the "heap pointer" closer to the beginning of the conveyor belt and further away from a page fault. The garbage collector rearranges things and makes it possible for the high-speed, infinite-free-heap model to be used while allocating storage.

To understand how this works, you need to get a little better idea of the way the different garbage collector (GC) schemes work. A simple but slow GC technique is reference counting. This means that each object contains a reference counter, and every time a handle is attached to an object the reference count is increased. Every time a handle goes out of scope or is set to **null**, the reference count is decreased. Thus, managing reference counts is a small but constant overhead that happens throughout the lifetime of your program. The garbage collector moves through the entire list of objects and when it finds one with a reference count of zero it releases that storage. The one drawback is that if objects circularly refer to each other they can have non-zero reference counts while still being garbage. Locating such self-referential groups requires significant extra work for the garbage collector. Reference counting is commonly used to explain one kind of garbage collection but it doesn't seem to be used in any JVM implementations.

In faster schemes, garbage collection is not based on reference counting. Instead, it is based on the idea that any non-dead object must ultimately be traceable back to a handle that lives either on the stack or in static storage. The chain might go through several layers of objects. Thus, if you start in the stack and the static storage area and walk through all the handles you'll find all the live objects. For each handle that you find, you must trace into the object that it points to and then follow all the handles in *that* object, tracing into the objects they point to, etc., until you've moved through the entire web that originated with the handle on the stack or in static storage. Each object that you move through must still be alive. Note that there is no problem with detached self-referential groups – these are simply not found, and are therefore automatically garbage.

In the approach described here, the JVM uses an *adaptive* garbage-collection scheme, and what it does with the live objects that it locates depends on the variant currently being used. One of these variants is *stop-and-copy*. This means that, for reasons that will become apparent, the program is first stopped (this is not a background collection scheme). Then, each live object that is found is copied from one heap to another, leaving behind all the garbage. In addition, as the objects are copied into the new heap they are packed end-to-end, thus compacting the new heap (and allowing new storage to simply be reeled off the end as previously described).

Of course, when an object is moved from one place to another, all handles that point at (reference) that object must be changed. The handle that comes from tracing to the object from the heap or the static storage area can be changed right away, but there can be other handles pointing to this object that will be encountered later during the "walk." These are fixed up as they are found (you could imagine a hash table mapping old addresses to new ones).

There are two issues that make copy collectors inefficient. The first is the idea that you have two heaps and you slosh all the memory back and forth between these two separate heaps, maintaining twice as much memory as you actually need. Some JVMs deal with this by allocating the heap in chunks as needed and simply copying from one chunk to another.

The second issue is the copying. Once your program becomes stable it might be generating little or no garbage. Despite that, a copy collector will still copy all the memory from one place to another, which is wasteful. To prevent this, some JVMs detect that no new garbage is being generated and switch to a different scheme (this is the "adaptive" part). This other scheme is called *mark and sweep*, and it's what Sun's JVM uses all the time. For general use mark and sweep is fairly slow, but when you know you're generating little or no garbage it's fast.

Mark and sweep follows the same logic of starting from the stack and static storage and tracing through all the handles to find live objects. However, each time it finds a live object that object is marked by setting a flag in it, but the object isn't collected yet. Only when the marking process is finished does the sweep occur. During the sweep, the dead objects are released. However, no copying happens, so if the collector chooses to compact a fragmented heap it does so by shuffling objects around.

The "stop-and-copy" refers to the idea that this type of garbage collection is *not* done in the background; instead, the program is stopped while the GC occurs. In the Sun literature you'll find many references to garbage collection as a low-priority background process, but it turns out that this was a theoretical experiment that didn't work out. In practice, the Sun garbage collector is run when memory gets low. In addition, mark-and-sweep requires that the program be stopped.

As previously mentioned, in the JVM described here memory is allocated in big blocks. If you allocate a large object, it gets its own block. Strict stop-and-copy requires copying every live object from the source heap to a new heap before you could free the old one, which translates to lots of memory. With blocks, the GC can typically use dead blocks to copy objects to as it collects. Each block has a *generation count* to keep track of whether it's alive. In the normal case, only the blocks created since the last GC are compacted; all other blocks get their generation count bumped if they have been referenced from somewhere. This handles the normal case of lots of short-lived temporary objects. Periodically, a full sweep is made – large objects are still not copied (just get their generation count bumped) and blocks containing small objects are copied and compacted. The JVM monitors the efficiency of GC and if it becomes a waste of time because all objects are long-lived then it switches to mark-and-sweep. Similarly, the JVM keeps track of how successful mark-and-sweep is, and if the heap starts to become fragmented it switches back to stop-and-copy. This is where the "adaptive" part comes in, so you end up with a mouthful: "adaptive generational stop-and-copy mark-and-sweep."

There are a number of additional speedups possible in a JVM. An especially important one involves the operation of the loader and Just-In-Time (JIT) compiler. When a class must be loaded (typically, the first time you want to create an object of that class), the **.class** file is located and the byte codes for that class are brought into memory. At this point, one approach is to simply JIT all the code, but this has two drawbacks: it takes a little more time, which, compounded throughout the life of the program, can add up; and it increases the size of the executable (byte codes are significantly more compact than expanded JIT code) and this might cause paging, which definitely slows down a program. An alternative approach is *lazy evaluation*, which means that the code is not JIT compiled until necessary. Thus, code that never gets executed might never get JIT compiled.

Because JVMs are external to browsers, you might expect that you could benefit from the speedups of some JVMs while using any browser. Unfortunately, JVMs don't currently interoperate with different browsers. To get the benefits of a particular JVM, you must either use the browser with that JVM built in or run standalone Java applications.

F: Recommended reading

Java in a Nutshell: A Desktop Quick Reference, 2nd Edition, by David Flanagan, O'Reilly & Assoc. 1997. A compact summary of the online documentation of Java 1.1. Personally, I prefer to browse the docs online, especially since they change so often. However, many folks still like printed documentation and this fits the bill; it also provides more discussion than the online documents.

The Java Class Libraries: An Annotated Reference, by Patrick Chan and Rosanna Lee, Addison-Wesley 1997. What the online reference *should* have been: enough description to make it usable. One of the technical reviewers for *Thinking in Java* said, "If I had only one Java book, this would be it (well, in addition to yours, of course)." I'm not as thrilled with it as he is. It's big, it's expensive, and the quality of the examples doesn't satisfy me. *But* it's a place to look when you're stuck and it seems to have more depth (and sheer size) than *Java in a Nutshell*.

Java Network Programming, by Elliote Rusty Harold, O'Reilly 1997. I didn't begin to understand Java networking until I found this book. I also find his Web site, Café au Lait, to be a stimulating, opinionated, and up-to-date perspective on Java developments, unencumbered by allegiances to any vendors. His almost daily updating keeps up with fast-changing news about Java. See *http://sunsite.unc.edu/javafaq/*.

Core Java, 3nd Edition, by Cornell & Horstmann, Prentice-Hall 1997. A good place to go for questions you can't find the answers to in *Thinking in Java*. Note: the Java 1.1 revision is *Core Java 1.1 Volume 1 – Fundamentals* & *Core Java 1.1 Volume 2 – Advanced Features*.

JDBC Database Access with Java, by Hamilton, Cattell & Fisher (Addison-Wesley, 1997). If you know nothing about SQL and databases, this is a nice, gentle introduction. It also contains some of the details as well as an "annotated reference" to the API (again, what the online reference should have been). The drawback, as with all books in The Java Series ("The ONLY Books Authorized by JavaSoft") is that it's been whitewashed so that it says only wonderful things about Java – you won't find out about any dark corners in this series.

Java Programming with CORBA Andreas Vogel & Keith Duddy (John Wiley & Sons, 1997). A serious treatment of the subject with code examples for the three main Java ORBs (Visibroker, Orbix, Joe).

Design Patterns, by Gamma, Helm, Johnson & Vlissides (Addison-Wesley 1995). The seminal book that started the patterns movement in programming.

UML Tookit, by Hans–Erik Eriksson & Magnus Penker, (John Wiley & Sons, 1997). Explains UML and how to use it, and has a case study in Java. An
accompanying CD–ROM contains the Java code and a cut-down version of Rational Rose. An excellent introduction to UML and how to use it to build a real system.

Practical Algorithms for Programmers, by Binstock & Rex (Addison–Wesley 1995). The algorithms are in C, so they're fairly easy to translate into Java. Each algorithm is thoroughly explained.

Index

Please note that some names will be duplicated in capitalized form. Following Java style, the capitalized names refer to Java classes, while lowercase names refer to a general concept.

specifiers, 31, 190, 202; within a directory, via the default package, 204

action( ), 597, 610, 619, 861; cannot combine with listeners, 675

ActionEvent, 641, 643, 665, 717

ActionListener, 641

actionPerformed( ), 644

ActiveX/Beans integration, 1027

adapters: listener adapters, 645

add( ), 613

addActionListener( ), 641, 714, 784

addAdjustmentListener( ), 641

addComponentListener( ), 641

addContainerListener( ), 641

addElement( ), Vector, 333

addFocusListener( ), 641

addItemListener( ), 641

addition, 100

addKeyListener( ), 641

addListener, 639

addMouseListener( ), 641

addMouseMotionListener( ), 641

addTab( ), 746

addTextListener( ), 641

addWindowListener( ), 641

AdjustmentEvent, 641, 643

AdjustmentListener, 641

adjustmentValueChanged( ), 644

Adler32, 484

aliasing, 98; and String, 579; during a method call, 543

align, 593

AlreadyBoundException, 902

analysis: & design, object-oriented, 58; requirements analysis, 60

AND: bitwise, 115; logical (&&), 105

anonymous inner class, 283, 380, 451, 649, 799, 954; and constructors, 287

appendText( ), 606

applet, 591, 850; advantages for client/server systems, 626; align, 593; and packages, 594; archive tag, for HTML and JAR files, 650; classpath, 594; codebase, 593; combined applets and applications, 646; creating a

Frame from within an applet, 700; destroy( ), 591; displaying a Web page from within an applet, 871; init( ), 591, 595; name, 593; packaging applets in a JAR file to optimize loading, 649; paint( ), 591; parameter, 593; placing inside a Web page, 592; restrictions, 625; start( ), 591, 595; stop( ), 591, 595; submitting a POST with an applet, 884; tag, for HTML page, 592; update( ), 591

Applet, 613; combined with application, 767; initialization parameters, 767

appletviewer, 593

application: application builder, 704; application framework, 298; combined applets and applications, 646; combined with Applet, 767; running an application from within an applet, 700; standalone windowed application, 631; windowed applications, 627

application framework, 590

archive tag, for HTML and JAR files, 650

argument: constructor, 149; final, 242, 452; passing a handle into a method, 542; variable argument lists (unknown quantity and type of arguments), 183

array, 324, 400; associative array, 345; bounds checking, 180; dynamic creation, 925; first-class objects, 325; initialization, 179; length, 325; multidimensional, 184; of Object, 732; of objects, 325; of primitives, 325; sorting, 391

ArrayList, 365, 370

ArrayMap, 377

Arrays, 391

Arrays.toList( ), 391

ArraySet, 374

assigning objects, 97

assignment, 96

associative array, 331, 345

auto-decrement operator, 102

auto-increment operator, 102

automatic compilation, 196

automatic type conversion, 219
available( ), 461
AWT: Abstract Window Toolkit, 587;
action( ), 597, 610, 619, 861;
action( ), cannot combine with
listeners, 675; ActionEvent, 641, 643,
665, 717; ActionListener, 641;
actionPerformed( ), 644; add( ), 613;
addActionListener( ), 641, 714;
addAdjustmentListener( ), 611;
addComponentListener( ), 641;
addContainerListener( ), 641;
addFocusListener( ), 641;
addItemListener( ), 641;
addKeyListener( ), 641; addListener,
639; addMouseListener( ), 641;
addMouseMotionListener( ), 641;
addTextListener( ), 641;
addWindowListener( ), 641;
AdjustmentEvent, 641, 643;
AdjustmentListener, 641;
adjustmentValueChanged( ), 644;
appendText( ), 606; Applet, 613;
applet advantages for client/server
systems, 626; applet restrictions, 625;
archive tag, for HTML and JAR files,
650; BorderLayout, 614, 648; Button,
596, 614; Button, creating your own,
620; Canvas, 620; CardLayout, 616,
745; Checkbox, 605, 606; Checkbox,
Java 1.1, 655; CheckboxGroup, 606;
CheckboxMenuItem, 628;
CheckboxMenuItem, Java 1.1, 660;
Choice, 607; Choice, Java 1.1, 657;
combining layouts, 616; Component,
591, 610, 613, 619;
ComponentAdapter, 645;
componentAdded( ), 644;
ComponentEvent, 641, 643;
componentHidden( ), 644;
ComponentListener, 641;
componentMoved( ), 644;
componentRemoved( ), 644;
componentResized( ), 644;
componentShown( ), 644; consume( ),
653; Container, 613;
ContainerAdapter, 645;
ContainerEvent, 641, 643;
ContainerListener, 641; controlling
layout, 613; DataFlavor, 703; desktop
colors, 692; Dialog, 631; dialog box,
631; Dialog, Java 1.1, 665;
dispatchEvent( ), 665; dispatching
messages, 665; dispose( ), 632, 699,
700; drawString( ), 592; drop-down
list, 607; East, 614; eliminating
flicker, 686; enableEvents( ), 686;
end( ), 699, event listener, 639; Event
object, 597, 610; event target, 597;
event-driven programming, 596;
FileDialog, 635; FileDialog, Java 1.1,
668; flavor, clipboard, 701;
FlowLayout, 613; Focus traversal,
692; FocusAdapter, 645; FocusEvent,
641, 643; focusGained( ), 644;
FocusListener, 641; focusLost( ), 644;
Font, 698; Frame, 613, 628;
getAlignment( ), 603;
getAppletContext( ), 599;
getContents( ), 703; getDirectory( ),
638; getFile( ), 638; getPrintJob( ),
699, 700; getSelectedItems( ), 609;
getState( ), 631; getText( ), 603;
getTransferData( ), 704;
getTransferDataFlavors( ), 703;
gotFocus( ), 619; graphics, 635;
Graphics, 591, 699; GridBagLayout,
618; GridLayout, 615; handleEvent( ),
598, 610, 619; inner classes, 639;
isDataFlavorSupported( ), 704;
isFocusTraversable( ), 692; ItemEvent,
641, 643, 655; ItemListener, 641,
655; itemStateChanged( ), 644; JAR,
packaging applets to optimize
loading, 649; KeyAdapter, 645;
keyDown( ), 619; KeyEvent, 641, 643;
KeyListener, 641; keyPressed( ), 644;
keyReleased( ), 644; keyTyped( ), 644;
keyUp( ), 619; Label, 602; layout
manager, 604; List, 609; list boxes,
609; List, Java 1.1, 659; listener
adapters, 645; lostFocus( ), 619;
match an event to the text on a
button, 599; Menu, 628; menu
shortcuts, 664; Menu, Java 1.1, 660;
MenuBar, 628, 665;
MenuComponent, 628; MenuItem,

628, 665; MenuItem, Java 1.1, 660; menus, 627; MouseAdapter, 645; mouseClicked( ), 644; mouseDown( ), 619, 635; mouseDrag( ), 620; mouseDragged( ), 644; mouseEnter( ), 620; mouseEntered( ), 644; MouseEvent, 641, 643; mouseExit( ), 620; mouseExited( ), 644; MouseListener, 641; MouseMotionAdapter, 645; MouseMotionListener, 641; mouseMove( ), 620; mouseMoved( ), 644; mousePressed( ), 644; mouseReleased( ), 644; mouseUp( ), 619; multicast, 717; multicast events, 672; multiple selection in a List, 613; new event model, 638; North, 614; paint( ), 620, 635, 693, 699; Panel, 616; print( ), 693, 699; PrintGraphics, 699; printing, 701; printing text, 698; PrintJob, 698; processEvent( ), 685; proportionally–spaced font, 604; radio button, 606; removeActionListener( ), 641, 714; removeAdjustmentListener( ), 641; removeComponentListener( ), 641; removeContainerListener( ), 641; removeFocusListener( ), 641; removeItemListener( ), 641; removeKeyListener( ), 641; removeMouseListener( ), 641; removeMouseMotionListener( ), 641; removeTextListener( ), 641; removeWindowListener( ), 641; repaint( ), 686; requestFocus( ), 692; setActionCommand( ), 664; setAlignment( ), 603; setCheckboxGroup( ), 606; setContents( ), 703; setDirectory( ), 637; setEditable( ), 601; setFile( ), 637; setLayout( ), 613; setMenuBar( ), 627; setText( ), 603; show( ), 637; showStatus( ), 599; South, 614; standalone windowed application, 631; StringSelection, 703; super.action( ), 598; super.handleEvent( ), 612; system clipboard, 701; target of an event, 598; TextArea, 601, 701; TextArea,

Java 1.1, 653; TextComponent, 600; TextComponent, Java 1.1, 653; TextEvent, 641, 643; TextField, 600; TextField, Java 1.1, 652; TextListener, 641; textValueChanged( ), 644; Toolkit, 700; TooManyListenersException, 672, 717; Transferable, 703; unicast, 717; unicast events, 672; update( ), 686; Web browser window status line, 599; West, 614; WINDOW_CLOSING, 665; WINDOW_DESTROY, 632; windowActivated( ), 644; WindowAdapter, 645; windowClosed( ), 644; windowClosing( ), 644; windowDeactivated( ), 644; windowDeiconified( ), 644; windowed applications, 627; WindowEvent, 641, 643, 665; windowIconified( ), 644; WindowListener, 641; windowOpened( ), 644

bag, 362

base 16, 117

base 8, 117

base class, 206, 222, 255; abstract base class, 264; base-class interface, 259; constructor, 308; constructors and exceptions, 226; initialization, 224

Basic: Microsoft Visual Basic, 704

BasicArrowButton, 728

Bean: integrating with ActiveX, 1027

beanbox Bean testing tool, 719

BeanInfo: custom BeanInfo, 720

Beans: and Borland's Delphi, 704; and Microsoft's Visual Basic, 704; and multithreading, 780; application builder, 704; beanbox Bean testing tool, 719; bound properties, 720; component, 705; constrained properties, 720; custom BeanInfo, 720; custom property editor, 720; custom property sheet, 720; events, 705; EventSetDescriptors, 711; FeatureDescriptor, 720; getBeanInfo( ), 708; getEventSetDescriptors( ), 711; getMethodDescriptors( ), 711;

CharArrayWriter, 474

Checkbox, 605, 606; Java 1.1, 655

CheckboxGroup, 606

CheckboxMenuItem, 628; Java 1.1, 660

CheckedInputStream, 482

CheckedOutputStream, 482

Checksum, 484

Choice, 607; Java 1.1, 657

class, 208; abstract class, 264; access, 209; anonymous inner class, 283, 451, 649, 799, 954; anonymous inner class and constructors, 287; base class, 206, 222, 255; browser, 209; class hierarchies and exception handling, 435; class literal, 521, 524; derived class, 255; final classes, 243; inheritance diagrams, 237; inheriting from an abstract class, 265; inheriting from inner classes, 294; initialization & class loading, 245; initialization of data members, 169; initializing members at point of definition, 170; initializing the base class, 224; inner class, 278, 653, 759, 925; inner class nesting within any arbitrary scope, 284; inner classes, 675; inner classes & access rights, 289; inner classes and overriding, 295; inner classes and super, 295; inner classes and the AWT, 639; inner classes and upcasting, 280; inner classes in methods & scopes, 282; inner classes, identifiers and .class files, 297; intializing the derived class, 224; loading, 247; member initialization, 219; order of initialization, 172; private inner classes, 301; public class, and compilation units, 191; read-only classes, 572; referring to the outer class object in an inner class, 293; static inner classes, 291; style of creating classes, 208; subobject, 224

Class, 730; Class object, 507, 518, 775; forName( ), 520, 987; getClass( ), 411; getConstructors( ), 534; getInterfaces( ), 530; getMethods( ), 534; getName( ), 530; getSuperclass( ), 530; isInstance, 526; isInterface( ), 530; newInstance( ), 530; printInfo( ), 530; reflection, 925; RTTI using the Class object, 528

ClassCastException, 320, 522

classpath, 97, 194, 594; and rmic, 903; pitfall, 199

cleanup: and garbage collector, 228; performing, 164; with finally, 427

client programmer, 30

client, network, 828

clipboard: system clipboard, 701

clone( ), 548, 922; and composition, 555; and inheritance, 561; Object.clone( ), 552; removing/turning off clonability, 563; super.clone( ), 552, 567; supporting cloning in derived classes, 563

Cloneable interface, 549

CloneNotSupportedException, 551

close( ), 460

CLSID, 1021

code: calling non-Java code, 997; coding standards, 17, 1051; extracting code listings, 958; organization, 202; re-use, 217

codebase, 593

coding: improving code with inner classes, 759

collection: class, 324, 331; Hashtable, 972; of primitives, 328

Collection, 362

Collections, 391, 396

collections library, new, 361

collision: name, 196

colors: desktop colors, 692

COM, 1019; Java/COM integration, 998

com.ms.com, 1026

com.ms.win32, 1011

combo box, 738

comma operator, 114, 134

comments: and embedded documentation, 86

common interface, 264

common pitfalls when using operators, 115

Common-Gateway Interface (CGI), 850
Comparable, 377, 394
Comparator, 377, 393
compare( ), 393
compareTo( ), 394
comparison: natural comparison
    method, 394
compilation unit, 191
compile-time constant, 238
compiling, automatic compilation, 196
complexity theory, Boids example, 988
Component, 591, 610, 613, 619, 746
component, and Java Beans, 705
ComponentAdapter, 645
componentAdded( ), 644
ComponentEvent, 641, 643
componentHidden( ), 644
ComponentListener, 641
componentMoved( ), 644
componentRemoved( ), 644
componentResized( ), 644
componentShown( ), 644
composition, 217, 358; and cloning,
    555; and design, 315; and design
    patterns, 909; and dynamic behavior
    change, 316; choosing composition
    vs. inheritance, 233; combining
    composition & inheritance, 226; vs.
    inheritance, 238, 470
compression: Java 1.1 compression
    library, 482
ConcurrentModificationException, 399
conditional operator, 113
conference, Software Development
    Conference, 6
console input, 478
const, in C++, 578
constant: compile-time constant, 238;
    folding, 239; groups of constant
    values, 275; implicit constants, and
    String, 578
constrained properties, 720
constructor, 148; and anonymous inner
    classes, 283; and exception handling,
    431; and exceptions, 424; and finally,
    431; and overloading, 150; and

polymorphism, 306; arguments, 149;
base-class constructor, 308; base-class
constructors and exceptions, 226;
behavior of polymorphic methods
inside constructors, 312; C++ copy
constructor, 568; calling base-class
constructors with arguments, 225;
calling from other constructors, 160;
default, 158; default constructor
synthesized by the compiler, 910;
default constructors, 152;
initialization during inheritance and
composition, 226; name, 148; no-arg
constructors, 152; order of
constructor calls with inheritance,
306; private constructor, 910; return
value, 150; static construction clause,
176
Constructor, 730; for reflection, 532,
    925
consulting & mentoring provided by
    Bruce Eckel, 19
consume( ), 653
Container, 613
container class, 324
ContainerAdapter, 645
ContainerEvent, 641, 643
ContainerListener, 641
content-type, HTML, 882
continue keyword, 135
control framework, and inner classes,
    298
controlling access, 31, 213
conversion: automatic, 219; narrowing
    conversion, 116, 157; widening
    conversion, 116
copy: deep copy, 547; shallow copy, 547
copy-constructor, in C++, 878
CORBA, 904, 1028
CORBA and Java, interfacing, 998
couplet, 759, 951
coupling, 409
CRC32, 484
createStatement( ), 889
creational design patterns, 911, 920

critical section, and synchronized block, 779

currentThread(), 754

daemon threads, 767

data: final, 238; primitive data types and use with operators, 119; static initialization, 173

database: flat-file database, 891; Java DataBase Connectivity (JDBC), 887; relational database, 892; URL, 888

DatabaseMetaData, 897

DataFlavor, 703

Datagram, 842, 851, 857; receive( ), 863; User Datagram Protocol (UDP), 842

DatagramPacket, 843, 847, 860

DatagramSocket, 843, 860

DataInput, 448

DataInputStream, 445, 460, 461, 462, 475, 959

DataOutput, 448

DataOutputStream, 447, 462, 476, 959, 972

DCOM, 904

dead, Thread, 785

deadlock, multithreading, 790, 797

decorator design pattern, 444

decoupling through polymorphism, 251

decrement operator, 102

deep copy, 547, 554; and Vector, 557; using serialization to perform deep copying, 559

default constructor, 152, 158; synthesized by the compiler, 910; synthesizing a default constructor, 225

default keyword, in a switch statement, 142

default package, 204

DefaultMutableTreeNode, 742

defaultReadObject( ), 503

DefaultTreeModel, 742

defaultWriteObject( ), 503

DeflaterOutputStream, 482

Delphi, from Borland, 704

dequeue, 361

derived: derived class, 255; derived class, initializing, 224

design, 25, 317; abstraction in program design, 908; adding more methods to a design, 214; analysis & design, object-oriented, 58; and composition, 315; and inheritance, 315; and mistakes, 213; library design, 190; of object hierarchies, 248

design patterns, 212, 907; behavioral, 911; creational, 911, 920; decorator, 444; factory method, 920; observer, 911; prototype, 922, 931; singleton, 212; structural, 911; vector of change, 908, 922; visitor, 944

desktop colors, 692

destroy( ), 591, 801

destructor, 163, 164, 427; Java doesn't have one, 228

development, incremental, 235

diagram, class inheritance diagrams, 237

Dialog, 631; Java 1.1, 665

dialog box, 631

Dictionary, 345

directory: and packages, 201; creating directories and paths, 454; lister, 449

dispatchEvent( ), 665

dispatching: double dispatching, 937, 946; multiple dispatching, 936

dispatching messages, AWT, 665

dispose( ), 632, 699, 700

division, 100

documentation: comments & embedded documentation, 86

Domain Name Service (DNS), 826

dotted quad, 826

double dispatching, 937, 946

double, literal value marker (D), 117

Double.valueOf( ), 929

do-while, 133

downcast, 238, 318, 522; type-safe downcast in run-time type identification, 522

drawString( ), 592

drop-down list, 607

FileInputStream, 441, 460

FilenameFilter, 449, 981

FileNotFoundException, 433

FileOutputStream, 443, 462

FileReader, 431, 474

FileWriter, 474

fillInStackTrace( ), 412

FilterInputStream, 442

FilterOutputStream, 443

FilterReader, 475

FilterWriter, 475

final, 268; and efficiency, 244; and
static, 239; argument, 242, 452;
blank finals in Java 1.1, 241; classes,
243; data, 238; keyword, 238;
method, 256; methods, 243; static
primitives, 240; with object handles,
239

finalize( ), 162, 231, 434; and
inheritance, 308; and super, 311;
calling directly, 165; order of
finalization of objects, 312;
runFinalizersOnExit( ), 167

finally, 228, 231; and constructors, 431;
keyword, 425; pitfall, 430

finding .class files during loading, 193

firewall, 863

flat-file database, 891

flavor, clipboard, 701

flicker, eliminating, 686

float, literal value marker(F), 117

floating point: true and false, 106

flocking, simulating behavior, 988

FlowLayout, 613

Focus traversal, 692

FocusAdapter, 645

FocusEvent, 641, 643

focusGained( ), 644

FocusListener, 641

focusLost( ), 644

folding, constant, 239

Font, 698

font, proportionally-spaced, 604

for keyword, 133

forName( ), 520, 987

FORTRAN, 117

forward referencing, 171

Frame, 613, 628; creating a Frame from
within an applet, 700

framework: application framework,
590; control framework and inner
classes, 298

friendly, 190, 280; and interface, 268

FTP: File Transfer Protocol (FTP), 593

functor, 450

garbage collection, 162, 165, 308; and
cleanup, 228; and native method
execution, 1005; forcing finalization,
231; how it works, 1067; order of
object reclamation, 231; setting
handles to null to allow cleanup, 301

generic, 337

Generic Collection Library for Java
(JGL), 360

GET, 864; CGI, 881; request, 867

get( ), Hashtable, 349

getAddress( ), 847

getAlignment( ), 603

getAppletContext( ), 599

getBeanInfo( ), 708

getClass( ), 411, 528

getConstructor( ), 730

getConstructor( ), reflection, 925

getConstructors( ), 534; reflection, 925

getContents( ), 703

getDirectory( ), 638

getDocumentBase( ), 870

getEventSetDescriptors( ), 711

getFile( ), 638

getFloat( ), 890

getInputStream( ), 830, 887

getInt( ), 890

getInterfaces( ), 530

getMethodDescriptors( ), 711

getMethods( ), 534

getModel( ), 742

getName( ), 530, 711

getOutputStream( ), 830, 885

getPort( ), 847

getPrintJob( ), 699, 700

getPriority( ), 802
getProperties( ), 353
getPropertyDescriptors( ), 711
getPropertyType( ), 711
getReadMethod( ), 711
getSelectedItems( ), 609
getState( ), 631
getString( ), 890
getSuperclass( ), 530
getText( ), 603
getTransferData( ), 704
getTransferDataFlavors( ), 703
getWriteMethod( ), 711
GNU C++ Compiler, 872
gotFocus( ), 619
goto: lack of goto in Java, 136
graphical user interface (GUI), 298, 587
graphics, 635; Graphics object, 591, 699
greater than (>), 103
greater than or equal to (>=), 103
GridBagLayout, 618
GridLayout, 615, 816
guarded region, in exception handling, 407
GUI: builders, 589; graphical user interface, 298, 587
GUID: Globally Unique IDentifier, 1020
guidelines, coding standards, 1051
GZIPInputStream, 482
GZIPOutputStream, 482
handle: assigning objects by copying handles, 97; equivalence vs object equivalence, 104; final, 239; finding exact type of a base handle, 518; handle equivalence vs. object equivalence, 552; null, 72
handleEvent( ), 598, 610, 619
handler, exception, 407
hardware devices, interfacing with, 997
has-a relationship, composition, 234
hashCode( ), 348, 374; overriding for Hashtable, 351
HashMap, 376
HashSet, 374

Hashtable, 324, 331, 345, 353, 362, 400, 470, 624, 972; combined with Vector, 972; used with Vector, 980
hasMoreElements( ), Enumeration, 339
hasNext( ), 365
herding, simulating behavior, 988
Hexadecimal, 117
hiding, implementation, 208
HRESULT, 1022
HTML, 850, 865; name, 766; param, 766; value, 766
Icon, 730
idltojava, 1031
if-else statement, 113, 131
IllegalMonitorStateException, 791
ImageIcon, 730
immutable objects, 573
implementation: and interface, 233, 268; and interface, separation, 31, 208; hiding, 208, 280
implements keyword, 269
import keyword, 190
increment operator, 102
incremental development, 64, 235
indexed property, 719
indexing operator [ ], 179
indexOf( ), 929, 970; String, 451, 534, 861
InetAddress, 860
InflaterInputStream, 482
inheritance, 206, 217, 221, 251; and cloning, 561; and design patterns, 909; and final, 244; and finalize( ), 308; and synchronized, 785; choosing composition vs. inheritance, 233; class inheritance diagrams, 237; combining composition & inheritance, 226; designing with inheritance, 315; extending interfaces with inheritance, 274; from an abstract class, 265; from inner classes, 294; inheritance and method overloading vs. overriding, 231; initialization with inheritance, 246; multiple inheritance in C++ and Java, 272; pure inheritance vs. extension, 316;

specialization, 234; vs composition, 470; vs. composition, 238

init( ), 591, 595

initialization: and class loading, 245; array initialization, 179; base class, 224; class member, 219; constructor initialization during inheritance and composition, 226; initializing class members at point of definition, 170; initializing with the constructor, 148; instance initialization, 177; instance initialization in Java 1.1, 288; member initializers, 308; non-static instance initialization, 177; of class data members, 169; of method variables, 168; order of initialization, 172, 314; static, 247; with inheritance, 246

inline method calls, 243

inner class, 278, 653, 675, 759, 925; access rights, 289; and super, 295; and overriding, 295; and control frameworks, 298; and the AWT, 639; and upcasting, 280; anonymous, 380, 954; anonymous inner class, 451, 799; anonymous inner class and constructors, 287; hidden reference to the object of the enclosing class, 290; identifiers and .class files, 297; in methods & scopes, 282; inheriting from inner classes, 294; nesting within any arbitrary scope, 284; private, 761; private inner classes, 301; referring to the outer class object, 293; static, 291; static inner classes, 291

input: console input, 478; file input shorthand, 463

InputStream, 440, 833, 852

InputStreamReader, 473, 474, 833

insertNodeInto( ), 743

instance: instance initialization in Java 1.1, 288; non-static instance initialization, 177

instanceof: dynamic instanceof, 526; keyword, 522

Integer: parseInt( ), 635

interface: and implementation, separation, 208; and inheritance, 274; base-class interface, 259; Cloneable interface used as a flag, 549; common interface, 264; graphical user interface (GUI), 298, 587; initializing fields in interfaces, 277; keyword, 268; Runnable, 763; separation of interface and implementation, 31; upcasting to an interface, 271; vs. abstract, 274; vs. implemenation, 233

interfacing with hardware devices, 997

internationalization, in IO library, 473

Internet: Internet Protocol, 826; Internet Service Provider (ISP), 593

interrupt( ), 797

InterruptedException, 754

Intranet, 627

Introspector, 708

IO: and threads, blocking, 786; available( ), 461; blocking on IO, 793; blocking, and available( ), 461; BufferedInputStream, 446, 460; BufferedOutputStream, 447, 462; BufferedReader, 431, 475, 970; BufferedWriter, 475; ByteArrayInputStream, 441; ByteArrayOutputStream, 443; characteristics of files, 454; CharArrayReader, 474; CharArrayWriter, 474; CheckedInputStream, 482; CheckedOutputStream, 482; close( ), 460; connecting to a non–Java program, 851; console input, 478; controlling the process of serialization, 495; data file output shorthand, 465; DataInput, 448; DataInputStream, 445, 460, 461, 462, 475, 959; DataOutput, 448; DataOutputStream, 447, 462, 476, 959, 972; DeflaterOutputStream, 482; deprecated, 440; directory lister, 449; directory, creating directories and paths, 454; exec( ), 852; Externalizable, 495; File, 441, 476, 972, 982; File class, 449; file input shorthand, 463; File.list( ), 449;

FileDescriptor, 441; FileInputStream, 441, 460; FilenameFilter, 449, 981; FileOutputStream, 443, 462; FileReader, 431, 474; FileWriter, 474; FilterInputStream, 442; FilterOutputStream, 443; FilterReader, 475; FilterWriter, 475; formatted file output shorthand, 464; from standard input, 465; GZIPInputStream, 482; GZIPOutputStream, 482; InflaterInputStream, 482; input, 440; InputStream, 440, 833, 852; InputStreamReader, 473, 474, 833; internationalization, 473; Java 1.1 compression library, 482; library, 439; lightweight persistence, 489; LineNumberInputStream, 446, 461; LineNumberReader, 475; mark( ), 448; mkdirs( ), 456, 972; nextToken( ), 982; ObjectOutputStream, 490; output, 440; OutputStream, 440, 442, 833, 852; OutputStreamWriter, 473, 474, 833; pipe, 441; piped stream, 793; PipedInputStream, 442, 466; PipedOutputStream, 442, 443, 466; PipedReader, 474; PipedWriter, 474; PrintStream, 447, 462; PrintWriter, 475, 833; Process, 852; pushBack( ), 982; PushbackInputStream, 446; PushBackReader, 475; RandomAccessFile, 448, 462, 476; read( ), 440; readChar( ), 462; readDouble( ), 463; Reader, 473, 474, 833; readExternal( ), 495; readLine( ), 434, 460, 462, 466, 475; readObject( ), 490; redirecting standard IO, 480; renameTo( ), 456; reset( ), 448; seek( ), 448, 463; SequenceInputStream, 442, 476; Serializable, 495; setErr(PrintStream), 480; setIn(InputStream), 480; setOut(PrintStream), 480; StreamTokenizer, 467, 475, 535, 981; StringBuffer, 441; StringBufferInputStream, 441, 460; StringReader, 474; StringWriter, 474; System.err, 465; System.in, 465, 478;

System.out, 465; text file manipulation, 958; transient, 499; typical IO configurations, 456; Unicode, 473; write( ), 440; writeBytes( ), 462; writeChars( ), 462; writeDouble( ), 463; writeExternal( ), 495; writeObject( ), 490; Writer, 473, 474, 833; ZipEntry, 486; ZipInputStream, 482; ZipOutputStream, 482

IP (Internet Protocol), 826

is-a, 317; relationship, inheritance, 234; relationship, inheritance & upcasting, 236

isDaemon( ), 768

isDataFlavorSupported( ), 704

isFocusTraversable( ), 692

isInstance, 526

isInterface( ), 530

is-like-a, 317

ISP (Internet Service Provider), 593

isPopupTrigger( ), 737

ItemEvent, 641, 643, 655

ItemListener, 641, 655

itemStateChanged( ), 644

iteration, during software development, 63

iterator, 337, 909

Iterator, 365

iterator( ), 365

J/Direct, 998

jactivex, 1023

JAR, 718; archive tag, for HTML and JAR files, 650; file, 192, 626; files, 678; jar files and classpath, 195; Java 1.1 JAR utility, 487; packaging applets to optimize loading, 649

Java: and classpath, 97; and pointers, 542; and set-top boxes, 108; C++ in contrast with Java, 873; capitalization style source-code checking tool, 974; comparing C++ and Java, 1039; connecting to a non-Java program, 851; crashing Java, 341; public Java seminars, 7; speed, 1067; versions, 18

polymorphic method calls, 918; protected methods, 235; recursive, 342; recursive method calls, 926; static, 162; synchronized method and blocking, 786

Method, 711; for reflection, 532

MethodDescriptors, 711

methodology, software development, 59

Microsoft, 749; Visual Basic, 704

min( ), 397

mistakes, and design, 213

mkdirs( ), 456, 972

modulus, 100

monitor, for multithreading, 775

MouseAdapter, 645

mouseClicked( ), 644

mouseDown( ), 619, 635

mouseDrag( ), 620

mouseDragged( ), 644

mouseEnter( ), 620

mouseEntered( ), 644

MouseEvent, 641, 643, 737

mouseExit( ), 620

mouseExited( ), 644

MouseListener, 641

MouseMotionAdapter, 645

MouseMotionListener, 641

mouseMove( ), 620

mouseMoved( ), 644

mousePressed( ), 644

mouseReleased( ), 644

mouseUp( ), 619

multicast, 717; event, and Java Beans, 781; multicast events, 672

multidimensional arrays, 184

Multimedia CD ROM for book, 15

multiple dispatching, 936

multiple inheritance, in C++ and Java, 272

multiple selection, AWT List, 613

multiple-document interface, 748

multiplication, 100

multitasking, 751

multithreading, 751, 837; and collections, 399; and Java Beans, 780; blocking, 785; deciding what methods to synchronize, 784; drawbacks, 820; Runnable, 814; stop( ), 861; when to use it, 820

multi-tiered systems, 672

name, 593; clash, 191; collisions, 196; creating unique package names, 193; spaces, 191

name, HTML keyword, 766

Naming: bind( ), 900; rebind( ), 902; unbind( ), 902

narrowing conversion, 116, 157

native code for connecting to a non–Java program, 851

native method interface (NMI) in Java 1.0, 998

natural comparison method, 394

natural logarithms, 117

network programming, 825; accept( ), 830; applet, 850; CGI GET, 881; CGI POST, 882; CGI programming in C++, 872; client, 828; Common-Gateway Interface (CGI), 850; connecting Java to CGI, 864; crash course in CGI programming, 864; datagram, 851, 857; Datagram.receive( ), 863; DatagramPacket, 843, 847, 860; datagrams, 842; DatagramSocket, 843, 860; dedicated connection, 837; displaying a Web page from within an applet, 871; DNS (Domain Name Service), 826; dotted quad, 826; firewall, 863; GET request, 867; getAddress( ), 847; getDocumentBase( ), 870; getInputStream( ), 830, 887; getOutputStream( ), 830, 885; getPort( ), 847; HTML, 850, 865; HTML content-type, in CGI programming, 882; identifying machines, 826; InetAddress, 860; intercepting results from a CGI program, 870; Internet Protocol (IP), 826; invoking a CGI program from Java, 866; Java DataBase Connectivity (JDBC), 887; local loopback IP address, 828; localhost,

828; multithreading, 837; openConnection( ), 885; port, 829; POST using an applet, 884; QUERY_STRING, 881; receive( ), 846, 861; reliable protocol, 842; server, 828; serving multiple clients, 837; Servlet Server, 905; servlet servers, 864; setAllowUserInteraction(false), 885; setDoInput(true), 885; setDoOutput(true), 885; showDocument( ), 871, 887; Socket, 836; stream-based sockets, 842; testing programs without a network, 828; Transmission Control Protocol (TCP), 842; unreliable protocol, 842; URL, 870, 872; URL openStream( ), 870; URLConnection, 885; URLEncoder.encode( ), 866; User Datagram Protocol (UDP), 842; Web application, 850

new collections library, 361

new operator, 162; and primitives, array, 180

newInstance( ), 730, 747; reflection, 530

newInstance( ), reflection, 925

next( ), 365

nextElement( ), Enumeration, 339

nextToken( ), 982

NMI: Java 1.0 native method interface, 998

no-arg: constructors, 152

non-Java: connecting to a non-Java program, 851

non-Java code, calling, 997

North, 614

not equivalent (!=), 103

notify( ), 786

notifyAll( ), 786

notifyListeners( ), 784

notifyObservers( ), 912, 914

null, 72, 327

NullPointerException, 416

numbers, binary, 117

object, 27; aliasing, 98; arrays are first-class objects, 325; assigning objects by copying handles, 97; assignment, 97; business object/logic, 672; Class

object, 507, 518, 775; creation, 149; equals( ) method, 104; equivalence, 104; equivalence vs handle equivalence, 104; final, 239; handle equivalence vs. object equivalence, 552; immutable objects, 573; lock, for multithreading, 775; object-oriented programming, 516; order of finalization of objects, 312; process of creation, 176; serialization, 489; web of objects, 490, 547

Object, 324, 348, 918; array of Object, 732; clone( ), 548, 552; getClass( ), 528

Object Request Broker (ORB), 998

object-oriented: analysis & design, 58

object-oriented programming, 25

ObjectOutputStream, 490

ObjectSpace, 360

Observable, 912

Observer, 912

observer design pattern, 911

Octal, 117

ODBC, 888

OMG, 1028

ones complement operator, 108

OOP, 208; protocol, 268

openConnection( ), 885

openStream( ), URL, 870

operator, 95; + and += overloading for String, 223; +, for String, 579; == and !=, 552; binary, 108; bitwise, 108; casting, 115; comma, 114; comma operator, 134; common pitfalls, 115; indexing operator [ ], 179; logical, 105; logical operators and short-circuiting, 107; ones-complement, 108; operator overloading for String, 579; overloading, 114; precedence, 96; precedence mnemonic, 119; relational, 103; shift, 109; ternary, 113; unary, 101, 108

operator overloading: in C++, 877

optimization, 1060

optional methods, in the Java 1.2 collections, 390

OR, 115; (||), 105
ORB (Object Request Broker), 998
order: of constructor calls with
    inheritance, 306; of finalization of
    objects, 312; of initialization, 172,
    246, 314
organization, code, 202
output: data file output shorthand, 465;
    formatted file output shorthand, 464
OutputStream, 440, 442, 833, 852
OutputStreamWriter, 473, 474, 833
overflow: and primitive types, 129;
    stack overflow, 342
overloading: and constructors, 150;
    distinguishing overloaded methods,
    152; lack of name hiding during
    inheritance, 231; method overloading,
    150; on return values, 157; operator
    + and += overloading for String,
    223; operator overloading, 114;
    operator overloading for String, 579;
    overloading vs. overriding, 231; vs.
    overriding, 263
overriding: and inner classes, 295;
    overloading vs. overriding, 231; vs.
    overloading, 263
package, 190, 917; access, and friendly,
    202; and applets, 594; and directory
    structure, 201; creating unique
    package names, 193; default package,
    204; names, capitalization, 80;
    statement and book chapter
    subdirectories, 97; visibility, friendly,
    280
paint( ), 591, 620, 635, 693, 699
Panel, 616
param, HTML keyword, 766
parameter, applet, 593
parameterized type, 337, 360, 940
parseInt( ), 635
pass: pass by value, 546; passing a
    handle into a method, 542
patterns, design patterns, 212, 907
performance, 1067; and final, 244
performance guidelines, 1057
persistence, 504; lightweight
    persistence, 489

pipe, 441
piped stream, 793
PipedInputStream, 442, 466
PipedOutputStream, 442, 443, 466
PipedReader, 474
PipedWriter, 474
planning, software development, 60
platform-independent file manipulation,
    959
pointers, and Java, 542
polymorphism, 251, 320, 516, 537,
    918, 934, 955; and constructors, 306;
    behavior of polymorphic methods
    inside constructors, 312
popup menu, 737
port, 829
portability in C, C++ and Java, 119
POST, 864; CGI, 882; using an applet,
    884
precedence: operator precedence
    mnemonic, 119
primitive: collections of primitives, 328;
    comparison, 104; data types, and use
    with operators, 119; dealing with the
    immutability of primitive wrapper
    classes, 573; final, 239; final static
    primitives, 240; initialization of class
    data members, 169; wrappers, 350
print( ), 693, 699
PrintGraphics, 699
printInfo( ), 530
printing, 701; text, 698
PrintJob, 698
println( ), 340
printStackTrace( ), 410, 412
PrintStream, 447, 462
PrintWriter, 475, 833
priority: default priority for a Thread
    group, 805; thread, 801
private, 31, 190, 202, 205, 235, 775;
    and the final specifier, 243;
    constructor, 910; inner class, 761;
    inner classes, 301
problem space, 27, 236
Process, 852
process, and threading, 751

resumption, termination vs. resumption, exception handling, 408

re-throwing an exception, 412

return: constructor return value, 150; overloading on return value, 157

reuse, 248; code reuse, 217; reusable code, 704

right-shift operator (>>), 109

RMI: AlreadyBoundException, 902; and CORBA, 1036; bind( ), 900; CORBA, 904; localhost, 901; rebind( ), 902; Remote, 898; remote interface, 898; Remote Method Invocation, 898; remote object registry, 900; RemoteException, 898, 904; rmic, 903; rmic and classpath, 903; rmiregistry, 900; RMISecurityManager, 900; Serializable arguments, 902; skeleton, 902; stub, 902; TCP/IP, 901; unbind( ), 902; UnicastRemoteObject, 899

rmic, 903

rmiregistry, 900

RMISecurityManager, 900

RNI: Raw Native Interface, 998

rollover, 732

RTI: Class, 730

RTTI: and cloning, 553; cast, 518; Class object, 518; ClassCastException, 522; Constructor, 532, 730; difference between RTTI and reflection, 532; downcast, 522; eliminating from your design, 936; Field, 532; getConstructor( ), 730; instanceof keyword, 522; isInstance, 526; meta-class, 518; Method, 532; misuse of RTTI, 918, 932, 952; newInstance( ), 730; reflection, 531; run-time type identification (RTTI), 319; type-safe downcast, 522; using the Class object, 528

runFinalizersOnExit( ), 311, 460

Runnable, 814, 857; interface, 763; Thread, 785

running programs and the classpath, 97

Runtime, 852

run-time binding, 256; polymorphism, 252

run-time type identification: (RTTI), 319; misuse, 537; shape example, 516; when to use it, 537

RuntimeException, 324, 416

rvalue, 96

safety, and applet restrictions, 625

scheduling, software development, 61

scope: inner class nesting within any arbitrary scope, 284; inner classes in methods & scopes, 282

section, critical section and synchronized block, 779

seek( ), 448, 463

selection, multiple selection in an AWT List, 613

seminars: public Java seminars, 7; training, provided by Bruce Eckel, 19

separation of interface and implementation, 31, 208

SequenceInputStream, 442, 476

Serializable, 489, 495, 499, 510, 717; readObject( ), 501; writeObject( ), 501

serialization: and object storage, 504; and transient, 499; controlling the process of serialization, 495; defaultReadObject( ), 503; defaultWriteObject( ), 503; RMI arguments, 902; to perform deep copying, 559; Versioning, 504

server, 828

server-side programming, 57

Servlet Server, 905

servlet servers, 864

servlets, 57

Set, 362, 374

setActionCommand( ), 664

setAlignment( ), 603

setAllowUserInteraction(false), 885

setBorder( ), 725

setChanged( ), 914

setCheckboxGroup( ), 606

setContents( ), 703

setDaemon( ), 768

setDirectory( ), 637

setDoInput(true), 885
setDoOutput(true), 885
setEditable( ), 601
setErr(PrintStream), 480
setFile( ), 637
setIcon( ), 732
setIn(InputStream), 480
setLayout( ), 613
setMenuBar( ), 627
setOut(PrintStream), 480
setPriority( ), 802
setSelectedIndex( ), 746
setText( ), 603
setToolTipText( ), 725
shallow copy, 547, 554
shape: example, 256; example, and run-
    time type identification, 516
shift operators, 109
shortcut, menu shortcuts, 664
show( ), 637
showConfirmDialog( ), 747
showDocument( ), 871, 887
showMessageDialog( ), 747
showStatus( ), 599
side effect, 96, 103, 157, 545
signed two's complement, 113
Simula-67, 208
simulation, 988
singleton, 909; design pattern, 212
size( ), Vector, 333
sizeof( ): lack of in Java, 119
skeleton, RMI, 902
sleep( ), 753, 773, 786, 788
slider, 739
Smalltalk, 26, 27, 162
Socket, 836
sockets, stream-based, 842
Software Development Conference, 6
software development, process, 59
sort( ), 391
sorting, 354
source code copyright notice, 16
South, 614
specialization, 234
specification: system specification, 60

specification, exception, 409
specifier: access specifiers, 31, 190, 202
speed, and Java, 1067
Spinner, 728
splitter control, 748
Springs & Struts, 748
SQL: stored procedures, 894; Structured
    Query Language, 887
stack: and object creation, 1060;
    overflow, 342
Stack, 324, 331, 344, 400
standard input: Reading from standard
    input, 465
Standard Template Library (STL) for
    C++, 360
standards: coding standards, 17, 1051
start( ), 591, 595
Statement, 889
static, 268; and final, 239; and inner
    classes, 291; block, 176; clause, 520;
    construction clause, 176; data
    initialization, 173; final static
    primitives, 240; initialization, 247;
    inner classes, 291; keyword, 162;
    method, 162; synchronized static,
    775
status line, Web browser, 599
STL: C++, 361; C++ Standard Template
    Library, 873; Standard Template
    Library for C++, 360
stop( ), 591, 595, 861; and deadlocks,
    797; deprecation in Java 1.2, 797
stored procedures in SQL, 894
stream-based sockets, 842
StreamTokenizer, 467, 475, 535, 981
String, 957; automatic type conversion,
    335; class methods, 577;
    concatenation with operator +, 114;
    immutability, 577; indexOf( ), 451,
    534, 861, 929, 970; length( ), 970;
    lexicographic vs. alphabetic sorting,
    393; methods, 581; operator +, 335;
    Operator +, 114; operator + and +=
    overloading, 223; replace( ), 971;
    substring( ), 970; substring( ), 929;
    toString( ), 219, 334; trim( ), 870,
    970; trim( ), 929

text: file manipulation, 958; processing, 957

TextArea, 601, 701; Java 1.1, 653

TextComponent, 600; Java 1.1, 653

TextEvent, 641, 643

TextField, 600; Java 1.1, 652

TextListener, 641

textValueChanged( ), 644

this keyword, 159

Thread, 751, 753; and Java Beans, 780; and Runnable, 814; blocked, 785; combined with main class, 761; daemon threads, 767; dead, 785; deadlock, 797; deciding what methods to synchronize, 784; destroy( ), 801; drawbacks, 820; getPriority( ), 802; interrupt( ), 797; IO and threads, blocking, 786; isDaemon( ), 768; new Thread, 785; notify( ), 786; notifyAll( ), 786; order of execution of threads, 757; priority, 801; properly suspending & resuming, 799; resume( ), 786, 789; resume( ) , deprecation in Java 1.2, 799; resume( ), and deadlocks, 797; run( ), 755; Runnable, 785; Runnable interface, 763; setDaemon( ), 768; setPriority( ), 802; sharing limited resources, 769; sleep( ), 773, 786, 788; start( ), 756; states, 785; stop( ) , deprecation in Java 1.2, 797; stop( ), and deadlocks, 797; stopping, 797; suspend( ), 786, 789; suspend( ) , deprecation in Java 1.2, 799; suspend( ), and deadlocks, 797; synchronized method and blocking, 786; thread group, 806; thread group, default priority, 805; threads and efficiency, 754; wait( ), 786, 791; when they can be suspended, 774; when to use threads, 820; yield( ), 786

throw keyword, 406

Throwable, 414; base class for Exception, 410

throwing an exception, 406

time-critical code sections, 997

TitledBorder, 726, 747

toArray( ), 387

token, 467

tool tip, 732

toolbar, 748

Toolkit, 700

TooManyListenersException, 672, 717

toString( ), 219, 334, 340, 353

training seminars provided by Bruce Eckel, 19

Transferable, 703

transient, 499

translation unit, 191

Transmission Control Protocol (TCP), 842

tree, 740

TreeMap, 377

trim( ), 604, 870, 929, 970

true, 105

try, 231, 427; try block in exceptions, 407

two's complement, signed, 113

type: finding exact type of a base handle, 518; parameterized type, 337, 940; primitive data types and use with operators, 119; type checking and arrays, 324; type safety in Java, 115; type-safe downcast in run-time type identification, 522

TYPE field, for primitive class literals, 521

type library, 1021

type safe sets of constants, 277

type-check coding, 918

type-conscious Vector, 335

UDP, User Datagram Protocol, 842

UML, Unified Modeling Language, 61

unary: minus (-), 101; operator, 108; operators, 101; plus (+), 101

unbind( ), 902

undo, 748

unicast, 717; unicast events, 672

UnicastRemoteObject, 899

Unicode, 473

unit testing, 223

Bruce Eckel's Hands-On Java Seminar Multimedia C
It's like coming to the seminar!
Available at http://www.BruceEckel.com

- Overhead slides and synchronized audio for all the lectures. Just play it to see and hear the lectures!
- Entire set of lectures are indexed so you can rapidly locate the discussion of the subject you're interested
- Special screen-formatted electronic version of *Thinki in Java* with hyperlinked index and table of contents